# *Anatomy*
# *of the Sacred*

# Anatomy
# of the Sacred

## An Introduction
## to Religion

Fifth Edition

James C. Livingston
*The College of William & Mary*

Upper Saddle River, New Jersey 07458

Library of Congress Cataloging-in-Publication Data

Livingston, James C.
  Anatomy of the sacred : an introduction to religion / James C. Livingston.— 5th ed.
    p. cm.
  Includes bibliographical references and index.
  ISBN 0-13-183564-5
  1. Religion.   2. Religions.   I. Title.

  BL48.L48 2004
  200—dc22

                                                                    2004011036

**Editorial Director:** Charlyce Jones-Owen
**Senior Acquisitions Editor:** Ross Miller
**Assistant Editor:** Wendy B. Yurash
**Editorial Assistant:** Carla Worner
**Production Liaison:** Fran Russello
**Production Editor:** Karen Berry/Pine Tree Composition, Inc.
**Marketing Manager:** Kara Kindstrom
**Marketing Assistant:** Jennifer Lang
**Manufacturing Buyer:** Christina Helder
**Cover Art Director:** Jayne Conte
**Cover Designer:** Bruce Kenselaar
**Director, Image Resource Center:** Melinda Reo
**Manager, Rights and Permissions:** Zina Arabia
**Manager, Visual Research:** Beth Brenzel
**Image Permission Coordinator:** Debbie Latronica
**Composition:** Interactive Composition Corporation
**Printer/Binder:** Courier Companies, Inc.
**Cover Printer:** Courier Companies, Inc.

Credits and acknowledgments borrowed from other sources and reproduced, with permission,
in this textbook appear on appropriate page within text.

Pearson Education LTD., London
Pearson Education Singapore, Pte. Ltd
Pearson Education, Canada, Ltd
Pearson Education–Japan
Pearson Education Australia PTY, Limited

Pearson Education North Asia Ltd
Pearson Educación de Mexico, S.A. de C.V.
Pearson Education Malaysia, Pte. Ltd
Pearson Education, Upper Saddle River,
  New Jersey

10  9  8  7  6  5  4  3
ISBN 0-13-183564-5

*To my grandchildren,*
*Max, Peter, Maria, and James,*
*heirs to a new pluralistic*
*world and its challenges*

# Contents

Preface    xiii

## Part I
## The Study of Religion    1

### 1   What Is Religion? How Is It Studied?    3

Overview    3
Defining Religion    4
Why Are Humans Religious?    11
Why Study Religion?    12
The Perspective of the Student—Commitment
    and Objectivity    15
The Ways Religion Is Studied    19
    Historiography    21
    Anthropology    21
    Sociology    23
    Philosophy    24
    Phenomenology    26
Interpreting and Explaining Religion    27
Notes    31
Key Words    32
Review Questions    32
Suggestions for Further Reading    33

# Part II
# Universal Forms of Religious Experience and Expression    37

## 2    *The Sacred and the Holy*    *39*

Overview    39
The Concept of Sacred Power    40
The Ambivalence of Sacred Power    40
The Holy as *Mysterium Tremendum* and *Fascinans*    42
Sacred Space and Sacred Time    46
 The Buddhist Stupa and Pagoda as Sacred Space    48
 Mount Zion as Sacred Space    51
Religion as Ultimate Concern    54
Notes    55
Key Words    56
Review Questions    56
Suggestions for Further Reading    57

## 3    *Sacred Symbol, Myth, and Doctrine*    *58*

Overview    58
Symbolic Communication    59
Religious Symbols    60
Metaphor, Parable, and Story    64
Religious Myth    68
 Functionalist Theory of Myth    70
 A Psychotherapeutic Theory of Myth    71
 A Phenomenological Interpretation    73
Models and Doctrines    74
Notes    77
Key Words    78
Review Questions    78
Suggestions for Further Reading    79

## 4    *Sacred Ritual*    *80*

Overview    80
Ritual Action    81
Types of Sacred Ritual    84
 Life-Cycle Rites    85
 Life-Crisis Rites: A Healing Ritual    91
 Calendar or Seasonal Rituals    92
Ritual and Sacrifice    95

Rituals as Sacraments   99
Notes   101
Key Words   102
Review Questions   102
Suggestions for Further Reading   102

## 5   *Sacred Scripture* *104*

Overview   104
The Pervasive Role of Sacred Scripture   105
Using the Term *Scripture*   108
Some Distinctive Features of Sacred Scripture   109
The Authority and Canonicity of Scripture   112
The Reception and Uses of Scripture   116
The Interpretation of Scripture   121
    Buddhist Interpretation   122
    Christian Biblical Interpretation   127
Notes   132
Key Words   133
Review Questions   133
Suggestions for Further Reading   134

## 6   *Society and the Sacred: The Social Formations and Transformations of Religion* *135*

Overview   135
The Reciprocal Relationship Between Religion
  and Society   136
Types of Religious Communities   137
    Natural Religious Communities   138
Voluntary Religious Communities   140
    Founded Religions   141
Protest and Change in Voluntary Religious
  Communities   143
    Reform from within the Church   144
    Separation from the Church-Type Community   146
The Sect   147
The Cult: New Religious Movements   149
    The New Age: Toward Self Discovery   151
    The Unification Church—the "Moonies"   156
Notes   159
Key Words   160
Review Questions   160
Suggestions for Further Reading   161

# Part III
# Universal Components of a Religious Worldview    163

## 7  *Deity: Concepts of the Divine and Ultimate Reality*    165

Overview    165
Polytheism and the Worship of Nature    166
    Sky Gods    168
    Mother Goddesses    169
Dualism    175
    Chinese *Yin-Yang*    175
    Dualism of Cosmic Struggle    176
Pantheism and Monism    179
Monotheism    183
Notes    192
Key Words    192
Review Questions    193
Suggestions for Further Reading    193

## 8  *Cosmogony: Origins of the Natural and Social Order*    196

Overview    196
The Practical Basis of Cosmogony    197
Emergence or Procreation from a Primal Substance or Being    199
The Sexual Union of a Primal Male and Female    200
Creation by Conflict and the Ordering of Chaos    202
Creation by a Divine Craftsman    207
Creation by Decree or from Nothing    209
The Rejection of Cosmogonic Speculation    213
Cosmogony Today    215
    The Anthropic Principle    217
Notes    220
Key Words    221
Review Questions    221
Suggestions for Further Reading    222

## 9  *Anthropology: The Human Problem*    223

Overview    223
Modern Views of Our Human Plight    224
Stoicism    226
Christianity    229

Theravada Buddhism   234
Confucianism   238
Notes   243
Key Words   244
Review Questions   245
Suggestions for Further Reading   245

## 10   Theodicy: Encountering Evil                                247

Overview   247
The Persistent Demand for Theodicy   249
Theodicy of "Mystical Participation"   250
A Future, This-Worldly Theodicy   251
Other-Worldly Theodicy   255
Dualism   257
The *Karma-Samsara* Theodicy   258
Monotheistic Theodicies   260
      Suffering as Recompense for Sin   261
      Suffering as a Test and as a Necessary Condition of "Soul-Making"   262
      A Theodicy of Submission: The Mystery of God's Sovereignty   265
      Process Theodicy   268
      A Theodicy of Protest   269
Notes   270
Key Words   271
Review Questions   271
Suggestions for Further Reading   272

## 11   Ethics: Patterns of Moral Action                           273

Overview   273
Virtues and Obligations   274
The Sources and Norms of Moral Authority   276
      Cosmic or Natural Law   276
      Charismatic Leaders   282
      An Ethics of Divine Command   288
Notes   297
Key Words   298
Review Questions   299
Suggestions for Further Reading   299

## 12   Soteriology: Ways and Goals
##        of Salvation and Liberation                               301

Ways of Salvation and Liberation   301
The Way of Grace through Faith   302
      Martin Luther   303
      Amida Buddhism—Shinran   306

The Way of Devotion   308
The Way of Action and Obligation   311
    Hinduism   312
    Islam   314
    Judaism   318
The Way of Meditation and Insight   320
    The Yoga Techniques of Patañjali   321
    Theravada Buddhism   323
Goals of Salvation and Liberation   325
Psychic Wholeness and a Healthy Social Order   326
    A Messianic, or Utopian, Age   330
    Ancient Israel's Messianic Hope   330
Resurrection, Immortality, and Eternal Life   334
    Immortality in Ancient Egypt and Greece   336
    Postbiblical Judaism and Christianity   338
*Samādhi* and Nirvana   342
    Hindu *Samādhi*   343
    Buddhist Nirvana   344
Notes   346
Key Words   348
Review Questions   349
Suggestions for Further Reading   350

# Part IV
# The Sacred and the Secular in Modernity   353

## 13   The Sacred and the Secular in Modernity   355

Overview   355
Secularization and Pluralism   356
The Reactions of Religious Fundamentalisms Today   358
The Characteristics of Contemporary Religious Fundamentalism   359
    American Protestant Fundamentalism   360
    Contemporary Islamic Fundamentalism   365
The Role of Women in Modern Christianity   376
The Role of Women in Islam   380
Notes   384
Key Words   386
Review Questions   386
Suggestions for Further Reading   387

Glossary   391

Index   403

# *Preface*

*Anatomy of the Sacred* is a comprehensive introduction to the nature and variety of religious belief and practice. Designed primarily for those who have not had a previous course in religion, it provides the student with an understanding of what religion is, of the universal forms of religious experience, and of the basic concepts that make up a religious worldview. By employing a comparative analysis across a rich range of ancient and modern religious traditions, this introduction allows students to see the ways in which certain classic forms of religious life appear in different societies over time, as well as to recognize the incredible diversity of human religious expression and belief.

The book is divided into four parts. Part I is concerned with such questions as the problem of defining religion, why it is important to study religion, and how one goes about the task, including the several disciplines or methods used in the study of religion. Each method is illustrated with specific examples from the work of eminent scholars in the field.

Part II is an introduction to the universal forms of religious experience and expression and includes discussions of the sacred and holy; religious symbolism, myth, and doctrine; sacred ritual; sacred scripture; and the social dimensions of religion.

Part III, which constitutes more than half of the book, consists of a comparative analysis of seven concepts, each one representing a fundamental structure or component of a religious worldview. A religious worldview is holistic, that is, it sees nature, human life, and the divine as interrelated and as forming a comprehensive vision of the world. A religion, therefore, includes a conception of sacred power and of an exemplary natural and social order. It offers an analysis of the breakdown or corruption of that order and of the human problem, but it also provides an answer to the ever-present threat of evil and chaos. Finally, a religious worldview affords an ethical pattern of action, a way of achieving liberation or enlightenment, and an ideal vision of the goal or end of human life. Part III thus includes analyses of such concepts as deity, cosmogony, the human problem, theodicy, ethics, the ways to salvation or liberation, and the end or goal of salvation. Again, each theme is illustrated by examples drawn from a wide variety of religious belief and behavior, ranging from primal and archaic cultures through the religions of the present.

Part IV addresses the question, What impact has Modernity, that is, the immense changes that have occurred in our social, political, legal, and economic institutions, as well as the wider access to education, the influence of science, technology, and mass communications, had on religious life and institutions today? It then examines the secularization thesis and raises questions about its validity. Finally, it explores contemporary religious Fundamentalism and the changing roles of women in religion and society as two different responses to these modern challenges facing religion today and in the future.

In preparing a new edition of this book I am especially aware of my debt to those teachers who were asked to evaluate the fourth edition and who offered excellent advice. I am, of course, also in the debt of many scholars whose highly specialized studies I was required to consult in updating substantive discussions in the text as well as the notes and suggestions for further reading. The important additions and revisions incorporated in this edition include an entirely new chapter on the response of religion to modernity; an extensive new discussion of the changing roles of women in religion; a new, substantive discussion of New Age religious movements and their significance; more illustrative material from contemporary religious life (e.g., an extended discussion of science and religion), and an extensive updating of the review questions and the suggestions for further reading. I would also like to thank the following reviewers: Linda J. Tessier, Youngstown State University; Scott Jansen, Chaffey College; Steven W. Godby, Broward Community College; Clark M. Brittain, Greenville Technical College; and Winston Davis, Washington and Lee University.

In preparing this edition I am particularly indebted to three individuals for their expert assistance: Tammy Cooper, secretary for the Department of Religion at the College of William and Mary, who kindly assisted with the preparation of early drafts; my wife Jackie, who, as always, has given me invaluable help as a copy editor; and my daughter Susannah, a professional editor, who assisted me in the final process of preparing the text. Her time and expertise were indispensable. I also thank Wendy Yurash, assistant editor at Prentice Hall, for her valuable assistance and her patience over many months, and Karen L. Berry for her excellent work and help. I am delighted to dedicate this edition to my grandchildren: Max, Peter, Maria, and James, young students on their way.

*J. C. L*

# Part I

## *The Study of Religion*

# 1

# *What Is Religion?*
# *How Is It Studied?*

## Overview

We begin our exploration of the anatomy of religion with the observation that religion is a universal and abiding dimension of human experience. This is followed, however, by a rather embarrassing admission, for when we attempt to define this phenomenon, we immediately run into difficulties. We look, then, at the problems connected with some of the influential definitions of religion. We will see that, while none of them is fully adequate, they do give us valuable insight into some essential aspects of religion.

The clue to the religious dimension of human life is likely to be found in those characteristics that set us apart from other living species. This leads us to a second question—"Why are we religious?"—and an attempt to answer the question by looking at some unique features of human self-consciousness, what is sometimes called our capacity for "self-transcendence" and what that means.

A further preliminary question explored in this opening chapter is why we should study religion, and why it is an important subject of study at this particular time in history. No doubt you will be able to come up with some additional reasons of your own.

This chapter concludes with a brief discussion of how we go about the study of religion, in this case, by looking at the question of whether a student of religion can or, indeed, should be a devout believer, a nonbeliever, or a neutral observer. The answer to this question may be more complex than we imagine. At any rate, it is a matter that we ought to think about as we begin our study of religion.

## Defining Religion

Few aspects of experience reveal the wealth, variety, and complexity that we encounter in a study of the religions of humankind. The playwright George Bernard Shaw once remarked, "There is only one religion, though there are hundreds of versions of it." We wonder, however, what Shaw had in mind when he spoke of *one* religion cloaked in a hundred forms. St. Augustine was closer to the mark when he observed, "If you do not ask me what time is, I know; if you ask me, I do not know." Religion, like time, is something we take for granted. We never doubt that we know what it is—until, of course, we start thinking about it. Then we encounter some uncertainties. There are, however, some things about which we are certain. One is that religion is as old as humankind. The evidence of **Neanderthal\*** and **Cro-Magnon** life—representing the earliest members of our own species *Homo sapiens*—is clear. From as long as 100,000 to 25,000 years ago, these humans practiced burial rites that indicate a belief in an afterlife. They also apparently practiced rites of ***propitiation\*\****, that is, made efforts to appease or conciliate spirits or powers. All cultures and societies about which we possess reliable information clearly reveal some form of this behavior. There do not appear to be any modern *societies* without religious beliefs and practices; however, there are individuals in modern societies who do not exhibit conventional religious activity. Nevertheless, anthropologists would agree that religion is a universal human phenomenon—a pervasive and, as we shall see, enduring reality. A human being is rightly called *Homo religiosus*, a religious animal.

If I speak so assuredly of the fact that humanity has practiced religion everywhere and at all times, we would expect that I should be able to identify the meaning of the term or at least to describe the range of phenomena to which the word *religion* applies. But here the difficulties already begin to appear. It is a strange quandary: Unless we can define religion—that is, unless we can indicate its reference range—it does not seem possible that we can begin to inquire into its nature or history. It is the definition that designates or delimits the type of phenomenon to be investigated. If we do not know what constitute observations of *religious* phenomena as opposed to other phenomena—say, kinship, politics, or medicine—how can we begin our study?

Religion has been studied extensively, but those studies, by and large, have been based on rather intuitive and conventional notions of what defines religion. To indicate something of the problem, we can look at several influential definitions or descriptions of religion. We will begin with two that assume some form of *theism* or belief in God or gods, but we will see that, in

---

\* Words in boldface type are defined in the Glossary.
\*\* Words in boldface italics are Key Words.

light of other definitions, these are not capable of serving as inclusive definitions. Here are our examples:

A. *Religion is the belief in an ever-living God, that is, in a Divine Mind and Will ruling the Universe and holding moral relations with mankind.*
—*James Martineau*

B. *Religion is an institution consisting of culturally patterned interaction with culturally postulated superhuman beings.*
—*Melford E. Spiro*

C. *The essence of religion consists in the feeling of an absolute dependence.*
—*Friedrich Schleiermacher*

D. *Religion is that which grows out of, and gives expression to, experience of the holy in its various aspects.*
—*Rudolf Otto*

E. *Religion is what an individual does with his solitariness.*
—*Alfred North Whitehead*

F. *Religion is the recognition of all our duties as divine commands.*
—*Immanuel Kant*

G. *The religious is any activity pursued in behalf of an ideal end against obstacles and in spite of threats of personal loss because of its general and enduring value.*
—*John Dewey*

H. *Religion is the state of being grasped by an ultimate concern, a concern which qualifies all other concerns as preliminary and which itself contains the answer to the question of the meaning of our life.*
—*Paul Tillich*

I. *Religion is comparable to a childhood neurosis.*
—*Sigmund Freud*

J. *Religion is the sign of the oppressed creature. . . . It is the opium of the people. . . . Religion is only the illusory sun which revolves around man as long as he does not revolve around himself.*
—*Karl Marx*

Each of these definitions or descriptions of religion is informative and each has been influential. However, not one of them strikes us as fully adequate. Obviously, they are not all compatible; some appear to be too *limited* in terms of what we know about the variety of historical expressions of religion. Certainly, James Martineau would limit religion to **monotheism** and thus would exclude the **polytheism** of much Greek and Roman religion, and popular Hinduism, as well as Theravada Buddhism and Confucianism,

Monk in solitary meditation by a Zen rock garden inside a Temple complex in Kyoto, Japan. This reflects the often-solitary dimension of religion. (*Source:* Courtesy of Catherine Karnow, Corbis/Bettmann.)

which are nontheistic. This is hardly an adequate definition. The anthropologist Melford Spiro is careful to avoid such a narrow conception by appropriating E. B. Tylor's classic definition of religion as "belief in Spiritual Beings." Spiro associates religion with belief in "superhuman beings," but note that he does not equate such beings with the supernatural. That is, religions may believe in ancestor spirits, powers, and processes that transcend the human, but that does not mean that these occupy a world beyond this natural one. That is an important corrective. But Spiro's definition may not capture some important characteristics of religion.

The definitions of theologians Schleiermacher and Otto focus on the *affective,* or emotional and feeling, dimension of religious experience that is so important. They point especially to the profoundly real and pervasive human experiences of finitude and dependence, awe, fear, and mystery as essential to religious life. They appear correct in what they affirm but again narrow in what they leave out. The critical place of belief and the ritually and ethically active dimensions of religion are left in the shade. In their different ways, the definitions of the philosophers Whitehead and Kant also are too narrow in scope. Kant perceives the profound moral dimension of religion, but he essentially reduces religion to the function of moral regulation; thus he leaves out important affective, aesthetic, social, and ritualistic dimensions of religious life. Whitehead's definition, like Kant's, appears too individualistic; furthermore, it is so vague as not to be very helpful.

The difficulty that we encounter in the valuable but problematic definitions of the philosopher Dewey and the theologian Tillich is that they may be *too* inclusive. Dewey says that "the religious" is a *quality* of experience, a quality that may be found in aesthetic, scientific, or political activity. For Tillich, the research scientist or the political zealot whose commitment represents a "state of being grasped by an ultimate concern" is, by his definition, religious. It was said of Dewey—not entirely in jest—that, for him, everything can be religious except religion! It does appear, however, that for Dewey and Tillich almost everything and anything is capable of being religious. But if everything human is religious, then it would seem to be synonymous with politics or artistic endeavor and not a very informative concept.

The definitions—or, rather, theories—of Freud and Marx suffer from different limitations. They are explanatory in intent; that is, they claim to explain why or how religion came into being or why it persists—in these instances, as a neurosis or as an illusory happiness. They are essentially reductive in that they seek to reduce religion to either psychological processes or socioeconomic factors. Such an approach can be guilty of the **genetic fallacy**, the confusing of the essence, value, or truth of religion with an explanation of its origin. They may also, of course, be considered prejudicial because they regard religion as something infantile and illusory that must be overcome.

This brief survey of influential definitions of religion has made us aware that any one definition will likely have its difficulties and that there are certain definitional characteristics that should be avoided. An adequate definition should, for example, avoid *narrowness,* that is, not overlook or dismiss features that are characteristic of religious traditions. *Vagueness,* a problem encountered with Whitehead's definition, is also to be avoided. An adequate definition should include both *distinctiveness* and *generality*; it should be distinctive enough for us to be able to distinguish religious phenomena from other forms of cultural life and expression, and yet it should be general enough to avoid being provincial, that is, relevant to only one religion or to religious life in one cultural setting or one time period. Monotheism would be an example of a definition that lacks appropriate generality. It is also important that a definition of the nature or essence of religion not be confused with a *causal explanation* of why humans are religious, as we saw with the descriptions of Marx and Freud. Finally, it should be evident that an adequate dèfinition of religion should avoid being *reductive* or *prejudicial.*

It has been said that defining religion is reminiscent of the fable of the blind men attempting to describe an elephant. "One touches its trunk and describes it as a snake; another touches its ear and describes it as a winnowing fan; another touches its leg and describes it as a tree; another its tail and describes it as a broom."[1] Perhaps the lesson to be learned is that we should give up the effort to define *religion.* Why, after all, should we think that the many religions of the world have some "essence" in common? There are legions of particular religions, but perhaps no such thing as "religion." This sounds plausible, but there are two good reasons to pursue the quest for a working definition.

First, many scholars in the field will argue that the various religions do share certain characteristics, structures, and analogies that set them apart as "religion," that is, as distinct from other human activities. Following the philosopher Ludwig Wittgenstein's influential discussion of language-games, it has been suggested that while the religions may not share a discernible substantive essence they, like languages or games, share a family resemblance or certain structural similarities. For instance, the philosopher John Hick draws the analogy between "games" and religions and points out that each game or religion is similar in important respects to some others in the family, though not in all respects. What they share is a network of overlapping similarities. In other words, "there are no characteristics that every member must have; but nevertheless there are characteristics . . . which together distinguish [religion] from a different family."[2] In the following chapters, numerous examples will be cited of the structural features or "family resemblance" shared by otherwise seemingly quite different religions.

A second reason to pursue a more adequate definition of religion is, quite simply, to avoid confusion and bias in an important field of study. If we are to study religion, we must have some sense of its defining features and boundaries. A scholar reminds us that definitions are simply "tools for bringing order to linguistic (and therefore conceptual) behavior," and that we should recognize that because "a tool may one day become obsolete or worn out is no ground for giving up the tool-making process."[3] Definitions, like hypotheses or working models, need not claim immutability or perfect universality.

Because our definitions must always seek greater precision, comprehensiveness, and adequacy, no definition can claim permanence. But that does not argue for falling back on conventional, unreflective, often inconsistent and biased, usage. The importance of the attempt to define *religion*—or science or art for that matter—is to bring some order, consistency, and clarity out of a chaos of unreflective confusion on a subject of great human significance.

We have argued the need for an adequate definition and have pointed out above the inadequacies of some influential definitions. At this point, the reader deserves some suggestions as to what might constitute an adequate working definition of religion before we turn to more particular forms of religious experience, behavior, and belief in the chapters that follow. Since there are some definitions that are currently attractive, we can begin by testing their appropriateness; then I will suggest a brief working definition of my own.

Students of religion often distinguish between *"substantive"* and *"functional" definitions*. An example of the former is E. B. Tylor's definition of religion as "belief in Spiritual Beings." We have already seen the difficulty involved in attempting to specify the singular essence or objective reference of religious activity and belief. This has persuaded many contemporary scholars to forgo the effort to define what religion *is* and to focus rather on its function, on what religion *does*. An excellent example of a widely cited functional definition is that proposed by the sociologist Milton Yinger. "Religion," Yinger writes, "can be defined as a system of beliefs and practices by means of which a group of people struggles with the ultimate problems of human life."[4]

Yinger, you will note, avoids any reference to the "sacred," the "divine," the "transcendental," or the "supernatural." A secular faith in science would fulfill, in Yinger's definition, the functions of a religion. It would appear that for Yinger every individual has, implicitly or explicitly, a set of beliefs and values that claim that person's intense faith and loyalty and by means of which he or she is able to struggle and to cope with the ultimate problems of life. Since everyone has some faith or center of value and loyalty, human beings are by nature religious. Here religion is indistinguishable from, say, a devout patriotism, or a faith in free-market capitalism, or an abiding loyalty to any cause.

I would propose that a functional definition, such as Yinger's, is deficient and therefore unsatisfactory, for the following reason. Religious persons explicitly affirm, or they tacitly assume, the independent reality of the object of their belief and behavior. That is, religions make claims about the Real, the Ultimate, the Ideal; they assume "beliefs about" some objective standard or independent reality and are not merely engaged in describing how belief functions subjectively for the individual or community. Functional definitions describe what religion does psychologically and sociologically independent of the truth or reality of its objective reference. I would insist that a definition that reduces a religion's beliefs exclusively to, say, sociological phenomena does not do justice to the full reality of religion as understood by its practitioners. A truly adequate *definition* must then take account of the language used by believers. This does not preclude the scholar from proceeding—indeed, it is his or her responsibility to proceed—beyond *description* to attempt to *explain* the belief and behavior of an individual or a religious group, explanations that may be neither apparent nor acceptable to the individual or group itself. We will discuss these issues.

A currently influential and rather more satisfactory definition of religion is one proposed by the anthropologist Clifford Geertz. It is primarily a functionalist definition, but one that also attempts to recognize the "realistic" character of the objects of religious experience without attempting to speculate about their status or nature. Geertz offers the following rich, manifold definition:

> Religion is (1) a system of symbols which acts to (2) establish powerful, pervasive, and long-lasting moods and motivations in [people] by (3) formulating conceptions of a general order of existence and (4) clothing these conceptions with such an aura of factuality that the moods and motivations seem uniquely realistic.[5]

This definition includes a number of noteworthy features. First, a religion is a holistic system, a many-faceted model or envisionment of the world and human life. Second, such a system of symbols profoundly influences the moral ethos, that is, human action, both in terms of the intensity of moral feeling and the direction of human behavior. Third, religion creates not only deep-felt moral dispositions and behavior but also a *cosmology*, that is, a set of rather simple beliefs or more developed conceptions of a general order of nature and society that satisfies our human need for explanation. Finally, a religion clothes its system of symbols in "an aura of factuality" that gives to the symbols their "realism" or quality of pointing to an objective order or reality outside of and independent of the subjective experience of the religious community. As a social scientist, Geertz naturally remains within the interpretive sphere of the human symbol system and does not philosophize about the symbol's transhuman nature or reality. But he recognizes this "aura of factuality" as crucial to any religious ethos.

A working definition of religion must then include some reference to its substantive reality, to what religion *is*. We cannot, however, ignore the fact that the reputed suprahuman reality to which the religions point and appeal as the ground, power, and goal of existence is extraordinarily diverse. The Ultimate, the Divine, the Real, the One, the Supreme, the Ideal not only go by different names—Brahman, Tao, mana, Samadhi, Allah, Zeus, Nirvana, Shiva, Grand Harmony, Father, to name a very few—but also symbolize often unique and incomparable realities. Any definition that includes reference to the object of religion, to its substantive reality, must take care to select a term that is of sufficient generality to take account of this diversity of religious objects. Scholars have used terms such as *God, the Divine, the Supernatural, the Eternal, the Transcendent,* and *the Sacred.* None of these are unproblematic or avoid some ambiguity, but the word *Sacred* strikes many as the most encompassing and workable term. It was given classic expression in the anthropologist Emile Durkheim's definition of religion as "a unified system of beliefs and practices *relative to sacred things*" (emphasis added).[6] That is, the religious object contrasts fundamentally with what individuals and communities associate with the common, everyday, and profane. This contrast between the sacred, or holy, and the profane is, as we will see, also the defining characteristic of the religious in the work of numerous scholars. This text adopts *the Sacred* as the term that best conveys, in the most general way, that objective reference or ultimate reality about which the religions speak or to which their symbols point. The working definition of religion that I then propose is the following: "Religion is that system of activities and beliefs directed toward that which is perceived to be of sacred value and transforming power."

Our exercise should have made it clear that defining religion is not a simple undertaking. I hope, however, that we are not left in quite the difficulty faced by St. Augustine when he was asked, "What is time?" At the least, we can offer several definitions that, taken together, may complement and supplement one another by pointing to several essential features of the phenomenon that we call religion. You may even venture, as I have done, the riskier task of attempting a single working definition.

## Why Are Humans Religious?

If we are correct that religion is both universally common and unique to our species, then we might expect to find the clue to why human beings are religious in those characteristics that distinguish us from other species. Through the centuries, thinkers have attempted to suggest what is unique about humankind. We are called *Homo sapiens,* a Latin term indicating that we humans are essentially sapiential, that is, possessed of wisdom or rationality. Others have spoken of *Homo faber,* human beings as makers or creators; *Homo ludens,* human beings as players or actors; or *Homo viator,* humans as those beings who hope.

All these terms imply that we humans possess a distinct form of self-consciousness. The human self is unique in that it can be an object to itself. We are not only conscious, like other animals, but also self-conscious. We can stand clear of ourselves, of our immediate environment, even of our entire world—and look at ourselves, our environs, and the cosmos and make judgments about them. We can contemplate and reflect not only about means but also about ends, about the meaning, value, and purpose of life. We can look about us and say, for example, "Vanity, vanity, all is vanity"; or we can come to a very different conclusion and rejoice, "God's in His Heaven and all's right with the world."

It is from this fact of self-consciousness, or *self-transcendence,* that the pressing questions of life come flooding in on us: "Why am I here?" "Why do righteous people suffer?" "To whom or what do I owe my ultimate loyalty and devotion?" "Is death the end?" These are what philosophers call the existential questions of life; they are universal and perennial; they are part of what it means to be human. To deny such questions concerned with life's meaning—moral obligation, guilt, injustice, finitude, and what endures—is to be less than human. That is why much recent talk about secularization or the widespread rejection of religious belief and institutions is, at a fundamental level, merely superficial.

We as human beings need sets of coherent answers to our existential questions as well as **archetypal** patterns of behavior and frames of reference because our lives, unlike those of other animal species, are not definable solely in terms of the satisfaction of the basic biological needs of food, shelter, and sex. While a fully human life obviously includes the satisfaction of these drives, they are not sufficient to satisfy such a life. We have other rational, moral, social, aesthetic, and religious needs that, strangely, have no limits and cannot easily be satisfied. We are a union of nature and spirit and our consciousness of the tension between our spiritual or religious aspirations and our finitude and creatureliness—that we are both free of nature and yet bound by nature—leads to our existential anxiety but also to our spiritual quests.

As humans, we are all too conscious of those things that challenge and threaten to destroy our deepest commitments and values—things such as moral failure, tragedy, inexplicable evil, and death itself. These realities can fill us with dread and terror, in part because they lie outside our ability to control. The sociologist Thomas O'Dea has spoken of religion as a response to three fundamental features of human existence: uncertainty, powerlessness, and scarcity. Religion is rooted, certainly, in a wider range of human experience and emotion than these, including such positive experiences as wonder, trust, love, and joy. But O'Dea is correct as far as he goes. The brute facts of our existence do bring us face to face with questions about which our normal practical techniques and scientific know-how are powerless to provide answers or solutions.

Unless these questions receive adequate answers—unless these "limit situations" of finitude, uncertainty, suffering, guilt, and failure are capable of being seen in some larger system of meaning or transcendent perspective—then morale may founder and cynicism and despair may begin to eat away at trust and hope. Religions are the vindicators of a holy and moral order in the face of the world's chaos and evil. If we ask, then, "Why are human beings religious?" the answer is that humans want to be delivered from the loss of meaning, from moral guilt, and from the threat of finitude and fatedness. Humans want to experience the joy and the moral animation accompanying the trust that we live in a spiritual world of moral meaning whose current leads not to death but to life and hope.

## Why Study Religion?

We began this chapter by asking "What is religion?" We found that the question does not lend itself to a simple answer and that it may be wiser for us first to describe a rather wide range of religious belief and practice before we try to say definitively what constitutes the essentials of religion. Why human beings are religious, we found, is more readily answerable, in view of our unique capacity for self-transcendence, which provokes those urgent and perennial existential questions about life, death, evil, and obligation.

Before we examine some of the classic forms of religious belief and expression as exhibited in diverse traditions, there are three additional questions that are important to consider. The first is *why* we should study religion and the second is *how* we should undertake the study of such a rich and manifold phenomenon. Third, we need to examine some of the issues that arise when we attempt to *interpret* and to *explain* religious belief and behavior. We will discuss the first question here and will explore the second at the end of this chapter.

There are some very good reasons why it is especially important, even crucial, to study religion at the present time.

1. *To understand* Homo religiosus. First, religion should be studied because we are *Homines religiosi*. As we have seen, part of what it means to be human is reflected in our capacity for spiritual self-transcendence. We ought, therefore, to study humans as religious beings just as we study humans as a biological

species, as political creatures, or as beings possessed of aesthetic sensibility—if we are to understand human life in its fullness.

2. *To overcome our ignorance.* Despite the rather high standard of education in Europe and North America, most of us remain surprisingly ignorant of the history and current beliefs and practices of the world's great religious traditions—even of our own. In high school or in college, we may have done advanced work in mathematics or chemistry, English literature or American history, but most students have not been exposed to a rigorous study of religion in its various manifestations. If we have grown up in a religious tradition, we may have attended Sunday school or have taken instruction for our **bar mitzvah,** but very often this proved too elementary and did not progress beyond our early teen years—and, of course, had little to do with religious traditions other than our own. We often have a narrow, **ethnocentric** view because we naturally tend to identify religion with experience of our own tradition or with those conventional forms of religious behavior that we observe in our own communities. We are reminded of Parson Thwackum in Henry Fielding's novel *Tom Jones:* "When I mention religion, I mean the Christian religion; and not only the Christian religion, but the Protestant religion; and not only the Protestant religion, but the Church of England." Needless to say, this can result in uninformed or poorly informed views, or, worse, in dangerously parochial or prejudicial attitudes.

3. *To comprehend our culture.* A third good reason for studying religion is to understand better our own history and culture as well as those of others. The American experience is not fully comprehensible without understanding, for example, the effect of Puritanism on the early history of the nation, the spread of the **evangelical** "Protestant ethic" westward in the nineteenth century, or the role of the Bible in shaping the life and character of the American South. Similarly, it is not possible to comprehend European or South Asian culture without appreciating how, in each instance, Christian or Buddhist ideas have informed cultural beliefs about nature, self, family, government, and work. We can easily forget that it is only in recent times, and outside the Third World, that there has been a conscious effort to distinguish between a society's religion and its culture. Religious beliefs nevertheless continue, largely unconsciously, to shape the values and institutions of a society that may no longer hold a common religion or maintain an established church. We may be fairly certain that the complex yet ordered fabric of any culture is woven from the loom of fundamental religious assumptions, loyalties, and hopes.

4. *To achieve a global perspective.* Due to the modern scientific and technological revolution—particularly in mass communication and transportation—we find ourselves today living in a rapidly shrinking world. Space exploration has made us acutely conscious of the fact that we are traveling on a small globe called Earth and that we humans may be endangering life itself on this remarkable planet. Technology certainly has proved ambiguous. The knowledge explosion can liberate human lives, but it can also create resentment, distrust, and fear. Nuclear power can warm our homes, and it can destroy civilization as we know it. Technology has made us more conscious of our human interdependence, but that can be threatening. If we are to maintain peace and establish a stable world order among the nations, it is imperative that we achieve a knowledge and understanding of and an empathy for beliefs and ways of life that we now find very foreign to our own. We cannot possibly understand another people or culture without a thorough knowledge and appreciation of the role of religion in its life. The failure of the U.S. government to grasp fully the religious dimensions of the conflicts in Southeast Asia and Iran explains, in part, our serious miscalculations and errors of judgment in those regions in recent history.

Many of the tragic conflicts in the world today are rooted in long-standing religious differences and animosities. We need only think of the conflicts between Arab and Israeli, Indian and Pakistani, and Protestant and Catholic in Northern Ireland.

It is paradoxical that our growing awareness of our proximity to, and dependence on, other peoples and nations has fueled disputes and wars at the same time that it has made us conscious that we are now living in a genuinely ecumenical, that is, worldwide or global, age. For the first time in history, there is a real opportunity for contact and dialogue among the great religious traditions of the world. True dialogue, however, demands a thorough knowledge of the other party and genuine willingness to be open and receptive to what that party is saying. It requires that all those engaged in dialogue seek real understanding. The effort to achieve such interreligious communication and a more global perspective on world affairs is not a mere luxury of a liberal-arts education. It is critically necessary to maintain world peace and to ensure human survival in the years ahead.

5. *To help us formulate our own religious belief or philosophy of life.* A final reason that can be suggested (this list is not exhaustive) for studying religion is that it can help us to reflect more systematically on some of the ultimate questions of life and death, and thereby it can help us to formulate our own religious beliefs or philosophy of life. Socrates was right in saying that "the unexamined life is not worth living," although Woody Allen pointed out that the examined life is not a bed of roses either. As persons who claim to be educated, we should make every effort to see that our fundamental beliefs and convictions about life are brought to consciousness, are made explicit, and then are carefully examined and critically tested.

It is not easy to be reflective about our own beliefs since these beliefs are often so basic as to be taken for granted. What is required is to step back and to see ourselves from a different perspective—to see ourselves, perhaps, as others see us. Unless we look at our beliefs from a fresh and different perspective, we may not even notice them. They remain unconscious and uncritical guides and energizers of our actions. We can learn a great deal about the strengths and deficiencies of our own religious beliefs and behavior by looking at them from other points of view, especially those of an honest and friendly critic. The Protestant can learn much about his own religion from a Catholic, as can a Catholic from the experience of a Protestant. The Buddhist, for example, can awaken Christians to the rich resources of meditation in their own tradition.

We are often hesitant to look at other faiths or to examine our own critically because we feel that, in so doing, we are being disloyal to our own deeply felt convictions. That is a natural and healthy reaction. And yet our beliefs are not worth very much if they cannot stand up to any scrutiny. Also, without examining our beliefs, without looking at them from new and different perspectives and possibilities, we cannot expect our minds and spirits to grow, or to move on to deeper levels of insight, understanding, and sympathy. It would be foolhardy in any other field of human endeavor to think that our knowledge and understanding should remain frozen at a particular stage or level of maturity. It is, in fact, rather presumptuous to think that we have already plumbed the depths of even our own religious tradition.

To be self-conscious and reflective about our beliefs does not mean, of course, that we become so open that our minds begin to resemble the proverbial sieve that cannot retain anything and through which all beliefs pass as though equally true and valuable. That is spiritual promiscuity. Our temptation today appears to be to fall into either an uncritical and slothful relativism or an uncritical and slothful dogmatism. To remain both committed and yet open, to hold a *critical* faith, takes real courage.

The honest exploration of others' beliefs usually will lead to a deepening and broadening of our own, but this is not a foregone conclusion. Honest exploration of a variety of religious beliefs and practices not only may cause us to reconceive our own religion in new ways, but also *may* force us to a painful reevaluation of long-held and deeply felt convictions and perhaps to a change of allegiance. It is a risk, but it is the risk of being educated and of living in a dynamic world of competing beliefs and values. The philosopher Nietzsche was correct when he said that real courage is not the courage of our convictions but the courage to examine our convictions.

## The Perspective of the Student—Commitment and Objectivity

A basic question that must be faced in any inquiry involving the selection and interpretation of any data is the relation between the scholar's own intellectual commitments and values and scholarly objectivity. Some would argue that persons cannot truly understand a system of religious beliefs and practices unless they do so from *within* that religion—from the sympathetic perspective of a participant and believer. Others would say that ardent faith or belief is not compatible with genuine knowledge and understanding. Both the devout believer and the detached, uncommitted observer have charged that the perspective of the other distorts what they are capable of seeing and interpreting. Are commitment and scientific objectivity opposed to one another? We will attempt to show that they need not be—but that a very real tension does and should exist between them—and that this tension does not admit of any easy solution one way or another. We can analyze this tension between commitment and detachment by looking at the question of the student's perspective along a continuum from naïve, partisan religious belief at one extreme to a standpoint of conscious, uncommitted relativity at the other.[7]

At the first extreme, we can envision a person who is not only a believer and active participant in a particular religion but also is unaware that there are other religious options. This is often the position, for example, of a tribesman in a *primal** society. The tribe's religious and cultural system is assumed to be the only "way things are." The possibility of adopting alternative beliefs or behavior is nonexistent. This could also be the position of a

---

*The word *primal* is used throughout this book to refer to preliterate human societies, either primordial or contemporary.

simple believer—for example, a young person who has not yet developed genuine individuality—in our own pluralistic culture today. The beliefs and moral norms of the family or the community are taken as self-evident. They are not yet open to reflection or to critical scrutiny. Such a person looks on or studies her or his religion as if none other existed. The sacred scriptures, the traditions, and the moral teachings of the individual's faith may be "studied," but only in the odd sense that these traditions and beliefs are learned and accepted as unquestioned authorities. Here the tension between commitment and objectivity does not exist.

In contemporary developed societies, it is much more difficult, if not impossible, to evade the shocks of cultural pluralism and the challenges of new and foreign ideas and values. Attempts on the part of some religious groups—for example, the Amish people in rural Pennsylvania or the Hasidic Jews in New York City—to isolate themselves and to keep outside influences at bay have proved only partially successful. Even in the most homogeneous of communities, there is the individual who will ask, "Why do we believe that?" or "Why should we do this?" Someone is certain to question the accepted way. When alternative beliefs and practices are proposed as reasonable options, the self-evidence, and thus the simplicity, of our own belief is gone. To become aware of another system of belief is, in a real sense, to have a new perspective on our own.

I suspect that this is where most of us find ourselves today. While we may identify ourselves as Jewish or Muslim, as Roman Catholic or Methodist, or as a secular humanist, we nevertheless have some sense of seeing ourselves as others see us. We are more self-conscious of our beliefs and aware that we might be called on to give an account of them. While our religious or ideological beliefs may still largely inform our system of values and our actions, we now must take into account other truths—scientific, moral, or social—alternative beliefs that may require us somehow to adapt our long-held beliefs to these newer insights. But how open and adaptable can a system or belief be allowed to be and yet have it maintain a coherent, recognizable shape? Here the tension between commitment to a set of beliefs and values and disinterested openness to new truth is often very great.

It sometimes happens—rather often these days—that a believer will feel more and more obliged to measure and to interpret her or his religious beliefs by norms or criteria taken from outside the religion itself. Often this step is taken in an effort to defend a religion against charges of being antiquated, to show, for example, that the religious beliefs are not inconsistent with current scientific thinking. The person, though remaining a believer, may—and perhaps not fully consciously—accept other standards of meaning or truth by which to measure or to interpret his or her own religious belief. This might be the case with a believer who also happens to be a philosopher or a historian. A philosopher may, for example, feel obliged to judge the credibility or adequacy of her religion based on some philosophical criterion of what counts as justified or reasonable belief. The historian, likewise, may reject certain teachings of his religion on the grounds that, based on certain historiographical criteria, there is not sufficient historical evidence to maintain them. The tension between commitment and objectivity may simply be slackening or, more likely, the tension between our religion and a new set of beliefs may be heightened. The passion or concern is just as real, although now it is divided between two possibly competing criteria of rationality or truth.

The final position on our hypothetical continuum is that of the completely detached and "objective" scholar who has no existential—that is, personal—interest in religion, including the religion under study. Often this is the position associated with the social scientist, the anthropologist, or sociologist. Social scientists are not supposed to be interested in the attempt to determine the truth of a religion or its general value. Rather, their aim is purely interpretive and explanatory, for example, to show how a religion functions in a certain social context in terms of the goals or ends it fulfills for that society. However, the "objective" observer can, often unconsciously, move from descriptive or interpretive statements of how a religion functions to normative judgments about standards of what is acceptable, good, or valuable. Notorious examples of this kind of false move in social science are the famous reports by Dr. Alfred Kinsey on the sexual behavior of American males and females. Kinsey purported simply to describe the actual sexual behavior of young Americans, but it was obvious to many astute critics that Kinsey's studies were not descriptively neutral. Rather, they gave the impression that certain sexual activity *ought* to be accepted as normative because it was widely practiced. The old maxim "Forty thousand Frenchmen can't be wrong" is sometimes hard to resist, but it is false. Simply because most people suffer from the common cold does not make it normative.

The question that needs to be explored, then, is whether a wholly disinterested neutrality is really possible. Can a person genuinely understand a foreign culture or another religion from the outside, from a perspective of complete detachment? Or is it even possible to speak of complete detachment and neutrality? Do we not bring to our observations and judgments certain preconceptions and unexamined assumptions about what is important, possible, or intelligible, or what constitutes evidence? Is not the gathering and organizing of data itself a process of selection? Are not some things overlooked or left in the shade? Do not the kinds or the forms of our questions set the boundaries and shape of the answers we can expect to receive?

The uncertain relationship between understanding and believing can be illustrated by looking at a work of the eminent anthropologist E. E. Evans-Pritchard. In his classic study *Witchcraft, Oracles, and Magic* among the African Azande, Evans-Pritchard insists that if we are to understand the African Azande's religious beliefs and practices, we must seek to understand them in terms of how they are taken by the Azande themselves—according to *their* form of life. Evans-Pritchard goes on, however, to maintain that the Azande belief in magic and witchcraft is, of course, illusory. He not only wants to urge that the Azande hold a different conception of reality than our Western scientific culture, but to go on "and to say, finally, that the scientific conception agrees with what reality actually is like, whereas the magical conception does not."[8] But why should we think that our concepts of rationality can provide the model by which to measure the truth of *all* other forms of belief? Critics of Evans-Pritchard argue that there is no *universal* norm of rationality. It follows that explanations or answers given to scientific questions require scientific answers, religious questions require religious answers. Religion, so the argument goes, can only be understood from within.[9]

A number of social scientists and philosophers have challenged the claim that a genuine understanding of a system of beliefs requires commitment to those beliefs. They point out, for example, that persons move from belief system A to a radically different belief system B and, having been a believer in system A, retain a "feel" for and a genuine understanding of that belief, although they are no longer committed to believing it. We might argue that, while it is imperative to begin a study of a religion from "within"—in terms of the way it understands itself—nevertheless, religious language and concepts are not wholly distinct or isolated from ordinary language and experience. A person might in turn reply, however, that this may be true of the way religious language and concepts function *within* a uniform cultural system, but that a witch doctor's concept of evidence or his test of what is real or true is, in fact, highly peculiar to many Western anthropologists. In other words, it is easy for the scholar studying another culture to assume the existence of some other, more universal, "norm of intelligibility" that transcends all particular cultures but, in fact, turns out to be the cultural norms with which he or she operates.

If we are really to appreciate different possibilities of making sense of human life, we may have to make a more rigorous effort to stand outside our own preconceptions and to enter empathetically into the culture or religion we are studying. But this is easier said than done. It demands not only an initial "suspension of disbelief" but also a thorough knowledge of how these seemingly alien beliefs and behaviors fit into a larger form of life taken as a whole. Such an effort at understanding can be made, nevertheless, without demanding that we be naïve believers or completely neutral observers. Commitment and understanding are not antithetical. Neither involves a total absence of criticism or a pure neutrality.

Let us suppose that there is an ancient religion that tells how the Earth was hatched from a giant bird's egg. Now, we can simply dismiss this out of hand as prescientific nonsense. On the other hand, we can make an effort to understand what might be conveyed by this marvelous tale. If we can do this, we probably possess the balance between empathy and objectivity required to study a complex variety of religious phenomena with both appreciation and critical understanding.

We already have covered some important ground in this opening chapter. We saw that the nature of religion is taken for granted—until, that is, we begin to analyze more carefully our assumptions and our definitions. We learned, however, that several of these influential definitions and theories, while inadequate when taken in isolation, can give us valuable clues to essential aspects and features of religion. We also learned something about why we humans are uniquely religious beings and why it is important, especially at this time in history, to study religion. Finally, we raised the question of how we go about the study of religion by briefly exploring the problem of scholarly perspective—that is, how our religious commitment or nonengagement may affect our ability genuinely to understand a religion. We concluded that religious commitment and objectivity, or the application of critical methods, are not incompatible; also, that we need not be a believer to understand a religion.

## The Ways Religion Is Studied

A final consideration, however, is the question, How does one go about the study of religion? We need to begin by pointing out that religion is not an academic discipline—in the sense that we can speak more easily of the scientific method or of the standards of historiography. Religion constitutes *a field of study* that includes many disciplines, including a variety of types of literary analysis or criticism, history, the tools of sociology, anthropology, psychology, philosophy, and many more subfields, such as archeology.

In our present culture, we often associate, even identify, religion with **theology** (from the Greek *logos*, "speech" or "inquiry," concerning *theos*, or the "gods"). We already encountered a difficulty in this equation since not all religions are theistic. Theology is, however, an accredited and respected academic pursuit in our society. A number of great universities have distinguished theological faculties or schools attached to them with renowned theologians engaged in scholarship and teaching. Is not theology, then, an appropriate subject within the broad academic field of religion? The answer, perhaps surprisingly, is a qualified yes. This requires some explanation.

For a subject to claim to be open to scholarly study, certain rules need to be agreed on. One critical scholarly rule is that persons studying a subject cannot appeal to criteria of analysis or evidence that are, in principle, unavailable to others who, though perhaps not believers, possess the requisite scholarly tools, empathy, and understanding. A second rule of academic scholarship is that a study should involve some form of critical analysis, that is, that it not consist merely of rote memorization, simple indoctrination, uncritical advocacy, or the effort to **proselytize**.

Furthermore, a *science* of theology cannot remain at the level of merely *describing* and *transmitting* the teachings of a religious tradition or community. As a science, theology must be prepared to deal with *explanatory questions* of various kinds. These impose certain requirements on the theologian: (a) No "limits can be set on who can participate in this examination, even though some may more qualify as experts than others . . .". (b) No solution can be based on privileged beliefs. "Clearly, we hold certain basic beliefs on which we base other beliefs. . . . But when basic beliefs are called into question, rational discourse requires that reasons be given on their behalf . . . (c) Consequently, *all* [scientific] beliefs must ultimately be treated as hypotheses. As hypotheses they must be internally coherent (consistent) and clearly criticizable."[10] Now, many departments or schools of theology are open to and employ those same academic tools and methods, such as literary and historical criticism, approved and used by scholars of religion. It would be perfectly legitimate, for example, to include in a department of religion a philosophical theologian—a person who, using beliefs and forms of experience drawn from her or his own religious tradition, applies to these materials the tools of philosophical analysis. The same would hold for a historical theologian who, a Catholic, for example, is an expert on the thought of Thomas Aquinas, or a Jew whose specialty happens to be nineteenth-century Jewish theology in Europe. What is crucial is that they be willing to apply to their own tradition the same critical tools and forms of analysis that they would apply to other, possibly quite alien, traditions. The scholarly legitimacy of their work depends, then, not on whether they are, for example, an agnostic or a Lutheran, but on their commitment to those scholarly tools and methods widely agreed on by scholars who work in the field.

There are, to be sure, some Bible and theological schools that reject the application of those literary, historical, and social-scientific methods that have come to be accepted by the scholarly community. They see their task as simply the uncritical transmission of a tradition or indoctrination. While such organizations have the fullest freedom to carry out their educational mission, this mission must not be identified or confused with the academic study of religion or with the critical study of theology.

A discipline is used in the study of religion because of its appropriateness and its fruitfulness in answering certain kinds of questions. For example, if we want to find out if a sacred text is the work of one or of several authors, we need to apply the tools of literary-documentary criticism. If we want to find out how a ritual functions in the larger cultural life of an African tribe, we would best employ the methods used by the anthropologist.

A rather brief description of some of the academic disciplines used in the study of religion is sufficient here to introduce you to these fields. (For further information, see the "Suggestions for Further Reading" for this chapter.)

*Literary criticism* is important in the study of religion because the events, beliefs, and authoritative teachings of a religion are often found in a collection of sacred writings, such as the Bible, the *Qur'an*, the Buddhist *Sutras*, or the *Analects* of Confucius. The literary critic asks certain highly important questions regarding these sacred texts or scriptures: Is it a version or translation of a more original and reliable text? Who was the author? When was the text composed? Where was it written and to what audience? What was the author's specific purpose? What types or genres of literature are used by the writer(s)? How was the work received, edited, interpreted, and passed on? If we can gain answers to these kinds of questions, we have come a long way toward understanding a particular sacred text.

## Historiography

The academic (critical) study of the history of religions essentially began in the nineteenth century. The historian's task is to establish the facts in an effort to reconstruct "what really happened." The "facts," of course, are selected from a vast array of possible sources. The historian *selects* the accounts or the evidence that she or he deems appropriate and relevant, based on some principle(s) of choice. The choice of relevant data will depend, in large part, on the kinds of questions the historian puts to the past. Some of these questions are the same as those that occupy the literary scholar: Who wrote what, when, why, and to whom? But, also, what social, economic, cultural, or environmental factors may have influenced a religion's beginnings, its development, or its geographical dispersion? The historian calls on nontextual sources as well, such as archaeology, geography, demography, or population statistics. More recently, the historian has used the tools and the findings developed in the social sciences of sociology, anthropology, and psychology in an effort to reconstruct and interpret "what really happened."

Modern historical science has helped the student of religion to distinguish historical occurrences from myths, legends, and tales, but also how religions have developed and how these traditions may differ from the earlier expressions of that religion. The historian's interests—religious, intellectual, economic, political—will, of course, be significant in his or her reconstruction and interpretation of the history of a religion, or of religion generally. A Marxist historian will likely argue that the origin and development of a religion can best be explained by material or economic considerations. Other historians will put greater weight on purely religious factors, or intellectual and social influences. This selectivity is not, as such, a bad thing for it can enable us to see the complexity of history and its interpretation and the interdependence of various factors in the origin and growth of a religion such as Islam or Buddhism.

Anthropology and sociology also trace their methodologies to the work of scholars in the nineteenth and early twentieth centuries.

## Anthropology

Anthropology has to do with the study of human beings and societies viewed primarily as both the creators and the creations of culture. Since religious institutions and practices are found in every known culture, the religious life of societies is of great interest to anthropologists. This is especially true because social institutions and beliefs never operate in a vacuum.

One of the giant totem poles on display at Thunderbird Park. Totems are of great interest to anthropologists since they are images of animals or other natural species that are associated with clans or tribes and their kinship and religious relations and rituals. (*Source:* Courtesy of Dorling Kindersley Media Library.)

Religious sentiments, ideas, and behavior shape and, in turn, are shaped by family organization, the economic system, law, and politics. Anthropologists also recognize that religion is an especially powerful factor in any culture because a society shapes and defines its world by reference to sacred stories, moral sanctions, and ritualized patterns of behavior.

The "father" of modern anthropology is Edward B. Tylor (1832–1917), and in his classic work, *Primitive Culture* (1871), he gave considerable attention to religion. This was also true of several others of the early anthropologists. However, it was the sociologist **Emile Durkheim** (1858–1917) who was most responsible for turning the interest of anthropologists to the study of the social functions of religion. **Functionalism** has been the method most widely used by anthropologists. As the term would indicate, the anthropologist is interested in the question of what functions particular institutions or activities serve in the total life of a community.

Applied to religion, functionalism asks how the religious beliefs and institutions of a society elicit acceptance of or sanction certain behavior, and how these factors assist in the integration and cohesion of that society. Since religion is (particularly in the premodern periods) so crucial to social integration and stability, it is given a very significant place in the work of many anthropologists.

## Sociology

The sociology of religion, like anthropology, focuses its attention on *social* behavior and the way in which religion interacts with other dimensions of our social experience. Sociology, however, is generally concerned with the religious life of modern, developed, literate societies. Early in the twentieth century there was a great flowering of interest in religion by eminent sociologists. These scholars perceived in religions an enduring human phenomenon. Earlier they were interested in exploring the social origins of religion, but soon they largely abandoned that quest and focused on *functional* questions (e.g., how the dynamics of human social life and institutions effect changes in religious life and, in turn, how religious belief and behavior act on and transform social behavior). This latter interest was dominant in the work of the influential sociologist *Max Weber* (1864–1920).

One of Weber's great contributions—turning on its head Marxist social analysis of religion—was the demonstration that forms of social life deeply *reflect* the decisive influence of religious belief and practice on a society. In his most notable study, *The Protestant Ethic and the Spirit of Capitalism* (1905), Weber analyzed how the Protestant ethic, which originated from the Reformation in sixteenth-century Europe, proved to be decisive in shaping the unique *spirit* of modern capitalist society. This religious ethic taught the importance of serving God in one's own vocation or work and emphasized the virtues of hard work, frugality, and the wise use of one's material resources—characteristics of modern capitalism.

*Psychology* is also a relatively recent academic study, having achieved the status of a scientific discipline only in the late nineteenth century. A noted, early explorer in this field was the American psychologist, and later philosopher, William James (1842–1910), whose *Varieties of Religious Experience* (1902) remains a classic. James explored the psychological dimensions of such religious phenomena as conversion, mysticism, and saintliness. Interest in this type of psychological research on religious experience soon was, in the popular mind, outstripped by the new explorations in psychotherapy, especially in the work of its best-known practitioners, *Sigmund Freud* (1856–1939) and Carl Jung (1875–1961). We will discuss Jung's understanding of the religious aspects of the human psyche, in Chapter 3.

Freud's psychological studies of religion—such as *Totem and Taboo* (1913) and *Moses and Monotheism* (1938)—were applications of his famous theory of the **Oedipus Complex** to primal religious history and institutions. Today scholars consider the scholarship in these books as questionable and the theories there offered equally dubious. However, Freud's theory of religious belief and behavior "as born of man's need to make his helplessness tolerable" and his view of humanity's tendency to anthropomorphize the powers of nature and spiritual experience in order to enter into relations with them need to be taken seriously. While not convincing as generalized explanations of religion, they do explain some forms of religious experience. Freud's view of religion is, however, fundamentally negative; he sees religion as rooted in human neuroses and calls religious beliefs "illusions, fulfillments of the oldest, strongest and most urgent wishes of mankind."[11]

Many of the more recent experimental-empirical psychological studies have pointed to the more positive and constructive aspects of religious life. An illustration is the work of *Gordan Allport,* especially his classic study of religion and prejudice in the United States. It was generally accepted as a fact that churchgoers were more prejudiced than non-churchgoers regarding ethnicity and race. Allport's several studies demonstrated that his was too simplistic a judgment. His research concludes that churchgoing has many motivations. There are those whose religion is what he call *extrinsic.* These churchgoers find religion *useful,* providing things such as solace, sociability, and social status. However, there are other churchgoers whose religious orientation is *intrinsic;* and these individuals have internalized their religion so that it is their "master motive." Such persons authentically *live* their religion. Allport found that persons with an extrinsic orientation more often tended to hold bigoted views while those persons with an intrinsic commitment to their religion more often exhibited ethnic and racial tolerance. Studies such as Allport's are valuable since they can warn us against too-simple conclusions about a subject such as religious belief and prejudice, or nonbelief and prejudice. Complex factors—social, psychological, geographic, economic, as well as religion—play a significant role in shaping a person's personality and beliefs.

## Philosophy

The philosophical scrutiny of religion is one of the oldest and most instructive ways of examining religious experience and belief. At least since the time of Plato (427?–347? B.C.), philosophers have reflected on religious stories and beliefs and have sought to establish their logical status, their meaning, and their truth.

The relationship between philosophy and religion has, however, varied significantly from century to century and from culture to culture. In India, philosophy emerged from and has remained intimately associated with historical developments in Hinduism. The same was true, at least until recently, in South and East Asia with regard to Buddhism and Confucianism. In the

West, from the appearance of the Christian Platonist Origen in the second century C.E. to the time of Thomas Aquinas (1225–1274), philosophy played the role of handmaiden to religion. By this we mean that the claims of Jewish, Christian, and Islamic revelation were, in part, justified and defended by appeals to the doctrines of the ancient philosophers themselves. Thomas Aquinas, for example, used the language and concepts derived from Aristotle's philosophy to mount his proofs for the existence of God.

Since the seventeenth century, philosophy has, not infrequently, been put to a different but, nonetheless, powerful service of religion. It can be called **agnosticism** in the service of **fideism,** that is, to question knowledge so as to allow a place for faith. The philosopher Immanuel Kant (1724–1804) supports this position in the celebrated preface to his *Critique of Pure Reason,* where he remarks that his task is "to deny knowledge in order to make room for faith." Modern critical philosophy, in its uncompromising scrutiny of the nature of reason, often has demonstrated the limits of rationality; that is, reason pushed far enough often reveals its own boundaries and contradictions.

By early in the twentieth century, philosophy's relation to religion was neither that of handmaiden nor that of philosophical skeptic making room for faith. The philosophical scrutiny of religion became more limited, analyzing the uses of religious language to test its logical status and meaning, as well as its claims to genuine knowledge and truth. It asked whether a particular religious expression has the status of a factual assertion, is simply performing an action ("I pronounce you husband and wife"), or is evoking the emotions. Philosophers believed that many problems and obscurities in religion are related to confusing these distinct uses of language. This philosophical clarification of religious discourse aimed to be neutral but, obviously, challenged conventional religious belief if, for example, a certain purported religious assertion of fact failed to pass the analytical test.

To illustrate this type of philosophical analysis of religion, we look at one philosopher's use of what is called the *falsification principle* to test the meaningfulness of certain religious *assertions.* Anthony Flew formulates the principle as follows:

> Suppose that we are in doubt as to what someone who gives vent to an utterance is asserting, or suppose that, more radically, we are skeptical as to whether he is really asserting anything at all, one way of trying to understand his utterance is to attempt to find what he would regard as counting against, or as being incompatible with, its truth.[12]

If *nothing* is incompatible with the truth of a statement, then, Flew argues, the statement does not assert anything. In other words, if there is nothing an assertion denies, then there is nothing that it asserts either. It really is not an *assertion* at all. Flew applies this principle to the claims or statements of theists who freely assert that "God has a plan" or that "God loves us." Flew inquires as to what would have to occur or have occurred to falsify such *factual* claims. If "God loves us" is made compatible with *any* present or *any* possible state of affairs, then, Flew insists, since nothing is incompatible with the statement, that is, does not deny anything, *nothing possible could happen* to entitle one to say, "God does not love us." Since "God loves us" is *not* falsifiable, it is not a real *factual* assertion at all. It may only be an emotional feeling or one of Freud's illusions based on a need or a hope, but it is not a fact.

More recently, philosophers have become critical of this type of religious language analysis practiced by Flew and others, the reason being that their analysis presupposes a rather narrow scientific understanding of what constitutes "facts" and true knowledge. Influenced by the work of the philosopher Ludwig Wittgenstein, philosophers today recognize that there are plural forms of discourse: scientific, moral, artistic, religious. And the *meaning* of a word is dependent on its particular use. Theistic language, for example, is a long-established form of discourse and conveys many clear meanings to those who participate in this theistic form of language and life. To participate in a particular form of life and language, whether it be scientific, moral, or religious, carries with it a certain *ultimacy* based on certain foundational or basic beliefs that constitute what is intelligible, compelling, and true. In the case of religion, one could say that the theist, the atheist, and the polytheist simply hold certain "basic beliefs" and forms of life. Wittgenstein points out that the religious belief in a Last Judgment may not appear a "reasonable" belief, but neither is it unreasonable to the theist. Why? Because its justifications (or "reasons") are not the same as scientific meteorological evidence that it will rain tomorrow. Nor is belief in a Last Judgment a blunder or mistake for, as Wittgenstein contents, "whether a thing is a blunder or not—it is a blunder in a particular system."[13] It is *within*, say, a science or a religion that beliefs and actions are to be judged logical or illogical. Not only philosophers but many other students of religion (for example, historians and anthropologists) often try to adhere to this interpretive principle. This leads us to consideration of another, and final, academic discipline widely used in the study of religion.

## Phenomenology

One of the recent and, in some respects, most illuminating approach to the study of religion is the *phenomenological method*. The word derives from the Greek *phainomenon*, meaning "that which appears." Phenomenology originated in the philosophical movement associated with Edmund Husserl (1859–1938). Husserl sought to concentrate on the data of experience as it directly presents itself to human consciousness. He was not concerned with explaining experience, for example, sociologically or psychologically, but with rigorous *description* only. He introduced the concept of *epoche* (from the Greek verb *epecho*, "I hold back"), or suspension of judgment, to indicate the "bracketing" from inquiry all attempts at explanation or all philosophical or theological questions of a phenomenon's truth. For example, the question to be inquired of in phenomenology is not "Does God exist?" or "When does belief in monotheism arise?" but, rather, "How is God present to human consciousness? What forms or characteristics do the experience of God exhibit?"

The goal of phenomenology is to portray religion in its own terms as a unique expression, a reality not to be reduced to or explained in other—for example, psychological or sociological—terms. To avoid intruding judgments of value or truth into this descriptive task, the phenomenologist must remain detached and impartial. Yet such insightful description and interpretation require a genuine feel for and empathy with religious experience. Phenomenology thus represents the effort to *reexperience* a certain religious phenomenon's essential character or structure. Phenomenology is, then, a study of the *morphology* (the structures or forms) of religion as manifested in and across different cultures and temporal periods. The forms that are studied vary, depending on each scholar's particular interest; they might be creation myths, rites of sacrifice, prayers, or forms of religious leadership. Parts II and III of this book undertake to exemplify such a comparative typology of universal or classic forms of religious experience, belief, and practice.

## Interpreting and Explaining Religion

We briefly explored the question of whether the student of religion can truly understand a religion from the perspective of an outside observer. We asked whether a convinced believer is capable of achieving the necessary empathy to do justice to another, foreign religion or, indeed, is able to see her or his own religion with sufficient objectivity. These questions touch on a related set of issues that are of current interest among scholars of religion. The issues have to do both with the role of understanding or interpretation and the role of explanation in the scholarly study of religion. These two topics frequently pit scholars in the humanistic-interpretive disciplines (literary, historical, and phenomenological studies) against those in the social sciences (anthropology, psychology) who often seek to apply the methods and criteria of the natural sciences. We close the discussion of *how* one goes about the study of religion with a brief analysis of these issues.

Religious experience and meanings are expressed and communicated through symbolic sounds and gestures, ritual dramas, architecture, and sacred texts. But these sources require an interpreter to convey the often richly complex and often mysterious meanings. The act or science of interpretation is called **hermeneutics** (from the Greek verb *hermeneuein*, "to interpret"). The interpreter of these various sources uses all the data and methods at hand, including those methods described in this chapter. But as we have seen, reading-off the meaning of a sacred text, for example, is not as simple as it might at first appear. Hermeneutics has to do, then, with the presuppositions of interpretation and understanding. It asks, what is required—what preconditions are necessary—to make the interpretation of these human cultural expressions possible and valid? Can we assume a commonality of human life that makes cross-cultural understanding and interpretation possible? Are the methods applied in the interpretation of these human cultural forms (such as religious rituals and texts) distinct from those applied in the natural sciences?

The first scholar to probe these questions deeply and systematically was the German philosopher and intellectual historian Wilhelm Dilthey (1833–1911). He sought to establish the foundations and methods for the study of those expressions of the human spirit that he believed were not subject or reducible to the laws and explanations of the natural sciences. For Dilthey, expressions of the human spirit reveal intentions, purposes, and meanings, knowledge of which requires *understanding*. This knowledge, he argued, is not reducible to scientific laws or to those modes of *explanation (Erklärung)* that are possible in the study of the nonhuman world.

What Dilthey proposed was a kind of imaginative reexperience or empathetic identification that results in a type of descriptive phenomenology of these human literary, artistic, or religious expressions. Human life and history, in its various manifestations, can thus be understood through these objectified forms—and they can open up for us new possibilities of envisioning human life. As you can see, Dilthey's hermeneutical method has much in common with phenomenology. Any human meaning must, first of all, be understood in its own terms from "within."

*Mircea Eliade,* an historian of religion, is one of many phenomenologists who is critical of all efforts to explain religious phenomena in nonreligious, that is, sociological or psychological, terms. To do so, he argues, is to fail to grasp the true meaning of the religious action or belief itself. "A religious datum," he contends, "reveals its deeper meaning when it is considered on its plane of reference, and not when it is reduced to one of its secondary aspects."[14] For Eliade, religion is, first and foremost, "an experience *sui generis,* incited by man's encounter with the sacred,"[15] and is therefore irreducible.

This insistence on understanding a religion from "within" seems entirely reasonable, since it merely seeks to describe a religion in terms of its own unique self-understanding. A religion does, of course, have numerous social and psychological meanings and functions, but for the believer it is also something more. The "inside" believer's and the "outside" observer's understanding therefore will likely differ at crucial points. As an anthropologist observes,

> As far as a study of religion as a factor in social life is concerned, it may make little difference whether an anthropologist is a theist or an atheist, since in either case he can only take into account what he can observe. But if either [the believer or non-believer] attempts to go further than this each must pursue a different path. The non-believer seeks for some theory—biological, psychological, or sociological—which will explain the illusion; the believer seeks rather to understand the manner in which a people conceive of a reality and their relation to it.[16]

The point is that a social or psychological explanation cannot *in itself* provide a complete *understanding* of religion, since it *explains* religion *only* as a social or psychic fact—and that may not be adequate. Explanation is, by its very nature, the attempt to reduce manifold phenomena to a more unified, inclusive, elementary theory or explanatory scheme. But, in doing this, it should not falsify the data of investigation.

Understanding must, then, be a precondition of explanation. However, that is not the end of the matter. We must be alert to the possibility that the "insider's" understanding may itself be partial, or distorted, or simply wrong. Furthermore, there are many reasons why persons exhibit specific forms of religious activity, and some of these may not only be unknown to the person but also purely secular, involving economic or social status, geographic coincidence, or psychic needs. Efforts to provide historical and social-scientific explanations of these forms of religious life cannot simply be dismissed or ignored. We have seen in the analysis of the various methods used in the study of religion that they are capable of explaining a great deal about various aspects of religious behavior.

It is not a question, then, of understanding *or* explanation but rather whether the explanation offered is partial, complete, or unjustifiably *reductionistic*. The distinction between **descriptive** and **explanatory reduction** is helpful here. Descriptive reduction is simply a failure to "identify an emotion, practice, or experience under the description by which the subject identifies it."[17] To *describe* a religious experience, for example, in nonreligious terms is to misdescribe it. A possible legitimate *explanatory reduction*, however, might involve offering "an explanation of an experience in terms [e.g., sociological] that are not those of the subject and might not meet with [her or] his approval."[18] To confuse these two forms of reductionism is to infer that the scholar-observer must employ *only* those concepts or explanations that would meet the believer's approval, and that the latter's description of her or his experience entails a compelling explanation. We would, I believe, be skeptical of a psychotic's explanation of his killing of his children as the result of a command received from God. Naturalistic explanations must not be dismissed categorically. They are crucial to an understanding of aspects of religion, if not essential components of some religions. Autobiography is, after all, often less reliable than biography.

Explanations of religion, like those in the fields of art, philosophy, or politics, will stand or fall according to how well they account for the complex data. One ought to be skeptical, however, of explanatory theories, for example, "childhood neuroses," "totemism," and so on, that claim to completely account for the complex origins or nature of religion itself, or of any religious tradition. Explanations often outrun the empirical evidence, for example, in the pseudo-historical explanations that Freud offers in *Totem and Taboo*.

The believer is justified in insisting, when the observer attempts to explain all of religious belief and practice in nonreligious terms, that the burden of proof is on the person offering such a comprehensive and self-sufficient explanation. Religious explanations must not be ruled out of court in principle any more than should nonreligious explanations. As one scholar has insisted,

> Participant explanations must always be seen, in the first instance, as legitimate rivals to observer or causal explanations . . . [an approach] that has been revitalized and fortified by a renewed understanding of the role of the participant observer in the social studies. The point of the participant observer is, according to many sociologists, crucially significant both for the collection of data *and* for its interpretation . . . [Unless] explanations in terms of concepts internal to the group are admitted as genuine explanations one has adopted, uncritically, a philosophical reductionism.[19]

It is perfectly reasonable, however, to suggest that multiple forms of explanation are not mutually exclusive; indeed, they may be complementary. It may well be the case that in order to fully interpret a religion, both intrareligious and extrareligious explanations are required to account for the complex levels of meaning observed. As one commentator has suggested,

> If in a given field of study we cannot find a theory general enough to explain all of the relevant data we have no alternative but to proceed piecemeal. We employ a variety of theories with limited explanatory scope even if a satisfactory overarching theory of the relationship among the partial theories is lacking. The absence of a general explanatory theory of *all* the *important* aspects of religions characterizes the current situation in the history of religions. Equally characteristic, but largely ignored, is the existence of a variety of fruitful explanatory theories of a limited scope of application, each of which is capable of contributing to the overall understanding of the complexity of religious history.[20]

We can summarize our explorations in this chapter as follows. The academic study of religion is a secondary activity that attempts to discover, describe, and explain the primary expressions of the religious life of a community—its rituals, its sacred texts, its institutions, beliefs, and behavior. This second-order academic endeavor requires the use of many disciplines and methods—history; linguistic and literary scholarship; the tools of anthropological, sociological, and psychological research; philosophical analysis, phenomenology, and many subdisciplines—if we are to uncover and understand the rich complexity of meanings, functions, and developments in the history of religions, or in any single religious tradition.

What these studies reveal is the universal and apparently enduring character of religious belief and behavior in human life. They also help us to appreciate how deeply embedded religions are in their social, cultural, and historical contexts, and that religious belief and practice cannot easily be severed from those contexts if we are to understand them in their many aspects. Religions are, then, holistic organisms that interact collaboratively with their culture and, in important ways, reflect their cultural milieu. Religion and culture are like soul and body, a psychosomatic unity. This, of course, has both positive and negative consequences—like any great treasure enveloped in an earthen vessel. Religions have been, and are today, not only the instruments of transcendent insight and supreme good but also of horrendous evil. They liberate our souls, raise us to heights of moral and spiritual wisdom and sanctity—but they are also capable of enslaving the human spirit, and legitimizing and sanctifying racial, ethnic, and sexual prejudice, hatred, and repression.

The academic study of religion can help us to see religion "whole," in its heights and depths—its inhumane and dark side as well as its human and sublime side. These scholarly disciplines also can help us as "insiders" to see aspects of our own religion about which we may be ignorant or "blind," or which we wish to deny. Through empathy, these studies can help us as "outsiders" to appreciate aspects of other religious traditions quite foreign to our own. They can teach us how, by an act of imagination, we can enter into, if only temporarily, an insider's perspective without actually adopting the belief of that insider. Finally, the several academic disciplines can teach us to understand that religions are complex entities that can be studied on different levels or from different perspectives, and that this can allow us to understand why they may appear so very different from different perspectives. Each of these perspectives, though partial, may provide us with insight, and from this we may learn some important things about the complexity of religion in the life of both individuals and groups.

## NOTES

1. Eric Sharpe, *Understanding Religion* (New York, 1983), 46–47.
2. John Hick, *An Interpretation of Religion* (New Haven, Conn., 1989), 4. See also, Robert McDermott, "The Religion-Game: Some Family Resemblances," *Journal of the American Academy of Religion* 6 (1970).
3. Frederick Ferré, "The Definition of Religion," *Journal of the American Academy of Religion* 38 (1970): 5.
4. J. Milton Yinger, *The Scientific Study of Religion* (New York, 1970), 7.
5. Clifford Geertz, "Religion as a Cultural System," in *Reader in Comparative Religion: An Anthropological Approach,* William A. Lessa and Evon Z. Vogt, eds. (New York, 1979), 79–80.
6. Emile Durkheim, *The Elementary Forms of Religious Life,* trans. Joseph Ward Swain (New York, 1963), 47.
7. For the general idea of this scheme, I am indebted to Winston King, *Introduction to Religion: A Phenomenological Approach* (New York, 1968).
8. For this discussion I am dependent on Peter Winch, "Understanding a Primitive Society," in *Rationality,* ed. Bryan Wilson (Oxford, 1970).
9. Peter Winch, *The Idea of a Social Science* (London, 1958), 87–88.
10. Philip Clayton, *Explanation from Physics to Theology: An Essay in Rationality and Religion* (New Haven, Conn., 1989), 161–62.
11. Sigmund Freud, *The Future of an Illusion,* tr. J. Strachey (London, 1927), 14, 26.

12. Anthony Flew and Alaisdair McIntyre, eds., *New Essays in Philosophical Theology* (London, 1955), 98.
13. Ludwig Wittgenstein, *Lectures and Conversations on Aesthetics, Psychology and Religious Belief,* ed. C. Barrett (Oxford, 1966), 89.
14. Mircea Eliade, *The Quest: History and Meaning in Religion* (Chicago, 1969), 6.
15. Ibid., 25.
16. E. E. Evans-Pritchard, *Theories of Primitive Religion* (Oxford, 1965), 121.
17. Wayne Proudfoot, *Religious Experience* (Berkeley, Calif., 1985), 195.
18. Ibid., 197.
19. Donald Wiebe, "Explanation and the Scientific Study of Religion," *Religion* 5 (1985), 39, 45.
20. John Y. Fenton, "Reduction in the Study of Religion," *Soundings* 53 (Spring 1970), 64.

## KEY WORDS

propitiation
theism
monotheism
polytheism
genetic fallacy
substantive and functional
   definitions of religion
cosmology
self-transcendence
existential
primal
theology
literary criticism
historiography

anthropology
Emile Durkheim
functionalism
sociology
Max Weber
psychology
Sigmund Freud
Gordon Allport
intrinsic and extrinsic religion
the falsification principle
the phenomenological method
hermeneutics
Mircea Eliade
descriptive and explanatory reduction

## REVIEW QUESTIONS

1. How would you have defined *religion* prior to reading this chapter? What factors do you think influenced your choice of this definition?
2. Why does the author think he needs to provide a working definition of *religion?*
3. According to the author, what are some of the problems with the definitions listed on page 5? Do you see these as problems?
4. What does the author think are the characteristics of an adequate definition of *religion?* Do you agree? Why or why not?
5. What is the working definition of *religion* proposed by the author?
6. Why does the author think human beings are religious? Can you think of other reasons? Do you think humans are inherently religious?

7. Summarize the five reasons that the author gives for studying religion. Can you think of other reasons?

8. Where would you place yourself on the spectrum of positions between a naïve commitment on the one extreme and the claim to uncommitted objectivity on the other? Why are these issues important for the study of religion?

9. Why may the study of theology not be the same as the study of religion? What conditions would be necessary for theology to be recognized as a scholarly field of study?

10. Why does the study of religion make use of so many different methods and academic disciplines?

11. What questions does the literary scholar of religious texts seek to answer? What are some of the questions that the historian of religion might attempt to answer?

12. Describe *functionalism* as a method of investigation of religion in anthropology and sociology. Try to give illustrations of a functional analysis of religion.

13. What kinds of questions interest the philosopher of religion? Describe the "falsification principle" as it is applied by Anthony Flew in his philosophical analysis of religion.

14. Describe some of the features of Freud's psychological interpretation of religious belief. Summarize the conclusions of Gordon Allport's empirical study of religion with regard to ethnic and racial prejudice.

15. Characterize the phenomenological method in the study of religion. How does it differ from the work of the sociologist or the philosopher?

## SUGGESTIONS FOR FURTHER READING

*For good analyses of the problem of defining and explaining the complex phenomenon of religion, the following studies are recommended:*

ALSTON, WILLIAM P. "Religion." In *The Encyclopedia of Philosophy*, vol. 7, ed. Paul Edwards. New York: Macmillan and Free Press, 1967.

BYRNE, PETER, AND PETER CLARKE. *Definition and Explanation in Religion*. Basingstoke, England: Macmillan, 1993.

GEERTZ, CLIFFORD. "Religion as a Cultural System." *The Interpretation of Cultures*. New York: Basic Books, 1973.

SPIRO, MELFORD E. "Religion: Problems of Definition and Explanation." In *Anthropological Approaches to the Study of Religion*, ed. Michael Banton. London: Tavistock Press, 1966.

*For interesting accounts of religion as intrinsic to what it means to be human, the following essays are recommended:*

BELL, DANIEL. "The Return of the Sacred." In *The Winding Passage*. New York: Basic Books, 1981.

TILLICH, PAUL. "Religion as a Dimension in Man's Spiritual Life." In *Theology of Culture*. New York: Oxford University Press, 1964.

*For interesting but advanced discussions of the problems involved in understanding another culture or religion, see the following:*

TAMBIAH, S. J. *Magic, Science, Religion, and the Scope of Rationality*. Cambridge: Cambridge University Press, 1990.

WILSON, BRYAN, ed. *Rationality.* Oxford: Oxford University Press, 1970.

*For an overview of various approaches to the study of religion in the scientific disciplines see the following:*

CAPPS, WALTER H. *Religious Studies: The Making of a Discipline.* Minneapolis, Minn.: Fortress Press, 1995.

CONNOLLY, PETER, ed. *Approaches to the Study of Religion.* London and New York: Cassell, 1999.

ELIADE, MIRCEA, ed. *The Encyclopedia of Religion.* 16 vols. New York: Macmillan, 1987. Excellent articles on "The Study of Religion," "Anthropology and Religion," "Philosophy of Religion," "Phenomenology of Religion," "Psychology of Religion," "Sociology of Religion," and so on.

PALS, DANIEL L. *Seven Theories of Religion.* New York: Oxford University Press, 1996. Excellent analysis and critique of Tylor and Frazer, Freud, Durkheim, Marx, Eliade, Evans-Pritchard, and Geertz. Also good on issues of interpretation and explanation.

SHARPE, ERIC J. *Comparative Religion: A History.* New York: Scribner's, 1975.

WAARDENBURG, JACQUES. *Classical Approaches to the Study of Religion* 2 vols. Berlin and New York: Mouton, 1983. Readings and commentary on important scholars.

*For short articles on the textual and literary criticism of the Hebrew Bible and the New Testament, see*

HAYES, JOHN H. ed. *Dictionary of Biblical Interpretation.* Vol. 2. Nashville, Tenn.: Abingdon Press, 1999, 541–551. Also, see articles and current bibliographies on Canonical, Form, Literary, Redaction, and Reader-Response Criticism.

*For a collection of essays by anthropologists and an analysis of themes and theorists in the anthropological study of religion, see the following:*

ELIADE, MIRCEA. See above.

LESSA, WILLIAM A., AND EVON Z. VOGT, eds. *Reader in Comparative Religion: An Anthropological Approach.* New York: Harper & Row, 1965.

MORRIS, BRIAN. *Anthropological Studies of Religion.* Cambridge, England: Cambridge University Press, 1987. A useful textbook.

*For essays on typical themes in the sociology of religion and works by both classical and contemporary sociologists of religion, see the following:*

BERGER, PETER. *The Sacred Canopy* New York: Doubleday, 1967.

ELIADE, MIRCEA. See above.

McGUIRE, MEREDITH. *Religion: The Social Context.* Belmont, Calif.: Wadsworth, 1994. A good introductory text.

WEBER, MAX. *The Sociology of Religion.* Boston: Beacon Press, 1963.

WILSON, BRYAN. *Religion in Sociological Perspective.* Oxford: Oxford University Press, 1982. Emphasis is on modern religious sectarianism and secularization.

*For a recent work in the psychology of religion and a comprehensive textbook on the psychology of religion see the following:*

BATSON, D. D. AND W. L. VENTIS. *Religion and the Individual.* Oxford: Oxford University Press, 1993.

WULFF, D. M. *Psychology of Religion, Classic and Contemporary Views.* New York: John Wiley and Sons, 1991.

*For the philosophical scrutiny of religion, see the following:*

CHARLESWORTH, M. J. *Philosophy of Religion: The Historic Approaches.* New York: Herder and Herder, 1972.

HICK, JOHN. *Philosophy of Religion.* Englewood Cliffs, N.J.: Prentice Hall, 1990.

PETERSON, M., W. HASKER, B. REICHENBACH, AND D. BASINGER, eds. *Reason and Religious Belief: An Introduction to the Philosophy of Religion.* Oxford: Oxford University Press, 1991.

*For examples of the comparative-phenomenological method and approach to the study of religion, see the following:*

ALLEN, DOUGLAS. "Phenomenology of Religion." In Mircea Eliade, ed. *The Encyclopedia of Religion,* 11. New York: Macmillan, 1987.

BLEEKER, C. J. "The Phenomenological Method." In *The Sacred Bridge: Researches into the Nature and Structure of Religion.* Leiden, Holland: E. J. Brill, 1971.

ELIADE, MIRCEA. *Patterns in Comparative Religion.* New York: Sheed and Ward, 1958.

VAN DER LEEUW, GERARDUS. *Religion in Essence and Manifestation.* New York: Harper and Row, 1963.

*For a discussion of issues in the interpretation and explanation of religion, see the following:*

CLAYTON, PHILIP. *Explanation from Physics to Theology: An Essay in Rationality and Religion.* New Haven, Conn.: Yale University Press, 1989. Advanced critical discussion of theories of interpretation and explanation.

PALS, DANIEL. See above.

PREUS, J. SAMUEL. *Explaining Religion: Criticism and Theory from Bodin to Freud.* New Haven, Conn.: Yale University Press, 1987. Advanced study.

# Part II

## *Universal Forms of Religious Experience and Expression*

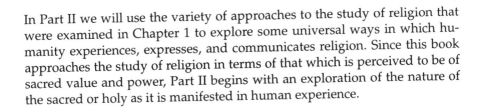

In Part II we will use the variety of approaches to the study of religion that were examined in Chapter 1 to explore some universal ways in which humanity experiences, expresses, and communicates religion. Since this book approaches the study of religion in terms of that which is perceived to be of sacred value and power, Part II begins with an exploration of the nature of the sacred or holy as it is manifested in human experience.

# 2

# *The Sacred and the Holy*

~~~~~~~~~~~~~~~~~~~~~~~~~~~~~~~~~~~~~~~~~~~~~~~~~~~

## *Overview*

When the scientific study of religion was fully established in the latter decades of the nineteenth century, one of its principal concerns was to trace religion back to its earliest expression in history. A number of influential theories about the origin of religion were proposed by scholars. Because the often-scanty evidence did not go back very far into human origins and was not capable of being applied universally to very different cultures, the search for *the* origin of religion soon lost credibility and died out.

It is clear, however, that the search for origins was closely related to the question of religion's essence. For example, when scholars sought the origin of religion in **animism** or **totemism,** or when Sigmund Freud traced the source of religion to infantile projection, these scholars were, at the same time, concerned with what they thought they had discovered to be the root of religious experience. This interest in the root nature of religion—that is, what, if anything, is its common, universal essence—remains a concern of scholars today. In Chapter 1, we encountered some of the difficulties in attempting general definitions of religion. Despite this problem, most scholars today agree that religion is a system of activities and beliefs directed toward that which is perceived to be sacred or of ultimate value and power. Such things—be they spiritual beings, cosmic laws, geographic places, persons, ideals, or ideologies—are thereby set apart as sacred or of ultimate significance.

Here we will discuss the sacred or the holy as the root of religious experience and practice. We will explore the nature of sacred power and the ambiguity of the sacred as **taboo** (from the Polynesian word *tapu,* meaning "to make separate or reserve"), that is, as the source of wonder and purity as well as of fear and danger. We will also examine the psychological or personal experience uniquely associated with the encounter with the holy, and how the sacred, or holy, is manifested in special places and times. Finally, we will explore a family resemblance between religion as the response to what is perceived as sacred and religion as commitment to what is held to be of ultimate meaning and value or as the source of ultimate transformation.

## The Concept of Sacred Power

In his phenomenological description of religion in *Religion in Essence and Manifestation,* the Dutch scholar Gerardus van der Leeuw points to the preconceptual experience of *sacred power* as the root of all religion. "The first affirmation we can make about the Object of Religion," he writes, "is that it is a highly exceptional and extremely impressive 'Other.' . . . This Object is a departure from all that is usual and familiar; and this again is the consequence of the Power it generates."[1]

In primal societies, almost any natural object or human artifact can be the bearer of sacred power. "During an important expedition, for example, an African negro steps on a stone and cries out: 'Ha! are you there?' and takes it with him to bring him luck. The stone, as it were, gives a hint that it is powerful."[2] The important role that **fetishes, amulets, *totems, icons,*** idols, as well as sacred personages, sanctuaries, temples, and sacraments play in the history of religion, points to them as special vehicles or bearers of sacred power. Certain persons—such as the king—and special times—such as the New Year's Festival—or specific activities—such as planting or sexual relations— are regarded as set apart and endowed with unique power, and therefore objects of awe, fear, and **taboo.** The distinction between such a uniquely effective power and that which is relatively powerless is, according to van der Leeuw, what characterizes the contrast between the sacred and the profane. It is *power* that creates for the sacred a special place and value all its own.

## The Ambivalence of Sacred Power

A unique characteristic of sacred power is the fact that it evokes a mixed response. A person's impulse, in the face of the awesome and mysterious, is instinctively one of avoidance; and yet the sacred possesses a magnetic attraction as well. "In the human soul," van der Leeuw writes,

> . . . power awakens a profound feeling of awe which manifests itself both as fear and as being attracted. There is no religion whatever without terror, but equally none without love. . . . Physical shuddering, ghostly horror, fear, sudden terror,

reverence, humility, adoration, profound apprehension, enthusiasm—all these lie *in nuce* within the awe experienced in the presence of Power.[3]

This ambivalent quality of sacred power especially needs to be underlined today, since modern life has tamed sacred power into something benign and benevolent. Modern society has little sense of the terror or dread of the sacred. In traditional societies, however, sacred power always shows itself ambiguously, simultaneously as awe and aversion, purity and danger. The sacred thus represents the two poles of a single dreadful domain: as both sanctity and defilement. The French sociologist Roger Caillois points out that the Greek word for "defilement" also means "the sacrifice which cleanses the defilement." So it is in primal cultures that the taboo experienced as awe in the presence of sanctity is not distinguished from the fear inspired by defilement. The sacred both fascinates and repels, eliciting feelings of both awe and aversion.

Caillois suggests that religion (that is, the realm of the sacred) is rooted in a primordial dual motive: the acquisition of purity and the elimination of defilement.

> Purity is acquired by submitting to a set of ritualistic observances. The point above all is to become separated from the profane world in order to make possible the penetration of the sacred world without peril. The human [profane] must be abandoned before the divine can be reached. That is to say, rites of **catharsis** are to the highest degree negations or abstentions. They consist of temporary renunciations of the varied activities typical of the profane world. . . . It is literally necessary to be purified in order to be worthy of approaching the domain of the Gods.[4]

A state of purity detached from the profane cannot, of course, be maintained for very long. Life requires a return to the profane, a world incompatible with sanctity. Hence, on leaving the sacred region, sacred vestments—for example, those of a priest—must be removed, or one must take a ritual bath, leaving the pure and consecrated life behind before emerging again into the region of the profane. This *must* be done, for contact with the sacred can also expose the profane community to the danger of supernatural defilement. Therefore, in many societies, holy persons such as kings, priests, or **shamans** must be kept from other members of the community lest the people be defiled. In Japan, for example, the utensils used in eating by the divine Emperor were destroyed, lest someone using them become infected.

> Everything that is touched by a holy person is consecrated by this very act and can only be used by them. . . . Contact with it is fatal. The divine and the accursed, consecration and defilement, have exactly the same effects upon profane objects. They render them untouchable, withdraw them from circulation, and communicate to them their formidable qualities.[5]

## The Holy as *Mysterium Tremendum* and *Fascinans*

The primal experience of sacred power with the accompanying feelings of awe, fear, purity, and danger, is pursued with great psychological insight by *Rudolf Otto* in his classic and influential study, *The Idea of the Holy*. Otto regards the holy as an experience peculiar to religion. He acknowledges that the holy often is associated with morality and that inevitably it does become conceptualized in the form of myths and doctrines. However, in Otto's view, the holy is fundamentally a nonrational and ineffable datum of human experience. In order to isolate the holy from either ethical or theological conceptions, Otto coined the word *numinous* to describe this uniquely religious phenomenon. The word comes from the Latin *numina* and refers to those powers or spirits that Latin farmers of ancient Italy associated with special places and functions.

Since Otto regards the numinous as unique, it is not reducible to any other more primary experience. He points out that the history of religion is, from one perspective, simply the history of the ways in which the numinous experience has been expressed in myth, ritual, and doctrine.

Considered subjectively, a person's encounter with the numinous evokes a profound "creature-consciousness" or "creature-feeling." Otto describes it as the emotion of a creature "submerged and overwhelmed by its own nothingness in contrast to that which is supreme."[6] Considered as an objective reality, the numinous can be suggested only in terms of the way it grips and stirs the human mind and emotions. Otto attempts to describe the most fundamental of these affective or emotional responses by the words *mysterium tremendum* and *fascinans*. Each of these terms requires some comment.

The *mysterium* is the experience of a reality that, when encountered, is perceived as lying beyond our capacity to comprehend or conceptualize fully; it is extraordinary, unfamiliar, and therefore mysterious. It is beyond our comprehension "not only because our knowledge has certain irremovable limits, but because in it we come upon something inherently 'wholly other,' whose kind and character are incommensurable with our own. . . ."[7]

The experience of the numinous can be better understood, however, if we also grasp what Otto seeks to convey by the words *tremendum* and *fascinans*. *Tremor* denotes fear but the *tremendum* is more than fear proper. It is a feeling of peculiar dread and awe. Otto believes that religious dread lies at the root of the religious experience of the numinous. "It first begins to stir," Otto observes, "in the feeling of 'something uncanny,' 'eerie,' or 'weird.' It is this feeling which, emerging in the mind of primeval man, forms the starting-point for the entire religious development in history."[8] Religion has, of course, transcended the worship of spirits and "daemons," that is, has advanced beyond animism or the worship of nature. Nevertheless, the peculiar feeling of the "uncanny" and "aweful" tremendum survives in more sophisticated expressions of theistic religion, reflecting the transcendence, the "otherness" and sublimity of the numinous.

Otto describes two qualities of the *tremendum* in addition to the sense of awe or dread. One is the aspect of "might" or "overpoweringness," which he signifies by the term *majestas* (majesty). In the experience of "aweful majesty," the human consciousness of creature-feeling is especially vivid. Furthermore, the *tremendum* reveals itself as an "energy" that often is felt as holy "wrath." It is symbolized by such expressions as a deity's vitality, passion, might, or will.

Encounters with the numinous are experienced not only by emotions of dread, awe, majesty, and wrath. The numinous is also positively attractive, fascinating, and even intoxicating. The positive feelings accompanying this captivating side of the numinous include love, pity, mercy, joy, peace, and beatitude. While the forms of worship that issue from the experience of "awe" and "dread" would include **expiation** and propitiation, the *fascinans* provokes expressions of joyful thanksgiving, praise, and adoration.

Otto points to the universal character of the experience of the holy by citing examples from a wide range of religious traditions, as well as from art, music, and poetry. A classic example is the biblical prophet Isaiah's awesome vision of the Lord God in the Temple of Jerusalem.

1. . . . sitting upon a throne, high and lifted up, his train filled the temple.
2. Above it stood the seraphims: each one had six wings; with twain he covered his face, and with twain he covered his feet, and with twain he did fly.
3. And one cried unto another, and said, Holy, holy, holy, is the Lord of hosts: the whole earth is full of his glory.
4. And the posts of the door moved at the voice of him that cried, and the house was filled with smoke.
5. Then said I, Woe is me! for I am undone; because I am a man of unclean lips, and I dwell in the midst of a people of unclean lips: for mine eyes have seen the King, the Lord of hosts.

*—(Isaiah VI)*

A similar numinous vision was experienced by Arjuna, the Hindu warrior-hero, as recorded in the *Bhagavad-Gita,* a sacred text. The *Gita* tells the story of Arjuna's request to Krishna—the God Vishnu in human form—that he, Arjuna, be allowed to see the Supreme Being Vishnu. Arjuna's wish is granted and the following terrible and yet majestic revelation is described:

9. Thus speaking Vishnu, the great Lord of the Rule, then showed to Pritha's son [Arjuna] his sovran form supreme . . .
12. If the light of a thousand suns should of a sudden rise in the heavens, it would be like the light of that mighty being . . .
14. Thereupon [Arjuna], smitten with amazement, with hair standing on end, bowed his head, and with clasped hands spoke to the God . . .
17. I behold Thee bearing diadem, mace, and disc, massed in radiance, on all sides glistening, hardly discernible, shining round about as gleaming fire and sun, immeasurable . . .

**20.** . . . Seeing this Thy fearful and wonderful form, O great-hearted one, the three-fold world quakes.

—*(Bhagavad-Gita, Ch. II)*

The experience of the holy often takes place in encounters with nature, especially in the silent presence of great mountains or the sea. It is a theme found in the writings of many nature mystics, in Romantic poetry, and in Chinese landscape painting. Otto cites the English art critic John Ruskin, who recounts the numinous experiences he had as a youth:

> . . . Although there was no definite religious sentiment mingled with it, there was a continual perception of Sanctity in the whole of nature, from the slightest thing to the vastest; an instinctive awe, mixed with delight; an indefinable thrill. . . . I could only feel this perfectly when I was alone; and then it would often make me shiver from head to foot with the joy and fear of it . . . when I first saw the swell of distant land against the sunset, or the first low broken wall, covered with mountain moss. I cannot in the least describe the feeling; but I do not think this is my fault nor that of the English language. . . . The joy in nature seemed to me to come of a sort of heart-hunger, satisfied with the presence of a Great and Holy Spirit. . . .[9]

From the first stirrings of primitive "daemonic dread" to the most sophisticated revelations of saints and mystics, the experience of the numinous remains, Otto insists, a unique, original experience. Our sense experience supplies the occasion for numinous experience; the experience itself does not arise *out* of sense experience but only by its means. In the evolution of the world's religions there is, of course, a process by which the numinous is variously named and conceptualized. Yet even in the most sublime flights of spiritual vision, the element of the wholly other, the nonrational and mysterious, is retained. Indeed, it is intensified, as an Isaiah or a Ruskin testifies. Nevertheless, the growth of human rationality is accompanied by a "schematization" of the nonrational *mysterium*, as is seen in the development of theological and moral concepts and systems. Otto points out that the *tremendum*, for example, "is schematized by means of the rational ideas of justice, moral will, and the exclusion of what is opposed to morality; and schematized thus it becomes the holy 'wrath of God.'" Similarly, the alluring *fascinans* "is schematized by means of the ideas of goodness, mercy, love, and, so schematized, becomes all that we mean by Grace. . . ."[10]

Otto cites the doctrine of atonement, a theme found in numerous religions, as an especially good example of this rationalizing process. Atonement is simply a more rational way of expressing the primal human feeling of the need for a shield or shelter from a sacred taboo.

As the human religious consciousness is filled out more and more with rational and moral elements, the nonrational primal experience of the holy may appear to be eclipsed, but it is never lost. If it were, according to Otto, the religious sense itself would be lost. Thus, Otto insists that the element of the nonrational numinous is always retained because it is the very essence of religion. "Revelation," he writes,

> does not mean a mere passing over into the intelligible and comprehensible. Something may be profoundly and intimately known in feeling for the bliss it brings or the agitation it produces, and yet the understanding may find no concept for it. To *know* and to *understand conceptually* are two different things.[11]

"Buddhist Monastery by Stream and Mountains." The great landscape painters of the Sung dynasty in China evoked the presence of sacred space and the infinite in their paintings of mountains, water, and mist. (*Source:* Courtesy of The Cleveland Museum of Art, gift of Katherine Holden Thayer.)

## Sacred Space and Sacred Time

*Mircea Eliade,* the historian of religion and phenomenologist, acknowledges Otto's contribution to an understanding of the numinous experience. However, he is critical of Otto's concentration on the psychological or emotional qualities of the numinous, such as the experience of the *tremendum.* Eliade wants to begin without any preconceptions about the qualities of the sacred and to explore how the sacred is manifested in the history of religions. He begins, therefore, with the simpler and more neutral distinction popularized by Emile Durkheim: the fundamental contrast between the sacred and the profane.

According to Eliade, this contrast represents the two fundamental modes of being in the world assumed by humankind throughout history. First, and most basically, the sacred always manifests itself as something nonordinary and thus wholly distinct from what is profane, common, or simply utilitarian. At the same time, Eliade points out that *anything*—a stone, a tree, or a building—can be set apart as disclosing the sacred. Both natural objects and human artifacts are capable of and have been transformed from a common use to a sacred presence. Eliade calls this *act of manifesting* the sacred a *hierophany* (from the Greek *hieros,* meaning "sacred," and *phanein,* meaning to "appear").

> It is a fitting term, because it does not imply anything further; it expresses no more than is implicit in its etymological content, i.e., *that something sacred shows itself to us.* It could be said that the history of religions—from the most primitive to the most highly developed—is constituted by a great number of hierophanies. . . .[12]

Eliade's extraordinary knowledge of the history of religions, including little-known primal and archaic religions, has enabled him to compare a rich variety of spatial and temporal manifestations of the sacred and to comment on their significance. For the religious, space is not uniform; some places are qualitatively different from others. Eliade points to the experience of Moses on Mount Sinai and then comments on its significance:

> "Draw not hither," says the Lord to Moses; "put off thy shoes from off thy feet, for the place whereon thou standest is holy ground" (Exodus 3:5). There is, then, a sacred space, and hence a strong, significant space; there are other spaces that are not sacred and so are without structure or consistency, amorphous. Nor is this all. For religious man, this . . . finds expression in the experience of an opposition between space that is sacred—the only *real* and *real-ly* existing space—and all other space, the formless expanse surrounding it.[13]

The break between sacred and profane space is what actually founds or establishes a world because sacred space reveals what the poet T. S. Eliot called "the fixed point of the turning world," a central axis or pivot around which the human world revolves. The revelation or discovery of a fixed point of sacred space is equivalent, **ontologically** as well as psychologically, to founding or creating a world. Through it, an orientation is given in the chaos of ordinary, profane space. Eliade points out, furthermore, that it is not possible to live in a completely profane, desacralized world. The setting apart and sacralizing of certain places is borne out in the behavior of modern, secular individuals as well as secular societies.

> There are, for example, privileged places, qualitatively different from all others—a man's birthplace, or the scenes of first love. . . . Even for the most frankly nonreligious man, all these places still retain an exceptional, a unique quality; they are the "holy places" of his private universe, as if it were in such spots that he has received that revelation of a reality *other* than that in which he participates through his ordinary daily life.[14]

Sacred space implies a hierophany, an opening to the holy or divine, a place where communication with sacred power is made possible. Eliade refers to such space as an ***axis mundi,*** the center of the world. It is the point around which, symbolically speaking, the world rotates. The founding of sanctuaries, shrines, and temples are illustrations of such sacred openings. The biblical story of Jacob's dream at Haran is a classic example. In his dream, Jacob sees a ladder set on the earth and reaching up to heaven, with angels ascending and descending on it. The Lord then speaks to Jacob, saying, "I *am* the Lord God of Abraham thy father. . . . The land whereon thou liest, to thee will I give it, and to thy seed." When Jacob awakes, he is afraid and cries out, "How dreadful is this place! This is none other but the house of

The Ka'ba, the House of Allah, in Mecca is the principal Islamic shrine and place of Pilgrimage. It is considered the geographic and religious center of the Muslim word. (*Source:* Courtesy of Woodfin Camp and Associates, Inc.)

God, this *is* the gate of heaven." Jacob then takes the stone that he had used as a pillow and sets it up as a pillar (monument) and pours oil on top of it. He then vows that the stone "shall be God's house" and "he called the name of that place Beth-el" (Genesis 28:12–22).

Consecrating a place is equivalent to founding a world, a cosmos out of chaos. Often, however, the sacred place, be it a simple altar or an elaborate temple, represents not only an "opening" to heaven but also a reproduction, on the human scale, of the cosmos or of Creation itself. It is an *imago mundi*, an image of the original world order. The symbolism of the altar or temple is often an explicit replica of the *cosmogony*—that is, a mirror of the original act of Creation, a prototype of the work of God or the gods. This is apparent in the symbolic construction of the ancient Hindu (Vedic) fire altar, consecrated to the god Agni. The ritual erection of the altar occurs, understandably, on the taking possession of a new territory.

> The water in which the clay is mixed is assimilated to the primordial water; the clay that forms the base of the altar symbolizes the earth; the lateral walls represent the atmosphere, and so on. And the building of the altar is accompanied by songs that proclaim which cosmic region has just been created. Hence the erection of a fire altar . . . is equivalent to a cosmogony.[15]

Every breakthrough to the sacred is effected by a hierophany, symbolized, for example, by a sacred pillar, tree, mountain, altar, temple, or city, perceived as the center of the world. For Jews, such a center is Mount Zion—Jerusalem; for Christians, it is the mount at Golgotha. Islamic tradition holds that the highest place on earth is the holy *ka'ba*, the small cubic building in the Great Mosque of Mecca that houses the sacred Black Stone, because, it is claimed, the Pole star bears witness that it faces the center of Heaven. The true world—sacred space—always lies at the Center, joining heaven and earth.

## The Buddhist Stupa and Pagoda as Sacred Space

An excellent example of a sacred *axis mundi* is the Buddhist *stupa* (India and Sri Lanka) or pagoda (Burma, China, and Japan). Stupas first appear within Buddhism in India as places where the cremated remains of the Buddha were interred as relics. They functioned as **reliquaries** in homage to the Buddha and later to Buddhist holy persons. Originally, they were simple mounds surrounded by railings with four cardinal gateways. In time, they became elaborate structures and temples symbolizing, in rich variety, the Buddhist cosmos and the path to enlightenment. Every aspect of the stupa plan conveys symbolic meanings and powers.

The point on the ground selected for the center of the stupa is symbolic, at the terrestrial level, of the transcendent sacred Center. The stupa is the symbolic *omphalos*, that is, the navel of the world. The axial point of the stupa thus represents the gateway between the several planes of existence: the terrestrial, the celestial, and the infernal realms. Furthermore, the orientation of the stupa plan is determined by the movements of the sun, and it represents a geometric diagram of the cyclical movements of the sun, the Center of the cosmos.

Most strikingly, the stupa is planned as a **mandala.** The Buddhist *mandala* is a circle, symbolizing the perfection of Buddhahood, inscribed within a square drawn in bright colors on the earth or as a painting on cloth or paper. The square of the *mandala* is subdivided into smaller squares, all expressing a model of the cosmic pattern of the universe. The *mandala* is, then, a compressed image of the total cosmos. The *mandala* that is marked out on the ground where the stupa is to be erected is a symbolic representation of the spiritual meaning of the completed three-dimensional monument.

Above the stupa's foundation are terraced levels representing a variety of Buddhist faculties and powers, for example, the four types of Mindfulness and the four types of Renunciation. The terraces are topped by a hemispherical dome. The Buddhists speak of the dome as the "womb" or "embryo," or

A typical domelike stupa found in Sri Lanka. (*Source:* Courtesy of Jack Van Horn.)

Buddhist monks paying homage to Mount Fuji. Every year, thousands of Japanese pilgrams climb the sacred mountain, where it is believed the shades of ancestors dwell. (*Source:* Courtesy of Burt Glinn, Magnum Photos, Inc.)

"egg." It is the "womb of the elements," that is, the creative source and power of the universe from whence all life flows. The dome is capped by a quadrangular *harmikā* that symbolizes the eternal sacrificial altar and often contains relics. It later became associated with the Buddhist Eightfold Path (see Chapter 12). The stupa is crowned by a vertical cone-shaped spire or tower. This elongated cone is often marked with several rings or umbrella-like notches that progressively diminish toward the apex. The stupa's spire represents the tree of life or tree of enlightenment on the summit of the sacred Mount Meru inhabited by the gods. The various notches of the cone-tree correspond to certain psychic faculties or stages of consciousness on the way to enlightenment. "Just as the Phoenix rises from the ashes, so the tree of life and enlightenment grow out of the ashes of the sacrificial altar [the harmikā] which crowns the dome, the monumental world-egg and womb of a new world."[16]

In the Buddhist countries of South and East Asia, the stupa appears in a variety of regional forms. The principal feature of the stupas of Sri Lanka is the beautiful bell-shaped dome. The terrace stupas of Tibet and Nepal do not feature the dome but appear rather like terraced pyramids. Tower-shaped pagodas are common in China and Japan. Their distinctive feature is the multiple stories set off by clearly articulated roofs. But whatever their form, the stupas and pagodas of Buddhist Asia represent the *axis mundi*, the sacred tree or cosmic mountain, that Center that joins earth and the realm of the transcendent and the real.

### Mount Zion as Sacred Space

In part through the stimulus of Eliade's work, scholars are now especially aware of the religious significance of geography, of space. The great geographically focused religions—such as the Egyptian, Babylonian, Indian, and Chinese—developed their mythic and ritual symbolism around the constants of their geographic space, around their sacred rivers, mountains, and cities. But sacred space also has played a formative role in the Western historical or "diasporic" religions—that is, those dispersed throughout the world—as testified to by the role of Jerusalem, Mecca, Golgotha, and Rome. Sacred mountains are especially common in the symbolism of the three Western biblical religions—Judaism, Christianity, and Islam—particularly the mountains and hills of Palestine and Arabia. It is noteworthy that the Hebrew word for mountain, *har*, appears 520 times in the Bible.

The pervasive symbolism of the cosmic mountain in Israelite and later Jewish religion can serve to illustrate the importance of geography on the religious imagination. Mountains are, of course, the nearest things to the sky and are obvious symbols of those transcendent powers "on high," that is, the gods and the dwelling place of the gods—such as the Greek Mount Olympus, the Japanese Mount Fuji, or the Indian Mount Meru. Since mountains are the abode of the gods, they are the natural places of worship. The Israelite tribes each had their shrine or sanctuary on a mountain—Dan in the north;

Schechem, Gibeon, Gilgal, and Bethel in the center of Palestine; and Hebron and Beersheba in the south. Mount Sinai, where Moses received the Law and sealed the Covenant with Israel's God, Yahweh, and Jerusalem (Mount Zion), the site of the monarchy of the great King David and the Temple, became especially sacred to Israel and to later Judaism.

The sacred mountains served the Israelites, first, as an image of security. There the people were protected from their enemies by Yahweh. But the mountains were a bulwark not only against the human enemy but also against the desolation and waste of the desert wilderness, against chaos. The mountain also symbolized authority. The Law was given to Moses on Mount Sinai, and it was on the mountains that Yahweh's spokesmen, the prophets, delivered the "Word of the Lord," God's warnings, blessings, and judgments. The antiquity, security, and authority of the mountain are joined in the image of the mountain as *axis mundi*, as the meeting place of heaven and earth and thus the sacred center, or navel, of the world. Moses goes up Mount Sinai to find God; there he receives the divine Law, which in turn creates Israel into a people bound by shared values and responsibilities.

Later, when King David brought the ark of the Covenant to **Mount Zion–Jerusalem**, it became *the* "holy mountain," a second Sinai—the *axis mundi* and center of security, authority, fertility, and blessing. Yahweh's dwelling in Jerusalem (Mount Zion) protected Israel against the encroaching powers of chaos:

> Great is YHWH and much to be praised
> In the city of our God is his holy mountain;
> The most beautiful peak, the joy of all the earth.
> Mount Zion is the heart [that is, the navel] of Zaphon
> The city of the great King.
> God is her citadel, has shown himself her bulwark. . . .
> God will make her secure forever.[17]
>
> —(*Psalm 48*)

The image of Mount Zion–Jerusalem as the Center of space is especially pronounced in later **rabbinic** literature and Jewish folklore. A famous rabbinic text maintains that

> . . . just as the navel is found in the center of the human being, so the land of Israel is found at the center of the world . . . and it is the foundation of the world. Jerusalem is at the center of the land of Israel, the Temple is at the center of Jerusalem, the Holy of Holies is at the center of the Temple, the Ark is at the center of the Holy of Holies and the Foundation Stone is in front of the Ark, which spot is the foundation of the world.[18]

Because Mount Zion, and especially its Temple, served as their *axis mundi*, pious Jews regarded them as essential to the maintenance of the cosmos. As long as the services in the Temple were performed, there were blessings in the world, the crops were plentiful, and man and beast ate and were satisfied. When the Jerusalem Temple was destroyed, God's blessings departed from the world. The Temple and its ritual were the two cosmic pillars—the sacred poles—that support the world.

The destruction of Jerusalem and the Temple and the exile of the Jews to Babylonia in the sixth century B.C.E. destroyed Israel's center and broke the link between heaven and earth. Disaster and chaos ensued. For orthodox Jews, the land of Israel, the city of Jerusalem, and Yahweh their God are inseparable. This fact points to the full tragedy of the 1900 years of Jewish exile from their Holy Land. For Jews, the overcoming of exile and chaos is traditionally accomplished through the commemorative rituals of the Sabbath and the high holy days during which there is a renewal of original, sacred time. However, the Zionist restoration of the land and the nation of Israel in 1948 represents the actual recovery of the Jewish center, of sacred space itself.

To summarize this theme, we can say that sacred space establishes a world, a cosmos, a fixed point in profane or chaotic space. Communication and passage are thereby opened between heaven and earth, a passage from one mode of being to another. Such a break in ordinary space creates a Center that makes orientation, hence meaning, possible. For the religious person, neither space nor *time* is ordinary. There are times as well as places set apart for festivals and holidays that break the unvarying and meaningless time of ordinary temporal duration. Through ritual, a person passes from ordinary, profane time into sacred time.

> One essential difference between these two qualities of time strikes us immediately: *by its very nature sacred time is reversible* in the sense that, properly speaking, it is a *primordial mythical time made present*. Every religious festival, any liturgical time, represents the reactualization of a sacred event that took place in the mythical past, "in the beginning."[19]

Since sacred time is mythical or primordial time, it is intimately connected with origins. In many primal and archaic religions, the cosmos is ritually re-created or reborn annually on New Year's Day by returning to and reenacting the mythical time of the creation "in the beginning" (see Chapter 8). Sacred space, the "house of god" or the "gate of heaven," represents not only the cosmos but also the year. This is again evident in the construction of the Hindu altar to the fire god Agni, referred to earlier. As Eliade explains it,

> The 360 bricks of the enclosure correspond to the 360 nights of the year, and the 360 *yajusmati* bricks to the 360 days. This is as much as to say that, with the building of each fire altar, not only is the world remade but the year is built too; in other words *time is regenerated by being created anew.*[20]

The mythic time portrayed in the original creation is the prototype or model for all other times. Therefore, the ritual reenactment of the Creation renews the cycle of the seasons and thereby restores time and preserves the temporal process from passage into chaos and death. Since the world does periodically retrogress toward stagnation and chaos, it must be ritually renewed. The New Year's ritual is just such an act of purification and restoration. The impurities and sins of the past year are purged away and the threat of returning to the chaos of nonbeing is forestalled.

Through the periodic ritual repetition of the original creation time is regenerated and temporal existence is restored and revitalized. Life can be renewed only by the regular ritual repetition of the originating events. In a similar way, the Christian, through participating periodically in the Eucharist or Holy Communion—which for the Christian reenacts an original yet eternal act of redemption through Christ—perceives that "old things are passed away," that sin is forgiven, life is renewed, and eternal life conferred.

We can conclude this topic by saying that Otto and Eliade are certainly correct that humankind has always lived in a sacred world of space and time. It is a world made real and sanctified by a break with ordinary time and space, making it possible to found a world and to model life after a sacred prototype, as it was "in the beginning." Eliade is right that the essence of religion is the desire to live in relation to a sacred order that is expressed in a prescribed pattern of behavior and belief. Such a sacred order, as we have seen, is distinct from the common or profane and is the source not only of meaning (value) but also of life-giving power. Such a sacred order, it should be pointed out, does not necessarily involve a division of the world into the "natural" and the "supernatural." Such a separation is common in some theistic religions that perceive reality as constituted by two distinct worlds, one a physical world governed by natural laws and the other a supernatural world of spiritual beings and powers. However, a sacred world need not be an order distinct from the natural world; rather, it can be seen as the natural world consecrated and made holy by special times and places.

## Religion as Ultimate Concern

Analysis of the sacred as the essence of religion can appropriately conclude with a few comments on a resemblance between Durkheim's and Eliade's contrast between the sacred and the profane and the theologian Paul Tillich's (1886–1965) more philosophical concept of religion as *ultimate concern.* Tillich does not conceive of religion in terms of a division between the natural and the supernatural nor as a distinct a priori faculty similar, for example, to our moral sense. Rather, he sees religion as the "depth dimension" of all human experience. By the use of the metaphor "depth," Tillich is pointing to what is ultimate in an individual's or a society's life—what gives that life meaning and what sustains it in being. There is, then, a certain equivalence in the role that the sacred plays in Durkheim's and Eliade's thought and the role of ultimate concern in Tillich's writings. According to Tillich,

> man is ultimately concerned about his being and meaning. "To be or not to be," in *this* sense is a matter of ultimate, unconditional, total and infinite concern. . . . Man is unconditionally concerned about that which conditions his being beyond all the conditions in him and around him. Man is ultimately concerned about what determines his ultimate destiny beyond all preliminary necessities and accidents.[21]

This quotation obviously betrays a more reflective, philosophical stage of religion than those that engage the interest of Durkheim and Eliade. Nevertheless, it shares a common concern for an order of meaning and a power of being that is set apart from what is of merely secondary or profane interest. Humans have sought ultimate security and meaning in a great variety of things, from totemic animals—such as the monkey in north India (the staple of life)—to divine kings, and to such sublime concepts as that of the Chinese Tao, the Indian Brahman, the Buddhist Nirvana, and the God of Western monotheism. But in each instance what is sacred is ultimate and what is ultimate is sacred, in that it does possess the power to threaten and to save our being, to empower life and give it a meaning which the vicissitudes of temporal existence cannot destroy.

It is appropriate, then, to speak of the object of religion as the holy or the sacred, or as an object of ultimate concern. But that object can only be pointed to, addressed, or communicated in the language and gestures of our own social and historical experience. We turn, therefore, in Chapters 3, 4, and 5 to a discussion of the distinct modes of religious expression and communication—to symbol, myth, ritual, and sacred text.

## NOTES

1. G. van der Leeuw, *Religion in Essence and Manifestation*, Vol. I (New York, 1963), 23.
2. Ibid., 37.
3. Ibid., 48.
4. Roger Caillois, *Man and the Sacred* (Glencoe, Ill., 1959), 38–39.
5. Ibid., 42.
6. R. Otto, *The Idea of the Holy* (New York, 1958), 10.
7. Ibid., 28.
8. Ibid., 14.
9. Ibid., 215.
10. Ibid., 140.
11. Ibid., 135.
12. Mircea Eliade, *The Sacred and the Profane*, trans. W. R. Trask (New York, 1961), 11.
13. Ibid., 20.

14. Ibid., 24.

15. Ibid., 30–31.

16. Lama Anagarika Govinda, *Psycho-cosmic Symbolism of the Buddhist Stupa* (1976), 30–31.

17. Translation of M. Dahood, *Psalms* (Garden City, N.Y., 1966), 288.

18. *Midrash Tanhuma, Kedoshim,* Vol. 10, quoted in A. Hertzberg, *Judaism* (New York, 1963), 143. For this and other citations on Mount Zion as Center, I am indebted to J. Z. Smith's excellent essay, "Earth and Gods," *The Journal of Religion* 49 (1969), 103–127.

19. Eliade, *The Sacred,* 68–69.

20. Ibid., 74.

21. Paul Tillich, *Theology of Culture* (New York, 1959), 7–8.

## KEY WORDS

| | |
|---|---|
| taboo | *axis mundi* |
| totems | *imago mundi* |
| icons | cosmogony |
| Rudolf Otto | stupa |
| numinous | mandala |
| *mysterium tremendum* and *fascinans* | Mount Zion–Jerusalem |
| Mircea Eliade | ultimate concern |
| hierophany | |

## REVIEW QUESTIONS

1. Why does the author begin the study of religious experience and forms of religious expression with a discussion of the sacred or holy? How does it fit in with the rest of the book?

2. What are some of the important characteristics associated with the experience of sacred power and what Rudolf Otto calls the "numinous" and the "*mysterium tremendum* and *fascinans*"?

3. Several scholars point to the fact that in much religious experience "the sacred both fascinates and repels." What does this mean? Do you think this is characteristic of the experience of the sacred in modern life? Why or why not?

4. In Mircea Eliade's discussion of sacred space, what does he mean by a hierophany, an *axis mundi*, and an *imago mundi*? Give an example of each of these forms of sacred space.

5. Cite some examples of other sacred places in other world religions. Are there some places in the United States that are, for Americans, sacred space?

6. Give examples of some sacred times that represent, for some of the world's religions, periods of atonement, purification, change, renewal, or rebirth.

7. How does the author relate the discussion of "ultimate concern" at the end of the chapter to the earlier discussion of sacred space and time? Can you think of examples of some nontraditional objects of "ultimate concern" that give individuals a sense of meaning, purpose, and hope?

## SUGGESTIONS FOR FURTHER READING

DURKHEIM, EMILE. *The Elementary Forms of the Religious Life.* New York: The Free Press, 1965.

ELIADE, MIRCEA. *The Sacred and the Profane.* New York: Harper & Row, 1961.

GIRARD, RENÉ. *Violence and the Sacred.* Baltimore, Md.: Johns Hopkins University Press, 1977.

NISBET, ROBERT. "The Sacred." In *The Sociological Tradition.* London: Heinemann, 1966.

OTTO, RUDOLF. *The Idea of the Holy.* New York: Oxford University Press, 1958.

TILLICH, PAUL. *Systematic Theology.* Vol. I. Chicago: University of Chicago Press, 1951.

———. "Religion as a Dimension of Man's Spiritual Life." In *Theology of Culture.* New York: Oxford University Press, 1964.

VAN DER LEEUW, GERARDUS. *Religion in Essense and Manifestation.* Vol. II. New York: Harper & Row, 1963.

*On sacred space and time*

See articles on "Sacred and Profane," "Sacred Space," and "Sacred Time" in *The Encyclopedia of Religion,* ed. Mircea Eliade. New York: Macmillan, 1987.

ELIADE, MIRCEA. *Cosmos and History: The Myth of the Eternal Return.* New York: Pantheon Books, 1954.

GASTER, THEODOR H. *Thespis.* Garden City, N.Y.: Doubleday, 1959. Sacred time in the ancient near eastern religions.

HOLM, JEAN WITH JOHN BOWKER, EDS. *Sacred Space.* London and New York: Pinter Publishers, 1994. Chapters on sacred space in the great world religions. Bibliographies on each religion.

SMITH, JONATHAN Z. *Map Is Not Territory: Studies in the History of Religions.* Leiden: E. J. Brill, 1978 (see pages 88–146).

WILLIAMS, PETER. *Houses of God.* Champaign: University of Illinois Press, 2000. Interesting treatment of the ways church architecture reveals different expressions of religion in America.

# 3

# *Sacred Symbol, Myth, and Doctrine*

## Overview

Religion has to do with what is considered sacred, holy, or ultimate. But we human beings either do not have direct access to the sacred or we cannot describe or communicate our experience of the sacred directly. We use human language, images, and gestures, that is, symbolic means of communicating our experience. This chapter therefore begins with a discussion of our uniquely human capacity for symbolic expression and then proceeds to explain different kinds of symbolic communication. This is followed by a number of illustrations of the ways in which religious symbols can bridge or "bring together," for example, the profane and the sacred, or varieties of religious meanings or concepts, or even entire religious communities around shared values and associations.

The chapter then explores several forms of symbolic communication—such as metaphor, parable, and story—and the unique ways in which they strike insight and communicate unexpected meanings about the sacred or holy. This is followed by an extended discussion of religious myth and its characteristics, and why it is considered an indispensable form of human expression. The study of religious myth is of great interest to anthropologists, psychologists, and literary critics, as well as to historians of religion. Special attention is given to the various ways in which these scholars interpret the meaning and significance of religious myth.

The chapter concludes with a discussion of religious doctrine, that is, with the need to translate the symbolic and mythic language of religious narrative into concepts and propositions. The purpose of doctrines is to achieve conceptual clarity, coherence, and comprehensiveness. In this regard, religious doctrine is compared to scientific models that seek to interpret experience in certain ways or according to certain patterns.

## Symbolic Communication

Every living creature feels and, through feeling, responds to the stimulus of the external world by means of gestures or sounds. A primal form of such response is the simple utterance. But, as one scholar points out, "even the cry of a hunted animal, the groan of a suffering or starving creature is a *symptom* of something, it is a *sign* of some motivated feeling." It is, however, only a sign of something, "not or not necessarily, a sign made *to* and intended *for* somebody."[1]

We should attend to the qualification, "or not necessarily." The lower animals not only *express* their responses to stimuli but also *communicate* through their piercing barks, repetitive songs, and anxious gestures. We refer to animal communication as a form of *signaling*. The communication is immediate, specific, and practical. In the case of human beings, communication takes on a new dimension because it is capable of *abstracting* from the immediate situation, forming judgments and concepts, generalizing, imagining, and fantasizing. The qualitative difference between animal and human communication lies in what students of language call our *symbolic* capacity—the distinction between mere signaling and human symbolizing.

*Signs* and *symbols* are both forms of expressing meaning. They point beyond themselves to something else. Animals are most susceptible to signs. A dog is alert to all kinds of signals from a master that denote "food" or "time for a walk." Susanne K. Langer, who has done more than any other philosopher to make us aware of the nature and role of symbolism, points out the pervasive character of *natural* signs:

> A sign indicates the existence—past, present, or future—of a thing, event, or condition. Wet streets are a sign that it has rained. A patter on the roof is a sign that it is raining. A fall of the barometer or a ring round the moon is a sign that it is going to rain. . . . A natural sign is part of a greater event. . . . It is a *symptom* of a state of affairs.[2]

The words *sign* and *symbol* are often used interchangeably, but they must be distinguished in terms of the relationship between the sign or symbol and the thing symbolized. We have spoken of signs as symptoms or natural reminders. Symbols are special kinds of signs. "We use certain 'signs' among ourselves," writes Langer,

> that do not point to anything in our actual surroundings. Most of our words are not signs in the sense of signals. They are used to talk *about* things, not to direct our eyes or ears or noses toward them. They serve to let us develop a

characteristic attitude toward objects *in absentia,* which is called "thinking of" or "referring to" what is not here. "Signs" used in this capacity are not *symptoms* of things, but *symbols.*[3]

Symbols are also sometimes distinguished as *representational* or *presentational.* **Representational symbols** tie together things that are distinct even when there may not be any natural or symptomatic connection between the symbol and the thing symbolized. The connection is due to custom or habitual practice. For example, the color green on the traffic light denotes "proceed." Why not the color blue? It would do as well, but conventional usage has come to associate green with "proceed." The point is that the meaning of representational symbols is determined by their cultural context and use. The image of an elephant may bring to the mind of an American businessperson thoughts of his or her political party or ideology; to a piously educated Indian, it represents a complex of meanings associated with a popular Hindu god. Many of our most common religious symbols—the eight-spoked wheel in Buddhism or the Jewish Star of David—are representational symbols. Their power to communicate meaning is clearly dependent on learned associations.

**Presentational symbols** are another important type of symbolization, one that often takes the form of an image or **icon.** Presentational symbols are more than signs or natural symptoms, and more than representative in a purely conventional sense. *They participate in, or are similar to, the thing they symbolize.* A secular example would be a map that resembles the geographical reality it depicts. Presentational symbols are especially powerful conveyors of religious meaning since they are more than reminders. They genuinely "participate in," manifest, or "make present" the holy or sacred. For this reason, presentational symbols cannot easily be changed or removed. Water and blood, for example, have qualities that are intrinsically associated with cleansing and new life, or with death and sacrifice. In the Eastern Orthodox Church, certain images or pictures called icons are believed not only to represent but also to "make present" the divine. They are similar to the sacramental actions of the priest in the Roman Catholic Church, actions through which the sacred is made present. In Buddhism, certain gestures—called **mudras**—disclose aspects of the Buddha spirit. Likewise, through certain sounds—called **mantras**—such as the Hindu chanting of OM, and the chant of the devotees of Hare Krishna, the sacred is actually, palpably present.

## Religious Symbols

Many symbols, including religious symbols, are objects or sounds that stand for something but are not intended to give us information about what they symbolize because we already have direct knowledge of the symbol's referent. Rather, the symbol functions as a kind of shorthand reminder or signal of some information or mode of action already known. The flag hoisted on holidays, such as on the Fourth of July, reminds us in one image of all that is

Common Buddhist *mudras* symbolizing (1) fearlessness, (2) appeasement, (3) worship, and (4) concentration. (*Source:* From E. Dale Saunders, *Mudra: A Study of Symbolic Features in Japanese Sculpture*, Bollingen Series 58. Copyright © 1960 by Princeton University Press. [Figures from Pictorial Index drawn by Mark Hasselriis.] Reprinted with permission of Princeton University Press.)

involved in patriotic pride and duty, but the flag itself does not inform us, it does not give us that information. In religious rituals, bells, incense, bodily gestures, and colors *remind* us of other things—meanings and values—already known, or they prompt us to some action.

Other symbols convey knowledge of the thing they symbolize, about which we would otherwise remain ignorant. To do this, the symbol must be *presentational,* it must in some manner *resemble* the thing symbolized. The way this is traditionally put is to say that there must be a genuine *analogy* between the symbol and that to which it points.

In Chapter 1, we spoke of the human capacity for self-transcendence, the fact that we live continuously on the threshold of something more. This is uniquely true of the human religious quest. Religiously, we stand on a threshold beyond which we can speak only by analogy, in symbols. The object of the religious quest is the Holy or sacred, that, while revealed through the world of sensory experience, at the same time is not wholly encompassed by the visible and imaginative signs and images by which we seek to glimpse and conceptualize it. Religious expression and communication is, then, pre-eminently symbolic, first because it points to and addresses a reality that is essentially transcendent, mysterious, and never fully plumbed. *We can speak of it, even depict it, but only symbolically and by analogy.* Religious language is then fundamentally the language of metaphor, poetry, myth, and ritual action, although, as we shall see at the close of this chapter, it is not *merely* poetic. To say "All flesh is grass" is both poetic and religious. It speaks by the use of a metaphor—it is not literally true—and yet it conveys a profound truth about the human condition.

Here a distinction may help. Most ordinary religious language—what is called primary or *"first-order" religious discourse*—is richly metaphoric and poetic in character. Yet, in literate societies, it does not remain at that level. The symbols, myths, and stories require interpretation, elaboration, and commentary. This leads to a *"second-order,"* a more abstract form of discourse that seeks greater clarity and coherence by translating the symbolic and mythic language into concepts and doctrines. But to return to our first point—the religious symbol is a necessary bridge erected between the finite and "the Something More."

The image of the bridge is especially apt because the word *symbol* is derived from the Greek verb *symballein,* meaning "to throw or bring together." We have spoken of the way in which the symbol analogically bridges, or "brings together," the image, gesture, or sound, taken from our ordinary experience, and the Holy, which remains elusive, mysterious, and ineffable. But a living symbol "brings together" in other important ways as well. A religious symbol, and especially certain *master symbols* or *root metaphors,* can "bring together" in the sense of literally creating and sustaining communities. For example, the Christian crucifix and the image of the reclining Buddha serve as master symbols, bringing together a rich complex of spiritual meanings for these two communities. The anthropologist Mary Douglas points to the way in which the eating of fish on Fridays by Irish Catholics and the abstinence from the eating of pork for Jews have served as "condensed symbols" for a complex pattern of meanings and associations that bind members of these religious communities. Religious symbols may express and help to sustain whole religious traditions.

What we can learn from a study of the symbol system of a religion is that it can illuminate the *deep* structure of sentiments and values that characterize a community and that may not be obvious on the surface. These master symbols point to the fact that religions are not merely a collection of discrete ideas and practices but that religions constitute an entire *form of life,* one that can only be understood by penetrating the meaning of these symbols and root metaphors. See the images of Christ and the Buddha on pages 63 and 64.

This is clear in the third way in which the religious symbol "brings together," namely, by joining in one, often simple, image a variety of events and meanings. A single example will suffice. A historian has shown that the sacred fish, a common symbol in the ancient pagan world, was also a pervasive image in the earliest Christian catacombs. The Greek acrostic for "fish"—arranged as below by taking the first letter of each line—means "Jesus Christ, God's Son, Savior." This hidden meaning was often inscribed in the catacombs. The transliterated Greek looks like this:

Iesous—Jesus
Christost—Christ
Theou—of God
Uios—the Son
Soter—Savior

The simple image ⤳⟝◯ also brings together symbolically a number of cardinal Christian meanings: Baptism, Holy Communion, Resurrection, and the **eschatological** Messianic Banquet in the Kingdom of God.

Matthias Grünewald's famous painting of the Crucifixion from the Isenheim Altar symbolizes the Passion and sacrifice as well as the anguish and ardor that we associate with Christianity. (*Source:* Courtesy of O. Zimmeman, Musée d'Unterlinden—Colmar.)

How did the fish represent these multiple meanings? An historian explains it as follows:

> When we consider the high significance of adult baptism in the Early Church, and the role that the baptism of Jesus played in the imagination of the early Christian, we can find a ready clue. . . . Jesus was the God revealed in the water. In the earliest strata of the Gospel the baptism of Jesus is the event which determines His mission, gives Him the awareness of the Kingdom as now present in some sense in Himself. . . . Indeed, the feast of Epiphany originally celebrated the baptism and certainly antedated the feast of Christmas. What connection would be more obvious than this: Jesus is the God revealed in the water, hence the sacred fish?
>
> But the fish is also food. The same God . . . descending again into the water at Christian baptism, is the heavenly food of the Eucharist [that is, Holy Communion]. Hence the consecration of the bread and wine is often depicted by the consecration of the sacred fish. . . .

The Paranirvana of the Buddha from Gal Vihara, Sri Lanka. This giant statue, portraying the Buddha in "complete nirvana," represents Buddhist deathlessness—perfect enlightenment, free of craving and delusion. (*Source:* Courtesy of Jack Van Horn.)

Yet the fish, as the sacrificial food, is also the food of the Heavenly Banquet. There is an eschatological note in the symbol. It looks toward the final consummation of the Kingdom in the Heavenly Banquet.... For the sacred fish is Leviathan of Jewish apocalyptic; and Leviathan is the main course at the Heavenly Banquet. ...

But we are not yet done. The fish is the symbol of Resurrection. The sign of Jonah, which perpetually recurs in the Catacombs, is the sign of Christ's resurrection, and of our own.[4]

Thus it is that this simple image >⊂⊃, which could be swiftly stroked in the sand as a means of identification, is capable of "bringing together" in one coherent symbol the central beliefs of the Christian faith.

## Metaphor, Parable, and Story

Before turning to a more extensive discussion of the role of myth in the life of religious communities, a few words must be said about other important symbolic forms.

*Metaphor* is a distinctive form of symbolic communication. A metaphor—"Time is a river"—is not a literal statement. It is, nevertheless, a basic form of our ordinary discourse. When we want to know the nature of something, we often ask "What is it like?" We live and speak

A contemporary Mexican pottery depicting the Last Supper and featuring a huge fish that, since early Christianity, has symbolized numerous basic teachings. (*Source:* Courtesy of the collection of John and Scottie Austin.)

through pointing out resemblances. Metaphor is then a basic means of communication.

What are characteristics of the symbolic form of metaphor? "The Lord is my shepherd" is, like other symbolic discourse, nonliteral; it also involves a comparison, it is like an analogy. But while analogy moves from the known ("shepherd") to the unknown ("The Lord") in a positive and proportional sense, a metaphor strikes insight by creating something entirely new, something both similar and dissimilar. The poetic metaphor "All flesh is grass" holds two different things together and thereby creates a novel meaning, a new insight.

In metaphorical speech, it is important that the tension between "the is and the is not" (the similarity in the difference) be retained in order to avoid slipping into literalism. Metaphor, by making us conscious of the symbolic and tentative character of our religious speech, protects against a mistaken literalism and idolatry, that is, a confusion of the sacred with the finite. Yet metaphor is not simply a "useful fiction." "All flesh is grass" reveals a genuine truth of our experience.

*Parable* is another distinctive form of religious discourse. It is essentially an *extended metaphor,* and it reveals the same surprise and openness to new insight that we have observed in a true metaphor. These qualities of the parable are present in the following definition:

> At its simplest, the parable is a metaphor or simile, drawn from nature or common life, arresting the hearer by its vividness or strangeness, and leaving the mind in sufficient doubt about its precise application to tease it into active thought.[5]

Because parables draw from the ordinary things of everyday experience, they have a homely way of communicating truth. But the surprise and vividness of the communication derives from the unexpected use, the difference, to which the commonplace image is put. The revelation of the story comes through the presence of the extraordinary in the ordinary. Jesus and Buddha, for example, made use of such ordinary images as rafts, lost coins, weddings, monkeys, elephants, mustard seeds, workmen in the field, and fire—but in unexpected and therefore illuminating ways. The Kingdom of God is like a mustard seed; the search for metaphysical answers is likened to blind men feeling an elephant. The impact of the parable lies in the simplicity and authenticity of the everyday event translated into a moral or spiritual truth.

Another feature of parable is its unity of content and form. Its reality and power lie in the fact that it is not an abstract discourse; like a story, it is vividly narrative in character. Furthermore, the hearer is addressed in his or her wholeness, since the feelings, emotions, and the human will are all engaged as forcefully as the conscious mind.

Many profoundly human experiences—such as death, suffering, guilt, and hatred—as well as "peak experiences" of a more positive nature—joy, peace, beatitude—require a language that is capable of illuminating them. Parable is such a language because it uses the ordinary to disclose the extraordinary.

We have spoken of the general features of parable; it is time to illustrate what has been said with specific examples. We select one parable from the Buddhist tradition and another from the Christian New Testament. Both are interesting, though baffling, stories; they can be viewed as "root metaphors," symbols of the central truths of these two great religions. The Buddhist parable, entitled "Visakha's Sorrow," is one of many that brings home powerfully the Buddha's teaching regarding the extinction of craving (*tanha*):

> Thus have I heard: Once upon a time the Exalted One was in residence at Savatthi, in Eastern Grove, in Visakha Mother of Migara's mansion. Now at that time Visakha Mother of Migara's granddaughter had died, and she was Visakha's darling and delight. And Visakha Mother of Migara, garments wet, hair wet, at an untimely hour approached the Exalted One. And having approached, she saluted the Exalted One and sat down on one side. And as she sat there on one side, the Exalted One said this to Visakha Mother of Migara: "Well, Visakha, how is it that you come here at such an untimely hour, approaching with garments wet, with hair wet?" "Reverend Sir, my granddaughter has died, and she was my darling and delight. That is why I approach at such an untimely hour, with garments wet, with hair wet." "Should you like, Visakha, to have as many children and grandchildren as there are human beings in Savatthi?" "I should like, Reverend Sir, to have as many children and grandchildren as there are human beings in Savatthi." "But, Visakha, how many human beings die every day in Savatthi?" "Reverend Sir, ten human beings die every day in Savatthi.... My granddaughter, Reverend Sir, is in no class by herself, apart from the other human beings who die in Savatthi." "What think you, Visakha? Should you ever, at any time, be without garments wet, without hair wet?" "No indeed, Reverend Sir."

"Verily, Visakha, they that hold a hundred dear, have a hundred sorrows; . . . ninety dear, have ninety sorrows . . . eighty . . . seventy . . . sixty . . . fifty . . . forty . . . thirty . . . twenty . . . ten . . . nine . . . eight . . . seven . . . six . . . five . . . four . . . three . . . two . . . one dear, have one sorrow. They that hold nothing dear, have no sorrow. Free from grief are they—free from passion, free from despair. So say I."[6]

We may not "like" the Buddha's parabolic message since it does assault our ordinary sense of social sympathy. It points, nevertheless, to the Buddha's hard teaching about the relation of desire and suffering.

In the New Testament parable of the workers in the vineyard, Jesus tells a story that also shocks a deep-seated human conviction, our sense of the necessity of justice. The parable makes nonsense of our notion of merit; it accentuates the scandal of grace:

And Jesus said to his disciples. . . . For the kingdom of heaven is like a house-holder who went out early in the morning to hire laborers for his vineyard. After agreeing with the laborers for a denarius a day, he sent them into his vineyard. And going out about the third hour he saw others standing idle in the market place; and to them he said, "You go into the vineyard too, and whatever is right I will give you." So they went. Going out again about the sixth hour and the ninth hour, he did the same. And about the eleventh hour he went out and found others standing; and he said to them, "Why do you stand here idle all day?" They said to him, "Because no one has hired us." He said to them, "You go into the vineyard too." And when evening came, the owner of the vineyard said to his steward, "Call the laborers and pay them their wages, beginning with the last, up to the first." And when those hired about the eleventh hour came, each of them received a denarius. Now when the first came, they thought they would receive more; but each of them also received a denarius. And on receiving it they grumbled at the householder, saying, "These last worked only one hour, and you made them equal to us who have borne the burden of the day and the scorching heat." But he replied to one of them, "Friend, I am doing no wrong; did you not agree with me for a denarius? Take what belongs to you, and go; I choose to give to this last as I give to you. Am I not allowed to do what I choose with what belongs to me? Or do you begrudge my generosity?" So the last will be first, and the first last.

—(*Matthew 20:1–16*)

Why do parables strike us as subversive, and yet as so real and authentically human? The answer lies, to a considerable degree, in their form as stories. A number of scholars have pointed to the fact that human life naturally takes the form of what can be called "the narrative quality of experience."[7] It has to do with our unique human experience of a past, present, and future. It is worth noting that what we call "the humanities" are not concerned with modes of abstraction and quantification, as in science, but with narrative forms of human experience: parable, epic, legend, myth, drama, and history. And this is because human life is inherently temporal. What unifies our experience are memory and anticipation. Our memory of the past and our anticipation of the future unite our experience into a narrative form—a sequence of before and after, that is, a story.

The stories that we hear and the ritual dramas in which we participate shape our own inner story, our own sense of place, and our own pilgrimage through time. There is nothing that pleases us, nothing that emotionally satisfies us more than a good story. The reason is that it corresponds with the narrative structure of our experience. The story moves us because it resonates in the depths of our own being; it rings true. Art imitates life, and the truly great stories are so true to life as to effect a shock of recognition, an emotional catharsis, and a spur to action. Most of the time, we are unconscious of the profound impression that the great archetypal stories and myths have in shaping our own sense of self, where we have come from, who we are, and where we are going. They also link us with others who share a common story—the American story, or the Jewish story, or the woman's story. That is why genuine conversion is both so agonizing and yet so liberating an experience. In religious conversion, we literally repudiate one story of our life and embrace another.

## Religious Myth

Another important religious form of symbolic narrative is myth. The word *myth* has long been open to ambiguity and confusion. In our common usage today, myth has come to mean what is *not* true. If we are told something that we have reason to doubt, we say, "Oh, that's just a myth." One reason for this skepticism is that traditional education in the West has long associated myth with the stories of the exploits of the Greek and Roman gods. In classical Greece and Rome, these mythic tales already were criticized as fictional "tall tales." Now, however, scholars reject the view that myth is to be understood simply as prescientific error and have concentrated on its complex nature and functions. Myth now is seen as a multileveled form of symbolic communication.

Like parable, myth tells a story. However, unlike parable, which discloses a moral or a singular meaning, myth can serve as a community's charter for its whole life-world, that is, it can explain or legitimize the natural order or a community's institutions and behavior. Many comparable definitions of myth are current; the following is a brief and highly serviceable one:

> Myth is to be defined as a complex of stories—some no doubt fact, and some fancy—which, for various reasons, human beings regard as demonstrations of the inner meaning of the universe and of human life.[8]

This definition points to the symbolic, narrative character of myth and to its service as a model or paradigm of the natural and human order, but the definition also expressly avoids the assumption that myth is untrue, "a mere tale." This is important because one of the concerns of recent students of myth has been to challenge any theory of myth that reduces it either to idle play or to crude scientific analysis. These scholars see myth, along with art and science, as basic, though distinct, forms of symbolic communication. Each has its own logic and intelligibility; neither is "truer" or "better."

Myth, however, does several things that science does not do, unless science itself takes on the form of a mythic vision—which, of course, sometimes happens. First, myths provide grids or models by which we can envision an entire world. The world is perceived as ordered, as having a meaning and purpose that is often portrayed mythically in a story of the original act of Creation itself or of certain archetypal events, such as Prometheus stealing the fire from the gods. Myth also shapes our sense of self, of who we are. The lives of certain exemplary persons—sages, saints, prophets, heroes—serve as root metaphors, as archetypes of what it means to be genuinely real and truly human. Myths therefore disclose and sanction models of behavior and moral norms, often for each stage in the human life cycle. Finally, myths portray why evil and chaos erupt and threaten our world and our own personal being—and what we must do to be saved, liberated, or renewed. We need not illustrate here the rich variety of myths about the creation and maintenance of cosmic order, human nature and destiny, or salvation since we will explore these in detail in Chapters 8, 9, and 12.

Myth is such a pervasive cultural form that many consider it to be indispensable as long as we continue to seek to make sense out of the deeply human questions that lie outside the province of technology or science. The anthropologist Malinowski speaks to this point. "A myth," he writes,

> is an indispensable ingredient of all culture. It is . . . a constant by-product of living faith, which is in need of miracles; of sociological status, which demands precedent; of moral rule, which requires sanction.[9]

The fact that myth, as well as science, is a primary and unique way of apprehending reality and charting the natural and human order suggests its indispensability. Evidence of the pervasiveness and inevitability of myth as a form of cultural life, even today, is apparent in the role it plays in modern literature and social thought, as well as in expressions of popular culture. We need not look only to the great classic works of Dante, Shakespeare, Milton, Goethe, or Melville for confirmation. André Gide makes use of the Theseus myth; the Nobel Prize–winning novelists John Steinbeck, Albert Camus, and William Golding all have recast mythic themes from Genesis: the Fall, the story of Cain and Abel, and the Tower of Babel; and T. S. Eliot has used Parsifal and the myth of the dying and rising God-King. James Joyce has employed the myths of Moses and Odysseus. It is also instructive that the two giants of modern psychotherapy, Freud and Jung, found it necessary to appeal to mythic figures and archetypal images—Oedipus, Eros, Thanatos, the Earth-Mother, the Divine Child, and so forth—in their attempts to express and to illustrate their theories.

Scholars have called attention to the reappearance of numerous archaic mythic patterns in contemporary popular culture, in science-fiction novels, in television commercials, and, of course, in movies. We see in Star Wars and in the James Bond books (over 10 million copies) and films examples of the deeds, sufferings, and testings of the archetypal mythical hero's journey in an age of technology:

> The Bond hero's journey involves a descent into Hades, the domain of evil, inhabited by the modern counterparts of malevolent magicians, sorcerers, witches, and warlocks whose guile and technological sophistication are many times greater than those of 007. Moreover, while he is alone almost all of the time, his enemies are many, organized into well-trained and blindly obedient corps of corruption. Yet James Bond willingly enters these labyrinths and seeks out their Minotaur-like ruler, as Theseus did in the famous Greek myth. He is willing to face torture and even death, never because of any personal reason or ambition, but simply because he is willing to suffer, to experience unspeakable agony in order to save the rest of us from disaster. . . . The greater the dangers he faces, the sufferings he undergoes for our sake . . . the more we will identify with him.[10]

Myth is indeed a perennial cultural form. But what are its purpose and function? How are we to interpret it? On these matters, there is considerable dispute. A number of distinct—though not necessarily mutually exclusive—theories currently attract significant followings among philosophers, anthropologists, psychologists, and theologians. Among the influential current theories are the *functionalist* theory of Bronislaw Malinowski and his followers; the *psychoanalytic* theory of Sigmund Freud and especially Carl Jung; and the *phenomenological* theory of Mircea Eliade.

### Functionalist Theory of Myth

The anthropologist **Bronislaw Malinowski** offers the clearest treatment of the functionalist approach in his book *Myth in Primitive Psychology.* We have remarked that Malinowski considers myth as an indispensable ingredient in all culture. Furthermore, he insists that myth or sacred tale is unique and must be distinguished from legend and fairy tale. Myth, he asserts, is regarded "not merely as true, but as venerable and sacred." "These stories live," he continues, "not by idle interest, nor as fictitious or even as true narratives; but are to the natives a statement of a primeval, greater, and more relevant reality, by which the present life, fates, and activities of mankind are determined."[11] In primal societies, myth is as much a reality as the biblical stories of Creation, the Fall, and the Redemption by Christ's Sacrifice on the Cross are to Christians. It governs faith and shapes conduct.

Malinowski not only rejects a "tall-tale" view of myth but also denies that it serves primarily as an explanation satisfying a scientific interest; rather, its meaning is to be understood in terms of its social function within a particular culture. This is stated explicitly in the following passage. "Myth," he writes, is

> but a narrative resurrection of a primeval reality, told in satisfaction of deep religious wants, moral cravings, social submissions, assertions, even practical requirements. It expresses, enhances, and codifies belief; it safeguards and enforces morality; it vouches for the efficiency of ritual and contains practical

rules for the guidance of man. . . . It is not an intellectual explanation or an artistic imagery, but a pragmatic charter of primitive faith and moral wisdom.[12]

Malinowski gives numerous examples of myths of origin, death and life, and magical power that reveal their profoundly practical, psychological, and social functions. A myth of the origin of death is representative:

> Once upon a time there lived in the village of Bwadela an old woman who dwelt with her daughter and grand-daughter. . . . The grandmother and granddaughter went out one day to bathe in the tidal creek. The girl remained on the shore, while the old woman went away some distance out of sight. She took off her skin which, carried by the tidal current, floated along the creek until it stuck on a bush. Transformed into a young girl, she came back to her grand-daughter. The latter did not recognize her; she was afraid of her and bade her begone. The old woman, mortified and angry, went back to her bathing place, searched for her old skin, put it on again, and returned to her grand-daughter. This time she was recognized and thus greeted: "A young girl came here; I was afraid; I chased her away." Said the grandmother: "No, you didn't want to recognize me. Well, you will become old—I shall die.". . . I shall not slough my skin. We shall all become old. We shall all die. . . . After that men lost the power of changing their skin and of remaining youthful.[13]

Malinowski points out that this myth is but a dramatization of the human loss of the power of rejuvenation and the reality of death, but its social function is

> to transform an emotionally overwhelming foreboding, behind which, even for a native, there lurks the idea of an inevitable and ruthless fatality. Myth presents, first of all, a clear realization of this idea. In the second place, it brings down a vague but great apprehension to the compass of a trivial, domestic reality. . . . Elements of fate, of destiny, and of the inevitable are brought down to the dimension of human mistakes.[14]

In this myth of the origin of death, we can see what Malinowski means by a sacred story "told in satisfaction of . . . social submissions . . . even practical requirements."

## A Psychotherapeutic Theory of Myth

*Carl Jung's* contribution to the scientific study of religion is centered on his theory of the archetypes of the collective unconscious, that is, on those firmly established symbolic and mythic images that reappear in a variety of cultures and historical periods. In these archetypes, Jung finds great significance for religious symbolism, myth, and psychic healing.

According to Jung, the human psyche consists of three layers—the conscious mind, the personal unconscious, and what he calls the "collective unconscious." The personal unconscious consists of all those contents "forgotten" or repressed from the conscious mind that are associated with the individual's own history. This level of the unconscious is not, however, the deepest layer. That belongs to the collective unconscious, which is the focus of Jung's attention.

The term *collective unconscious* has been generally misunderstood. Jung does not mean by it a collective inheritance of images and myths that are a joint possession of the human race; rather, he means that the unconscious includes materials that are psychically real prior to their personal appropriation. They are inherent potentials in the psychic structure of all individuals. These unconscious psychic contents are archetypal in character; what Jung calls "forms or images of a collective nature which occur practically all over the earth as constituents of myths. . . ."[15] They are "primordial images" that can be seen to recur throughout human history. They are not, however, inherited conscious ideas. "The archetype is," Jung writes,

> on the contrary, an inherited *tendency* of the human mind to form representations of mythological motifs—representations that vary a great deal without losing their basic pattern. . . . The inherited tendency is instinctive, like the specific impulse of nest-building, migration, etc. in birds. One finds these *representations collectives* practically everywhere, characterized by the same or similar motifs. They cannot be assigned to any particular time or region or race. They are without known origin, and they can reproduce themselves even when transmission through migration must be ruled out.[16]

The motifs studied by Jung include the Divine Child, Mother Earth, the Hero, the number four, and the *mandala*. Jung sees Christ, for example, as exemplifying the ancient hero motif:

> The idea of Christ the Redeemer belongs to the world-wide and pre-Christian motif of the hero and rescuer who, although devoured by the monster, appears again in a miraculous way, having overcome the dragon or whale or whatever it was that swallowed him. How, when, and where such a motif originated nobody knows. . . . Our only certainty is that every generation, so far as we can see, has found it as an old tradition. . . . The hero figure is a typical image, and archetype, which has existed since time immemorial.[17]

For Jung, the importance of an *archetype*, such as the hero, lies in its psychic efficacy or therapy. The universal hero myth, for example,

> shows the picture of a powerful man or god-man who vanquishes evil in the form of dragons, serpents, monsters, demons, and enemies of all kinds, and who liberated his people from destruction and death. The narration or ritual repetition of sacred texts and ceremonies, and the worship of such a figure . . . grip the audience with numinous emotions and exalt the participants to identification with the hero. If we contemplate such a situation with the eyes of a believer, we can understand how the ordinary man is gripped, freed from his impotence and misery, and raised to an almost superhuman status.[18]

Jung points out that participation in the ritualization of the hero myth can shape and create whole communities around the life-world of the hero.

However, Jung is interested not only in the archetype's social function but also in its power of individual psychic healing, which he calls *individuation* or "self-realization." According to Jung, the development of genuine self-hood is not the same as what we mean by individuality. The latter "means deliberately stressing and giving prominence to some supposed peculiarity, rather than to collective considerations and obligations." Individuation, on the other hand, "means precisely the better and more complete fulfillment of the collective qualities of the human being."[19] Individuation is neither the loss of the self in favor of some social role or persona nor the giving of one-self over to some primordial image. It is, rather, the development of a self that involves the integration of the personal ego *with* archetypes of the un-conscious. An example of what Jung means by individuation is a believer's identification with the archetypal Christ-hero in the Catholic Mass.

> Looked at from the psychological standpoint, Christ, as the Original Man (Son of Man, second Adam) represents a totality which surpasses and includes the ordinary man, and which corresponds to the total personality that transcends consciousness. . . . So the mystery of the Eucharist transforms the soul of the empirical man, who is only a part of himself, into a totality, symbolically ex-pressed by Christ. In this sense, therefore, we can speak of the Mass as the *rite of the individuation process.*[20]

Jung perceives myth as vitally significant for *it represents the deepest level of the psychic life of humankind.* To refuse to take myth seriously is to imperil the soul, to court neurotic and even psychotic disorders. Jung concludes that "The mythology of a tribe is its living religion, whose loss is always and everywhere, even in the *case of a civilized* man, a moral catastrophe."[21]

### A Phenomenological Interpretation

In Chapter 2, we discussed Mircea Eliade's distinction between the sacred and the profane. That theme relates directly to his theory of myth be-cause myth is an account of a sacred history, a primordial time in which real-ity as we now know it came into being. Eliade describes myth as follows:

> Myth narrates a sacred history; it relates an event that took place in primordial time, the fabled time of the "beginnings." In other words, myth tells how, through the deeds of Supernatural Beings, a reality came into existence, be it the whole of reality, the Cosmos, or only a fragment of reality—an island, a species of plant, a particular kind of human behavior, an institution. Myth, then, is always an account of a "creation"; it relates how something was pro-duced, began to *be.* . . . The actors in myths are Supernatural Beings. They are known primarily by what they did in the transcendent times of the "begin-nings". . . . It is this sudden breakthrough of the sacred that really *establishes* the World and makes it what it is today.[22]

From this description, only a few points need to be stressed. First, religious myth has to do with the acts of the gods or supernatural beings.

Second, myth is, for Eliade, always an account of origins; it tells us how something came into existence. Myths are thus the exemplary models of all natural and human life and activity. This relates to the third, or existential, role of myth. "Myth," Eliade insists, "constitutes the paradigms for all significant human acts."[23] "Myth teaches [humankind] the primordial 'stories' that have constituted [humans] existentially . . . [their] legitimate mode of existence. . . ."[24] Myth thus answers our most urgent questions about existence. It gives us a sense of orientation and meaning in the face of the threat of chaos and **anomie,** hence, it serves a unique and universal role.

Since myth is the universal response to humankind's experience of limit situations such as finitude and moral guilt, it is possible to carry out a crosscultural phenomenological comparison of the myths of many cultures. Finally, myth is "true" because it is concerned with reality; that is, it effectively answers such existential questions as why we are mortal, why there are social relations of hierarchy and subordination, or why there is suffering. By knowing the myth, we know the origin and nature of things—a knowledge not abstract but "living," for it is constantly reexperienced through ritual reenactment.

It is interesting to note that the three theories we have outlined—those of Malinowski, Jung, and Eliade—all perceive myth as not simply a vestige of the prelogical mind but as in some sense universal, indispensable, and displaying its own distinctive logic. They all wish to defend the idea that myth is in some sense "true."

## Models and Doctrines

To this point, the subject of this chapter's discussion has been focused on what we have called primary or "first-order" religious discourse. But "the symbol gives rise to thought."[25] This is the philosopher Paul Ricoeur's striking way of indicating that in literate societies the symbolic and mythic language of religion naturally calls for interpretation, for conceptual clarification and translation into propositional language. The product of this "second-order" interpretive process is often what we call *doctrines* and dogmas. The move toward conceptual clarification and generalization is a necessary one because a myth can "tell many little lies in the service of a great truth."[26] The lie would be, for example, a literal or scientific reading of the accounts of Adam and Eve in the Garden of Eden. On the other hand, the truth of that myth would be the experienced fact of human dependence, finitude, sin, and the inordinate human desire to be like God. Because we live in a literal, scientific age, the symbolic language of the Genesis myth of the Creation and the Fall must, therefore, be *interpreted;* it must be "demythologized," that is, reinterpreted to bring out the universal and existential meanings that lie within the mythopoetic story. Conceptual language can facilitate such an understanding. However, religious language is fundamentally symbolic and analogical since it speaks about that which eludes literal statement. The translation from symbolic to conceptual and propositional language (doctrine) can, therefore, actually hinder understanding if it results in a literalness that denies the intrinsically metaphoric, analogical nature of religious expression and communication. Ricoeur reminds us that "the dissolution of the myth as explanation is the necessary way to the restoration of the myth as symbol."[27] He states both the interpretive problem and its goal: "Between the concept which kills the symbol and pure conceptual silence, there must be room for a *conceptual* language which preserves the character of symbolic language."[28] Second-order conceptual language, interpretation, must allow us to *hear again* the meaning of the primary symbol.

It is appropriate to speak of religious language as *metaphysical poetry*. Like metaphysics, it does make factual assertions; it therefore must meet the demands for coherence, comprehensiveness, and criteria by which its truth-claims can be tested. On the other hand, religious language is *poetic*, symbolic, and analogical. A way of seeking both conceptual clarity and comprehensiveness, while protecting religious language against a mistaken literalism, is to conceive of master symbols, root metaphors, and myths as *models*, functioning in a manner similar to scientific models.

As employed in science, a model seeks to construe certain patterns in observable data. It is an image that attempts to organize or restructure our interpretation of the world. While not literal, a scientific model does lead to theories that can be tested by observations. Similarly, religious models (symbols and myths) lead to conceptual beliefs or doctrines that construe or interpret experience in certain ways, according to certain patterns or exemplary paradigms. A scholar characterizes the role of religious models as follows:

> Models can represent the enduring structures of the cosmic order which myths dramatize in narrative form. Images which originated in religious experience and key historical events are extended to interpret other areas of individual and corporate experience. As models of an unobservable gas molecule are later used to interpret other patterns of observation in the laboratory, so models of an unobservable God are used to interpret new patterns of experience in human life. Ultimate interpretive models . . . are organizing images which restructure one's perception of the world. One may notice features which might otherwise have been ignored.[29]

A religious model is able to take account of a wide range of experience or phenomena; it is, therefore, authenticated in experience. A model might be likened to an especially illuminating sentence in an otherwise profuse, complex book. We can make no sense of the narrative until we come on the sentence or image that enlightens everything that has come before and that will follow later.

Models are ways of experiencing what is not observable straight off and so are symbolic representations. But, as many philosophers of science would also insist, there simply are no bare uninterpreted data. All data assume some implicit theory. We do not simply experience; we "experience as": "In the act of perception, the irreducible 'data' are not isolated patches of color or fragmentary sensations, but total patterns in which interpretation has already entered. Our experience is organized in the light of particular interests"[30]—or in the light of a certain grid, pattern, or model.

Where religious models differ most from scientific ones is in the fact that they serve numerous noncognitive functions—such as deeply felt social and psychological needs and ideals. They also provide norms and motivations for ethical action. In other words, religious models engage our deepest human concerns. This does not mean, however, that religious models lack cognitive significance. The religious beliefs and doctrines that we derive from our models and paradigms also must "give a faithful rendition" of those areas of our experience that are humanly significant, especially our "religious and moral experience and key historical events."[31] Thus, *extensibility* of application (comprehensiveness) and *fruitfulness* are, according to Barbour, essential criteria for the truth or adequacy of any religious doctrine or assertion.

The symbols, myths, and models that serve as the source of religious doctrine and belief are, however, never verifiable in the same sense that scientific theories are testable. But that does not mean that religious doctrines are not communicable and therefore testable to a degree. If various religious or ideological communities shared no language, concepts, or experience in common, then, indeed, their several claims would be incommensurable and untestable. There are, in fact, widely shared human experiences and profound symbolic and conceptual similarities to be found in the world's religions. Therefore, Barbour would appear to be correct that "persons in diverse traditions can appeal to facets of each other's experience and can discuss together their interpretive frameworks. Intelligible reasons can be offered, rather than arbitrary 'leaps of faith.' "[32]

Two things can be said by way of conclusion: (1) Religious language is unique and resists scientific modes of verification, and (2) all religious communities take for granted that their religious language makes assertions, that is, it refers to what is most true and real. Religious discourse is, then, fundamentally mythopoetic—but with a difference. W. M. Urban rightly remarks that the mythopoetic "is present in all genuine religious language, only . . . it is heightened and deepened in a peculiar way. It is, so to speak, poetry transposed to another scale."[33] The crucial point here is the phrase "transposed to another scale." This is what distinguishes religious language from either aesthetic or emotive discourse. Rather than disengaging from the question of fact and truth, and settling for a world of fairy tale and imagination, religion, in the words of the anthopologist Clifford Geertz,

> deepens the concern with fact and seeks to create an aura of utter actuality. It is this sense of the "really real" upon which the religious perspective rests and which the symbolic activities of religion as a cultural system are devoted to producing, intensifying, and, so far as possible, rendering inviolable.[34]

The "transposition to another scale" means that religious language not only symbolizes (for that it must) but also *asserts* nonsymbolic truth—it makes doctrinal claims that are not *merely* poetic. What makes mythopoetic discourse uniquely *sacred* or religious is, then, the fact that it is believed to be true. It is this alone that gives religious communication its power. Religious symbol, parable, and myth all assert, implicitly if not explicitly, that human values are grounded in what is ultimately real.

We have attended in some detail to the symbolic nature of religious communication, especially to its verbal, narrative forms in parable, story, and myth. In the past century, equal—if not more—attention has been given to the study of ritual action as a primary form of religious expression and communication. To that subject we now must turn.

### NOTES

1. Erich Kahler, "The Nature of the Symbol," in *Symbolism in Religion and Literature,* ed. Rollo May (New York, 1960), 50.
2. Susanne K. Langer, *Philosophy in a New Key* (New York, 1951), 45–46.
3. Ibid., 24.
4. C. Richardson, "The Foundations of Christian Symbolism," in *Religious Symbolism,* ed. F. Ernest Johnson (New York, 1955), 6–8.
5. C. H. Dodd, *The Parables of the Kingdom* (London, 1935), 16.
6. *Udana,* Vol. VIII, 8; 91–92, in *Buddhist Parables,* trans. E. W. Burlingame (New Haven, Conn., 1922), 107–108.
7. For what follows I am especially dependent on the seminal essay by Stephen Crites, "The Narrative Quality of Experience," *Journal of the American Academy of Religion* 39 (Sept. 1971).
8. Alan Watts, *Myth and Ritual in Christianity* (London, 1953), 7.
9. B. Malinowski, *Myth in Primitive Psychology* (London, 1926), 125.
10. Raphael Patai, *Myth and Modern Man* (Englewood Cliffs, N.J., 1972), 292–293.
11. Malinowski, *Myth,* 39.
12. Ibid., 81–83.
13. Ibid., 104–105.
14. Ibid., 76–77.
15. C. G. Jung, *Psychology and Religion* (New Haven, Conn., 1938), 63.
16. C. G. Jung, "Symbols and the Interpretation of Dreams," in *The Collected Works of C. G. Jung,* Vol. 18 (Princeton, N.J., 1977), 228.
17. Ibid., 231–232.
18. Ibid., 238.
19. C. G. Jung, "Two Essays in Analytical Psychology," in *The Collected Works of C. G. Jung,* Vol. 6 (Princeton, N.J., 1977), 171–172.
20. C. G. Jung, "Transformation Symbolism in the Mass," in *The Collected Works of C. G. Jung,* Vol. 11, 273.
21. C. G. Jung and C. Kerenyi, *Essays on a Science of Mythology* (New York, 1963), quoted in Patai, *Myth and Modern Man,* 23.
22. Mircea Eliade, *Myth and Reality* (London, 1964), 5–6.

23. Ibid., 18.

24. Ibid., 12.

25. Paul Ricoeur, *The Symbolism of Evil* (Boston, 1969), 348.

26. Reinhold Niebuhr, "The Truth in Myths," in *The Nature of Religious Experience*, ed. Eugene Bewkes (New York, 1937), 129.

27. Ricoeur, *Symbolism*, 350.

28. Paul Ricoeur, "Biblical Hermeneutics," *Semeia* 4 (1975), 36.

29. Ian G. Barbour, *Myths, Models, and Paradigms* (New York, 1974), 49.

30. Ibid., 120.

31. Ibid., 143.

32. Ibid., 145–146.

33. W. M. Urban, *Language and Reality* (London, 1939), 572.

34. Clifford Geertz, "Religion as a Cultural System," in *Reader in Comparative Religion*, 2nd ed., ed. William A. Lessa and Evon Z. Vogt (New York, 1965), 213.

## KEY WORDS

signs

symbols

representational symbols

presentational symbols

analogy

first-order religious discourse

second-order religious discourse

metaphor

parable

myth

Bronislaw Malinowski

Carl Jung

collective unconscious

archetype

individuation

doctrines

models

## REVIEW QUESTIONS

1. Why does the author treat this material after the chapter on the sacred and the holy and before the chapter on sacred ritual?

2. Define a sign and a symbol. What is the difference between representational symbols and presentational symbols? Can you think of other examples of both kinds of symbols? Can symbols be easily or quickly changed?

3. What are three ways that symbols can "bring together"? Describe some of the different things that are brought together in the Christian symbol of a fish.

4. What is a metaphor and how can it function as a religious symbol? What is a parable and what are some of its distinctive characteristics? How do the Buddha's parable of Visakha's sorrow and Jesus' parable of the workers in the vineyard illustrate these characteristics of parable?

5. Why are stories, such as parables and myths, important for religion?

6. What are some of the characteristics of myth as a form of religious expression and communication? What is the difference between a myth and a parable? How would you describe the difference between the functionalist, the psychotherapeutic, and the phenomenological interpretations of myth?

7. What does the author mean when he writes that doctrines and dogmas are "second-order" religious discourse in contrast to "first-order"?

8. If religious discourse (parable, myth, and so forth) is fundamentally symbolic and analogical and cannot be tested by scientific modes of verification, by what criteria, if any, can religious claims (doctrines) be tested for their truth or adequacy?

## SUGGESTIONS FOR FURTHER READING

LANGER, SUZANNE. *Philosophy in a New Key.* New York: New American Library, 1954.

*For discussions of metaphor, parable, and models, see the following:*

BARBOUR, IAN. *Myths, Models, and Paradigms: A Comparative Study in Science and Religion.* New York: Harper & Row, 1974.

CRITES, STEPHEN. "The Narrative Quality of Experience." *The Journal of the American Academy of Religion* 39 (September 1971).

McFAGUE, SALLIE. *Metaphorical Theology.* Philadelphia: Fortress Press, 1982. (This book and Barbour's include references to the best current literature on the subject of the use of metaphor, parable, and models in religious discourse.)

SOSKICE, JANET M. *Metaphor and Religious Language.* Oxford: Oxford University Press, 1985. An excellent philosophical analysis.

TeSELLE, SALLIE. *Speaking in Parables.* Philadelphia: Fortress Press, 1975.

*For the study of myth, see the following:*

CAMPBELL, JOSEPH. *The Masks of God: Primitive Mythology.* New York: Viking Press, 1959.

DUNDES, ALAN. *Sacred Narrative: Readings in the Theory of Myth.* Berkeley: University of California Press, 1984.

ELIADE, MIRCEA. *Cosmos and History: The Myth of the Eternal Return.* New York: Harper Torchbooks, 1959.

———. *Myth and Reality.* New York: Harper & Row, 1964.

JUNG, CARL G. *Psychology and Religion.* New Haven, Conn.: Yale University Press, 1938. See also *The Collected Works.* Vols. 7, 11, 18.

KIRK, G. S. *The Nature of Greek Myths.* New York: Penguin Books, 1974. (Chapter 3, "Five Monolithic Theories," raises critical questions about universal theories.)

MALINOWSKI, BRONISLAW. *Myth in Primitive Society.* New York: Norton, 1926. Reprinted in *Magic, Science and Religion.* Garden City, N.Y.: Doubleday, 1954.

NIEBUHR, REINHOLD. "The Truth in Myths." In *The Nature of Religious Experience,* ed. Eugene Bewkes. New York: Harpers, 1937.

STRENSKI, IVAN. *Four Theories of Myth in Twentieth Century History: Cassirer, Eliade, Lévi-Strauss, and Malinowski.* Iowa City: University of Iowa Press, 1987.

*On the cognitive status of religious language: Most of the books cited deal with this problem directly or indirectly, but for a more philosophical analysis the following are recommended as introductions:*

FERRÉ, FREDERICK. *Language, Logic, and God.* New York: Harper & Row, 1961. This book surveys a number of positions and is a good introduction to the issues.

GEIVETT, DOUGLAS R., AND BRENDAN SWEETMAN, eds. *Contemporary Perspectives on Religious Epistemology.* New York: Oxford University Press, 1992.

HICK, JOHN. *An Interpretation of Religion.* New Haven, Conn.: Yale University Press, 1992.

# 4

# *Sacred Ritual*

## *Overview*

Here we continue our investigation on forms of symbolic expression and communication of the sacred with an exploration of the nature of sacred ritual. We begin with a definition of religious ritual and the reasons why ritual has played such an essential role in religious life. This is followed by a discussion of several approaches to the study of religious ritual, including the relationship between ritual and myth, the social functions of ritual, and the connections and resemblances between ritual and human drama and play.

The discussion then turns to an analysis of two classic types of sacred rituals. The first type are those rites that are connected to the human life cycle—such as birth, marriage, and death—and to human crises—such as illness. These rituals often reflect a distinctive structure that is analyzed and illustrated in rites associated with birth, puberty, and initiation into a religious vocation.

A second classic type of sacred rite is associated with fixed points in the yearly calendar and is connected either with the changing of the seasons or with the commemoration and rehearsal of a momentous historical event, for example, God's Covenant with Israel on Mt. Sinai or the Passion of Christ. Here, again, a distinct ritual pattern often can be discerned, and it is illustrated in an analysis of the ancient Babylonian New Year festival and in the Roman Catholic Mass.

A striking feature of many sacred rites is the offering of a sacrifice. The various purposes of sacrifice are discussed and particular attention is given to rituals of atonement for defilement, transgression—or sin—and the critical role played by the sacrificial representative—or scapegoat—as sin remover. This theme is illustrated from the earliest account of the Jewish Day of Atonement that is found in the Book of Leviticus. According to some recent scholars, rites of sacrifice, which go back to the Palaeolithic age, are at the root of all religion and are an outlet or a means of escaping violence by transferring human aggression outside the community, thereby maintaining peace and solidarity.

The chapter concludes with a discussion of rituals as sacraments and how sacraments reflect some of the most characteristic features of sacred ritual.

## Ritual Action

Rituals are found in every human community and are a primary means of social communication and cohesion. The Greek word for *rite* derives from *dromenon*, meaning "a thing done" to achieve a specific end. If a symbol is a meaningful sign, a ritual can be called a significant *action*. Rituals range from simple gestures, such as bowing or shaking hands, to elaborate ceremonial dramas, such as the Eastern Orthodox liturgy or a British royal coronation. The Confucianist sage Hsün Tzu spoke of the significant role of ritual in the following memorable words:

> When rites are performed in the highest manner, then both the emotions and the forms embodying them are fully realized. . . . Through rites Heaven and earth join in harmony, the sun and the moon shine, the four seasons proceed in order . . . and all things flourish; men's likes and dislikes are regulated and their joys and hates are made appropriate. Those below are obedient, those above are enlightened, all things change but do not become disordered; only he who turns his back upon rites will be destroyed. Are they not wonderful indeed?[1]

A *religious ritual* can be defined as *an agreed-on and formalized pattern of ceremonial movements and verbal expressions carried out in a sacred context.* One of the interesting things about religious rituals is that they can serve as "condensed symbols." Friday abstinence, until recently, was such a symbol of the Christian life for Roman Catholics, just as certain dietary practices remain for observant Jews a condensed symbol of their faith. Rituals are capable of expressing and communicating several levels of meaning, in a fashion similar to our description of the fish symbolism in Chapter 3. Moreover, the meanings or functions of a ritual may not be "manifest" or obvious, but only "latent," or hidden to the participants themselves.

Many scholars would concur that ritual is the very heart and soul of religion and that ritual must be viewed as both prior to and more fundamental than either myth or doctrine. The biblical scholar W. Robertson Smith (1846–1894) was among the first to hold this view and to insist that myth is merely an explanation of ritual and, therefore, of secondary importance. This perception of ritual as constituting the essence of religion was reinforced by Emile Durkheim, and it remains a fundamental conviction of his followers at the present time.

Robertson Smith, Durkheim, and their contemporary followers may be quite wrong in their effort to derive myth from ritual. However, they are unquestionably right in emphasizing the central role of ritual in the life of religion. It is critical to point this out in our present context, since persons brought up in a Western, secularized culture are likely to approach religion intellectually—that is, see it as a system of beliefs—and to undervalue the bodily and behavioral aspects of religious life. Ritual is primordial and universal because it appeals to the whole person, weaving together bodily gesture, speech, and the senses—the sight of colors and shapes, the sounds of chants or *mantras*, the tactile feel of water and fabric, and the smell of incense or the aroma of symbolic foods. Through its appeal to bodily movement, verbal chants and responses, and our multiple senses, ritual is symbolic in the most profound sense, for it "brings together" the mind, the body, and the emotions and, at the same time, binds us to a community of shared values.

Social scientists often focus their attention on the *functions* that ritual plays in the life of individuals and communities. They point out that society is like an organism—for example, like a human body. In a body, all the organs function together to maintain the whole organism. So it is with society: All parts of the system work together to ensure the continuity of the social organism. According to the functionalists, religious ritual is critical to this task. Furthermore, ritual actions may be continued in a society for reasons not wholly consistent with their apparent purpose. For example, rituals may be enacted to dispel forms of anxiety or to strengthen the social order, even if these functions are not apparent to the participants themselves.

Rituals clearly serve many important psychological and social functions; here we can mention a few of the most basic. Rituals of initiation, such as the Jewish bar mitzvah, can legitimize the transition from one stage of life to another. In so doing, they can, like liturgical rites, also serve an important identity function. Rituals can also routinize behavior and help reduce the anxiety and uneasiness associated with the loss of clear boundaries or the experience of dislocation. Similarly, rituals can help to resolve social tensions due, perhaps, to the scarcity and arbitrary distribution of life's material goods or the seeming injustice in the apportioning of social positions. A scholar speaks of this ritual function in his study of the natives of the small island of Tikopia:

> One can assume that every individual has emotional dispositions and tensions arising from his relation to the external world, including members of his own society. . . . What ritual has done is to provide routinization and canalization for such tensions. These are not left for random expression, but are assigned their time and place for explicit mention and acting out.[2]

Rites that allot social duties or offices, such as the investiture of a bishop or tribal chief, or rites that allow for and channel the expression of pent-up emotion at certain times in socially accepted ways, such as Mardi Gras, would be examples.

Rituals also serve to dramatize and therefore to articulate a community's archetypal patterns of belief and behavior and, in so doing, to legitimize those beliefs and actions. In ritual, these patterns are perceived as established by the gods or as having a sacred or divine sanction. Related to this is the fact that the ritual is performative; that is, it accomplishes something or reinforces the belief or behavior by the very fact of its periodic repetition. It has been said, "man is what he eats" or, to put it another way, we become what we habitually do.

These and other functions of ritual will be more obvious when we describe a number of specific rituals. Suffice it to say, the functionalists have greatly increased our appreciation of the place, indeed the indispensability, of ritual in human social life. However, it would be wrong to reduce religious ritual solely to functional analysis if that meant viewing it as simply or primarily serving some *other*—secular, psychological, or social—purpose. In other words, the danger of functionalism is in its reduction of a *religious* phenomenon, such as ritual, to a purely psychic or social reality. Such a reduction is an impoverishment, for it fails to do full justice to the *religious* dimension of the ritual itself. Needless to say, while all action has a function or purpose, there are social scientists who have shown far greater interest in and sensitivity to the specifically religious meaning of ritual action. The work of the anthropologist Victor Turner, discussed later, is a case in point.

A nice counterbalance to an extreme functionalist interpretation is the observation that rituals, like some other types of human activity, do not always serve a practical purpose. A good deal of human behavior is not instrumental, that is, is not a means to some other end but is, rather, an end in itself. Games and play are good examples. Another way, then, that ritual has been investigated is exploring the analogies between it and human play. The foremost work in this field is Johan Huizinga's influential *Homo Ludens: A Study of the Play Element in Culture.* Huizinga summarizes the formal characteristics of play as follows:

> We might call it a free activity standing quite consciously outside "ordinary" life as being "not serious," but at the same time absorbing the player intensely and utterly. It is an activity connected with no material interest, and no profit can be gained from it. It proceeds within its own proper boundaries of time and space according to fixed rules and an orderly manner. It promotes the formation of social groupings which tend to surround themselves with secrecy and to stress their difference from the common world by disguise or other means.[3]

Huizinga points out how primal and archaic religious ritual is closely related to play, and in this he is supported by the ethnographers who have demonstrated the sacred origin of many games. We observe that ancient religious ritual often is marked by play-acting and "make believe" in which the distinction between empirical reality and imagination actually breaks down. In ritual or play, fantasy and imagination are not sharply distinguished from the empirically real. In tribal rituals, for example, men carve monstrous masks, which stand for ghosts, and scare both themselves and the women of the tribe. Yet both the men and the women know that behind the masks are their own relatives. Both play and religious ritual have this dramatic and imaginary quality about them; both are "different from ordinary life." This perhaps explains the interest people take in the ritualized pageantry associated with the British monarchy. The colorful costumes from another era, the pomp, and the solemnity are all touched with an aspect of fantasy and festivity. Ritual, like play, introduces us to the imaginative possibilities of "another world."

From what we know about our human capacity for self-transcendence, it makes a good deal of sense to see ourselves as *homo ludens,* as the player or the ritualist. Essential to our nature is the expressive need to act, to imagine new possibilities, and to engage spontaneously in festivity and celebration—the goal of which is in the activity itself. Without pressing the connection perhaps as closely as Huizinga has done, we can nevertheless appreciate the family resemblance that does exist between human play and religious ritual and how both reflect an indispensable dimension of human life.

## Types of Sacred Ritual

We have looked at some of the ways in which ritual has been studied and interpreted. We now can examine the principal forms of religious ritual and illustrate these types with specific examples from a variety of traditions, both archaic and modern. There is no agreed-on typology or study of types of religious ritual, one reason being that rituals often overlap, both in form and in meaning. Nevertheless, there are some helpful distinctions that can be made. Rituals sometimes are differentiated by whether they are corporate, domestic, or personal. Another possible contrast is between rituals based on the cycle of nature and the seasons—for example, agricultural festivals or celebrations of the New Year—and those rituals that commemorate or re-create a historical or mythological event—for example, the birth of Christ or the Jewish Passover.

Another type of ritual consists of nonperiodic rites connected with the human life cycle, or rites of passage, as they have come to be called. These include rituals associated with such events as birth, initiation into adulthood, marriage, and death. Some scholars have distinguished these noncyclical rites of initiation and passage from other occasional rituals associated with the "life crisis" of an individual or community. Examples would be healing rites or rainmaking rites. In this chapter, we will analyze all these various types in terms of two paramount forms: (1) nonperiodic life-cycle and life-crisis rites and (2) periodic festivals based on calendar-fixed seasonal or historical events.

### Life-Cycle Rites

The significance of rituals connected with critical events in the life of individuals was brought to the attention of scholars by Arnold van Gennep in *The Rites of Passage*. Van Gennep noted that there are numerous rituals that accompany life's stages and crises.

> The life of an individual in any society is a series of passages . . . so that a man's life comes to be made up of a succession of stages with similar ends and beginnings: birth, social puberty, marriage, fatherhood, advancement to a higher class, occupational specialization, and death. For every one of these events there are ceremonies whose essential purpose is to enable the individual to pass from one defined position to another.[4]

What life-cycle rituals do, according to van Gennep, is help individuals through the difficulties of such critical transitions, as well as assist society in accepting significant changes in the status or the loss of their members. Other scholars would, however, give greater attention than does van Gennep to the sacred symbolism of these rites, which reveal the most profound values of a community. For example, it is through puberty rites, Eliade contends, that the individual passes "beyond the natural mode—the mode of the child—and gains access to the cultural mode; that is, he is introduced to spiritual values."[5]

Van Gennep called attention to the striking fact that *rites of passage* often reveal a common pattern, consisting of three distinct elements: separation, transition, and reincorporation. The first stage removes individuals from their old status. This is often shown by actual physical separation from other members of the society or by a simulation of death itself. The transition stage is frequently marked by some form of social isolation and a condition of statuslessness, a kind of limbo. During this time, the initiate—whether an adolescent girl or an elder, grieving son—is prepared for her or his new station. The third stage of reincorporation signals the passage to a new status or to normal social life, often symbolized by the wearing of new attire, a ring, or other forms of insignia.

Victor Turner has developed van Gennep's insight into the three stages of life-cycle rites by giving special attention to the transitional, or *liminal* (*limen*, signifying "threshold" in Latin), *stage* and its social and religious significance. Turner sees societal life as a process involving successive periods of structured differentiation, forms of hierarchy, and times of what he calls *communitas,* or the spontaneous bond of communion between members of a society. Life-cycle rites exhibit this alternating process in the life of both individuals and groups.

The liminal, or threshold, stage is a transitional one, and thus, according to Turner, it represents antistructure. It is likened to being in the wilderness, to darkness, and to death. In the liminal stage, the initiate is stripped of status, symbolized by uniform dress, loss of rank, and submissiveness. A rite of the African Ndembu tribe, undertaken for the installation of their chief, is a good example of Turner's understanding of the role of liminality. The Ndembu chief is, in fact, a condensed symbol for the tribe itself because he represents its territory, its community, and its fecundity. But before the chief-elect can be installed, he must be stripped of his status and reduced to that of the commonest tribesman. The Ndembu liminal rite begins with the construction of a hut known as the *kafu*, which means "to die," and it is here "that the chief-elect dies from his commoner state."[6]

The chief-to-be is clad in nothing but a ragged waistcloth and is led, with a ritual wife, to the *kafu*, as if they were infirm. In the hut, they sit crouched in a posture of shame and submissiveness and undergo a tirade of rebuke and humiliation by fellow tribesmen:

> Be silent! You are a mean and selfish fool, one who is bad-tempered. You do not love your fellows. . . . Meanness and theft is all you have! Yet here we have called you and we say you must succeed to the Chieftainship. Put away your meanness, put aside anger, give up adulterous intercourse, give them up immediately.[7]

Anyone in the tribe wronged by the chief-elect is entitled to revile him during this liminal period. The chief, by being ritually stripped of his status, is being prepared to facilitate the achievement of *communitas*, the sense of sharing a common humanity, a profound fellow feeling required of a chief. Turner points out that the elevation to a new status must be preceded by such a status reversal. In a real sense, the first must be last before becoming first. By so doing, human communion and fellow feeling are achieved.

The attainment of *communitas* is considered holy or sacred because it "breaks through the interstices of structure" and "transgresses or dissolves the norms that govern institutionalized relationships."[8] But rites of passage do not conclude in the liminal stage; they also include the rites of incorporation back into a structured society, revitalized by the experience of *communitas*. Turner argues that it is only the achievement of a sacred communion that makes ongoing social life possible.

The profound attraction of many of the world's great religious leaders lies, perhaps, in the fact that their lives can be viewed as condensed symbols of this ritual process. Buddha, Jesus, and Gandhi come to mind. During Holy Week, the Pope often visits an Italian prison where he washes the feet of some of society's outcasts, thus showing his bond with all of suffering humanity.

Life-cycle rites can be observed in every religion because of their importance not only to the individual, but also to the larger community. However, the number of rites and the importance of specific types of rites of passage vary greatly among the religions. In some cultures, marriage rites play a critical role whereas in others—for example, the Zuni Indians—it is absent or nearly so. Buddha once recommended 40 rites connected with life's

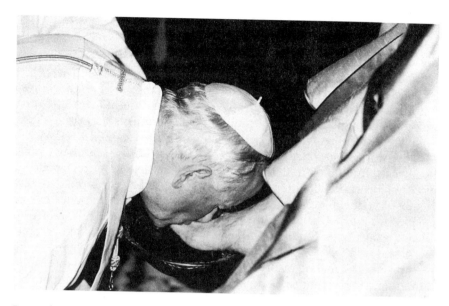

Pope John Paul II washing and kissing of an Italian prisoner's feet, often undertaken during Holy Week, is an example of what the anthropologist Victor Turner calls the ritual achievement of *communitas*. (*Source:* Courtesy of AP/Wide World Photos, Inc.)

stages. Today, devout Hindu Brahmans observe 16 *samskaras*, or sacraments. These are rites accompanying such events as conception, name-giving, **tonsure,** and the beginning of formal study, as well as those associated with birth, marriage, and death. It is striking that four of the seven authorized sacraments of the Roman Catholic Church are rites of passage: baptism; confirmation; matrimony; and extreme unction or anointing of the sick. Here we confine our examples of life-cycle rites to three classes: social puberty, rites of initiation into special societies or vocations, and marriage and funeral rites.

    *Social Puberty—Initiation into Adulthood* Initiation rites are among the most important religious rituals and include not only initiation into adult status in society, but also entrance into secret societies and admission to a special vocation, such as the enthronement of a king or the ordination and consecration of a nun, priest, or bishop.

    In primal and archaic societies, transition to adult status often coincides with physical puberty or sexual maturity. However, initiation into adulthood does not always take place at the time of physical puberty, especially in the case of boys. Nevertheless, social puberty rites have to do with the transition from the asexual world of childhood to an adult society that is differentiated by sexual roles. Rites marking the transition to adulthood reveal a rather common pattern in which the initiates are socially isolated and their behavior restricted, undergo certain ordeals to test their ability to take on their new responsibilities, are instructed in the secret knowledge of the community and shown the sacred objects, and finally are given the insignia of their new status and formally recognized as having made the transition. It is worth noting that this pattern may still be recognized in contemporary college fraternity initiations as well.

Isolation and restricted behavior are common to the initiation rites of both girls and boys. Ordeals are a somewhat more typical feature of rituals for boys, although girls often do undergo such ordeals as fasting, sitting motionless, and even whipping. Boys frequently are required to prove their physical prowess and their hunting feats. Another feature of puberty rites is the physical mutilation of the body, which marks the separation from childhood and incorporation into adult life. In the case of boys, this often involves circumcision or subincision, a slitting of the underside of the penis. In some societies, a ritual act, called clitoridectomy, is performed on girls. It often involves a painful excision of the clitoris, part of the female genital organ. It is interpreted as an act of purification and initiation into adult membership. Other means of signaling incorporation include removing a front tooth, filing teeth to points, piercing ear lobes and the septum for the insertion of ornaments, tattooing and scarifying the body, ornamenting the body with special clothing and bracelets, and haircutting and dressing.

Another important component of puberty rites is the instruction of the adolescents in the tribal law and in the sacred knowledge of the community.

> In this religious perspective, initiation is equivalent to introducing the novice to the mythical history of the tribe; in other words, the initiated learns the deeds of the Supernatural Beings, who, in the dream times, established the present human condition, and all the religious, social, and cultural institutions of the tribe. All in all, to know this traditional lore means to know the adventures of the Ancestors and other Superhuman Beings when they lived on earth.[9]

The ordeals and instruction of the young are frequently accompanied by a dramatic ceremonial and dance—including the use of frightening masked figures and bull-roarers, which emit a roaring sound when whirled through the air—all intended to impress on the adolescents a sense of the *tremendum*, the sacredness of the occasion, which they are never to forget.

*Vocational Initiation Rites*   In many societies, there are, in addition to the usual social puberty rites, initiation ceremonies for special groups or fraternities that consist of an elite class of persons who have demonstrated that they possess a special capacity to understand the sacred mysteries or are gifted with unique spiritual powers. Membership in a sacred society often cuts across tribal or social boundaries, and entrance can involve a series of rites extending over several years. However, the pattern of initiation is similar in, for example, North America, Oceania, and Africa.

Intiation into a special religious vocation—be it that of a monk, nun, or priest—follows the pattern of separation, transition, and reincorporation. In Chinese Buddhism, this can be observed in the ritual known as *tonsure*, in which a monk shaves the head of a layman, often a youth, who thereby enters

An adult baptized by immersion in a pool that represents the waters of the Jordan. Baptisms universally represent ritual purification as well as incorporation into the religious community. (*Source:* Courtesy of Camera Press Ltd.)

the *sangha,* or congregation of Buddhist monks or nuns. The ceremony in the shrine hall is simple but replete with symbolic meaning. A sermon is read by the master to the kneeling candidate, relating how Sakyamuni, the Buddha, stole out of his palace, cut off his hair, and renounced lay life. The candidate waves to his parents, symbolizing "leaving the home" and accepting an older monk as his new master. The young candidate then faces the altar and makes nine prostrations, lying face down, to the Three Jewels: the Buddha, the Dharma (the doctrine or teaching), and the Sangha. At that point, the master sprinkles the candidate's head with holy water and then receives a razor from the candidate, who beseeches: "I, your disciple . . . today beg Your reverence to be the Teacher who shaves my hair. . . . I wish to renounce lay life as your dependent."[10]

The master shaves all but the top tuft of hair, reminding the youth that it is not too late to withdraw from his vows. The candidate then answers: "I have made up my mind to renounce lay life and I will never regret or withdraw." Three times the question is put to the youth, and three times he replies. The master then cuts off the remaining hair, cutting off the candidate from all previous ties. The youth then dons a monk's gown, prostrates himself before the Buddha image, and joins the other monks in a chant. The ceremony ends with the novice returning to his family and the other spectators to receive their congratulations. From that day forward, he will begin to live like a monk and train for ordination, although he may not actually be ordained for several years at the age of 20.

*Marriage and Funeral Rites*  The classic features of life-cycle rites that we have observed so far are also evident in marriage ceremonies and in funeral or mortuary rites. As a "holy estate," marriage is hedged around by numerous taboos and customs, such as the throwing of rice or grain at the bride to ensure her fertility, the seclusion of the bride and groom for a period, the changing of clothing before the marriage, and the tying of knots and the exchanging of rings to strengthen the marriage bond.

Funeral rites also reflect the threefold pattern of separation, transition, and reincorporation. For most religions, death is viewed as a threshold leading from one mode of existence to another, a liminal period before rebirth to a new status. Similarly, mourning rites represent a time of separation and transition for the deceased's family and friends. The greater the role played by the deceased in the community—a ruler, for example—the more elaborate and extended are the funeral and mourning rites. The variety of rituals surrounding death are legion, and their features depend to a considerable degree on the society's attitude toward the role of the deceased in the afterlife state. Fear of the dead often means elaborate rites of purification or efforts to appease and to placate the spirit of the dead. The body may be removed from the house by special means to ensure that it will not return, or a stake may be driven through the corpse for the same purpose. In China, elaborate mortuary rites ensure both a safe and speedy journey of the deceased spirit to Heaven and its well-being in Paradise. The extraordinary number and the duration of these rites impress the living kinsmen of the importance of the ancestors for the ongoing cohesion, health, and happiness of the family. The sage Hsün Tzu points to the unique importance of rites connected with both birth and death:

> Rites are strictest in their ordering of birth and death. Birth is the beginning of man, death his end. When both beginning and end are good, man's way is complete. Therefore the gentleman is reverent in his treatment of the beginning and careful in his treatment of the end, regarding both with the same gravity.[11]

## Life-Crisis Rites: A Healing Ritual

Another prevalent type of nonperiodic ritual is a *life-crisis rite* undertaken to meet a specific crisis in the life of an individual or a community, such as illness, miscarriage, failure in the hunt, or drought. Understandably, the concern for health is of particular urgency, and all religions—especially those in nonliterate societies—have rituals that invoke or ward off supernatural powers as a means of curing disease.

In primal societies, it is generally believed not only that health is supernaturally given but also that disease is often supernaturally caused. Thus, the crucial dealing with illness, the loss of soul, or evil possession is left to the work of religious professionals: diviners, medicine men, **shamans, exorcists,** and priests, since it is often believed that they possess special powers for dealing with the supernatural.

The shaman is uniquely able to undergo altered states of consciousness and to leave his body and travel to the other world of the spirits, and thereby to serve as intercessor and healer. The word *shaman* is Siberian, and it is in the northern regions that shamanism can be observed in its classic form. It is, however, found throughout the world and is a common feature of native American Indian religious life. The shaman protects the community by warding off demons and disease.

An illustration of a life-crisis healing rite that focuses on the prominent role of the shaman is found among the Iban or Sea Dayaks, a people of western Borneo, now a part of Malaysia. The Iban shaman is called a *manang*, and his principal concern is caring for the psychic welfare of his Iban clients. The Iban believe that every person has a separable soul that can leave the body and wander about in the world of the spirits and therefore become ensnared by an evil spirit. Sickness is most often diagnosed as some misfortune that has befallen the soul, and, it is believed, the shaman can heal the soul by freeing it from a malevolent spirit or by slaying the evil spirit.

The infant mortality rate among the Iban is very high, and most women in the community have suffered the loss of a child. Child loss is widely attributed to the work of an incubus, or evil demon, who descends on persons in their sleep, especially to seek carnal intercourse with women. In their dreams, the incubus appears to Iban women as a handsome and alluring male whose advances they are unable to resist. However, the incubus is really a guise for an animal, such as the monkey, that is metamorphosed to assume an attractive human shape.

The intercourse with the evil spirit leads, of course, to fatal consequences for the women's offspring, as well as for the family. High infant mortality is a powerful threat to the entire community. Slaying the incubus and restoring a woman to health is one of the Iban shaman's most important and formidable tasks. While most shamans can perform rituals to ward off an incubus, only the exceptional shaman can actually ritually slay an evil demon. Manang Bungai, an Iban shaman, possessed such extraordinary powers.

Through elaborate divinatory rites he was able to subdue and destroy these life-threatening demons.

Similar healing rituals are found in most tribal societies. Eskimo shamans, for example, go on spirit flights for the purpose of curing illness and retrieving lost souls. The belief in the intrusion of disease-causing objects is especially widespread among native American Indians. The Sia Pueblo Indians have special medicine societies whose job it is to carry out elaborate rituals for the purpose of extracting foreign, disease-producing objects—thorns, sticks, or pebbles—from the bodies of the Sia who are in need of cures.

## Calendar or Seasonal Rituals

All over the world, from time immemorial, societies have marked the seasons and important events in the cycle of the year with public rituals. These *seasonal and calendar rites* are closely associated with the rhythmic changes of nature; with the cycles of the sun and moon; with winter, spring, summer, and autumn; as well as with seed time and harvest. In agricultural societies, rites connected with planting, the first fruits, and the harvest are universal. On the other hand, in historical religions such as Judaism and Christianity, fixed calendar rites serve to commemorate and to represent archetypal historical events. Even some of these rites—Christmas and the Jewish Passover, for example—trace their roots to the annual cycle of the seasons.

Seasonal ritual is always directed to securing the well-being of both the community and the individual. It tends to follow a common ritual structure in which the evil, pollution, and eclipse of life's vitality, connected with the old year, are purged away. The pattern is marked by mortification and lenten austerities and rites of emptying (*kenosis*), followed by rites of revitalization, or the giving of new life, fertility, and prosperity. A scholar rightly observes that, for the ancient community, "life is not so much a progression from cradle to grave as it is a series of leases annually or periodically renewed."[12]

These "leases on life" follow a more or less uniform structure that are described in terms of four principal movements:

> First come rites of MORTIFICATION, symbolizing the state of suspended animation which ensues at the end of the year, when one lease of life has drawn to a close and the next is not yet assured.
>
> Second comes rites of PURGATION, whereby the community seeks to rid itself of all noxiousness and contagion, both physical and moral, and of all evil influences which might impair the prosperity of the coming year and thereby threaten the desired renewal and vitality.
>
> Third comes rites of INVIGORATION, whereby the community attempts by its own concerted and regimented effort, to galvanize its moribund condition and to procure that new lease of life. . . .
>
> Last comes rites of JUBILATION, which bespeak men's sense of relief when the new year has indeed begun and the continuance of their own lives. . . . is thereby assured.[13]

A wealth of evidence from primal and ancient religion has been amassed to support this general pattern. For purposes of illustration, we will focus on one classic example, the *New Year (Akitu) Festival* of the ancient Babylonians. We will see, however, that the pattern is also discernible in a historical—calendric rite such as the modern Roman Catholic Mass.

The Akitu was celebrated at the beginning of each year at the vernal equinox, during the first 12 days of the month of Nisan (March–April). The rites centered around the temple (called Esagila) of the god Marduk in Babylon and the ritual dramatization of the creation story, the *Enuma elish,*\* and Marduk's victory over Tiamat and the forces of chaos. The Akitu Festival is a threshold rite marking the transition from one status to another. You will note that the themes discussed by van Gennep and Turner are prominent. However, the ritual is an exemplary model of the seasonal pattern so common among agricultural societies. The seasonal theme is nonetheless tied closely to the political concern of ensuring the life and prosperity of the social order.

The first four days of Nisan are somber and melancholy, expressing a sense of the desolation of the winter season, the defilement of the people, and the impotence of the king. These are days of lenten *mortifications* and prayer. On the second day of the rite, the priests entreat Marduk

> [Have pity] upon the city, Babylon
> Turn thy face towards Esagila thy temple;
> Give freedom to them that dwell in Babylon, thy wards.[14]

Marduk is thought to be "bound" and the king is deposed or symbolically slain. On the evening of the fourth day, the entire *Enuma elish* is recited, marking the beginning of the passage from winter to spring, from chaos to cosmic renewal.

The fifth day of Nisan ushers in the rites of *purgation* on the Day of Atonement. The temple is purified, sprinkled with water, and fumigated with incense. Incantations are recited by an exorcist, and a sheep is beheaded and its body rubbed against the temple walls to absorb all the pollution of the previous year. The head and body of the sheep, or scapegoat, are then thrown in the river, and both the officiating priest and the executioner are sent into quarantine in the desert for the remainder of the festival. This purging is followed by a ritual abdication of the king. The king's crown, ring, and scepter are removed, and the priest strikes the king across the face. The sovereign is forced to kneel and make an act of penitence and expiation in the presence of Marduk, offering a "negative" confession declaring his innocence:

> I have not sinned, O Lord of the lands . . .
> I have not neglected the temple of Esagila . . .
> I have not rained blows on the cheek of a subordinate . . .
> I have cared for Babylon; I have not broken its walls.[15]

---

\*For a discussion of the Babylonian creation myth, the *Enuma elish,* see Chapter 8.

The king is then reinvested and resumes his regal status. During the king's divestiture in the temple, there is a carnival atmosphere in the streets of the city, accompanied by ritual combats symbolizing the ascendancy of chaos. The social order is overturned, slaves become masters and masters become slaves, and a criminal is enthroned as carnival king. However, once the king is restored and Marduk is ritually released by his son Nabu, the rite moves into its third phase with ceremonies of *invigoration*.

From the sixth to the eighth day of Nisan, the ritual liberation of Marduk, his victory over the evil Tiamat, the assembly of the gods, and Marduk's enthronement are all enacted. On the ninth day of Nisan there occurs a triumphant procession of Marduk and the king from Esagila to the House of the New Year's Feast accompanied by a joyful populace. New life is assured. On the next day, a sumptuous banquet is held for the king, the gods, the priests, and their attendants. That night, Marduk and the king return to Esagila where a sacred marriage is consummated between the king and a sacred female temple slave. This signals the return to fertility, the impregnation of Mother Nature, and the restoration of life. The rite ends with the couple emerging from "the chamber of the bed" to partake of a final elaborate feast of *jubilation* for the new life won:

> Around the shoulders of his beloved bride he has laid his arms . . .
> The king, like unto the sun, sits beside her,
> A sumptuous meal is placed before her . . .
> The palace is in fest[ive mood], the king is glad,
> The people are passing the day in abundance.[16]

Seasonally, the Akitu Festival marks the fertility of the new year but, politically, it also ensures divine approval of the king and the assurance of his vitality and authority—the return to cosmic order.

Vestiges of the fourfold seasonal pattern can be noted in some of the calendric rituals of the later historical religions. It can be seen, for example, in the Roman Catholic Mass, particularly in the pre-Vatican II (1965) liturgy. The liturgy begins with prayers of entreaty, confession, and acts of mortification. The priest and the people say the *confiteor,* a public confession of sin, which includes the following:

> I have sinned exceedingly in thought, word, and deed / (striking the breast three times as a sign of contrition), through my fault, / through my fault, / through my most grievous fault.[17]

At the conclusion of the first movement of the Mass, the priest leads the people in the *Kyrie,* a triple supplication: "Lord have mercy on us, / Christ have mercy on us, / Lord have mercy on us."

The second movement, that of *purgation*, begins, as does the Akitu ritual, with a reading from sacred scripture (the Bible, like the *Enuma elish*, is the archetypal Word), a homily or sermon on the readings from the Bible, and the recitation of the Creed. The central rite of the purgation, and the holiest point in the Catholic Mass, is the offering of the sacrifice at the altar, where the priest represents both the sacrificial offering of the people and Christ's eternal sacrifice on the cross at Golgotha. The priest offers the bread (signifying Christ's body), saying

> Accept, O holy Father, / almighty and eternal God, / this host for the all-holy sacrifice, / which I, Thy unworthy servant, offer unto Thee, / my living and true God, / to atone for my numberless sins of willfulness and neglect; / on behalf of all here present, / and likewise for all faithful Christians, living and dead, / that it may profit me and them / as a means of salvation unto life everlasting. Amen.[18]

Similar words are said at the offering of the chalice (wine) signifying Christ's blood.

Following the priest's consecration of the elements of the bread and the wine and the eucharistic sacrifice itself, the people join in the sacred meal, which introduces a series of rites of *invigoration*. This is indicated by a number of prayers, including the following offered by the priest:

> Most humbly we implore Thee, Almighty God . . . that those of us who, from this sharing in the heavenly sacrifice, shall receive the most sacred Body and Blood of Thy Son, may be filled with every grace and heavenly blessing . . .[19]

The Mass concludes with rites of *jubilation:* prayers of thanksgiving, sung Psalms and hymns, and benedictions. Grace has been conferred, the mystical union with God effected, and eternal life assured.

## Ritual and Sacrifice

A random study of seasonal and calendric rituals reveals a striking feature that these religious rites share: So many of them include ritual acts of sacrifice. This feature has long been noted by scholars, and a number of interesting and influential ideas about the origin and the purpose of ritual sacrifice have been suggested.

What is the religious intention or purpose of presenting offerings and sacrifices? Obviously, innumerable human emotions can be expressed in these actions, including fear, guilt, adoration, gratitude, and homage. Three dominant purposes have been highlighted by scholars. Early commentators focused on what is called the rule of *do-ut-des*—"I give that thou mayest give." In other words, offerings signify a simple bargain or exchange, expressed succinctly in a Hindu ritual: "Here is the butter; where are thy gifts?"

The anthropologist E. B. Tylor (1832–1917) believed that sacrifice evolved through three stages: gift giving; homage; and abnegation, or renunciation.[20] Gift giving clearly can express *do-ut-des*—the giver obligating the receiver (the god) to act in kind. Tylor saw the same rule at work in homage. The person paying tribute seeks to gain the king's or the god's goodwill and protection. Renunciation, however, expresses only self-denial and, Tylor believed, is free of crudely practical motives. He therefore considered such acts of renunciation as expressing higher forms of sacrifice. Common to *do-ut-des*, or Tylor's first function of sacrifice, is **propitiation.** To propitiate means to cause to become favorably inclined, to appease or conciliate another. From the dawn of human life, offerings have been made to propitiate the spirits or gods, to achieve their favor, and to minimize their hostility.

W. Robertson Smith (1846–1894) focused on a second important purpose of sacrifice: the securing of a social bond. Smith perceived that ancient Semitic sacrificial rites were often accompanied by a sacred feast or meal. The meal served to establish a covenant, or a mystical union, between the god—symbolized by the sacrificial elements consumed—and those participating in the meal. The ritual also strengthens the bond between the members of the community itself. According to Smith, it is the establishing of community and not barter or propitiation that is the central purpose of sacrifice.

A third, and most important, function of sacrifice is expressed by the term *expiation*—the making of amends or *atonement*—for defilement or transgression. According to this view, sacrificial rites of expiation assume some offense against the sacred or divine. In their most primal form, rites of expiation are directed at the removal of pollution, release from which, it is believed, can free the community and the individual from deadly contagion. What is of critical importance to expiatory rites, however, is the belief that life can be restored not simply by ethical good works but only by costly self-sacrifice. Life must be offered in order that life may be preserved. Moreover, the focus of attention is not on the individual but rather on the transgression that affects the entire society. The community is defiled, and reconciliation needs to be effected. The defiled and sinful life therefore must be offered, sacrificed, and destroyed so that new life might be given.

The way in which corporate purgation and atonement is usually achieved is through the community's representative, or scapegoat. The word *scapegoat* has, in recent times, come to refer to someone who is blamed for someone else's errors and who bears the burden of blame, but this is a distortion of its original intention. Both primal societies and the ancient world shared a more profound sense of society's corporate nature than we do today. It is sometimes called the sense of "corporate personality"—the belief that one person, perhaps the king or a totem animal, can *represent* the entire tribe or nation and can thereby be its sin bearer. The following passage points to the real function of the scapegoat as representative:

> The essential point about the scapegoat is that it removes from the community the taint and impurity of sins *which have first to be openly confessed.* There is no question of transferring to it either blame or responsibility; the sole issue is how to get rid of the miasma of transgression which one freely acknowledges. [Yet] there can be no assurance that every single person will indeed undergo that process; latent impurity may therefore remain. . . . There is thus only one

method of securing clearance, namely, to pronounce a *comprehensive,* blanket confession of sins and to saddle the *comprehensive* taint upon some person, animal or object which will be forcibly expelled and thereby take it away.[21]

The representative is the sin remover, and expiation usually involves the offering—the sacrifice and death—of the victim, which removes or covers the pollution and sin. The Hebrew word for such rites of purgation or covering is *kippurim,* and the holiest day of the Jewish year is **Yom Kippur,** or the Day of Atonement. Originally, the rites of Yom Kippur focused exclusively on the removal of pollution, but in the later Temple and synagogue rites, it became more closely associated with the atonement of sins, understood in terms of the Jewish community's moral obligations under the Covenant with their God.

The earliest account of Yom Kippur is in Chapter 16 of the Book of Leviticus, where it is said to be instituted by Moses in connection with the tabernacle. The ritual is performed by the high priest called Aaron. Its purpose is to purify the priests, the sanctuary, and the people once a year. It consisted of numerous rites of fumigation; ablutions, or washings; and burnt offerings and sacrifices, culminating in a rite that sends into the desert a scapegoat bearing the collective sins of the people.

> And when he has made an end of atoning for the holy place and the tent of meeting and the altar, he shall present the live goat; and Aaron shall lay both his hands upon the head of the live goat, and confess over him all the iniquities of the people of Israel, and all their transgressions, all their sins; and he shall put them upon the head of the goat, and send him away into the wilderness by the hand of a man who is in readiness.
>
> The goat shall bear all their iniquities upon him to a solitary land; and he shall let the goat go in the wilderness.
>
> —(*Leviticus 16:20–22*)

Aaron then removes his garments and bathes in a holy place before again dressing. Thereafter, he offers burnt offerings to make atonement for himself and for the people. The text concludes with the following "everlasting statute":

> And it shall be a statute to you forever that in the seventh month, on the tenth day of the month, you shall afflict yourselves . . . for on this day shall atonement be made for you, to cleanse you; from all your sins you shall be clean before the Lord.
>
> —(*Leviticus 16:29–30*)

Rites of expiation or atonement follow another threefold structure that can be observed on Yom Kippur. The rite begins with a ceremonial *offering.* Here something costly is selected, and a spiritual union is effected between the offerer and the offering. The offering is a genuine representative. This initial rite is followed by the actual *sacrifice.* The representative dies, which symbolizes the offerer's sacrifice of self and death. Life must be given if life is to be received and renewed. The third movement of the rite is the *receiving of new life,* resurrection and regeneration. This is often symbolized by the participation in a common meal or feast, or by the putting on of new garments or other insignia. It is well known that the Christian liturgy of Holy Communion, or the sacrifice of the Mass, is rooted in the ancient Israelite atonement rites. In the liturgy of the Mass, Christ is the people's representative before the throne of God, paradoxically both the offering and the offerer.

More recently, a striking theory of sacrifice has been suggested, based on the thesis of Konrad Lorenz's *On Aggression:* Violence is deeply rooted in human behavior and serves an essential function in human society. The classicist Walter Burkert has built on Lorenz's idea that group demonstration of aggression toward outsiders creates a sense of close personal community. Burkert suggests that human solidarity was, in the primal and ancient world, achieved through a sacred crime—that is, bloody, violent killing—which required amendment for the wrong. The **Paleolithic** Age was, after all, the age of the hunter with its indelible effects on all of humankind.

> Man can virtually be defined as "the hunting ape." . . . The age of the hunter, the Palaeolithic, comprises by far the largest part of human history. No matter that estimates range between 95 and 99 percent: it is clear that man's biological evolution was accomplished during this time. By comparison, the period since the invention of agriculture—10,000 years, at most—is a drop in the bucket. From this perspective, then, we can understand man's terrifying violence as deriving from the behavior of the predatory animal, whose characteristics he came to acquire in the course of becoming man.[22]

According to Burkert, humanity's explosive aggression was transferred and released "in the dangerous and bloody hunt"; that is, in the hunting ritual, aggression between humans was redirected toward animal quarry, assuring order and peace within the community. However, this primordial human violence provoked feelings of fear and guilt that called for amendment; hence the emergence of the ritual of sacrifice. "Sacrificial killing," Burkert concludes, "is the basic experience of the 'sacred.'" *Homo religiosus* acts and attains self-awareness as *homo necans* [from the Latin *necare,* "to kill"].[23]

Burkert's theory has much in common with one proposed by René Girard in his important study *Violence and the Sacred.* Girard also sees violence as the matrix of *all* ritual, and hence religion:

> In a universe where the slightest dispute can lead to a disaster—just as a slight cut can prove fatal to a hemophiliac—the rites of sacrifice serve to polarize the community's aggressive impulses and redirect them toward victims that may be actual or figurative, animate or inanimate, but that are always incapable of propagating further vengeance. The sacrificial process furnishes an outlet for those violent impulses that cannot be mastered by self-restraint. . . . The sacrificial process prevents the spread of violence by keeping violence in check.[24]

Girard has developed an elaborate theory concerning the relationship between the original human victim and the ritual surrogate or substitute victim, the scapegoat. Ritual victims are ambivalent figures, both belonging and yet not belonging to the community. Hence, the surrogate victim often is a slave or livestock. The fundamental point, however, is that the scapegoat keeps violence *outside* the community. It keeps the sacred at bay because, according to Girard, the sacred is not a beneficent power but the *tremendum,* a force of peculiar dread. It represents all those powers—tempests, forest fires, and plagues— that are outside our human mastery. Chief among these is the chaotic threat of human violence—a power, according to Girard, that is "seen as something exterior to man and henceforth as a part of all other outside forces that threaten mankind. Violence is the heart and secret soul of the sacred."[25]

Girard makes the extraordinary claim that *all* religious ritual has its origin in the representative sacrificial victim and that all our great human institutions are founded on religious ritual. The sacrificial victim is, then,

> . . . the ideal educator of humanity, in the etymological sense of *e-ducatio,* a leading out. The rite gradually leads men away from the sacred [as malevolent power]; it permits them to escape their own violence, removes them from violence, and bestows on them all the institutions and beliefs that define our humanity.[26]

There appears, however, to be no agreement on the origin or meaning of sacrifice, and it is likely that none of the theories we have surveyed fully explains this primordial and universal human phenomenon. It is a reasonable conjecture that there are multiple sources of ritual sacrifice and that its practice in any particular context may include several overlapping meanings. In any case, acts of renunciation, the covering or purging of impurity or sin, the strengthening of the bonds of community, and the warding off of violence are deeply human and are not to be dismissed as merely the aberrant actions of ancient peoples.

## Rituals as Sacraments

It will be helpful to conclude this analysis of sacred ritual with a brief consideration of ritual as *sacrament.* By so doing, we can summarize some of the most salient characteristics of sacred rite. Broadly speaking, all *religious* ritual is sacramental in that it concerns the *presence* of the sacred or holy. Sacraments make use of temporal things—words, gestures, and objects—for a spiritual purpose, to make manifest the sacred or the supernatural. A classic definition of a sacrament, found in the catechism of the Anglican *Book of Common Prayer,* states that it is "an outward and visible sign of an inward and spiritual grace." An important addition would be that sacraments do not, like symbols, simply signify or represent the sacred; they also *work.* Effective action is essential to sacraments. The following underlines this point:

> The water cleanses, the bread and wine feed, the oil anoints, the imposition of consecrating hands conveys new character, the marriage act unites; and all this

in the interior and spiritual as well as in the exterior and natural sense. . . . *A valid sacrament, therefore, always leaves the situation diffirent from what it was before.* (Italics added.)[27]

Sacraments, like initiation ceremonies, are *performative* in the sense that they actually accomplish something; they change the status or condition of the participants. In many sacramental religions, such as Roman Catholicism, the efficacy of sacramental rites is not fundamentally dependent on the individual's subjective condition or feelings. The sacrament functions, according to Catholic doctrine, *ex opere operato* ("by the work worked"); that is, the rite itself has a causal power or efficacy beyond its subjective or psychological effects. The anthropologist Mary Douglas registers this performative character of sacraments in her comments on the Roman Catholic **Eucharist.** "Symbolizing," she writes

> does not exhaust the meaning of the Eucharist. Its full meaning involves . . . sacramental efficacy. . . . The crux of the doctrine is that a real, invisible transformation has taken place at the priest's saying of the sacred words and that the eating of the consecrated host has saving efficacy for those who take it and for others.[28]

Sacraments do, of course, have profound psychological and sociological effects, as do all rituals. The function of *catharsis,* or the clarification and purification of the emotions in ritual action, should not be underestimated. Nor should the wider sociological effects of sacraments be minimized in the least. Sacraments, like all rituals, bring attitudes and beliefs to a heightened state of consciousness, thereby strengthening these convictions and, in turn, fortifying the community. As the Chinese Confucianist would say, "Men become truly human as their raw impulse is shaped by *li* [ritual]." However, since social scientists have given such elaborate attention to the emotional and social functions of ritual, it is worth emphasizing their purely sacramental or spiritual efficacy.

Sacramental rites are *performative,* but related to this is their *repetitive character.* Sacramental action must be undertaken periodically at certain specified times of the season, the life cycle, or the liturgical calendar. The habitual, recurrent, and rhythmical character of sacramental ritual is crucial to its effect. Sacraments cannot simply be random and unfamiliar because they are based not only on what is believed to be a venerable tradition but also—more important—on an exemplary model, on an authorized, sacred, archetypal pattern of behavior.

Another characteristic of sacraments is the *meticulous accuracy of their performance,* which is often considered essential to their efficacy. Therefore, the form of a sacramental ritual becomes uniform, fixed, and conventional. Departure from the traditional "way" can cause anxiety as to whether the rite is actually achieving its effect. For this reason, sacramental rites are the most conservative aspect of a community's religious life and can be a source of weakness if the rituals become too conventional and routinized and lose their vitality and relevance. This is the cause of periodic antiritual protests by religious prophets and puritans against the dead monotony of formal liturgical routine, of "going through the paces."

Such forms of antiritualism are probably a sign that a certain deadness has, indeed, set in. But authentic ritual is neither lifeless nor unfeeling; quite the contrary, we have seen that it engages both individuals and communities at the deepest levels of their being. We can conclude, then, by calling to mind Mary Douglas's claim and warning that "ritual structure makes possible a wordless channel of communication."[29] Put another way, ritual can represent or create a structure of meaning that is capable of binding us together; of reviving our sense of participation in a larger human, even cosmic, drama; and of restoring us to genuine *communitas*.

We turn next to an examination of sacred scripture which, we shall see, also serves numerous religious purposes.

## NOTES

1. Hsün Tzu, "A Discussion of Rites," in *Basic Writings of Mo Tzu, Hsün Tzu and Han Fei Tzu*, trans. Burton Watson (New York, 1967), 94.
2. Raymond Firth, *The Work of the Gods in Tikopia* (New York, 1967), 25, 23.
3. Johan Huizinga, *Homo Ludens* (Boston, 1950), 13.
4. Arnold van Gennep, *The Rites of Passage* (Chicago, 1960), 2–3.
5. Mircea Eliade, *Rites and Symbols of Initiation* (New York, 1958).
6. Victor Turner, *The Ritual Process* (Chicago, 1969).
7. Ibid., 101.
8. Ibid., 128.
9. Eliade, *Rites and Symbols*, 39.
10. Holmes Welch, *The Practice of Chinese Buddhism* (Cambridge, Mass., 1967), 274.
11. Hsün Tzu, "Discussion of Rites," 96.
12. Theodore Gaster, *Thespis: Ritual, Myth, and Drama in the Ancient Near East* (New York, 1961), 23.
13. Ibid., 26.
14. Henri Frankfort, *Kingship and the Gods* (Chicago, 1948), 319.
15. Ibid., 319.
16. Ibid., 296.
17. The Rev. Richard E. Power, *Our Mass: A Manual for the Dialogue Mass* (Collegeville, Minn., St. John's Abbey, 1956), 5.
18. Ibid., 26–27.
19. Ibid., 44–45.
20. E. B. Tylor, *Primitive Culture*, Vol. II (New York, 1958), 461–62.
21. Theodore Gaster, *Festivals of the Jewish Year* (New York, 1974), 142–43.
22. Walter Burkert, *Homo Necans: The Anthropology of Ancient Greek Sacrificial Ritual and Myth* (Berkeley, Calif., 1983), 20.
23. Ibid., 3.

24. René Girard, *Violence and the Sacred* (Baltimore, Md., 1977), 113.

25. Ibid., 31.

26. Ibid., 306.

27. Evelyn Underhill, *Worship* (New York, 1957), 43.

28. Mary Douglas, *Natural Symbols* (New York, 1970), 47–48.

29. Ibid., 33.

## KEY WORDS

| | |
|---|---|
| religious ritual | seasonal and calendar rites |
| rites of passage | New Year Akitu Festival |
| liminal stage | propitiation |
| *communitas* | expiation (atonement) |
| social puberty rites | scapegoat |
| life-crisis rites | Yom Kippur |
| shamans | sacrament |

## REVIEW QUESTIONS

1. How does this chapter fit into this book? Why does it come where it does?

2. Define a religious ritual. Why are rituals so common and important?

3. Scholars who apply a functional analysis to their study of religious rituals refer to their *social values*. Can you think of social values (including some unconscious ones) that some specific rituals may serve in our society?

4. What are some similarities between religious ritual and human play?

5. What are life-cycle rites? Give three examples of different types of life-cycle rites. Describe the three-fold pattern of many life-cycle rites. What is the significance of what Victor Turner calls the "liminal" period?

6. Try to describe the symbolic meanings of some of the religious rituals still present in our society, such as baptisms, bar mitzvahs, ordinations, weddings, and funerals.

7. What are life-crisis rites? Describe a life-crisis rite with which you are familiar and indicate its purpose.

8. What is a calendar or seasonal ritual? Describe the fourfold ritual structure that is characteristic of many calendar and seasonal rituals such as the Babylonian Akitu Festival.

9. What are some of the meanings or functions of ritual sacrifice?

10. What is a sacrament and what are some of the characteristics of the sacramental rituals?

## SUGGESTIONS FOR FURTHER READING

BELL, CATHERINE. *Ritual Perspectives and Dimensions.* New York: Oxford University Press, 1997. Emphasis on the complexity of ritual action and limitations of comprehensive theories.

ELIADE, MIRCEA. *Rites and Symbols of Initiation.* New York: Harper and Row, 1958.

GASTER, THEODOR H. *Thespis: Ritual, Myth, and Drama in the Ancient Near East.* New York: Doubleday, 1961.

GRIMES, RONALD L. *Beginnings in Ritual Studies.* Columbia: University of South Carolina Press, 1995. (Parts I–IV)

RAPPAPORT, RAY. *Ritual and Religion in the Making.* Cambridge: Cambridge University Press, 1999. Incorporates material from a range of disciplines. A comprehensive study of ritual in the life of humankind.

SMITH, JONATHAN Z. *To Take Place: Toward a Theory of Ritual.* Chicago: University of Chicago Press, 1987.

TURNER, VICTOR. *The Ritual Process.* Chicago: Aldine Publishing, 1969.

ZUESSE, EVAN. "Ritual." In Mircea Eliade, ed., *The Encyclopedia of Religion,* 12, pp. 405–22. New York: Macmillan, 1987.

*For rites of passage, see the following:*

"Rites of Passage." In Mircea Eliade, ed., *The Encyclopedia of Religion,* 12, pp. 380–403. New York: Macmillan, 1987. Overview and articles on Hindu, Jewish, and Muslim rites.

HOLM, JEAN, WITH JOHN BOWKER. *Rites of Passage.* London: Pinter, 1994.

VAN GENNEP, ARNOLD. *The Rites of Passage.* Chicago: University of Chicago Press, 1960.

*For discussions of ritual and sacrifice, see the following:*

CARTER, JEFFREY, ed. *Understanding Religious Sacrifice: A Reader.* New York: Continuum, 2002. An excellent collection of essays that relate sacrifice to such issues as religious origins, magic, symbolism, ritual, and violence.

GIRARD, RENÉ. *Violence and the Sacred.* Baltimore: John Hopkins Press, 1977.

HASTINGS, JAMES, ed. *Encyclopedia of Religion and Ethics.* Edinburgh: T. and T. Clark, 1912–1918. See essays on "Expiation and Atonement" and "Sacrifice."

HENNINGER, JOSEPH. "Sacrifice." In Mircea Eliade, ed., *The Encyclopedia of Religion,* 12, pp. 544–557. New York: Macmillan, 1987.

HUBERT, HENRI, AND MARCEL MAUSS. *Sacrifice: Its Nature and Function.* Chicago: University of Chicago Press, 1982.

# 5

# *Sacred Scripture*

## *Overview*

Chapter 4 called attention to the power of religious ritual and its many functions in both personal and communal life. Here we will examine another pervasive form of religious expression and communication: sacred scripture. Most readers of this book who live in North America or Europe are likely to take two things for granted in beginning this chapter. The first is the assumption of literacy as a commonplace, with all that that implies. The second is a preconception of what scripture is because of the significant role that the Bible has played in Western civilization. You will see that these suppositions that often shape Western ideas about sacred scripture may need considerable qualification and revision with regard to the use of scripture in other religions.

An important feature of the great living religions of the world is the fact that they all possess sacred texts, and that these are set apart from other religious literature as especially normative for worship, teaching and doctrine, and as a guide for daily life. We begin this chapter by pointing out that, while most religions have sacred scriptures, these scriptures vary in important ways. Some scriptures are relatively short and rather uniform in their literary style and genre. The sacred scriptures of other religions are enormous, constituting essentially a library of volumes and including a rich diversity of literary types: poetry, history, law, philosophy, magical chants, and so on. Some religions possess a variety of sacred scriptures but may assign them different levels of authority. Furthermore, some religions have very fixed boundaries as to which texts are included in their scriptures, whereas in other religions the boundaries have remained open and fluid over the centuries. It is also true that not all religions are as scripturally centered as are Judaism, Christianity, and Islam, the three "religions of the book."

Despite this diversity, the sacred scriptures of the world's religions do share certain features, which we describe in this chapter in some detail. All sacred scriptures, for example, are regarded by their particular communities as possessing sacred power and as having a transforming effect upon the devout reader or hearer. Many religious traditions also believe that their sacred scriptures are the earthly expression of what is a preexistent and eternal Divine Word. For this and other reasons, it is not surprising that sacred scriptures are revered, venerated and, in some instances, worshiped as an object possessing spiritual or magic power. And, of course, all sacred scriptures are regarded by their devotees as authoritative and a normative guide for life. In the discussion of the variety of types of scripture and their common features, you will also be introduced to the ways in which some of the world's influential scriptures originated and how they developed over time and, in many cases, achieved canonicity, that is, were limited to a fixed number of writings or books.

We turn next to the various uses of scripture in the history of religion. It may surprise Western readers that most scriptures were passed on orally for long periods, even centuries, before they were written down, and that they were initially composed for very practical purposes, most often for oral use in worship and ritual. These oral as well as written texts were also used for instruction and educational purposes, a function that is given special prominence in the three Western monotheistic faiths but is an important feature of scripture in most traditions. Another use of scripture is for religious meditation and devotion, both in private and in community, for example, in the daily spiritual exercises of monks and nuns. Sacred scripture can be used both as a guide or a means of promoting the devotional life and also as an object of devotion. In the latter case, the scripture may become the object of worship itself or may be used in a quasi-magical way, for example, to bring about some effect such as to heal or to drive away evil spirits.

In the final segment of this chapter we explore the important subject of scriptural interpretation. We begin by examining some of the reasons why the interpretation of scripture is essential, including some important reasons that may not be obvious. This is followed by two rather full discussions of the methods of interpretation in both Buddhism and Christianity. This discussion will reveal why the interpretation of scripture is both a necessary task and one often fraught with contention.

## The Pervasive Role of Sacred Scripture

A significant feature of the religions of literate societies is the fact that they possess a body of sacred literature. It is also the case, however, that the number of texts that these religions consider sacred and authoritative and the variety of literary genres and uses made of their sacred literature vary significantly. Some sacred texts are meant to be read or recited only in the original language which is considered especially holy. The Hindu *Vedas,* for example, are recited and transmitted only in Sanskrit. Similarly, in Islam and in Orthodox Judaism the *Qur'an* and the *Hebrew Bible* are to be read, recited, studied, and transmitted only in Arabic and Hebrew, respectively. Translations are discouraged in Judaism and regarded as impossible in Islam, though "interpretations" in other languages are permissible.

Some sacred scriptures are relatively uniform in literary type and style. Others, such as the Hebrew and Christian Bibles and the Buddhist sacred books, encompass a vast range of literary genres: historical and legendary narratives, myths and tales, wisdom sayings, law, philosophic discourse, poetry, parables, oracles, and ritual prescriptions. Religions differ as well in the number of books that are considered *canonical* and uniquely normative for the community. For many religions, for example Buddhism, the boundaries between canonical and other sacred texts remain rather fluid, and what are considered canonical texts may differ from school to school. Most religions, however, attempt to distinguish the uniquely normative scriptures from other holy and venerated literature. Islam distinguishes between the unique revelation found in the *Qur'an* and the *Hadith,* the latter having to do with the traditions concerning the teachings and actions of Muhammad. But while these two texts are distinguished in order of authority, in actual practice they are closely connected, and both are clearly separated from other sacred literature in Islam with regard to their authority.

Similarly, in Judaism the *Written Torah* or Five Books of Moses (Genesis, Exodus, Leviticus, Numbers and Deuteronomy) is distinguished from the *Oral Torah,* or Torah commentary, but in practice many Orthodox Jews believe that the Oral Torah was also given to Moses on Mt. Sinai, and since antiquity the two have been understood by the rabbis as interdependent. There are, nevertheless, many other holy books in Judaism that do not possess the same authority. Confucianism also established two categories of sacred literature, distinguishing *ching,* or the Classics (scripture), from *shu,* or sacred books. The number of Confucian Classics has varied over the centuries, at different times consisting of groupings of Five, Six, Nine, Twelve, and Thirteen Classics. During the Han dynasty (206 B.C.E.–220 C.E.) the emperor Han Wu-ti established the Five Classics as essential. These include the *I-Ching* or *Book of Changes* (see Chapter 7), the *Book of Poetry,* the *Book of History,* the *Book of Rites,* and the *Spring and Autumn Annals.* The Neo-Confucian revival in the Sung dynasty (960–1279 C.E.) brought to prominence the Four Books which, with the Five Classics, have achieved *canonical authority.* The Four Books include the *Analects* of Confucius, the *Mencius,* named after its author, the great Confucianist philosopher (see Chapter 9), the *Great Learning,* and the *Doctrine of the Mean.* Since the Sung dynasty, the *Four Books and Five Classics* have been considered uniquely authoritative and possess the canonical status of *ching*, although Neo-Confucianists generally regard the practical and ethical teachings of the Four Books as having primacy over the Five Classics.

Among the great world religions, the vast body of sacred literature of Hinduism perhaps reveals the most elastic boundaries. Another feature of the Hindu sacred texts is the fact that much of this literature was not written down for hundreds of years and was intended to be used orally in ritual. The oldest Sanskrit text, the *Rg-Veda*, was not printed as a book until 1854.

Classical Hinduism, like Confucianism, also makes a distinction between two types of sacred literature: *Sruti*, that is, "what is heard" by the ancient sages and transmitted orally, and which includes a large body of Vedic literature; and *smirti*, or "what is remembered." By about 100 C.E. the *sruti* literature had come to be regarded as the "eternal word" in both content and form and, it is believed, was not composed by any human. The earliest layers of this literature are the four *Vedas*. The *Rg-Veda* consists of ten books of 1,028 hymns to various Hindu deities, such as Indra and Agni, the god of fire. The *Sama-Veda* is a collection of songs and chants based on the *Rg-Veda* and used in ritual recitation. The *Yajur-Veda* consists of additional hymns used in ritual, and the *Atharva-Veda* is a compilation of hymns and formulae that are concerned with magical healing and other matters of more popular religious interest.

A second body of Vedic *sruti* are the *Brahmanas*, which are prose manuals used by the Brahman priests and which contain rules and explanations of the Vedic ritual. The *Aranyakas*, or forest books, are meditations on the meaning of the ritual sacrifice, thus reflecting a greater philosophical and contemplative interest. This latter concern is fully developed in the fourth group of Vedic texts called the *Upanishads*, which is often translated as "sitting near" and suggests a disciple sitting at the feet of a master teacher or guru. The *Upanishads* are philosophical treatises concerned with that knowledge or mystical insight that will achieve the release of the soul from the cycle of birth and death (see Chapter 12). The *Upanishads* thus reflect a move away from ritual performance to a philosophical knowledge that itself leads to salvation. The earliest *Upanishads* date from about the eighth century B.C.E. However, later literature also called by the name *Upanishad*—but not possessing the authority of the classical texts by that name—continued to be produced in the modern period. This illustrates the often rather open and shifting notion of sacred scripture in Hinduism. The concept of *sruti* is therefore not fixed. The four classic categories of revealed Vedic literature do, nevertheless, focus on two concerns: (1) the ritual recitation of the eternal word, for example, in the *Vedas* and (2) the search for philosophical knowledge in the *Aranyakas* and, especially, in the *Upanishads*.

Hindu sacred literature also includes, as earlier suggested, a vast body of texts of human authorship, the *smrti* literature ("that which is remembered") which, nevertheless, is important in the everyday religious life of the Indian populace. Millions of Hindus are unfamiliar with the classic

Vedic literature, but their religious imaginations are steeped in the stories and polytheistic myths of the popular Indian epics and the *Puranas* (400–200 B.C.E.) or "ancient lore." The two great popular epics are the *Mahabharata* (500 B.C.E.–400 C.E.) and the *Ramayana* (750–500 B.C.E.). The *Ramayana* tells the story of Rama, an incarnation of the god Vishnu, and the rescue of his wife Sita from the Demon Ravana. The *Mahabharata* is an enormous work that includes the *Bhagavad Gita (Song of the Lord)*, the popular text that teaches the need to follow one's caste duty *(dharma)* and thereby, with true devotion to God, achieve release *(moksha)* from the cycle of reincarnations. While the *Gita* is classified as *smirti*, it is actually venerated as *sruti*, which, again, points to the fluidity of this enormous collection of sacred writings. The *Mahabharata*, the story of the Bharata dynasty, centers on an account of the god Krishna's assistance to the Pandava clan in its conflict with the rival Kaurava clan. Both epics are organized around the two popular heroes, Rama and Krishna, both of whom are incarnations of the great god Vishnu.

## Using the Term *Scripture*

Here, in brief compass, we have illustrated the fact that while the world's great religions look to a specific text or, more often, to a body of texts as uniquely revealed, they also acknowledge a body of later literature (the *Hadith*, the Oral Torah, the *Mencius*) as crucial and as having authoritative status. Some religions—Hinduism here serves as our example—have allowed the distinction between revealed texts and other later and popular sacred literatures to remain open and indeterminate. The fact that so many of the historical religions possess an enormous body of sacred texts, and the relative authoritativeness of the component texts is not always evident, or may not even be a matter of importance, raises the question whether it might be better to forgo the use of the term *sacred scripture* and use the broader and less precise designation, *sacred writings* or *sacred texts*.

The word *scripture* is, after all, a Western term derived from the Latin *scriptura*, meaning "a writing." *Scripture* is, then, a written text. But here we encounter a problem. The sacred texts in most religions were initially both circulated and used in oral form. Indeed, in some religious traditions, most strikingly in Hinduism, the oral use and transmission of sacred texts is normative. As noted earlier, the Hindu sacred Vedas have been passed on orally for over three thousand years, and this oral transmission is preferred to the written form of the "text." And, we must remember, the vast majority of persons in most of the world's religious communities were, for centuries, illiterate. Furthermore, these "scriptures" were communicated largely in ritual settings and were received orally—even if the meaning of the written text was not fully comprehended by those hearing it. It is noteworthy that the word *Qur'an* signifies that which is "recited." Yet the term *oral scripture* is misnamed, since scripture means "something written."

Despite the misconceptions that the Western word *scripture* may convey, many scholars agree that it remains the best term to use to convey the idea of a body of sacred, authoritative, and normative texts, whether their use is primarily oral and auditory, for example, in ritual, or as "holy writ," and intended to be used for doctrinal and moral instruction in a number of contexts, for example, preaching, teaching, or private study and meditation. The problem with the use of the term *sacred text* is that it refers to a very much broader body of religious literature that may not possess the authority or normative character of "scripture." Furthermore, the term *sacred text* might well convey to Western readers the idea that other religions may have their sacred literatures while Muslims or Christians have "holy Writ," implying that the latter alone is divinely revealed or of heavenly origin, and thus uniquely authoritative.[1] It is also true that since Max Müller's publication of the 50 volumes of the *Sacred Books of the East,* beginning in 1879, the word *scripture* has come to be applied more widely to the sacred writings of the East as well as those of the West.

## Some Distinctive Features of Sacred Scripture

When sacred texts achieve a normative or canonical status, they take on certain features that they share, to a greater or lesser degree, with other sacred scriptures. Some of these features are recognized, of course, only by those within the particular community of believers. A Christian, for example, would not normally acknowledge that the *Rg-Veda,* the *I Ching,* and the *Qur'an* have a divine or heavenly origin, are eternal, and possess sacred, transformative power. But many scriptures possess just these features for the believer. In Chapter 2 we pointed out that at the root of every religion is the experience of sacred power which sets the religious object—be it a person, place, image, sound, or book—apart from the ordinary and profane. *Sacred scripture possesses, first of all, this quality of sacred power* and thus it becomes an object of reverence and veneration.

Related to this first feature is scripture's *transformative effect.* For a high-caste Hindu, the *Vedas* are not only intrinsically holy; the recited words also possess a transformative power. Nor does that power rest necessarily in the intelligibility of the words but, rather, in the very hearing of the sounds which represent aspects of an eternal cosmic order. For example, the sound of the **mantra** Om is regarded as uncreated and eternal. The *Katha Upanishad* speaks of Om as "imperishable Brahman: this syllable indeed is the end supreme." By hearing and chanting this *mantra,* one is joined "to the basic sound or vibration of the universe. By a continual hearing and chanting one purifies and transforms one's life until it is vibrating in harmony with the Divine, which is itself pure sound."[2]

The sacred sound of the Word is powerful and transformative because it points to another quality: *that which is eternal and unchanging.* Muslims similarly view the *Qur'an* as the earthly expression of an eternal cosmic reality. The Sunni majority believe that the *Qur'an* is uncreated and preexistent, God's eternal Word in human history. An analogy has been drawn between the Christian taking on the divine Christ in the Holy Eucharist and the activity of the Muslim "memorizer" or reciter. The latter, it is suggested,

> has in some sense appropriated [the *Qur'an*] to himself, has interiorized it in a way that could conceivably suggest to a Christian some analogy with what happens when the Christian in the Communion Service appropriates to himself the body of Christ Who in his case is the mundane expression of God, the supernatural-natural, the embodiment of eternity in time.[3]

In orthodox Judaism the written Torah is not only the repository of divine law that is to be studied, commented on, and taught by the rabbis with the assistance of a long oral tradition; the Torah is also the eternal, divine Wisdom, an uncreated aspect or plan of God that was manifest before the creation of the world.[4] In Proverbs 8:27–30 we read: "When He [God] established the heavens I [Wisdom] was there, . . . when He marked out the foundations of the earth, then I [Wisdom] was beside Him as an artisan." The great Hellenistic Jewish philosopher Philo Judaeus (20 B.C.E.–50 C.E.) joins the Greek concept of the *Logos* (Word or Reason) to the Jewish Torah, which he conceives as the eternal divine pattern or reason from which the earthly world is copied, as well as being the living sacred power present in the cosmos and which serves as the intermediary between God and human beings.

The early rabbis also spoke of the Torah not only as the preexistent divine plan and instrument by which the world was created, but they also taught that the world was created for the sake of the Torah. In both early rabbinic and in later medieval Jewish mysticism, the Torah is personified, even hypostasized, that is, conceived as a living, substantial reality joined or in union with God. The rabbis describe how this eternal Divine Wisdom, God's co-worker in creation, came to the earth embodied in the words of the Written Torah. Divine Wisdom thus makes its home on earth. Rabbinic commentaries compare the Torah's descent to earth to a marriage ceremony "in which the Torah as the bride of Israel departs from the home of her father on high and makes her abode with her spouse on earth":

> Thus the Holy One, blessed be He, said to Israel, "I have given you a Torah from whom I cannot be separated, and yet I cannot say to you, 'Do not take her.' However, in every place to which you go make for me a house wherein I may dwell."[5]
> —(*Exod. R. XXXIII.1.*)

Thus it is taught that the Torah descended to earth and is not only the Written Torah but God's own real presence with Israel. Therefore, the Torah is not simply meant to serve the purposes of ritual and ethical guidance; it is to be studied and venerated for its own sake—and by so doing one is in the very presence of God.

In the Christian tradition the Bible is seldom treated with the same reverence as the *Qur'an*, the Torah, or the *Guru Granth Sahib*, the eternal holy book of the Sikhs in India, which is enthroned every morning, draped with richly embroidered cloths, opened with appropriate ceremony, and approached with covered head, prostrations, and offerings. Because Christianity looks to Jesus as the divine incarnation and mediator between God and humanity, the Bible is not venerated in quite the same manner as the holy scriptures of many other religions, despite its being recognized as inspired and authoritative. Nevertheless, in those Christian churches with a rich liturgical tradition, such as the Eastern Orthodox, Roman Catholic, and Anglican churches, the Bible is revered in worship. For example, it is held high by the priest in a solemn procession before the reading of the Gospel lesson. But it is also true that in some nonliturgical Protestant churches, especially those characterized by Pentecostal fervor and revivalism, the Bible often is treated as an **icon,** or *as possessing miraculous power,* such as healing. The minister, holding a large Bible in the palm of his hand, can be observed thrusting the Bible high in the air, at arm's length, while praying, preaching, or healing.

We have been discussing particular features of scripture that, for many religious communities, make the sacred book itself an object of veneration. This sacredness is conveyed by its divine or heavenly origin, by the fact that, while it is written, it is also considered uncreated and eternal, preexistent

The American evangelist Billy Graham is here pictured with his arm extended, holding up the Bible as if it had talismanic religious power. (*Source:* Courtesy of Getty Images, Inc.—Hulton Archives Photos.)

before its earthly embodiment. Furthermore, the sacred book possesses transformative power when studied, read, or recited. Sacred scripture is, for these reasons, set apart from profane texts and is revered and venerated in the same manner as a holy seer or a sacred place would be, as manifesting a sense of what Rudolf Otto calls the numinous (see Chapter 2). A further and quite obvious feature of sacred writ is its *normative authority and canonicity* in matters of belief and practice. Because this feature of scripture is being given such renewed prominence recently in religious resurgence movements, such as the fundamentalist movements in both Christianity and Islam, and because this feature bears upon the critical question of the interpretation of scripture, it deserves special attention. This discussion will also offer an opportunity to present a few examples of what is called "canon formation."

## The Authority and Canonicity of Scripture

Holy scriptures are, among other things, considered religiously authoritative for the community that has set them apart from other, profane, literature. This "setting apart" implies that these writings are to serve as a measure of what is authoritative in belief and practice. The English word *canon* comes from the Greek *kanon,* and it refers to a measuring rod or a rule. Oftentimes, scriptural canons form very slowly and by a process of consensus, perhaps over centuries of oral tradition. Also, as we have mentioned, there often are levels of authority recognized within a body of authorized, that is, canonical writings. An example is the distinction yet interdependence between the Written Torah and the Oral Torah in Judaism. The Written Torah is "inspired," while the same claim may not be made for the Oral Torah; nevertheless, because both have come to be accepted as authoritative for practice and belief, they both have essentially achieved canonical status. Frequently, as in Confucianism, a canon will grow over centuries, as when the Four Books were added to the Five Classics, and in certain Confucian schools the canon continues to remain open. These examples show that the authority and normativeness of some texts may be widely acknowledged long before they achieve, or may never achieve, official canonization, that is, inclusion on a closed, communally recognized list of texts.

There are a few examples in the history of religion in which a fixed canon of scripture was established by the founder of the religion, or very shortly after the founder's death. One instance is that of the teacher Mani (216–277 C.E.), the founder of Manicheanism, a religion composed of elements of Zoroastrianism, Judaism, and Christianity. Manicheanism was one of Christianity's greatest rivals in the third and fourth centuries (see Chapter 7). As founder, Mani claimed to be inspired by the Holy Spirit; he joined elements of other scriptures into his own texts that came to comprise his one "Great Wisdom." What is striking is that this book, in its original literary form, attained canonical status during Mani's lifetime.

The Muslim's *Qur'an* is unique among the scriptures of the Abrahamic, that is, biblical religions, because it is not a collection of books, as are the Hebrew Scriptures and the Christian New Testament, both of which were brought together over time and then canonized. Islam teaches that the *Qur'an* was orally dictated piecemeal directly to the prophet Muhammad and that the *Qur'an* is the eternal message of God spoken to Muhammad through the Archangel Gabriel. The *Qur'an* is simply "the Book," not, like others, a collection of sacred texts. Furthermore, as the speech of God, it is dictated in the heavenly language which ensures its verbal inspiration, inerrancy, and perfection. It is God's "standing miracle."

> Truly it is the revelation ["sent down"] of the Lord of all Being, brought down by the Faithful Spirit [Gabriel] upon thy heart, that thou mayest be one of the warners, in a clear, Arabic tongue.
> —(*Sura 26: 193–195*)

As it exists today, the *Qur'an* consists of 114 chapters or *suras* and is not quite the length of the Christian New Testament. Its present form is not, however, as it existed in Muhammad's lifetime, since the ordering of the *suras* and other important editorial work was carried out by Muhammad's disciples. Nonetheless, the text of the *Qur'an* was essentially settled within 23 years of the prophet's death. The need for further instruction, hence interpretation, of the *Qur'an's* meaning, led, of course, to collecting the prophet's teachings and practice, which constitute the **Hadith.** In time it became authoritative and normative.

The Hebrew Bible and the Christian New Testament are examples of sacred scriptures that evolved over significant periods of time, consist of a rich variety of types of literature, and were finally made canonical, with officially marked textual limits. Even so, there were some books that became more authoritative than others, for example, the Five Books of Moses for Judaism. In the case of the Christian New Testament, some writings that were accepted into the canon quite late have never been regarded as authoritative as the others; such has been the status of the Book of Revelation in the Eastern Orthodox churches.

The ancient Israelites possessed a body of literature for centuries before the concept of a canonical scripture became urgent in the life of the community. This literature included many stories and legends; accounts of the kings of Judah and Israel; oracles of the great prophets from Moses, Samuel, Elijah, and Jeremiah to the so-called minor prophets such as Hosea, Amos, and Malachi. Much of this literature was transmitted orally for generations, and it spans at least fifteen hundred years from the second millennium B.C.E. to the last biblical books, Daniel and Esther, that were written in the second century B.C.E.

During the reign of King Josiah (639–609 B.C.E.) of Judah, a book was found in the Jerusalem Temple that was the nucleus of the Book of

Deuteronomy, which was attributed to Moses. This was the beginning of the Jewish Torah or Law. Editors gradually combined Deuteronomy with other sources of literature that were to constitute the first five books of the Hebrew Bible. These Five Books of Moses, or the **Pentateuch** (from the Greek *pente* meaning "five"; *teuchos*, meaning "book"), as it is often called, was completed about 400 B.C.E.

By this time the Jewish community possessed a number of other books, including prophetic oracles, that were popular but not yet considered divinely inspired. These were later to constitute that section of the Hebrew Bible known as the Prophets. Scholars conclude that by 200 B.C.E. these works were considered divinely inspired. A book entitled Ecclesiasticus, written about 180 B.C.E., attests to the fact that the Prophets had, by this time, been accorded the status of revealed sacred scripture along with the Torah. The third section of the Hebrew Bible, known as the Writings, consists of such books as the Psalms, the Wisdom literature (Job, Proverbs, Ecclesiastes), Esther, Daniel, Ezra, and Nehemiah. Scholars are not certain when all of these writings became scripture, but certainly it was by early in the second century C.E.

The destruction of the Jewish Temple in Jerusalem by the Romans in 70 C.E. was a significant event for the future direction of the Jewish religion, for it made imperative the need for an authoritative book. The razing of the Temple was accompanied by the decline of the priestly class and the emergence of the role of the rabbis to a place of enormous significance. This, and the evangelistic activity of the early Christians in Palestine, led the rabbis to establish an official canon of scripture which was accomplished at the Councils of Jamnia in 90 and 118 C.E. While the rabbis may have decided that only 24 books—those now present in the Hebrew Bible—should be included as holy scripture, debates concerning the status of some of the Writings, such as the book of Ecclesiastes, Proverbs, and Esther, continued for decades. It was noted earlier that Orthodox Jews do not consider the Prophets and the Writings as authoritative as the Torah.

There is another feature of Jewish sacred literature in late antiquity that also became important in the formation of the Christian scriptural canon. The Jews in the Diaspora—that is, those living in the Greco-Roman world outside of Palestine—did not believe that prophecy had ended with Ezra and Nehemiah. Therefore, many Jewish works that would later be excluded in the Hebrew Bible were included along with those canonical books; together they were translated from Hebrew into Greek in Alexandria in Egypt, a work called the **Septuagint**. In the Christian churches, the *Septuagint* became the most influential of the Greek versions of the Old Testament, despite the fact that it comprised books not included in the Hebrew Bible, for example the Wisdom of Solomon, Ecclesiasticus, Judith, and I and II Maccabees. These writings are called the **Apocrypha** (from the Greek *apokryphos* meaning "hidden" things). In the fifth century C.E. the Christian scholar St. Jerome translated the *Septuagint*, including these apocryphal works, into Latin, thus providing Christians with an expanded Latin version of the Old Testament.

This became part of the approved Roman Catholic version (the *Vulgate*) of the Bible that was officially so designated at the Council of Trent in 1546. At the time of the Protestant Reformation in the early sixteenth century, Protestant churches returned to the canon of 24 books that had long served as the official Hebrew text of the Jewish Bible. Therefore, the Roman Catholic and Protestant texts of the Bible differ in the number of books included. This variation in the number of books included in the Christian canon is not unique to the Catholic and Protestant canons, as we will see.

The *New Testament* is the name that is given to the 27 writings that were, over a period of four centuries, circulated with other Christian literature in the churches. Finally, these 27 writings were fixed as canonical by general consensus in the fourth and fifth centuries. This process of canonization was slow, and it did not take place uniformly among the churches that were widely dispersed throughout the Greco-Roman world. Jesus and his disciples, of course, already had their scriptures, the authoritative Hebrew writings that were expounded in the synagogues in Palestine in the first century C.E. There is no evidence that Jesus wrote anything, but after his death the story of his teachings and mighty acts, and accounts of his crucifixion and resurrection, were circulated orally among his disciples. By 40–45 C.E. it is likely that there was a collection of Jesus' sayings in circulation.

The earliest surviving writings that were later to be included in the New Testament are the letters of the apostle Paul (ca. 48–64 C.E.) that were written to specific churches (e.g., Thessalonica, Corinth, Galatia, Rome) to address their particular concerns. It was not until early in the second century C.E. that a collection of these letters was in wide circulation and was known as the "letters to seven churches." The earliest surviving Gospels were, in part, made up of oral and some written traditions about Jesus that were shaped in certain stylized forms. The four New Testament Gospels (Mark, ca. 65–70; Matthew and Luke, ca. 80–90, and John, ca. 90–100) were widely known and in use by 120 C.E. Other writings were composed and later regarded as apostolic (i.e., written by the apostles of Jesus) and therefore authoritative. These include the Book of Revelation (ca. 90–100) and the Pastoral epistles (e.g., I and II Timothy and Titus [ca. 100–150, and perhaps later]).

The idea of a Christian scripture distinct from the Hebrew Bible or the *Septuagint* did not fully emerge until about 100 C.E., or somewhat later. There were several practical reasons for establishing a Christian canon. Christianity had, by then, separated itself from Judaism; there was need for authoritative writings for use in worship and instruction and, most importantly, as a defense against heresy. There were many writings in circulation by the second century C.E. that claimed to be Christian. Several reflected the considerable influence of Hellenistic or Greek ideas on some Christian communities, ideas that came to be recognized as antithetical to Christian teaching. There were, for example, Christian communities that were teaching **Gnostic** doctrines (see Chapters 7 and 11). These Gnostic-Christian communities possessed gospels and other writings that competed with those writings that were later to be included in the New Testament canon. One such Gnostic gospel, entitled *The Gospel of Thomas*, was written in the second century by a Gnostic Christian. It depicts the five-year old Jesus as an infant prodigy and miracle worker:

> 3.1. But the son of Annas the scribe was standing there with Joseph; and he took a branch of a willow and (with it) dispersed the water which Jesus had gathered together. 2. When Jesus saw what he had done he was enraged and said to him: "You insolent, godless dunderhead, what harm did the pools and the water do to you? See, now you also shall wither like a tree and shall bear neither leaves nor root nor fruit." 3. And immediately that lad withered up completely . . .
> —*(The Gospel of Thomas, I:3–4)*

One can see that the question of which Christian writers were genuinely Spirit-endowed, and which writings should be authorized, became acute for the growing and far-flung Christian churches. Therefore, church leaders in the late second century began a process of framing their own lists of official scriptures. Anthanasius, the Bishop of Alexandria in Egypt, sent an Easter letter to his churches in 367 C.E. listing 27 writings that alone were to comprise the Christian scriptures. This list corresponds to the 27 books presently in the New Testament. By then it was generally held that the sacred scriptures of the New Testament were the writings authored by those who had been closely associated with Jesus, that is, the apostles. We know from historical investigation, however, that few of the New Testament writings could have been authored by the apostles themselves, although many of them reflect apostolic teaching to a considerable degree.

## The Reception and Uses of Scripture

In the earlier discussion of various features of sacred scripture, we made the point that those highlighted are not characteristic of all sacred scriptures. Nevertheless, they remain important features of a great many of the scriptures of the world's living religions. Canonicity, we have seen, is especially important in the three Western "Abrahamic" faiths. Yet all of the sacred scriptures we have discussed achieved some measure of religious and moral authority and serve as normative guides in their communities. They also serve many and varied uses or functions, and an account of some of these will be instructive.

One fairly obvious use of sacred scripture is for *instruction and educational purposes*. As we will see, in Buddhism, religious doctrine and, more so, religious practice, hold priority, but neither can be separated from the explicit teachings of the Buddhist sacred texts. All doctrine and practice are, finally, based on those authoritative sacred texts and their interpretation. Interpretation, of course, requires expertise and, with written scriptures, high literacy and scholarly discernment. In Judaism, Islam, and Buddhism a

A *kuttāb*, or school, in the courtyard of an eighteenth-century mosque in Tunisia where children are learning the *Qur'an* by recitation. (*Source:* Courtesy of Caroline Williams.)

special class of scribes, exegetes, and interpreters emerged: the Jewish rabbis, the Muslim *ulamā* ("learned") or *fuqahā* (men of insight, jurists), and the monks of the Theravada Buddhist *sangha* or community. As in Christianity, these experts in scriptural **exegesis** and interpretation often established schools for teaching youth and the laity the language, recitation, and interpretation of scripture. In most religions, differing schools of scriptural interpretation developed to guide the community in correct belief and behavior. For instance, several important schools (see Chapter 11) of legal interpretation in Islam have been established to help the community attain *fiqh* or insight into the divine Law. Some of these Muslim schools are literalist or fundamentalist. Others, such as the Hanafis, apply reason and practical considerations when instructing believers on their duties toward the Law and allow for various "permissible" legal opinions.

A second, and critically important, use of scripture is its role in *public worship and ritual*. In some religions the explicit guidance for the performance of public ritual or worship is given definitively in the community's sacred scriptures, such as in the ritual instructions in the Hindu *Brahmanas*. A community's scriptures are also recited and read as central elements of worship itself. In both Hindu and Islamic daily worship the recitation of the divine word is essential. The Hindu *Laws of Manu* clearly state that a male Brahman, that is, a member of the priestly class, is obligated every morning and evening to recite certain verses from the *Veda*, preceded by the holy syllable Om. And those Indians not "twice-born" (of the three higher classes) are not meant to hear the sacred *Veda* recited.

The Hindi popular words for worship are *pūjā-pāṭha; pūja* refers to devotional offerings and *pāṭhā* means recitation or recital of the sacred texts. It is believed that through this recital of the sacred sounds of the Veda—the power of speech *(Vāc)*—that the hearer makes contact with ultimate reality or Brahman. The sacred Vedic speech embodies the creative power of the universe itself. The significance of the spoken word is thus indicated in the phrase, "wherever there is *brahman*, there is *Vāc*, wherever *Vāc*, there is *brahman*."[6] In the *Ṛg Veda*, the word *brahman* means both the sacred utterance of truth and the word of power.

In many seasonal or calendar rituals, sacred scriptures are read as essential to securing the renewal and the well-being of the community and its members, as we have observed in both the Babylonian New Year's Festival and in the Roman Catholic Mass (see Chapter 4). In these and other instances the reading or reciting of sacred scripture serves a truly *performative* function in that the rehearsal of the sacred word is instrumental in effecting a real change in the condition of the participants in the ritual. Passages from the community's holy scriptures additionally serve as texts for sermons, for chants and hymns, and for set prayers used in worship. Examples in Christian worship are sermon texts, the **lectionary** of daily scriptural readings, musical settings for the singing of the Psalms, and the communal recitation of the Lord's Prayer.

Another important use of sacred scripture is for *meditation* and *devotion*. Scriptures are almost universally used for private meditation and contemplation, that is, in spiritual exercises carried out by priests, nuns, and monks, as well as by laypersons, that are directed to a contemplation or union with God. A passage of scripture may be recited audibly or silently or simply dwelt upon and visualized by the mind. In Islam, the Sufi mystics visualize certain words from the *Qur'an* or may repeat certain scriptural passages as a means of achieving a rapturous, mystical union with God. Meditation on scripture by oral reading and hearing has also been a central aspect of the life of Christian monastics. This is also true of monastic life in Buddhism, which includes daily periods of recitation, chanting, and meditation on the Buddhist scriptures.

Often closely associated with the meditative and contemplative use of scripture is its use as an *object of religious devotion.* We remarked earlier that most religions treat their scriptural books with great care and reverence, even veneration. This use of sacred scripture is, perhaps, most conspicuous in the **Sikh** religion in its devotional veneration of its canonical scripture, the *Guru Granth Sahib* (also referred to as *Adi Granth*). This holy book is called **Guru,** for the Sikhs teach that when the succession of the ten living *gurus,* in the line of the poet Guru Nanak (1469–1539) ended, their revered teachings became resident in the book which became *the Guru,* the source of the revealed word of God.

The *Guru Granth Sahib* ("the Honorable Book Guru") is essential to and dominates all Sikh ceremonies, including regular worship and the various rites of passage such as marriage. Wherever the *Guru Granth Sahib* is installed, it is kept in its house called the *Gurdwara* ("doorway to the Guru"). *Gurdwaras* vary from elaborate temples, such as the Golden Temple at Amritsar in the Punjab region of north India, to a simple cabinet in its own special room in a modest Sikh home today in London. When a Sikh enters the *Gurdwara,* he or she is in the real presence of the *Guru.* A commentator describes the devotional elements that characterize such a visit or "audience" (*darśan*) with the *Guru Granth Sahib:*

> It is placed on a cushion, covered by a canopy and wrapped in special clothes. It is physically located so that it will be in the most elevated position, and when being moved it is carried on the head, all to indicate its exalted status as *Guru.* . . . The book is ritually put to bed and awakened. Before entering a *Gurdwara* one must have bathed, removed one's shoes, and covered one's head. Offerings are placed before the enthroned book and after worship a *prasad* [holy food] is eaten. For many Sikhs the very sight of the scripture is a means of receiving grace.[7]

Sikh congregational worship begins with the ceremonial opening of the *Guru Granth.* The hymns that accompany worship also are taken from the *Guru Granth,* and there are readings from it. Often these readings are unbroken and last for two days, each worshipper reading for a few hours. Another distinctive feature of Sikh worship occurs at its conclusion when the *Guru Granth* is opened randomly and a verse is read to the congregation for their guidance. Sikhs often randomly consult their own copy of the *Guru Granth* to seek counsel for their daily lives. Thus the *Guru Granth* also functions as an *oracle* or messenger of God. This feature leads us to another, and final, aspect of the use of sacred scripture, namely, its *transactional* and *magical* uses as an object possessing sacred power in itself.

Because sacred scripture is regarded as the source of spiritual truth and authority, the physical text or book itself is often perceived as possessing supernatural power and is therefore worshiped. This worshipful veneration of the physical scripture, or a passage of scripture heard chanted as a **mantra,** is found in many scriptural religions, and it takes many forms in Hinduism, Buddhism, Judaism, Christianity, and Islam. A common quasi-magical form already mentioned is the random opening of scripture to find guidance or assistance. This is a common religious practice. In some traditions the copying, chanting, or even the reverent holding of scripture in one's hands is itself believed to convey sanctity or merit. In Buddhism especially, the hearing of a *sutra* chanted can convey spiritual power. In Islam the final two *surahs* (*surahs* 113, 114) of the *Qur'an*, "that deliver from evil," consist of charms or **talismanic** recitations that are meant to ward off witchcraft and black magic. **Amulets** were worn by the ancient Israelites to ward off danger, and modern

In the Sikh Golden Temple of Amritsar in India, an official reader recites from the holy scripture, the *Guru Granth Sahib*. An attendant waves a horsehair fan in veneration of the book. (*Source:* Gunter Reitz/Barnaby's Picture Library.)

Jews affix to their doorpost a *mezuzah*, a small cylinder containing passages from the Books of Moses, for similar purposes. Under the guidance of a Brahman priest, a high-caste Hindu householder will utter scriptural **mantras** with the intention of driving away demons and protecting the household from evil.

In the many ways that we have illustrated, sacred scripture is used in performative ways for the purpose of bringing about some transaction. This might include the transfer of karmic merit to one's departed kinsfolk to assist them in their progress toward Nirvana or enlightenment; or to secure protection against evil spirits; or to assist the individual in the carrying through of virtuous tasks for others; or for the purpose of covering past evil actions and securing greater sanctity; and so on. What is significant, however, is that it is through the actual performative uses of these sacred texts that these transactions are achieved.

We have now covered a great many, but certainly not all, of the functions and uses of scripture. It is now time to turn to an analysis of a most interesting, but also contentious, aspect of our subject: the interpretation of scripture.

## The Interpretation of Scripture

Every sacred scripture requires interpretation. **Hermeneutics** is the inquiry concerned with the presuppositions and rules of interpretation. There are several reasons why interpretation required. First, scripture is written and passed on in human language. And because language is human it is always embedded in a specific temporal and cultural context, a context that conveys particular meanings and often reflects culture-specific ideas or presuppositions. Hence, the reader of a scriptural text should not only be familiar with the language and grammar in which the particular text is written but should also possess a knowledge of the cultural and historical context of the text in order to rightly understand the writer's intention and meaning. Otherwise the reader will be prone to read *into* the text meanings that reflect the reader's—rather than the writer's—own ideas or preconceptions. Some scholars seriously question whether it is even possible to thoroughly understand a text or an artifact from a culture radically different from one's own. Moreover, it is a fact that words and meanings often change significantly over time even within the same culture. That is why, for example, so many words in Shakespeare's plays require an editorial explanation at the bottom of the page to indicate that the word had a different meaning for Shakespeare than it has for us today.

Many of the world's sacred scriptures also consist of compilations of books or texts written over centuries, even millennia. As mentioned earlier, these comprise a vast range of literary genres, including history, legend, poetry, philosophy, and so on. One thinks, for example, of the scriptures of both Judaism and Buddhism. When these collections of often quite dissimilar texts are read as sacred scripture, it is almost inevitable that one will come across what appear to be, or are, contradictions and puzzling obscurities. Sacred texts therefore require interpretation to clarify these problems.

A further reason why interpretation is a crucial task is that many of the world's sacred scriptures, like the great classics of literature, possess a rich variety of possible meanings. This is especially true when a body of sacred texts achieves canonical authority, for then its meaning is not meant solely for its own time and context, but for later readers as well, and for every age. Thus sacred scriptures are not only open to different levels or depths of meaning; they may also be indeterminate in their meanings; that is, they possess spiritual truths that the reader may not readily be prepared to see or to understand. As these meanings and truths may transcend a straightforward, literal reading of the text, the reader must, then, probe further and allow the text to reveal other, possibly crucial, meanings. Most important, sacred scripture must be "brought home," so to speak. It must speak to the contemporary—for example, the modern—reader so that it does not simply remain archaic, relevant only to a past time and place. In order to plumb such levels of meaning in the Christian scriptures and to clarify ambiguities or obscurities, the Medieval interpreters proposed several possible readings of the Bible. One may, for example, need only discern the plain or literal meaning, such as its historical or philosophic teaching. However, the deeper meaning of an historical event or legendary tale may be found in its not so self-evident moral meaning. Beyond that, the meaning of the sacred text may lie in its allegorical meaning, that is, it may point to a profound spiritual truth hidden beneath the literal historical account.

Here we will illustrate in some detail the role of interpretation in both Buddhism and Christianity, two religions that possess sacred scriptures that include an enormous variety of forms of literature that were composed over many centuries. In Chapter 11 we also illustrate the ways in which both the Jewish rabbis and the Muslim *ulamā* interpret their respective sacred scriptures with regard to certain ethical questions that have, over the centuries, required clarification for their faithful.

## Buddhist Interpretation

The Buddhist approach to the authority and interpretation of the tradition's collected sacred texts is rather paradoxical. None of the world's religions possesses such an overwhelming body of sacred writings as is found in Buddhism. Buddhism is the world's earliest missionary religion, and during its twenty-five hundred years of existence it has traveled from its home in India to the south to Sri Lanka (Ceylon), north to Tibet and Central Asia, east to China, Korea, and Japan, and south-east into Thailand, Cambodia, and Vietnam. In the past two centuries it has made its way into the West. In most of these distinct cultures Buddhism has both adapted to and has become a formative power in its new home. Thus many distinctive Buddhist canons developed: the Pali (India), Chinese, Tibetan, Mongolian, Korean, and Japanese. It is likely that no Buddhist or scholar of Buddhism has ever read all of the texts in these multiple canons. Oftentimes a sacred text, for example, a *sutra*, or text of the teachings of Buddha, is superseded over time by one or more popular commentaries. Furthermore, in many of the Mahayana schools of Buddhism the question of what constitutes their canonical or collected sacred texts remains open and growing, although classical Theravada Buddhism would not agree.

This openness is related to the distinctive, quite ambivalent, attitude of Mahayana Buddhism toward its own sacred writings and their authority. This is traceable to a central tenet of the Buddha' own teaching. Near the time of Buddha's death, Buddha's disciple Ananda asked him who would guide and teach his followers after his death, assuming that the disciples would need some authoritative text or interpreter. Buddha responded, "henceforth, be ye lamps unto yourselves and be ye refuges unto yourselves, seek no other refuge; let the *dharma* [teaching] be your lamp and your refuge, and seek no other refuge." Buddha here proposed that the texts that comprise his *dharma* be the disciples' "lamp" and "refuge," yet it is also clear that the Buddha set this admonition side by side with, and inseparable from, his first teaching that his disciples must be "lamps unto yourselves," and rely on nothing else.[8] After achieving enlightenment in c. 529 B.C.E., Gautama, the Buddha, spent a half-century teaching others—the aim being to help all sentient beings achieve enlightenment. The Buddha used no single method toward this end. Rather, he adapted a variety of methods that are called "skill in means" or techniques. He therefore refused to teach a single, dogmatic doctrine. And the Buddha's use of many means, or "rafts," as they often are called, to help others reach the farther shore of enlightenment is also consistent with his rejection of a single text or collection of sacred texts. He allows a plurality of "turnings of the wheel of the Dharma," or aids to enlightenment. (On the Buddha's teachings see Chapters 9, and 12.) This is illustrated in an often-cited parable that appears in the famous *Lotus Sutra* about a man with many children who are playing in a burning house:

> They will not listen to his warnings at first, too absorbed in their play, so he changes his tack and instead tells them he has some marvelous toys for them outside and they should come and see. Knowing what each one likes, he tells some he has deer-carts for them, some he has horse-carts, and some bullock-carts. Out they rush pell-mell, only to discover that after all the man has only bullock carts for them to ride in. At the cost of a slight disappointment, they all escape the burning house in this way.[9]

The Buddha thus offers many "means" to the one goal of the cessation of suffering. The "means" may even contradict one another, but they all retain their status as sacred scripture so long as they lead the individual to enlightenment. Thus the text in itself is not authoritative, but only in so far as it is a true means to the goal. It is the teaching (the *Dharma*) and *not* the text or teacher that is authoritative. Furthermore, the words of the Buddha in his human form may not be the only *buddha-vacana* or "word of the Buddha"; it may also be found in the words of his disciples or later sages, or in the heavenly buddhas who speak "with the mind of enlightenment." Thus the **Buddha's Dharma** is understood to have many sources that have multiplied over time with the growth of diverse Buddhist schools.

There is, then, no single canon of Buddhist scriptures. It would be better to refer to the entire body of Buddhist sacred texts as a library of canonical literature. Major geographical (India, China, Tibet) and sectarian groups (Theravada or the "Tradition of the Elders" and Mahayana or the "Greater Vehicle") developed their own compilations or canons, and they vary significantly from one another in both content and size.

Buddhist tradition teaches that after Buddha's death a council was convened and Ananda, Buddha's disciple and attendant, was called upon to recite, in the company of 500 *arahants*, or enlightened monks, all the discourses or teachings of the Buddha. These teachings constituted the *Sutra* literature (*Suttapitaka*), the first division or "basket" of the official Theravada or Pali canon, later called the *Tripitaka*. Tradition also holds that another expert monk reported on all of the rules of the Buddhist monastic community (the *Sangha*), and these rules constituted the *Vinayapitaka*, the second "basket" of the *Tripitaka*. Later the third "basket," the *Abhidharmapitaka*, was included in the canon. It consists of a body of exegesis and philosophical literature that organizes the teaching of the *Sutras* into certain categories. This Pali canon then was transmitted orally for a long time and, according to Theravada tradition, was not committed to writing until 29 B.C.E. Buddhism in Sri Lanka, Burma, and Southeast Asia regard the Pali canon as the official canonical language and, in most cases, are loath to translate it.

Mahayana schools of Buddhism emerged about the beginning of the Christian era. Because they introduced new teachings—but claimed that these were original teachings of the Buddha hidden for centuries—these Mahayana groups began producing their own collection of *sutras*. Among the most influential of this vast literature are the Perfection of Wisdom (*Prajnaparamita*) scriptures, composed over a period of one thousand years, beginning about 200 B.C.E. A principal theme of these texts is the doctrine of emptiness or the nonsubstantiality (*sunyata*) of all things. Many of these Indian texts were taken to China and translated into Chinese. A large body of indigenous Chinese Mahayana literature was also produced that claimed to be the "word of the Buddha" and, together with the original Indian texts, constituted the distinctive and influential Chinese canon that itself became the foundation of the Mahayana schools and canons in Korea and Japan.

Another late, but astonishingly large, body of sacred texts are those of Tantric or Esoteric Buddhism, referred to as the *Vajrayana* ("Diamond Vehicle"). These texts, from roughly the fifth century C.E. and later, are based on the Mahayana tradition but go well beyond the bounds of Mahayana teaching. This Tantric form of Buddhism found some interest in East Asia but it is most influential in Tibet. Tibetan *tantric* literature is organized into four categories, each one concerned with specific elements of tantric practice. They deal with the ritual worship of tantric deities, with "inner yoga" and certain magical practices associated with it, and with highly esoteric mystical treatises that feature sexual symbolism and iconography that are antithetical to the monastic Theravadin tradition. Beyond these three distinctive canonical collections there are many popular texts, such as the *Dharmapada* and the *Jataka* tales, the latter of which relate aspects of the previous lives of Gautama Buddha before he achieved enlightenment. These popular works nurture Buddhist piety and ethics.

Each of these canonical collections (the Theravada, Mahayana, and Tantric) claims to be founded on *buddha-vacana* and became authoritative because they satisfied this principle of authenticity, namely, they were consistent with the teaching of the Buddha's *Dharma*. Nonetheless, the existence of such an enormous library of sacred writings compiled over the centuries and coexisting, still raised the question of how a particular text was to be understood and interpreted. The attempt in the *Abhidharmapitaka* to organize and interpret the Pali *sutras* is an example of an early interpretive effort. The authority of a text, it became clear, did not finally rest on its antiquity or on the historical person of Gautama the Buddha but, rather, on the authenticity of the teaching *and* its efficacy in leading the individual to enlightenment.

In time an interpretive guide was proposed in a work called the **Sutra on the Four Reliances** which became of critical importance in Buddhist **hermeneutics**. The "four reliances" can be stated as follows:

1. The *dharma* is the refuge, not the man.
2. The *meaning* is the refuge, not the letter.
3. Those *sutras* which are *direct* in meaning are the refuge, not those which are indirect in meaning.
4. *Direct intuition* is the refuge, not discursive thought.[10]

We will look briefly at each one of these interpretive principles. The first establishes that it is the Buddha's *dharma* or teaching that is primary, not the person of Gautama the historical Buddha. That does not mean that there is no value in the person of Gautama, for he is the necessary, though relative, means which made possible the final refuge of his *dharma*. The Buddha's achievement of enlightenment and his teaching (*dharma*) as conveyed to his disciples are thus interdependent.

The second principle addresses the question, What is the *meaning* of the *dharma*, a meaning that may not be transparent in the literal words of the text? The Buddhists speak of the external and the internal dimensions of *dharma*. The external dimension is, of course, the literal text, while the internal *dharma* is the true understanding or "personal realization" of its meaning. But again, while the two are distinguished, the external and internal *dharma* cannot be separated, since the external, literal text is a crucial "means" to the "personal realization" of *dharma*. The literal text is the relative, pedagogical *dharma*, while the internal *dharma* is its ultimate, realized dimension.

Buddhism teaches that attention to the literal text which claims to be the "word of the Buddha," has great merit, for one cannot achieve true understanding (the "right view") if one does not adhere to the literal text. A mere "parroting" of the literal text without understanding may seem a poor way of achieving enlightenment; nevertheless, while it is not the goal, a reverence for the literal text may well prepare one for greater insight into its spiritual truth. In some instances the letter must, however, be sacrificed to the spirit; in fact, Buddhism teaches that ultimately all "means" or "supports" must be let go. But if one casts off the literal text prematurely, before it is fully known, how can one know what one is abandoning and that it must be abandoned?

To say that the meaning of the *sutra* is ultimately more important than the letter of the text still leaves a vital issue unanswered, namely what *is* the meaning of "the word of the Buddha"? Buddhism, after all, consists of several diverse traditions. How does one account for and deal with the diversity, the seeming contradictions? The third reliance—those *sutras* which are *direct* in meaning are the refuge, not those that are indirect in meaning—acknowledges that there are important differences among the schools, and that these differences have to do with the question of the ultimacy or definitiveness of any particular view. Therefore, one should rely on those texts and "words" which express the definitive meaning of the Buddha, rather than on those that merely point to it, or are partial and require interpretation, that is, are indirect and only implicit.

The distinction between *sutras* that are *direct* in meaning and those that are *indirect* in meaning allows each of the three great Buddhist traditions (Theravada, Mahayana, and Tantra) and their schools to claim the definitiveness or ultimacy of their *sutras* and teaching while allowing for the usefulness of other Buddhist teachings and texts. However, each school does conceive a hierarchy of teachings, in that each claims a degree of ultimacy or perfection of teaching, while the teachings of other schools can be regarded as valuable stepping stones on the path to enlightenment. Thus the scriptures of the various schools can be distinguished and variously graded, so to speak, without engaging in exclusion.

The fourth and final interpretive principle is crucial and points to the essential, practical teaching of Buddhism: Direct intuition or knowledge is the refuge, not discursive thought. The interpretive process begins by determining the authenticity of a sacred text and then proceeds to the recognition that it is the *dharma* and not the person, Gautama the Buddha, that is primary. One must then master the *letter* of the sacred text before one can rightly discern its meaning. Next, one must recognize the great diversity of texts and their teaching *and* how each can be viewed as a useful and valuable step on the path to enlightenment.

The final and essential step remains, namely, to pass beyond discursive teaching and consciousness and to achieve direct knowledge of reality or enlightenment. Ultimately, no person, no text, no doctrine, no verbal formula can be pointed to as authoritative, for they all remain in the domain of the discursive consciousness. The following passage points to the supremely practical and experiential goal and authority of Buddhism and envisions sacred scripture, finally, as a skillful means to achieving that goal:

> Ultimate reality eludes encompassment in any concept, no matter how hallowed, and hence the hermeneutician would betray his craft if he were to rest forever on the intellectual plane, no matter how refined his understanding. Thus the Buddhist hermeneutical tradition is a tradition of realization, devoid of any intellect/intuition dichotomy. Authority here gives way to intellect, yet never lets intellect rest in itself, as it were, but pushes it beyond toward a culminating nondual experience.[11]

## Christian Biblical Interpretation

The earliest disciples of Jesus were Aramaic—a Semitic dialect—or Greek-speaking Jews living in Palestine. They continued to attend the Jewish synagogue, and they used the *Septuagint,* the Greek translation of the Hebrew scriptures. The idea of a Christian canon of scriptures, distinct from the Jewish scriptures, did not emerge until about 100 C.E. or later. As we noted earlier, by the second century C.E. a number of Christian writings were in circulation, and concerns arose that some of these writings were not in accord with the teachings of Jesus and the early apostles. The circulation of such questionable writings caused the Christian churches to seek to establish a canon of authentic apostolic writings, that is, writings authored by those thought to have associated with Jesus.

Once the Christian canon of the Old and New Testaments was essentially closed, the issues shifted to questions of exegesis and interpretation. As we have learned, the Christian scriptures were originally written for specific occasions and were intended to meet particular practical needs. Yet by achieving their status as sacred canon, and their incorporation into a sacred book, the Bible, these texts were read as having an enduring and universal meaning and application. Moreover, the Christian community regarded the New Testament as the fulfillment of the Old, the latter being a foreshadowing and preparation for the coming of Christ. Therefore, the Old Testament was to be read from the perspective of Christ's message and work. But how, then, was the Christian to interpret specific passages in the Old Testament? Or how was one to deal with contrasting accounts of the same events narrated in the New Testament Gospels, or how was one to interpret the seemingly conflicting doctrines found in, for example, the Epistle of James and the apostle Paul's Letter to the Romans? Or how is one living in a much later age to be confident that he or she understands the original intention or meaning of such a complex work as the Book of Revelation? These and many other questions required the skills of an interpreter. An account of some of the ways that Christians have interpreted their Bible will be instructive.

*Traditional Christian Interpretation* Once the early Christian writings had gained authority as divinely inspired and canonical, the leaders of the churches and the theologians began to propose ways in which these works should be read and interpreted. We must appreciate the fact that these early interpreters did not possess the same kind of historical consciousness or interests that many readers take for granted today. Nevertheless, they read many of the narratives of the Old and New Testaments realistically, that is, historically or literally. But these interpreters were also aware of the difficulties and the error of reading all of the narratives literally or historically. They recognized that the Bible also contained poetry and wisdom sayings and legislation and parables and, moreover, that the deepest meaning of the historical narratives often lay in their spiritual or moral meaning. In the course of time a *fourfold method of biblical interpretation* was accepted and it remained popular throughout the Middle Ages. It was a system of interpretation through which it was possible to find any of four senses or types of meaning in a particular text or passage: the literal, the allegorical, the moral, and the anagogical. A sixteenth-century verse suggests the meaning of each sense:

> The letter shows what God and our fathers did;
> The allegory shows us where our faith is hid;
> The moral meaning gives us rules of daily life;
> The anagogy shows us where we end our strife.

The letter was, of course, the literal or historical sense, which may in some instances be necessary but not sufficient to plumb the real or vital meaning of a passage. The allegorical or symbolic meaning was often the deepest meaning. For example, Christian exegetes found the true meaning of many Old Testamemt events as hidden allegorical types or symbols that pointed to certain Christian teachings, the event itself being of secondary importance. For example, the Hebrew prophet's reference to the captivity of Israel and its return to Palestine was read as an allegory of the captivity of the soul and its return to Christ. Without allegory, many of the Old Testament texts would, for the Christian, simply remain unclear. The anagogical meaning of a passage referred to its hidden **eschatological** meaning, that is, to what it teaches about the future or God's purposes.

Christian theologians such as Origen (185–254 C.E.) and St. Augustine (354–430 C.E.) were fond of using allegorical interpretations, but in the late Middle Ages a reaction set in against the excesses to which allegory had been taken. Theologians such as St. Thomas Aquinas (1225–1274) insisted that the literal meaning should be the basis of all other interpretations. The allegorical or parabolic or spiritual senses are, however, often contained in the literal, since the literal sense has to do with the *meaning* of words, and words can be used not only literally, but also figuratively and metaphorically. For example, the Bible speaks of God "walking" in the Garden of Eden in the cool of the day (Gen. 3:8), but it does not mean that God has feet; rather, that God is as present to Adam and Eve as is another person. The literal sense in this case is not the metaphor ("walking") but what it means. The emphasis on the literal meaning (whether it be historical, metaphorical, or moral) gave impetus to more scientific (i.e., historical-literary) investigations of the Bible in later centuries.

The great Reformers of the Protestant Reformation of the sixteenth century, Martin Luther (1483–1546) and John Calvin (1509–1564), attacked many medieval church traditions and teachings and called for a return to the authority of Scripture alone (*sola Scriptura*). They also defended the priority of the literal or historical sense in the interpretation of the Bible. While it has been said that they both upheld a theory of the divine, plenary (meaning "full") inspiration of the Bible, it is clear that the Reformers did not mean by "full" inspiration that the Bible was inerrant in every respect. Both Luther and Calvin recognized discrepancies in Scripture, for example, regarding matters of geography or historical accuracy. Both Luther and Calvin also drew a distinction between the Word of God and the written Scriptures. God's Word is found *in* the Scriptures as a letter is found in an envelope—but the letter and the envelope are not identical.

For the Protestant Reformers, the Bible is the Word of God only by the inner testimony of the Holy Spirit. Those persons who are inwardly taught by the Spirit of God will thus find the Bible self-authenticating, that is, it will carry its own evidence.[12] Without the inspiration of the Holy Spirit the words of Scripture will likely remain incomprehensible. By appealing to the convergence of the words of Scripture *and* the Holy Spirit, Luther and Calvin can hold that the Bible is spiritually authoritative yet not worry about historical errors or apparent contradictions.

Due in large part to the rise of modern science to ascendancy and authority in the seventeenth century and beyond, both Protestantism and Catholicism turned away from the interpretive traditions of the Middle Ages and those of the Protestant Reformers and embraced a rigid theory of the Bible's verbal inspiration and inerrancy. It is an interpretive theory that continues to the present day in many fundamentalist Protestant churches. This new theory insists that the Bible's inspiration and inerrancy extend to every written word of the text. This position is well-stated by a seventeenth-century representative of Lutheran orthodoxy, the theologian J. A. Quenstedt. He writes,

> The Holy Spirit not only inspired in the prophets and apostles the content and sense contained in Scripture, or the meaning of the words ... but the Holy Spirit actually supplied, inspired and dictated the very words and each and every term individually.[13]

This view of the Bible's full verbal inspiration and inerrancy came in conflict with the findings of modern biblical scholarship and natural science and this ushered in the notorious "warfare" between science and theology in the nineteenth and early twentieth centuries.

More recently, both Roman Catholic and Protestant interpreters acknowledge that no person or community comes to the interpretation of the Bible without presuppositions. The scholar or the layperson may come to the Bible with certain scientific or theological preconceptions that may shape his or her reading of the Bible. Or the scholar or layperson may come with certain key Christian beliefs that shape the way he or she reads the Bible as the Church's authoritative book. Consciously or not, every reader brings to the Bible some interpretive principles or guidelines. Therefore, the call for "Scripture alone" is more complex than it may first appear. People do not read the Bible with an impartial eye; rather, they read it with the help of some interpretive key. Consciously or not, Christian interpretations of the Bible also follow a principle similar to that employed in Buddhist hermeneutics: Certain doctrines or normative teachings are essential to understanding the literal text.

In the twentieth century, scholarly interpreters of the Christian Bible have not only benefited from almost two hundred years of intense historical and literary study of the biblical texts. They have also seen the emergence of numerous interpretive approaches that reflect the influence of contemporary cultural and social currents on the reading of the Bible. The feminist movement has, for example, produced a considerable body of literature that interprets the biblical texts from the distinctive perspective of women's experience. A similar interpretive perspective has emerged in the African-American community whose scholars and clergy have focused on those prophetic themes in the Bible that speak forcefully about oppression and liberation. Here we select an example from the work of the African-American Old Testament scholar, Renita Weems.

*An African-American Womanist Interpretatiom*   African-American Christians look at the Bible with considerable ambivalence. The Bible has been an extraordinarily influential force in the American black community, but that community also knows that the Bible was used to legitimize slavery and that it still continues to be used to foster prejudice and injustice. In the case of black women, the Bible has been a source of dual oppression—both with regard to race and gender. And yet, as the African-American biblical scholar Renita Weems acknowledges, the Bible has also been a source of black women's inspiration and identity. Here we will examine briefly how Weems approaches the question of biblical interpretation from a black woman's perspective.

Weems adopts an interpretative approach to the reading of the biblical texts that is called *reader-response criticism*. This method of literary analysis explores the implications of the fact that no individual or community ever approaches a text—especially such an authoritative text as the Bible—without bringing to it some sociocultural preconceptions that exert a powerful influence on *why* and *how* they read a text and *what* they read, for example, in a large collection of texts such as the Bible. The scholarly insistence that the reader "allow the text to speak for itself," though theoretically admirable, is never a simple matter, since one never comes to a text in a vacuum, that is, without interests. And this is particularly true in the reading of a sacred text for the purpose of seeking spiritual meaning and moral guidance.

Weems points to a historical factor in the life of African-American slaves that proved determinative and liberating for them and for later generations of African Americans, especially black women. Slaveholders did not permit their slaves to read, but this, unintentionally, reinforced an aural tradition of listening to and retelling stories that were learned through public readings from the Bible and through the hearing of sermons.

> The very material they forbade the slaves from touching and studying with their hands and eyes, the slaves learned to claim and study through the powers of listening and memory. That is, since the slave communities were illiterate, they were, therefore, without allegiance to any official text, translation, or interpretation; hence once they heard biblical passages read and interpreted to them, they in turn were free to remember and repeat in accordance with their own interests and tastes.[14]

African Americans raised in such an aural culture experienced both the deep influence of the Bible on their community *and* a resistance to those passages in the Bible that were used by the dominant slaveholding culture to legitimize the slavery and oppression of blacks. Contemporary African-American women approach the Bible in a similar manner, applying an analogous "aural hermeneutic":

> This hermeneutic enables them to measure what they have been told about God, reality, and themselves against what they have experienced of God and reality and what they think of themselves as it has been mediated to them by the primary community with which they identify. The community of readers with whom they identify as they read tends to influence how they negotiate the contents and contexts of the Bible.[15]

The experience of their community's slavery and its continuing oppression plays a significant role in how black women read the Bible and how they resist those parts of the Bible that are used by others to legitimize a marginalized, demeaning, and unjust role in society for African-American women. On the other hand, their experience of marginalization and oppression has allowed African-American women to find the Bible passages which capture their imagination and which speak profoundly about their own existential condition and hope, for these passages

> speak to the deepest aspirations of oppressed people for freedom, dignity, justice, and vindication. Substantial portions of the Bible describe a world where the oppressed are liberated, the last become first, the humbled are exalted, the

despised are preferred, those rejected are welcomed, the long-suffering are re-warded. . . . And these are passages, for oppressed readers, that stand at the cen-ter of the biblical message and, thereby, serve as a vital norm for biblical faith.[16]

Weems points out how African-American women will therefore differ from the dominant white male exegesis in their interpretive stance toward, for example, the New Testament writings of the Apostle Paul. First, the black woman will be more alert to how the social position and context of Paul are reflected in his teachings on women and slavery, and thus on his vision of a reconstituted humanity in Christ. Second, the black woman's experience will make her more aware of those subgroups within early Christianity whose marginalized status likely shaped their vision of humanity and of Christian-ity differently from that of those Christians in positions of social dominance.

Until now, we have been exploring the concept of the sacred and some of the forms that it has taken in the expression and communication of reli-gion, such as symbols and myths, rituals, and authoritative sacred scriptures. We will shortly examine seven classic dimensions of religion that together frequently make up a religious worldview. Before we do so, we must look at some of the ways in which religion is both shaped by society and shapes society and its institutions.

## NOTES

1. For a succinct and insightful account of the problems associated with the use of the word "scripture" in a comparative perspective and its justification, see Miriam Levering, "Introduction: Rethinking Scripture," in *Rethinking Scripture: Essays from a Comparative Perspective,* ed. Miriam Levering (Albany N.Y., 1989), 1–17.

2. Harold Coward and David Goa, *Mantra: Hearing the Divine in India* (New York, 1996), 4.

3. Wilfrid Cantwell Smith, "Some Similarities and Differences between Christianity and Islam: An Essay in Comparative Religion" in *The World of Islam: Studies in Honor of Philip K. Hitti,* ed. James Kritzeck and R. Bayly Winter (New York, 1959), 57.

4. For a detailed and helpful analysis of this eternal, creative conception of the Torah in biblical and rabbinic texts, on which I am dependent, see Barbara A. Holdrege, "The Bride of Israel: The Ontological Status of Scripture in the Rabbinic and Kabbalistic Traditions," in Levering, *Rethinking Scripture,* 180–261.

5. Ibid., 215–16.

6. Cited in William A. Graham, *Beyond the Written Word: Oral Aspects of Scripture in the History of Religion* (Cambridge, 1993), 71.

7. Coward and Goa, *Mantra,* 29.

8. On this paradoxical point, see Reginald Ray, "Buddhism: Sacred Text Written and Realized," in *The Holy Book in Comparative Perspective,* ed. Frederick M. Denny and Roderick L. Taylor (Columbia, S.C., 1985).

9. Robert A. F. Thurman, "Buddhist Hermeneutics," *Journal of the American Academy of Religion* 46, no. 1 (March 1978): 22–23. For this point, and other matters regard-ing Buddhist hermeneutics, the author is much indebted to Thurman's insightful article.

10. For my elucidation of the Buddhist interpretive scheme set out in the "Four Reliances," I am especially dependent on Ray's lucid discussion in "Buddhism;" 160–75.

11. Thurman, "Buddhist Hermeneutics," 35.

12. J. K. S. Reid, *The Authority of Scripture* (London, 1962), 69.

13. J. A. Quenstedt, *Theologia dedactico-polemica* (1685), Vol. I, 72. Cited in ibid., 85.

14. Renita J. Weems, "Reading *Her Way* through the Struggle: African American Women and the Bible," in *Stony the Road We Trod: African American Biblical Interpretation,* ed. Cain Hope Felder (Minneapolis, Minn., 1991), 61.

15. Ibid., 66.

16. Ibid., p. 70.

## KEY WORDS

| | |
|---|---|
| *Vedas* | *Septuagint* |
| *Qur'an* | *Apocrypha* |
| Hebrew Bible | *Vulgate* |
| Written and Oral Torah | New Testament |
| canon (canonical authority) | *Guru Granth Sahib* |
| *Analects* | hermeneutics |
| Four Books and Five Classics | Buddha's *Dharma* |
| scripture | *Sutra of the Four Reliances* |
| *Logos* | fourfold method of biblical |
| icon | interpretation |
| *Hadith* | *sola Scriptura* |
| *Pentateuch* | |

## REVIEW QUESTIONS

1. How does this chapter fit in with what has been discussed in Chapters 2–4?

2. What are some common characteristics of sacred scripture? What are some of the differences that you have observed regarding the various scriptures described in this chapter?

3. What is meant by a canon? What are some reasons why religious communities develop a canon of sacred scripture? What are some of the common features of canonical texts?

4. What comparisons and contrasts can you make between the scriptures of Western or Abrahamic religions and those of Eastern religions?

5. What are some common ways in which scriptures are used or function within religious traditions?

6. Is it necessary to interpret scripture? Why or why not? If you disagree with the reasons given for the need for interpretation, be able to explain why you think interpretation is not necessary.

7. Try to outline the basic interpretive rules that Buddhists use in the interpretation of their rich and varied body of sacred scripture.

8. Describe the interpretive principles that were used in the Middle Ages to interpret the Christian Bible. What principle guided the Protestant Reformers Luther and Calvin in their use of the Bible?
9. What principle guides the interpretation of the African-American biblical scholar Renita Weems?

## SUGGESTIONS FOR FURTHER READING

COWARD, HAROLD. *Sacred Word and Sacred Text.* Maryknoll, N.Y.: Orbis Books, 1988. Chapters dealing with scripture in Christianity, Islam, Hinduism, Sikhism, and Buddhism, with an emphasis on the oral uses of scripture.

DENNY, FREDERICK M., AND RODNEY L. TAYLOR, eds. *The Holy Book in Comparative Perspective.* Columbia: University of South Carolina Press, 1985. Not a comparative study, but helpful chapters on aspects of scripture in nine religious traditions, with a fine concluding chapter on nonliterate oral traditions and the "performative" use of sacred writings.

GRAHAM, WILLIAM. *Beyond the Written Word: Oral Aspects of Scripture in the History of Religion.* Cambridge: Cambridge University Press, 1987. An important study of the oral and aural experience and use of holy texts, especially in the Judeo-Christian, Muslim, and Hindu traditions. Valuable notes and bibliography. Also, see Graham's excellent article, "Scripture," in M. Eliade, ed., *The Encyclopedia of Religion* Vol. 13, 133–45.

GRANT, ROBERT, with DAVID TRACY. *A Short History of the Interpretation of the Bible.* 2nd ed. Philadelphia: Fortress Press, 1984. A readable survey of the Christian interpretation of Scripture from Jesus' interpretation of the Old Testament to the present day.

HOLM, JEAN, with JOHN BOWKER., eds. *Sacred Writings.* London: Pinter Publishers, 1994. Similar to Denny and Taylor, with helpful chapters on the important facts about the sacred writings in eight living religious traditions.

LEVERING, MIRIAM, ed. *Rethinking Scripture: Essays from a Comparative Perspective.* Albany: State University of New York Press, 1989. An excellent introductory essay by the editor, laying out the scholarly issues related to rethinking the nature and uses of scripture in the world religions. Followed by valuable essays on aspects of scripture by leading scholars.

SMITH, WILFRED CANTWELL. *What Is Scripture? A Comparative Approach.* Minneapolis, Minn.: Fortress Press, 1993. An important study that poses and explores the critical issues in the comparative study of scripture with chapters devoted to Muslim, Jewish, Hindu, Buddhist, Chinese, and Christian instances. Valuable notes.

*For current articles and bibiographies on the interpretation of the Hebrew Bible and New Testament, for example, Form, Canonical, Literary, Reader Response, and Redaction Criticism, see*

HAYES, JOHN H., ed. *Dictionary of Biblical Interpretation.* Nashville, Tenn.: Abingdon Press, 1999.

*There are numerous anthologies of the world's sacred scriptures. For a recent, well-organized collection with a helpful introduction, see*

VAN VOORST, ROBERT E. *Anthology of World Scriptures.* Belmont, Calif.: Wadsworth Publishing Co., 1994.

# 6

# *Society and the Sacred: The Social Formations and Transformations of Religion*

## Overview

We human beings are not isolated individual units or islands. To be a human being means, fundamentally, to be a social being. The wild boy of Aveyron, raised with animals and isolated from human community, was not considered fully human. In this chapter, we look at some—but by no means all—social expressions of religion and some of the important ways in which religion and society relate, often in a reciprocal or symbiotic way. Differences in the structures of societies both affect the forms of religious belief and behavior and these structures, in turn, are shaped by religion. We will begin with the debate over whether religion is essentially a reflection of more fundamental social realities or whether religion is a powerful independent creator of profound social values, institutions, and behavior.

The focus of this chapter, however, is an analysis of a variety of types of religious societies and the social and religious dynamics of their development, change, and dissolution. One basic type of religious society is the natural community, that is, one based on kinship ties, race, nationality, or geography. A second type is the voluntary religious group whose membership is based on common beliefs, special functions, or sacred powers that extend beyond the natural ties of kinship or geography. These include secret societies that often maintain close affiliation with the kinship group while, at the same time, remaining autonomous.

Another type of voluntary group is the "founded" religion. It is established by a charismatic seer or prophet who brings a new revelation or spiritual message and whose authority commands disciples. The "founded" religious community faces unique problems on the death of the founder, and the means employed by the community to sustain itself and to grow are discussed.

The church-type voluntary religious community is another example. It also experiences special strains and challenges often not encountered by natural religious communities. We will explore the ways in which the church-type religion manages protest and reform, both from within—for example, the church-within-the-church and monasticism—and by secession. This will lead us to an extended analysis of the sect-type religious group, a form of voluntary religious community that is found throughout the world. The ideal features of the sect-type are discussed, as are the distinctive features of several different groups that share sect characteristics. Finally, we describe those features common to religious groups known as cults and those diverse movements that today represent the quest for a New Age Spirituality.

## The Reciprocal Relationship Between Religion and Society

There is little doubt that social systems influence the form and even the substance of religion. It also is obvious that religious beliefs and values have served as critical forces in social and cultural change and stability. The question, of course, has to do with the relative importance that is given to social and material conditions and, conversely, to the role of religious beliefs and human agents as causal factors in human history.

An example of the perspective of Emile Durkheim and his followers can be seen in *The Birth of the Gods* by sociologist Guy Swanson. Swanson claims to have discovered definite correlations between certain social structures—primarily political sovereignty—and specific types of religious belief—monotheism, polytheism, reincarnation, and so on. He begins his study by asserting that "we assume that insofar as a group has sovereignty, it is likely to provide the conditions from which a concept of spirit originates."[1] He insists that people experience supernatural qualities because specific types of social relationships "inherently possess the characteristics we identify as supernatural," that is, certain "constitutional arrangements" that are often unconsciously taken for granted.[2] "Constitutional structures, and especially those of sovereign groups . . . are what men often conceptualize as personified and supernatural beings."[3]

Swanson is, of course, correct that religious ideas and structures often are drawn from and mirror social relations. We need only consider the use of family imagery in many religious traditions, for example, the metaphor of Father in Christian language about God ("Our Father who art in Heaven") and its use of Father and Son in describing the relationship between God and Jesus Christ. It is also evident that the structure of the Roman Catholic Church reflects the organization of the old Roman Empire into parish, diocese, and province. Sexual relations and roles are another instance. In a religion such as

Islam, the sexual patterns of Arab society—in this case, a strongly patriarchal social structure—are mirrored by the limited role of women in the religion itself. Having recognized the obviously formative role of society on religion, it would nevertheless be wrong to assume a one-way social determinism.

Religious beliefs and practice also play a critical role in the change and evolution of societies. This was one of the sociologist *Max Weber's* most important contributions to the study of religion. For Weber, religion is a powerful causal factor influencing social action and social structures. In this, he countered Karl Marx's influential idea that religion is merely an epiphenomenon, that is, a mere reflection of more fundamental social realities. In his book *The Protestant Ethic and the Spirit of Capitalism*, Weber argues that the ethic of Protestantism preceded the emergence of *modern* capitalism and was a crucial factor in its development. In his study of the religions of China, India, and ancient Israel, he further demonstrated that varying religious conceptions of salvation shape economic behavior and other practical choices and decisions—and hence the fundamental value structure or ethos of these societies. An example is the influence of the Hindu belief in reincarnation on the practice of caste duty in India.

Weber did not, however, propose that religion is a wholly independent variable—as if it were free of, or only marginally influenced by, material conditions and social structures. For Weber, religious ideals and values and socioeconomic structures are interactive; the relationship is complex and dependent on many variables. Ideas are rooted in and shaped by material and social conditions, yet these beliefs are not static; they are embodied in persons and persons are not passive, inert things. As the carriers of ideas and values, persons participate in the process of social change. Religious prophets, sages, and saints often introduce quite unexpected new disclosures of truth and reality. While remaining at one level continuous with their social world, they introduce something radically new. One thinks of the great eighth and ninth century (B.C.E.) prophets of Israel, of Jesus within Judaism in the first century C.E., and of Gautama Buddha in sixth century (B.C.E.) India.

The dynamic, interdependent relationship between society and religion means that religion often can functionally serve society in a number of ways that will conserve and strengthen the traditional social structure, some of which we have mentioned in our discussion of sacred ritual. Conversely, religion can be a disintegrating factor for a society, serving as an engine of radical social change, even revolution. The same religious belief or activity can be viewed as functional or dysfunctional, good or bad, according to one's religious or secular beliefs.

## Types of Religious Communities

It is evident that, at both the ideational (ideas and values) and the institutional levels, religions are shaped in significant ways by their material and social environments. Since all religions involve some form of community or fellowship, it is worth exploring the relationship between social structures and types of religious groups, as well as the dynamics of change in these communities.

## Natural Religious Communities

There are important differences to be observed between "natural" and "founded," or voluntary, religious groups. In *natural religious communities* there is little differentiation between the religious and the sociocultural life of the community: family life, polity, the economy, warfare, medicine, and so forth. Religion is interwoven into all of these activities. Furthermore, natural religious groups are joined by biological-blood relations, kinship (clan and tribe), geography (region and nation), or culture. The individual is born into or marries into the group. On the other hand, "founded" religions are dependent on the unique authority of a charismatic leader, on the teachings or ideology that he or she professes, and on personal conversion to that teaching or doctrine. It is therefore voluntary rather than based on natural ties of blood or kinship.

The distinction is not quite this neat, however, since natural religious groups do contain special subgroups that are based on the possession of certain gifts, powers, or functions. Conversely, voluntary religions often divide into smaller subcommunities that, while based on commonly shared beliefs, nevertheless become so identified with blood and family ties that they are indistinguishable from natural religious communities. This has often been the case in Christian history, for example, in some ethnic groups within Eastern Orthodoxy (e.g., the Russian and Greek Orthodox churches) and Roman Catholicism and in communities such as the **Amish** and **Hutterite Brethren.** These groups make no effort to evangelize those outside and seek to perpetuate the community through procreation and nurture. In time, little distinction is made between cultural ethos and religion.

Because natural religions are maintained through blood, kinship, race, or nation, great attention is devoted to rites of passage and especially to the religious significance of fertility and procreation, puberty, marriage, death, and ancestor veneration or worship. All these rites represent vital links in maintaining the family bond over the generations. In voluntary religions, the members are bound by doctrines and ethical ties that do not require the same attention to rites ensuring the perpetuation of the extended family. Hence, in contemporary Western religion, birth and puberty rites are often marginal, if not wholly absent, and marriage and death rites are frequently quite private affairs, certainly no longer communal rites of immense importance. Such is not the case in natural religious groups, either primal or modern. An imperative is marrying within the clan, tribe, or racial group. For example, Abraham, father of the 12 tribes of Israel, expressed deep concern that his son Isaac not marry a daughter of the Canaanites (Genesis 24:2ff). Again, in the religious reforms carried out under the Israelite king Josiah in the seventh century B.C.E. (Deuteronomy 7:3–5) and during the restoration of Judea by Ezra and Nehemiah two centuries later, the matter of marriage is a central motif:

> In those days also I saw the Jews who had married women of Ashdod, Ammon, and Moab; and half of their children spoke the language of Ashdod, and they could not speak the language of Judah, but the language of each people. And I contended with them and cursed them and beat some of them . . . and made them take oath in the name of God, saying, "You shall not give your daughters to their sons, or take their daughters for your sons or for yourselves."
> —*(Nehemiah 13:23–25)*

Another way natural religious communities join the family, clan, or nation in kinship is through ancestor veneration. Here, the deceased are bound together with the living in a seamless web of generations. This is a crucial aspect of caste Hinduism, Japanese Shinto, and Chinese Confucianism. It is also the central motif in the life of the Dahomey tribal nation of West Africa. It is believed that the ongoing life and well-being of each Dahomey sibling group or extended family is dependent on the appropriate care and veneration of the dead ancestors through the carrying out of costly, elaborate, and lengthy funeral ceremonies for all dead adults, as well as through rites in which the descendants are properly "established," or deified. This is because it is believed that the ancestors, though departed, continue to exert an influence on the sibling community, as do the living on their descendants. During the ceremonial funeral dance of the siblings, they are reminded:

> Your fathers and your kinsmen
> Shall never wear torn clothes because of the neglect of their children who
>     remain in life;
> And when fine clothes are worn,
> Your ancestors shall appear in *lubik pa*.[4]

Every sibling family is called on to build a special house in which the worship of the ancestors is held, including the conduct of sacrifices to provide for their care. If the deification ritual is not fulfilled, members of the family begin to die, the head of the community being the first. It is critical, therefore, that the ceremony of "establishing" the ancestors be completed by each of the Dahomey sibling groups.

The largest natural religious community is the race nation or nationality. The nation—or folk, as it is sometimes called—is not technically based on race. Nevertheless, the people believe that they share a common ancestry, history, and tradition. Here, the symbiotic relation between society and religion is especially striking because religion finds in the national-cultural institutions powerful means for its expression. Society, in turn, sees in religion the sacred legitimation of its order, its values, and its destiny.

National religions often trace the nation and its people back to a sacred origin, even as descendants of the gods, and view the king or emperor as representative or incarnation of deity itself. Here, there is a perfect symmetry between the divine cosmic order and the political order, between the macrocosm and the microcosm. This type of national religion was dominant in the ancient Near East, for example, in Egypt, Babylonia, and Assyria. In each instance, the king served as the god's representative. This type was also present in ancient Rome, where the emperor not only took on the high priestly role of Pontifex Maximus but also, finally, was deified as a god incarnate.

Examples of national religion are not, however, a thing of the archaic past. *Japanese State Shinto* is a vivid illustration of its presence in the twentieth century. According to Japanese mythology, the Japanese islands were created by the sexual union of two gods, the primal male and primal female (see Chapter 8), and the first human emperor, Jimmu Tenno, is portrayed as descended from the sun-goddess, Amaterasu. According to tradition, Jimmu Tenno established his capital on the island of Honshu in 660 B.C.E. Here, then, are the ingredients of a national religion: a divinely created land, people, and emperor—and a divine destiny.

Japanese Shinto was not, however, highly nationalistic until quite recently. Shinto's latent nationalism became manifest with its political restoration by the Emperor Meiji in 1868. The focus of public attention was placed on reverence for and obedience to the emperor and on Japan's unique national destiny. An imperial decree on education (1890) joined obedience to the emperor with unswerving loyalty to the Japanese state and empire: "Always respect the Constitution and observe the laws: Should emergency arise, offer yourselves courageously for the State; and thus guard and maintain the prosperity of Our Imperial Throne coeval with heaven and earth."[5] Shinto thus emerged from the Meiji period as a cult of nationalistic patriotism. It contributed, in the years before World War II, to a growing Japanese militancy and war fever. Schools taught young Japanese that Japan stood high above the other nations of the world and that her people excelled other peoples. Here, religion was serving the national political interests of an expansive military power.

The uses of religion for political ends are not, of course, unique to natural religious communities; the history of Christianity and Islam makes this point indelibly plain. We see in natural religious groups, however, a most powerful weaving of the natural, the societal, and the religious into an often seamless fabric.

## Voluntary Religious Communities

The relation between religion and the natural and social environment is never without some tension, even in the most stable and homogeneous of natural religious groups. There are unpredictable spiritual strains and demands.

Closer communion with sacred power may be called for, which requires special talents or spiritual gifts, for example, an elite fraternity of priests or shamans. In an extreme case, certain social institutions may come to be seen as impediments to a genuine access to the sacred or the transcendent. Some religious fraternities may therefore separate or even break away from the larger natural group. It may even reach the point where the new group regards the larger society and its cultural values as of little import or, indeed, as actually evil.

A growing consciousness of "inwardness," of a new and distinct spiritual life, which challenges the customary bonds of society, is an important factor leading to voluntary religious groups even within the natural community. The new spiritual association is set off from other members of the same sex, kin, or race.

The *voluntary religious community* has certain distinct features. First, there is at least a partial break with the natural ties. The new spiritual unity often is based on religious function—for example, priesthood—but also, and more often, on a new spiritual insight or experience of the sacred or of spiritual power. This may entail a feeling of regeneration or conversion, not only deepening a sense of intimacy with the new fellowship but also loosening the ties with the natural kin who do not share in this sacred experience. The old natural ties of blood and kinship may now even count for naught.

Where the break with natural bonds becomes relatively complete, as in the universal voluntary religions such as Islam, Buddhism, or Christianity, those social relations that were essential to the natural religious community may also lose their hold. Marriage within the group, for example, may no longer be important. What is important is union with another person who is committed to the same spiritual doctrine or experience; or chastity and vows of celibacy may be considered the highest spiritual ideal—that of priest, monk, or nun—as in the case of Roman Catholicism and Theravada Buddhism. The religion is no longer sustained merely by procreation but, rather, by evangelization, proselytization, and conversion.

In voluntary religions, rites centering on the veneration of the ancestors also play little or no role. In fact, the Buddhist monk ritually severs ties with his natural family. Jesus turned to the multitudes following him and asserted, "If any one comes to me and does not hate his own father and mother and wife and children and brothers and sisters, yes, and even his own life, he cannot be my disciple" (Luke 14:26). It is often remarked how Islam's radical monotheism transcends ethnic, racial, and national boundaries.

### Founded Religions[6]

Among the voluntary type of religious community is the "founded" religion with its own distinctive characteristics. As the name implies, the community is established through the unique role of a religious leader. This person is variously called a prophet, reformer, teacher, or master. He or she is, first, a *witness* to a new revelation or a new spiritual wisdom. The witness then speaks of this new spiritual truth as a prophet or enlightened master. But no founder produces a new religion de novo; he or she is usually a powerful reformer, building on the foundation of an existing religion. Zoroaster, Buddha, Jesus, and Muhammad were all reformers in this sense. But they were also more than reformers; what they established was also something new. What is distinctive about the founder is a decisive religious experience followed by the enlisting of disciples. The founder possesses a unique and compelling authority, usually both in his or her person and teaching. Max Weber spoke of this distinct power as *charisma,* "a certain quality of an individual personality by virtue of which he is set apart from ordinary men and treated as endowed with supernatural, superhuman, or at least specifically exceptional powers or qualities."[7]

It is this special charisma possessed by the prophet or seer that captivates disciples and sparks the new religious movement. The disciples are drawn together by their shared religious insight, which is interpreted to them by the founder. Their commitment to the founder and to the fellowship may demand a sharp break with the natural community, with the ties of family and kinship, and with the civil authority. It is this severing of kinship bonds, the claim of doctrine over blood, that Max Weber considers the achievement of the great universal, "ethical" religions.

The companions of the founder—who are also apostles spreading the new teaching—face a horrendous crisis at the death of their master. What is to be done when the personal charismatic authority of the leader is no longer present? How is the spiritual authority to be preserved and passed on? How are questions to be answered? Who or what is to guide and to inspire? Many voluntary religious groups do not survive their leader's death. Two twentieth-century examples are the Father Divine Peace Mission in New York and the Peoples Temple in Jonestown, Guyana; these communities collapsed with the death of Father Divine (1965) and the Reverend James Jones (1978).

On the death of the founder, the future of the spiritual fellowship rests on its message and its organization, rather than on the leader's personal charisma. The community has reached a turning point. If it is to survive and be spared divisive conflicts among the followers, a number of things, characteristically, are to be done. First, the oral teachings and the practices of the founder must be collected, systematized, and established as an official canon of sacred writings. To simplify teaching and to establish conditions of membership, a standardized rule of faith or creed is often produced. The community frequently must defend its ongoing life in the wider society; hence, the necessity of creating apologetical writings, that is, arguments defending the religion. Worship and discipline must also be standardized, based on the teachings and practices of the founder. Most important, the *ecclesia,* or fellowship, must organize itself more formally, establishing a constitution, clear functions, and lines of authority. For example, in the early Christian *ecclesia,* there soon emerged deacons, presbyters, and bishops. As the authority of spiritu-ally (charismatically) gifted persons declined, or became problematic for the community, a clearer distinction was made between "clergy" and "laity." All of this process is what Weber calls *"the routinization of charisma"*—the stan-dardizing of doctrine, discipline, worship, and organization.

The English word *church* (from the Greek *ekklesia,* meaning "people called by God") has a definite Christian origin. Not all large-scale voluntary religious communities have evolved organizational structures similar to that of the Christian Church. The Buddhist Sangha ("assembly"), or monastic order, does not include laymen and therefore is, in some respects, more like a Catholic monastic order. The Muslim *ummah* (the entire community of those "surrendered" to Allah) has more in common, perhaps, with the Christian church. What they all share, however, when compared to the Hindu caste or Confucian family, is a break with natural religious ties and, at least ideally, commitment to a spiritual message and life *universal* in its outreach. As they developed, Islam, Mahayana Buddhism, and Christianity all were required to develop organizational structures different from those of the early spiri-tual brotherhood, the inner circle of disciples. These larger structures, con-cerned with maintaining doctrine, discipline, and cult, can properly be called church-type organizations.

## Protest and Change in Voluntary Religious Communities

All human organizations experience the stresses and strains brought on by discord among their members concerning beliefs and practice. Even the most closely knit kinship group will find within it both the highly zealous and the relatively indifferent, the orthodox conformist and the questioner. Further-more, different persons have different needs and goals. This explains, in part, the emergence of special subgroups and secret societies in almost all natural religious communities.

Discord, protest, and calls for reform and change are, however, especially prevalent in voluntary religious groups, that is, in church-type communities. From the beginning, there is the tension between the "true believers" and those prone to lapse in their discipleship. There are the inevitable disagree-ments over the interpretation of scripture or doctrine, over cultic practice, and over authority. All these tensions make the church-type community more vul-nerable to protest, conflict, and even division.

Protest, reform, and renewal can either be individual or collective and can either take place within the community or result in withdrawal from it. If the reformer is to be socially effective, he or she must gain followers and can do so only by exhibiting the requisite authority. Here, we will describe suc-cessful reforms that were achieved *within* the larger voluntary church-type community and then those that were accomplished only through separation from the original church.

## Reform from within the Church

Calls for reform or more radical change may be handled *within* the community in a number of ways. The dissidents may be shown the error of their ways and brought back into conformity with the majority. In the Roman Catholic Church, many priests and bishops who in the 1860s vigorously opposed the majority's wish for an official declaration by the Church on the infallibility of the pope, were reconciled to this development when it was, in fact, declared a dogma in 1870. Often, a compromise is struck by which the protesters are somehow accommodated within the larger community.

*The Ecclesiola in Ecclesia*　It often happens that a small group within the church becomes concerned about the community's "laxity" or carelessness with regard to doctrine, discipline, or worship. Yet the protesters do not wish to secede. This was true of Philipp Jacob Spener (1635–1705), the father of the movement within German Lutheranism called Pietism, and of John Wesley (1703–1791), the founder of Methodism, who organized Methodist societies *within* the established Church of England in order to renew the spiritual life of the people. What both men wished to do was to establish a spiritual "leaven" within the larger church community—a little church (*ecclesiola*) within the larger church (*ecclesia*). These men were not finally successful since their followers withdrew from the mother churches and organized the separate Moravian and Methodist church-type communities that exist today.

Spener introduced into Lutheranism small meetings for the purpose of prayer, devotions, and Bible study. He called for less emphasis on the difference between clergy and laity. He was not interested in the finer points of Lutheran theology but, rather, in the deepening of personal piety, sanctity, and devotion. Spener called these small meetings "colleges of piety" (*collegia pietatis*). Similar "churches within the Church" were found in early Puritanism and the early Society of Friends (Quakers) and also in such pious and mystical movements as **Hasidism** within orthodox Judaism and Sufism in Islam. These "colleges of piety" have been described as follows:

> [It] is a loosely organized group, limited in numbers and united in a common enthusiasm, peculiar convictions, intense devotion, and rigid discipline, which is striving to attain a higher spiritual and moral perfection than can be realized under prevailing conditions.[8]

What is also common to the *ecclesiola in ecclesia* is, of course, an explicit protest against the larger church that, if too pronounced and too prolonged, may lead to division.

*Monasticism*　Another classic form of protest and reform from within is the institution of monasticism. In the Roman Catholic Church, this has been perhaps the best-known form of resolving conflict and of accommodating always-new eruptions of spiritual zeal and calls for a stricter discipline. As early as the third century C.E., anchorites—or desert hermits—joined in Christian communities to develop a strict rule of spiritual life and work. In Western Christianity, the rules of the monastic community were classically formulated by St. Benedict in the sixth century C.E. Monasticism, however, is a common feature of many of the great religious traditions. In early Buddhism, it *was* the primary religious community (the Sangha).

Unlike the *ecclesiola in ecclesia*, which includes families engaged in worldly activities, the monastic community calls for a more fundamental rejection of worldly compromise; indeed, it calls for a denial of, or near denial of, the world and its ways—and thus a more radical spiritual ideal. Some monastic orders, like the Cistercian Trappists (men) and the Strict Observance Carmelites (women), require a relatively severe discipline of self-denial, but most Catholic orders follow the moderate rule established by St. Benedict.

While restrained in its discipline, *the Benedictine rule* nevertheless does require a more demanding spirituality than would be possible for the average layperson. The monks' day is divided among worship, work, study, and prayer. They share everything; dress cheaply and simply; and eat twice a day on a diet of bread, vegetables, and fruit. Silence is enjoined at all times. Poverty, chastity, and obedience are required. The simplicity and rigor of the rule is evident in Benedict's 72 precepts, among which are the following:

> Not to be fond of pleasures.
> To become a stranger to the ways of the world.
> Not to be fond of much talking.
> Often to devote oneself to prayer.
> Not to give way to the desires of the flesh; and to hate one's own will.
> In all things to obey the abbot's commands, even though he himself should act otherwise.[9]

Later ventings of spiritual zeal and devotion in the Catholic Church were legitimized through the establishment of new religious orders, each one meant to direct certain spiritual gifts into official channels: the Franciscans (providing humanitarian service, especially to the poor), the Dominicans (preaching the faith), the Jesuits (defending the faith against heresy and performing missionary work), and the Trappists (encouraging liturgical worship, study, and silent contemplation).

The enthusiasm or the integrity of a movement within the church-type community may become so powerful and the resistance so strong as to propel the reformers beyond the pale of the church into dissent and secession. Such a move may be long coming and undertaken regretfully. Other forms of withdrawal may come, however, as a joyful liberation from "Babel," from a sense that the older community has lost its integrity and hence its capacity to save genuinely.

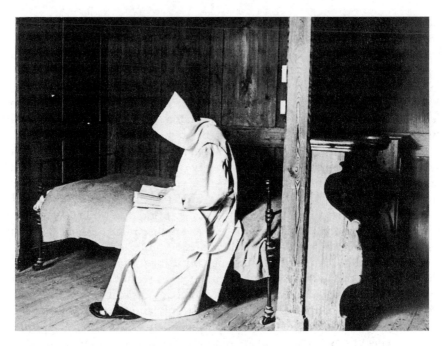

A Carthusian monk sits reading and in contemplation in his cell at St. Hugh's Charterhouse monastery in Sussex, England. The monk passes most of his life praying, studying, eating, and working in solitude. (*Source:* Courtesy of Religious News Service.)

## Separation from the Church-Type Community

When the new community breaks irrevocably with the original church, it is because (1) it has discovered in the original teachings norms of belief and practice once delivered to the saints, but that are now overlooked or denied, or (2) it claims a new, independent revelation or teaching that stands as a challenge to both the church and the larger society and culture. In either case, the new teaching becomes the standard of the new-founded community. The voluntary and universal nature of the church-type religious community invites such movements of "renewal," as well as further "revelations" that often, in turn, claim to be the definitive teaching forbidding new developments.

Examples of the first kind of secession would be the establishment of independent Lutheran, Calivinist, Nonconformist (e.g., Baptist), and Anglican churches *within* Christianity at the time of the Protestant Reformation in Europe in the sixteenth century; the division *within* Judaism between Orthodoxy and the modern movements of Conservatism and Reform Judaism; or the emergence *within* Islam and Buddhism of several schools or movements—each of which claims a new spiritual insight, teaching, or norm of authority. Examples of the second and more radical type of protest would be the early Christian community's break with Judaism, involving the former's claim to be the New Israel; Buddhism's emergence out of and yet rejection of some of the fundamental doctrines of Hinduism; or the claims of Mormonism and Christian Science to have new revelations and new authoritative scriptures (the *Book of Mormon* and *Science and Health*) other than the Christian Bible. In all of these latter instances, as well as in some of the former, the reformer (Jesus, Buddha, Joseph Smith, and Mary Baker Eddy) caused his or her followers to secede from the mother community and to establish an independent, separatist school, sect, or church.

## The Sect

The word *sect* has long carried a disparaging connotation, implying something strange and deviant, perhaps even contemptible. It was, indeed, originally used by churches to describe heretical and schismatic groups. However, the word is used today by scholars simply to distinguish sociologically certain types of voluntary religious communities from others with different sociological features, for example, from the *ecclesia*, or established churches; from the *ecclesiola in ecclesia*; and from a more recent ecclesiastical institution, the **denomination.**

In *The Protestant Ethic and the Spirit of Capitalism*, Max Weber first noted the distinction between church and sect and discussed the factors involved in their development. These differences were explored more extensively by Weber's colleague Ernst Troeltsch, in his study *The Social Teachings of the Christian Churches*. Since these two epochal studies, sociologists have worked on refining a **typology** of religious groups and, more important, on determining the social as well as the religious factors involved in the origin, development, and change of specific types of religious communities, especially the sect-type.

*Sects* differ from churches and denominations in a number of ways. While no sect perfectly exemplifies the ideal type, scholars are agreed that the sect is distinct in joining the following characteristics:

1. The sect tends to be exclusive.
2. The sect claims to have a monopoly on the religious truth.
3. The sect tends to be lay-organized and to reject or downplay a religious division of labor. Religious obligations are equal and shared by all in the group.
4. The sect is strongly marked by voluntarism; that is, each member is usually required to show some knowledge or change of life in order to be accepted.
5. The sect demands the total allegiance of the member in all areas of life; hence, membership in the sect is the individual's most important means of personal identification.
6. The sect exercises sanctions against the wayward to the point of expulsion of the deviant from the sect.
7. The sect is a protest group, not only against the church but also against the wider culture and the state.[10]

No sect conforms perfectly to all these features. Sects do tend, however, to be small, rigorous, and selective rather than broad and inclusive, as are established churches. Unlike churches, sects often are not deeply involved in the wider society; sects not infrequently are alienated from the surrounding culture. The rigor and alienation of sects also may express themselves in non-conformist dress or in what is considered a deviant style of living.

Some scholars have theorized that genuine sects are short-lived and be-come **denominations** in the course of one generation. If a sect, as a radical protest group, does not wither away, the upward social and economic mobil-ity of its members and the change from voluntary membership to second-generation membership through birth will cause the sect to move to the status of a denomination. If it survives, the sect must focus on the nurture and education of its young, on organization, and on the acquisition and man-agement of property. Moreover, the second generation rarely holds the con-victions with the zeal of their parents; secular commitments and the desire for social respectability intrude. The sect thus becomes "denominational-ized"; it becomes a form of church-type community that is limited by bound-aries of social class, race, and ethnicity or region and that displays more liberal and tolerant attitudes toward other religious groups, greater accom-modation to the "secular" world, and rather more formality in worship and leadership.[11] The denomination, it was observed, is a dominantly American type of religious association, although it has become common in other parts of the English-speaking world. This points to a weakness in this type of sect analysis. It mistakes the sequence of development of a certain type of American "conversionist" sect for a universal and inevitable social process of sect growth and change.

More recently, sociologists have demonstrated that these earlier sect typologies reflect too-narrow preoccupations with Western Christian forms of religious community. They fail to do justice to the sect-type groups that are found in other religious cultures and in Western culture since the decline in the special status of the older European established churches. *Bryan Wilson* is prominent among those sociologists who have suggested a new typology of sect-type communities.[12] Wilson believes that the sect is a universal form of religious community, far more pervasive than the dominantly Western church or denomination. Furthermore, there are a number of distinctive types of sects or religious movements, some prone to "denominalization" while others are apparently immune to the alternatives of denominational development or dissolution.

Wilson proposes a typology of several types of sects, each one expressive of a distinctive "response to the world." Among them is the *conversionist sect*, which is characteristic of fundamentalist and pentecostal groups within Protestant Christianity, especially in America. These groups have little or no interest in programs of social reform. What is called for is a highly emotional, personal spiritual conversion experience. The evil of the world is transcended by this radically new, subjective experience of salvation here and now.

The *revolutionist sect* believes that salvation will come soon, but only with the destruction of the present natural and social order. This process of destruction will be supernaturally wrought, although the believers may participate in the process. What is looked for, however, is a new order that is seen as historically imminent. Salvation will come only by divine action. An American example of this type of sect is the Jehovah's Witnesses or, perhaps, the Branch Davidian community in Waco, Texas in the early 1990s. Wilson sees the revolutionist sect as one of the most distinctive sect movements in contemporary less-developed countries.

A very different kind of religious movement is what Wilson calls the *gnostic* or *manipulationist sect.* What is distinctive about this kind of group, sometimes called a cult, is the fact that it fully *accepts* and pursues what others would see as worldly goals. What it seeks is not withdrawal from or an indifference toward the world but, rather, appropriation of the right spiritual means or techniques by which to cope with or to achieve worldly goals. Liberation essentially means health, happiness, success, status, wealth, or long life. Salvation is a present, immediate possibility. Group fellowship in some of these movements is minimal. Examples are many of the New Age movements (see below) such as est, the human potential movement, ritual healing, Wicca and Witchcraft, Deep Ecology, Scientology, and Transcendental Meditation.

Wilson's last type is the *utopian,* a very complex sect. Unlike the revolutionist, it does not look to the violent overturn of the present world; rather, it looks to the human reconstruction of the world on a communitarian basis and according to a divinely given plan. It is more radical than the reformist groups in that it calls not only for social improvement and reform but also for a total social reorganization in which evil is eliminated. The Oneida Community in nineteenth-century western New York, the Brüderhof communities, the Peoples Temple in Guyana, and a few of the New Age movements are examples of this type of religious society.

The varied characteristics of these sect types—in terms of ideology, organization, and response to the world—make some more vulnerable than others to change, development, and dissolution. Some can remain relatively stable over time while others, such as the conversionist type, are vulnerable to external influences that often bring rather rapid modifications in belief and organization and transformation into a denomination.

## The Cult: New Religious Movements

Before we conclude this analysis of religious communities, attention needs to be given to one other type of religious group. The emergence of new religious movements is one of the more striking developments on the contemporary religious scene—not only in North America but also in Africa, Japan, Melanesia, and Latin America. In the past three or four decades, there has been something of an explosion of new religious movements worldwide. They display a luxuriant diversity of religious experience, and they derive from many different sources. Some, like the recent highly charged forms of fundamentalist and pentecostal Christianity, are essentially new expressions of sectarian Protestantism, although they also reflect the influences of contemporary popular culture and communications technology. Others, like the Unification Church, the Rajneesh Foundation, the Divine Light Mission, and Krishna Consciousness (Hare Krishna), have their roots in various Asian traditions. A third type of new religious movement represents an eclectic mix of American pop psychology, older forms of therapeutic mind-cure, elements of Eastern mysticism and meditation, a return to the wisdom of the earth, and systems of astrology, witchcraft, and magic, all found in the New Age movement.

Many of these new religious movements do not conform to the dominant characteristics of traditional sects. They appear to be new and loose-knit, and they are often a mixture of religious beliefs and practices. For these and other reasons, they frequently are referred to as cults. The term, however, is much disputed. None of these movements has emerged de novo but, it is argued that all enduring religions also admit to some degree of admixture. In time, cults often take on the features of older religions. Nevertheless, the term serves to designate those new movements that appear to represent estrangement from, or indifference to, the older religious traditions; indeed, many do not at all resemble sectarian secession from an older tradition.

These new movements also often display a more private and subjective religiosity and a highly secular, practical, therapeutic character. It should be noted, however, that some students of these recent developments prefer to refer to them as "new religious movements" rather than as cults, since they insist it is not clear that the term *cult* encompasses features wholly distinct from those of sects. In any case, these cults, or new religious movements, represent a proliferation of diverse, innovative, voluntary forms of religious life.

Not surprisingly, these new movements do appear to mirror aspects of cultural change at the turn of the new millenium. They call attention to the rather widespread disaffection with the older, mainline churches and traditional orthodoxies. As one scholar has noted, cults arise "when religions fail . . . when the institutional framework of religion begins to break up, the search for direct experience which people can feel to be 'religious' facilitates the rise of cults."[13] They also reflect the growing pluralism and individualism of modern life, even in those societies that only now are showing the influences of modern technology, urbanization, and bureaucratization. Many scholars have pointed out how these new movements appear to be responses to the secularization of modern society (see Chapter 13). Many of the new cults—but by no means all—reveal the breakdown between the private and public character of traditional religions in that these new movements often are characterized as a privatized religiosity that lacks a civic dimension and a concern with social issues and public affairs.

Other observers of the new religious movements see their proliferation as a refutation of the secularization thesis, and as proof of the enduring human need to seek some form of spiritual transformation or transcendent meaning. However one may judge this question, it is clear that many of these new cults reflect two other features of our contemporary life: the prestige of psychic therapies in our psychologically conditioned culture and the obsessive search for genuine community in an increasingly pluralistic, socially dislocated society. The cults clearly minister to these two concerns.

Caught in increasingly complex and impersonal institutional structures, individuals feel that they have lost personal control, spontaneity, and spiritual freedom. Many cults offer therapies that emphasize the primacy of consciousness, mind control, and taking responsibility for one's own thoughts so as to "control" external events and enhance one's own capabilities, even one's worldly success. As traditional structures—the family (especially the extended family), neighborhoods, and churches, for example—lose their hold, many persons, and especially the young, feel dislocated and lonely. Some of the new cults promise their followers genuine kinship and community that will give them the acceptance, love, and moral nurture for which they long.

It is not possible here to introduce the numerous examples of these new religious movements. Students of this phenomenon have, however, discerned two somewhat contrasting types of cults that have responded to the spiritual needs newly created by our contemporary cultural dislocations. In describing these two types, we select two movements for fuller attention. The first type is represented by the therapeutic, mystical, and generally world-affirming movements that include Transcendental Meditation, est, Scientology, and the various quasi-religious groups in the Human Potential Movement. What all these movements share is a disillusionment with traditional forms of knowledge, whether religious or scientific, and the belief that liberation comes from acquaintance with some special knowledge or technique that can free the latent powers of the self. These movements emphasize liberation of the self by the self, here and now.

## The New Age: Toward Self Discovery

The *New Age* spiritual search for the inner self, psychic healing, and new, creative possibilities follows many paths. In describing the New Age, a spokesperson offers the metaphor of a "flea market" or "county fair"—to contrast these movements with the image of the "cathedral" of traditional religion. The "county fair" indicates the richness, openness, and vitality of the New Age spiritualities, and their bewildering variety of tents including "jesters and tricksters, magicians and shamans, healers and mystics, and the inevitable hucksters eager for a quick sale."[14]

The sources appealed to in these cults include the wisdom of ancient Egypt, Indian Yoga meditation, Zen Buddhism, Native American rituals, astrology, Earth goddess spirituality, shamanism, herbalism and nutrition, and various popular psychotherapies such as Jungian (see Chapter 3 on myth) and Transpersonal psychology, as proposed by Abraham Maslow (see Chapter 11), to name but a few. What links these various "tents" together is the fact "that each of them offers a challenge or an alternative to the dominant materialistic, patriarchal paradigm of contemporary Western industrialized culture. They each offer an image or *process of transformation.*"[15] Many of these "paths" or useful "means" assist in the perception of the union or interdependence of all living things and our human relationship to the earth—indeed to the entire cosmos—as the key to personal freedom and wholeness. The New Age leaders frequently speak of the "paradigm shift," the revolution that is taking place or that must take place, in human consciousness required to usher in a New Age, replacing the older authoritarian, rationalistic, mechanistic, patriarchal, industrialized civilization, the fruits of which have been an intense competition ("rat-race"), repression, estrangement, emptiness, and the "terror"—political, genocidal, nuclear—that marked the twentieth century.

These various spiritual paths and movements share a good deal in common, despite their enormous variety. First, the New Agers are, on the whole, optimistic about the future, for they are confident that the emergent Age of Aquarius offers the potential for new creative transformation—personal, earthly, even cosmic—that is, a New Age. They see some signs of its emergence in the new internationalism, in racial and religious pluralism, in the feminist revolution, in a growing ecological-environmental consciousness, and in new developments and insights in science. The various devotees of the New Age do not simply want to return to premodern ways of life. Nor do they reject modern science and technology, as do some contemporary religious fundamentalists.

While they are extraordinarily diverse, the New Age movements do reveal some important common characteristics and themes. These features are important in understanding the movement as a whole.

1) First, the New Agers feel their personal lives and our Western civilization are on a destructive path. One New Ager refers to the situation as a dysfunctional "melodrama which goes on in many of our heads most of the time, the fear, anxiety, guilt and recrimination; the burden of the past which continues to dominate our present responses, and produces exaggerated or inappropriate responses to current circumstances."[16] There is a deep sense that one must be freed of this destructive accumulated "baggage" through a transformative experience. And the means or paths to freedom are many, and complimentary, being offered out there in a motley "county fair."

2) The focus of most of these New Agers is on the *individual* and his or her *physical and spiritual healing or transformation.* A worshipping community, such as a church is not common. Interpersonal relations are, more

characteristically, between the seeking initiate and a spiritual director, a *guru* or teacher, be it a master of Yoga, a spirit-possessed medium, or a psychotherapist. The goal of the numerous techniques or therapies is to get in touch with one's "inner" or "higher" self, one's innate divinity. This idea owes much to the teachings of contemporary transpersonal psychology. Similarly, the practice and goal of *channeling*—of consulting a medium or spirit-filled person—is not so much an effort to make contact with an ancient wise teacher or a transcendent being (e.g., God) but, rather, to connect with hidden dimensions of one's own psyche. The channeling or messages are therapeutic, offering personal healing, insight into the "higher" self, and inspiration. This is also true of the practice of contemporary **shamanism.** The author of *Maps of Ecstasy: Teaching of an Urban Shaman* writes, "Everybody has a shaman side. Waiting for a wake-up call. . . . Shamanic healing is a journey . . . stepping out of our habitual roles . . . to unleash the body, heart, mind, soul . . . to discover the healer within."[17]

3) A third, and quite distinctive feature of much New Age thought is the attention given to what is called a universal "vibrational energy." It is related to the insight of quantum physics that matter and energy are systematized as a network of vibrational patterns. Some physicists have speculated that the vibrational changes of physical phenomenon are associated with consciousness as the organizing principle of these transformations—hence postulating an essential link between matter and mind or consciousness. The higher the consciousness is raised the nearer one comes to the true cosmic consciousness or Reality.

Neo-pagan earth rituals and festivals, such as **Wicca,** or white witchcraft associated with the feminine principle, the Goddess imminent in all of nature, stress this energy. The Wicca coven, or group, ideally of thirteen, believes that its ritual raises a "cone" of earth energy and power that can be harnessed for healing as well as for beneficial activity in the world. In other New Age cults this universal "energy" goes by various names—mana, prana, the ch'i, holy spirit, and mind, all of which can be released, through appropriate rituals or therapies, to energize and heal the body and the mind.

4) Another feature of the New Age movements is the high regard for currents of modern science, and their use of scientific language—quark symmetries, implicate orders, chaos theory—and their claims that their beliefs are congruent with recent scientific hypotheses and breakthroughs. They see their movement as a sign that we are experiencing—to use the term made famous in Thomas Kuhn's *The Structure of Scientific Revolutions*—a new *paradigm change* from the old mechanistic and dualistic (body/spirit, matter/consciousness, thinking/feeling) model of the world to a cosmology more holistic, vitalistic, and spiritual. New Agers look to the work of some eminent scientists whose views, they see, as corresponding to the metaphysical speculations of New Age writers. These scientists have, themselves, often shown an interest in the New Age movement. We can illustrate this

dimension with an example of the work of the physicist David Bohm. He has proposed a hypothesis called the "holographic paradigm." The hologram is a three-dimensional image of objects that Bohm converts into frequency patterns; their importance is the holistic insight that the peculiar characteristic of each fragment of intermediate frequency pattern contains the information of the whole object. Bohm thus suggests that, similarly, the whole of the universe is implicit in each of its parts—a theme central to New Age spirituality and cosmology.[18]

5) A feature of much New Age thought and discussion, alluded to previously, is its attention to the earth and the interdependence of all living things. This is closely related to the movement's interest in our earth's natural environment and to the wider development of an environmental-ecological consciousness worldwide. Unity, as a central principle of the New Agers, finds expression in a vision and expectation of the coming unity and peace among the world's religions and the peoples of the earth that will supercede the past tribal, racial, and national parochial ideologies and loyalties. This also reflects the concern to extend an appreciation of our natural world globally and to reverse the destruction of our planet, its animals and birds, its rain forests, rivers, and air. Crucial to its sense of the sacredness of nature and the interconnectedness of its elements is then the expansion of humanity's ecological mindfulness.

One contemporary cult will serve to exemplify *some* of the characteristics of the New Age movements that we have discussed, especially their individualistic, therapeutic, and optimistic, world-affirming features.

*Scientology* Though it has met with considerable opposition from governments in both the United States and abroad, the **Church of Scientology** is one of the most enduring of these New Age movements. It was founded by L. Ron Hubbard, who as a very young man was introduced to psychotherapy and had traveled to Japan, China, and Indonesia. In his early twenties he began writing fiction, largely popular westerns and supernatural fantasy. Later he was a screenwriter in Hollywood. After service with the Navy in World War II, Hubbard's energies were turned to researches on the human mind. These were influenced by his knowledge of depth psychology, Oriental religions, and the occult. In 1950 he published *Dianetics: The Modern Science of Mental Health,* which immediately made the *New York Times* bestseller list. Scientologists mark the publication of *Dianetics* as not only the founding event of their movement but a major turn in the possible transformation of humankind. From a legal perspective Scientology became a religion with the founding of the Church of Scientology in 1954 as a tax-free institution.

A crucial development in Hubbard's scientific explorations of the mind was the development of the electropsychometer, called the E-meter or "lie-detector," which claims to measure changes in the mind, hence quantifying the psychological processes basic to Hubbard's program. For Scientologists it gave Dianetics a scientific credibility.

According to Hubbard's early analysis, individuals possess four *dynamics*—the urge or desire to survive, the desire of sex or the procreation of children, the desire for the group, and the desire for humankind—in an ascending scale. Positive actions toward these achievements yield pleasure, while destructive actions lead toward failure, suffering, and death. What causes the inhibition of these pleasures are certain psychological pathologies that Dianetics is able to cure. It represents a form of "mind-cure" characteristic of many New Age cults. According to Hubbard, the distortions of the mind are traceable to the way we process data. Each moment of experience is stored as an image, taken together they are called the "time-track."

In the case of our waking-consciousness, or analytical mind, the mind takes in these images, analyzes them, and makes survival-oriented decisions. However, there is also the unconscious mind that is operative, in many cases, when our analytical-conscious mind is turned off (sleep) or is distorted by certain events. It is on these occasions that the unconscious, or what Hubbard calls the *reactive mind*, also stores mental data. These collective images are called *engrams* and lack the conscious mind's analytical or rational operation. Hence when the traumatic, negative images of the unconscious-reactive mind are recalled they can cause destructive responses: pain, depression, humiliation, and so on.

The process of mental therapy Hubbard offers is called "auditing," which serves to eliminate the destructive effects of the engrams. Trained counselors, called "auditors," are skilled in the process of bringing these engrams to the consciousness of the person being counseled (the individual is called a pre-clear). This process leads the person to an awareness of these negative factors, through the skillful means of the auditor. The end is awareness, enlightenment, or being "clear"—somewhat analogous to the Buddhist release (*moksha*) and enlightenment. The auditor's use of the E-meter simply modernizes and enhances this process by measuring the pre-clear's mental states and the changes in the response to the engrams as they are recalled and then eradicated.

Hubbard's early Dianetics program did not promise any "transcendental" rewards, as do many religions. However, new spiritual and metaphysical ideas were introduced with the founding of the Church of Scientology and the publication of Hubbard's *Scientology: The Fundamentals of Thought*. Beyond the body and the mind Hubbard now introduced the idea of the spirit or immortal soul, which can leave and exist apart from the body. This soul is called a *thetan*; and with this new spiritual entity, Hubbard extends the chain of engrams to include images from "past lives and past deaths." He also increased the four dynamics of Dianetics to eight, including the desire for the species "to seeking to survive through identification with the universe, spirituality, and infinity or the Supreme Being."[19] Here Scientology's metaphysics is rather similar to Hindu monistic meditation and philosophy (see Chapters 7 and 12).

Scientology is a worldwide movement and hundreds of thousands of people have taken counseling courses, including such celebrities as the movie stars Tom Cruise and John Travolta. In 1993 the Church of Scientology won a long battle with the Internal Revenue Service and received the U.S. government's sanction as a religion. The future of Scientology, like that of the other cult-type religious movements, is difficult to judge. Scientology—and other cults with the similar features—has been harshly criticized but also praised by outside observers. Critics point to what they see as the "narcissism" and self-absorption of these private spiritual "shoppers." The aforementioned sociologist Bryan Wilson writes dismissively that these privatized cults "have no real consequence for other social institutions. . . . They add nothing to any prospective reintegration of society, and contribute nothing towards the culture by which a society might live."[20] Others disagree and believe that many of the New Age movements, despite their deficiencies, represent a serious call for an awakening, a transformation and revisioning of the self and our world. In the words of one advocate, the New Age can

> inspire us with the knowledge that we can cocreate the world . . . a revisioning of our images of God, the transformation of our imagination to embrace a deeper and broader definition of the sacred, one that is cosmic, ecological, cocreative, and wild in the sense of being beyond the control of human interests and preferences.[21]

### The Unification Church—the "Moonies"

What distinguishes this movement is its focus on communal and political values, and on idealistic sacrifice of the self for the achievement of social, even world, unity and peace. While the therapeutic cults are generally adaptive and world-affirming, this second type often finds itself militantly contending against the corruptions of society, thus evoking the suspicion and hostility of the larger society. This type of group is morally dualistic: It sees certain forces in society or the wider world as the enemy, as the "devil."[22]

The *Unification Church* was founded in Korea in 1954 by the Reverend Sun Myung Moon. The movement is known by several names, such as the Holy Spirit Association for the Unification of World Christianity, the Moon Organization, and, more popularly, the "Moonies."

Moon was born in 1920 and raised in a Korean family that had converted to Presbyterian Christianity. Moon claims that on Easter Day 1936, Jesus appeared to him and revealed that God had chosen him to establish His Kingdom of Heaven on Earth. For the next decade Moon received revelations through meditation and the study of various religious scriptures, and claims to have entered into communications with Jesus, Moses, Buddha, and God Himself. These revelations were written down by Moon's disciples and published in 1957. A subsequent text, translated into English as *Divine*

*Principle,* is now used as the basis for the official teachings of the Unification Church. The Church says that further revelations will be released as progress is made toward establishing the earthly Kingdom.

Moon's early evangelistic efforts in Korea met with considerable opposition. He was imprisoned several times and spent two and a half years in a communist labor camp in North Korea. His sufferings, persecution, and endurance served to enhance Moon's renewed religious efforts after he was released from prison by United Nations forces in October 1950. In the late 1950s some of Moon's missionaries went to Japan and the West; however, it was not until the early 1970s, when Moon himself took up residence in the United States, that the movement rapidly began to grow.

The attraction of the Unification Church is primarily among the young and is due principally to its messianic, New Age idealism that promises moral renewal and the imminent coming of the Kingdom of God on earth. The main beliefs, which include a cosmology, soteriology, and eschatology, or vision of the future, are all found in the *Divine Principle.* The focus of the Church's activities, other than raising funds for its recruitment program, is on lectures and discussions of the *Divine Principle.*

The teachings of the *Divine Principle* cannot be easily summarized, and what is said here does not do justice to the full teaching. What I point out are those doctrines that are most distinctive and, to outsiders, most controversial. The Unification Church teaches that the *Divine Principle* is the fulfillment of the Christian Bible and of other scriptures. God created the world into polar, complementary (positive–negative or male–female) elements, like the Chinese *yin* and *yang* (see Chapter 7). These polar units are themselves first engaged in a reciprocal action and then engaged with larger units, ultimately forming a whole. Divine love ("Heart") is fundamentally unitive. The goal of history is, then, the increasing unity effected by this growing love.

According to Moon, the Fall destroyed God's original plan for Adam and Eve, which was for them to pass through certain necessary stages and then to be joined in marriage. As "True Parents," Adam and Eve, through their children and their children's children, would populate a perfect world. Unfortunately, the angel Lucifer grew jealous of God's love for Adam and had an illicit spiritual (though sexual) relation with Eve. Eve, in turn, persuaded Adam to have a physical sexual relationship with her. This Lucifer-inspired premature union resulted in the Fallen Nature that since has been transmitted to the entire human race. History is the record of the efforts of God and men to restore the world to its original perfection and to establish the Kingdom of God on Earth.

The *Divine Principle* teaches that the restoration of the world to its original perfection can only be accomplished by the Messiah, who with his wife will take on the roles of the original Adam and Eve. The Messiah will be a man born of human parents but free of original sin. Jesus was such a person but, because of the fault of John the Baptist, he was executed before he could marry and carry out God's earthly plan. Jesus thus offers only spiritual, not

Four thousand two hundred members of the Unification Church are married in Madison Square Garden in New York, 1982. The Reverend Moon decided which individuals would be joined together. (*Source:* Courtesy of Tannenbaum, Corbis/Sygma.)

earthly, physical salvation. Physical restoration must wait for another Messiah, the Lord of the Second Coming.

At the center of Unification theology is its messianic reading of history. It teaches that the present time is ripe for the Second Coming of the Messiah. Here it reflects the dominant aspects of classic *millenarian-messianism*. The separation between good and evil, which is signaled by the actions of Adam and Eve, Cain and Abel, and then by the later estrangement of whole peoples and nations, has now reached the point of international conflict between the two world powers of communism (evil) and democracy (good). The Moonies teach that an ultimate showdown is inevitable. If the battle cannot be won by persuasion, then Satan (communism) must be defeated by force. In either case, an ideology of true love must then be spread abroad.

According to the "Conclusion" of the *Divine Principle*, entitled "The Second Coming," the Messiah will not come supernaturally on the clouds of heaven. Rather, he will be born here on earth and will be the ideal human person. The Church's calculations indicate that, while the exact date of the

Messiah's coming is unknown, he should have been born between 1917 and 1930. Also, his birth must be in the East, in a nation that has experienced great suffering, one where many religions have lived together, and where two powers of evil (communism) and good (democracy) are now locked in conflict. All indications point to the claim that the Messiah was born in Korea. While the Moonies say that their attention is focused on the coming of the New Age, the vast majority in the movement also believe that Sun Myung Moon and his wife are the "True Parents" and that he is the long-awaited Messiah.

Scholars have pointed out that cults, like the Moonies, serve crucial mediating roles in a society suffering from the breakdown of traditional social and family structures. The Unification Church provides a familylike community, a surrogate family which, moreover, emphasizes universal spiritual values that are deeply attractive to idealistic youth. These young recruits see themselves engaged selflessly in a struggle to achieve universal harmony and peace in a loveless, immoral, cynical world. The idealistic zeal of the Moonies, however, often reflects their "totalism," that is, a militancy and dogmatic moral dualism that alienates them from the larger society. As a result, the Unification Church is frequently looked upon with hostility and accused of coercion and "brainwashing" techniques and with political extremism. Many governments have taken special legal measures against the Unification Church which the Moonies—and many other new religious movements—see as a highly selective form of religious prejudice and persecution.

A complete discussion of religion and society would, of course, include a number of other significant themes beyond the ones we have explored in this chapter—for example, the relation of religion to economic and racial status, that is, to social stratification. (On the issue of gender, see Chapter 13.) It is time now, however, to turn from the analysis of some of the universal forms of religious expression given in Chapters 2–6 to a consideration of some classic forms of belief and practice that make up a religious worldview.

## NOTES

1. Guy E. Swanson, *The Birth of the Gods* (Ann Arbor, Mich., 1960), 21.
2. Ibid., 22.
3. Ibid., 26–27.
4. Melville J. Herskovits, *Dahomey: An Ancient West African Kingdom*, Vol. I (Evanston, Ill., 1967), 202.
5. F. H. Ross, *Shinto: The Way of Japan* (Boston, 1965), 140.
6. This discussion of founded religions is dependent on Joachim Wach, *Sociology of Religion* (Chicago, 1944).
7. Max Weber, *The Theory of Social and Economic Organization* (New York, 1947), 358–59.
8. Wach, *Sociology of Religion*, 175.

9. *The Rule of Saint Benedict,* trans. Cardinal Gasquet (London, 1925), 17–22.
10. For this ideal-type characterization I am dependent on Bryan Wilson, *Religion in Sociological Perspective* (Oxford, 1982), 91–92.
11. H. Richard Niebuhr, *The Social Sources of Denominationalism* (New York, 1929).
12. Bryan Wilson, *Religious Sects* (London, 1970); *Magic and the Millennium* (London, 1973), 18–31; and "The Sociology of Sects," in *Religion in Sociological Perspective.*
13. Daniel Bell, "The Return of the Sacred? The Argument on the Future of Religion," *British Journal of Sociology* 28 (1977), 443.
14. David Spangler, "The New Age: The Movement Toward the Divine," in Duncan S. Ferguson, ed., *New Age Spirituality* (Louisville, 1993), 80.
15. D. Spangler, "The New Age," 81.
16. Roy Wallis, *The Elementary Forms of the New Religious Life* (London, 1984), 32.
17. Gabrielle Roth, *Maps of Ecstasy: Teachings of an Urban Shaman* (Wellingborough, 1990), 3.
18. For a more extensive discussion of New Age Science, on which this brief discussion is dependent, see Wouter J. Hanegraaff, *New Age Religion and Western Culture* (Albany, 1998), Chapter Three.
19. J. Gordon Melton, *The Church of Scientology* (Signature Books, 2000), 31. Melton's concise, accurate account of Scientology has been especially helpful in my brief delineation of this movement.
20. Bryan Wilson, *Contemporary Transformations of Religion* (Oxford, 1976), 68.
21. David Spangler, "The New Age: The Movement Toward the Divine," in Duncan S. Ferguson, ed., *The New Spirituality: An Assessment* (Louisville, 1993), 105.
22. See Eileen Barker, *The Making of a Moonie* (Oxford, 1984). I am dependent on Barker's analysis for much of my discussion.

## KEY WORDS

Max Weber
natural religious communities
Japanese State Shinto
voluntary religious communities
"founded" religions
charisma
"the routinization of charisma"
*ecclesiola in ecclesia*
monasticism
the Benedictine rule

the denomination
Bryan Wilson
the conversionist sect
the revolutionist sect
the gnostic or manipulationist sect
the utopian sect
New Age
Church of Scientology
The Unification Church
millenarian-messianism

## REVIEW QUESTIONS

1. Why is a chapter devoted to the social formations of religion?
2. From the discussion in the text, give examples of the way religion *mirrors* social beliefs and practice. Give an example of a society whose religious beliefs have been important in *changing* social beliefs and behaviors.

3. What are the differences between natural and voluntary religious communities? Give examples of each type.
4. What special problems does the founded religion face? How does it deal with these problems?
5. What is meant by "church-type" religious organization? Describe, with examples, the forms that religious protest and reform take within the voluntary religious community and how they have been resolved. Give some examples of protest and reform that have led to secession from the original church-type community.
6. Describe the chief characteristics of the sect-type religious group. What are the distinctive features of the conversionist type sect, the revolutionist sect, the gnostic sect, and the utopian sect?
7. Characterize some of the chief features of the New Age movements.
8. In what ways do Scientology and the Unification Church represent two distinct types of cults or new religious movements?

## SUGGESTIONS FOR FURTHER READING

BERGER, PETER. *The Sacred Canopy.* New York: Doubleday, 1967.

McGUIRE, MEREDITH. *Religion: The Social Context.* Belmont, Calif.: Wadsworth, 1994.

NIEBUHR, H. RICHARD. *The Social Sources of Denominationalism.* New York: Henry Holt, 1929.

WEBER, MAX. *The Protestant Ethic and the Spirit of Capitalism.* New York: Scribners, 1930. Advanced study.

WILSON, BRYAN. *Religious Sects.* New York: McGraw-Hill, 1971.

———. *Religion in Sociological Perspective.* Oxford: Oxford University Press, 1982.

*On the new religious movements, see*

BARKER, EILEEN. *New Religious Movements: A Practical Introduction.* London, HMSO, 1989.

BAINBRIDGE, WILLIAM S. *The Sociology of Religious Movements.* New York, 1996.

FERGUSON, DUNCAN. *New Age Spirituality: An Assessment.* Louisville: Westminster/John Knox Press, 1993.

HANEGRAAFF, WOUTER. *New Age Religion and Western Culture.* Albany: State University of New York Press, 1998. An encyclopic study.

HEELAS, PAUL. *The New Age Movement.* Oxford: Blackwell, 1996.

# Part III

## *Universal Components of a Religious Worldview*

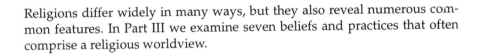

Religions differ widely in many ways, but they also reveal numerous common features. In Part III we examine seven beliefs and practices that often comprise a religious worldview.

# 7

# *Deity: Concepts of the Divine and Ultimate Reality*

## *Overview*

In this chapter, we will describe a variety of ways in which deity or sacred power and value have been experienced and conceived in the history of religion. We will organize our exploration along a continuum through various forms of *polytheism, pantheism, dualism, monotheism,* and *monism.* A scheme such as this can be useful as long as it is not taken as representing a series of mutually exclusive types. Many religions reflect a curious mix of **animistic,** pantheistic, and theistic beliefs or tendencies. Neither must the scheme be thought to represent an evolutionary or progressive development from, say, primal **mana** to sophisticated philosophical conceptions of monism or monotheism. We know that high gods are present in the oldest societies and that animistic spirits, totems, and other deities are not uncommon in the religious life of present cultures.

As we will see, when the human imagination begins to reflect on deity, tensions and paradoxes arise between, for example, the immanence (meaning "to dwell within") and the transcendence (meaning "above of apart from") of the sacred, or between the rich plurality of sacred power and the quest for a primordial sacred unity or oneness.

The way in which deity is humanly experienced raises questions of momentous importance because it points to the deepest sources of human security, social order, and moral action. The perception of deity deeply affects a society's understanding of nature, of the human condition, and of what constitutes human salvation or liberation.

We have learned that sacred power is the ultimate object of religion. We also know that sacred power can be present in any object, person, or spiritual

**165**

being when it is approached in awe and fear, or when it is perceived as the source of both purity and danger. Our oldest ancestors are one with us in our common awareness of a distinction between what is ordinary and profane and what is "other," sacred, and set apart as holy. Primal societies, however, were not as prone as we are to draw sharp distinctions between the "natural" and the "supernatural." Any object or event that elicits unique feelings of awe and aversion possesses sacred power. It is set apart as having special import, although it is present in such a seemingly earthy object as a bear's skull or a stone weapon; sacred power is always particular, immediate, and tangible, even though it may be ineffable.

## Polytheism and the Worship of Nature

Until relatively recently (2000 B.C.E.), the religious life of most prehistoric and primal societies was *polytheistic*. These deities were often associated with certain realms and forces of nature—the sun, the sky, the earth, and the waters—as well as with totem plants and animals, all of which represented sacred power, the giver, sustainer, and destroyer of life.

We know little of the religion of prehistoric humans—our Neanderthal and Cro-Magnon hominid ancestors—but some things appear evident. The early Neanderthal hunters, who inhabited the lands skirting the Alps, treated the fearsome cave bear—which they stalked and killed—with great reverence. We are relatively sure that they deposited the undamaged head of the bear, with the brain intact, in an altar-like stone chest in the dark recesses of the caves that they inhabited. These hidden chambers, with their bear skull niches, are, we believe, the earliest human sanctuaries and shrines.[1] The reverence shown the bear points to its deity, to its sacredness as the dispenser of hunting fortune and providence. The bear cult is practiced even today by tribes in the sub-Arctic regions of northern Asia.

For the hunters of the late **Paleolithic** period, as for primal societies today, the hunter and the hunted joined in a mysterious and magical relationship. The animal is providence, the source of life, but it is also humankind's feared adversary. The later Paleolithic hunters adorned their caves and weapons with pictures of their game animals. In the presence of these images, they performed magical rituals and sacrifices meant to ensure the success of the hunt. These pictures—such as the one of the "great sorcerer" in the Trois Frères cave at Ariège, France—are evidence of the belief in spirits that personified sacred, magical power.

The religious practice of the **Neolithic** Age (7000–3000 B.C.E.) reflects the different life of the farmer and the tiller of the land. The traces of religion that exist from this period are symbols and images associated, in the main, with the polytheistic worship of nature—the sun, the sky, and the earth—the fundamental realities for the farmer. Sky and earth, representing the primal pair of male and female, are common in the nature cults of the Neolithic Age.

The sky is the supreme deity in some cults; in others, worship centers on the Great Goddess of earth and vegetation. Together, however, the two deities represent cosmic fertility. The theme is expressed in the hymns of the Pleiades of Dodona:

> The Earth is our mother, the Sky is our father. The Sky fertilizes the Earth with rain, the Earth produces grains and grasses.

Polytheistic cults are generally characteristic of primal and Neolithic religion. Each cult reflects the practical needs and concerns of these early societies. A French scholar has shown, for example, that the earliest Indo-European communities were divided into three classes—priests, warriors, and animal breeders or farmers—and that each class possessed a distinctive religious cult; for example, one was devoted to the gods of martial power and another to the gods representing nature's fecundity. There were sky gods of creation and order; gods of the storm and of might and force; and maternal gods of the earth.

Paleolithic mural from a cave in France depicting an owl-masked shaman arrayed in reindeer antlers and animal skins. He is probably leading a magical hunting ceremony, the animal features representing the objects of the hunt that the shaman seeks to subject to his power. (*Source:* Image # 329853, Courtesy of the Department of Library Services, American Museum of Natural History.)

## Sky Gods

More needs to be said about the distinctive role of the *sky gods* of cosmic order and sovereignty, as well as about the female goddesses of earth and fertility. The school of ethnology associated with Wilhelm Schmidt discovered sky or high gods among primal societies to be so universal as to argue for the existence of a primal monotheism. While serious objections can be raised about calling belief in high gods monotheism, Schmidt and his disciples are quite right in claiming an almost-universal belief in a creator god who dwells in the sky and who fertilizes the earth with his life-giving rain. This supreme god—for instance, among many African tribes—is often regarded with indifference because he has withdrawn into the sky, his work of creation already accomplished. In some instances, it is evident that the sky god is the personification of an abstract concept, the first cause, for example, to explain the origin of the cosmos. The African cults tend to center around the lower gods whose sacred powers impinge on the tribe's daily activities. Here, we see a characteristic phenomenon of all religions: the move away from the otherness or absolute transcendence of the sacred and toward more immanent, dynamic, and accessible forms of sacred power, especially in rites and sacraments.

However, when sacred power becomes too localized, as in the belief in mana or in animism, the pendulum often moves in the opposite direction, toward more transcendent, less localized expressions of deity. Ascendance and dominion are quite naturally associated with the sky, and so it is intelligible why the sky became the abode of the all-knowing supreme Creator.

When we move from primal religion to the great polytheistic religions of the historical civilizations of Greece, Egypt, and Mesopotamia (present-day Iraq), we observe that the sky god is connected not only with creation but also with sovereignty—a rather new conception of sacred power that guarantees cosmic order. The Indo-European peoples worshiped a sky god under various names derived from the same root word that meant both sky and "to shine." In Latin, the word is *deus*; in Sanskrit, *deva*; and in Iranian, *div*. In the Indian Vedic hymns, he is the god Varuna, who is "visible everywhere" and who sees all. Varuna, it is said, "even counts how often men wink their eyes." It is he "who knows all, spies out all secrets, all deeds and intentions" (*Rig Veda* VIII, 41, 3; 1, 25). Varuna rules as king since it is the common characteristic of these later sky gods that they see all and know all, and are keepers of the law.

Perhaps the best known of the sky gods of antiquity is **Zeus**, head of the Greek **pantheon**. Homer, in the *Iliad*, says that "the portion of Zeus is the broad heaven, in brightness and in cloud alike" (XV, 192). Zeus not only dwells in the sky but is also spoken of as the sky itself. It is Zeus who sends the rain and hurls the lightning and the thunderbolts. He is ruler and father, although his sovereignty is achieved after considerable struggle. This is recounted in Hesiod's *Theogony*, which chronicles Zeus' rise to supremacy among the Greek gods. According to Hesiod, after much intrigue and family fighting among the gods, his brothers offered Zeus the thunder and the lightning, with which Zeus henceforth commanded "both mortals and immortals." Through a series of marriages and liaisons with Hera, Demeter, and Leto, among others, Zeus both absorbed and replaced these popular goddesses in both power and popular veneration. Here, then, begins the unification of divine power in one god, Zeus, which leads to what can be called *monarchical polytheism,* a form of polytheism, as seen in Homer, featuring one triumphant and superior god—"the father of gods and men" (*Iliad* I, 544). The sovereign Zeus is invoked in a variety of aspects: as Zeus Chthonios (god of agriculture), as Zeus Herkeios (god of the hearth and household), as Zeus Polieus (god of the city-state), as Zeus Katharsios (god of purification), and so on. Zeus' mastery and omnipotence are illustrated in the *Iliad* in his challenge to the other Olympian deities:

> Then you will see how far I am strongest of all the immortals. Come, you gods, make this endeavor, that you may learn this. Let down out of the sky a cord of gold; lay hold of it all you who are goddesses, yet not even so can you drag down Zeus from the sky to the ground, not Zeus the high lord of counsel, though you try until you grow weary.[2]

## Mother Goddesses

If the sky is our father, the earth is our mother. If sky gods can be traced back to the earliest societies, so also do we find a primeval worship of female earth deities. This is attested to in the discovery of prehistoric female figurines with exaggerated breasts, thighs, and abdomen—for example, the Paleolithic image of the Venus of Laussel discovered in a rock shelter in the Dordogne, France. Though universal, the worship of the "Great Mother" Earth is especially pronounced in the ancient Mediterranean and Near Eastern religions. So conspicuous is her cult that we can see traces of it still in the simple worship of the Virgin Mary in some Roman Catholic and Orthodox communities in southern Europe and the East. From Cyprus we have this vivid illustration:

> In honour of the Maid of Bethlehem, the peasants of Kuklia in Cyprus anointed lately, and probably still anoint each year, the great corner stones of the ruined temple of the Paphian Goddess. As Aphrodite was supplicated once with cryptic rites, so is Mary entreated still by Moslems as well as Christians, with incantations and passings through perforated stones, to remove the curse of barrenness from Cypriote women, or increase the manhood of Cypriote men.[3]

The Neolithic discovery of agriculture radically changed the nature of religious life from that of the previous era of Paleolithic hunters. A new relationship was divined between the human community and vegetation, centering on the mysteries of birth, death, and rebirth. The fertility of the earth and the harvest were perceived as bound up with feminine sexual fecundity. Women are associated with the earliest practice of agriculture, and, of course,

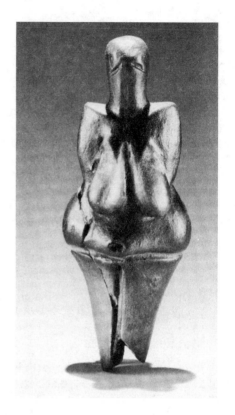

The Paleolithic "Venus" of Laussel, with exaggerated breasts and hips, symbolizes fertility, the central feature of the prehistoric mother-goddess cults. (*Source:* Neg. # 329316, Courtesy of the Department of Library Services, American Museum of Natural History.)

it is natural that women should be connected with birth and creation. However, it was also understood that the birth of vegetation requires the "death" of the seed before a new birth is ensured. Human life was thereby assimilated into the cyclical drama of the agricultural year.

The slow transformation of the feminine Mother Earth into the Great Goddess of life and rebirth can be observed in the influential religions of the ancient Near East: in the history of the Mesopotamian goddess Ishtar; the Syrian Astarte (meaning "womb"); the Egyptian Isis; and the Greek Demeter. Isis was the most important of the Egyptian goddesses. She was adored in her role both as wife and as mother and was called the "divine mother." She personified the feminine creativity of the earth and was represented nursing the infant god Horus, who was sitting on her lap.

In Egyptian mythology, Isis is depicted as the daughter of Geb and Nut, the primal earth and heaven, and as the wife of her brother Osiris. According to the myth, Osiris is murdered by his evil brother, Set, but his dismembered body is recovered by Isis. She embraces her husband, who then revives briefly and impregnates her with the god Horus. Horus, in turn, defeats Set and rules as lord of the upper world. Horus is able to bring his father back to life. However, Isis is perceived as responsible, if indirectly, for the revival of the divine king Osiris, the most popular of the Egyptian deities.

The *cult of Isis-Osiris,* associated as it was with the themes of death and rebirth, had deep human appeal and spread far beyond Egypt. Isis became assimilated to and identified with a number of Semitic, Greek, and Roman goddesses. She became the object of the most fervent adoration, especially during the Roman period, and, despite the Christian prohibition against the feast of Isis in 394, the mysteries of Isis continued to be celebrated until as late as the sixth century of the Christian era.

Ishtar played a role in Mesopotamia similar to that of Isis in Egypt and Rome. Ishtar is the mother and lover of the young god Tammuz, who represents the spring vitality whose vigor fades with autumnal vegetation. In the Akkadian myth *The Descent of Ishtar to the Nether World,* the theme of the "dying and rising" god is vividly enacted. The young god Tammuz dies and goes to the land of the dead, where he is rescued by Ishtar. In reviving Tammuz, Ishtar also gives new birth to nature and to humankind.

The myth ends with these words of Ishtar:

> On the day when Tammuz *welcomes* me
> When with him the lapes flute (and) the carnelian ring welcomes me,
> When with him the wailing men and wailing women welcome me,
> May the dead rise and smell the incense.[4]

The myth of *Tammuz-Ishtar* personifies the ceaseless movement of the seasons, life coming to fruition, its decline in the summer heat, its death, and its restoration again in the springtime. Ishtar was but one of the many goddesses representing the fecundity and life-giving powers of Mother Earth.

The ancient association of the earth goddess with life-giving fertility remains alive in folk religion to the present day. It would be quite wrong, however, to think that female deities simply represent the fecundity and nurturing of Mother Earth as a manifestation of early matriarchal forms of human social organization. Today, scholars largely reject the idea of the priority of matriarchal society. Nor is it possible to predict the type or role of female deities in a particular historical context from an analysis of that community's social structure. For example, there is no necessary correlation between the presence of exalted female goddesses and the high social status of women—or the reverse. There are too many historical, environmental, and socioeconomic variables for us to be confident with such simple correlations. Therefore, it is important to recognize the multiple and often ambivalent characteristics of mother goddesses. They are pregnant with life but also virginal; they are chaste and yet promiscuous; they are matrons of suffering but also demanders of blood sacrifice; they create but also destroy; and they protect and unify yet also fiercely divide by conflict. This ambivalence can be perceived in the goddesses of the ancient Near East and Mediterranean world but, perhaps, even more graphically in the popular myth and devotion of India.

The Egyptian goddess Isis, here nursing her son Horus, is the
exemplar of motherhood, the patroness of childbearing, the
protector of children, and the symbol of immortality. (*Source:*
Courtesy of the Fitzwilliam Museum, Cambridge University.)

Among the most popular of Indian religious cults are those known collectively as *śakti* (meaning "energy"). They are distinct in conceiving sacred power as manifest and paramount in the wife of the god or in the female consort. The *śakti cults* render devotion to all that is associated with the eternal female, which often is perceived as *the* active principle of the universe. Some Hindu sects stress the maternal nature of deity, the Mother Goddess, such as Umā, the wife of the god Śiva. Others focus on *śakti* as the personification of the tender and devoted wife, for example, the beautiful Pārvati, another consort of Śiva's. *Śakti* also symbolizes female voluptuousness, sexual desire, and sexual joy. The sexual union of female energy with the male is a common theme of *śakti* imagery and devotion. The eternal virgin is a popular theme as well, represented by a girl in her middle teens. Finally, there is *śakti* in the form of terror, cruelty, destruction, and death. Here, *śakti* is best personified by the goddess Kali, or Durga. But *Kali* also reflects the multiple and ambivalent character of the Hindu goddesses. She is represented as the power of creation, protection, and destruction as well as the power in which all things rest after their dissolution, the power beyond life and death, the One, the Supreme.

As goddess of terror and destruction, Kali brings bloodshed, pestilence, and death. She is black and pictured wearing a necklace of human

The fearsome Kali stands on the body of the god Śiva, her lord. (*Source:* Courtesy of Jack Van Horn.)

skulls. In two of her multiple hands, she carries a sword and dagger; in another is the head of a demon dripping with blood. Blood also trickles down her chin and neck. In the past, human sacrifices were offered to Kali; today, in Bengal, she is pacified with the blood of goats. As a young man, Sri Ramakrishna, one of the great leaders of the modern Hindu renaissance, became attached as chief priest to the Dakshineswar Kali temple near Calcutta. His devotion to Kali, as divine Mother and representative of cosmic power, was the source of his own intoxicated mystical visions and his profound spiritual insight.

A few words by way of conclusion are necessary before we turn to other forms of sacred power. The religious life of humankind, until approximately 2000 B.C.E., was largely animistic and polytheistic. A belief in high or sky gods and mother goddesses was common even in the earliest societies. However, between the Neolithic Age and the emergence of our historical period, a move toward greater organization and even abstraction in the conception of sacred power can be observed in a number of cultures. In place of the myriad spirits—dwelling in every tree, rock, or river—one god is often given dominion over a particular aspect of nature or department of life; Poseidon is god of the seas, Aphrodite is goddess of love, and Ares is god of war. The great sky gods and representatives of Mother Earth often assimilate the roles of local deities and replace their cult. Zeus and Isis are good examples of this process.

Roughly at the time (800–600 B.C.E.) when the Hebrew prophets were reproving the Israelites for their worship of idols and false gods, speculative minds in Greece were challenging the all-too-anthropomorphic depiction of the gods of the Homeric pantheon. "Is the ultimate, is sacred power," they asked, "to be identified with the mental limitations and the moral crudities of animals or of humans writ large?" Humans, wrote the Greek philosopher Xenophanes, erroneously portray the gods in their own likeness:

> Homer and Hesiod have ascribed to the gods all things that among men are a shame and a reproach—theft and adultery and deceiving one another.
> Mortals think that the gods are begotten, and wear clothes like their own, and have a voice and a form.
> If oxen or horses or lions had hands or could draw with them and make works of art as men do, horses would draw the shapes of gods like horses, oxen like oxen; each kind would represent their bodies just like their own forms.
> The Ethiopians say their gods are black and flat-nosed; the Thracians that theirs are blue-eyed and red-haired.[5]

Xenophanes was confident that deity was "one god greatest among gods and men, not like mortals in form, not yet in mind. He sees all over, thinks all over, and hears all over."[6] In both Greece and India, the protest against forms of polytheism often moved toward pantheistic and monistic conceptions of deity. However, before commenting on these, we must look at a rather different idea of sacred power, namely, forms of cosmic dualism.

# Dualism

*Dualism* perceives the world as constituted by or as living under the ordering of two coequal, and often coeternal, sacred powers. Some forms of dualism, as in certain ancient Chinese texts, conceive the world as *balanced* between dual polar forces that are neither antithetical nor hostile to one another. In other forms of dualism—for example, in late expressions of Iranian Zoroastrianism—the two coequal powers are locked in an eternal conflict.

## Chinese *Yin-Yang*

The *yin-yang* dualism of China is very ancient and reflects a benign, complementary conception of two primordial sacred cosmic forces or principles. The origin of *yin-yang* is traced to ancient occult or magical teachings, but it later was taken up by Confucian and Taoist writers. It is reflected, for example, in the Confucian appendix to the *I-Ching*, or *Book of Changes*, written during the Ch'in and Han periods (221 B.C.E.–9 C.E.) by Hsi Tz'u. The original *I-Ching* was produced between 900 and 700 B.C.E. It was made up of eight trigrams, each consisting of broken and unbroken lines:

Originally, the trigrams, in their multiple combinations, were but symbols of actual changes in nature. Later, the trigrams were invested with real *power* by which, it was thought, changes actually did occur. The trigrams became the basis of Chinese cosmogony, science, and even social ethics. The unbroken line stands for the power of *yang*, the broken line for *yin*. *Yang* is male, light, dry, hard; *yin* is female, shadowy, moist, soft. Together, they represent the bipolar forces of nature, rather like positive and negative electrical charges. According to this bipolarity, nature, including human nature, requires and operates through the interplay of such forces as light and darkness, heat and cold, and male and female.

In Hsi Tz'u's "Great Appendix," the trigrams *Ch'ien* (☰ = Heaven) and *K'un* (☷ = Earth)—made up entirely of undivided and divided lines, respectively—are the representations par excellence of the *yang* and *yin*. It is believed that the other six trigrams were produced through the intercourse of *Ch'ien* (father) and *K'un* (mother). The process of universal change is described as follows in the "Great Appendix" to the *Book of Changes*:

> Heaven is high, earth is low; thus the *ch'ien* and the *k'un* are fixed. As high and low are thus ordered, honorable and humble have their places. Movement and rest have their constancy; according to these strong and weak are differentiated. Ways coincide according to their species and things fall into classes. Hence good fortune and bad fortune come about. In the heavens phenomena appear;

on earth shapes occur. Through these, change and transformation becomes manifest. Therefore the strong and the weak [lines in the trigrams] interplay, and the eight trigrams act and react upon each other. Things are roused by thunder and lightning; they are fertilized by wind and rain. Sun and moon revolve on their courses with a season of cold and then a season of heat. The way of the *ch'ien* constitutes the male, the way of the *k'un* constitutes the female. The *ch'ien* knows the great beginning; the *k'un* gives things their completion.[7]

Chinese thinkers perceived a perpetual interplay between the negative, passive, dark, feminine *yin* and the positive, active, light, masculine *yang*. These bipolar powers are mutually related phases in the ceaseless transformation of nature. They interact harmoniously, each one necessary to the proper functioning of the other. The Chinese sages even saw the *yang* and *yin* as embodying the two schools of Confucianism (representing the active, like *yang*) and Taoism (representing the passive, like *yin*), symbolizing the complementary principles of the Chinese tradition. In an imaginary dialogue, the Taoist philosopher Chuang Tzu (365–290 B.C.E.) tells Confucius of his having voyaged to the world's beginning and relates what he saw:

> I saw Yin, the Female Energy, in its motionless grandeur; I saw Yang, the Male Energy, rampant in its fiery vigour. The motionless grandeur came out of the earth; the fiery vigour burst out from heaven. The two penetrated one another, were inextricably blended and from their union the things of the world were born.[8]

### Dualism of Cosmic Struggle

There is a quite different form of cosmic dualism that reflects an enduring conflict, rather than a harmony, between two primordial sacred powers. It can be seen in the religions of Egypt, Mesopotamia, and India, as well as in some aspects of ancient Judaism and Christianity. They all reflect dualistic tendencies, but they rarely, if ever, adopt a thoroughgoing dualism. In Egypt, for example, Re, the sun-god, representing life and truth, is pitted against Apophia, the serpent of darkness. In Babylon, the god Marduk struggles against Ti'amat, the monster of chaos (see Chapter 8) while, in the Bible, the final victory of God over the powers of darkness is portrayed in God's victory over the sea monster Leviathan. In each case, the satanic power of darkness and chaos is overcome by the God of light and life who, in victory, establishes the Divine kingdom or rule.

In *Zoroastrianism,* the ancient religion of Persia (Iran), we have a good example of the development of a more radical cosmic dualism of conflict. The founder of the religion was the prophet Zoroaster (or, more properly, *Zarathustra;* the former is a Greek corruption of this Iranian name) who, according to Persian tradition, was born in the seventh century B.C.E. Some scholars contend that, if not legendary, Zarathustra may have lived as early as 1000 B.C.E. In any case, tradition relates how he was brought before the celestial assembly and was instructed by *Ahura Mazda* (later Ohrmazd), the supreme deity and Wise Lord of Light, in the true religion. The result of this encounter was Zarathustra's reform of ancient Persian polytheism, transforming it into a tempered form of monotheism centered on the worship of Ahura Mazda.

What is significant about Zarathustra's prophetic revolution, however, is his dramatic portrayal of a cosmic struggle between the dual forces of good and evil, that reaches a climax in a titanic **apocalypse** at the end of time. According to Zarathustra, Ahura Mazda's supremacy and his Good or Holy Spirit (Spenta Mainyu) are constantly challenged by *Angra Mainyu*, the Bad Spirit, and his satanic *daevas*, or evil spirits.

The hymns compiled by Zarathustra, called the *Gathas*, portray the entire world as divided between these good and evil powers and between moral right and wrong. According to the *Gathas*, this cosmic moral division occurred in the beginning when Ahura Mazda created the world and gave his creatures, including the two Spirits, freedom of choice:

> Now the two primal Spirits, who revealed themselves in visions as Twins, are the Better and the Bad in thought and word and action. And between these two the wise one chose aright, the foolish not so. And when these twin Spirits came together in the beginning, they established Life and Not-Life, and that at the last the Worst Existence (Hell) shall be the followers of the Lie, but the Best Thought (Paradise) to him that follows Right. Of these twain Spirits he that followed the Lie chose doing the worst things; the holiest Spirit chose Right.[9]

Zarathustra did not himself teach a thoroughgoing dualism, for he had no doubt about the ultimate issue in the struggle between the two powers. In the fullness of time, Ahura Mazda would triumph over evil. Centuries later, however, Zoroastrianism resorted once again to older polytheistic gods and from this there evolved a more radical dualism. According to the *Bundahishn*, a text from the ninth century C.E., in the beginning light and darkness existed together with no link between the two powers:

> Ohrmazd [a later form of Spenta Mainyu] was on high in omniscience and goodness; for Indefinite Time he was ever in the light. That light is the Space and place of Ohrmazd; some call it the Endless Light . . .
> Ahriman [a later form of Angra Mainyu] slow in knowledge, whose will is to smite, was deep down in the darkness: he was and is, yet will not be. The will to smite is his all, the darkness is his place: some call it the endless Darkness.[10]

In the *Vendidad*, a priestly text also of the ninth century C.E., Ohrmazd is portrayed as creator of all that is good, while Ahriman is seen as creator of all that is evil and noxious—the two creators being coequal. Ahriman, unlike satan or the devil in the Christian and Muslim traditions, creates his own *daevas* and all other harmful creatures: snakes, wolves, locusts, as well as evil men and their vices and lusts.

The power of Ahriman and his army of evil spirits is portrayed as finally regnant over this world. Water, earth, and plants are all defiled. Even

Righteous Man, who held Ahriman at bay for 3,000 years is, finally, unable to withstand the Evil One. Ahriman is pictured exulting in his power and the ruin he has wrought:

> Perfect is my victory: for I have rent the sky, I have befouled it with murk and darkness, I have made it my stronghold. I have befouled the waters, pierced open the earth and defiled it with darkness. I have dried up the plants, and have brought death to the Bull, sickness to Gayomart. Against the stars have I set up the planets, frought with darkness. I have seized the kingdom. On the side of Ohrmazd none remains to do battle except only man; and man, isolated and alone, what can he do?[11]

This late Zoroastrian dualism profoundly affected the other religions of the ancient Near East with its pessimism and sense of engagement in an intractable struggle against formidable powers of evil. None of the great monotheistic faiths of the West that came in contact with Persian religion—Judaism, Christianity, and Islam—succumbed fully to its radical dualism and pessimism. We know, however, that in the centuries just prior to the beginning of the Christian era, dualistic tendencies and historical pessimism found their way into Judaism. Philo, a Jewish philosopher of this time, speaks, although briefly, of God creating the world by means of two divine powers, one the creator of good and the other the creator of evil. According to the Rule of Qumran—one of the important scrolls from Dead Sea caves—two spirits were created by God, the Prince of Darkness and the Prince of Light, and together they rule this world.

Radical dualism came closest to capturing Christianity in the first two centuries of its life. The challenge came primarily from *Gnosticism* (from the Greek *gnosis*, meaning secret knowledge), a religio-philosophical movement of the Greco-Roman world, comprising many sects within paganism, Judaism, and Christianity. Gnosticism was thoroughly dualistic. It taught that this world was created by a Demiurge who was inferior to the Supreme Being. The human soul, a spark of the divine, had fallen from its heavenly home and was imprisoned in a mortal, material body. The soul could be saved from its horrible state only by acquiring true knowledge (*gnosis*), which would free it to return to its heavenly home. The Gnostic Christians rejected the Genesis account of Creation and taught that the true God of light had nothing to do with this vile and evil material world. According to the Gnostic Christians, this world was created and is now ruled by inferior powers, including the Old Testament God, Yahweh. Gnostic doctrine was widespread within Christianity by the second century, but it was then condemned by the Church at Rome in the middle of that century. Thereafter, its influence waned.

*Manicheanism* is a third historically influential form of radical dualism in the West. For a century, it was Christianity's chief rival. Manicheanism was founded in the third century C.E. by a Mesopotamian teacher named Mani. An eclectic thinker, Mani wanted to combine Gnostic Christianity with elements of Zoroastrianism and Greek philosophy. The world, according to Mani, is ruled by two independent, eternally opposing powers: Light, which he associates with the soul, and Darkness, or matter. Mani relates how Darkness attacked Light, causing the two to be mixed and the soul to be befouled. Mani further tells how the soul can be freed from the Darkness, its material prison. Some historians believe that the writings of St. Augustine (354–430 C.E.), which are so infused with strong, dualistic contrasts, were deeply, if unconsciously, influenced by Manichean doctrine. St. Augustine had been a Manichee for nine years before his conversion to Christianity.

Hellenistic-Gnostic and Persian ideas are unquestionably present in early Christian writers—St. Paul and St. John, for example—and most obviously in the apocalyptic worldview that dominated Christianity in the first and second centuries. However, like Judaism and Islam, Christianity also came to view dualism as a mortal threat to both its doctrines of God and creation and repudiated it as a heresy. However, in Chapter 10 we shall see that as a **theodicy,** or explanation for the reality of evil, dualism has had great appeal.

## Pantheism and Monism

Earlier, it was pointed out that the protest against animism and polytheism often took the form of **pantheism** and even **monism.** Pantheism (from the Greek words for "all" and "God") is the belief that all existing things are in some sense divine. Pantheism and monism (from the Greek word for "single") are often indistinguishable if, for example, it is believed that there is only one divine Being or Reality and that all finite things are simply modes or appearances of that One.

The Greek Stoic philosophers were pantheists. They attacked popular polytheism and taught that there is but one sacred Being, which they called the **Logos,** or Reason. They identified this divine Logos with an element, the ether, or with the basic element, fire. They further taught that each person is a spark of this divine Logos and participates in the Logos through the exercise of reason (see Chapter 9). Perhaps to satisfy more popular religious sentiments, some Stoics did personify the Logos, calling it Zeus and offering it hymns and prayers.

A more significant religious move from polytheism to pantheism and monism can be observed in the historical development of Hinduism, that family of religions of India. It is most evident in the contrast between the ancient Vedic hymns and the later speculations found in the writings called the *Upanishads.* The religion of early Hinduism is that of the ancient Aryans and is reflected in four collections of hymns: the *Rig-Veda,* the *Sama-Veda,* the *Yajur-Veda,* and the *Atharva-Veda,* used by different groups of priests. This Vedic religion was polytheistic, and its pantheon included many gods, the most prominent being Indra, Varuna, Agni, Soma, Rudra (later Śiva), and

Vishnu. Indra, the most popular and often invoked, is the warrior-king and god of the storm. Varuna is the guardian of *rta*, the law or cosmic order, while Agni and Soma are clearly associated with the sacred Vedic ritual sacrifice. Both Śiva and Vishnu emerge as the great Supreme Beings of later Hinduism.

As was the case in Greece, the earthy, life-affirming but simple polytheism of the ancient Vedic period was, in time, found wanting:

> Toward the end of the Rig-Vedic period, it becomes clear that a plurality of gods becoming ever less distinguishable from each other was beginning to be an embarrassment, for these later Vedic seers were becoming increasingly interested in what constituted the unitary and unifying principle of the universe, and in this quest the multiplicity of gods was a scandal. . . . So according to the new way of thinking the personalities of the various gods shrank and became little more than mere names marking a single reality. This 'they called Indra, Mitra, Varuna, Agni. . . . What is but one the wise call by manifold names,' (Rig-Veda 1.164–46). Here Vedic polytheism is already slipping into classical Hindu pantheism.[12]

By the end of the Vedic period, the many gods are perceived "as but marking a single reality." The thrust of this reflection is carried further along in the *Upanishads* (meaning "sitting near a teacher"), the great Hindu speculative treatises, often in the form of dialogues written between 700 and 300 B.C.E. The *Upanishads* include a mixture of theistic and pantheistic tendencies, but the latter is characteristic of many texts. In reflecting on the origin and explanation of the phenomenal world, the Indians first posited fire as the primal element, then space, and then the more abstract notions of being and nonbeing. But the conception that finally gained ascendancy in the *Upanishads* is called **Brahman.**

In the *Rig-Veda, brahma* is interpreted as meaning "hymn," "prayer," or "sacred knowledge." However, it also came to signify the sacred *power* inherent in the hymn or in knowledge; it was then associated with the world-ground, with the power that pervades and upholds the cosmos, in which all things live and have their being. In the *Brihad-Āranyaka Upanishad*, it is written: "As a spider might come out with his thread, as small sparks come forth from the fire, even so from this Soul [Brahman] came forth all vital energies, all worlds, all gods, all beings."[13]

All things, including the human soul, are actual only through their participation in Brahman. The *Chāndogya Upanishad* declares, "Verily this whole world is Brahma. Tranquil, let one worship It as that from which he came forth, as that into which he will be dissolved, as that in which he breathes."[14] Here, we encounter the first explicit statement of Indian pantheism, but it is latent in much earlier speculation.

According to the *Chāndogya Upanishad*, the human soul, all that is subjective, is merely a mode or phase of Brahman, the One. The term that came to be used for the soul or inner self, in contrast to the body, is *Ātman.* "Yajnavalkya," asks an inquirer, "explain to me him who is the Brahman present and not beyond our ken, him who is the soul of all things." The answer is that Brahman "is your soul":

> He who dwelling in the earth . . . in the waters . . . in the fire . . . in the atmosphere . . . the wind . . . the sky . . . the sun. . . . He who dwelling in all things, yet other than all things, whom all things do not know, whose body all things are, who controls all things from within—He is your Soul, the Inner Controller, the Immortal.[15]

The soul is spoken of here as Brahman, but this form of Hindu pantheism is not fully monistic. As the *Brihad-Āranyaka Upanishad* makes plain, finite entities are the body of Brahman who is "yet other than all things." The world, including the soul, is divine since Brahman is immanent in all things. However, there is not a perfect unity or monism but rather a plurality in unity. This is evident in the well-known parable of the bees and the honey, which is found in the *Chāndogya Upanishad.*

> As the bees, my dear, prepare honey by collecting the essences of different trees and reducing the essence to a unity, as they are not able to discriminate "I am the essence of this tree," "I am the essence of that tree"—even so, indeed, my dear, all creatures here, though they reach Being, know not "We have reached Being." . . .
> That which is the finest essence—this whole world has *that* as its soul. That is Reality. That is Ātman (Soul). That art thou, Svetaketu.[16]

While Ātman and Brahman are one, because the individual soul loses its individuality in Brahman, distinctions do remain. Nevertheless, a tremendous change has taken place. The goal of religion now is knowledge of the pantheistic unity of the soul and world in Ātman–Brahman. The diligent performance of ritual sacrifice to the many Vedic gods is perceived as crude and a fraud: "So whoever worships another divinity [than his Self], thinking 'He is one and I another,' he knows not."[17]

Classical Hinduism did not remain entirely satisfied with the ambiguous relationship between the One and the world of plural beings that characterized Indian pantheism. In the relatively late *Māndūkya Upanishad*, the move to a thoroughgoing monism is evident. It is a state beyond waking, beyond dreaming, or even beyond dreamless sleep. It is spoken of as a fourth state, that

> . . . has cognizance neither of what is inside nor what is outside, nor of both together; it is not a mass of wisdom, it is not wise nor yet unwise. It is unseen; there can be no commerce with it; it is impalpable, has no characteristics, is unthinkable; it cannot be designated. Its essence is its firm conviction of the oneness of itself; it causes the phenomenal world to cease; it is tranquil and mild, devoid of duality. . . .[18]

This extreme form of monism, or absolute nonduality, was developed in the *Vedanta Sūtra* (*Vedanta* meaning "the end of Vedas") in the first century before the Christian era. The Indian philosophy of nonduality thus came to be called the **Vedanta.** However, the greatest systematizer of radical Hindu *Advaita* (nondualism) *Vedanta* was a later thinker named Śankara (788–820 C.E.). Śankara begins his teaching with the assertion of the *Māndūkya Upanishad* that the Ultimate or Real is "unthinkable" and "cannot be designated"; that is, it has no attributes. According to Śankara, it follows that the phenomenal world of subjects and objects, the world of plurality, "ceases" or, rather, is an illusion or appearance. Śankara introduces the concept of *māyā* to signify the illusory phenomenal world, which gives us only an "apparent" and not a real knowledge of the relationship of the One and the many. According to Śankara, belief that the objects of our sense experience are real is the work of ignorance. In one of his favorite similes, he says that *māyā* is like perceiving a rope as a snake in the twilight. The "snake" is simply imposed on the rope through our ignorance. Likewise, it is the work of ignorance to believe in the independent and contingent reality of the individual self or soul. True knowledge is achieved only when we realize that the self, Ātman, and Brahman are not distinct, that the soul is identical with Brahman, which alone exists, timeless and eternal. Such knowledge is liberating, but it cannot be described because it transcends the limits of space and time. The Hindus call it *sat chit ānanda*, "being-awareness-bliss."

A type of pantheism, with liberating effects not unlike those described by exponents of Vedanta, is observable in certain forms of "natural mystical experience." Numerous examples are cited in William James's *The Varieties of Religious Experience.* The recollection of the English poet Alfred Lord Tennyson is typical:

> I have never had revelations through anaesthetics, but a kind of waking trance—this for lack of a better word—I have frequently had, quite up from boyhood, when I have been all alone. This has come upon me through repeating my own name to myself silently, till all at once, as it were out of the intensity of the consciousness of individuality, individuality itself seemed to dissolve and fade away into a boundless being, and this not a confused state but the clearest, the surest of the sure, utterly beyond words—where death was an almost laughable impossibility—the loss of personality (if so it were) seeming no extinction, but the only true life. I am ashamed of my feeble description. Have I not said the state is utterly beyond words?[19]

Tennyson's experience of the dissolving of individuality and the sense of death being "an almost laughable impossibility" is not unlike the Vedantist's efforts to describe the ineffable bliss of "the One without a second."

If we review our comparison of forms of deity, we see that pantheism and monism are located at one extremity of the spectrum and animism at the other. The two, however, join in the conviction that sacred power is immanent in and through all things. Polytheism appears to conceive of sacred power as more fully personalized, as in the youth and beauty of the god Apollo, although some forms of polytheism appear to be indistinguishable from animism. As we have seen, the polytheistic religions of the ancient Mediterranean world and the Near East also tend to move toward hierarchical patterns, exhibiting a division of labor within the pantheon of gods, with one god (e.g., Zeus) becoming preeminent in power and authority. On occasion, the various gods are simply the names for one supreme deity.

While the problem in the East was how to reconcile the fact of a world of plurality with the intuition of a single world-soul or ground, the problem for the Western historical religions was how to reconcile the presence of sacred power *in* the world with its wholly otherness or *transcendence of* the world. The crisis that faced Greco-Roman religion, and the Semitic religions as well, came at the point when their pantheon of gods began to appear all too earthly and human. The gods' moral weaknesses and errors exposed their lack of genuine transcendence. In the East, the move against polytheism often—but by no means always—took the form of pantheism and monism. In the West, the protest against and reform of polytheism usually took the form of *monotheism,* or the worship of one god.

## Monotheism

*Monotheism* is not the same as belief in a high god or even a creator god in the sky. In primal religion, the high god often is considered superior, but his remoteness frequently results in the god's eclipse by more popular gods of the local polytheistic cult. Marduk was "a great king above all gods" in Babylon, but, even in ancient Mesopotamia, the other gods of the pantheon also had their dominions and functions. Monotheism, as we know it today, is a rather late development in the history of religions and is most appropriately associated with the emerging faith of ancient Israel. However, proto-monotheistic tendencies are present in a number of movements that sought to reform polytheism, for example, by Zoroaster in ancient Iran and, perhaps most notably, in Egypt for a brief time under the Pharaoh Amenhotep IV about 1375 B.C.E.

Amenhotep was a devotee of the sun god, Aton, and when he ascended the throne he suppressed all polytheistic cults and had the names of all gods erased from the monuments. He set up a new priesthood and changed his own name to Ikhnaton (meaning "profitable to Aton"). He declared Aton to be "the sole god whose powers no other possesseth," the Creator and Sustainer, ruling the entire cosmos. No cult image was allowed, other than the simple sun disc with its emanating rays. The singing of hymns and the giving of offerings were the principal acts of worship. The simplicity of Ikhnaton's theism is reflected in an inscription in one of the tombs at El-Amarna:

> Beautiful in thine appearing in the horizon of heaven, thou living sun, the first who lived!
> Thou riseth in the easter horizon and
> Thou fillest every land with thy bounty. . . .

Thy rays, they compass the lands, so far as all that thou hast created. . . .
Though thou art far away, yet are thy rays upon earth;
Thou art before their face—thy going.[20]

Ikhnaton's religious reform was short-lived, however, and after his death in 1350, the Egyptians returned to their earlier polytheistic ways. It is therefore correct to say that *monotheism*, as we understand the term, has its origin in the great Semitic religions of the West, principally in Israel, and later in Judaism, Christianity, and Islam, all of which began as protests against polytheism.

The religion of the early Israelite tribes was not monotheistic. Before the ninth century B.C.E., the patriarchs and the kings of Israel did not worship a universal Creator god but, rather, a tribal god who was nevertheless conceived as unique in power and moral authority. *Henotheism* perhaps best describes the religion of Israel in both the Patriarchal and the Mosaic periods. Henotheism refers to those religions that, while recognizing the reality of many gods, worship and believe in the asendancy of only one god. The early Israelites lived in a polytheistic environment, but from the time of Moses they considered their God *Yahweh* as unique in power and authority.

The ancient Israelites did not arrive at a knowledge of Yahweh by examining the order of nature or by rational speculation, as did the Greeks.

King Ikhnaton and Queen Nefertiti presenting offerings to the Egyptian sun god, Aton, the one Creator and Sustainer. Aton is transcendent, yet his rays encompass the entire earth. (*Source:* )

Rather, Yahweh was revealed to Israel through her historical experience and, most notably, through the Exodus from Egypt, the Covenant sealed at Mount Sinai, and the exile in Babylonia. According to the account in the Book of Exodus, Moses was tending the flock of his father-in-law, Jethro, in the desert when an angel of the Lord appeared to him in a flaming bush that was not consumed:

> God called to [Moses] out of the bush, "Moses, Moses!" And he said, "Here am I." Then he said, "Do not come near; put off your shoes from your feet, for the place on which you are standing is holy ground." And he said, "I am the God of your father, the God of Abraham, the God of Isaac, and the God of Jacob." And Moses hid his face, for he was afraid to look at God.
> Then the Lord said, "I have seen the affliction of my people who are in Egypt, and have heard their cry because of their taskmasters; I know their sufferings, and I have come down to deliver them out of the hand of the Egyptians, and to bring them out of that land to a good and broad land, a land flowing with milk and honey. . . . Come, I will send you to Pharaoh that you may bring forth my people, the sons of Israel, out of Egypt. . . ." Then Moses said to God, "If I come to the people of Israel and say to them, 'The God of your fathers has sent me to you,' and they ask me, 'What is his name?' What shall I say to them?"

The answer Moses received is a most significant event in the history of religions. God said to Moses, "I am who I am." And he said, "Say I am [YHWH\*] has sent me to you" (Exodus 3:4–14).

Whether the divine name Yahweh predates Moses is a matter of dispute, but it is generally agreed that Moses' interpretation of the **theophany** both in the desert and later on Mount Sinai gave birth to a new conception of deity. It is not a fully conceived monotheism but a henotheism that, for all intents and purposes, can be called "practical monotheism." Yahweh is a transcendent, holy God who nevertheless enters into a solemn covenant with the people Israel, promising them peace and prosperity for their strict loyalty. Yahweh also is "a jealous God" (Exodus 20:5; 24:14), a conviction associated with the first commandment of the Decalogue or Ten Commandments: namely, that Israel will have "no other gods before me" (Exodus 20:3). Yahweh demands exclusive worship and no idols or images are to be made of God. However, the period of Israel's history, from the entrance into Canaan (the thirteenth century B.C.E.)—rife with polytheistic cults—to the religious reforms of King Josiah (621 B.C.E.), testifies to Israel's violent struggle against pagan idolatry (see Judges 2:11–13; II Kings 16:3–4).

The great Prophets of the ninth to the sixth centuries B.C.E. enlarged Israel's understanding of the meaning of Yahweh's "jealousy" to include God's sovereignty and providential care over the entire creation. The prophet Isaiah heaped scorn on the gods of the nations as worthless idols and warned Israel of the wrath of God. He saw Yahweh as no tribal god but

---

\* The divine name YHWH is here connected with the verb hayah, to be. In ancient Hebrew texts only consonants and not vowels were written to reproduce the name.

as the Lord of all the nations that are subject to God's decrees. Yahweh even uses the enemy nations to chasten unrighteous Israel:

> Oh, Assyria, the rod of my anger, the staff of my fury!
> Against a godless nation I send him and against the people
> of my wrath I command him.
>
> —(Isaiah 10:5–6)

A century later, the prophet Jeremiah denounced the gods as simply "no gods" (2:11; 5:11) and worthless:

> They are both stupid and foolish; the instruction
> of idols is but wood! . . .
> But the Lord is the true god;
> he is the living God and the everlasting King.
> At his wrath the earth quakes,
> and the nations cannot endure his indignation.
>
> —(Jeremiah 10:8, 10)

During the Exile in Babylon, Israel's God speaks through the prophet known as Second Isaiah, in terms that are unquestionably monotheistic.

> I am the Lord and there is no other,
> beside me there is no God;
> I gird you [Cyrus, King of Persia], though you do not know me,
> that men may know, from the rising of the sun
> and from the west, that there is none beside me;
> I am the Lord, and there is no other.
> I form the light and create darkness.
> I make weal and create woe,
> I am the Lord, who does all these things.
>
> —(Isaiah 45:5–7)

A genuine monotheism can thus be observed evolving in Israel in the period from the Exodus from Egypt (1250 B.C.E.) to the Exile in Babylon (sixth century B.C.E.). Israel's understanding of God developed out of the nation's experience of Yahweh's loving care, providential intervention, and wider sovereignty over all the nations. Yet underlying this experience of God's providence were certain convictions about God's other attributes or character. Yahweh was, first, a *personal* God, not a remote sky-god, but a God who intervenes in human affairs—a *personal providence*. Furthermore, there was neither a time when Yahweh was not nor a time when God will not be. God is from everlasting to everlasting, *eternal*. All things come from God's hand as *Creator*. Yahweh is also wise and benevolent, whose councils will not, finally, be thwarted—that is, God is what the theologians later will call **omniscient** and **omnipotent**. These rather abstract concepts were, of course, only tacit in Israel's faith in God, but they were later fully defined by the theologians in all three of the great monotheistic traditions. The distinctiveness of Western theism, as well as some of its unique problems, is connected, as we shall see, with this rather elaborate philosophical development of biblical monotheism. Classical Western monotheism is, in fact, the result of the joining of biblical theism and Greek philosophical speculation, especially in the centuries between the Jewish thinker Philo (20 B.C.E.–54 C.E.) and the great Catholic theologian St. Thomas Aquinas (1225–1274 C.E.).

Before describing in detail God's attributes as defined by theologians in the West, we can get a sense of their conceptual dexterity and of the complexity of philosophical monotheism by listening to one of them. Our example is the orthodox Islamic theologian and mystic, al-Ghazālī (1058–1111 C.E.), a contemporary of the equally brilliant Christian theologian, St. Anselm. Al-Ghazālī's statement joins all the elements of classic monotheism:

> 81. Praise be to God, the Creator.... He is one in essence, unequalled, unique, sole, incomparable, alone without opponent or rival. He exists from the beginning, without predecessor, from all eternity, beginningless; he endures, none follows him, he is everlasting without end.... He is no substance and there are no substances in him; he is not an accident and there are no accidents in him.... He is high above heaven and earth, and yet is "closer to man than his own arteries" ... for his presence is not like that of a body ... he is not in things nor are things in him.... He is exalted above change and alteration; for him there are no happenings, no misfortune can befall him, but rather he possesses everlastingly the properties of his majesty, beyond the reach of decay, and for the attributes of his perfection he needs no growth or process of perfection.
>
> 82. He knows all things knowable.... He knows the inward motives and impulses and the most secret thoughts, with an external knowledge which he has had before all time.... He wills all that exists, and determines events.... What he wills takes place and what he does not will, does not take place.... From eternity he willed the existence of things in the times appointed for them, and they come into being at those times and no others, precisely in accordance with his knowledge and will.
>
> 83. He brought forth the creation to reveal his power ... not as though there were for him any necessity or need for the creation.... It is proof of his generosity, and not a necessity, that he showers mercy and good things upon his servants, a pure gift on his part, for he could have punished his servants with every possible affliction, suffering, and illness.[21]

Viewed in isolation, each of the divine attributes described by al-Ghazālī appears abstract, the product of intellectual analysis; however, each one is the result of reflection on the religious experience of believers who, in the first instance, personally felt the reality of standing in the presence of an unseen and awesomely majestic God. The classical attributes of God derive, then, from a more primal experience of God's overwhelming *holiness*. As the Qur'an says, "He is *the* God, other than whom there is none; He is the knower of the seen and unseen ... the Sovereign, the Holy" (59:22).

God's holiness is traditionally symbolized by the spatial imagery of height. Height stands for God's transcendence, for the fact that God is above and distinct, although not remote, from the world. Unlike pantheism, monotheism insists that the world is not a part of God; God and the world remain distinct. Furthermore, God's holiness reflects God's self-sufficiency. God does not need the world. Why God created the world, except as an act of love, remains a mystery. One fundamental aspect of God's holiness and transcendence is the fact that "his ways are not our ways." The holy God remains, finally, mysterious and not fully knowable.

A primary tenet of *mono*theism is that God is *one*—the belief in the unity of God. It became a critical doctrine for both Judaism and Christianity in their encounters with Greco-Roman polytheism between roughly 300 B.C.E. and 300 C.E., and later, of course, for Islam. Defenders of these religions argued that God is, by definition, the object of absolute devotion, but that a god who *shares* being and powers with other gods cannot be such an object. St. Thomas Aquinas later insisted on the self-evidence of God's oneness, simplicity, or unity on the grounds of his perfection:

> For God, as we have seen, embraces in himself the whole perfection of existence. Now many Gods, if they existed, would have to differ. Something belonging to one would not belong to the other. And if this were a lack the one God would not be altogether perfect, whilst if it were a perfection the other God would lack it. So there cannot be more than one God. And this is why philosophers in ancient times, bowing, so to speak, to the truth, held that if the source of things was unlimited it could not be many.[22]

Implied in God's perfection is the further belief that God is not limited as are all finite creatures. God is *infinite*—that is, nonfinite. This emphasis can be observed in efforts at all costs, especially in Islam and Judaism, to avoid **anthropomorphism,** or the tendency to view God in too human terms. This can be seen in the writings of the Mu'tazilites, Islamic thinkers of the ninth century C.E., who sought to speak of God by denying all concrete terms:

> The Mu'tazila agree that God is one; there is no thing like him . . . he is not a body, not a form, not flesh and blood, not an individual, not substance nor attribute . . . no movement, rest, or division . . . no place comprehends him, no time passes over him . . . he is not comparable with men and does not resemble creatures in any respect . . . he is unlike whatever occurs to the mind or is pictured in the imagination.[23]

Since monotheists deny that God suffers all those limitations common to finite, created beings, it is understandable that negative predicates often must be used in speaking of God, for example, that God is *immutable*. However, the term most used by Medieval theologians to refer to God's infinity is his *aseity* (from the Latin *a se esse*, meaning "being from oneself"), self-existence or necessity. God is not dependent on any other reality. God is not created, nor is there anything that can limit or destroy God. According to Aristotle, the essence of finite *homo sapiens* is not existence since we all one day will die. Humans are essentially rational, though finite, beings. But God's

A portrait of St. Thomas Aquinas, the thirteenth-century
philosopher and theologian whose influence on later Western
Christian thought has been profound. He is most famous,
perhaps, for his five proofs of the existence of God. (*Source:*
Courtesy of the French Government Tourist Office.)

unique essence is, indeed, to exist—God alone possesses *aseity*, necessary
existence. It follows from God's infinity and aseity that God is *eternal*. God is
without beginning or end; if God had a beginning, there obviously would
have to be another being or prior cause that brought God into existence. This
would deny God's infinity, independence, and perfection. However, God's
eternity is not to be confused with everlastingness, as in a temporal series.
God is outside the temporal series; God is timeless.

Three additional divine attributes follow from God's infinity and aseity.
First, monotheism must conceive of God as the Creator of all that exists. The
biblical doctrine of creation is discussed at length in Chapter 8, and so we
need refer to it only briefly here. For monotheism, creation means creation
*ex nihilo*—creation out of nothing—since there can be nothing that is prior
to God or that God is required to create. God does not form a preexistent

material into an ordered cosmos. God and the creation, the world, are distinct, the latter being wholly dependent on the former. Creatures are dependent on God not only for their being but also for their continued existence. God's creative activity is continuous.

In this latter respect, classical monotheism differs from *deism*, which teaches that God created the world but no longer has any commerce with it; rather, that God simply allows the world to continue according to the laws which God originally established. This conception of deity was popular in the eighteenth century, both in Europe and in America, among freethinkers who were offended by miracles and the orthodox claim that God intervened directly in worldly events on special occasions. According to the Deists, as they were called, belief in God is a rational necessity because it is required to explain the existence of a world of contingent or non-self-existent beings. The Deists argued that without a first cause or first mover, the world remains inexplicable; out of nothing comes nothing (*ex nihilo nihil fit*). This deistical conception of God is analogous to that proposed by Aristotle (384–322 B.C.E.) in his proof of the necessity of an unmoved mover:

> 18. . . . . all things that are in motion must be moved by something.
>
> Now this may come about in either of two ways. Either the movent is not responsible for the motion, which is to be referred to something else which moves the movent, or the movent is itself responsible for the motion. Further, in the latter case, either the movent immediately precedes the last thing in the series, or there may be one or more immediate links, e.g., the stick moves the stone and is moved by the hand, which again is moved by the man . . .
>
> If then everything that is in motion must be moved by something, and the movent must either itself be moved by something else or not, and in the former case there must be some first movent that is not itself moved by anything else. . . . (for it is impossible that there should be an infinite series of movents, each of which is itself moved by something else, since in an infinite series there is no first term)—if then everything that is in motion is moved by something, and the first movent is moved but not by anything else, it must be moved by itself . . .
>
> 22. . . . . the following considerations will make it clear that there must necessarily be some such thing, which, while it has the capacity of moving something else, is itself unmoved and exempt from all change.[24]

Aristotle is arguing that the fact of a world process, without beginning or ending, requires either that the process itself be necessary (but the finite and contingent cannot be necessary) or that such a process implies an agent whose existence is itself necessary and eternal. The Aristotelian argument became the foundation of Western natural theology and what is called the **cosmological proof** of the existence of God.

In Aristotle's work, classic monotheism found an intellectual resource of incomparable value. However, monotheism could not accept the idea of an "absentee" God, one who sets the world in motion but has since left it to run on its own. Monotheism asserts that God's *creativity is continuous.*

Thomas Aquinas, for example, argues that every being remains in existence through the immediate and continuous creativity of God alone:

> Since the infinite must be everywhere and in all things, we have now to consider whether this applies to God. God is in all things, indeed, as part of their essence, or as a quality, but in the manner that an efficient cause is present to that on which it acts. An efficient cause must be in touch with the product of its action immediately, and this by its own power. Now since God's very essence is his existence, created existence is his proper effect. This effect God causes, not only when things first begin to be, but so long as they continue to be. While a thing endures, therefore, God must be present to it according to its mode of being. Existence is most intimate to each and deepest in all reality since it is the heart of all perfection. Hence, God is in all things, and intimately.[25]

Two additional divine attributes are implied by God's creativity, as well as by God's infinity and aseity. One such perfection is *omniscience*, or the belief that God is all-knowing. We finite humans develop our knowledge piecemeal through experience. We are fallible. According to monotheism, God knows all things perfectly. There is nothing that falls outside God's preknowledge or is not dependent on God's will. Events that come to be in future time are already known to God but, according to Aquinas, without God imposing on them the necessity of existing. God is omniscient, but the creation is also given a relative freedom or autonomy.

Finally, God's infinity and creativity imply *omnipotence*, the belief that God is able to do all things within the Divine nature. The last three words are important, since omnipotence does not mean that God can act contrary to the very laws God has created. Monotheists, therefore, insist that it is only reasonable to believe that God's power of action is always within God's own, so to speak, self-imposed limits—limits imposed, for example, by creating this world rather than some other and by creating human beings with genuine freedom.

The attributes of omniscience and omnipotence are, however, problematic for monotheism when they are joined with God's infinite *goodness and love*—qualities essential to monotheistic belief. This question naturally arises: If God is both omnipotent and infinitely good and loving, then why does God permit evil? We will not pursue the question here since we will do so at length when we consider the various responses to the problem of evil and suffering in Chapter 10, on types of theodicy.

In this chapter, we have observed the many ways in which human beings have experienced the reality of sacred power and value—from animism and polytheism through highly philosophical conceptions of monotheism and monism. As we have seen, any object, person, or event—from a stone or a bear's skull to the world itself, or the power that infinitely transcends this created world—can be and have been the object of religious awe and worship. Another universal religious concern has been the origin and order of the natural and human world. Cosmogony, or accounts of the origin and order of the world, is our next subject of study.

## NOTES

1. For this account, I am dependent on J. Maringer's *The Gods of Prehistoric Man* (New York, 1960).
2. *The Iliad of Homer,* trans. Richmond Lattimore (Chicago, 1951).
3. D. G. Hogarth, *A Wandering Scholar in the Levant* (London, 1896), 179–80. See, for example, "An Italian Religious Feast," in *Mother Worship,* ed. James J. Preston (Chapel Hill, N.C., 1982), 95–122.
4. James B. Pritchard, ed., *Ancient Near Eastern Texts* (Princeton, N.J., 1950), 108–9.
5. F. M. Cornford, ed., *Greek Religious Thought from Homer to the Age of Alexander* (London, 1923), 85.
6. Ibid., 87.
7. *I-Ching,* Hsi Tz'u, Vol 1. As cited in W. T. deBary, ed., *Sources of the Chinese Tradition* (New York, 1960), 211–12.
8. Arthur Waley, *Three Ways of Thought in Ancient China* (New York, 1956), 16.
9. James Hope Moulton, *Early Zoroastrianism* (London, 1913), 349.
10. *Greater Bundahishn,* Vol. 2:12–36. Cited in R. C. Zaehner, *The Dawn and Twilight of Zoroastrianism* (London, 1961), 248.
11. Ibid., 264.
12. R. C. Zaehner, *Hinduism* (London, 1966), 39.
13. Robert E. Hume, trans., *The Thirteen Principal Upanishads* (London, 1921), 95.
14. Ibid., 209.
15. Ibid., 110–11.
16. Ibid., 246.
17. Ibid., 84.
18. *Māndūkya Upanishad* Vol. 7. Translated and cited in R. C. Zaehner, *Hinduism,* 56.
19. William James, *The Varieties of Religious Experience* (London, 1902), 384. See R. B. Martin, *Tennyson: The Uniquiet Heart* (Oxford, 1980), 28–29.
20. Norman Davies, *Rock-Tombs of El-Amarna* (London, 1903–8). Cited in E. O. James, *The Concept of Deity* (London, 1950), 94–95.
21. Al-Ghazālī, *Resuscitation of the Sciences of Religion.* Trans. and cited in C. Hartshorne and William L. Reese, *Philosophers Speak of God* (Chicago, 1953), 107.
22. Thomas Aquinas, *Summa Theologica,* Blackfriars ed. (London, 1964), 1a, 11, 3.
23. Montgomery Watt, *The Formative Period of Islamic Thought* (Edinburgh, 1973), 246–47.
24. *The Works of Aristotle,* trans. and ed. J. A. Smith and W. D. Ross (Oxford, 1912), 256a, 2–20, 258a, 14–23.
25. *Summa Theologica* 1a, 8, 1, in Thomas Gilby, ed., *Philosophical Texts* (Oxford, 1951), 234.

## KEY WORDS

polytheism

sky gods

Zeus

monarchical polytheism

mother goddesses

cult of Isis-Osiris

Tammuz-Ishtar

śakti cults

Kali

dualism

*yin-yang*

Zarathustra

Zoroastrianism

Ahura Mazda (Ohrmazd)

Angra Mainyu (Ahriman)

Gnosticism

Manicheanism

pantheism

monism

Logos

Brahman

Ātman

Vedanta

Śankara

māyā

monotheism

henotheism

Yahweh

anthropomorphism

aseity

deism

## REVIEW QUESTIONS

1. How did changes in human society from the Paleolithic period to the Neolithic Age relate to changes in religions during this same period?

2. Why do you think sky gods and mother goddesses figure so prominently in early civilizations? What is the religious significance of the great mother goddesses Isis and Ishtar and the cults of Isis-Osiris and Ishtar-Tammuz in ancient Egypt and Mesopotamia, respectively?

3. What is cosmic dualism in the conception of deity or ultimate reality? Contrast the dualism of Chinese *yin-yang* with forms of dualism in late Zoroastrianism and in Gnosticism.

4. What is meant by pantheism? What is meant by monism? Describe how the monism of Hindu Advaita Vedanta differs from forms of pantheism in, for example Stoicism and some earlier Hindu texts such as the *Upanishads*.

5. How do monotheistic conceptions of God differ from other views of deity or ultimate reality? Describe how the Hebrews' conception of God evolved from the Exodus and early life in Canaan (thirteenth century B.C.E.) to the time of the Exile in Babylon in the sixth century B.C.E.

6. What are some of the attributes of God assumed by monotheistic religions? How do some of these attributes, taken together, pose theological problems for monotheistic religion?

7. How would you describe the difference between monotheism and deism as the latter is described by Aristotle and some eighteenth century writers?

## SUGGESTIONS FOR FURTHER READING

*On primal and ancient conceptions of deity or ultimate reality, see*

ELIADE, MIRCEA. *A History of Religious Ideas, I. From the Stone Age to the Eleusinian Mysteries.* Chicago: University of Chicago Press, 1978.

GUTHRIE, W. K. *The Greeks and Their Gods.* London: Methuen, 1950.

HULTKRANTZ, AKE. *The Religions of the American Indians.* Berkeley: University of California Press, 1979.

JAMES, E. O. *The Ancient Gods.* London: Weidenfeld and Nicholson, 1960.

————. *The Concept of Deity.* London: Hutchinson, 1950.

MARINGER, JOHANNES. *The Gods of Prehistoric Man.* New York: Alfred A, Knopf, 1960.

MBITI, JOHN. *Concepts of God in Africa.* New York: Praeger Publishers, 1970.

*On mother goddesses, see*

HAWLEY, JOHN S. AND DONNA WULFF, eds. *The Divine Consort: Radha and the Goddesses of India.* Berkeley: University of California Press, 1983.

JAMES, E. O. *The Cult of the Mother Goddess.* New York: Praeger Publishers, 1959.

NEUMANN, ERICH. *The Great Mother: An Analysis of the Archetype.* Princeton, N.J.: Princeton University Press, 1955.

OLSON, CARL, ed. *The Book of the Goddess: Past and Present.* New York: Crossroad, 1986.

PRESTON, JAMES, J., ed. *Mother Worship.* Chapel Hill: University of North Carolina Press, 1982. (The essays in this volume call in question the generalizations of James, Neumann, and others.)

STONE, MERLIN. *When God Was a Woman.* New York: Dial Press, 1976.

*On non-Western forms of polytheism, dualism, theism, and monism, see*

BHATTACHARJI, S. *The Indian Theogony.* Cambridge: Cambridge University Press, 1970.

DANIELOU, ALAIN. *Hindu Polytheism.* New York: Pantheon Books, 1964.

DAS GUPTA, S. N. *A History of Indian Philosophy.* 5 vols. Cambridge: Cambridge University Press. This and the Radhakrishnan work, cited below, are a mine of information on Indian Vedantic monism.

NEEDHAM, JOSEPH. *Science and Civilization in China,* Vol. II. Cambridge: Cambridge University Press, 1956. An account of Chinese *yin-yang* dualism.

O'FLAHERTY, W. D. *Hindu Myths.* Baltimore, Md.: Penguin Books, 1975.

RADHAKRISHNAN, S. *Indian Philosophy.* 2 vols. New York: Macmillan, 1923.

WARD, KEITH. *Images of Eternity: Concepts of God in Five Religious Traditions.* London: Darton, Longman, and Todd, 1987.

ZAEHNER, R. C. *The Dawn and Twilight of Zoroastrianism.* New York: Putnam, 1961. On classic Iranian dualism.

*On studies of Western theism, see*

EICHRODT, WALTHER. *Theology of the Old Testament.* 2 vols. Philadelphia: Westminster Press, 1961. The beginnings and development of Hebrew monotheism.

HARTSHORNE, CHARLES, AND, WILLIAM L. REESE. *Philosophers Speak of God.* Chicago: University of Chicago Press, 1953. An excellent anthology of texts representing classical forms of theism, pantheism, and panentheism.

HICK, JOHN. *The Existence of God.* New York: Macmillan, 1964. An excellent collection of classic texts on the ontological, cosmological, teleological, and moral arguments for theistic belief and contemporary theistic problems.

KAUFMANN, YEHEZKEL. *The Religion of Israel.* Trans. and abridged by Moshe Greenberg. Chicago: University of Chicago Press, 1970. Argues that monotheism was Mosaic and the belief of Israel from earliest times.

OWEN, H. P. *Concepts of Deity.* London: Macmillan, 1971. A study of Western theism, pantheism, process theology, and the view of contemporary theologians.

PRESTIGE, GEORGE L. *God in Patristic Thought.* London: S.P.C.K., 1956.

WENSINCK, A. J. *The Muslim Creed.* New York: Barnes and Noble, 1965.

*Two classic Western texts are*

AQUINAS, ST. THOMAS. *Summa Theologica,* Vol. I. Questions 1–26, *Basic Writings of Saint Thomas Aquinas.* Ed. Anton C. Pegis. New York: Random House, 1945.

CALVIN, JOHN. *Institutes of the Christian Religion.* Book I. Philadelphia: Westminster Press, 1936.

*For brief scholarly treatments of God in the Hebrew scriptures, the New Testament, Postbiblical Judaism, earlier Christianity, and Islam, see*

ELIADE, MIRCEA, ed. *The Encyclopedia of Religion,* Vol. 6. New York: Macmillan Publishing Company, 1987, pp. 1–35. For goddess worship, see 35–66.

# 8

# *Cosmogony: Origins of the Natural and Social Order*

## Overview

Religions associate their concepts of deity with their other religious beliefs. And among humanity's most persistent concerns is the question, "How did our world and its natural and social order come into being?" This chapter explores a variety of religious responses to this question. A *cosmogony* is an account of the emergence or creation of world order (from the Greek *kosmos*, meaning "world," and the root of *gignestai*, meaning "to be born"). As we shall see, interest in beginnings is not the result of idle speculation; it is intimately tied to basic concerns about the natural and social order, the status of the gods and humankind, and human action.

We will begin by underlining this practical basis of cosmogony, and then we will present a typology of cosmogonic myths, some found in primal and archaic societies and others prominent among the ancient Greeks and Hebrews. We will conclude, however, by reflecting on the mythic elements in modern, "scientific" **cosmology** or characterizations of the cosmos and an example of how contemporary physicists are again raising religious questions regarding our knowledge of the origins and nature of the cosmos.

Our typology includes accounts of generation or procreation from a primal substance(s), the sexual union of a primal male and female, and the ordering of a primal chaos through the conflict of divine forces. Sometimes, as in Chinese Taoism, the world is viewed as an ongoing, infinite process of becoming, with no conception of a fixed or final sacred order. A pervasive cosmogonic theme is that of divine craftsmanship, the ordering of the world of preexistent matter through the agency of a god or, as in the philosopher

Plato's speculation, through the creative work of an intelligent and purposeful Mind, or *Nous*.

The crucial differences between the Greek and ancient Hebrew (Genesis) accounts of creation are discussed, including the very different implications of each conception for such important matters as the nature of God and the problem of evil. These very problems have, however, convinced some religions—for example, Jainism in India and certain schools of Buddhism—to insist on the futility of cosmogonic speculation and to focus their attention on the practical matter of achieving liberation from evil and suffering.

The chapter concludes with an examination of cosmology in our scientific age and with a critical analysis of the effort, by Creation Science, to claim a *scientific* basis for a particular religious cosmogony.

## The Practical Basis of Cosmogony

The creation of a world, in the sense of an original beginning, is an idea that many Westerners take for granted. A number of our unwitting assumptions about cosmology—that is, about the nature of the world and our place in it—are derived from the Bible. Also, we may not be conscious of the fact that the idea of *a beginning* of the world is a relatively sophisticated idea, involving some sense of detachment from our environment and the capacity to imagine a state of affairs radically different from what we experience daily. It would be quite natural to think of our world as always the way it is now observed to be. Primal societies did, nevertheless, speculate about the origin and ordering of the world. The rudiments of such imaginative thinking can be found in efforts to answer questions about the origin of some regularly observed feature of nature or social life, such as tribal kinship.

Until the emergence of Greek and Indian philosophic speculation in the first millennium B.C.E., cosmogony was cloaked in the vivid, concrete imagery of myth. For the purpose of our discussion here, we can refer again to Mircea Eliade's comment that "myth narrates a sacred history; it relates an event that took place in primordial Time, the fabled time of the 'beginnings.' "[1] Of special interest is Eliade's claim that myth is related to a creation, to how something came into existence. Furthermore, Eliade insists that myths of origin are not primarily concerned with conveying scientific knowledge of a first cause; rather, they are interested in putting us in touch with those sacred orders or those exemplary patterns that are presupposed before any meaningful activity can be undertaken.

Cosmogonic myth often represents the exemplary model for every future creative act, and therefore many **etiological** (meaning the description of the cause or reason of a thing) myths begin with a rehearsal of the original cosmogony. Only after such a rehearsal does the mythic narrative go on to relate, for example, the genealogy of the royal family, the history of the tribe, or the origin of one of its institutions. Eliade illustrates the point by a custom of the Osage Indians:

> When a child is born among the Osages, "a man who had talked with the gods" is summoned. When he reaches the new mother's house he recites the history of the creation of the Universe and the terrestrial animals to the newborn infant. Not until this has been done is the baby given the breast. Later, when it wants to drink water, the same man—or sometimes another—is called in again. Once again he recites the Creation, ending with the origin of Water. When the child is old enough to take solid food, the man "who had talked with the gods" comes once more and again recites the Creation, this time also relating the origin of grains and other foods.[2]

We see that the interest here is not at all speculative. It is quite necessary to reestablish contact with the sacred time of the original "beginning" in order to ensure the renewal of nature, ongoing human life, or social institutions.

While it is true that existential anxiety about the maintenance and renewal of the natural world and the social order is the essential interest underlying archaic cosmogonic mythology, an intellectual element is not wholly absent and, as previously stated, this requires a certain detachment from the environment. The origins of cosmogonic speculation are uncertain, but some conditions would appear to have been critical and formative.[3] The archaeological evidence of the Paleolithic (or Old Stone) Age, especially of the female figurines with exaggerated maternal features, points to the phenomenon of birth as perhaps supplying the initial conception of a "beginning." But Paleolithic art does not reveal any interest in the larger natural environment. However, the subsequent Neolithic revolution (c. 4500 B.C.E.) changed humans from food gatherers and hunters to cultivators and agriculturalists. Humans became acquainted with the generative powers of Nature and its fertility.

The Neolithic Age also saw the invention of the craft of potterymaking, and we later see the image of the fashioning of a lump of clay as a recurring one in depictions of world beginnings. But whatever the sources of such speculation, cosmogonic myths were little developed before the third millennium B.C.E., when the earliest known creation texts appear. The imagery found in these texts varies considerably. Surprisingly, many of them reflect, if crudely, modern theories of catastrophic and continuous creation. The dominant themes, however, are those of sexual fecundity and union, fertilization, procreation, and generation. Conflict, conquest, and the ordering of chaos are other common subjects, as is craftsmanship. It is worth noting, however, that some of these ancient myths also depict creation as resulting from a divine thought or will—an idea we often erroneously associate exclusively with the emancipation of thought from nature mythology in the great historical religions. The typology of cosmogonic myths here employed is necessarily selective; nevertheless, it gives some sense of the variety of imaginative conceptions of creation and order that we find in the history of the world's religions.

## Emergence or Procreation from a Primal Substance or Being

The ancient Egyptians, like so many archaic and primal cultures, accepted many accounts of the creation and felt no need to reject one for another. Among the earliest Pyramid Texts (c. 2400 B.C.E.) are various accounts of life emerging from the primordial watery abyss (Nun). The sun and creator-god, *Re-Atum,* according to one text, appears on the "primeval hillock," produced by the silt of the flooding Nile River. Re-Atum is self-created: "I am Atum when I was alone in Nun; I am Re in his (first) appearances, when he began to rule that which he had made. . . . 'I am the great god who came into being by himself.' "[4]

Re-Atum proceeds to engender the first male and female pair of gods, Shu and Tefnut, by several means. In one text, the creation of air (Shu) and his consort, moisture (Tefnut), is accomplished by a violent sneeze:

> O Atum-Kheprer, thou wast on high on the (primeval) hill; thou didst arise as the *ben*-bird of the *ben*-stone in the *Ben*-House in Heliopolis; thou did spit out what was Shu, thou did sputter out what was Tefnut. Thou didst put thy arms about them as the arms of a *ka* [the vital force of Atum].[5]

A common theme in archaic cosmogonies is this form of emanation of the primal elements or beings from a watery chaos or nonbeing, or from a primeval being—a god or being itself. As we have seen, in the Egyptian Pyramid texts Atum appears out of the watery abyss and creates through his own fecundity. In the Greek Orphic religion (600 B.C.E.), the first god, Protagonos, is also androgynous and bears within himself the seeds of all the future gods and men. A more sophisticated version of this theme is found in the *Chandogya Upanishad,* the Hindu philosophical text written about 700 B.C.E. The *Upanishads* are consumed with the question of the relation of being to nonbeing. In the following passage, emergence from the abysmal waters of nonbeing is rejected, for how could something come from nothing? Being is everexistent and the manifold world is the result of Being's own procreation:

> In the beginning, my dear, this world was just Being, only one, without a second. To be sure, some people say: "In the beginning this world was just Non-being, one only, without a second; that from Non-being Being was produced."
>
> But verily, my dear, whence could this be?, said he. How from Non-being could Being be produced? On the contrary, my dear, in the beginning this world was just Being, one only, without a second.
>
> It bethought itself: "Would that I were many! Let me procreate myself!" It emitted heat. The heat bethought itself: "Would that I were many! Let me procreate myself!" It emitted water. Therefore whenever a person grieves or perspires from the heat, then water . . . is produced.
>
> That water bethought itself: "Would that I were many! Let me procreate myself!" It emitted food. Therefore whenever it rains, then there is abundant food. So food for eating is produced just from water.[6]

The Egyptian Sky God, Nut, held apart from the earth, Geb, by the god of air, Shu. (*Source:* From the William Sturgis Bigelow Collection. Courtesy of the Museum of Fine Arts, Boston.)

## The Sexual Union of a Primal Male and Female

In many religions, the appearance of the elements, the seasons, and the myriad beings that make up the natural environment are the result of the sexual union of a primeval male and female. It represents the coming together of the primal opposites—often the earth and the sky. This can be seen in the interaction of *yin* (the earth, female) and *yang* (the sky, male) in Chinese mythology, as well as in the primal role of Uranos, the sky-Father, and Gaea, the earth-Mother, in Greek myth—for example, in Hesiod's *Theogony*.

One of the most elaborate expressions of creation by sexual union is found in the Japanese *Kojiki* ("Records of Ancient Matters," 712 C.E.) and *Nihongi* ("Chronicles of Japan," 720 C.E.). These texts include most of the themes we have surveyed so far. In the beginning, there is chaos, but gods spontaneously appear, including the primeval male and female. The interest in the gods and the origin of the cosmos is, however, only preliminary to the central interest of this Japanese chronicle: the divine creation and destiny of the Japanese islands and the emperial state. The *Kojiki* speaks of an original chaos from which numerous deities appear, either spontaneously or from a reed shoot in the mud. However, the *Nihongi* begins—as does the Chinese myth of the creator god, P'an Ku—with the feminine and masculine principles not yet divided but forming a great cosmic egg:

> Of old, Heaven and Earth were not yet separated, and the In [feminine] and Yo [masculine] not yet divided. They formed a chaotic mass like an egg, which was of obscurely defined limits, and contained germs. The purer and clearer part was thinly diffused and formed Heaven, while the heavier and grosser element settled down and became earth. . . . Heaven was therefore formed first, and Earth was established subsequently. Thereafter Divine Beings were produced between them.[7]

The eighth generation of the gods produced *Izanagi* (the male-who-invites) and *Izanami* (the female-who-invites), who create the Japanese islands:

> Izanagi and Izanami stood on the floating bridge of Heaven, and held counsel together, saying:
> "Is there not a country beneath?" Thereupon they thrust down the jewel-spear of Heaven, and groping about therewith found the ocean. The brine which dripped from the point of the spear coagulated and became an island which received the name of Ono-goro-jim—the pillar of the world.[8]

The *Nihongi* further relates the birth of the eight Japanese islands. It is then that Izanagi and Izanami join in creating the rivers, the mountains, and the wind that blows away the mists covering the world. Izanami's last child is the god of fire, who accidentally but fatally scorches his mother, who descends to Yomi (Hades). In his grief, Izanagi searches for Izanami and begs her to come back to the land of the living. She forbids him to look on her decaying body. But Izanagi refuses and, in her fury, Izanami pursues the terror-stricken husband, who endeavors to escape to the light of day.

At the entrance to Yomi, the two gods swear their divorce. Thereafter, Izanagi rules over the earth until his creative work is done. Izanami rules over the land of the dead. Here we see a critical subtheme that has parallels in many, especially Near Eastern, religions. The changing aspects of the seasons, and the crisis of Japanese rice farming in times of drought, is enacted in this segment of the Shinto myth cycle. Scorched by heat, Izanami loses her life-giving powers and descends to the underworld, like Ishtar or Persephone. Unlike the Near Eastern myths, Izanami remains in Hades. However, in an early Japanese ritual used in a fire-subduing ceremony, the story is told how Izanami returns to earth and gives birth to children who will aid in the return of vegetation:

> Then she taught Izanagi saying, "Whenever the heart of the evilhearted child becomes violent, subdue it with the Deity of Water, with Gourd, with Clay Mountain Lady, and with River Leaves."[9]

Our attention here, however, is focused on the political meaning of the *Kojiki* and the *Nihonshoki*. When Izanagi escapes from Hades, he undertakes elaborate bathings in the river to wash away the pollution and decay of death. From this purifying bath, many things are born. From his left eye is born Amaterasu, the sun goddess and giver of life. From *Amaterasu* come the Japanese emperors, the divine source of political authority, and the divine, emperial destiny of the Japanese people (see Chapter 6).

The chronicle then tells of the end of prehistory and the coming of the first human emperor, Jimmu Tennō, as the direct descendent of the Sun-Goddess through her grandson (660 B.C.E.). The mythic and legendary history of Jimmu Tennō and his successors has played a crucial role in the development of the Shinto concept of the divine origin of the emperial house and the Japanese people. A *Teacher's Manual of National History for Primary Schools*, published in Japan in 1931, reveals the import of this national cosmogony on the moral imagination of the Japanese people:

> *The Sacred Virtue of Amaterasu-Omikami.* From these two [Izanagi and Izanami] *kami* was born Amaterasu-Omikami. From the beginning it was determined that she should be the person who should be the ruler of the realm . . . She allotted the divisions of water and land, she taught the cultivation of the five cereals. . . .
>
> *The Benevolence of the Imperial Family.* From that time onward generation after generation of Emperors, in a single dynasty unbroken for all ages, have handed on the three sacred treasures as the symbols of the Imperial Throne . . .
> *The Splendor of the National Life.* Thus the antiquity of the establishment of our state is already seen as superior to that of any other country . . . Here the Deity of the Sun has handed on her eternal rule . . . We, the people of the nation, must realize the nature of the splendor of our national organization and must be more and more zealous in the expression of loyalty and must exert ourselves in the patriotic protection of the state.[10]

## Creation by Conflict and the Ordering of Chaos

In the Japanese cosmogony, we observed that sexual union is a dominant theme. However, unlike some other myths to which we have referred, the union is not basically quiescent and harmonious; on the contrary, it is turbulent and ends in conflict and violence. The Japanese myth reveals the practical concern with the struggle between the powers of chaos, darkness, and death and those of life and order. This is a most important cosmogonic motif because in this type of myth the cosmos is created or, rather, *ordered* through a battle with the terrible powers or monsters—the Dragon, the Serpent, or the Leviathan—that symbolize chaos and disorder, or even repressive order.*

We observed earlier that in the Egyptian myth creation emerges from the primal, boundless, deep waters (Nun), but that the waters appear motionless and entirely benevolent. However, even here, according to some texts, cosmic order is threatened by Apophis, the dragon or water monster symbolizing hostile darkness. The sun's rising each day on the eastern horizon heralds the victory of Amon-Re and the pharaoh (the image of Amon-Re) over chaotic darkness (Apophis). As we might expect, each day in the Temple of Amon-Re the Egyptians ritually recited the myth "The Repulsing of

---

*Not all myths depicting the struggle with chaos represent the latter in purely negative terms, for example, meaningless nonbeing or complete disorder. Recent studies of both ancient Near Eastern and Chinese creation mythology have made it clear that chaos can be the source of creativity itself. See, for example, the brief discussion of the Taoist *hun-tun* (Chaos) at the conclusion of this section.

The Japanese god Izanagi about to thrust his spear into the ocean; the Japanese islands were created from the drippings off his spear. (*Source:* "Izanagi Creating the Japanese Islands," Kobayashi Eitaku, Japan, 1843–90. Hanging scroll; ink and color on silk. 125.7 × 54.5 cm. From the William Sturgis Bigelow Collection. Courtesy, Museum of Fine Arts, Boston.)

the Dragon" as a spell against Apophis. The recitation included the following triumphant declaration:

> He Is One Fallen To The Flame, Apophis with a knife on his head. He cannot see, and his name is no more in this land. I have commanded that a *curse* be cast upon him. . . . He is fallen and overthrown. . . .[11]

The Babylonian creation epic, ***Enuma elish*** ("When on high"), is a classic example of a cosmogony involving conflict and the bringing of order out of chaos. The epic comes from the middle of the second millennium B.C.E. It was introduced briefly in Chapter 4 in the discussion of the Babylonian Akitu or New Year's Festival and temple ritual. The creation myth itself deserves attention here. The text primarily honors Marduk, the Babylonian high-god, ruler of the lesser gods and creator of heaven and earth. But the conflict of the elements and the ordering of the cosmos serves as the background and justifies Marduk's rise to sovereignty.

The myth begins with watery chaos, consisting of three elements: Apsu, representing the sweet water; *Ti'amat*, the sea; and Mumma, their son, the mist. As yet, there is neither sky nor firm ground, although in time the union of Apsu and Ti'amat brings forth Lahmu and Lahamu, representing the silt formed by waters. From a later pair, Anu, the sky-god, is born; Anu, in turn, engenders Nudimmut—also known as Enki—and Ea—the wise god of the subterranean sweet waters, but also here representing the earth itself. The practical import of the myth is not difficult to discern at this point. Mesopotamia is a land produced by the soil of the flooding Tigris and Euphrates rivers, which is deposited at the meeting of the sea on the Persian Gulf. The silt is formed where the fresh water meets the salt water.

The myth proceeds to tell the manner in which the primal elements are ordered and how a cosmic government is established and assured. This is accomplished through a prolonged conflict between two principles: the older gods representing primordial inactivity and the younger gods symbolizing movement, energy, and activity. Restlessly surging back and forth, the young gods disturb Ti'amat and Apsu, who respond:

Their ways are verily loathsome unto me.
By day I find no relief, nor repose by night.
I will destroy, I will wreck their ways,
That quiet may be restored. Let us have rest.[12]

The young gods dash about in panic and only Ea proves equal to the challenge. He casts a sacred spell on Apsu, who falls into a profound sleep. Ea then removes Apsu's royal crown—and in so doing possesses his might and splendor—and kills him, imprisoning his son, Mummu. On Apsu, Ea established a spacious dwelling and here **Marduk** is born, endowed with awe-inspiring majesty.

The older gods chide Ti'amat for failing to come to the aid of Apsu, urging her to avenge her spouse's death. Ti'amat finally yields, chooses the wicked Kingu to be her spouse, and entrusts him with command of the army and authority over "the tablets of destinies." A formidable demonic and chaotic power now threatens the young gods. Ea this time is no match for Ti'amat—even his powerful spell fails him. Anu, the sky-god, then proceeds against Ti'amat with the combined approval and authority of the gods, but he also fails. Authority alone cannot defeat the mighty Ti'amat. In desperation, the gods ask Ea to seek out his son, Marduk, "whose strength is mighty." Marduk is prepared to do battle, but he demands a high price:

If I indeed, as your avenger
Am to vanquish Ti'amat and save your lives
Set up the Assembly, proclaim supreme my destiny
When in Bushukinna jointly you sit down rejoicing,
Let my words, instead of you, determine the fates.
Unalterable shall be what I may bring into being;
Neither recalled nor changed shall be the command of my lips. . . .[13]

The gods agree to Marduk's terms and confer on him kingship: political authority joined with the power of physical force. The gods plead, "Go and cut off the life of Ti'amat." Arrayed in his dazzling and terrifying might, Marduk is challenged to battle by the fearsome and angry Ti'amat. Marduk, however, shoots an arrow through Ti'amat's jaws, piercing her heart and killing her. Marduk takes from Kingu the "tablet of destinies" and fastens it on his own breast. Finally, Marduk cuts the body of Ti'amat in two, lifting up one half to form the sky and fashioning the earth with the other half. Marduk then establishes Anu, Enlil, and Ea in their appropriate dominions. The conflict between Marduk and Ti'amat again explains a realistic feature of life in Mesopotamia. The battle has to do with the spring flooding of the Mesopotamian plain and the contest between the waters and the wind. In spring, the land reverts to a watery chaos until the winds can fight back the waters and bring back dry land.

The creation myth concludes with Marduk assigning all the gods their stations and their duties, organizing the calendar, and creating and organizing the heavenly bodies. On plea from the gods, the new king agrees to relieve them of all toilsome and menial tasks. He addresses Ea:

Blood I will mass and cause bones to be,
I will establish a savage, "man" shall be his name.
Verily, the savage-man I will create.
He shall be charged with the service of the gods,
That they might be at ease.[14]

Marduk in battle with Ti'amat. The winged Marduk attacks Ti'amat with double tridents. Wings outstretched, the fierce Ti'amat retreats. (*Source:* Wall panel in the palace of Ashur-nasiripal II, 885–860 B.C.E. © The British Museum.)

Ea has another plan. He suggests that the gods in assembly determine which of the prisoners was guilty of contriving to make Ti'amat rebel. The gods declare that the guilty one is Kingu. He is executed, and from his blood mankind is created under Ea's supervision.

> They imposed upon (Kingu) his guilt and severed his blood (vessels). Out of his blood they fashioned mankind.[15]

Humankind, it is important to note, is created for the purposes of serving the gods and relieving them of burdensome work. The epic poem ends with an account of the gods—toiling for the last time—building for their king the city of Babylon and a temple in his honor. The focus of the *Enuma elish* is not primarily on the origin of the physical cosmos but, rather, on the more pressing issue of establishing a social order. The myth describes both the rise of Marduk to kingship and the establishment of a political organization. First, there is a semidemocratic assembly of the gods, each with their role and duties, but that is replaced by a monarchy in which the young king Marduk takes on the task of political organization as emperor, assigning all the gods their tasks. Scholars point out that the myth dramatizes the political crises of Mesopotamian history, from primal warring communities to city-states, and finally to empire. What is significant is that the myth sees the emerging political structure as the human-social reflection of the order already achieved by the pantheon of the gods. As the *Enuma elish* says of Marduk, there is to be "a likeness on earth of what he has wrought in heaven."[16]

We noted earlier that not all cosmogonic myths conceive of chaos as unambiguously evil or as representing the powers of death and destruction. Ancient Chinese **Taoist cosmogony** is a case in point. The early Taoist sages taught that the reality of Tao or "the Way," as it is often translated, is an "uncarved Block." By this they meant that it was not to be thought of as an already determinate order but, rather, a becoming, a process capable of infinite possibility. The Tao, they said, is both "nameless" and "nameable"; that is, the Tao as creative process is a joining of "nonbeing" and "being." The *Tao Te Ching* says: "Being and non-being produce each other"—in other words, they are the polar aspects, the *yin* and *yang*, of Tao. "This is but to say that only becoming (coming into being which illustrates some mixture of being and non-being) is; not-becoming (either being or non-being abstracted from its polar relation with its opposite) is not."[17]

The Taoist sages intuited that there is no simple, final, and permanent order; there is no privileged rational order among lesser orders or disorder. As one commentator has written, the Taoist "does not feel obliged to single out any specific order as the true one. His vision of nature is as if it were an uncarved block, a matrix of actualizable orders, passive to infinite patterning. The primary fact about the Taoist universe is that it is the sum of all orders. . . . There are as many actualizable worlds as there are events in the process of becoming."[18]

In the Taoist cosmogony, chaos (nonbeing) is a polar element with cosmos (order, being) in Becoming itself (*Tao*), the harmonious *yin-yang* of the creative process of nature. In some Near Eastern myths, the monster representing chaos is similarly a source, not only of disorder but also of ongoing creativity, and the battle with the monster chaos is a necessary and perennial aspect of life itself.

## Creation by a Divine Craftsman

To this point, we have used the words *cosmogony* and *creation* interchangeably. However, an important distinction needs to be made. The cosmogonic accounts we have surveyed are not, strictly speaking, mythic expressions of *creation;* rather, they are imaginative narratives of *generation, procreation,* or *ordering* from some primal substance(s) or being—the abysmal waters, the divine body, the embryonic egg, and so on. Technically, creation means **creatio ex nihilo,** or creation by decree or out of nothing. Such an idea was unthinkable in many primal and archaic cultures. It was even inconceivable to the Greeks. *Creatio ex nihilo* finds its most distinctive expression in the later theologies of the three Western monotheistic faiths—Judaism, Christianity, and Islam—and is derived from their interpretations of the Creation story in the book of Genesis.

Greek cosmogony employed, among others, the image of the *creative artisan* or *craftsman*—which is often, although erroneously, associated with the idea of creation. It will be instructive to look first at myths of the divine craftsman before we turn to accounts of *creatio ex nihilo.* Examples of the former are common in Egyptian and in North American Indian texts, but the following illustrations are taken from the Greeks.

It is common to hear it said that the Greeks were responsible for the transition from mythological cosmogony to philosophical and scientific cosmology. The problem with such a claim is not only that it leaves out of the account the important philosophic and scientific developments in other ancient civilizations, but also that it distorts the history of Greek thought itself. It is wrong to speak of a movement "from myth to reason" in Greek thought if it implies that the later Greeks wholly supplanted mythic thinking with scientific explanation.

The earliest Greek philosophers—the Ionians, Thales, Anaximander, and Anaximenes (sixth century B.C.E.)—attempted to establish that the world evolved from a single material substance, without reference to the elaborate cosmogonic and theogonic myths of Homer and Hesiod. Nevertheless, neither these pre-Socratic philosophers nor Plato could avoid the use of mythic imagery in their cosmological speculations. They conceived the world animistically as a living, divine organism, and they spoke of the origin and evolution of the cosmos in images of piloting and craftsmanship that implied intelligent direction and design.

Thales held that water is the primary stuff from which all things evolve. Aristotle conjectured that Thales formed the idea from the fact that the seeds of all things are moist and from the fact that evaporation and freezing may, after all, turn water into air and perhaps even earth. Anaximenes thought the prime element was air, or breath, while for Heraclitus the essence of all things was fire, which symbolized the strife and tension immanent in all existence. What these Ionian philosophers discovered was the fact that, despite all change and becoming, there must be something permanent, which may undergo change but itself exists eternally. What they did *not* explain was motion, or the *cause* of cosmic evolution. They assumed that the primal substance possessed its own inherent power. Empedocles (fifth century B.C.E.) and Anaxagoras (fifth century B.C.E.) went further and tried to explain the *power* responsible for the order and evolution of the cosmic process. In mythic fashion, Empedocles posited the forces of Love and Hate, or Harmony and Strife. Love, he said, brings the four primal elements of earth, air, fire, and water into a cosmic harmony. Hate and Strife separate the elements, causing discord and the cessation of individual existences. The world process moves, then, in periodic cycles of unity and dissolution—an idea common to Hindu and Buddhist cosmology as well.

*Anaxagoras* introduced a radically new principle—*Nous,* or Mind—to explain motion and cosmic evolution. *Nous* does not create matter, for that is eternal; rather, *Nous* sets matter in motion. *Nous* is a kind of Deus ex machina (literally "a god from a machine," that is, a thing introduced to solve a difficulty), says Aristotle, brought in to explain change and the origin of all particular things. Anaxagoras spoke of *Nous* as infinite and alone. Yet *Nous* is also present in all living things. Anaxagoras obviously is seeking to distinguish an intelligible principle, that is, mind—the source not only of movement but also of intelligent design—from brute matter, an effort that reaches its highest development in Greek cosmology in Plato's (428/7–348/7) *Timaeus.*

*Plato* wrote *Timaeus* in part to show that the cosmos is the work of intelligence, "that Mind orders all things." Plato did not, however, think it possible to give an exact scientific account of cosmic origins. He presented his own mythic vision as, in his own words, a most "likely account." Plato believed that the material world of becoming requires some eternal cause that he called the divine *Demiurge* or Craftsman. This god is good, and "he desired that all things should come as near as possible to being like himself."

> Desiring, then, that all things should be good and, so far as might be, nothing imperfect, the god took over all that is visible—not at rest, but in discordant and unordered motion—and brought it from disorder into order, since he judged that order was in every way the better. . . . Taking thought, therefore, he found that, among things that are by nature visible, no work that is without intelligence will ever be better than one that has intelligence. . . . In virtue of this reasoning, when he framed the universe, he fashioned reason within soul and soul within body, to the end that the work he accomplished might be by nature excellent and perfect as possible.[19]

This important passage requires several comments. First, we should note that Plato's Demiurge is divine, creative Reason, but it *is not a Creator God*. According to Plato, the Demiurge "took over" preexisting material and fashioned it as perfectly *as possible* "so far as might be." The Demiurge is not to be confused with an omnipotent Creator but must instead be seen as a persuasive power working on disordered, stubborn material. Later in the dialogue, Plato speaks of the generation of the cosmos as "a mixed result of the combination of Necessity and Reason." Necessity is also called the Errant Cause, and it represents the purposelessness or the chance element in existence that is not informed by Reason. The cosmos is fashioned "by the victory of reasonable persuasion over Necessity."

For Plato, the Demiurge's creative work is limited by two additional eternal realities. One is "the Receptacle—as it were, the nurse—of all Becoming." The Receptacle is not matter but the Space in which all the material elements of the world of becoming appear. The Demiurge thus takes over the Receptacle (Space) and the material elements and fashions the cosmos after the model of the *Forms*, the other coeternal reality. Plato writes that the Demiurge "took thought to make, as it were, a moving likeness of eternity (the Forms)." Here we see Plato portraying an eternal Craftsman persuading and shaping a somewhat resistant, purposeless Necessity into a cosmos, according to preexistent, eternal Forms or Ideas. One result of Plato's mythic cosmogony is that he escapes the difficult problem of attributing imperfection and even natural evil in the world to God, a problem faced by the believer in an omnipotent Creator. The Western monotheist insists, of course, that God is perfect but also that the Creator is omnipotent and cannot be limited, like the Demiurge, by any other *coeternal* matter or form.

## Creation by Decree or from Nothing

When we turn to the idea of creation by decree or from nothing, it is important to mention that many creation accounts, quite independent of Genesis, conceive of the deity as creating by divine *fiat*, that is, simply by word of command or by will. The Quiche Maya, a great tribe of the southern branch of the Mayan civilization, spoke of the two powers—Tepeu and Gucumatz, or sun-fire—as existing in the beginning in the dark waters. The cosmos is then perceived as emerging from their deliberation and word.

> There was only immobility and silence in the darkness, in the night. Only the Creator, the Maker, Tepeu, Gucumatz, the Forefathers, were in the water surrounded with light. . . . By nature they were great sages and great thinkers. In this manner the sky existed and also the Heart of Heaven, which is the name of God and thus He is called.
> Then came the word. Tepeu and Gucumatz came together in the darkness, in the night, and Tepeu and Gucumatz talked together. They talked then, discussing and deliberating; they agreed, they united their words and their thoughts.

> Then while they meditated, it became clear to them that when dawn would break man must appear. Then they planned the creation. . . .
>
> Thus let it be done! Let the emptiness be filled! Let the water recede and make a void, let the earth appear and become solid; let it be done. Thus they spoke. Let there be light . . . Earth! they said, and instantly it was made. . . . So it was that they made perfect the work, when they did it after thinking and meditating upon it.[20]

In this Mayan creation story, the cosmogony is a deliberative and willed action and is not conceived solely in terms of procreation, involuntary emergence, or craftsmanship.

The role of divine forethought and will has at least some analogy to the Creation narrative in the book of Genesis, the text that became the classic source of the doctrine of *creatio ex nihilo*.

Scholars agree that there are two distinct accounts of the Creation in Genesis. One is found in Chapters 1–2:4a and is the work of a rather late hand, a *Priestly (P) writer* of the middle of the fifth century B.C.E. The second account, in Chapters 2:4b–25, is the work of two sources, the *Jahwist (J) and Elohist (E)*, representing the southern kingdom of Judah and the northern kingdom of Israel. The J and E sources are woven together in Genesis into one continuous narrative. They can, however, be distinguished on various grounds, not only by their different viewpoints but also by the fact that the two writers use different names for God: Jahweh (Yahweh) and Elohim. The interests of the later Priestly and the earlier J and E writers are markedly different, and this is reflected in the central focus and the order of their respective Creation narratives. These differences can be seen most easily by setting them out in parallel columns.[21]

| P (Genesis 1–2:4a) | J–E (Genesis 2:4b–25) |
|---|---|
| The original state of the earth is a watery chaos. | The original state of the earth is a waterless waste, without vegetation. |
| The work of creation is divided into six separate operations, each assigned to one day. | No note of time is introduced into the account. |
| The order of creation is | The order of creation is |
| (a) Light. | (a) Man, made out of dust. |
| (b) The firmament-heaven. | (b) The Garden, to the east, in Eden. |
| (c) The dry land-earth. Separation of earth and heaven. | (c) Trees of every kind, including the Tree of Life, and the Tree of the knowledge of Good and Evil. |
| (d) Vegetation—three kinds. | |
| (e) The heavenly bodies, sun, moon, and stars. | |
| (f) Birds and fishes. | (d) Animals, beasts, and birds (no mention of fish). |
| (g) Animals and man; male and female together. | (e) Woman, created out of man. |

It is evident that the J–E tradition focuses on the creation of man and woman, their dependence on and obedience to God, the Tree of the knowledge of Good and Evil, and later the Temptation, the Fall, and Paradise Lost. We will discuss this narrative in detail in Chapter 9, where we compare accounts of the human problem. Here we concentrate on the distinctive cosmogonic features of the Priestly narrative. First, we note that the geographical background of the Priestly account is not an uninhabitable waste, without rain and vegetation (the Palestine of J–E), but is, rather, an original watery chaos, representing the point of view of the Mesopotamian myths, especially the Babylonian creation epic. Scholars point out that the Hebrew word for chaos of waters, *tehom*, is a corruption of the name *Ti'amat*, the chaos-monster slain by Marduk. The rending of sky and earth from one another also resembles the splitting of Ti'amat's body in two. There also is a general resemblance to the Babylonian order of creation in the Priestly narrative of the six days. A common Near Eastern, especially Babylonian, background is clearly present, and yet, as we will see, the Priestly writer transforms this material in significant ways.

At first glance, the opening chapter of Genesis does not appear to support the later theological idea of *creatio ex nihilo*. We read: "In the beginning God created the heavens and the earth. The earth was without form and void, darkness was upon the face of the deep and the Spirit of God was moving over the face of the waters" (1:1–2). Reference to "the deep" and to "the waters" would indicate the presence of a coeternal, uncreated substance. However, in the total context of the Priestly story, scholars agree that God is perceived as the sole agent in creation and is a being who exists entirely transcendent, free and independent, of his creation. This is affirmed both in the first verse—"In the beginning God created the heavens and the earth"—and by the imposition of the divine fiat again and again in the successive acts of creation. For instance, the statement that "God made the firmament and separated the waters . . ." (1:7) is preceded by "God said, let there be a firmament . . . and let it separate the waters" (1:6). The same pattern is followed throughout the successive creative acts. Thus, while the inclusion of the second verse appears to express an idea not entirely consistent with *creatio ex nihilo*, the fact is that "the deep" (*tehom*) apparently plays no role in the account of the creation. Creation is achieved by divine command.

To summarize the Genesis account, we can point out some of the distinctive features in the biblical cosmogony. They shaped the worldview and the ethical ethos of ancient Israel, also the theology of later Judaism and Christianity, indeed, that of Western consciousness. First, in Genesis, there is no theogony, or account of the creation of the god(s). As we have seen, the creation of the gods is a common theme in the cosmogonies of many cultures. While Israelite religion was not initially monotheistic, the supremacy of Yahweh was paramount early in its history. Theological reflection was later to underline the theistic and moral implications of the early verses of Genesis as well as the cosmogonic motifs in the Psalms, in the great prophets, and in the Wisdom literature, such as Job. The doctrine of *creatio ex nihilo* also implied that no other reality whatsoever was coeternal with God. This finite world is wholly dependent on God and therefore *not* of the same substance or identical with God; in other words, the world is not divine.

Furthermore, in the Hebrew myth there is no struggle between the Creator and any other beings in the act of bringing forth cosmic order. This, again, contrasts with numerous myths of creation by conflict, such as is found in the *Enuma elish* where Marduk must slay the deities Ti'amat and Kingu before either the natural cosmos or humanity can be formed. In Genesis, the *tehom* ("the deep") offers no resistance to Yahweh. Similarly, in the Book of Job (Chapters 40–41), the evil powers, Behemoth and Leviathan, are depicted as mere playthings in Yahweh's hands. The biblical-creationist model implies, then, that God alone is self-existent, creates sovereignly by Divine wisdom and will, is not engaged in any struggle, and relates to a world that is wholly dependent on divine creative and providential activity.

The biblical cosmogony also sets beside its account of the creation of the world and all its life, a parallel narrative telling the story of the origin, unique status, task, and indictment of humanity. This, too, has distinctive features, discussed in detail in Chapter 9. Briefly, humanity is given a very high status.

Michelangelo's portrayal of the Creation of Man "in the image and likeness of God," from The Sistine Chapel, Vatican City, Rome. (*Source:* Courtesy of Alinari/Art Resource, NY.)

In Genesis, human life is created neither out of evil or rebellious substances, nor with a fated tragic flaw, as in Greek tragedy, nor as burdened with a divided body and soul, the latter yearning to escape to its supramundane home, as in Gnosticism. Rather, humans enjoy a unity of body and soul, a unity that is declared "very good." Humanity also is bestowed with a free will to judge and to act independently. Indeed, to humanity falls the task of dominion over the entire earth, a rule analogous to that of the Creator. The indictment, as portrayed in Genesis 3, is that these same humans, despite God's gift and will, misuse that unique gift and status for prideful and evil purposes.[22]

The biblical cosmogony, like others, entails a vision of a social and moral order, and certain ethical directives. First, the creation is brought forth according to God's will and order and is declared "good." Implied in the Hebrew *tob* ("good") is the wider sense that the world and humanity are founded on a divine righteousness, justice, love, and constancy. The "good creation" is considered ordered, reliable, moral, and just. Moral evil and disorder are brought about by humanity itself through its own prideful rebellion and alienation from God. Moral evil, therefore, has no prehuman independent existence; humanity is accountable for the moral evil in the world.

This evil, nevertheless, is no mere nuisance. As portrayed in the legends of Genesis 4–11, moral evil escalates at a sinister pace, and it is obstinate and enduring. The suffering and oppression of the world are due, however, not to God's creation but to the human perversion of the original Creation. In the biblical myth, the cosmos created by God is then a righteous and just one, ruled by moral cause and effect: goodness yielding blessings, evil sowing suffering and disorder. But is it always so? The question, as we shall see, reaches its height in Job's cry of anguished protest against God for allowing the righteous to suffer. Is the Creator God's almighty power, wisdom, and steadfast love compatible with the horrific suffering and evil evident in the world?

## The Rejection of Cosmogonic Speculation

Before we leave the subject of cosmogony, a few additional points need to be discussed briefly. The first has to do with the fact that not all religions possess cosmogonic myths, or, if they do, they play a less significant role in the religion's thought and life. The highly imaginative and speculative character of cosmogony is reason enough why some practically minded religions have remained indifferent to or skeptical of accounts of world beginnings, particularly toward the idea of *creatio ex nihilo*. **Jainism,** a religion that began in ancient India as a protest against Hindu ritualism, is an example. The goal of Jainism is to free the soul from its imprisonment in karmic matter and the cycle of rebirth, which is a result of its attachment to the material world. The Jain path leading to release regards cosmogonic speculation not only as full of contradictions but also as irrelevant to salvation and therefore to be avoided:

> Some foolish men declare the Creator made the world.
> The doctrine that the world was created is ill-advised,
>     and should be rejected . . .
>
> How could God have made the world without any
>     raw material?
> If you say he made this first, and then the world,
>     you are faced with an endless regression.
> If you declare that this raw material arose naturally
>     you fall into another fallacy, For the whole universe
>     might thus have been its own creator, and have
>     arisen equally naturally . . .
>
> If he is ever perfect and complete, how could the will
>     to create have arisen in him? . . .
> If, on the other hand, he is not perfect, he could no more
>     create the world than a potter could . . .
>
> If out of love for living things and need of them he
>     made the world,
> Why did he not make creation wholly blissful,
>     free from misfortune? . . .
>
> Good men should combat the believer in divine creation,
>     maddened by an evil doctrine.
>
> Know that the world is uncreated, as time itself is,
>     without beginning and end . . .
>
> Uncreated and indestructible, it endures under the
>     compulsion of its own nature.[23]

In the sixth century B.C.E., Gautama, the Buddha (meaning the "Enlightened One"), also voiced his disapproval of cosmogonic theorizing. His antimythological and antimetaphysical temperament has since characterized Theravada Buddhism in Southern Asia. Gautama's religious teaching (see Chapters 9 and 12) is essentially a spiritual therapy directed at freeing persons from the suffering caused by ignorant, egoistic desire or craving. The story is told of Malunkyaputta, a monk and disciple of Gautama, who was addicted to speculation. One day, as he sat in meditation, he began to fret about whether or not the world was eternal and how, if not, it had begun. He went to the Buddha to seek answers to these puzzlements. Gautama replied,

> Well, Malunkyaputta, anyone who demands the elucidation of such futile questions which do not in any way tend to real spiritual progress and edification is like one who has been shot by an arrow and refuses to let the doctor pull it out and attend to the wound. If the wounded man were to say, "So long as I do not know who the man is who shot me . . . until then I will not allow the arrow to be pulled out or the wound to be attended to"—that man, Malunkyaputta, will die without ever knowing all these details.[24]

Buddha was advising his disciple that the wise man will seek to be treated immediately and in a practical way by a physician and will not demand answers to secondary and futile questions that cannot contribute to his present need.

"A holy life, Malunkyaputta," the Buddha continues,

> does not depend on the dogma that the world is eternal or not eternal and so forth. Whether or not these things obtain, there still remain the problems of birth, old age, death, sorrow . . . all the grim facts of life—and for their extinction in the present life I am prescribing this Dhamma [Doctrine]. Accordingly, bear it in mind that these questions which I have not eludicated . . . I have not elucidated purposely because these profit not, nor have they anything to do with the fundamentals of holy life nor do they tend toward Supreme Wisdom, the Bliss of Nibbana [Nirvana].[25]

Buddha's advice to his disciple sounds very modern in its indifference to metaphysical questions about cosmic beginnings or endings, questions that appear irresolvable. But below the surface of Buddha's brilliant analysis of the human plight in the world lie, of course, fundamental assumptions about the essential nature of things and the implications for human action. Humankind's perennial resort to cosmogonic reflection—to myth and metaphysics—is, many will insist, inherently human. For cosmogony, as we have seen, has to do with judgments about what is real, the fundamental order of the world, the status and duties of humans, and the purposes of the gods.

## Cosmogony Today

There is one final question. The cosmogonies surveyed in this chapter are, in every case, imaginative and intuitive efforts to answer etiological questions about the origin of the primal elements, the cosmos itself, its natural and political order, or human institutions and duties. Whether or not they were originally understood literally, in our modern sense, is not the critical point. Clearly, they were taken as "true stories" because each cosmogony offered a structure of meaning and value that adequately accounted for the perennial features of life as observed—for example, the annual victory over the spring floods, the intelligible order and design of nature or the social order, the institution of kingship, or humankind's lowly status or dominion over the earth.

Today, we are living in a scientific age in which few educated persons still think of cosmology in such mythic terms. Or do we? Certainly, the scientist setting forth the nebular hypothesis, the "big bang" theory, or the theory of "continuous creation," attempts to avoid poetic and anthropomorphic language. However, the scientist is not always successful; human language is intractably anthropomorphic. Charles Darwin, despite his materialist doctrine of natural selection and evolution, could not always avoid using human language of purpose and intelligent design in discussing natural evolution in

*The Origin of Species.* Scholars perceive in Marxist dialectical materialism implicit cosmogonic assumptions that inform the Marxist theory of history and ethical action, for example, the role of labor, the processes of production, and the proletarian revolution.

Most revealing, perhaps, are the cosmogonic suppositions to be found in that most modern of "scientific" theorists, Sigmund Freud. We know that Freud was a severe critic of all religious cosmogonies. He believed they revealed an unhealthy wish to find the world congenial to and supportive of our human values, desires, and hopes. Freud asserts, quite beyond doubt, that the *world* has no meaning. That does not, however, prevent him from producing his own quite remarkable and imaginative vision—in *Civilization and Its Discontents*—of those primal forces at work in the world that, it turns out, are to guide our behavior.

As Freud sees it, everything is ruled by two cosmic forces: what he calls Eros, or the life-instinct, and Thanatos, or death-instinct. The latter is the drive to aggressive destructiveness. Freud describes our condition dramatically:

> And now, I think, the meaning of the evolution of civilization is no longer obscure to us. It must present the struggle between Eros and Death, between the instinct of life and the instinct of destruction, as it works itself out in the human species. This struggle is what all life essentially consists of, and the evolution of civilization may therefore be simply described as the struggle for life of the human species. And it is this battle of the giants that our nursemaids try to appease with their lullaby about Heaven.[26]

Freud realizes, of course, that civilization is imperiled by the aggressive death-instinct. As he sees it, the only means that civilization can employ to inhibit socially destructive Thanatos is to turn aggression toward others into aggression against the self:

> His aggressiveness is introjected, internalized; it is, in point of fact, sent back to where it came from—that is, it is directed towards his own ego. There it is taken over by a portion of the ego, which sets itself over against the rest of the ego as **superego**, and which now, in the form of "conscience," is ready to put into action against the ego the same harsh aggressiveness that the ego would have liked to satisfy upon other, extraneous individuals. The tension between the harsh superego and the ego that is subjected to it, is called by us the sense of guilt. . . . Civilization, therefore, obtains mastery over the individual's dangerous desire for aggression by weakening and disarming it . . .[27]

In Freud's vision, civilization is purchased at the heavy price of individual neurotic illness, that is, aggression toward one's own self. In this somber view, human ethical activity is fundamentally pathological.

Our brief discussion of Freud can serve to alert us to the fact that mythic visions of nature's order or our human plight are not foreign to our present scientific culture. They can be found lurking, often unconsciously, in the background of what purports to be scientific claims, or at least claims free of religious or metaphysical assumptions.

While traditional religious cosmogonies do, quite naturally, fail to meet our scientific explanations, some ancient cosmogonic mythic conjectures are surprisingly, though quite coincidentally, similar to modern geological and cosmological theories. Both the Egyptians and the Incas believed, for example, that the Earth was a creation of the sun. Anaxagoras spoke of the heavenly bodies "breaking off" from a revolving mass of hot matter. The ancient Mesopotamian cosmogony spoke, as do modern evolutionists, of life beginning in the abysmal ocean.

It is also true that today there are theoretical physicists and cosmologists who are raising interesting questions about design and purpose (teleology; Greek *telos*, "end" or "goal") in the universe. In so doing they have posed some important religious and theological issues. One example will suffice to show this renewed interest in the religious dimensions of current cosmogonic speculation, namely, what some physicists call the *anthropic principle*.[28]

## The Anthropic Principle

Simply put, this principle refers to the recognition by some physicists of the extraordinary fine-tuning observed and required to explain our natural world as we know it.

This fine-tuning entails a convergence of many constraints and constants in our universe's beginnings that were required for the emergence of our particular world. And this convergence of constants appears to defy all probabilities. One such cosmological constant is hydrogen. If this constant had been slightly smaller, hydrogen would have been the only element in the universe; hence life would not have emerged, since life is impossible without some hydrogen being converted to carbon by fusion. If the constant were slightly larger, hydrogen would have converted to helium, the result being no enduring formation of stars which are essential to the emergence of life. Similarly, if the electromagnetic structural constraint had been smaller, the stars would have burned out too soon to allow life; if larger, the stars would not be at sufficiently warm temperatures to maintain life as we know it. And so on.

This amazing fine-tuning has led a number of scientists to consider anew the possibility of a "designed" universe, challenging a long-standing contention (for example, of the Darwinians) that our world emerged as a mere random evolutionary possibility among others, a universe without direction or purpose. The famous astrophysicist Stephen Hawking, author of *A Brief History of Time*, writes that "the odds against a universe like ours emerging out of something like the Big Bang are enormous"; he continues, "I think there are clearly religious implications."[29] The astronomer Fred Hoyle, popularizer of the Big Bang theory of cosmic beginnings, goes further: "I believe," Hoyle writes, "that we are the emergence of software that has basically been designed *by another intelligence*, probably to represent itself. In a way, software is the soul."[30]

Some proponents of the anthropic principle insist that beings similar in complexity to our human race were potentially realizable from the beginning and, therefore, it is quite natural to expect such beings to evolve at some point in time. Against evolutionary biologists, such as Jacques Monod, who proclaims that this universe is a meaningless accident, the Nobel Prize biologist Christian de Duve writes,

> My reason for seeing the universe as meaningful lie in what I perceive as its built-in necessities. . . . It gives chance the same role, but acting within such a stringent set of constraints as to produce life and mind obligatorily, not once but many times. To Monod's famous statement "The universe was not pregnant with life, nor the biosphere with man," I reply: "You are wrong. They were."[31]

There were, so it is argued, inbuilt teleological tendencies in the evolution of life, including human life, in this universe—tendencies that beg for some metaphysical explanation.

Although the physicist Freeman Dyson acknowledges that this finely wrought "architecture of the universe" does not prove the existence of God, he, too, believes that it is consistent with the hypothesis that *mind* plays an essential role in its functioning.[32]

It is important to point out that those scientists who see the anthropic principles as an impressive idea do regard it as a *hypothesis,* but one raising important scientific and religious questions. It does not offer proof of the existence of the God of Western monotheism. Nonetheless, these scientists maintain that the anthropic principle can be viewed as *consistent* with a theistic worldview. And, for some religious persons, this new development in cosmological theory reinforces the scientific credibility of a theistic vision of the cosmos.

One can conclude that none of the hypotheses regarding the random chance, or necessity, or design of our universe are experimentally testable; design does, however, appear as plausible as the other explanations. Three fundamental questions of cosmology appear to be beyond the scope of physical science: (1) Why is there a universe at all?; (2) Why are the regularities in nature amenable to our human comprehension through physical laws?; and (3) Why have the regularities and laws of nature taken the *particular* improbable form that they do (the issue posed by the anthropic principle)? All of these appear to require the resort to metaphysical modes of thinking.[33]

A final consideration: The attempt to harmonize the *mythic* cosmogonies of the past with modern scientific cosmogony is not a fruitful endeavor. The attempt to do so has often discredited religion in the minds of many. The conflict between science and religion has, unfortunately, been rekindled through the attempt, by those who espouse **Creation Science**, to legally require the teaching of the biblical account of Creation *as science* in science courses in the public schools. On examination, the creation scientists' argument appears strangely negative. Rather than offering compelling reasons as to how a scientist might establish a comprehensive *scientific* explanation of cosmology based on the Genesis account of a *divine, miraculous Creation,* the creationists simply attempt to show that the received scientific view of evolution (for example, Darwinism) faces a number of serious problems. These are especially associated with the mechanism of Darwinian natural selection and with the gaps in the fossil record, which raises questions about the gradual development of new forms of life. The argument seems to be this: If the scientists cannot agree on the details of evolution, then divine Creation must be a preferable *scientific* theory.

The scientific community has, perhaps, contributed to popular questioning of evolution by long conveying the impression that Darwinian evolution is a sufficient and incontestable hypothesis. As one historian of science has commented,

> Clearly evolution is not a "fact" in the sense that the man in the street understands the word. . . . A scientific theory is not a fact; it is a working hypothesis of great explanatory power employed because it continues to guide research along fruitful lines. . . . If ordinary people can be persuaded to adopt this more sophisticated view of scientific activity, they will realize that evolutionists cannot be expected to answer all the questions put to them. They will also realize that a decision to abandon evolutionism in favor of creationism could be justified if creationism shows that it can be elaborated into a comprehensive explanatory system that can serve as a better guide to research.[34]

As it turns out, Creation Science is not a science but a religious belief of a very specific kind. Members of the Creation Research Council acknowledge subscribing to a statement of faith committing them to belief in special, miraculous creation; to a worldwide Noahic Flood, and to opposition to evolution as being contrary to the teaching of the Bible. It is difficult to see how these creation scientists can describe their methodology as scientific if they start with several extrascientific conclusions and refuse to change them, regardless of any possible evidence to the contrary. Furthermore, since it is clear that biblical Creation is a particular religious belief, there is no reason why it, rather than the Japanese or the Babylonian account of creation, should be singled out to be taught in U.S. public schools—in view of the constitutional separation of church and state.

After reading this chapter, we should be wary of any claim that there is only one or, at most, two possible "models" of cosmogony. Scientific evolution can teach us much but so, in different ways, can those mythopoeic accounts that we have explored in this chapter. They can provide us with profound insights into the human moral and spiritual world. They are not scientific; they are poetry and myth but, as such, are uniquely able to illuminate dimensions of our existence. Human beings not only are interested in giving scientific explanations but also have engaged and continue to engage in value judgments about the meaning and significance of the natural and social world and the cosmic process itself.

## NOTES

1. Mircea Eliade, *Myth and Reality* (London, 1964), 5–6.
2. Ibid., 33.
3. The following discussion is dependent on S. G. F. Brandon's essay, "The Dawning Concept of Creativity," in *Creation Legends of the Ancient Near East* (London, 1963).
4. James B. Pritchard ed., *Ancient Near Eastern Texts Relating to the Old Testament* (Princeton, N.J., 1955), 3–4.
5. Ibid., 3.
6. Robert E. Hume, ed. and trans., *The Thirteen Principal Upanishads* (London, 1971), 214–15, 241.
7. W. G. Aston, trans., *Nihongi,* I. (Yokohama, Japan, 1896), 1ff.
8. Ibid.
9. Quoted in D. C. Holtom, *The National Faith of Japan* (New York, 1965), 116.
10. *Teacher's Manual of National History for Primary Schools* (Tokyo, 1931), 1–6. Cited in Holtom, *National Faith of Japan,* 128–29, 131–32.
11. Pritchard, *Ancient Near Eastern Texts,* 7.
12. Pritchard, *Ancient Near Eastern Texts,* 61.
13. Ibid., 65.
14. Ibid., 68.
15. Ibid.
16. Ibid., 69.
17. David L. Hall, "Process and Anarchy—A Taoist Vision of Creativity," *Philosophy East and West* 28 (1978): 276.
18. Ibid., 278.
19. F. M. Cornford, *Plato's Cosmology: The "Timaeus" of Plato Translated with a Running Commentary* (London, 1937), 33.
20. Adrian Recinos, trans., *The Popal Vuh.* Cited in Sproul, *Primal Myths* (London, 1980), 289–90.
21. The parallelism is taken from S. H. Hooke, *In The Beginning* (Oxford, 1947), 21.
22. See Douglas A. Knight, "Cosmogony and Order in Hebrew Tradition," *Cosmogony and Ethical Order,* ed. Robin W. Lovin and Frank E. Reynolds (Chicago, 1985), 133ff.
23. *Mahapurana.* Cited in W. Theodore de Bary, ed., *Sources of Indian Tradition* I (New York, 1966), 76–78.
24. *Majjhima Nikaya* I, 1966. Cited in Kenneth Morgan, ed., *The Path of the Buddha* (New York, 1956), 18.
25. Ibid., 19.
26. Sigmund Freud, *Civilization and Its Discontents* (New York, 1961), 77.
27. Ibid., 78.
28. The scientific discussions of the anthropic principle are highly technical and the principle has variations. See, e.g., J. D. Barrow and F. J. Tipler, *The Anthropic Cosmological Principle* (Oxford, 1988). For less technical discussions, see Nancey Murphy and George F. R. Ellis, *On the Moral Nature of the Universe: Theology, Cosmology, and Ethics* (Minneapolis, 1996), Chap. 3.
29. Stephen Hawking, quoted in John Boslough, *Stephen Hawking's Universe* (New York, 1985), 121.
30. "An Astronomer Sees the Light," interview with Fred Hoyle, *New Scientist,* 21 (November 1983): 49. Hoyle's "cosmic designer" is an impersonal intelligence,

not the personal intelligence of monotheism; it is, nevertheless, transcendent of the elements and forces that make up the physical universe.

31. Christian de Duve, *Vital Dust* (New York, 1995).

32. Freeman Dyson, *Disturbing the Universe* (New York, 1979).

33. For a good analysis of this point, see Nancey Murphy and George F. R. Ellis, *On the Moral Nature of the Universe: Theology, Cosmology, and Ethics* (Minneapolis, 1996), Chap. 3.

34. Peter Bowler, *Evolution: The History of an Idea* (Berkeley, Calif., 1984), 341–42.

## KEY WORDS

| | |
|---|---|
| cosmogony | Anaxagoras |
| Re-Atum | *Nous* |
| *Kojiki* and *Nihongi* | Plato's cosmology (*Timaeus*) |
| Izanagi and Izanami | Demiurge |
| Amaterasu | the Forms |
| *Enuma elish* | Priestly (P) writer |
| Ti'amat | Jahwist (J) and the Elohist (E) writers |
| Marduk | Jainism |
| Taoist cosmogony | the Anthropic principle |
| *creatio ex nihilo* | Creation Science |

## REVIEW QUESTIONS

1. What practical concerns of human beings might have contributed to the creation of cosmogonic myths? Can you give examples of such concerns expressed in some of the cosmogonies described in this chapter?

2. How does a cosmology of emergence from a primal substance differ from a cosmology based on the union of a primal male and female?

3. How might the cosmogonic myths in the Japanese *Kojiki* and *Nihongi* have affected later Japanese society?

4. In what specific ways is the Babylonian *Enuma elish* creation story an example of creation by conflict and the ordering of chaos?

5. Is creation by a divine craftsman the same as creation by decree or creation from nothing? How, if at all, do they differ?

6. What significant features of the natural world, human life, and God are reflected in the Genesis account of creation?

7. Why do some religions, such as the Jain religion in India, reject cosmogonic speculation?

8. Recent scientific discussion has renewed interest in the religious aspects of cosmology. What is the anthropic principle and what is its religious significance?

9. The movement called Creation Science claims that the biblical account of creation in Genesis should be taught *as science* in public schools. Do you agree? Why or why not?

## SUGGESTIONS FOR FURTHER READING

ANDERSON, BERNHARD W. *Creation versus Chaos: The Reinterpretation of the Mythical Symbolism in the Bible*. New York: Association Press, 1967.

———, ed. *Creation in the Old Testament*. Philadelphia: Fortress Press, 1984.

BRANDON, S. C. F. *Creation Myths of the Ancient Near East*. London: Hodder and Stoughton, 1963.

ELIADE, MIRCEA. *Gods, Goddesses, and Myths of Creation*. New York: Harper & Row, 1974.

FRANKFORT, H., H. A. FRANKFORT, ET AL. *Before Philosophy: The Intellectual Adventure of Ancient Man*. Harmondsworth, Middlesex: Penguin Books, 1951.

GIRARDOT, N. J. *Myth and Meaning in Early Taoism: The Theme of Chaos*. Berkeley: University of California Press, 1983.

GUTHRIE, W. K. C. *In the Beginning: Some Greek Views of the Origin of Life and the Early State of Man*. Ithaca, N.Y.: Cornell University Press, 1957.

LINCOLN, BRUCE. *Myth, Cosmos, and Society: Indo-European Themes of Creation and Destruction*. Cambridge, Mass.: Harvard University Press, 1986.

LONG, CHARLES. *Alpha: Myths of Creation*. New York: Collier Books, 1963; Scholars Press, 1983.

LOVIN, ROBIN W., AND FRANK E. REYNOLDS, eds. *Cosmogony and Ethical Order*. Chicago: Chicago University Press, 1985.

PRITCHARD, JAMES B., ed. *Ancient Near Eastern Texts Relating to the Old Testament*. Princeton, N.J.: Princeton University Press, 1950.

SPROUL, BARBARA C. *Primal Myths: Creating the World*. London: Rider, 1980.

*On modern scientific cosmology and the anthropic principle, see*

ALEXANDER, DENIS, *Rebuilding the Matrix: Science and Faith in the 21st Century*. Oxford: Lion, 2001.

BARBOUR, IAN G. *Religion and Science: Historical and Contemporary Issues*. San Francisco: Harper and Row, 1997, Chap. 8.

REES, MARTIN. *Before the Beginning. Our Universe and Others*. Reading, Mass.: Addison-Wesley, 1997, Chap. 15.

# 9

# *Anthropology: The Human Problem*

## Overview

In this chapter, we will explore the ways in which religious traditions understand the root of the human problem. While we may seriously disagree on the cause of human ignorance, distress, and strife, most human beings agree that life is not what it should be. We are often overwhelmed by a sense of our own weakness and inadequacy, by feelings of hostility and estrangement, or by a profound disquiet provoked by shame, moral guilt, and failure. We seek enlightenment, reconciliation, forgiveness, and peace.

We begin by looking briefly at some modern, secular theories and asking whether they have probed the human problem at its deepest level. We then turn to four classic diagnoses of the human problem—the Stoic, the Christian, the Buddhist, and the Confucianist—and discuss each one in some detail. While they are strikingly different, each one insists that the cause of the human problem and its cure can be understood only in terms of the human self's relation to a primordial or ultimate sacred order.

As you think about these alternative accounts of the human problem, keep in mind certain questions about what is at stake. What are the assumptions concerning the self, human nature, and human freedom—for example, about the human capacity to know the truth or the good and to do it? Are different conceptions of nature and of deity, or the ultimate, reflected in these contrasting views of the human problem and the true goal of human existence, that is, in their accounts of salvation or enlightenment? Conceptions of the human problem are usually inextricably related to beliefs about cosmogony and about deity, or the ultimate.

## odern Views of Our Human Plight

In 1961, Richard Alpert was a young, up-and-coming professor of psychology at Harvard University. He was, by any measure, a success. Suddenly, his life, despite its outward glitter, turned empty and meaningless. This is how he described his situation:

> I had an apartment in Cambridge that was filled with antiques and I gave charming dinner parties. I had a Mercedes-Benz sedan and a Triumph and a Cessna 172 airplane and an MG sportscar. But I felt that something was wrong with my world and that all the stuff I was teaching was just like little molecular bits of stuff, but they didn't add up to a feeling of wisdom.[1]

Alpert tried LSD, but he said it was like coming into the kingdom of heaven and then being cast out again and again. He began to feel depressed. He gave up drugs, went to India to study under a guru, and found deep spiritual insight. He changed his name to Ram Dass and became "a new man." Now, we might say that Richard Alpert was simply one of those overdriven, discontented intellectuals, but the fact is that other examples come easily to mind—middle-aged corporate executives, for instance, whose lives suddenly turn empty and who begin to question the mad scramble for wealth and power. Why are we humans so driven to seek pleasure, status, and knowledge and yet so frequently disappointed and anxious? The answer has to do with the fact that we are self-transcendent and therefore are insatiable in our desires and never fully satisfied with those temporal aspirations that prove precarious, transient, and ultimately negligible. Because we are spiritual as well as biological creatures, we are a problem to ourselves.

A number of modern secular theorists have probed the human problem and have tried to discover the reasons for our persistent anxiety and alienation. Karl Marx argued that we are alienated and unhappy because, in an industrial, capitalist society, our work and the objects we produce are alien to us. Humans are estranged and miserable, according to Marx, because they find no satisfaction in their productive work. This may be true, as far as it goes, but we have to wonder whether Marx touches the human problem at its deepest level.

As we have seen, Sigmund Freud perceived human unhappiness and neuroses in the discontent brought about by the conflict between the individual's drive to express his or her libidinal, erotic energies and the frustrating demands of society and civilization that thwart those essential drives. Freud's rather antisocial characterization of human nature is similar, in this respect, to Konrad Lorenz's theory of innate human aggression, as proposed in his book *On Aggression*. Both Freud and Lorenz hold out guarded hope for the future of humanity, based on our ability to exercise those rational capacities that just might redirect our aggressive antisocial behavior along more socially constructive lines. However, whether reason is the cause or the cure of our seemingly intractable problem has been questioned by some of the great religions, as we shall see.

Whatever the cause of our unease and strife, few thoughtful persons would deny that we humans have, over the millennia, sensed a tragic flaw, a falling short of our potential, a missing the mark of life as it was meant to be or should be. Something, we feel, is "out of joint." We recognize that we are ignorant, estranged, anxious, or morally guilty, and are in need of enlightenment, reconciliation, salvation, or atonement. And so we ask, "What is it about human consciousness and behavior that causes us such unrest and suffering? What is it that can free us from this tragic plight?" To provide answers to these questions is a primary function of the world's religions. The differing views of human nature that these religions propose naturally result in different conclusions about the character of the problem and the variety of prescriptions for its cure.

The classical Greek philosophers saw humankind's problem as essentially ignorance. According to Plato, virtue—and, therefore, happiness—is a matter of the exercise of intellect and is to be found in a knowledge of what is perfect and unchanging, rather than in mere appearances or opinion. The individual, therefore, must be brought out of the shadowy cave of ignorance and into the light of knowledge and truth. In *The Republic*, Plato offers his blueprint for a perfect state. Since only the highly educated have attained true knowledge and can discern truth from opinion, it is they who must rule if social harmony is to be secured. "There will be no end to the troubles of states, or of humanity itself," writes Plato, "till philosophers become kings in this world, or till those we now call kings and rulers really and truly become philosophers" (*Republic*, 473).

*Plato's* prescription for humankind's ills is called *rationalism* because he assumes that the solving of our problems lies in overcoming ignorance and in acquiring knowledge *and* virtue through the employment of reason. He further assumes that human nature is capable of discerning the unchanging Truth from what is relative and perhaps self-serving, and that humans are able to act virtuously once the nature of true virtue is understood. For Plato and all rationalists, reason is redemptive.

While offering very different solutions, both classical Chinese Confucianism and contemporary Marxism would say that the human problem lies in unnatural, corrupt, or alienated social relationships. We are essentially "what we eat"; that is, we are products of our habits and our social relations. While we are basically human-hearted and social, we are nevertheless corrupted by false habits and relations. By returning to the way of the ancients or, in the case of Marxism, to truly productive relationships—that is, by a reorganization of society as we now know it—envy, acquisitiveness, strife, and suffering will be largely rectified, if not eliminated.

Judaism and, more particularly, Christianity see the genesis of the human problem neither in ignorance nor in unnatural social relations as such, for these are more fundamentally traceable to a hardened heart and a sinful will. The problem is rooted in our rebellion against and disobedience of God's will. Our redemption and reconciliation can come only through confession of our moral guilt and through repentence and conversion, or the turning of the will from self to God.

Buddhism's answer to the human problem is perhaps the most radical of all because it sees the self as, in fact, illusory and this deception as the source of human suffering and social unrest. According to Buddhism, our illusion about a permanent self is the root of our craving and egoistic desire, and hence of our unease and pain. Only by the rigorous adoption of a spiritual discipline can we hope to achieve that enlightenment by which egoistic craving is overcome, desire stilled, and peace achieved.

Every religion, of course, holds some conviction about life and its predicament, even if only unconsciously and inarticulately. Here, we select four distinct and explicit theories of human nature and the source of the problem to illustrate the range of possibilities. Our examples are taken from Stoicism, Christianity, Theravada Buddhism, and Confucianism.

## Stoicism

*Stoicism* was founded by Zeno about the year 306 B.C.E. in Athens. The golden age of Greece and of Athens was past by then. The noble order of independent Greek city-states had fallen before the military empire of Alexander and his generals. The old moral guides and confidence were now gone. There was need of a new philosophy and religion for the Hellenistic age, one that could stand firm against the rising chaos. Until the coming and triumph of Christianity, Stoicism filled that role.

The burning question for Greco-Roman society remained the ethical one: How persons should live, because to many it appeared that human hopes and plans were at the mercy of impersonal, unpredictable forces. Chance, the great god Tyche, seemed to rule the world. And Tyche was a capricious deity, lifting people to the heights one day and dashing their hopes the next. Men and women saw themselves as playthings of fate, of powers outside their control. This world may be our only home, but it appeared to many to be an alien, even a hostile, place. For the educated Greek, Stoicism offered a noble response to this sense of fatedness, a means of spiritual liberation in a time of historical uncertainty and change.

According to Stoicism, this world is not a meaningless chaos, as we might surmise; on the contrary, the world is an ordered whole, governed and permeated by a Divine Reason, Law, or God. The evolutionary process is not chaotic, the Stoics argued, but is under the rule of a Divine Purpose by which all things—from the smallest worm to the human intellect—are governed. The Stoics called this law of growth *Phusis,* or Nature. *Phusis* is what shapes living things into their perfect form, and each thing is a germ or spark of this *Divine Logos* or Reason. The Stoics viewed the world pantheistically as a divine organism, each thing a microcosm of the animating, germinating Divine Reason. To live according to nature is to live according to this Divine Nature, or God.

Since we are a part or a spark of the Divine, the nature of the ethical life is clear. Goodness is living in accordance with Nature, or fitting our aims and conduct so they may be in accord with Divine Reason. The Stoics insisted that happiness cannot be found in the pursuit of pleasure, because pleasure often means the rule of passion over reason. Personal happiness can come only when we adjust our hopes and actions to the laws of Nature. To do otherwise is to resist the inevitable—and to be miserable. If evil befalls a person, it is, after all, only temporary; indeed, seen in the long run, it is not even evil because all events are but parts of a larger Whole.

The Stoic was thereby able to accept dispassionately both pain and pleasure, poverty and fortune, and health and sickness. The human soul, being a spark of the divine, has the same freedom as God. Therefore, it can act either with or against Nature, or God. However, to act against Nature is to court disaster, for true freedom is to live according to Nature. Freedom is not the rejection of all restraints; that is simply license. On the contrary, true freedom is the voluntary acceptance of the natural law, Reason or Fate, that must be obeyed whether we will to or not. "The Fates," writes Seneca, "lead him who is willing; they constrain him who is unwilling." The Stoics teach that a person must accept the apparent adversities of life and bad fortune—such as bereavement, pain, poverty, and death—because every person, although a slave or poor, can be spiritually free. Death is, of course, inevitable and therefore must be accepted calmly as Nature's law. So writes the great Stoic philosopher *Epictetus:*

> We act very much as if we were on a voyage. What can I do? I can choose out the helmsman, the sailors, the day, the moment. Then a storm arises. What do I care? I have fulfilled my task: another has now to act, the helmsman. Suppose even the ship goes down. What have I to do then? I do only what lies within my power, drowning if drown I must, without fear, not crying out or accusing heaven, for I know that what is born must needs also perish. For I am not immortal, but a man, a part of the universe as an hour is part of the day. Like the hour I must be here and like an hour pass away. What matters it then to me how I pass . . . for by some such means I must needs pass away.[2]

According to the Stoics, true goodness, and thus happiness, is to know that we must live according to Nature or, to put it another way, to recognize the difference between what lies within our nature or power and what lies beyond it. Things that lie outside our nature must be of no concern. Such "externals" are to be regarded with indifference, with *apatheia,* since we cannot control them. Now, such things as our physical appearance, our mental gifts, our ethnicity, our nationality, and, of course, death itself lie outside our control, and thus it is folly to fret and fuss about them.

The wise person, therefore, sees the vanity of much worldly, human striving since so much that happens lies outside our capacity to change or is merely temporary and passing. The great Stoic emperor Marcus Aurelius counseled the following:

> Think often on the swiftness with which things that exist and are coming into existence are swept past us and carried out of sight . . . all is as a river in ceaseless flow. . . . Is he not senseless who in such an environment puffs himself up, or is distracted or frets as over a trouble lasting and far reaching?[3]

On brief reflection, it would appear that the counsel of *apatheia* conflicts with the Stoic appeal to civic duty. How can we work diligently for the welfare of humanity if so much of our effort is, in the long run, vain striving? Why work to increase our wealth and prosperity if worldly goods are in themselves worthless and to be regarded with indifference? The Stoic reply is forthright: Every created thing, from the acorn to the cobbler to the king, is created for a function, a purpose. Nature shapes everything to achieve its form or end—for example, the end of the acorn is to be an oak tree.

> A good bootmaker is one who makes good boots; a good shepherd is one who keeps his sheep well; and even though good boots are, in the Day of Judgment sense, entirely worthless . . . yet the good bootmaker or good shepherd must do his work well or he will cease to be good. To be good he must perform his function; and in performing that function there are certain things that he must "prefer" to others, even though they are not really good. He must prefer a healthy sheep or a well-made boot to their opposites. It is thus that Nature, or Phusis, herself works when she shapes the seed into the tree, or the blind puppy into the good hound. The perfection of the tree or hound is in itself indifferent, a thing of no ultimate value. Yet the goodness of Nature lies in working for that perfection.[4]

Epictetus taught that life is like a drama or a game. The role of the actor or the athlete is to play the part well, no matter whether the play is insignificant or the game is lost:

> Remember that you are an actor in a play, and the Playwright chooses the manner of it: if he wants it short, it is short; if long, it is long. If he wants you to act a poor man you must act the part with all your powers; and so if your part be a cripple or a magistrate or a plain man. For your business is to act the character that is given you and act it well; the choice of the cast is Another's.[5]

The person capable of cultivating *apatheia* is free and thus happy; no "externals" can assail her or him, neither poverty nor riches, neither health nor sickness. It is, finally, the way we take things that make them good or evil.

What disturbs our minds, according to Epictetus, is not events but the view we take of events. For instance, death is nothing dreadful, or else Socrates would have thought it so. The only dreadful thing about death is our judgment that it is dreadful. The person who achieves this knowledge, who cultivates indifference to externals, is a wise man or woman and is freed of anxiety, fear, envy, and desire.

Stoicism sees the human problem as rooted in ignorance. The cure it proposes is essentially naturalistic and psychological because the healing of human distress is achieved by knowledge, by self-education, and by the attainment of wisdom. The Stoic expects no change in external conditions; liberation involves a change of mental and emotional viewpoint, not a change of the world. There will not be any reward for Stoic self-sacrifice and its contempt for pleasure by a promise of recompense in another life or in another world—which, the Stoic would say, is only to postpone the pleasure for a time. To follow Nature or God suffices for the Stoic. "Shall not the fact," writes Epictetus, "that we have God as maker and father and kinsman relieve us from pains and fears?"

The Stoics' noble and selfless creed was admired by many of the early Christian Fathers, including St. John Chrysostom and St. Augustine. Epictetus's *Enchiridion* was adapted for monastic life in the Middle Ages. But, as we will see, the Christian diagnosis of the human condition, its problem, and its solution is strikingly different.

## Christianity

The Christian view of human nature and the human predicament is rooted in the biblical portrayal of man and woman, especially as it is found in the early chapters of the Book of Genesis. To be human, according to Christianity, is to be in a sense both angel and devil. Pascal called us "a monster, a chimera, the glory and the shame of the universe." This paradoxical vision of what it is to be human may be clarified by a brief analysis of the story of the Creation and human Fall in Genesis.

The first thing that is evident in Genesis 1–2 is the fact that man (the Hebrew *ha'adam* means man in the generic sense of humankind or human being) is a finite creature. Being human does not entail any notion that we are naturally divine or immortal. "The Lord God formed man of dust from the ground, and breathed into his nostrils the breath of life, and man became a living being" (Genesis 2:7). Human life is *created* and therefore is derivative and dependent. Human beings do not choose life, and they cannot prevent its end in death. God has the power over human breath—life and death are, according to the Bible, "in God's hands." To be human, then, is to be a part of nature, created from the dust of the earth to which we will return. Human life does not have an existence in and of itself; life is a gift of God.

While human life entails radical finitude and dependence, it is not for that reason worthless or evil. For, according to Genesis, God "saw everything that he had made, and behold, it was very good" (Genesis 1:31). There is nothing essentially evil about human creatureliness and finitude. The ancient Hebrew did not consider the body as distinct from or inferior to the soul or spirit, or evil as such. For the ancient Hebrew, there is no sharp dualism between the body and the soul, as we find in certain Hellenistic religions, for example, Gnosticism. To be human is to be "a living being," a psychosomatic (*psyche* means "soul" and *soma* means "body") unity. Finite human life is declared good.

Not only is human existence good but also, according to Genesis, humankind is given a unique place in God's creation. Humanity is the crown and the glory of God's work. This is indicated by the fact that "God created man in his own image, in the image of God he created him; male and female he created them" (Genesis 1:27). To be created "in the image and likeness of God" is to be given a unique status, one in which all creation is placed under human dominion:

> And God blessed them, and God said to them, "Be fruitful and multiply, and fill the earth and subdue it; and have dominion over the fish of the sea and over the birds of the air and over every living thing that moves upon the earth."
> —*(Genesis 1:28)*

Human dominion—or, better, vice-regency over creation—is further underlined by the fact that we are called on to name all the animals, which in ancient Israel implied a power and authority over what is named.

Human life is given a unique status in the biblical cosmogony. Man and woman are *like* God—but they are *not* God. It is just this "likeness" that is humanity's glory; but it is also the root of the human problem. The human "image and likeness" is the source of the temptation to play God, and thus to rebel against God. From the early years of Christianity until the time of the Protestant Reformation, theologians saw the image of God (the *imago Dei*) as essentially present in the human exercise of *reason*. Roman Catholic theology has traditionally distinguished between two conceptions of the human "likeness" to God. One has to do with those special supernatural endowments that are associated with sanctifying grace and that were lost as a result of the *Fall*. However, there is also the natural gift of reason, essential to what it means to be *homo sapiens* (like wisdom). Reason is intrinsic to our being human, and it is *not* lost in the Fall. This twofold nature of the *imago Dei* is described by a contemporary Roman Catholic philosopher in a summary of the teaching of the medieval theologian Thomas Aquinas:

> The quality of being the image of God is co-essential to man because it is one with the rationality of his nature. To be a mind is to be *naturally capable of knowing and loving God*. To be able to do this is one with the very nature of thinking. It is as natural for man to be the image of God as to be a rational animal, that is, as to be man. [But there is also a special supernatural endowment.] *The first effect of grace is, therefore, to perfect this resemblance of man to God* by divinizing his soul, his mind and consequently his whole nature. From the moment he has grace, man can love God with a love worthy of God since his love is divine in its origin. [Italics added.][6]

According to Roman Catholic teaching, our nature is "wounded" as a consequence of the Fall and thus susceptible to sin and evil; however, it is not so deep a wound as to destroy our natural human power of reason and free will.

Classical Protestant theology—for example, in the thought of Martin Luther and John Calvin—has rejected the Roman Catholic distinction between the two forms of the divine likeness and has claimed that the Fall did, indeed, involve the loss of something essential to human existence. According to Luther, the divine image that was lost in the Fall is *the freedom of the human will.* You can see how these opposing views of the image of God and the effects of sin would have important implications regarding the way to salvation (see Chapter 12).

In non-Roman Catholic Christianity, the *imago Dei* has been identified with unique human characteristics other than reason—for example, with human creativity, such as in the mastery of nature and in artistic genius, or in humanity's unique addressability or moral response and responsibility. One of the most compelling modern views of the *imago Dei* is the idea of human *self-transcendence.* It is most fully developed in the writings of the Protestant theologian Reinhold Niebuhr (1892–1971). According to Niebuhr, humans are unique in their capacity to stand clear of their actions, even their world, and to judge them from beyond the self. For example, humans alone write histories and conceive of systems of ultimate and universal value. The self is capable of transcending the processes of nature and even its own rationality:

> The human spirit has the special capacity of standing continually outside itself in terms of indefinite regression. . . . The rational capacity of surveying the world, of forming general concepts and analyzing the order of the world is thus but one aspect of what Christianity knows as "spirit." The self knows the world . . . because it stands outside both itself and the world, which means that it cannot understand itself except as it is understood from beyond itself and the world.[7]

Human self-transcendence involves self-determination or freedom, which is the key to genuine selfhood. Nevertheless, self-transcendence or self-determination is the source not only of human creativity, but also of human destructiveness. This is why, Niebuhr would argue, it is not possible to identify virtue with reason as such. Self-transcendence can make humans both saints and devils. Humans can be more deadly than the brute animals just because they can transmute the brute's instinctive will to survive into an egocentric will to power; that is, freedom allows humans, encompassed by natural limits, to attempt to defy those limits with infinite ambitions and pretensions. It is just this ambiguous situation that makes humans conscious of their vulnerability and insecurity and that leads to anxiety, the root and precondition of what Christianity calls *sin* or destructive self-assertion.

According to Christianity, sin is the human propensity to put our own egoistic interests at the center of things. This can be seen in the variety of ways Christianity has attempted to describe sin. In the Old Testament, sin is seen largely as a turning away from God, disobedience or distrust—a hardening of the human heart. The prophets thus saw sin as a straying from God, a faithlessness and a breaking of the Covenant that had been sealed at Mount

Sinai. The medieval theologians tended to see sin as less a turning away from God than a turning in, self-absorption. They called sin *concupiscence,* or lust. It was often associated with sexual or fleshly lust, but it should be seen as having a wider application. Concupiscence is also a lusting of the mind (for example, in the figure of Faust) or the spirit. It is a never-satisfied egoistic striving.

Christian theologians have seen all these forms of egoistic sin—disobedience, the hardening of the heart, concupiscence, and sensuality—as derived from and best described in terms of human *pride. St. Augustine* so defined sin:

> For "pride is the beginning of all sin." And what is pride but an appetite for in-ordinate exaltation. Now, exaltation is inordinate when the soul cuts itself off from the very Source to which it should keep close and somehow makes itself and becomes an end to itself. This takes place when the soul becomes inordinately pleased with itself.... and falls away from the unchangeable Good which ought to please the soul far more than the soul can please itself.[8]

Subsequently, St. Augustine's view of sin dominated Western orthodox Christianity, and we find the Protestant Reformers Luther and Calvin also describing sin in Augustinian terms as a self-love and a false confidence. Calvin writes of human sin:

> They worship not him, but a figment of their own brains in his stead. This depravity Paul expressly remarks: "Professing themselves to be wise, they become fools." He had before said "they become vain in their imaginations." But lest any should exculpate them, he adds that they were deservedly blinded, because not content with the bounds of sobriety, but arrogating to themselves more than was right, they willfully darkened and even infatuated themselves with pride, vanity and perverseness. Whence it follows, that their folly is inexcusable, which originates not only in a vain curiosity, but in false confidence, and in immoderate desire to exceed the limits of human knowledge.[9]

Christianity views sin as not primarily connected with the body or finitude but with the spirit—that is, associated with human freedom or, rather, with a perverted exercise of the human will or desire. So pervasive and inevitable (though not necessary) is sin that St. Augustine spoke of it as *original sin.* Augustine found explicit biblical warrant for viewing sin as an inevitable human defect in St. Paul's association of sin with Adam, the first man: "Therefore as sin came into the world through one man and death through sin, and so death spread to all men because all men sinned" (Romans 5:12). While sin is a certainty, in that no person can claim to be free of its taint, it is not necessary because, if it were, it would deny human responsibility. Augustine thus follows St. Paul in affirming sin's original or universal character while insisting on human responsibility: "So they are without excuse; for although they knew God they did not honor him as God or give thanks to him.... Claiming to be wise, they became fools"

Polish Roman Catholics at confession. Each person must confess his or her sins privately before the priest, who may prescribe certain penances before absolution of sin is given. (*Source*: Courtesy of Elliot Erwitt, Magnum Photos, Inc.)

(Romans 1:21–22). St. Augustine joins these two convictions of sin's inevitability and human moral responsibility in the following passage:

> Man's nature, indeed, was created at first faultless and without any sin; but that nature of man in which every one is born from Adam, now wants the Physician, because it is not sound. All good qualities, which it still possesses . . . it has of the Most High God, its Creator and Maker. But the flaw, which darkens and weakens all those natural goods, . . . it has not contracted from its blameless Creator—but from that original sin, which it committed by free will.[10]

St. Augustine maintains that sin condemns humankind to ignorance and prideful lust, and that sin is not merely a psychological state but a condition of being. This is the stark reality of the human predicament. Before the Fall of Adam, humans possessed both the ability not to sin (*posse non peccare*) and the ability to sin (*posse peccare*). But since the Fall, humans are capable only of the latter and are justly condemned to damnation. Traditional Christianity has consistently maintained that the cause of humanity's unease and tragic plight is an evil, disordered will, a turning to self rather than to God—and that humankind can do nothing to save or deliver itself from this bondage to sin and the sting of death. Only God's grace, freely bestowed, can redeem and liberate the self from its sin. This is expressed by St. Augustine at the conclusion of the passage cited above:

> The grace, however, of Christ, without which neither infants nor adults can be saved, is not bestowed for any merits, but is given *freely*, on account of which it is also called, *grace*.[11]

Many modern Christian theologians have rejected the Augustinian implication that every human inherits biologically not only the propensity to sin but also Adam's guilt. However, they, too, affirm the belief contained in the Adamic myth of the Fall: that we humans are all born into a social matrix of sinful pride and egoism. The individual cannot escape this tendency to sin and should not search for scapegoats in evil social institutions or in other persons—for example, Hitler. Christian theologians would insist that, while there surely is an inequality of personal guilt for evil, the taint of egoism is universal and every human is to some extent personally responsible for evil. Thus, while rejecting literal interpretations of St. Augustine's doctrine of the Fall and original sin, modern Christian thinkers maintain a belief in the universal reality of sin and the necessity of God's prior action or grace in freeing the individual of moral guilt. How Christianity, in both its Catholic and its Protestant forms, understands the ways to and the goal of redemption or salvation is discussed in Chapter 12.

## Theravada Buddhism

Buddhism has given the world a radical and an influential body of teachings regarding the human problem. *Siddhartha Gautama—the Buddha* (563?–483? B.C.E.), or enlightened one—lived in north India, the son of a ruler of the kingdom of the Sakyas. He taught how we should live in order to avoid pain and achieve supreme happiness and bliss, but knowledge of the right path requires that we know what is the true nature of human life and the truth about the processes of nature itself.

At the heart of Buddha's teaching is the Indian doctrine of *karma* (or *kamma* in Pali). The word means "action," "doing," or, more accurately, "volitional action." According to Buddhism, every living being exists by virtue of an individual force or energy peculiar to that being—the *karma* of each living thing. *Karma* is the way each being manifests itself in its own unique way and thus creates a self or personality. Now, our volition or action may be relatively good or bad. Good *karma* produces good "fruits," or effects, and bad *karma* produces bad effects. In every moment of a being's life, that individual is fashioning the life that will follow. Each being, the Buddha taught, is the architect of his or her own destiny: "The self is Lord of the self, who else is the Lord?" asked the Buddha.

The *law of karma* should not, however, be confused with the theistic idea of "moral justice," which implies a Supreme Being who metes out divine rewards and punishments. The law of *karma* is simply the law of cause and effect, and good and bad karma will continue to manifest themselves in another life after the death of this individual existence.

We have said that each being is an individual, something that is. It is more accurate, however, to say that Buddhism teaches that each being is a *becoming*, an event, a process. The cause of this process is *karma*. Every cause is the effect of a previous cause, world without beginning or end. Thus, Buddha taught what is called the "dependent origination" of all things. However, beings are not only in a state of becoming or process but also in a state of *compoundedness* and *conditionedness*. Every becoming is simply a compounded process that can be analyzed into the several elements or conditions of which it is composed. These elements are called *dhammas,* meaning that which "bears" certain qualities. According to Buddhism, these elements, which are both corporeal and mental, are found in five aggregates called **khandhas.** The *khandhas* are described as follows:

> The five aggregates together constitute what is called the "I" or "personality" or the "individual." The aggregates are not parts or pieces of the individual but phases or forms of development, something like the shape, color, and smell of a flower. . . . There is no "stuff" or substratum as such but only manifestations, energies, activities, processes. . . . Every living being, since it is a process, is described as a flux, a flowing, a stretching forth, a continuity, or, more frequently, as a combustion, a flame. There is no "substance," no "self" or "soul," underlying the process, unifying it.[12]

Buddhism teaches that nothing in reality corresponds to what we in the West call "I" or "self." The self is simply an abstraction of what, in fact, is a compoundedness of energies and activities. There is no enduring, substantial self beyond or underlying this aggregate of energy processes. This implies the Buddhist doctrine of **an-atta** (**an-atman** in Sanskrit), or the not-self. Buddha taught that what we call the enduring self, soul, or ego is in reality only an aggregate of phenomenal processes.

The not-self doctrine leads naturally from an analysis of the self or, rather, of its unreality, to the discussion of the human problem. According to Buddhism, the belief in a self is the indispensable condition for the emergence of suffering, which is the root of all unhappiness and sorrow. Buddha addressed the reality of suffering, and its cause and cure, in his famous sermon given near Benares immediately after his enlightenment. Because this discourse contains the **Four Noble Truths** that are the foundation of Buddha's *Dharma*—Truth or teaching—it is important that we quote the first part of the sermon in full:

> Thus have I heard: at one time the Lord dwelt at Benares at Isipatana in the Deer Park. There the Lord addressed the five monks:
> These two extremes, monks, are not to be practised by one who has gone forth from the world. What are the two? That conjoined with passions and luxury, low, vulgar, common, ignoble, and useless, and that conjoined with self-torture, painful, ignoble, and useless. Avoiding these two extremes the Tathagata ["one who has found the Truth," that is, Buddha] has gained the enlightenment of the Middle Path, which produces insight and knowledge and tends to calm, to higher knowledge, enlightenment, Nirvana.
> And what, monks, is the Middle Path? . . . This is the noble Eightfold Way, namely right view, right intention, right speech, right action, right livelihood,

right effort, right mindfulness, right concentration. This, monks, is the Middle Path . . .

1. Now this, monks, is the noble truth of pain [*dukkha*]: birth is painful, old age is painful, sickness is painful, death is painful, sorrow, lamentation, dejection and despair are painful. In short the five groups of grasping [*khandhas*] are painful.
2. Now this, monks, is the noble truth of the cause of pain [*tanhā*]: the craving, which tends to rebirth, combined with pleasure and lust, finding pleasure here and there, namely, the craving for passion, the craving for existence, the craving for non-existence.
3. Now this, monks, is the noble truth of the cessation of pain: the cessation without a remainder of craving, the abandonment, forsaking, release, non-attachment.
4. Now this, monks, is the noble truth of the way that leads to the cessation of pain: this is the Noble Eightfold Way.[13]

The First Noble Truth of the Buddha is the reality of *dukkha,* usually translated as pain or suffering. *Dukkha* should not, however, be understood simply as ordinary pain, sorrow, and suffering; it includes the deeper sense that imperfection and impermanence are constitutive of life. According to Buddha, whatever is impermanent is *dukkha,* and since nature itself is constituted by change and conditionedness, it is permeated by *dukkha.* Buddha insisted this includes the aggregates that make up the "individual": "The five aggregates of attachment are *dukkha.*"

*Dukkha* includes, then, the sense of impermanence, imperfection, and incompleteness that life exhibits—the persistent conflict between our desires and hopes and our actual attainments. It involves a sense of unease, of anxiety, of what the American writer Thoreau (1817–1862) described as our lives of "quiet desperation." Buddhism would contend that most of us try to minimize these unpleasant facts of life. Edward Conze refers to this tendency:

> Most of us are inclined by nature to live in a fool's paradise, to look on the brighter side of life, and to minimize its unpleasant sides. To dwell on suffering runs normally counter to our inclinations. Usually we cover up suffering with all kinds of "emotional curtains." . . . This is illustrated by the widespread use of "euphemisms" which is nothing but the avoidance of words that call up disagreeable associations. . . . A man does not "die," but he "passes away," "goes to sleep" . . . etc.[14]

Conze suggests that a special effort of meditation is needed to realize the great amount of concealed suffering in what we unwittingly consider pleasant. For example, we frequently experience pleasure at the expense of others. Wealth, for instance, often is achieved at the expense of poverty-stricken laborers. Furthermore, pleasure is tied to unconscious anxiety because we are concerned about losing it—for example, wealth or youthful beauty. This is called "suffering from reversal." It is what the poet Shelley meant by "that unrest which men miscall delight." Buddha speaks of six occasions when suffering is present: birth; sickness; old age; the phobia of

Tibetan Buddhist *mandala* depicting the Wheel of Life, which symbolizes the causes of suffering. The black monster embracing the Wheel is Impermanence, which devours existence. (*Source:* Neg. #329316. Courtesy of the Department of Library Services, American Museum of Natural History.)

death; association with what we dislike or abhor, such as a personal weakness; and separation from what we love—for example, a friend, child, or a beloved environment.

Buddhists insist that to focus on *dukkha* is not to be pessimistic but, rather, to be *realistic*, to see things as they truly are. Only by facing the reality of *dukkha* can a person understand its cause and achieve its cessation. A Buddhist, they point out, is not gloomy and melancholy but is like the Buddha himself—serene, contented, and happy. However, before *dukkha* can be overcome it is essential to understand its cause. This is the Second Noble Truth.

When asked how "individuality" arises, Buddha replied by pointing to the Second Noble Truth, the cause of *dukkha:* It "is that craving [*tanhā*]," he said, "which gives rise to ever fresh rebirth and bound up with pleasure and lust, now here, now there, finds ever fresh delight."[15] ***Tanhā*** is thirst, craving, unsatisfied longing, a will to live that gives rise to and upholds the continuity of the ego or "self." Buddhists often describe *tanhā* by using the image of heat or a flame, a burning desire. However, it is important to realize that *tanhā* is not only egoistic craving for sense pleasure, wealth, or power. It is also a thirst for

> and attachment to ideas and ideals, views, opinions, theories, conceptions, and beliefs. According to the Buddha's analysis, all the troubles and strife in the world, from little personal quarrels in families to great wars between nations and countries, arise out of this selfish "thirst." From this point of view, all economic, political and social problems are rooted in this selfish "thirst."[16]

The Third Noble Truth is that there is liberation from suffering through a cessation of craving. Where there is no craving, there is no suffering. The goal of enlightenment, ***Nirvana,*** is known by the term *Tanhākkhaya,* or the "Extinction of Thirst." The Fourth Noble Truth is the truth of the Way leading to the cessation of suffering, of the ***Eightfold Path*** that leads to enlightenment and Nirvana. The Eightfold Path and the goal of Nirvana are discussed in Chapter 12.

Before we consider a fourth tradition, note that both Christianity and Buddhism see the human problem as rooted in anxiety and egoistic desire, although they hold radically different notions of the true nature of the "self." Also, as we will see in Chapter 12, Christianity requires a profoundly metaphysical solution—redemption through God's grace—to the human problem, while Theravada Buddhism renounces such a solution altogether. A very different conception of human nature and the human problem is found in Confucianism in traditional China.

## Confucianism

Confucianism's this-worldly, practical view of the human problem and its resolution have led some scholars to deny that Confucianism is in any proper sense a religion; rather, that it is merely a humanistic code of manners. But that view fails to appreciate the sacred dimension of China's ancient way. Confucius's fundamental doctrine of *li*—of social rite or ceremonial, the "rules of social propriety"—is perceived by Confucians as a sacred Rite or Way. *Li* involves the acquiring of a human virtue and power *consistent with the Mandate or Approval of Heaven.* It is heaven brought down to earth.

Confucianism is known in China as the "way of the ancients," or the "way of the sages," a rule of behavior that the pre-Communist Chinese assumed had existed from time immemorial. ***Confucius*** was not regarded as the founder of the "Way" but nevertheless was spoken of reverently as the First Teacher, foremost in rank among the ancient "sages." He saw himself, however, as only a "transmitter" of the "way of the ancients."

Confucius was born around 551 B.C.E. in the province of Lu (now Shantung) and died in 479. He spent most of his life as a tutor to the sons of the ruling class and never achieved his ambition of holding a high government position, whereby he might have put his precepts into practice. What we know of Confucius is largely derived from the *Analects,* or "Selected Sayings," written by him and his disciples. During the Sung Dynasty (960–1279 C.E.), the *Analects* and the *Book of Mencius* (written by a later idealistic Confucian) were added, among others, to the ancient, hallowed Six Classics.

What was the human problem that afflicted the China of Confucius's time, and what did he prescribe for its cure? The Master, as he was called, lived in a period of terrible social and political instability, resulting from the disintegration of the feudal society typical of the early Chou Dynasty (1122–249 B.C.E.). China was divided by a number of independent, warring states, each pursuing its own interest. Confucius believed that the solution to the incessant strife was a return to the Golden Age, to the social rites and the values of the earlier Chou rulers who, Confucius taught, had won the Mandate of Heaven because of their virtuous and peaceable ways. Confucius believed that a society perseveres through the instilling of a correct pattern of behavior. The pattern is exemplified in the lives of those in authority and is thereby passed on to others as a "pattern of prestige." Confucius devoted himself to transmitting this ancient Grand Harmony. "I transmit," he wrote, "but do not create. I have been faithful to and love antiquity."[17]

The Confucian sage Hsün Tzu (298–238 B.C.E.) also traced the human problem to an unrestrained pursuit of personal desire and to the undoing of the ancient rules of social propriety:

> Whence do the rules of decorum arise? From the fact that men are born with desires, and when these desires are not satisfied, men are bound to pursue their satisfaction. When the pursuit is carried on unrestrained and unlimited, there is bound to be contention. With contention comes chaos; with chaos dissolution. The ancient kings disliked this chaos and set the necessary limits by codifying rules of decorum and righteousness. ... It is through rites that Heaven and earth are harmonious. ... He who holds to the rites is never confused in the midst of multifarious change; he who deviates therefrom is lost.[18]

It follows from the Confucian analysis of the human problem that its cure lies in education. Assimilation of the ancient rites is the following of antique ways not simply for nostalgia's sake but rather for the specific purpose of modifying social conduct. Every aspect of life—the school, the theater, entertainments, public ceremonies, the lessons of history, and manners in the home—must be pressed into the service of nurturing the traditional values and patterns of behavior. The American social philosopher Walter Lippmann describes the social imperative of such a process and the dire consequences of its failure. Social life

> has to be transmitted from the old to the young, and the habits and the ideas must be maintained as a seamless web of memory among the bearers of the tradition, generation after generation. . . . When the continuity of the tradition of civility is ruptured, the community is threatened. Unless the rupture is repaired, the community will break down into factional . . . wars. For when the continuity is interrupted, the cultural heritage is not being transmitted. The new generation is faced with the task of rediscovering and reinventing and relearning by trial and error most of what [it] needs to know. . . . No generation can do that.[19]

According to Confucianism, learning is essentially the imitation of exemplary models, the teacher providing a direct, living model of virtuous behavior. Confucius therefore taught that "a gentleman . . . who associates with those who possess the Way and is rectified by them, may be said to be fond of learning."[20] It is evident that Confucianism is optimistic about human nature because it contends that every person has an innate capacity to learn virtue and that education should be available to all.* Moreover, it believes that persons of wisdom and virtue, from whom we can learn the way, are always to be found among us. "In the presence of a worthy man, think of equaling him. In the presence of a worthless man, turn your gaze within."[21]

It is critical, of course, that we associate with the wise and worthy and not with the unworthy person since our patterns of behavior are picked up, often unconsciously, from our environs. Therefore, it is important to live in the right locality. "It is humaneness which is the attraction of a neighborhood. If from choice a man does not dwell in the midst of humaneness, how can he attain to wisdom?"[22] Confucius would say that "man is what he does," that we are shaped by our actions and habits. For this reason, he saw ritual (*li*) as the foundation of the educative process.

The word *li*, usually translated "ritual," originally meant "to sacrifice" and had to do with ritual sacrifices in a religious context. Later, the word came to mean ceremonious activity on special secular occasions; finally, it came to be associated with the "social propriety" or decorum expected in all human relationships. The Confucian sages believe that social unrest and war are the result of a decline in social ritual and that its restoration will result in a harmonious social order. Ritual, they teach, humanizes our relationships; therefore, it is the essential means of governing a society. The ruler is the model from whom others take their cue:

> Yen Hui asked about humaneness. The Master said: "To subdue oneself and return to ritual is humane. If for one day a ruler could subdue himself and return to ritual, then all under Heaven would respond to the humaneness in him."[23]

---

*Confucius and Mencius held optimistic or Idealist views of human nature. However, Hsün Tze was a Realist and taught that "the nature of man is evil; his goodness is acquired training"—a product of moral learning.

The sage Confucius lecturing to his pupils, passing on the "way of the ancients" through precept as well as through his own example of virtuous living. (*Source: Courtesy of Howard Sochurck, Life* Magazine, © 1955 TimePix.)

A statement attributed to Confucius in the *Record of Rites* underlines the preeminent place he gave to ritual in the amelioration of human strife:

> Of all things to which the people owe their lives the rites are the most important. If it were not for the rites, they would have no means of regulating the services paid to the spirits of Heaven and Earth; if it were not for the rites, they would have no means of distinguishing the positions of ruler and subject, high and low, old and young; if it were not for the rites, they would have no means of differentiating the relations between male and female, between father and son, and between elder and younger brother, and of linking far and near by the ceremony of marriage.[24]

Westerners often are skeptical of the formality of oriental "bowing and scraping." We consider it perfunctory and rather inauthentic. However, this is to fail to recognize the true depths of Confucian ritual behavior. Beneath the seemingly excessive outward formality is a genuine inward and spiritual grace, the interrelation of action and sentiment. Ritual action shapes behavior and therefore character, and, in turn, character reinforces action. "Manners," the adage rightly declares, "make the man."

Confucius suggests a number of means by which *li* and the social virtues associated with "propriety" are to be advanced. One is the *rectification of names.* What Confucius meant by this term is linguistic clarity regarding the use of words—a clarity that issues in moral exactitude and order. Semantic confusion results when *li* is forsaken, because then we have "no means of differentiating the relations between male and female, between father and son," and so on. Confucius said that if names—for example, ruler, son, and elder brother—are not correct, then language cannot be in accord with the true nature of things. A father cannot be a true father or a son a true son. As long as our words are askew, our actions will be incorrect, and strife and unhappiness will prevail. In a stable social order, names must have clear meanings. It is necessary that we know what it means to be a father *and* that a father *be* a father. The Confucian gentleman is known to embody the supreme virtue of humaneness (*jen*), but Confucius says, "If a gentleman abandons humaneness, how can he fulfill the name?"[25]

Confucius considered the rectification of names to be the first order of government. When Duke Ching of Ch'i asked his advice about government, Confucius replied, "Let the prince be a prince, the minister a minister, the father a father, and the son a son."[26]

To govern means to rectify not only names, but also the realities to which they correspond. Confucius believed that true government begins, literally, at home. The regulation of the home depends on the cultivation of personal life. In turn, the ordering of national life is accomplished only by the humanizing of home life. Thus, a second means of advancing *li* and social order is through the ***Five Great Relationships.*** They have to do with the rights and responsibilities of ruler and subject, father and son, husband and wife, elder brother and younger brother, and elder and younger friends. At the heart of these relationships are the rules governing the family—the foundation of Confucian society. The key to the family is the child's respect for his or her parents, or ***filial piety.***

Confucianism demands the deference and respectful obedience of the young toward their elders, and especially toward their parents. The Chinese are surprised at the West's exaltation of youth and are horrified at our neglect of the aged. A Confucian son's obligations to his father are extraordinarily demanding, including a period of over two years of mourning and retirement from normal activities following the death of the father. In this regard, it is interesting to note that Confucianism did not reject ancestor worship, despite its this-worldly, practical approach to life. The ancestral shrine remained at the center of the Confucian home, a sign of family solidarity. Confucius regarded the moral discipline and example of filial piety as, once again, essential to government. When someone asked why he did not take part in government, Confucius replied,

> What does the *Book of History* say about filial piety? "Only be dutiful towards your parents and friendly towards your brothers, and you will be contributing to government."[27]

Confucius taught that the moral ideal is exemplified in the ***chun-tzu,*** the gentleman or superior person. It is he or she, and not the skillful administrative expert, who should hold the reins of government. The *chun-tzu*—poised, sincere, and adequate for every occasion—rules by *te*, the virtue and power of moral character. Confucius taught that the good society is achieved neither by law nor by physical power, but through the example of moral virtue and character. Confucius said,

> If you lead the people by means of regulations and keep order among them by means of punishments, they will be without conscience in trying to avoid them. If you lead them by virtue [*te*] and keep order among them by ritual [*li*], they will have a conscience and will reform themselves.[28]

The power of *te* is what we today might call *charisma* in the sense that it represents "the power of a specific person to accomplish his will directly and effortlessly through ritual, gesture, and incantation."[29] Confucius speaks of this in another aphorism in the *Analects*; "He who rules by means of virtue may be compared to the pole-star, which keeps its place while all the other stars pay homage to it."[30]

Compared to St. Augustine or Freud, Confucius was highly optimistic about human nature and the cure of social strife. He believed that there is an ancient Harmony and order in the world and that it is possible for human beings to understand it and to recover it by adopting a code of social behavior. Unlike St. Augustine or Luther, Confucius did not consider human nature "fallen" or the will in bondage and requiring divine grace. He taught that the "way of the ancients" is open to all since every person is born with the innate capacity to develop humaneness (*jen*), even to become a sage.

A number of striking differences have been noted in the Stoic, Christian, Buddhist, and Confucian understanding of the human problem. Despite these fundamental differences, all four contrast with their modern secular substitutes in the conviction that there is, beyond the appearances of this empirical world and the present time, a sacred order. That order—*Phusis*, the Kingdom of God, Nirvana, and the Grand Harmony—is the only true goal of human striving and, they insist, the only real hope for eradicating our pain and suffering, our illusions, and our anxious guilt.

## NOTES

1. Richard Alpert, *Be Here Now*. Cited in William G. McLaughlin, *Revivals, Awakenings, and Reform* (Chicago, 1978), 204.
2. Epictetus, *Discourses*, Vol. II, in *The Stoic and Epicurean Philosophers*, ed. Whitney J. Oates (New York, 1940), 288–89.
3. Marcus Aurelius, *Thoughts* (Oxford, 1948).
4. Gilbert Murray, "The Stoic Philosophy," in *Essays and Addresses* (London, 1921), 100.
5. Epictetus, *Enchiridion*, in Oates, *Stoic and Epicurean Philosophers*, 472.
6. Etienne Gilson, *The Christian Philosophy of St. Thomas Aquinas* (London, 1957), 345–46.

7. Reinhold Niebuhr, *The Nature and Destiny of Man*, Vol. I (New York, 1941), 13–14.

8. St. Augustine, *The City of God*, Book XIV, Chap. 13 (New York, 1958), 308–9.

9. John Calvin, *The Institutes of the Christian Religion*, Book I, Chap. 4 (Philadelphia, n.d.).

10. St. Augustine, "Treatise on Nature and Grace," Chap. 3 in *The Nicene and Post-Nicene Fathers*, Vol. V, ed. Philip Schaff (Grand Rapids, Mich., 1971), 122.

11. Ibid.

12. G. P. Malalasekera, "The Status of the Individual in Theravada Buddhism," *Philosophy East and West* 14 (July 1964), 147. I am dependent on Malalasekera for much that follows.

13. *Samyutta-Nikaya*, Vol. V, 420. Cited in Bhikshu Sangharakshita, *A Survey of Buddhism* (Boulder, Colo., 1980), 113–14.

14. Edward Conze, *Buddhism: Its Essence and Development* (New York, 1959), 44.

15. *Digha-Nikaya*, Vol. XXII, cited in Sangharakshita, *A Survey of Buddhism*, 98.

16. Walpala Rahula, *What the Buddha Taught* (New York, 1962), 30.

17. Confucius, *Analects* (7.1), cited in Raymond Dawson, *Confucius* (New York, 1981), 11.

18. Hsün Tzu, Vol. XIX, 3. *Sources of Chinese Tradition*, ed. William T. de Bary et al. (New York, 1960), 122–23.

19. Walter Lippmann, *The Public Philosophy* (Boston, 1955). Cited in Huston Smith, *The Religions of Man* (New York, 1959), 164. I am indebted to Smith for this striking passage. The reader may wish to consult Smith's brilliant and sympathetic treatment of Confucianism in the above volume.

20. *Analects* (1.14), in Dawson, *Confucius*, 10. (Dawson's exposition of Confucius's teaching has been very helpful.)

21. *Analects* (4.17), in ibid., 16.

22. *Analects* (4.1), in ibid., 17.

23. *Analects* (12.1), in ibid., 30.

24. Dawson, *Confucius*, 32.

25. *Analects* (4.5), in ibid., 56.

26. *Analects* (12.11), in ibid., 57.

27. *Analects* (2.21), in ibid., 67.

28. *Analects* (2.3), in ibid., 73.

29. Herbert Fingarette, *Confucius—The Secular as Sacred* (New York, 1972), 3.

30. *Analects* (2.1), in Dawson, *Confucius*, 73.

## KEY WORDS

Plato's rationalism

Stoicism

*Phusis* (Nature)

Divine Logos

Epictetus

*apatheia*

*imago Dei*

self-transcendence

the Fall

sin

pride

St. Augustine

original sin

Siddhartha Gautama—the Buddha

law of karma

*khandhas*

*an-atta (an-atman)*  
Four Noble Truths  
*dukkha*  
*tanhā*  
*Nirvana*  
The Eightfold Path  
*li*

Confucius  
*Analects*  
rectification of names  
*jen*  
Five Great Relationships  
filial piety  
*chun-tzu* and *te*

## REVIEW QUESTIONS

1. Do you agree that there is a "human problem"?
2. How is a religious interpretation of the human condition (anthropology) related to the conceptions of *deity* or *ultimate reality* and *cosmogony*? Give two examples from those discussed.
3. What is the source of the human problem according to Plato, Marx, and Freud?
4. Describe the Stoic view of the cause and cure of the human problem, including such concepts as Divine Logos (Reason), *Phusis*, and *apatheia*.
5. What is the root of the human problem according to Christianity? How do the Roman Catholic and the Protestant views of the *imago Dei* and the Fall differ? What are some of the ways that sin is described in Christianity? What does "original sin" mean?
6. Describe the cause and cure of the human problem as described by the Buddha in the famous Deer Park sermon, referring to such concepts as the *khandas, an-atta (an-atman), dukkha, tanhā*, and Nirvana.
7. According to Confucianism, what is the root of the human problem? How does the appreciation of such means as *li*, the rectification of names, the five great relationships, and filial piety lead to a cure of the human problem?
8. Do any of the four views of the human problem discussed in this chapter agree in any way about the source of the human problem? What would you say are the foremost differences in the four analyses of the human problem and its cure?

## SUGGESTIONS FOR FURTHER READING

*For studies of several religious and secular views of human nature and the human problem, see the following:*

RADHAKRISHNAN, S., AND P. T. RAJU. *The Concept of Man: A Study in Comparative Philosophy*. London: George Allen and Unwin, 1966.

STEVENSON, LESLIE. *Seven Theories of Human Nature*. Oxford: Clarendon Press, 1974.

———. *The Study of Human Nature*. Oxford: O.U.P., 1986.

*For a discussion of the religious views of the human condition treated in this chapter, see the following:*

*Stoicism*

COPLESTON, FREDERICK. *A History of Philosophy*, Vol. I. London: Burns Oates, 1956.

MURRAY, GILBERT. "The Stoic Philosophy." In *Essays and Addresses*. London: Allen and Unwin, 1921.

*Christianity*

AQUINAS, ST. THOMAS. *Basic Writings of St. Thomas Aquinas.* Questions 75–79 from the *Summa Theologica.* New York: Random House, 1948.

AUGUSTINE, ST. "Nature and Grace" and "On Original Sin." In *Basic Writings of St. Augustine,* Vol. I. New York: Random House, 1948.

CALVIN, JOHN. *Institutes of the Christian Religion.* Philadelphia: Presbyterian Board of Christian Education, n.d.

NIEBUHR, REINHOLD. *The Nature and Destiny of Man.* Vol. I. New York: Scribner's, 1964.

*Buddhism*

MALALASEKERA, G. P. "The Status of the Individual in Theravada Buddhism." In *Philosophy East and West,* Vol. 14. Honolulu: University of Hawaii Press, 1964.

RAHULA, WALPALA. *What the Buddha Taught.* Chaps. 2–4 and 6. New York: Grove Press, 1962.

SANGHARAKSHITA, BHIKSHU. *A Survey of Buddhism.* Chap. I, XII–XVI. Bangalore: Indian Institute of World Culture, 1966.

*Confucianism*

DAWSON, RAYMOND. *Confucius.* New York: Hill and Wang, 1981.

FUNG YU-LAN. *A History of Chinese Philosophy.* 2d ed. Trans. by Derk Bodde. Princeton, N.J.: Princeton University Press, 1952.

LIU, WU-CHI. *A Short History of Confucian Philosophy.* Harmondsworth, England: Penguin Books, 1955.

SMITH, HUSTON. "Confucianism." In *The World's Religions.* San Francisco: Harper and Row, 1991.

# 10

# Theodicy: Encountering Evil

## Overview

We have discussed the variety of ways that religions conceive of deity, or sacred power and value, the origin and order of the natural and social world, and accounts of the human problem. Here we explore religious theodicy or explanations of evil in the world. The word *theodicy* comes from the Greek words *theos* and *dike* ("God" and "justice") and means "justifying the ways of God" in the face of the chaos and evil in the world. The word was coined by the philosopher Leibniz in an influential work entitled *Essais de Théodicée* (1710). Since then, the term has been principally employed in Christian theology and refers to the attempts of theologians to justify the goodness and omnipotence of God in the face of the world's real evil.

More recently, social scientists have adopted the term *theodicy* to describe a wide range of religious and ideological explanations or legitimations of the anomic, that is, the chaotic and evil experiences faced by both individuals and societies. Here, the word *theodicy* will be used in this broader sense, and we will include in our discussion religions that, while offering explanations for evil and suffering, do not hold monotheistic assumptions—for example, God's goodness or omnipotence. Our analysis will follow rather closely a typology introduced by the sociologist Peter Berger.[1]

Theodicies derive from the fact that evil and chaos must not only be endured but also be explained if a sense of fatedness, meaninglessness, and despair are to be held at bay. The world's religions propose a variety of explanations or legitimations for the fact of evil, many of which have proven enormously compelling and have endured in very different times and places.

The power of these theodicies lies in their capacity to provide convincing explanations for the awful reality of suffering and evil. Perhaps surprisingly, what humans seek most is not happiness but the assurance that, evil notwithstanding, life has meaning and purpose.

The first type of theodicy we examine is one in which persons lose all sense of individuality through complete identification with the larger community—the tribe, nation, or race—or through absorption in some larger cosmic reality. The prototype is often found in primal religion, where the life of the individual is subsumed within and indistinguishable from that of the ongoing life of the community. Personal suffering is minimized in face of the assurances of the continuing life and prosperity of the clan or tribe. In mysticism, the individual's mundane suffering becomes insignificant, even laughably unreal, through the rapturous loss of self in union with the One or God.

A very common type of theodicy is one in which compensation for present suffering is perceived as coming imminently in the future here on earth. Present sufferings can be endured because they are relativized in the expectation of a future change of fortune. This form of theodicy is common in the West—for example, in ancient Israel, in some of the radical sects of the Protestant Reformation, in Marxism, and even in the Islamic revolutionary movements today. However, it is a type that is also associated with what anthropologists call Cargo Cults that are found throughout the Third World.

Perhaps the most common religious theodicy is that which looks to the reversal of present suffering and evil in a future life beyond this earth in Heaven or Paradise. It is prominent in Western theism and also in certain schools of Mahayana Buddhism. Cosmic Dualism offers a rather different explanation for evil. As we saw in Chapter 7, dualism often regards this world as created by and presently under the rule of satanic powers. Since the God of Light did not create this earth, he cannot be held accountable—as is often the case in monotheism—for present evil. Dualism looks to the end of this earthly suffering only in a distant cosmic victory of the God of Light over Darkness.

The sociologist Max Weber regards the classical theodicy of India, of *karma* and *samsara*, as the most rational or plausible of all religious explanations of present evil. According to this theodicy, our present existence is simply the result of our past karmic actions. We reap, inescapably, those effects of our past actions while we sow those karmic seeds that will determine, unalterably, our future destiny on the wheel of rebirth or reincarnation. We have no one to blame but ourselves. We will illustrate this theodicy with citations from both Hinduism and Theravada Buddhism.

Western monotheism faces unique problems in its justification of evil since it teaches that the God who created the world *ex nihilo* is also omnipotent, omniscient, and perfectly good or benevolent. Why, then, is there so much evil and pain? In the final segment of this chapter, we explore a number of theistic justifications or explanations of evil, using the Book of Job as our basic source. As we will see, theologians have regarded suffering as a punishment for sin, as a test of faith, and as a necessary condition for "soul-making." More recently, they also have challenged traditional notions of God's omnipotence. Finally, though, theism calls for both agonizing protest *and* faith before the mystery of God's ways that pass human understanding.

## The Persistent Demand for Theodicy

Suffering and evil have always tortured and oppressed the human body and the human spirit. In the sixth century B.C.E., a Greek by the name of Kallinos lamented, "There is no wit in man. Creatures of a day we live like cattle, knowing nothing of how the god will bring each one to his end. . . . Thus evil is with everything. Yea ten thousand dooms, woes and grief beyond speaking are the lot of mankind."[2]

The French writer Albert Camus estimated that 70 million human beings were displaced, enslaved, and killed *in the twentieth century alone*. The figures have risen dramatically since Camus wrote. Drought and famine persist in Ethiopia and the Sudan. The holocaust of the innocent did not end with the Nazi horror in Eastern Europe; it continued with the Khmer Rouge in Cambodia and elsewhere. Wars persist and grow more deadly, starvation recurs, and humanity's inhumanity and the injustices of life are ever-present to us on the evening television news. The sick horror that we all feel in the presence of evil, injustice, and suffering raises for us, as for countless millions in the past, the problem of theodicy.

Basically, what a theodicy does is to place our own life, which may be riven with tragic suffering and the threat of chaos, in a larger framework of meaning that bestows a sense of order, purpose, and even repose. Peter Berger explains how rites of passage often involve an implicit theodicy:

> Social ritual transforms the individual event [the crises encountered at various stages of life] into a typical case, just as it transforms biography into an episode in the history of society. The individual is seen as being born, living and suffering, and eventually dying, as his ancestors have done before him and his children will do after him. As he accepts and inwardly appropriates this view of the matter he transcends his own individuality as well as the uniqueness, including the unique pain and the unique terrors, of his individual experience. . . . He is made capable of suffering "Correctly." . . . In consequence, the pain becomes more tolerable, the terror less overwhelming.[3]

The religious legitimation of suffering and evil often is unconscious. So, while theodicies may entail rather complex metaphysical doctrines, as in Buddhism and Christianity, they as often represent the unsophisticated convictions of ordinary people. When such a person explains a drought as a judgment of God, he or she is engaging in theodicy. For example, take the simple and moving testimony on television of a young American soldier whose legs had been blown off by a land mine in Vietnam. He had been involved, to his own deep remorse, in the annihilation by flame throwers of an entire Vietnamese village, including the death of innocent women and children. Some time after that event, he suffered his own tragic, crippling injury. He saw it, however, as God's judgment on his own monstrous crime and a merciful release. His personal suffering strangely satisfied his sense of justice, and he accepted his condition, not grudgingly or stoically, but with an apparent sense of relief, satisfaction, and peace. The young man was engaging, unawares, in theodicy.

## Theodicy of "Mystical Participation"

A common way of justifying the "slings and arrows of outrageous fortune" is for individuals to see themselves as a "typical case." Berger describes how this often takes place in rites of passage, but also through the loss of self in mystical participation or absorption in a larger social or spiritual reality. In such cases, what defines the self is not its unique individuality but, rather, its participation in and identification with a corporate group, clan, tribe, nation, or race. Thus, the Chinese Confucian father could die a "happy death" knowing he lived on in his sons and their sons. The soldier can sacrifice his life in battle with the assurance that, spiritually, he lives on in his tribe or nation.

This form of theodicy is especially common in primal societies where a heightened sense of individuality is not developed. The sociologist Lucien Levy-Bruhl (1857–1939) called this identification, or merging of the self with others, the "law of participation." He maintained that individuals in primal societies suffered less from personal anomie or misfortune because of their *"mystical participation"* in the ongoing life of the tribe and of nature itself. The individual may suffer personal loss, but the tribe lives on and nature is immortal:

> Every individual *is* both such and such a man or woman, alive at present, a certain ancestral individual, who may be human or semihuman . . . and at the same time he *is* his totem, that is, he partakes in mystic fashion of the essence of the animal or vegetable species whose name he bears. The verb "to be" . . . encompasses both the collective representation and the collective consciousness in a participation that is actually lived, in a kind of symbiosis effected by identity of essence.[4]

The continuity of individual–society–nature places the "individual's" birth, growth, and death within the larger life and rhythm of the tribe and of nature itself. The sting of our own misfortune and death is thus relativized by a form of *"objective immortality"* in the ongoing life of the family or clan. Such a sense of "corporate personality" was an essential feature of life among, for example, the ancient Semitic tribes, including Israel. In ancient Israelite psychology, the "soul" was considered to be more than the individual, conscious ego; it was everything that we associate with a name—renown, property, progeny, and so forth. The "soul" may thus live on even when the individual ego dies.

Theodicies of "participation" are present in all those forms of mysticism that emphasize the absorption or annihilation of the self in its union with the divine. In this form of mystic union, all sense of ego and individuality is lost in union with the All or the One. In the blissful passivity that accompanies such an "oceanic" experience, the individual's own sufferings and trials become as nothing, trivial and unreal. The symbolism of the ocean is prominent in this form of mysticism, as is evident in the reminiscence of a German mystic:

> I was alone upon the seashore as all those thoughts flowed over me, liberating and reconciling. . . . I was impelled to kneel down . . . before the illimitable ocean, symbol of the Infinite. I felt that I prayed as I had never prayed before, and knew now what prayer really is: to return from the solitude of individuation into the consciousness of unity with all that is, to kneel down as one that passes away, and to rise up as one imperishable. Earth, heaven, and sea resounded as in one vast world-encircling harmony. It was as if the chorus of all the great who had ever lived were about me. I felt myself one with them, and it appeared as if I heard their greeting: "Thou too belongest to the company of those who over came."[5]

Such a "consciousness of unity," of escape from "the solitude of individuation," leaves the soul "imperishable," free of mundane anxieties and threats. They now are seen as inconsequential, even imaginary.

## A Future, This-Worldly Theodicy

It is common to associate the religions of the biblical tradition—Judaism, Christianity, and Islam—with the belief that the evils and sufferings of this life will be compensated for and that justice will be meted out in a future life in heaven or, as the case may be, in hell. Indeed, it can be claimed that this form of theodicy has been the dominant one in at least two of these biblical faiths. We know, however, that in early Israel there was no belief in a future life; that Israel's hope lay in the promise that their God, Yahweh, would redeem Israel from the oppression and injustice of its enemies and, in the future, would establish it in triumph and prosperity. Palestine was envisioned as a new Eden, a Paradise regained, which would be established through a "righteous remnant." Once holy Zion was secure, a world reign of justice and peace would ensue; the desert would bloom; the poor would be rewarded; and flocks, corn, and fruit would multiply. This hope of early Israel was sorely tested through the centuries. Out of Israel's travail, there emerged a radically different but essentially *this-worldly eschatology*. This shift in eschatology is discussed in Chapter 12.

Western consciousness has been deeply influenced by the biblical vision of a peaceable Kingdom or new age on earth, where all will live in justice and harmony. The animals and native American Indians appear apprehensive about the arrival of the newcomers. (*Source:* Courtesy of Abby Aldrich Rockefeller Folk Art Museum, Williamsburg, Virginia.)

In the centuries prior to the Christian era, Israel began to look to the intervention of a supernatural figure, called "the Son of Man," who would put down the ever-growing power of Satan and would establish a kingdom of his saints. This form of supernatural, yet this-worldly, hope persisted long after the vision weakened its hold on the Jewish imagination. A scholar describes, as follows, the features of this eschatological theodicy:

> The world is dominated by an evil, tyrannous power of boundless destructiveness—a power moreover which is imagined not as simply human but as demonic. The tyranny of that power will become more and more outrageous, the sufferings of its victims more and more intolerable—until suddenly the hour will strike when the Saints of God are able to rise up and overthrow it. Then the Saints themselves, the chosen, holy people who hitherto have groaned under the oppressor's heel, shall in their turn inherit dominion over the whole earth. This will be the culmination of history.[6]

What is distinctive about this *millenarian* form of theodicy is that compensation for the suffering of the present time is postponed into the future, but *a future realized on this earth* and not in some other-worldly heaven. Moreover, the coming justice is imminent; it will come soon and it will be total. That is, there will be a *revolutionary* transformation in which the just will be rewarded and the unjust will be put down. Supernatural intervention will be accompanied by human action. For the "saints," the present sufferings can be endured because they are relativized in relation to the expectation of an imminent, future change of fortune.*

Historical experience would appear to confirm that such a future, this-worldly theodicy is most likely to attract support during times of natural disaster and social upheaval, when a sense of present historical injustice and pessimism is widespread. The period between the eleventh and sixteenth centuries in Europe was just such a time. Europe witnessed a number of social convulsions associated with the breakup of feudal society and with the horror brought on by the Black Death, the Crusades, and the various peasant uprisings before and during the Protestant Reformation. Examples from the Czech and German peasant revolts are especially revealing of this type of future-oriented theodicy.

In the early fifteenth century, a socioreligious reform known as the Hussite movement burst forth in Bohemia, the area of the present Czech Republic. It soon joined zealous religious reform with social revolution. In the 1390s, the writings of the English reformer John Wycliffe (d. 1384) became known in Prague. They particularly influenced the Czech preacher John Hus (1372–1415), who later was burned at the stake by the Roman Church for his heretical teachings. Hus's mantle was soon taken up by more radical leaders. In 1419, a large gathering of disaffected Czech peasants met on a hilltop that they identified as the biblical Mount Tabor, the place of Christ's transfiguration and the renewal of the Church. The *Taborites,* as they came to be called, soon broke all ties with the feudal order and organized into a new society that stressed a sharing of all goods in common. They taught that a new age of the Holy Spirit was about to dawn: All feudal institutions and their lords and priests would be destroyed. So began a series of savage wars against the authorities. A member of the Taborite community, John of Pribram, who later opposed the movement, describes the incendiary teachings of the prophets of Tabor:

> And they said that the elect of God would rule in the world for a thousand years with Christ, visibly and tangibly. And they preached that the elect of God who fled to the mountains would themselves possess all the goods of the destroyed evil ones and rule freely over all their estates and villages. And they said, "You will have such an abundance of everything that silver, gold, and

---

*This kind of realized millenarian theodicy can be observed in the Shi'i movement that is distinctive of Iranian revolutionary Islam under the recent leadership of the Imām Khomeini. Traditional Shi'i Islam is more other-worldly, as we will soon see. According to this recent Iranian Shi'ism, the coming of the Imām at the end of time to initiate a thousand years of peace and justice, and to redress the wrongs of individuals and the community, is believed to be occurring at the present time. Through its revolution, the Iranian people had taken on a kind of Imāmic function in bringing about the fulfillment of a golden age here on earth. The evil world of suffering is now being transformed, and justice and virtue will be rewarded in this life as well as the next. The hope for a future Paradise for the martyr and the righteous is present but is balanced by a more-earthly, revolutionary theodicy.

money will only be a nuisance to you." They also said and preached to the people, "Now you will not pay rents to your lords any more, nor be subject to them, but will freely and undisturbedly possess their villages, fish-ponds, meadows, forests, and all their domains."[7]

Implicit in the Taborites' *apocalyptic* message was the promise that despite the injustice and suffering of the present time, the Elect peasants would soon be vindicated and consoled, and the unjust brought down and punished.

Similar millenarian, this-worldly theodicies are found within Islam. From time to time, Islamic peasant movements have nourished the belief that a time of justice and well-being on earth was imminent and would be ushered in by, for example, the return of the Mahdi or savior who would triumph over the Evil One. It is a prevalent theme in the Shi'ite tradition of Islam today. A similar millenarian theodicy is found in movements that may have little relation to ancient biblical apocalypticism, for example, in the Taiping Rebellion in China and in numerous Cargo Cults.

The phenomenon of Cargo Cults is of great interest to anthropologists because they represent a curious, often bizarre response to conditions of rapid socioeconomic change and deprivation. In these cults, a prophet appears to announce the imminent end of the world that will result from a series of apocalyptical disasters. With the destruction of the old order, a savior figure arrives to bring all the goods that previously had been denied. During the interim, the people are called on to prepare for the Golden Age by building storehouses and depots to receive the goods, known as "cargo." In the period of waiting, the cult members' actions reflect a complete break with the old order; pigs and cattle are slaughtered, all savings are squandered, and work ceases. Often, an **antinomian** spirit prevails, with boisterous revelries and ecstatic dancing.

The *John Frum Cargo Cult* was just such a movement in the southern island of Tanna in the New Hebrides. The cult is described, with many others, by Peter Worsley in *The Trumpet Shall Sound*. The islands of the New Hebrides had long suffered from labor recruiters who had taken the natives from their islands, often by force, to work on plantations in Australia and elsewhere. In 1940, a native named John Frum began to prophesy. The natives came to regard him as the earthly manifestation of Karaperamun, the island's highest mountain. Here is Worsley's description of the movement:

John Frum prophesied the occurrence of a cataclysm in which Tanna would become flat, the volcanic mountains would fall and fill the riverbeds to form fertile plains, and Tanna would be joined to the neighboring islands of Eramanga and Aneityum to form a new island. Then John Frum would reveal himself, bring in a reign of bliss, the natives would get back their youth, and there would be no sickness; there would be no need to care for gardens, trees or pigs. The Whites would go; John Frum would set up schools to replace the mission schools and would pay chiefs and teachers. . . .

Natives now started a veritable orgy of spending in European stores in order to get rid of the European's money, which was to be replaced by John Frum's with a cocoanut stamped on it. Some even hurled their long-hoarded savings into the sea, believing that "when there would be no money left on the island the white traders would have to depart." . . .[8]

John Frum was soon arrested by the authorities, but the movement continued and new leaders came along to proclaim themselves to be John Frum. Worsley reports that the activity of the cult varied in intensity during the following decade, depending on the changing social and economic conditions of the island.

One of the obvious weaknesses of a future, this-worldly theodicy is its possible empirical disconfirmation. The Millerites—followers of the New England farmer William Miller—predicted that, according to the Bible, the end of the world would occur in 1843. The end did not come. New predictions were then forthcoming. Finally, the day was set for October 22, 1844. That day also passed, and there was no deliverance. This failure caused the collapse of the Millerite movement. However, not all millenarian movements die out as quickly. Various explanations—miscalculations, claims that the time is not yet ripe or that God is testing the group's faith—can be advanced. The response to the failure of prophecy is examined by Leon Festinger in *When Prophecy Fails* (1956), an exploration of how people cope with such conditions of "cognitive dissonance." Festinger studied, firsthand, a group in Lake City, Minnesota, that claimed to have received a message—from a planet called "Clarion"—of a great Deluge that would destroy the world. The group's rationalizations and responses to disconfirming evidence were striking but not unexpected. The classic example of a this-worldly theodicy is Marxism.

## Other-Worldly Theodicy

The form of theodicy that would appear to be most common among the great religions—certainly the three missionary religions, Christianity, Islam, and certain schools of Mahayana Buddhism—is one that looks to a recompense for the evil and injustice of this life in a life after death in a blessed Heaven or Paradise. It is voiced, for example, in the famous hymn "Jerusalem the Golden":

1. Jerusalem the Golden, With milk and honey blest,
   Beneath thy contemplation Sink heart and voice oppressed;
   I know not, O I know not What joys await us there,
   What radiancy of glory, What bliss beyond compare. . . .

4. O sweet and blessèd country, The home of God's elect!
   O sweet and blessèd country, That eager hearts expect!
   Jesus, in mercy bring us, To that dear land of rest,
   Who art, with God the Father, And Spirit ever blest.

The vision of a Heaven or Paradise is prominent in much of the devotional and even some of the great poetical literature of the West. Dante's *Paradiso* is the supreme example. We need not illustrate the theme with numerous examples, but a particularly apt type is found in the *Shi'i tradition* of Islam. It is especially appropriate because the conventional Shi'i theodicy so strongly underlines the compensation for present suffering, and especially for martyrdom, in an other-worldly Paradise.

The Shi'i movement arose over a dispute concerning the succession to the Prophet Mohammad. The causes of the sectarian division are complex but, essentially, the Shi'i claim that only members of Mohammed's family should be considered his legitimate successors separates it from the larger Sunni tradition in Islam. Ali—the fourth caliph, or supreme ruler, and a cousin of Mohammad—is considered by Shi'is to be the first legitimate successor. They regard the assassinations* of Ali and his two sons, Hasan and Husain, to be glorious and revered martyrdoms. The role of the sacrificial death of the innocent has since profoundly shaped the Shi'i understanding of suffering and theodicy. The dramatic reenactment of the historic martyrdoms—called passion plays—gives special prominence in Shi'i Islam to a future reward for present suffering in an other-worldly Paradise. The theme is prominent in the play honoring Husain. As he faces death, Husain offers the following reflections:

> *Husain:* Trials, afflictions and pains, the thicker they fall on man, the better dear sister, do they prepare him for his journey heavenward. We rejoice in tribulations, seeing they are but temporary, and yet they work out an eternal and blissful end. Though it is predestined that I should suffer martyrdom in this shameful manner, yet the treasury of everlasting happiness shall be at my disposal as a consequent reward. Thou must think of that, and be no longer sorry. . . .

At the play's end, the angel Gabriel, through Mohammad, gives Husain the keys to Paradise, which he had desired. Gabriel speaks: "Peace be unto thee, O Muhammad the elect, God hath sent thee a message saying, 'None has suffered the pain and afflictions which Husain has undergone. None has like him, been obedient in my service.'" Husain then replies: "O my friends, be ye relieved from grief, and come along with me to the mansions of the blest. Sorrow has passed away, and it is now time for joy and rest; trouble has gone by, it is the hour to be at ease and tranquility."[9]

The Shi'i can face martyrdom joyful not only in the assurance that his or her suffering hastens the day when the Imām will come but also in the promise of immediate heavenly bliss.

---

*While the historical evidence is lacking for the death by assassination of all the successors, such martyrdoms are held as an article of belief.

# Dualism

*Dualist theodicy* is not a prevalent doctrine in the modern world religions, either East or West. However, as indicated earlier, its appeal was very great in the centuries just before and after the beginnings of Christianity, in Zoroastrianism, Mithraism, Manichaeism, and Gnosticism. Its attraction in certain forms of contemporary popular Gnosticism is still clearly discernible. We have learned that, according to dualism, all evil and suffering are to be ascribed to powerful, satanic forces that created and now rule this world, including our bodily existence. The god of light and truth did *not* create this material world and therefore cannot be held accountable for our earthly suffering. The earth, by its very nature, is a realm of darkness and disorder. The victory of order over chaos and the defeat of evil and suffering will take place, as in Zoroastrianism, in a distant cosmic victory of Light over Darkness or, as in Gnosticism, in a return to a world of Light wholly beyond this material world.

The Mandeans were one of the Gnostic sects of late antiquity, and a few thousand Mandeans live today in religious communities along the rivers of southern Iraq and Iran. In the Mandean *Ginza*, or "Treasure," the vivid contrast between the world of Light and Darkness is portrayed:

> 278. In the name of the great Life! I cry to you, I instruct you, and I say: (you) true and believing men (you) perceiving and separate ones: separate yourselves from the world of imperfection which is full of confusion and replete with error. First I gave you instruction about the King of Light, blessed be he in all eternity. And I told you about the blessed worlds of light in which there is nothing perishable. . . . Now I will speak to you about worlds of darkness and what is in them, hideous and terrible whose form is faulty.
>
> Beyond the earth of light downwards and beyond the earth Tibil southwards is the heart of darkness. . . . Darkness exists through its own evil nature, (is) a howling darkness, a desolate gloom which knows not the First or the Last. But the King of Light knows and perceives the First and the Last, that which is past and that which is to come. And he knew and perceived that evil was there, but he did not want to cause it harm, just as he said: "Harm not the wicked and the evil, until it has done harm itself." Its own evil nature exists from the beginning and to all eternity. The worlds of darkness are numerous and without end. He (the King of Light, or: One) said: "Broad and deep is the abode of evil, whose peoples showed no fidelity to the place which is their endless habitation, whose kingdom came into being from themselves. Their earth is black water and their heights gloomy darkness."[10]

Because this world is a realm of desolation, sin, and darkness, earthly existence is radically devalued—to the point that moral license and promiscuity are often encouraged as indifferent. Such a profound earthly pessimism, which considers evil as the natural condition of this earthly life, does not have enduring popular appeal. However, as a theodicy it does resolve the nagging question that confronts the monotheistic faiths: How can a good and omnipotent Creator God allow the presence of so much unspeakable suffering and sorrow? But before surveying forms of monotheistic theodicy, we need to examine what Max Weber calls the most rational of all the religious answers to the presence of evil: the *karma–samsara* doctrine found in Hinduism and later in Buddhism.

## The *Karma–Samsara* Theodicy

The classical Indian theodicy is built on two related doctrines: **samsara** and **karma**. *Samsara* is the wheel of rebirth, or reincarnation, the doctrine that each soul passes through a sequence of bodies. The soul's human embodiment brings with it self-consciousness, freedom, and responsibility. Every human thought and action thus have their effect and—as the Bible also affirms—"as a man sows, so shall he reap." The law of *karma*, we have learned, is the law of cause and effect. Each person is the effect of the actions of a previous embodiment and, in turn, is the architect of their own habits and character, and hence of his or her destiny in a future rebirth. As the Hindu *Chandogya Upanishad* asserts,

> . . . those who are of pleasant conduct here—the prospect is, indeed, that they will enter a pleasant womb, either the womb of a *Brahmim* [priest], or the womb of a *ksatriya* [warrior], or the womb of a *vaisya* [trader and agriculturist]. But those who are of stinking conduct here—the prospect is, indeed, that they will enter a stinking womb, either the womb of a dog, or the womb of a swine, or the womb of an outcast [*candala*].
>
> —(V.X.7)

Most of us would prefer to deny such a doctrine and to claim that our present and future lives are not of our own making but are rather the work of fate, or of "social conditions," or lie "in the hands of God." The Hindu* rejects all such "excuses" that would place the blame elsewhere. The Hindu would repudiate Job's protestations of innocence before God and would side with Job's friends, who tell him that his suffering is the result of his own unrighteousness. However, for the Hindu, Job's suffering may be the effect not only of his present life but also of his previous lives: The acts done in former births never leave any creature. Since all deeds are under the control of *karma*, we must always have in mind how we can restore the balance and rescue the self from evil consequences.

Hinduism teaches that rescuing oneself "from evil consequences" cannot be achieved by pretending that they are not real. It is thus essential to fulfill the obligations of our present state. Progress between stages of rebirth depends in large measure on fulfilling the **dharma** or law appropriate to our present condition or caste. The Hindu is assured that, if called on to carry out

---

*We speak here of classical Hinduism. In the popular Hindu cults, *karma* has been essentially replaced by theism.

what appear to be evil actions associated with his or her caste duties, no evil *karma* will attach to such actions. The warrior thus need not fear that being a good soldier will result in the sowing of more evil effects in a future existence. *Dharma* is dutiful action without attachment to consequences.

The point is made dramatically in the *Bhagavad Gita* (the *Gita*), the much-loved, popular Hindu scripture. Two related families, the Kauravas and the Pandavas, are about to engage in battle, and the Warrior Arjuna recoils from fighting his own people. He turns to his charioteer, Krishna (the human incarnation of the god Vishnu), and tells him that it is not right for him to slay his kinsmen. Arjuna casts away "his bow and arrow, his spirit overwhelmed by sorrow." However, Krishna advises him that his real duty is to fulfill his *dharma*—so long as he does so with detachment:

> Further, having regard for thine own duty, thou shouldst not falter; there exists no greater good for a *ksatriya* [warrior] than a war enjoined by duty. . . . Therefore, arise, O Son of Kunti [Arjuna], resolve on battle. Treating alike pleasure and pain, gain and loss, victory and defeat, then get ready for battle. Thus thou shall not incur sin.[11]

The rationale of this Indian theodicy is plain to see since the individual has no one to praise or to blame for successes or for misfortune and suffering. The law of *karma* assures a completely intelligible explanation for both happiness and evil. However, it is also true that, joined with the doctrine of *dharma*, this Indian theodicy constitutes an extraordinary justification of a gender and socioeconomic status quo. (see Chapter 13 on religion and gender.)

The most radical form of the *karma–samsara* theodicy is found in another, heterodox Indian religion, Theravada Buddhism, an offshoot of Hinduism. We have learned that the Buddha's teaching about the cause and cure of human suffering is the foundation of early Buddhism. Buddha's insight into human pain (*dukkha*) and his theodicy is briefly summarized in his famous Four Noble Truths. You will recall that when his disciple, Mālunkyaputta, asked him the answer to some puzzling metaphysical questions, Buddha dismissed them as a waste of time. For whatever views we hold on such questions, there remains "old age, decay, death, sorrow, pain, grief, distress."

Buddha connected his profound realism about suffering with the doctrines of *karma* and *samsara*. In the Wheel of Life, there is that inexorable chain of causation, the dependent origination of all things. And since nothing exists independently, all beings are the effect of previous causes. Every action produces its effect and the pleasant and painful consequences cannot be escaped:

> Even a flight in the air cannot free you from suffering after the deed which is evil has been committed. Nor in the sky nor in the ocean's middle, nor if you were to hide in cracks in mountains, can there be found on this wide earth's corner where Karma does not catch up with the culprit. . . . The iron itself creates the rust, which slowly is bound to consume it. The evil-doer by his own deeds is led to a life full of suffering.[12]

*Karma* ensures that everything that comes to us is the fruit of previous seeds. The Buddha thereby explained the apparent inequalities of life to a puzzled king:

> The King said: "Revered Nagasena, what is the reason that men are not all the same, some being shortlived, some weakly, others healthy, some ugly, others comely, some of few wishes, others of many wishes, some poor, others rich, some belonging to low families, others to high families . . . ?"
>
> The Elder said: "But why, sire, are trees not all the same, some being acid, some salt, some bitter, some sharp, some astringent, others sweet?"
>
> "I think, revered sir, that it is because of a difference in seeds."
>
> "Even so, sire, it is because of a difference in *kammas* [*karmas*] that men are not all the same."[13]

The doctrines of *karma* and *samsara* give us the clue to the profound sense of rightness that is so distinctive of the Buddhist theodicy. It is captured in the words of a Burmese Buddhist philosopher:

> We must never forget that *kamma* [*karma*] is always just—it neither loves or hates, it does not reward or punish, it is never angry, never pleased. It is simply the law of cause and effect.
>
> *Kamma* knows nothing about us. It does not know us any more than fire knows us when it burns us. It is the nature of fire to burn, to give out heat; and if we use it properly it gives us light, cooks our food—but if we use it wrongly it burns us and our property. . . . It is foolish to grow angry and blame fire when it burns us because we made a mistake. In this respect *kamma* is like fire.[14]

Theravada Buddhism strips religion of all its usual elements—gods, demons, saviors, cosmologies, heavens, and hells. What is left are a few fundamental laws—*dukkha, karma,* and *samsara*—that explain why things are the way they are. There can be no excuses, no appeal to blind chance or to the prevenient action of an omniscient God. Buddhism says, in effect, you have made your bed, now you must lie in it—unless and until you find enlightenment and release. A modern apologist for Buddhism sums up the matter:

> Only *Karma* can explain the mysterious problem of Good and Evil, and reconcile man to the terrible *apparent* injustice of life. For when one acquainted with the noble doctrine looks around him, and observes the inequalities of birth and fortune, of intellect and capacities; when one sees honour paid to fools and profligates, and their nearest neighbor, with all his intellect and noble virtues, perishing of want and for lack of sympathy . . . that blessed knowledge of Karma alone prevents him from cursing life and men, as well as their supposed Creator.[15]

## Monotheistic Theodicies

Ethical monotheism presents a very different complex of beliefs and issues. For Western monotheism, the problem of theodicy is sharply put by the philosopher David Hume: "Is he [God] willing to prevent evil, but not able: then he is impotent. Is he able, but not willing? then he is malevolent. Is he both able and willing? whence then evil?"[16]

The great theistic faiths of the West—Judaism, Christianity, and Islam—all recognize the stark reality of both moral and natural evil and innocent suffering. They also affirm the sovereignty, providence, and benevolence of God. How can they hold all these beliefs at once? Are they not required to deny either God's all-powerfulness, his benevolence, or the reality of evil? The response to this dilemma has been varied, and there is no better source for their study than the biblical **Book of Job**. At least four theodicies are suggested in Job; we will explore three here and the fourth at the end of the chapter.

## Suffering as Recompense for Sin

One justification of suffering is to see it as a punishment for sin. This was the traditional answer of the biblical Deuteronomic historians who completed a compilation of ancient Hebrew historical works after the exile in Babylon in 587 B.C.E. They interpreted the history of the kings and the people of Israel and Judah, especially in their relations with their foreign neighbors, strictly in terms of divine reward and punishment. The story of King Manasseh is a good example. In the sixth century B.C.E., the king allowed idolatrous practices to be performed in the Jerusalem temple. The historian of II Kings records the consequence:

> And the Lord said by his servants the prophets, "Because Manasseh, King of Judah, has committed these abominations . . . and has made Judah also to sin with his idols; therefore thus says the Lord, the God of Israel, Behold, I am bringing upon Jerusalem and Judah such evil that the ears of every one who hears of it will tingle."
>
> —(21:10–12)

This is the view that is taken by Job's three friends, Eliphaz, Bildad, and Zophar, who maintain that Job's sufferings are the result of his sin. When Job challenges God to justify the enormity of the affliction that he has borne—miseries that "outweigh the sands of the seas"—the friends are horrified at his impiety. They find Job's questioning of God's justice intolerable. Bildad expresses their reaction:

> How long will you say these things and the words of your mouth be like a great wind? Does God pervert justice? Or does the Almighty pervert the right? If your children have sinned against him he has delivered them into the power of their transgression.
>
> If you will seek God and make supplication to the Almighty, if you are pure and upright, surely then he will rouse himself for you and reward you with a rightful habitation. And, though your beginning was small, your latter days will be very great.
>
> —(Job 8:2–7)

Job's three friends insist that his suffering is punishment for his sins, but Job resists their explanation. (*Source:* "The Just Upright Man is laughed to scorn" [Job xii. 4], by William Blake. From the Rosenwald Collection, courtesy of the National Gallery of Art, Washington, D.C.)

This traditional explanation of suffering is, as we will see, challenged by the whole movement of the poem of Job. Nevertheless, its perfect symmetry has always lent it a popular appeal—in Christianity and Islam as well as in Judaism.

### Suffering as a Test and as a Necessary Condition of "Soul-Making"

The belief in a just balancing of righteousness and prosperity, of evil and suffering, although possibly attractive in the abstract, does not long stand up to the test of experience. Another possible explanation of evil is offered in Job: Suffering is a divine test or a trial of faith. In the prologue to the long poetic dialogue between Job and his friends, God is portrayed as allowing Satan to "entice" him to allow all manner of evil to be heaped on a God-fearing Job to test his faith:

> And the Lord said to Satan, "Have you considered my servant Job, that there is none like him on the earth, a blameless and upright man, who fears God and turns away from evil?" Then Satan answered the Lord, "Does Job fear God for nought? Hast thou not put a hedge about him and his house and all that he has on every side? Thou hast blessed the work of his hands, and his possessions have increased in the land. But put forth your hand now and touch all that he has, and he will curse thee to thy face." And the Lord said to Satan, "Behold, all that he has is in your power . . ."
>
> —(*Job 1:8–12*)

God's only request is that Satan spare Job's life. Satan proceeds to smite Job with the loss of all his possessions and his sons and his daughters and finally afflicts him with running sores from head to foot. At this extremity, Job's wife calls on him to "curse God and die!" But Job answers, "You talk as any wicked fool of a woman might talk. If we accept good from God, shall we not accept evil?" Throughout the ordeal, Job does not voice one sinful word. Seated among the ashes, he utters his final resignation, "Naked I came from my mother's womb, and naked shall I return; The Lord gave and the Lord has taken away; blessed be the name of the Lord" (Job 1:21).

The Job depicted here passes the divine trial of faith, but we may find it difficult to admire him fully. He does not strike us as a genuine flesh-and-blood human being. What is perhaps worse is the depiction of God! The Almighty allows Job to be stricken with the most harrowing and painful evil, and all *gratuitously*, that is, without just cause. God's motive appears hardly fitting for a loving father; it strikes us as more like the sadistic pleasures of a tyrant. The Job and the God who are portrayed in the long dialogue itself are very different.

Despite the grotesqueness of the prologue's test of Job's faith, the idea that the believer can be purged and refined in the crucible of suffering is a deep-felt and universal religious conviction. It plays an important role in Islamic piety. The *Qur'an* is quite explicit:

> Surely We [Allah] will try you with something of fear and hunger, and diminu-
> tion of good / and lives and fruits, yet give thou good tidings / unto the patient /
> who, when they are visited by an affliction, / say, "Surely we belong to God,
> and / to Him we return."[17]

The *Qur'an* also points to the necessity for enduring an immediate pain to achieve a greater good. The eminent Muslim theologian al-Ghazālā gives us, as example, the ancient practice of blood-letting (cupping) of an infant:

> The mother feels tender concern for the little one and forbids cupping, but the
> father who is intelligent, inflicts it forcibly on him. The ignoramus thinks that
> the mother, and not the father, is the compassionate one. But the reasonable per-
> son knows that the father's infliction of cupping on the child represents perfect
> compassion . . . and that the mother is (the child's) enemy in the guise of a
> friend.[18]

To see the trial of faith only as a cruel test imposed by a less-than-beneficent God is to fail to recognize the other elements that enter into any profound divine-human encounter. These would include the "medicinal" role of suffering, and the place of suffering in shaping character and in teaching individuals such virtues as humility, patience, and fellow-feeling. Furthermore, there is in the presence of evil the attendant experience of the divine mystery, which places our suffering beyond our finite comprehension. Before we turn to this latter theme, we need to look more deeply into the relationship between suffering and the forming of character.

Those monotheistic theodicies that focus on God's limitless power and sovereignty tend to place the blame for moral evil on the fact of the Fall of Adam and the ever-present intractable character of human sin. After all, a good deal of suffering—even pestilence and famine—can be traced to human sloth and hard-heartedness. When confronted with the inexplicable fact of natural evil, these same theodicies—for example, Islam and Calvinism—appeal to radical faith in the face of the divine mystery. However, there is another tradition in Western monotheism that takes a different tack. It sees God's purpose as including the creation of finite, imperfect creatures who, through their own freedom, can develop personal spiritual insights and moral character. According to this theodicy, human moral growth requires the kind of world that includes the reality of pain and loss. This position is found in the writings of a number of Christian theologians, including the early Church Father St. Irenaeus (120–202 C.E.) and the important liberal Protestant theologian Friedrich Schleiermacher (1768–1834). A contemporary formulation is developed by the philosopher John Hick.

Hick begins by acknowledging it is not possible to show that all human pain serves God's purpose. However, he does believe it is possible to show that the divine purpose could not be advanced in a world that was "designed as a permanent hedonistic paradise," that is, in an environment where the end was simply human pleasure and comfort. This, he argues, is exactly the assumption of the skeptic. Since this world does indeed include hardship, danger, and pain, the nonbeliever concludes that the world could not have been created by a perfectly benevolent and omnipotent God. Hick points out the crucial difference:

> An essential premise of this argument concerns the nature of the divine purpose in creating the world. The skeptic's assumption is that man is to be viewed as a complete creation and that God's purpose in making the world was to provide a suitable dwelling-place for the fully formed creature. Since God is good and loving, the environment which he has created for human life to inhabit is naturally as pleasant and comfortable as possible. . . .
>
> Christianity, however, has never supposed that God's purpose in the creation of the world was to construct a paradise whose inhabitants would experience a maximum of pleasure and a minimum of pain. The world is seen, instead, as a place of "soul-making" in which free beings, grappling with the tasks and challenges of their existence in a common environment, may become "children of God" and "heirs of eternal life."[19]

Having set out these alternative conceptions, Hick proceeds to make the case for his *"negative theodicy."* He asks us to suppose that the world is a hedonistic paradise, that is, free of all possibility of pain and suffering. What kind of world would it be? Hick argues that it would, to say the least, be quite extraordinary and, finally, not very appealing:

> For example, no one could injure anyone else: the murderer's knife would turn to paper or his bullets to thin air . . . fraud, deceit, conspiracy, and treason would

somehow always leave the fabric of society undamaged. Again, no one would ever be injured in an accident: the mountain climber, steeplejack, or playing child falling from a height would float unharmed to the ground. . . .

To make possible this continual series of individual adjustments, nature would have to work by 'special providences' instead of running according to general laws which men must learn to respect on penalty of pain or death. The laws of nature would have to be extremely flexible: sometimes gravity would operate, sometimes not . . . there could be no sciences, for there would be no enduring world structure to investigate. . . .

Courage and fortitude would have no point in an environment in which there is, by definition, no danger or difficulty. Generosity, kindness, the *agape* aspect of love, prudence, unselfishness, and all other ethical notions which presuppose life in a stable environment, could not even be formed. Consequently, such a world, however well it might promote pleasure, would be very ill-adapted for the development of the moral qualities of human personality. In relation to this purpose it would be the worst of all possible worlds.[20]

If, indeed, it is within God's purpose to create human beings who, though imperfect, can develop free and uncoerced into more perfect children of God, then this present world of danger and pain is a more plausible environment for such a purpose than is a hedonistic paradise. The great monotheistic faiths would agree that this is, in fact, God's purpose and that both moral and natural evil are, therefore, compatible with belief in a God who is both omnipotent and perfectly good.

If we keep our attention trained on *individual* "soul-making," much can be said for such a theodicy. But the innocent suffering that we have witnessed in the twentieth century—the Jewish Holocaust, Hiroshima, the bloodbath in Cambodia, and the thousands of starving infants in Ethiopia— these forms of demonic evil strike us as somehow radically incompatible with any notion of individual "soul-making." Can God's purpose include such unspeakable, large-scale suffering? Or even the innocent suffering of a single infant?

Hick fully acknowledges that a theodicy of "soul-making" never can be *emotionally* satisfying in view of human genocide or the torture of a single child. He insists, nevertheless, that it remains *intellectually* compelling since we cannot expect God to revoke our freedom when its wrong exercise becomes intolerable to us. Finally, however, the theist must fall back on a radical trust that the mystery of present suffering will be lifted and God's action justified in the *eschaton*, the end time of resurrection and final judgment.

## A Theodicy of Submission: The Mystery of God's Sovereignty

In the last analysis, John Hick appeals to faith in the face of God's mysterious ways that pass human understanding. This is, no doubt, the monotheist's ultimate refuge, whatever intellectual explanations may appear as plausible justifications of God and evil. The *locus classicus* is again the Book of Job.

After his three friends gave their brief for Job's suffering as his recompense for sin, Job presents the final defense of his own case. Once again, he portrays himself as a pious and righteous man, indeed as something of a paragon of virtue. He ends his plea:

> Let me call a witness in my defense!
> Let the Almighty state his case against me!
> If my accuser had written out his indictment,
> I would not keep silence and remain indoors.
> No! I would flaunt it on my shoulder and wear
> it like a crown on my head; I would plead the whole record
> of my life and present that in court as my defense.
> —*(New English Bible, Job 31:35–37)*

Job's persistent self-justification does not cause God to remove his rod of suffering. Neither does God feel called on to reply to Job's questions or to defend his own conduct; rather, the Almighty appears to Job in the whirlwind, brutally pressing him with questions and convicting him of his ignorance. What Job receives in reply is neither recompense nor comfort, but anger, sarcasm, and mockery:

> Who is this whose ignorant words cloud my design in darkness? Brace yourself and stand up like a man; I will ask questions, and you shall answer. Where were you when I laid the earth's foundations? Tell me if you know and understand. Who settled its dimensions? Surely you should know. Who stretched his measuring-line over it? On what do its supporting pillars rest? Who set its cornerstone in place, when the morning stars sang together and all the sons of God shouted aloud? . . . Have you descended to the spring of the sea or walked in the unfathomable deep? Have the gates of death been revealed to you? Have you ever seen the door-keepers of the place of darkness? Have you comprehended the vast expanse of the world? Come, tell me all this, if you know. . . . Brace yourself and stand up like a man; I will ask questions and you shall answer. Dare you deny that I am just or put me in the wrong that you may be right?
> —*(New English Bible, Job 38:2–7, 16–18; 40:7–8)*

Job challenges the very government of the universe while, at the same time, he sits in self-absorption, riveted on the injustice of his own condition. God calls on Job to cast his view beyond his own parochial horizon. Job, after all, is not God's only concern—nor is man. Finally, then, in the presence of the wondrous mystery of the whole, vast creation, Job forgets his case; his focus is suddenly and profoundly widened and deepened:

> Then Job answered the Lord: I know that thou canst do all things and that no purpose is beyond thee. But I have spoken of great things which I have not understood, things too wonderful for me to know. I knew of thee then only by report but now I see thee with my own eyes. Therefore I melt away, I repent in dust and ashes.
> —*(New English Bible, Job 42:1–6)*

Job does not repent of any sins that had brought affliction on him. He is vindicated before his three friends. Suffering as a recompense for sin can only be, at best, partially true. Job repents of his ignorant charges against God and of his lack of faith. No longer does he cry out to be delivered from innocent suffering. Job can only put his hand to his mouth and confess his error in speaking of things beyond his comprehension. Suffering is, in a sense, dissolved as a problem before God's sovereign majesty and mystery.

Job's experience is essentially the normative theodicy of the Western monotheistic faiths. In Islam, the problem of evil and suffering is always seen in the perspective of Allah's providential will. The Arabic word *aslama* means "to submit" to Allah, the Lord of the Universe. For the pious Muslim, the most certain thing in life is that all occurs with Allah's omnipotent but mysterious will. Any denial of complete predestination seems to imply a power other than God controlling the universe.

Al-Ghazālī points out that all explanations of evil are, finally, inadequate. We must accept the mystery of God's predestination:

> Do not doubt in any way that God is the most compassionate of the compassionate . . . for beneath this is a mystery, disclosure of which the law forbids. Be content then with prayer, do not hanker after disclosure! You have been informed by hints and signs if you are among his people. Reflect! . . . for I deem you one endowed with insight into God's secret of predestination.[21]

Despite all appearances of evil to the contrary, submission to Allah teaches the Muslim both patience and endurance. God, after all, is in perfect control. All comes from God, whether it be good fortune or seeming calamity. This kind of spiritual resignation can, of course, translate into a divine determinism and fatalism, as it did in some forms of Islamic theology. In orthodox Islamic thought, this extreme determinism is, however, balanced with doctrines of human freedom and divine compassion.

Preoccupation with the divine unity, omnipotence, and predetermination may appear to outsiders as strange, even inhumane. On the contrary, such a faith has given millions of theists a deep sense of cosmic order, of the moral *rightness* of things, and a profound spiritual repose—in the midst of recurrent evil and innocent suffering.

What underlies the experience of divine sovereignty and omnipotence is a profound religious sentiment. Job and Al-Ghazālī and John Calvin are telling us that, despite all appearances to the contrary, God cannot but have chosen the best. Not that evil and suffering are unreal; rather, that the pain and sorrow will somehow be used by God or, in the *eschaton*, be shown by God to be justified. Faith rests in that assurance.

The three types of monotheistic theodicy that we have explored so far hold in tension the reality of evil and the perfect goodness and omnipotence of God. Some critics would argue that some monotheists have so emphasized the sovereignty of God as possibly to call into question God's goodness and compassion. God's omnipotence is sustained but, seemingly, at the terrible price of denying any plausible meaning to the attribute of divine love. God's love and goodness have no analogy to what we know as human love and goodness. No monotheistic theodicy has, of course, explicitly denied God's goodness, and few (Christian Science may be a modern exception) deny the reality of evil. However, in the past two centuries, a number of Western philosophers and theologians have called for a thorough examination and revision of the idea of divine omnipotence. It is, they believe, the only way of making theism intelligible in a world of real suffering and evil.

## Process Theodicy

The most impressive arguments for the incoherence of the classical view of divine omnipotence are offered by theologians who have appropriated the doctrines of twentieth-century Process philosophy, particularly those of Alfred North Whitehead (1861–1947) and Charles Hartshorne (b. 1897). According to these Process philosophers, all reality is constituted by process and change, from the least to the greatest, God not excluded. Furthermore, this process is social, that is, the world consists of entities—again, from mere particles of matter to God—that freely respond to and are responded to by the free activity of other entities. Nothing whatever, not even God, *wholly* determines the being of something else. This doctrine has important implications for the idea of "power," because power here is, by its very nature, social; that is, it presupposes free relationships between distinct individuals or agents, including the relationship between God and his creatures.

*Process theodicy* therefore argues that nothing, not even God, can *wholly* determine the being of others. A contemporary theologian puts it as follows:

> This means that even the greatest possible power over other things—even the omnipotent power than which no greater can be conceived—could not be all the power there is but only all the power that any one actual thing could be conceived to have, consistently with there being other actual things having lesser power over which its omnipotent power could alone be exercised. . . .
>
> The conclusion seems obvious, then, that the coherent meaning that "all-powerful" or "omnipotent" could have is not all the power there is—since nothing can have that . . . but only all the power that any one individual could conceivably have consistently with their being other individuals who as such must themselves also have some power, however minimal.[22]

Process theologians argue that such a conception of divine power is more in keeping with the biblical picture of God's relations with his creatures; moreover, that it certainly is more consistent with the idea of divine love and omnibeneficence that, they insist, must presuppose the real freedom and responsibility of finite selves. Process theology can accept the real existence of evil as in no way incompatible with belief in a God *whose power and goodness alike are the greatest conceivable* "since such evil as exists may be attributed to decisions other than God's own for which God cannot be reasonably held responsible."[23] God cannot eliminate evil; God can only minimize it while maximizing the possibilities for good.

Many contemporary theists have found this to be an attractive solution to the problem of evil. Others, however, regard it as quite unsatisfactory because God's action appears to be only a persuasive one. God does not seem to be fully in control; God's will and purposes can be frustrated, or, indeed, defeated. A finite or limited God struggling to maximize good may be admirable but, say the critics, this God is no match for the earthly power of evil and thus not the proper object of our ultimate trust and hope.

### A Theodicy of Protest

Many sensitive theists will insist that philosophical arguments justifing God in the face of evil are not only shallow but also downright diabolical. Intellectual arguments, they contend, end up legitimating evil. These believers are wary of all answers. While remaining believers, they engage in a *theodicy of protest,* more properly, an *antitheodicy.* They agree with Dostoevsky's Ivan Karamazov in refusing to approve any theodicy that entails acceptance of the torturing to death of even one terror-stricken, innocent child. Surely, much evil is the result of human freedom and sin, but, they argue, God cannot so easily be removed from responsibility. The cost in evil for human freedom is too high. God allows far too much suffering and waste.

These protesters are also repelled by the notion of a "limited" God who, so to speak, "holds his breath" while we humans foolishly act out our carnage, a God who then tries to make the best out of a bad job. Such a God, they claim, is not worth bothering about. God, they insist, is the Lord of Creation. God cannot be exonerated because of human freedom. God, too, is guilty; God, too, must bear a large share of responsibility for evil. God must be put in the dock and interrogated, and called to account.

To put God on trial may appear blasphemous—but, in fact, it may be paying God the highest compliment. To contest against God is at least to take God's reality seriously. It would, in some ways, be much easier to deny that God exists and have done with it. The believing protester wants both to interrogate God and to resist despair. The most powerful expression of this form of angry, faithful quarrel with God is found in the novels and essays of the Jewish writer **Elie Wiesel,** who experienced the Holocaust firsthand. His testimony and protest express a long tradition of Jewish faith going back to Job.

Wiesel learned from one of his teachers that the Jew alone realizes that "he may oppose God as long as he does so in defense of his [God's] creation."[24] In his play *The Trial of God,* Wiesel tells of the aftermath of a *pogrom,* the organized massacre of Jews, in Russia in 1649. God is put on trial for his crimes against humanity by Berish, one of only two Jewish survivors. Sam, a brilliant attorney, offers all the usual defenses of God: God has reasons that are beyond our understanding, and so forth. But Berish will not hear of it and responds:

> I lived as a Jew and it is as a Jew that I shall die—and it is as a Jew that, with my last breath, I shall shout my protest to God. And because the end is near [another pogrom is imminent], I shall shout louder! Because the end is near, I'll tell Him that He's more guilty than ever![25]

This rejection of all attempts to "justify the ways of God to man" may not be satisfying to the philosophic mind, but Berish's "No!" to all forms of consolation can also strike one as refreshing and real. But the "No!" is only penultimate. There is the other side of the quarrel, voiced by Job: "Though he slay me, *yet will I trust in him*" (Job 13:15). This side is beautifully related in a tale told by Wiesel. It may sum up the ultimate stance of any profound theistic belief. A family of Jews is left in the desert without provision of food or drink.

> One evening they collapsed with fatigue. They were four to fall asleep; they were three to rise. The father dug a grave for his wife, and the children recited the **Kaddish.** And they took up their walk again.
>
> The next day they were three to lie down; only two woke up. The father dug a grave for his older son and recited the *Kaddish.* And with his remaining son he continued the march.
>
> Then one night the two stretched out. But at dawn only the father opened his eyes. He dug a grave in the sand and this is how he addressed God: "Master of the Universe, I know what you want—I understand what you are doing. You want despair to overwhelm me. You want me to cease believing in You; to cease praying to You, to cease invoking Your name to glorify and sanctify it. Well, I tell you: No, no—a thousand times no! You shall not succeed! In spite of me and in spite of You, I shall shout the *Kaddish,* which is a song of faith, for You and against You. This song you shall not still, God of Israel."[26]

## NOTES

1. The sociologist Max Weber was the first to use the term *theodicy* in this wider sense and the one who developed a useful typology of theodicies. More recently, the American sociologist Peter Berger has adapted and expanded upon Weber's work in his book *The Sacred Canopy* (New York, 1967). The account of theodicy in this chapter is heavily dependent on Weber and Berger, especially the latter's distinctive typology.

2. W. K. C. Guthrie, *The Greeks and Their Gods* (London, 1950), 130–31.

3. Berger, *Sacred Canopy,* 54–55.

4. Lucien Levy Bruhl, *How Natives Think,* trans. L. A. Clare (London, 1926), 91.

5. William James, *The Varieties of Religious Experience* (New York, 1902), 395.

6. Norman Cohn, *The Pursuit of the Millennium* (London, 1970), 21.

7. Howard Kaminsky, *A History of Hussite Revolution* (Berkeley, Calif., 1967), 340–41.

8. Peter Worsley, *The Trumpet Shall Sound: A Study of "Cargo" Cults in Melanesia* (London, 1957), 154–55.

9. Lewis Pelly, *The Miracle Play of Hasan and Husain,* Vol. II (London, 1879), 347f.

10. Werner Foerster, *Gnosis: A Selection of Gnostic Texts,* Vol. II, trans. and ed. R. McL. Wilson (Oxford, 1974), 159.

11. *Bhagavadgita,* Vol. II, 31, 37–38, in S. Radhakrishnan and C. A. Moore, *A Source Book in Indian Philosophy* (Princeton, N.J., 1957), 108–9.

12. *Dharmapada Karmavarga,* Vol. IV, 4-5, 8, 19, cited in John Bowker, *Problems of Suffering in Religions of the World* (Cambridge, Eng., 1970), 248.

13. *Milindapanha,* Vol. 65, cited in Bowker, *Problems of Suffering,* 249.

14. U. Thittila, "The Fundamental Principles of Theravada Buddhism," in Kenneth W. Morgan, ed., *The Path of the Buddha* (New York, 1956), 86–87.

15. Christmas Humphreys, *Karma and Rebirth* (London, 1943), 54f.

16. David Hume, *Dialogues Concerning Natural Religion,* ed. N. K. Smith (Oxford, 1935), 244.

17. Arthur J. Arberry, *The Koran Interpreted,* Vol. II (London, 1955), 48.

18. Abu Hamid al-Ghazālī, *al-Maqsad al-asnā* (Beirut, 1971), 68–69. Cited in Eric L. Ormsby, *Theodicy in Islamic Thought* (Princeton, N.J., 1984), 253.

19. John Hick, *Philosophy of Religion* (Englewood Cliffs, N.J., 1964), 44.

20. Ibid., 45.

21. Al-Ghazālī, in Ormsby, *Theodicy,* 69–70.

22. Schubert Ogden, "Evil and Belief in God: The Distinctive Relevance of a 'Process Theology,'" *The Perkins Journal* (Summer 1978), 32–33.

23. Ibid., 33.

24. Elie Wiesel, *A Jew Today* (New York, 1978), 6.

25. Elie Wiesel, *The Trial of God* (New York, 1979), 157.

26. Wiesel, *A Jew Today,* 135–36.

## KEY WORDS

theodicy

"mystical participation"

"objective immortality"

this-worldly eschatology

millenarian eschatology

Taborites

apocalyptic

John Frum Cargo Cult

Shi'i Islam

dualist theodicy

*karma–samsara*

Hindu *dharma*

Book of Job

John Hick's "negative theodicy"

Process theodicy

theodicy of protest

Elie Wiesel

## REVIEW QUESTIONS

1. What is theodicy? Can you give examples of theodicy from your own experience or observations?

2. Describe the characteristics of a theodicy of "mystical participation." Give some examples.

3. What are some of the features of a millenarian, this-worldly theodicy, such as that of the Taborites or the John Frum Cargo Cult?

4. How does a radically dualistic theodicy, such as Gnosticism and Mandeanism, differ from millenarian or monotheistic theodicy?

5. Explain the Hindu theodicy in terms of the *karma–samsara–dharma* complex of doctrines. Why is this theodicy called the most "rational"?

6. Many monotheistic religions defend human suffering and "testing" as a necessary condition of "soul-making." Can you describe John Hick's defense of what he calls a "negative theodicy"?

7. How do different understandings of deity or ultimate reality relate to the theodicies with which they are associated?
8. Explain why the monotheistic conception of deity presents problems for the monotheistic faiths with regard to the problem of evi. How does Process theology attempt to address these problems?
9. Which theodicy makes the most sense to you, or is the most satisfying to you. Why?

## SUGGESTIONS FOR FURTHER READING

*For a general discussion of evil theodicy in the world's religions, see*

BERGER, PETER. *The Sacred Canopy.* Chapter 3. New York: Doubleday, 1967.

BOWKER, JOHN W. *Problems of Suffering in Religions of the World.* Cambridge: Cambridge University Press, 1970.

CENTNER, WILLIAM, ed. *Evil and the Response of World Religion.* St. Paul, Minn., 1997.

HEBBLETHWAITE, BRIAN. *Evil, Suffering, and Religion.* London: Sheldon Press, 1976.

HERMAN, ARTHUR L. *The Problem of Evil in Indian Thought.* Delhi: Motilal, Banarsidass, 1976.

*On the problem of evil in the context of Western monotheism, see*

CAMUS, ALBERT. *The Plague.* New York: Vintage Books, 1948.

DAVIS, STEPHEN, ed. *Encountering Evil.* Atlanta: John Knox Press, 1981. An interesting collection of essays and critiques by five philosophers.

DOSTOEVSKY, FYODOR. *The Brothers Karamazov.* Trans. Constance Garnett. Book V, Chapter 4. New York: Modern Library, n.d.

HICK, JOHN H. *Evil and the God of Love.* London: Macmillan, 1966.

HUME, DAVID. *Dialogues Concerning Natural Religion.* Book XI. Ed. Kemp Smith. Indianapolis: Bobbs Merrill, n.d.

GRIFFIN, DAVID. *God, Power, and Evil: A Process Theodicy.* Philadelphia: Westminster, 1976.

ORMSBY, ERIC L. *Theodicy in Islamic Thought.* Princeton, N.J.: Princeton University Press, 1984.

PETERSON, MICHAEL L., ed. *The Problem of Evil: Selected Readings.* Notre Dame, Ind.: University of Notre Dame Press, 1992. Includes an extensive bibliography.

WIESEL, ELIE. *Night.* New York: Avon Books, 1969. (Wiesel's account of his own experience in Birkenau, Auschwitz, Buna, and Buchenwald concentration camps.)

———. *The Trial of God.* New York: Random House, 1979. A dramatic portrayal of the Jewish "quarrel with God," in the context of a seventeenth-century pogrom in Russia.

# 11

# *Ethics: Patterns of Moral Action*

## Overview

In the previous two chapters we have learned that religions are deeply aware of our human deficiencies and the reality of evil. They are confronted with the question: "How are we to live in relation to the Sacred and our fellow human beings?" A distinctive feature of all religious communities is therefore the shaping and transmission of a moral tradition. This includes a complex of obligatory moral rules and taboos, time-honored moral virtues, and social values that often are transmitted through sacred narratives and texts, and codified in ethical or legal traditions and in ritualistic behavior. As we have seen, many would argue that action, what people *do*, is more important than what they believe. In any case, moral action that is clearly sanctioned by sacred authority is a crucial dimension of a religious worldview.

In many religions, there is no sharp demarcation between ritual, legal, and ethical requirements. The Jewish *halakhah*, the Muslim *sharī'a*, and the Hindu *dharma* (see Chapter 12) involve a totality of ritual directives, moral commands, and civil obligations and punishments. What distinguishes religious ethics from secular morality is that the former involves a complex of moral dispositions, principles, and practices based dominantly, if not solely, on the *acceptance of a sacred authority*. The authority may be located in the commands of a sacred book—the Hebrew Scriptures, the New Testament, or the *Qur'an*—in cosmic law—*rta* or *dharma* (Hinduism), or the *tao* (Confucianism)—in the teachings and example of a charismatic leader—Jesus or Buddha—or, more often, in a combination of these.

The religious person's sense of obligation and right action is shaped by and conforms to a regulative or normative sacred authority. Conformity may be largely personal and demand an essentially interior or dispositional response—as is found, for example, in certain classical passages in the Hindu *Bhagavad Gita* and in the writings of the Protestant reformer Martin Luther. Other ethical obligations may be more focused on the community and be largely consequential, that is, measured by certain social goals. The sacred moral obligation may also involve degrees of possibility, success, and failure. The transgression of or failure to fulfill the sacred duty may result in a variety of problems for the individual and for the community that require improvement (see Chapter 9). Transgression or failure may bring a sense of defilement, shame, guilt, or remorse, all of which require purification, amendment of life, redemption, or liberation (see Chapter 12).

This chapter examines some important aspects of religious ethics from a comparative perspective. It begins by suggesting some differences between an ethics of virtue and an ethics of duty. Considerable attention is then given to the distinctive *sources* of religious ethics and how, from these sources, the religious traditions develop principles, norms, and models of the moral life. First, we discuss the concept of cosmic or natural law, with examples of this source and its normative application in both Confucianism and Roman Catholicism. Charismatic leadership is another source of moral authority that has served as a powerful energizer of moral action in the religious traditions. A brief characterization of charismatic leadership is followed by two examples: the great Indian sage and reformer Mohandas Gandhi and the ancient Judean prophet Amos. A third source of the religious moral life is what we refer to as an "ethics of divine command," that is, an ethics based on commands or laws that are divinely revealed, recorded in a sacred scripture, and commented upon down through the years by a clerical class of legal and moral experts. Here, considerable attention is given to an analysis of both Jewish and Islamic law and ethics, for they are critical to an understanding of these two great religious traditions. The discussion of Jewish ethics focuses on the example of abortion; Islamic ethics is illustrated through an analysis of the moral obligation of Muslims to engage in *jihād*, or holy war.

## Virtues and Obligations

Before we embark on a broader discussion of the sources of moral action in the religious traditions, a special word needs to be said about an ethics of virtue and an ethics of obligation or duty. Generally speaking, for the Greeks and the early Christians, as well as for Confucianism in China, an *ethics of virtue*—of what is morally commendable or ideal—was the chief concern of moral discourse. However, since the Enlightenment in the West, an *ethics of obligation*—of what ought to be done—has dominated ethical reflection. An ethics of duty is essentially concerned with how to establish those general principles that can guide persons when they are confronted with a broad range of actions—principles such as benevolence or justice; or it is concerned with specifying more particular rules that can guide persons in more concrete actions, for example, why a woman may or may not undertake a therapeutic abortion.

Unlike an ethics of duty, an ethics of virtue is not principally concerned with establishing general principles or specifying rules by which to guide moral action. Rather, it looks to and seeks to emulate the kind of person who is considered good—the ideal moral character—and to those qualities such as self-giving love, fidelity, and courage that form the character of the moral exemplar. Here, the judgment of one's actions has to do with the motives, the inner dispositions, the habits and traits of character of a person or group of persons, especially as those traits are realized in compelling moral exemplars: Socrates, Jesus, the Buddha, Muhammad, the martyrs, and the saints. Virtuous actions derive their merit from virtuous motives and not from the external performance itself. The moral guide here is "be this" rather than "do this."

Most religious traditions have focused attention on certain *cardinal virtues*, and these often reflect the character traits of the religious founder or of a venerated sage or saint. The Greeks thought there were four cardinal virtues: wisdom, courage, temperance, and justice. Buddhism has emphasized the virtues of love, compassion, joyful sympathy, equanimity, and patience. Christianity traditionally has spoken of seven cardinal virtues: the three "theological" virtues of faith, hope, and love; and the four "human" virtues of prudence, fortitude, temperance, and justice. What these traditions have rightly intuited is that morality is more than the adding up of a certain number of duties accomplished; rather, morality has to do with the formation of a self, of a character of a certain kind that aspires to a moral ideal that goes far beyond what is merely required. In fact, one could argue that duty is only made possible through a habitual virtuous intent. Furthermore, a person of virtue is necessarily dutiful. Not to be so would be to fail to be virtuous. The virtuous person therefore will seek out those principles and norms by which to guide their action in specific cases. The cultivation of virtue and the following of certain rules are, in the last analysis, complementary rather than conflicting.

The virtuous hero or saint often dominates the life of popular, lay religion in most of the traditions. These saints and heroes are the subjects of legends and stories, and they are depicted in popular art and iconography. The **Bodhisattva** is the central hero and moral exemplar or pattern in the Mahayana (Great Vehicle) school of Buddhism in East Asia. The Sanskrit term *bodhisattva* conveys the sense of "a being whose mind and effort is directed toward enlightenment." What the Mahayana *sūtras* or texts focus on, however, are the Bodhisattva's heroic feats of compassion on behalf of all creatures. While the Theravada *arhant* seeks to secure enlightenment for himself in monastic isolation, the Bodhisattva is deeply moved by the sight of the sufferings of all sentient beings and vows to become a Buddha in order to relieve others of their distress, no matter how many aeons this might require. In Mahayana, the qualifications for becoming a Bodhisattva are drastically reduced and therefore may be open to any person who is willing to make the effort to alleviate the suffering of the world. The Bodhisattva, it is said, is like a shepherd who enters the safety of the fold only after all the sheep have been brought in—a sign of willingness to postpone liberation for the sake of others.

*Avalokitésvara* (*Kuan-yin* in China; *Kannon* in Japan) is the Bodhisattva singled out as the perfect embodiment of compassion and is perhaps the most popular figure in the East Asian Buddhist pantheon. Depicted in a male or female form, he or she watches over all suffering beings and heeds their cries of pain and distress. Avalokitésvara is portrayed as a male Bodhisattva in India but frequently assumes the form of a female deity—as Kuan-yin and Kannon—in China and Japan. The latter are among the most popular of the "celestial" Bodhisattvas, and devout lay Buddhists look to Kuan-yin (or Kannon) as the perfect moral embodiment of compassion, praying to her for help in living the virtuous life and for protection against a host of dangers and calamities.

In China, Kuan-yin is referred to as the "Goddess of Mercy." She often is depicted as the White-Robed Kuan-yin, a slender figure carrying a white lotus in her left hand. She is also depicted with a small child in her arms or at her feet. The famous *Lotus Sutra* portrays Kuan-yin as the savioress of this distressed world, relieving the suffering of all who call out her name. There she appears in seven female forms as a nun, a Buddhist laywoman, a woman, a housewife, an officer's wife, a Brahman woman, and a young girl—in each instance she takes on the appropriate form that can, through selfless action, save the distressed.

## The Sources and Norms of Moral Authority

### Cosmic or Natural Law

*Cosmic* or *natural law* is one of the important sources of ethical guidance. Natural law theory holds that human moral action is grounded in the essential structure of reality itself. The Roman statesman-philosopher Cicero (106–43 B.C.E.) summarized it well in *The Republic:*

> True law is right reason in agreement with nature; it is of universal application, unchanging and everlasting; it summons to duty by its commands, and averts from wrongdoing by its prohibitions.... It is wrong to alter this law or to repeal any part of it.... Neither senate nor people can free us from its obligation, and we need no one outside ourselves to expound or interpret it.[1]

*Cosmic Law in Confucianism*　　In China, the law that underlies and directs the natural world and the law of the moral and social order traditionally

The White Robed Kannon, the popular female Bodhisattva, the perfect embodiment of compassion and self-sacrifice. (*Source:* Courtesy of the Cleveland Museum of Art, John L. Severance Fund, 51.540.)

have been joined. This is true of both Confucianism, especially certain schools of Neo-Confucianism, and of Taoism, the other great native religious tradition of China. The word *tao* is used to refer to cosmic or natural law in both Confucianism and Taoism.

*Tao* literally means road or pathway, but it also came to mean "the way to do" something, hence as moral guide or truth. Confucius used the term *tao* only to refer to the ethical path that was to guide both the individual and society, the following of which would produce order, happiness, and peace. He referred to the *tao* as following the way of the "ancients" (see Chapter 10). Implicit in Confucius's thought, however, is the link between *tao* as universal natural law and its presence in all individual things by which their particular innate character or essence is shaped. This is fully developed by later Confucianist writers such as Mencius.

Meng-Tzu (391–308 B.C.E.), or *Mencius* as he is known in the West, is the moral philosopher who developed a more idealistic theory of morality than did Confucius, in whose tradition he stands. The Chinese regard Mencius as their Second Sage. What we know of him and his thought is found in the *Mencius*, a book of sayings and dialogues between Mencius and his disciples. Mencius taught that all humans are born with an innate "childlike heart"—what he called *hsin* ("heart-mind")—which is the basis of all morality. **Hsin** is a natural, innate capacity for moral discrimination. Mencius insisted that human morality was natural and not simply a culturally learned response, and he often used metaphors taken from nature to refer to it. He spoke, for example, of goodness as planted in "good soil" and of moral "sprouts" that should be cultivated like plants.

A critic of Mencius, Kao Tzu, said that human nature was like a swift current of water. "If led eastward, it will flow eastward; if led westward it will flow westward." In other words, human nature is not disposed either to good or evil but can be directed simply by habit or indoctrination. Mencius, however, disagrees: "It is true that water is neither disposed to east nor west, but is it neither disposed to flowing upward nor downward? The tendency of human nature to do good is like that of water to flow downward. There is no man who does not tend to do good."[2]

Mencius was convinced that when left to follow their natural feelings, humans will do what is honorable, proper, and good. He wrote,

> Why I say all men have a sense of commiseration is this: Here is a man who suddenly notices a child about to fall into a well. Invariably he will feel a sense of alarm and compassion. And this is not for the purpose of gaining the favor of the child's parents, or seeking the approbation of his neighbors and friends, or for fear of blame should he fail to rescue it. Thus we see that no man is without a sense of compassion, or a sense of shame, or a sense of courtesy, or a sense of right and wrong. The sense of compassion is the beginning of humanity [*jen*]; the sense of shame is the beginning of righteousness [*i*]; the sense of courtesy is the beginning of decorum [*li*]; and the sense of right and wrong [*chih*] is the beginning of wisdom. Every man has within himself these four beginnings just as he has four limbs.[3]

Later Neo-Confucian thinkers were to extend Mencius' teaching and to emphasize the fact that the person who understands his or her mind understands nature itself. The words, in fact, mean one and the same; they represent only verbal differences. Hence, one must turn within to rediscover the "child's-mind" with which all humans are endowed by nature or Heaven.

The Neo-Confucian teacher Lu Hsiang-shan (1139–1192 C.E.), who lived during the Sung dynasty, taught that the mind *is* li or "principle," which he associated with *tao*. To be at one with the ultimate principle of things is simply to return to one's own moral nature, for "all things are already complete in oneself." Lu Hsiang-shan writes,

> The moral principle inherent in the human mind is endowed by Heaven and cannot be wiped out. Those who are clouded by material desires so as to pervert principles and violate righteousness, have become so because they do not think, that is all. If they can truly return to their true selves and think, their sense of right and wrong and their ability to choose right and wrong will have the qualities of quiet alertness, clear-cut intelligence, and firm conviction.[4]

Lu Hsiang-shan, though a Confucian, advocated "quiet-sitting" and meditation, much in the manner of Ch'an Buddhism which had been introduced into China only a few centuries before. Ch'an, or the Meditation School of Buddhism, is better known in the West by the Japanese word *Zen.* Ch'an taught, as did Lu, a "direct pointing to the human mind" and the sudden enlightenment or realization that one's own mind is one with the ultimate, one with the natural law that underlies everything. For Lu, however, this sudden insight is *ethical,* not principally metaphysical. What it involves is the rediscovery of one's own moral nature. In Lu's form of Neo-Confucianism, we also see certain affinities with Taoism which also taught that moral wisdom is found in the *Tao,* or the Way. It is, however, a very different path from that of the Confucianists, one that is essentially passive and receptive—even "quietistic"—rather than active. The Taoist sage Lao Tzu (604–531? B.C.) exemplifies what we refer to below as "charismatic" leadership. He saw the power of personal example and recognized that we are chiefly moved by a person's character and style of life. By his or her personal attraction, the Taoist causes others to want what he or she wants, to be what he or she is. The Sage relies on "actionless activity," for the Tao is the way of those who would "achieve without doing":

> Therefore the Sage
> Puts himself in the background; but is always to the fore.
> Remains outside; but is always there.
> Is it not just because he does not strive for any personal end
> That all his personal ends are fulfilled?[5]

*Natural Law in Roman Catholicism*   The Neo-Confucian sages taught that when humans follow their essential nature, they follow what is ordained of Heaven, a natural, moral law. This is also the teaching of the Roman Catholic Church. *St. Thomas Aquinas,* the greatest of the Catholic teachers, wrote that "Natural law is nothing other than the participation of eternal law in rational creatures." For St. Thomas, the moral law is God's divine plan for human beings impressed upon their own natural reason. Catholic natural law doctrine has its roots in earlier Greek philosophy, principally in the Stoic's admonition to "live according to Nature" (see Chapter 9), and in Aristotle. However, early Jewish and Christian writers also spoke of God's law as not only specially revealed in the Scriptures but also manifest in unwritten form in the minds and hearts of all human beings. St. Paul, for example, in his Letter to the Romans, writes,

> When the Gentiles who have not the law [Biblical] do by nature what the law requires, they are a law to themselves, even though they do not have the law. They show that what the law requires is written on their hearts.
> —*(2:12–16)*

It remained for St. Thomas Aquinas, however, to fully develop the Catholic natural law doctrine and to give it an authoritative stamp in modern Catholic teaching on ethics. In 1879, in a papal encyclical entitled *Aeterni Patris,* Pope Leo XIII called upon the Church to "restore the golden wisdom of Thomas and spread it far and wide for the defense and beauty of the Catholic faith." Since then, Aquinas has held a preeminent place among Catholic moral theologians.

What did Aquinas teach regarding natural law and the moral life? Law, Aquinas remarks, is a measure or rule of human acts conceived by reason with a view to the common good. This would appear to coincide with secular, positive law. But Aquinas wishes to establish the moral and positive law on a theological foundation. He begins with the idea of the eternal law of God. God's eternal law does not, however, suggest to him that all human law must depend on some particular command of God. Rather, according to Aquinas, God creates all creatures with their specific essence, or end, and the means of achieving those ends. And the divine wisdom, which moves all things in the achievement of their ends, is the eternal law. "Accordingly, the eternal law is nothing else than the exemplar of divine wisdom, as directing all actions and movements of creatures."[6] Creatures below the level of humanity participate unconsciously in the eternal law, whereas humans can, by the exercise of reason, discern the essential needs of their nature and determine the natural moral law, that is, those commands of reason that promote human good and avoid evil. These would include precepts of natural law having to do with such things as self-preservation, the procreation and care of offspring, and so on:

> The order of the precepts of the natural law is according to the order of natural inclinations. For there is in man, first of all, an inclination to good in accordance

with the nature which he has in common with all substances ... as every substance seeks the preservation of its own being, according to its nature; and by reason of this inclination, whatever is a means of preserving human life, and of warding off its obstacles, belongs to the natural law. Secondly, there is in man an inclination to things that pertain to him more specially ... such as sexual intercourse, the education of offspring and so forth. Thirdly, there is in man an inclination to good according to the nature of his reason, which nature is proper to him. Thus man has a natural inclination to know the truth about God, and to live in society; and in this respect, whatever pertains to this inclination belongs to the natural law.[7]

Aquinas was confident that humans, exercising their reason, could move from these general principles to discern more particular precepts for their practical moral guidance. For example, he taught that suicide is wrong and monogamy is right, not simply because God prohibits or commands them. Rather, they are prohibited or commanded by God because they are contrary to or in accord with natural moral law, hence divine, eternal law. Suicide, Aquinas argues, is contrary to our natural inclination to self-preservation; monogamy is required for the propagation and proper care of children.

The Catholic Church has followed rather faithfully Thomas Aquinas's teaching on natural law as it applies to a vast range of subjects from civil liberty and the relations of church and state to complex issues of biomedical ethics such as contraception. An example is the Church's condemnation of *contraception,* or the artificial interruption of human fertility, as intrinsically immoral for interfering with the natural *telos,* or goal, of sexual intercourse. The unequivocal rejection of contraception was enunciated in Pope Pius XI's encyclical letter *Casti Connubii,* issued on December 31, 1931. The pope permits the confining of conjugal acts to known infertile periods (the rhythm method), but he condemns contraception as unnatural:

> No reason, however grave, may be put forward by which anything intrinsically against nature may become conformable to nature and morally good. Since, therefore, the conjugal act is destined primarily by nature for the begetting of children, those who in exercising it deliberately frustrate its natural power and purpose sin against nature ...[8]

The Roman Catholic teaching on birth control has been defended in a variety of ways, but most of these are based on inferences derived from natural law. A typical argument proceeds as follows:

1. It is wrong to impede the procreative power of actions that are ordained by their nature to the generation of new human life.
2. Contraception impedes the procreative power of actions that are ordained by their nature to the generation of new human life.
3. Therefore, contraception is wrong.[9]

### Charismatic Leaders

The word *charisma* derives from the Greek *charis*, and it suggests the possession of a spiritual gift with special, often extraordinary, endowments. Its use has gained currency in the contemporary study of religion since its introduction by the sociologist Max Weber in his studies of types of authority and of moral and religious leadership. Regarding his use of the word, Weber wrote:

> The term "charisma" will be applied to a certain quality of an individual personality by virtue of which he is set apart from ordinary men and treated as endowed with supernatural, superhuman, or at least specifically exceptional powers or qualities. These are such as are . . . regarded as of divine origin or as exemplary, and on the basis of them the individual concerned is treated as a leader.[10]

Charismatic leadership is not unique to religious and moral authority, but it has been a potent source of such authority in the history of religions. Many of the great founders, leaders, and prophets—Zoroaster, Buddha, the Hebrew prophets, Jesus, Muhammad, Gandhi—are recognized as marked by distinctive charismatic features. These include "signs" or "wonders," which guarantee both the leader's authentic charisma and her or his empowerment of those "called" to be followers or disciples. The leader's charismatic moral authority also lies outside the realm of any purely rational, legal, or practical justification. It is therefore revolutionary, holding up a radically new, transcendent moral vision, one that calls for a break with the established order. The charismatic prophet says in effect: "It is written . . . but I say unto you." He or she is viewed as a special vessel or instrument of the Divine will or the Ultimate, and the followers feel a duty to follow the leader's moral summons at whatever cost. Charismatic moral authority can be expressed either in the passionate action of the leader and her or his command over others, or in an extraordinary passivity that reflects a serene self-possession.

Weber suggests that there are two kinds of charismatic religious leaders, the one represented by, for example, the Buddha and the other by Muhammad. Weber calls the former type "exemplary"; it is found most characteristically in India and East Asia. The latter type of charismatic leader is the "ethical prophet" who proclaims the command of God and is typically found in the religions that have their origin in the Near East. Weber's scheme may be too neat, but it is useful in illustrating the different types of charismatic moral authority. Our example of the "exemplary" type of charismatic authority is the twentieth-century Indian holy man, *Mohandas K. Gandhi.*

*Mohandas K. Gandhi*   Gandhi (1869–1948), known to his followers as the Mahatma or "Great Soul," is considered by many to be the greatest religious leader and political and social reformer of modern India, perhaps of the modern world. He is best known in the West for his philosophy of nonviolence, rooted in his teachings of *satyāgraha,* which he defined as "soul-force" or "the force which is born of truth and the love of nonviolence." Gandhi associated *satyāgraha* with the Indian concept of *ahimsa* (noninjury), although he expanded *ahimsa* to include prohibitions not only against physical violence but also against all coercion, even the depreciating of any other forms of life.

Born and schooled in India, Gandhi went to London at 19 to study law. He returned to Bombay to practice law but, shortly after returning, he sailed for South Africa to serve as a lawyer for an Indian client. There, he found himself subjected to racial intolerance and decided to stay in South Africa to fight racial injustice. In 1906, he began his first *satyāgraha* campaigns against the discrimination of those of color. For these actions, he was jailed many times. It is estimated that during his lifetime he spent 2,338 days in prison for his nonviolent civil disobedience. In 1914, he returned to India where he continued his nonviolent campaigns and his fastings against the injustices of British rule. He soon was looked upon as the leader of the Indian independence movement and of the effort to achieve a reconciliation between Hindu and Muslim. He became the guide and hero of the Indian masses and the liberator of the untouchables, whom he called *harijans,* meaning "people of God." His efforts to achieve religious tolerance led to his assassination on January 30, 1948, by a fanatical member of the Hindu right wing. After Gandhi's cremation, there were 13 days of national mourning. The ceremonies accompanying the immersion of his ashes at the confluence of the sacred rivers at Allahabad were witnessed by 4 million people. At the time, a disciple wrote in the press:

> For me there were only two, God and Bapu [Gandhi]. And now they have become one. When I heard the news something deep, deep down within me opened—the door to the imprisoned soul—and Bapu's spirit entered there. From that moment a new sense of the eternal abides with me. . . . Now must we move heaven and earth to fulfill the task which Bapu has left us.[11]

When asked for his message to humankind, Gandhi declared, "My life is my message." Indeed, Gandhi exhibits those characteristics that personify the *"exemplary"* charismatic **moral leader,** that is, one who teaches by her or his powerful personal example. We recall that the Chinese Confucians (see Chapter 9) insist that morality is taught, neither by legal obligation nor by physical force, but by the virtuous (*te*) example of a great personality. As we have seen, a similar doctrine was taught by the sage Lao-Tzu in the great classic *Tao Te Ching.*

Gandhi was the living embodiment of all the ancient virtues—courage, duty, self-renunciation, self-control, *ahimsa*—admired by ordinary Hindus. They felt, however, that without his powerful influence they were incapable of realizing those virtuous ideals. Gandhi energized the masses by becoming one with them: dressing in a loincloth and sandals, speaking their dialects,

The Indian leader Mohandas Gandhi working imperturbably at his spinning wheel while several Indian officials surround him. (*Source:* Courtesy of the Library of Congress).

living in a mud hut, eating the simplest of diets, and engaging in manual labor. Of leadership, he wrote,

> My co-workers and I never hesitated to do sweeping, scavenging and similar work, with the result that others took it up enthusiastically. In the absence of such sensible procedure, it is not good issuing orders to others. All would assume leadership and dictate to others, and there would be nothing done in the end. But where the leader himself becomes a servant, there are no rival claimants for leadership.[12]

Taking on his ascetic, lowly status, Gandhi achieved what Victor Turner (see Chapter 4) calls *communitas*. By breaking through and transgressing the routine order, Gandhi dissolved the norms of conventional social life, living out a deeper, transcendent truth. In so doing, he established a sacred communion with the disaffected masses that led to a powerful collective effort of hundreds of thousands of followers who sought to establish a new social order.

Another feature of the charismatic moral leader, one prominent in Gandhi's life and action, is an intense sense of being in direct contact with God or the Ultimate. Gandhi called this his "Inner Voice." Many of his most radical actions, his fastings and *satyāgraha* campaigns, for example, were undertaken after periods of quiet meditation that resulted in the bidding of the "Inner Voice." Like Jesus, Gandhi was aware, however, that the voice of God was a dangerous call. He wrote: "The 'Inner Voice.' may mean a message from God or from the Devil, for both are wrestling with the human beast." It is, he insisted, engagement alone that can judge. "Acts determine the nature of the voice."[13] Despite the dangers, Gandhi was emboldened to lead his people into costly "experiments" with truth. A powerful illustration of Gandhi's moral charisma was his famous 200-mile Salt march undertaken in 1930 to the Arabian Sea and the village of Dandi. In accord with the British-imposed Salt Act, Indians were prohibited from manufacturing, possessing, or selling contraband salt, or carrying away natural salt deposits from the sea—all this, despite the fact that this commodity was easily available all along the thousands of miles of Indian seashore. The British made a profit of £25 million a year as a result of this tax which affected millions of India's poor. By 1930, the Indian Congress Party was calling for complete independence from Britain within a year, the nonpayment of taxes, and a movement of massive civil disobedience. However, it agreed to allow Gandhi to determine the nature and the time of the new *satyāgraha* campaign.

On March 12, Gandhi and 78 disciples began the 12-day, 200-mile march to Dandi. A biographer describes some of the drama of the march:

> Peasants sprinkled the roads and strewed leaves on them. Every settlement in the line of the march was festooned and decorated. . . . For miles around, peasants gathered to kneel by the roadside as the pilgrims passed. . . . In the area traversed, over three hundred village headsmen gave up their government jobs. . . . Young men and women attached themselves to the marching column; when Gandhi reached the sea at Dandi on April 5th, his small ashram band had grown into a non-violent army several thousand strong.[14]

The entire night of April 5, Gandhi and his followers prayed. In the early morning, they accompanied Gandhi into the sea, and, on returning to the beach, Gandhi picked up some salt, thereby breaking the British law. In true charismatic fashion, by this small symbolic gesture, Gandhi had communicated to an entire nation. It is said that every villager along India's vast coast waded into the sea with a pan to make salt. Soon, many prominent Indian leaders, including Gandhi and the future president of India, Jawaharlal Nehru, were sentenced to terms in prison. It is estimated that over a hundred thousand persons were imprisoned for civil disobedience. But the heaviest price was yet to be required of Gandhi's devoted followers. It was borne by 2,500 disciples during a nonviolent raid on the Dharasana Salt Works north of Bombay. Their leader exhorted: "Gandhi's body is in jail but his soul is with you. . . . You must not use any violence under any circumstances. You will be beaten but you must not resist. You must not even raise a hand to ward off blows."[15]

Technically, legally nothing had changed. India was still a British colony. But for the Indians independence from Britain was now secure, for Gandhi had given his people the conviction and resolve that they would be free. Gandhi's charismatic march to the sea and his courageous lifting up of a few grains of salt had empowered an entire nation of millions to act nonviolently—even unto death.

*Amos—A Hebrew Prophet*   In the life and work of Gandhi we have a vivid portrayal of the "exemplary" charismatic leader. The *ethical prophet* shares a number of features with the "exemplary" moral leader, but the prophet also is distinctive in several important respects. The classic depictions of the charismatic prophet are those found in the prophetic books of the Hebrew Bible, for example in the portraits and oracles of Amos, Hosea, Isaiah, and Jeremiah. Here, we will focus on the prophet *Amos* to illustrate this type of charismatic moral authority.

The English word that we use for the Hebrew prophets is derived from the Hebrew *nabi*, which means "one who speaks for another." The Hebrew prophets were so possessed by the spirit of God that they no longer felt in control of their own words or actions. They were compelled to proclaim God's word. Many of the prophets were what we would call "ecstatics," in that they experienced visions, heard voices, and felt that they had no control over the oracles that they were called upon to prophesy. The Israelite priest Amaziah, for example, dismissed the Judean Amos on this very charge; Amos was merely a professional visionary and not an accredited prophet. But it was divine possession that compelled Amos to deliver God's message, whether or not it was received, or at what cost. Amos answered Amaziah:

> I am no prophet, nor a prophet's son; but I am a herdsman, and a dresser of sycamore trees, and the Lord took me from following the flock, and the Lord said to me, "Go, go prophesy to my people Israel."
> —*(Revised Standard Version, Amos 7:14–15)*

Amos simply had no choice:

> The lion [the Lord] has roared;
>     who will not fear?
> The Lord has spoken:
>     who can but prophesy?
>
> —*(Revised Standard Version, Amos 3:8)*

Amos was a shepherd from Tekoa, a village near Bethlehem in the southern Kingdom of Judah. Yet he was called by Yahweh, his God, to deliver the divine oracles of judgment against the northern Kingdom of Israel. Under the long reign of Jeroboam II (circa 786–746 B.C.E.), Israel had reached the pinnacle of political power, material prosperity, and territorial expansion—and of spiritual pride. And the outraged court priest, Amaziah, wanted no word of criticism from the lowly herdsman from the south. But Amos responded, nevertheless:

> Now therefore hear the word of the Lord.
> You [Amaziah] say, "Do not prophesy against Israel,
> And do not preach against the house of Isaac."
> Therefore thus saith the Lord:

"Your wife shall be a harlot in the city, and your sons and your daughters shall fall by the sword, and your land shall be parceled out by line; you yourself shall die in an unclean land, and Israel shall surely go into exile away from its land."

—*(Revised Standard Version, Amos 7:16–17)*

What had provoked the anger of the Lord God against Israel? Israel was prosperous, filled with plenty, but there was no justice in the land. Amos breaks through this complacency and proclaims God's terrible moral judgment and doom on the people:

Woe to those who are at ease in Zion, and those who feel
    secure on the mountain of Samaria . . .
Woe to those who lie on beds of ivory, and stretch themselves upon
    their couches, and eat lambs from the block, and calves from the
    midst of the stall; who sing idle songs to the sound of the harp,
    who drink wine in bowls, and anoint themselves with the finest
    oils, but are not grieved over the ruin of Joseph!
Therefore, they shall be the first of those to go into exile, and
    the revelry of those who stretch themselves shall pass away.

—*(Revised Standard Version, Amos 6:1, 4–7)*

Amos's moral denunciation is directed especially against an Israelite piety that assumes that sacrifice and temple ritual will cover injustice and iniquity.

I hate, I despise your feasts, and I take no delight in your
    solemn assemblies.
Even though you offer me your burnt offering and all your cereal
    offerings, I will not accept them, and the peace offering of your
    fatted beasts I will not look upon.
Take away from me the voice of your songs;
    to the melody of your hands I will not listen.
But let justice roll down like waters, and righteousness like an
    ever flowing stream.

—*(Revised Standard Version, Amos 5:21–24)*

Amos's blunt and fierce "Word of the Lord" to Israel is that there can be no life in God, no light, no peace, no hope, without righteousness. God and righteousness are inseparable.

The mark and authentication of the Hebrew prophets' moral authority were, first and foremost, the signs of genuine spirit possession, which often was accompanied by dramatic symbolic actions; for example, Jeremiah's smashing a pot before his listeners to dramatize the destruction of Jerusalem, and Isaiah's walking naked through Jerusalem's streets. Ezekiel's drawing of a picture of the besieged Jerusalem appears to have actually brought about the siege, by means, perhaps, of sympathetic magic. The authority of genuine prophecy required certain marks of traditional prophetic behavior, but often a prophet's authority was authenticated by the fact that his words came to pass. Later, the moral authority of the prophet's oracles is passed on to future generations through their canonization in holy scripture. This is the process referred to by Max Weber as the *"routinization of charisma."* The moral power of the original charismatic authority is not lost, although it may be weakened by being institutionalized in a closed book. The courageous, radical ideal lives on, perhaps diminished in intensity as it is accommodated to the complexities of ongoing life. Exegetes and commentators, like the rabbis in Judaism and the *fuqahā'*, or jurists, in Islam, succeeded the charismatic moral authority of the prophets' revelations to ensure their ethical applicability in changing social and historical conditions. Here, we actually enter into another, more common, source of ethical authority, namely, moral duties that are established through the pious study of religious experts based on authoritative precedents. These precedents usually are found in a revealed body of sacred scriptures (the Hebrew Bible, the *Qur'an*), but they may also include precedents developed in the ongoing historical life of the religious community—interpretations that may in time appear rather far removed from the original positive commands.

### An Ethics of Divine Command

For the three historical monotheistic religions—Judaism, Islam, and Christianity—the sources and the norms of moral obligation are derived from commands or instructions that are revealed through or dictated to a divine intermediary or a messenger (Moses, Jesus, Muhammad) and set down in a sacred scripture. The standard of right and wrong is so *because* it is commanded or forbidden by God.

In Plato's *Euthyphro*, Euthyphro proposes just such a claim, namely, that what *makes* an action right is simply the fact that it is commanded by God. But, Socrates asks him, "Is something right because God commands it or does He command it because it is right?" Euthyphro replies that, of course, God commands it because it is right. Most theologians would agree. If they did not, it would appear that if God commanded cruelty or injustice for their own sake these things would have to be judged right (moral) and obligatory. However, God would not, the argument goes, command cruelty, since it is against his nature. God's love and goodness are simply presupposed. Some writers have not, however, taken this tack, on the grounds that to do so is to measure God's moral goodness and commands by an all-too-human standard. The classic case often cited, for example, by the Christian philosopher Soren Kierkegaard (1813–1855) is God's command to Abraham that he sacrifice his son Isaac (Genesis 22). Most monotheists, however, would disagree with Kierkegaard that there can be a divine suspension of the ethical. They would say that while it is not logically impossible that God could command cruelty for its own sake, his will as revealed in the Bible or the *Qur'an* taken as a whole is that of a God "committed" to loving kindness, justice, and mercy. In other words, one can trust that God's command is righteous, that a monotheistic religion never could deny or subordinate morality to a divine caprice.

*Jewish Law and Ethics*    The ancient Israelites perceived God's revealed will and command to be the ultimate source and sanction of law and morality. There was no sharp distinction between religious and moral duties and prohibitions, and what we today might consider to be secular ones. For the God of Israel is intimately concerned with all aspects and orders of his creation—the religious cult, the family and sexuality, property and the economy, matters of state, criminal activity, and so on. In Israel, law and morality are inextricably joined, rooted in the command of Yahweh as that command is set forth in the Books of Moses. A violation of law—be it related to the status of women, the role of the king, property inheritance, or theft—is understood not only as an offense against civil society but also as a sin, a violation of God's command.

Because of God's deep concern and loving kindness for his people—who are created in his own image and called to respond to him—he has revealed his will and command through his messenger Moses, through whom the moral covenant between God and Israel was sealed at Mount Sinai:

> Moses came and told the people all the words of the Lord and all the ordinances; and all the people answered with one voice, and said, "All the words which the Lord has spoken we will do." And Moses wrote all the words of the Lord. . . . And he sent young men of the people of Israel, who offered burnt offerings and sacrificed peace offerings of oxen to the Lord. . . . Then he took the book of the covenant, and read it in the hearing of the people; and they said, "All that the Lord has spoken we will do, and we will be obedient." And Moses took the blood and threw it upon the people, and said, "Behold the blood of the covenant which the Lord has made with you, in accordance with all these words."
>
> —*(Revised Standard Version, Exodus 24:3–8)*

The Israelites spoke of God's law as "commandment" (*mitzvah*) and as "instruction" (*torah*), and, as mentioned, it covered all aspects of Israelite, and later Jewish, life. There were, for example, specific instructions regarding the poor. One should not, it is written, impose usury on loans to the poor (Exodus 22:25). On the seventh year, the poor were to be further relieved, since all debts were to be canceled (Deuteronomy 15:1–2). By the end of the first century C.E., the written books of the Torah were canonized and became the Hebrew Bible as we know it today. As we also know, however, by then the word *torah* referred not only to the written scriptures but also to an unwritten tradition of moral and legal instruction that both interpreted and supplemented the written torah. This came to be called the oral law.

It was perfectly natural that such an oral tradition should emerge. Over time, the written law could not easily cover the various contingencies faced by the Jewish community as it found itself in new circumstances. In some cases, the written law did not specify clearly enough what exactly was prohibited, for example, the types of work prohibited on the Sabbath. In the postexilic period, and especially during the periods of Greek and Roman rule in Palestine, radically new conditions had to be faced. New interpretations, explanations, and commentaries on the Torah of Moses were required. An example of the need for such interpretation is the relief of debts (Deuteronomy 15:1–2) referred to earlier. In the first century C.E., Jewish commercial life in Palestine was expanding. The command regarding the relief of debts understandably aroused great uncertainty concerning commercial transactions. Therefore, a rule was enacted by a famous rabbi named Hillel, allowing for a declaration, made before a court of law by a creditor, guaranteeing that the loan in question would not be relieved under the terms of the seventh-year law.

As we have learned in Chapter 5, a rich tradition of oral law thus grew up alongside the written law. At first, its authority was established by its connection with a specific text of Scripture, but soon the oral law took on an authority independent of the written Torah. Tradition soon maintained, however, that it was part of the original revelation given to Moses at Sinai—and therefore as binding as the written law. This was the background of all later rabbinic commentary and what we have come to know as rabbinic or *Talmudic Judaism.* Ethics in Judaism has been linked to this tradition of rabbinic study and commentary on the Mosaic law. Though detailed and complex, the regulations of the law are not regarded by the observant Jew to be a heavy yoke. Rather, they are a divine gift to be followed in gratitude and joy. The observance of the commandments (*mitzvot*) link the Jew to God in every aspect of daily life.

We close this discussion of Jewish ethics with an example of how, in the Jewish community today, the divine commandments are interpreted ethically, that is, made to apply in very different historical contexts. In our contemporary period especially, Judaism has had to confront "modernity." The result is that Judaism does not speak with one voice on such ethical questions as abortion, the status of women, homosexuality, or capital punishment. Reform Judaism, a movement originating in the nineteenth century, holds the Talmudic tradition of commentary in reverent regard but generally does not consider it to be singularly normative on issues such as those just cited. Rather, it looks also to the ethical teachings of the prophetic literature (Amos, Jeremiah, Hosea, etc.) for the moral "essence" and norms of Judaism. The contemporary discussion of abortion offers a timely illustration of both the divergent approaches taken and the conclusions reached by an Orthodox and a Reform Jew in their handling of this contentious question.

The Orthodox commentator builds his case against abortion on demand and the conditions justifying therapeutic abortion by a strict appeal to the citations and precedents found in the Hebrew Bible, the Talmud, and the Rabbinic commentaries. First, he points out that "murder in Jewish law is based on Exodus 21:12 where it is written: 'He that smiteth a man so that he dieth shall surely be put to death.' The word 'man' is interpreted to mean a man but not a fetus. Thus, the destruction of an unborn fetus is not considered murder."[16] The commentator then turns to the Talmudic sources. The *Mishnah* in *Tractate Oholoth* 7:6 asserts, "If a woman is having difficulty in giving birth (and her life is in danger), one cuts up the fetus within her womb and extracts it limb by limb, because her life takes precedence over that of the fetus. But if the greater part was already born, one may not touch it, for one may not set aside one person's life for that of another."[17]

Many Talmudic commentaries consider the "greater part" to be the newborn's "head." Once the head of the child has come out, the child is considered fully born and cannot be harmed. To kill the newborn at this point is considered infanticide. The Talmud clearly explains that the embryo is part of the mother's body and has no identity of its own. Prior to 40 days after conception, a fertilized egg is considered "mere fluid" and "need not take into consideration the possibility of a valid childbirth" (*Mishnah Niddah* 3:7). However, after 40 days, the fetus is deemed formed and any abortion thereafter requires that the Jewish laws of ritual uncleanliness be observed (*Mishnah Niddah* 3:2–6). On the basis of these Talmudic sources, the question naturally may be asked: Why do most Rabbinic authorities still prohibit abortion on demand, except when there is a threat to the mother's life, if the unborn fetus does not have the status of a person (*nefesh*)? In the numerous commentaries, a considerable variety of answers are given: The fetus does, in fact, have some status, that of a "partial person," indicated by the laws regarding impurity (*Responsa Tzofnat Paneach*, I, no. 49); one is prohibited from wounding oneself (*Bava Kamma* 91b); the act of vaginal abortion entails danger, and, according to Jewish law, one is prohibited from placing oneself in danger (Deuteronomy 4:15); the fetus, even prior to 40 days, is considered a potential human being, and so on.

On the basis of an exhaustive citation of these and other legal precedents, the Orthodox commentator draws his more conservative conclusions as to what constitutes normative guidance for Jews on the question of abortion on demand and legitimate therapeutic intervention:

> Prior to forty days following conception, the fertilized egg is considered by some Rabbinic authorities as nothing more than "mere fluid." For forty days until birth, the fetus is not considered a living person (*nefesh*) but is regarded as part of the mother's flesh and aborting it might not be considered murder. However, the destruction of an unborn fetus without sufficiently strong indication is still condemned for a variety of reasons. Abortion is permitted by most Rabbinic authorities where a medical or psychiatric threat to the mother's life exists. . . . A small minority of Rabbinic opinion allow therapeutic abortions for reasons such as incest, rape and fear that a malformed child may be born. Justification for this position rests on the grounds of concern for the mother. . . . This latter viewpoint is not subscribed to by most Rabbinic authorities, however.[18]

It is interesting to compare the above with the position on abortion taken by a leader of Reform Judaism. It is evident that he, too, cites evidence that the fetus in the womb is not a person (*nefesh*) and that, nevertheless, the

A pro-choice advocate takes hold of a pro-life advocate's bullhorn during a confrontation over abortion outside the U.S. Supreme Court. (*Source:* Courtesy of Reuters/Bettmann.)

unborn fetus, while not a person, still has some status. But the Reform rabbi does not mention the numerous citations advanced by the Orthodox scholar for opposing abortion except in clear cases of threat to the mother's life or health. He focuses, rather, on the fact that "nowhere does [the Law] state that killing the fetus by premature artificial termination of pregnancy is prohibited," and "that Jewish law does not consider abortion murder."[19] Furthermore, the Reform commentator's appeal is based essentially on more general moral considerations having to do with the sanctity of the human person—person being understood as unambiguously postnatal—and the inviolability of the individual conscience. "It is precisely because of this regard for that sanctity," he writes,

> that we see as most desirable the right of any couple to be free to produce only that number of children whom they felt they could feed and clothe and educate properly. . . . It is precisely this traditional Jewish respect for the sanctity of human life that moves us now to support that legislation which would help all women to be free to choose when and under what circumstances they would elect to bring life into the world.[20]

Here, you will notice that general, overarching moral principles are appealed to in determining what is right. They are applied to this special instance as broad norms whereas in the Orthodox case moral conduct regarding abortion is justified by appeal to a very specific tradition of Jewish *halakhah*.

*Islamic Law and Ethics* We turn now to another important example of an *ethics of divine command* based also on a tradition of legal–ethical commentary, one that guides the lives of millions of observant Muslims throughout the world today. It is often remarked that the characteristic feature of the Islamic community is its deep sense of Divine Law prescribed by God, the source and guide of action to which the faithful "commit." For Muslims there is little, if any, distinction between what is legal, ethical, and religious. It is quite natural then that the expositions of Islamic law all begin with elaborate consideration of religious duties, such as ritual purity, prayer, and pilgrimage.

*Sharī'a* is, as we have learned, the Arabic name for Divine Law, and its original reference suggests the "right path" to the source of water. Finite beings, of course, cannot know every aspect of God's immutable and transcendent Law; humans can only have insight, *fiqh,* into the Divine Law. Thus, *fiqh* is our human knowledge or understanding of the Divine Law. The word refers also to Islamic jurisprudence, or the legal rules established by the Islamic jurists (*fuqahā'*) through their pious scholarship.

There are different systems of *fiqh,* or "ways to the water." Traditionally, in **Sunni Islam,** jurists acknowledged that no ruling could be an infallible statement of Divine Law. All rules proposed by qualified jurists, based on a careful study of the sources, are considered equally valid. A clear distinction was thus drawn between God's Law and *fiqh,* and toleration of differences was accepted. Modern resistance to Westernization has been accompanied, however, by a growing intolerance of competing schools of interpretation, especially of those that appear to accommodate Western ideas, and this, in turn, has led to an increase of "fundamentalist" movements in Islam, as we shall see.

While the **Qur'an** contains many references to God's laws and commands, these often are general admonitions, rather than specific and detailed commands, hence the need for elaboration and interpretation. Over time, classical Sunni jurisprudence established four sources of the *sharī'a.* First, of course, is the *Qur'an.* Sunni Muslims hold that divine revelation ceased with the death of Muhammad. But the Prophet was possessed not only of the inspiration of the written "book" but also the inspired "wisdom" by which to guide the interpretation and application of the Divine Law. So it was that the detailed traditions or "customs" (*sunna*) of the Prophet, derived from his words and deeds, were collected and transmitted. The **Sunna of the Prophet,** the record of his words and action, thus became a second source, and the *Qur'an* and the *Sunna* of the Prophet have unique status since they both are considered to be divinely inspired and infallible. Because of human fallibility, the moral law can be known only by divine revelation. However, neither the *Qur'an* nor the *Sunna* of the Prophet may offer detailed application of the law that later came to be required. Where questions of lawful action arose that were not covered in the *Qur'an* or the *Sunna* of the Prophet, a third source was appealed to, called *analogical deduction.* Because this kind of analogical reasoning involved the imposition of human judgment, many jurists rejected analogy as a true source.

To meet the urgent need for specific rules and applications, an elaborate science of legal interpretation emerged in the second and third centuries. This, in turn, produced a clerical class of legal experts that achieved a status similar to that of the rabbinate in Judaism. These clerics are the *ulamā'*, or "learned," and the *fuqahā*, the jurists. In time, the authority of the *ulamā'* was accepted by the Islamic community. In fact, as early as the second century after Muhammad the "Consensus of the Community," represented by the *ulamā'*, had authoritative force in Sunni Islam. *Ijmā'*, or "consensus," thus became the fourth source of the law, since the majority must be right in a community guided by God. Some schools simply identified the *Sunna* of the Prophet with the consensus of the legal authorities. *Ijmā'* thus integrates all the parts of the system into a seamless whole:

> It is obvious that *ijmā'* underlies the whole imposing structure and alone gives it final validity. For it is *ijmā'* in the first place which guarantees the authenticity of the text of the Koran and of the Traditions. It is *ijmā'* which determines how the words of their texts are to be pronounced and what they mean and in what direction they are to be applied. But *ijmā'* goes much further; it is erected into a theory of infallibility, a third channel of revelation.[21]

In its role as authoritative teaching, the *ijmā'* is somewhat analogous to the *magisterium*, or teaching authority, in the Roman Catholic Church. The "consensus," as determined by the *ulamā'*, represents the legal and moral authority of the Islamic community. One could say that it follows the principle that "the will of the sovereign is the law," in this case, the Will of God as revealed through the Prophet and as authenticated and applied through the interpretations of the *ulamā'*.

The Divine Law (the *sharī'a*) is both positive law and moral obligation. This is evident in the way that the jurists classify human acts and duties in moral terms. Most actions do not come within the law as we in the West conceive law in our secular terms. How one must act morally may not have any worldly legal validity but, at the same time, may come under the strict sanction of Islamic law. The moral character of legal actions is classified according to a fivefold scheme:

1. Actions mandatory on believers
2. Actions recommended or desirable
3. Actions neutral or indifferent
4. Actions objectionable or blame-worthy, but not forbidden
5. Actions prohibited

This scheme helps devout Muslims to follow "the right way to the water," that is, the course of duty that will ensure their entry into Paradise on the Day of Judgment.

For us to understand this complex system of Islamic law and ethics, which involves textual study, interpretation, classification, and so on, another development requires mention, namely, the emergence of the legal schools during the third Islamic century (the ninth century C.E.). Among these several schools, the four dominant ones are the Hanafī, Māliki, Shafi'i, and Hanbalī. Each school is associated with a particular authoritative teacher, and their differences have to do with certain supplementary legal principles that are brought to bear on legal decisions. For example, the Māliki school allows for rules to be formulated based on public utility or the common good as standards by which to determine the ultimate purposes of the Divine Law.

The first three of these schools all recognize the traditional sources—*Qur'an, Sunna, analogy,* and *Ijmā'*—and they consider each other's systems acceptable. These schools generally recognize the tentative nature of the "striving" of the jurists to achieve "opinion" on the complex issues of the law, and this has resulted in a certain caution about dogmatism. The Hanbalī school, however, represents a fundamentalist reaction against the "innovations" of the other schools, and it is less tolerant toward them. Threats of Westernization in modern times have brought about an increase of this conservative reaction. This is especially evident in **Shi'i Islam,** which is dominant in Iran. In *Shi'i* theory, the sources recognized by the *Sunni* jurists are modified to include the sayings of the Twelve Imams, the spiritual heads of the community until 874. The *Shi'i* community considers the **Imam** no less infallible and authoritative than the Prophet. Therefore, in *Shi'i* Islam, there is not the same tolerant latitude; there is only one valid legal source, that of the Prophet and the Imams.

We have sketched some of the main features of the Islamic legal and ethical system. We now need to see how such an ethics of divine command works in practice. We select for illustration the important, and often misunderstood, Islamic obligation of **jihād** (from the Arabic verb *jāhada* meaning "to strive," "to exert," or "to struggle"). In Western minds, it is associated exclusively with the duty of Muslims to engage in military warfare with their enemies, whereas in Islam it has had a much broader religious application.

*The Duty of Jihād*   The Muslim's duty of *jihād* is, in its widest meaning, simply the exertion of one's religious effort, more particularly, in the spread of belief in Allah and of Islam throughout the world. It does not necessarily imply military warfare. The spread of Islam can be undertaken peacefully, as is indicated in the *Qur'an,* sura 16:125: "Call thou the way of the Lord with wisdom and admonition, and dispute with them in the better way." This is referred to as the "*jihād* of the tongue" or "*jihād* of the pen." These forms of peaceful persuasion and personal righteousness in combating evil have long been emphasized by certain movements and circles within Islam. Based on the *Hadīth* of the Prophet, these are spoken of as the "greater *jihād*": "Once, having returned from one of his campaigns, the Prophet said: 'We now returned from the lesser *jihād* [military effort] to the greater *jihad.*'" It is wrong, therefore, to associate *jihād* exclusively with the idea of a "holy war."

It is true, nevertheless, that the Muslim jurists concur that there is a duty of *jihād* "by the sword," that is, a duty of military action against unbelievers. In Shi'ite doctrine, all enemies of the faith—both within (heretics and rebels) and without—are objects of *jihād* through the prosecution of war. The majority of the references to *jāhada* in the *Qur'an* do refer to warfare, and scholars point to an evolving tradition on *jihād* as military effort in the *Qur'an* itself and in the developing tradition. Some *Qur'anic* verses appear to place qualifications on *jihād* by the sword, making it conditional upon some overt provocation or aggression: "And fight in the way of God with those who fight with you, but aggress not. God loves not aggressors" (*Qur'an* 2:190). Other verses, however, appear to give unconditional command to permanent war against unbelievers: "Then, when the sacred months are past, slay the idolaters wherever you find them, and take them and confine them, and lie in wait for them at every place of ambush" (*Qur'an* 9:34).

The "sword verses" thus are considered authoritative in establishing the classic tradition in Islamic law on warfare, a tradition that recognizes military *jihād* as the collective duty of all Muslims who are called upon to engage in the universal spread of Islam. While not an end in itself, *jihād* is a means to a "good," namely, to rid the world of evil and unbelief, and so it is "good" in its purpose. It is also considered a perpetual duty "until the day of the resurrection" and the end of the world.

In Islamic law, the world can be viewed as divided between *dār al-Islām*, the territory under Muslim rule, *dār al-sulh*, or territory on peaceful terms with Islam, and *dār al-harb*, the territory of war, that is, the communities hostile to Islam, the world of unbelievers. Since the aim of Islam is the universal spread of the faith and "the extirpation of unbelief," the *dār al-harb* is, at least in theory, the object of Muslim warfare whether by persuasion or by the sword. What the requirements of *jihād* demand in particular contexts is a matter at issue among the *ulamā'* and the legal schools. If an enemy attacks Muslim territory, military *jihād* becomes the duty of all the able-bodied inhabitants necessary to repel it, and those who die in *jihād* are considered martyrs and are promised eternal life in Paradise. The chapters in the legal handbooks dealing with military *jihād* understandably contain elaborate rules for the conduct of warfare, offensive or defensive. For example, they address the question as to when warfare may commence or not; when revolt against a ruler is legitimate; and the questions of military methods, of the protection of noncombatants and prisoners of war, and of the disposition of the spoils of war.

Since the eighteenth century especially, with the rise of Islamic resistance to Western colonialism, the duty and doctrines of *jihād* have often dominated Muslim discussion. Militant *jihād* movements, such as the *Tanzīm al-Jihād*, responsible for the assassination of the Egyptian president Anwar Sadat in October 1981, have grown in numbers throughout the Muslim world. More recently we have read or seen reports on television about the militant Islamic groups Hamas and Hizbollah, and Al Qa'ida led by Osama bin Ladin (see Chapter 13). These movements are dedicated to maintaining the purity of traditional Islam and to spreading its belief—to a "permanent revolution of Islam." On the other hand, the modern period has also seen the emergence of "modernist" Islamic scholars who have sought to interpret *jihād* in marked contrast to the classic doctrine. Ongoing ethical conflicts between Muslim traditionalists and modernists are, in many respects, similar to those that one observes today in Christianity and Judaism.

Many modernist Islamic apologists emphasize the defensive role of *jihād* in warfare, especially applying it to the right of Islam to engage in war against foreign colonialists who have aggressively invaded Islamic territory for political or economic gain. They take as their norm those commands of the *Qur'an*, such as the following: "Fight in the way of God those who fight you, but do not provoke hostility; verily God loveth not those who provoke hostility" (2:192). The fundamentalists, however, see the struggle for the islamization of all of society as legitimate *jihād*, and the most radical groups among them also advocate the use of violence against their fellow Muslims who they consider to be heretics and betrayers.

In the examples that we have selected—from Judaism and Islam— we have seen that the source and norms of ethical action are derived from those divine commands that are set down in the sacred books of the Bible and the *Qur'an*. We have noted, however, that in both cases it has been necessary for the two communities to develop traditions of systematic interpretation of these revealed commands and obligations, so that they might be applied to new and complex historical situations. And this has led, in turn, to the proliferation of various schools of interpretation that, in many instances, appear to interpret the divine commands in strikingly divergent, indeed incompatible, ways.

Perhaps the greatest challenge to the great world–historical religious traditions today is how to deal with the rich diversity of their own sectarian developments over time (see Chapter 13). The ethical question that they all face is, To what extent can the moral claims that we make—for example, with regard to abortion or warfare—remain elastic? Can they be stretched to accommodate different interpretations without sheer sophistry, without simply licensing incompatible moral behavior? This is a critical source of the struggle today between Orthodox and Reform Jews, between fundamentalist and liberal Christian groups in the United States, and between similar factions throughout the Muslim world.

## NOTES

1. Cicero, *The Republic.*
2. *The Mencius,* VI, A:3, cited in Wm. Theodore deBary et al., eds., *Sources of Chinese Tradition* (New York, 1960), 102–3.
3. *The Mencius,* II, A:6, cited in ibid., 105.
4. *Hsiang-Shan ch'üan-chi,* cited in deBary, *Sources of Chinese Tradition,* 568.
5. *Tao Te Ching,* VII, in Arthur Waley, *The Way and Its Power* (New York, 1958), 150.

6. Thomas Aquinas, *Summa Theologica,* Ia IIae, 93, 1, in Anton Pegis, ed., *Basic Writings of Saint Thomas Aquinas,* Vol. II (New York, 1945), 749.

7. Ibid., 94, 2, in ibid., 775.

8. Pope Pius XI, *Casti Connubii* (Boston, n.d.), 28.

9. The literature on *Humanae Vitae* and the birth control debate is immense. Among the best studies and anthologies are: In defense: John C. Ford, S. J., Germaine Grisez et al., *The Teaching of Humane Vitae: A Defense* (San Francisco, 1988); William E. May, *Contraception, "Humane Vitae,"* and *Catholic Moral Thought* (Chicago, 1984). Critical of *Humanae Vitae:* Andrew Bauer, ed., *The Debate on Birth Control* (New York, 1969); Daniel J. Callahan, ed., *The Catholic Case for Contraception* (New York, 1969).

10. Max Weber, *The Theory of Social and Economic Organization,* trans. A. M. Henderson and Talcott Parsons (New York, 1964), 358–59.

11. "Homage from Mirabehn," in Homer A. Jack, ed., *The Gandhi Reader* (New York, 1956), 491–92.

12. Louis Fischer, ed., *The Essential Gandhi* (New York, 1962), 107.

13. Louis Fischer, *The Life of Mahatma Gandhi* (New York, 1950), 264.

14. Fischer, *Life of Gandhi,* 267–68.

15. Jack, *Gandhi Reader,* 249.

16. Fred Rosner, "The Jewish Attitude Toward Abortion," in *Contemporary Jewish Ethics,* ed. Menachem Marc Kellner (New York, 1978), 258.

17. Ibid.

18. Ibid., 266.

19. Balfour Brickner, "Judaism and Abortion," in Kellner, *Contemporary Jewish Ethics,* 282.

20. Ibid., 282–83.

21. H. A. R. Gibb, *Mohammedanism* (New York, 1962), 96.

## KEY WORDS

| | |
|---|---|
| ethics of virtue | Amos |
| ethics of obligation | routinization of charisma |
| Bodhisattva | *mitzvah* |
| Avalokitésvara (Kuan-yin; Kannon) | torah |
| cosmic or natural law | Talmudic or rabbinic Judaism |
| *tao* | *Sharī'a* |
| Mencius | *fiqh* |
| *Hsin* | Sunni Islam |
| St. Thomas Aquinas | *Qur'an* |
| contraception | *Sunna* of the Prophet |
| charisma | *ulamā'* |
| Mohandas K. Gandhi | *Ijmā'* |
| *satyāgraha* | Shi'i Islam |
| exemplary moral leader | *Imam* |
| ethical prophet | *jihād* |

## REVIEW QUESTIONS

1. How does this chapter fit in with the organization of this book? Why does it come where it is?
2. Contrast a religious ethic of virtue with a religious ethic of obligation. Give an example of a religious leader or hero who has served as a virtuous model. What specific virtues does he or she exemplify?
3. Characterize natural law as a source of moral guidance. Give an example of the way that Roman Catholicism applies natural law to a specific social or ethical issue.
4. Describe the several sources and features that are components of the Jewish tradition of *halakhah* that serves as the foundation of Jewish ethics.
5. Describe the sources of the Islamic *sharī'a* or Divine law. Explain how, through an appeal to these sources, various Islamic legal interpreters might arrive at different judgments regarding a moral obligation such as *jihād*.
6. How do you go about making moral decisions? Are you more inclined to follow a virtue ethic? A charismatic moral leader? An ethic based on the conception of natural laws? An ethic of revealed divine commandments? Some other method? Or simply your own feelings and intuitions?

## SUGGESTIONS FOR FURTHER READING

*On comparative religious ethics, see*

CHIDESTER, DAVID. *Patterns of Action: Religion and Ethics in a Contemporary Perspective.* Belmont, Calif.: Wadsworth, 1987.

LITTLE, DAVID, and SUMNER B. TWISS. *Comparative Religous Ethics.* San Francisco: Harper & Row, 1978. For the advanced student.

*On Buddhist ethics, see*

KING, WINSTON L. *In the Hope of Nibbana: An Essay on Theravada Buddhist Ethics.* La Salle, Ill.: Open Court, 1964.

PREBISH, CHARLES S. *Buddhist Ethics: A Cross-Cultural Approach.* Dubuque, Iowa: Kendall-Hunt Publishers, 1992.

"Buddhist Ethics." In *Encyclopedia of Religion.* Vol. 2. New York: Macmillan, 1987, 498–504.

*On Confucian ethics, see*

FINGERETTE, HERBERT. *Confucius—the Secular as Sacred.* New York: Harper & Row, 1972.

LIU, WU-CHI. *A Short History of Confucian Philosophy.* Harmondsworth: Penguin, 1955.

FUNG, YU-LAN. *A History of Chinese Philosophy.* Princteon, NJ.: Princeton University Press, 1952. See relevant chapters of this multivolume work.

*On Hindu ethics, see*

HINDERY, RODERICK. *Comparative Ethics in Buddhist and Hindu Traditions.* India: South Asia Books, 1979.

SHARMA, I. C. *Ethical Philosophies of India.* Lincoln, Nebr.: Johnson Publishing, 1965.

*On Islamic ethics, see*

*Encyclopedia of Religion.* Vol. 7. New York: Macmillan, 1987. Since Islamic ethics is closely allied to discussions of law (*sharī'a*), see the article and bibliography on "Islamic Law."

DONALDSON, D. M. *Studies in Muslim Ethics.* London: S.P.C.K., 1953.

*On Jewish ethics, see*

*Encyclopedia of Religion.* Vols. 6, 8. New York: Macmillan, 1987. Since Jewish ethics is closely related to discussions of law (*halakhah*), see the articles and bibliographies on "Halakhah" and "Jewish Ethical Literature."

KELLNER, MENACHEM MARC. *Contemporary Jewish Ethics.* New York: Sanhedrin Press, 1978. A fine collection of essays on morality, law, and religion, and on specific ethical issues. Helpful bibliography.

*On Christian ethics, see*

*Encyclopedia of Religion.* Vol. 3. New York, Macmillan, 1987, 340–48.

GUSTAFSON, JAMES M. *Protestant and Roman Catholic Ethics.* Chicago: University of Chicago Press, 1978. Describes convergences and differences.

HÄRING, BERNARD. *The Law of Christ.* 3 vols. Westminster, Md., 1961–66. Volume 1 contains a good historical survey of moral theology. An important Catholic contribution.

HAUERWAS, STANLEY. *Vision and Virtue: Essays in Christian Ethical Reflection.* Notre Dame, Ind.: Fides Publishers, 1974. A good statement of virtue ethics.

NIEBUHR, H. RICHARD. *Christ and Culture.* New York: Harper & Row, 1957. A classic study of how varieties of Christian ethics reflect differing attitudes toward society and culture.

TROELTSCH, ERNST. *The Social Teachings of the Christian Churches.* 2 vols. Chicago: University of Chicago Press, 1981. Though dated, it is still an influential study.

# 12

# Soteriology: Ways and Goals of Salvation and Liberation

## Ways of Salvation and Liberation

Human life is burdened by a tragic moral and spiritual discontent. At least that is what the great religions teach. Viewed realistically and without illusion, they tell us that life is marked by anxiety, estrangement, and a sense of failure, defilement, moral guilt, shame, pain, and unease. Our empirical self, or ego, compares pitiably with our potentially real or spiritual self. Life, it is felt, is in need of liberation, healing, transformation. The conditions from which we humans need to be delivered range from the most basic physical threats—for example, an absence of food and bodily safety—to the spiritual need to sacrifice our finite, private self to that which is truly supreme and enduring.

The ways or means of achieving liberation or salvation have varied greatly in the history of religion and range from coercive magic, used to foil an enemy or to ensure a harvest; to acts of passionate entreaty and ecstatic devotion; to highly disciplined ethical patterns of behavior; to pure mystical flights of union with the divine. There are, however, three or four discernible "paths" or ways that can be observed in all the historical religions and are recognized as classic types. These are the way of *faith*, the way of *devotion*, the way of *disciplined action*, and the way of *meditation* and *insight*. While these patterns can be distinguished, they obviously are often combined. For example, the devout Muslim may reveal a highly patterned life of ethical and devotional behavior, but the Muslim discipline also reflects a life of radical faith and trust in Allah's providential care and goodness—and, perhaps, may be accompanied by occasional flights of mystical insight. The fact is that the great religions—Hinduism, Christianity, Buddhism, Judaism, and Islam—have at one time or another, in one or another tradition or school, emphasized one of these traditional ways over the others as normative, as *the* way. However, these paths are not mutually exclusive, and in religious traditions such as Hinduism and Roman Catholicism all three or four ways may coincide.

Personal needs and temperaments differ greatly, and it is obvious that different persons are drawn to one or another way as religiously more suitable and effective. Some persons are attracted to highly emotional expressions of religion, as in certain forms of revivalistic Protestantism; other persons require a daily discipline of activities, of prayer and good works, carried out in a ritualistic manner that may appear merely routine to the emotionally charged temperament; and there are those rarer types who are neither very emotional nor practical but are essentially contemplative and meditative and who seek spiritual wisdom or insight largely in private.

It is true, however, that certain religions do appear to favor or to reflect one way of salvation as more characteristic of its normative life. Protestantism, for example, is characterized by the ways of faith and devotion, is less drawn to disciplined sacramental action, and gives almost no attention to the way of mystical insight. Both orthodox Judaism and Islam reflect a very practical religious life, one that is punctuated by a daily pattern of religious acts. Theravada Buddhism, on the other hand, is normatively meditative and reflects the way of knowledge or insight.

## The Way of Grace through Faith

It would appear obvious that any religion holding a belief in a transcendent sacred power, be it personal or impersonal, must assume an act of faith on the part of the believer. It may be that we live, move, and have our true being in and through Sacred Power, but such a reality is not necessarily transparent in the world of sensory experience or demonstrable in the same sense as a physical object. *Faith,* therefore, can mean the mental assent to the existence of such an unseen reality. In such a case, faith is synonymous with belief, the intellectual apprehension of a religious truth. However, the faith we are speaking of here is not intellectual assent (*assensus*) alone but, rather, the total response of a person—heart, mind, and will. It is what the theologians call trust (*fiducia*), a total, confident reliance on divine grace, on unmerited love and dependence.

Faith in this second sense implies that the believer feels incapable of taking any action that can lead to liberation from the condition binding him or her to sin, craving, or ignorance. The self has reached a condition of complete helplessness and abasement; the will is in bondage to evil or ignorance and is wholly dependent on the grace and love of the divine for its release. The way of faith is common in all three of the Western monotheistic traditions but is, perhaps, most often associated with Protestantism. Since its beginnings in the Reformation, Protestantism has accentuated the stubborn reality of human sin. It logically follows that the deeper the sense of sin, the greater is the need for help from beyond the self. Because the individual can do nothing to be saved—not the least good work—he or she must eradicate every vestige of self-assertion and humbly cast the self before the mercy-seat of God. The believer is liberated or saved by divine grace through faith alone. However, the way of faith is not exclusive to Western religion. It is present in both popular Hinduism and in some traditions of Mahayana Buddhism in China and Japan.

### Martin Luther

The Protestant reformer *Martin Luther* (1483–1546) represents the classic expression of the way of faith in the West. Before his break with Rome, Luther was a diligent Augustinian monk. But, despite his devotion, Luther was plagued by the fact that he felt incapable of attaining the righteousness of God—that is, of standing morally satisfied before a righteous and demanding God. He could not know God as a merciful and forgiving God because of his own unrighteousness. "How," he asked, "can I find a gracious God?" The more this afflicted him, the more he tried to prove his righteousness and merit, by which he would be worthy of eternal life. He tried every possible spiritual and ascetic discipline: fasting, good works, pilgrimage, self-denial, and austerity. Nothing relieved his doubts. He could not acquire the monastic ideal of a proper balance between spiritual "dread" of God's righteous judgment and "security" in God's loving mercy. In desperation, he came to believe that Christianity was a cruel hoax. He felt he was eternally lost and fell into an abyss of despair.

Luther came to hate the word *righteousness*. He interpreted it as meaning God's demand of justice and his punishment of the sinner for his or her unrighteousness. However, as he studied the apostle Paul's Letter to the Romans, he came on this statement: "the righteous shall live from faith to faith" (Romans 1:17). Here, righteousness was disclosed not as demanding justice by God but as a gift from God, as disclosing the mercy of God. Luther later wrote of his new discovery:

> Now I felt exactly as if I had been born again and believed that I had entered Paradise through widely opened doors. As violently as I had formerly hated the expression "righteousness of God" so I was now as violently compelled to embrace the new conception of grace, and thus for me the expression of the Apostle really opened the Gates of Paradise.[1]

About the same time, Luther made a second discovery. The Latin Vulgate (the official Roman) version of the Gospels read, "do penance, for the Kingdom of God is at hand." However, the great scholar Erasmus produced a new Greek text that rendered the passage as "repent, for the Kingdom of

God is at hand." For Luther, the words *penance* and *repent* represented radically different spiritual worlds. His great discovery was that believers are *made righteous by grace through repentance and faith*, not through good works. Luther no longer saw God as a severe, demanding judge but as a loving Father whose will was to forgive the unrighteous. Righteousness is the undeserved gift of divine grace which is to be received by faith alone.

For Luther, any thought of persons meriting righteousness and salvation is utterly out of the question; indeed, it is a blasphemy. The "merit-mongers," he says, "refuse to receive God's grace freely, which is the glory of His divinity, but rather seek to deserve God's grace by their own works."

While the law or good works, such as ensuring public order and justice, has its function in the maintenance of civil society, it has no role whatsoever in personal redemption. In fact, Luther sees works and the law—that is, what is commanded—as the "hammer of God," breaking down human pride and self-reliance, that "rebellious, obstinate, stiff-necked beast." God has need, writes Luther, "of a mighty hammer, that is to say, the law." God uses the law to teach us how miserably we have failed and have "transgressed all the commandments of God." The law only strikes "a terror into the conscience so that it feeleth God to be offended and angry indeed, and itself to be guilty of eternal death."[2]

Luther's radical rejection of the way of works as a means of salvation might raise the questions of whether good works have any place in the religious life or what motivation there is in doing good works. According to Luther, these very questions show that one is still mired in an egoistic perspective. The religious life remains motivated by thoughts of heavenly joy and the fear of hell, that is, by our own advantage. For Luther, to be blessed means only "to will the will of God and His glory and to desire nothing of one's own either here or hereafter." The pious do everything that may redound to God's glory alone. The Christian serves God for God's sake, simply because He *is* God. Otherwise, Luther believed, the Christian does not serve God but only himself or herself. In such a God-centered perspective, there is no consideration of meritorious action, for one is set free to pursue good works for their own sake. To ask why the Christian, saved by grace through faith, should do good reveals a total miscomprehension of what it means to have the burden of one's sin removed by God's grace.

> It is as absurd and stupid [Luther declares] to say: the righteous ought to do good works, as to say: God ought to do good, the sun ought to shine, the pear-tree ought to bear pears; . . . it follows without commandment or bidding of any law, naturally, willingly, uncompelled. . . . Just so, we do not have to tell the righteous that he ought to do good works, for he does so . . . without any commandment or compulsion, because he is a new creature and a good tree.[3]

Luther's joyous experience of being freed from the bondage of sin and condemnation and of being lovingly accepted by a gracious God has been duplicated in the lives of millions. The heart of the way of faith is the

The reformer Martin Luther's rediscovery that the believer is saved through faith by God's grace alone remains a bulwark of Protestant Christianity today. (*Source:* Lucas Cranach, courtesy of Giraudon/Art Resource.)

profound sense of blessedness, even ecstasy, that comes with the feeling of an awful burden removed, in spite of one's absolute inability to do anything on one's own behalf. It is expressed in the popular Protestant hymn, "Just as I Am":

1. Just as I am, without one plea
   But that thy Blood was shed for me,
   And that thou bidd'st me come to thee
   O Lamb of God, I come, I come. . . .

3. Just as I am, though tossed about
   With many a conflict, many a doubt,
   Fightings and fears within, without,
   O Lamb of God, I come. . . .

5. Just as I am, thou wilt receive,
   Wilt welcome, pardon, cleanse, relieve;
   Because thy promise I believe,
   O Lamb of God, I come.

## Amida Buddhism—Shinran

It was mentioned earlier that the way of faith, while typical of Protestant Christianity, is also a popular way of liberation in Hinduism and Buddhism. It is especially typical of the Buddhist Pure Land sects in China and Japan. The description of Buddhist doctrine in Chapter 9 focused on the original teachings of Gautama the Buddha as they are found in the earliest Pali texts and interpreted by the elite Theravada monks. *Theravada* means the "Way of the Elders." Like Christianity, Buddhism experienced a celebrated split into two principal schools. Roughly about the beginning of the Christian era, popular devotional Hinduism (known as *bhakti*) began to influence Indian Buddhism in decisive ways. For example, the Buddha came to be represented as an image and to be worshiped. A revolutionary movement within Buddhism, called the **Mahayana** or the Greater Vehicle, was the result, in part, of this penetration of popular *bhakti*. Over the centuries, the Mahayana Buddhism of faith and devotion became the dominant form of Buddhism in China and Japan. Theravada remained the normative expression of Buddhism in Sri Lanka (Ceylon) and in Southeast Asia.

**Theravada** Buddhism centers on the highly disciplined, rather elite life of the monk who renounces life in the world. Conversely, Mahayana is a religion of laypersons that teaches the universality of salvation. While Theravada Buddhism considers each person to be an individual who must work out his or her own salvation, Mahayana sees the fate of each individual as linked with that of all others. Associated with this belief was the development of *parināmanā*, the transfer of merit, whereby the meritorious action of those enlightened can assist those weaker beings enslaved to passion and attachment in this degenerate age. Note that such a transfer of merit runs counter to the strict Theravada doctrine regarding the pitiless workings of the law of *karma*. While Theravada stresses the original teaching of Buddha and considers him a great sage, a man among men, Mahayana focuses on the life of Buddha, especially on his selfless compassion (*karuna*), and looks to the Buddha as a savior of others. Mahayana removed the distinction between ignorant laypeople and the learned monk, between saint and sinner, and made salvation equally accessible to all. The ideal of Theravada remained the *arhant* (perfect being), the disciplined monk who, through concentrated meditation, seeks only his own enlightenment and Nirvana. As we have seen, the ideal type in Mahayana is the **Bodhisattva,** previous incarnations of the Buddha who, having achieved enlightenment and on the brink of Nirvana, return to the world to make salvation possible for others.

According to Mahayana, Gautama is a Bodhisattva, the last of many compassionate Buddha saviors. In later years, Mahayana came to teach that other Buddha saviors were yet to come, most notably Maitreya. As the tradition developed, the world was seen as full of Bodhisattvas, each one an emanation of the Buddha-essence and each one seeking the liberation of other beings. However, the Pure Land sects of Mahayana taught that, while there were many emanations of the original Buddha-essence, the heavenly Buddha most concerned with earthly beings is Amitabha (Amida), the Buddha of Infinite Light who dwells in the Western Paradise, the Pure Land.

In medieval Japan, Pure Land or *Amida Buddhism,* as it is called, became the most popular and influential school. In a time of bewildering change and strife, it offered the weary soul hope for eternal bliss in the Western Paradise. Amida had vowed that all would be saved who simply called on his name, saying *Namu Amida Butsu* with wholehearted trust and devotion. This fervent repetition of Amida's name became known as Nembutsu. It originally signified the work of meditation on the name of Amida but took on the rather different connotation of radical reliance on the saving power of Amida alone.

It was Honen (1133–1212) who, more than any other Buddhist sage, called for mutual tolerance in the use of methods of achieving enlightenment and taught that rebirth in heaven is achieved by recitation of the Nembutsu while relying on the grace of Amida. It was Honen's disciple, *Shinran* (1173–1262 C.E.), however, who carried the logic of the way of faith to its conclusion. He came to believe that recitation of the Nembutsu was itself an act of merit and therefore self-assertion. He advanced a radical doctrine of salvation by grace through faith in Amida. His rejection of merit deepened his own sense of the ineradicable character of human sin and lostness to the point that he believed that wicked persons were more acceptable to Amida than righteous men and women, because the wicked were more aware of their need to throw themselves entirely on Amida's mercy.

Shinran concluded that it was impossible for a person to do good works. All acts are tainted with self-centeredness. He saw no bridge between the holy, pure Amida and humankind's petty, egoistic deeds.

> However good a man may be, he is incapable, with all his deeds of goodness, of effecting his rebirth in Amida's Land of Recompense. Much less so with bad men. . . . Good deeds are of no effect and evil deeds of no hindrance as regards rebirth. Even the rebirth of good men is impossible without being helped by Amida's specific Vow issuing from his great love and compassion which are not at all of this world.[4]

Shinran taught that the way of faith, while seemingly easy, is the most difficult of all paths because human pride always tempts individuals to seek their own salvation, rather than to rely on the Buddha. For Shinran, all spiritual merit proceeds *from* the Buddha—including the gift of faith itself.

The experience of "acceptance," despite our being unacceptable, is central to the way of faith and is a pronounced feature of devotional hymns and literature in Protestantism, as well as in the True Pure Land sect. The sentiment is conveyed by the words of the hymn "Just as I Am," cited earlier. Because one is accepted by the mercy of God or by the compassion of Amida, one finds rest and peace, a "nonchalance of faith," the taking of life as we find it, without fear or anxiety. The profound sense of release that accompanies

Amida's "acceptance" wells up in expressions of joy and gratitude. For Shinran, as for Luther, all attempts to gain some practical benefit from religion must be rejected. True religion rests, finally, on a recognition of our own moral failure; on our nothingness; and on the infinite, unspeakable mercy of God or Buddha. It is this overflow of thankfulness and love that often is expressed in acts of devotion.

## The Way of Devotion

The joy and feeling of exaltation that accompany the experience of divine grace impel the believer to acts of devotion. These acts are not, however, only grateful responses to divine mercy. They may also be a *means*, a discipline, directed at achieving enlightenment, redemption, or even union with the divine. In this latter sense, devotion has more in common with the way of action or deeds. It is hardly distinguishable from either sympathetic magic or from the way of ritual action discussed in earlier chapters and observed, for example, in certain Hindu or Catholic sacramental practices. Devotion may also be an integral component of mystical insight, as in the case of the Hindu saint Ramakrishna, or the Catholic mystic St. Teresa of Avila. As such, it often is considered a distinct path and has been called *devotional mysticism*.[5]

The point that needs to be underlined here is that *the way of devotion* is found, more often than not, in company with the ways of faith, action, and insight and is either an integral means or a natural outcome of those classic paths. The way of devotion is, then, an inclusive way of salvation. Nevertheless, it does have distinctive features that deserve brief analysis.

The intensity of devotional religion is often regarded with disfavor by those who follow the more prosaic way of obligation and duty, and by those who take the arduous path of wisdom and insight. An example is the horror expressed by the Hindu temple priests on encountering Ramakrishna's childish devotional excesses before the image of the Divine Mother, the goddess Kali, or the revulsion of the sober and inexcitable Protestant when confronted with the ecstatic shouting and dancing of a Pentecostal revival. The first mark of devotionalism is its deep feeling and emotion. It often reflects a dissatisfaction with the formal, unfeeling character of traditional religion. Devotionalism involves an effervescence of emotion that is often absent in older, established churches.

Closely related to its emotional character is the deeply personal quality of devotion. Here, again, it reflects a reaction against the dispassion, even detachment, of much traditional religious practice. Devotionalism expresses a deeply felt personal encounter with the divine. God is felt as a profound presence, vividly experienced in a revelatory encounter that leaves the devotee radically changed.

On occasion, this direct, intense personal encounter with the divine issues in a rapture in which the devotee actually feels transported out of the

The emotional and ecstatic aspects of much religious devotionalism are reflected in a revival meeting. The woman experiences the personal presence and power of the Holy Spirit. (*Source:* Courtesy of Stock, Boston, Inc.)

body or to another spiritual plane. This is often the case with the great mystics, such as the Spanish nun *St. Teresa of Avila* (1515–1582). *Ecstasy* (from the Greek *ekstasis*) literally means being outside oneself. St. Teresa describes such a transport:

> In these raptures the soul seems no longer to animate the body, and thus the natural heat of the body is felt to be very sensibly diminished; it gradually becomes colder, though conscious of the greatest sweetness and delight. No means of resistance is possible. . . . Often it comes like a strong, swift impulse, before your thought can forewarn you of it or you can do anything to help yourself; you see and feel this cloud, or this powerful eagle, rising and bearing you up with it on its wings. . . .
>
> The majesty of Him who can do this is manifested in such a way that the hair stands on end, and there is produced a great fear of offending so great a God, but a fear overpowered by the deepest love, newly enkindled, for One Who, as we see, has so deep a love for so loathsome a worm that He seems not satisfied by literally drawing the soul to Himself, but will also have the body, mortal though it is.[6]

St. Teresa's frequent reference to the divine love is also characteristic of devotionalism. In fact, the divine–human encounter is often described in terms reserved for a lover's desire—words such as *rapture, ecstasy,* and *thirst for union.* Ramakrishna insisted that "extreme longing is the surest way to God-vision," and he often used the explicit language of passionate desire in expressing his encounters with the divine. This personal intimacy of devotionalism is pronounced in the ardent words of a Muslim **Sufi** poet:

A fever burns below my heart
And ravages my every part;
It hath destroyed my strength and stay,
And smouldered all my soul away. . . .

So passionate my love is, I do yearn
To keep His memory constantly in mind;
But O, the ecstasy with which I burn
Sears out my thoughts, and strikes my memory blind.[7]

In the West—for example, in Catholicism or Islam—devotional mysticism will occasionally blur the distinction between the human devotee and God. Normally, however, Western devotion maintains the distinction and remains within the bounds of theistic orthodoxy. Only rarely does it reach the explicit eroticism of Hindu **bhakti**. The following is an excerpt from popular Bengali devotional lyrics offered to the god Krishna. He is depicted as a noble warrior and a divine lover, and the lyrics express the erotic longing of the beautiful young Radha as she waits for Krishna's return:

When my beloved returns to my house
I shall make my body a temple of gladness,
I shall make my body the altar of joy
    and let down my hair to sweep it.
My twisting necklace of pearls shall be the intricate
    sprinkled design on the altar
    my full breasts the water jars,
    my curved hips the plantain trees
    the twinkling bells at my waist the young
    shoots of the mango.
I shall use the arcane arts of fair women in
    all lands
    to make my beauty outshine a thousand moons. . . .
The moon has shown upon me,
    the face of my beloved.
O night of joy![8]

The rapturous and erotic devotionalism of Hindu *bhakti* and some Sufi mysticism does appear occasionally, though more covertly, in Christian devotion. It is evident, for example, in some of the language used by devotees of the Roman Catholic cult of the Sacred Heart. One of the leaders of the cult, Mother Louise Margaret de la Touche (1868–1915), in her *Book of Infinite Love*, exhorts Catholics to adore the eucharistic Host, the wafer or bread, and to lovingly kiss the consecrated paten, or plate holding the wafer. Students of Protestant **revivalism** have also pointed to the veiled erotic imagery in some Pentecostal sermons and hymns. However, Protestant devotionalism does not express so much erotic union as it does the warm personalism of friendship. God is spoken of in the intimacy of a real human friend. The dominant feeling of Protestant devotionalism is expressed in the popular hymn "What a Friend We Have in Jesus":

What a Friend we have in Jesus
All our sins and griefs to bear!
What a privilege to carry
Everything to God in prayer.

O what peace we often forfeit,
O what needless pain we bear
All because we do not carry
Everything to God in prayer!

Can we find a friend so faithful
Who will all our sorrows share?
Jesus knows our every weakness
Take it to the Lord in prayer.

## The Way of Action and Obligation

The human body and mind need to be active. This is a deep human compulsion. We are anxious and discontent when, involuntarily, we are inert and passive. It is no wonder, then, that activity is also central to the religious life of humankind. In fact, the way of action is the most universal and popular of the paths to salvation. Dramatic conversion experiences, mystical flights to the One, even devotional ecstasy are relatively infrequent events, the experiences of a religious elite. The vast majority of believers express their religious convictions and hopes through rather prosaic patterns of religious activities—rites, sacraments, and obligatory moral duties.

There are certain characteristic features of the way of action. First, it reflects a very *practical*, everyday, nondramatic approach to religion. It is the secular as sacred or, more accurately, the secular round of life punctuated by habitual religious duties. It is a deep, if unconscious, conviction of the way of action that the cosmos or reality is sustained by a rehearsal of the "way of the fathers," the Grand Harmony. Without these actions, it is felt that the world will degenerate further and may even return to chaos.

A second feature of the way of action is its *patterned character*. What is striking about religious rite and duty—pointed out in Chapter 4—is the regular nature of this form of religious life—down-to-earth, ordered, and disciplined, usually lacking the ecstasy and effervescence of the devotional mystic. The way of action is typically conservative and institutional. This relates to a third feature, namely, the *traditional* character of religious action. It is the way not only of orthodoxy (correct opinion) but also of **ortho-praxis** (correct practice). Right duty or action means following the path established by the gods or the fathers "in the beginning." The way of action is suspicious of innovation; it demands a conformity of behavior as essential to community survival. The way of action is basically the only way found in primal and archaic religion because the function of religious rite is to sustain social, even cosmic, order. It is natural that this way is also characteristic of the orthodox traditions in the historic religions: Orthodox Judaism and Islam, traditional Roman Catholicism, and caste Hinduism. Chapter 4 introduced the main features of the way of action as observed in the practice of religious ritual and sacrament. Here, we will concentrate on those aspects of religious action exhibited in the full range of obligatory duties expected of the faithful in Hinduism, Islam, and Judaism.

### Hinduism

Orthodox caste Hinduism places great emphasis on the performance of duties associated with one's class and stage of life. These are formulated in ancient sacred codes of behavior, especially in a series of law books called the *Dharma Shastras.* The most ancient and authoritative of these texts is the *Manu Smriti,* or **Code of Manu.** The practice of duty—or **dharma,** as it is called—is the heart of orthodox Hinduism and, it is believed, will lead to a happy and moral life. Some also would see the fulfilling of *dharma* as leading to **moksha,** or liberation. In the Vedas, the word *dharma* stood for an eternally fixed moral law that underlies the universe. In the later law books, *dharma* came to refer specifically to the duties and obligations of social life. In the *Code of Manu,* for example, these duties are elaborately formulated in terms of two social patterns: the duties of the four classes, or castes (*varnas*), and the duties of the four stages (*ashramas*) of life.

Hinduism looks on social life as a complex and fragile organism. Complexity involves danger. It is possible that if there is a breakdown in one part of the organism, the whole social body will be endangered. Unless each strand of the social fabric is maintained and makes its proper contribution, the whole will unravel. And so Hinduism teaches that the functioning of the four classes—the Brahmans (priests), Kshatriyas (warriors), Vaishyas (farmers and producers), and Shudras (laborers)—is essential to the perfect ordering of society. So also is the right functioning of thousands of other caste groupings that are distinguished by occupation, family, geography, cult practices, and so on. Hinduism considers it entirely natural and realistic to recognize fundamental differences in sex, age, type, and status—and that to confuse the station and duties of various classes and stages of life is to invite chaos. The *Bhagavad Gita* describes the consequence of such social confusion:

> When the religious laws of the family are destroyed, then lawlessness destroys the whole family. Because lawlessness prevails, the women of the family become corrupted, and when women are corrupt, intermingling of caste follows. Intermingling of caste leads to hell, both those who destroy the family as well as the family itself. The ancestors also fall into hell for they are deprived of the offerings of food made to them.[9]

The *Code of Manu* describes in detail the duties of the four classes, including the sacraments appropriate for each stage (*ashrama*) of life. It points out that "it is better to discharge one's own appointed duty incompletely than to perform completely that of another,"[10] because to do otherwise is to introduce the confusion that results in social chaos. Therefore, in the beginning the Lord

> for the sake of the prosperity of worlds, created the Brahman, the Kshatriya, the Vaishya, and the Shudra. . . .
> To Brahmans he assigned teaching and studying (the Veda), sacrificing for their own benefit and for others, giving and accepting (of alms).
> The Kshatriya he commanded to protect the people, to bestow gifts, to offer sacrifices, to study (the Veda), and to abstain from attaching himself to sensual pleasures;
> The Vaishya to tend cattle, to bestow gifts, to offer sacrifices, to study (the Veda), to trade, to lend money, and to cultivate land.
> One occupation only the lord prescribed to the Shudra, to serve meekly even these (other) three castes.[11]

The *Dharma Shastras,* or law books, describe the sacramental as well as the social obligations that accompany each of the first three stages of life for the males of the three "twice-born" classes. The *Gautama Dharma* alone lists 40 sacraments, although there are 16 principal ones. The numerous obligations and rites of the male of the "twice-born" classes differ from stage to stage and therefore depend on the stage in life he has reached.

The first stage—after a young man undergoes initiation, including the investiture of the sacred cord—is that of a celibate student living with his master, or guru. This *ashrama* begins between the ages of 8 and 12 and lasts for 12 years, although today this first stage is not as exacting as the one described here in part:

> Now follow the rules for the studentship.
> He shall obey his teacher, except when ordered to commit crimes which cause loss of caste.
> He shall do what is serviceable to his teacher, he shall not contradict him. . . .
> He shall not eat food offered at a sacrifice to the gods or the Manes,
> Nor pungent condiments, salt, honey, or meat. . . .
> He shall preserve his chastity. . . .
> Bringing all he obtains to his teacher, he shall go begging with a vessel in the morning and in the evening, and he may beg from everybody except low-caste people unfit for association with Aryas [Aryans].[12]

The second *ashrama* begins with marriage, when a man's interests are turned to family, occupation, and the wider community. Begetting children, studying the Vedas, and performing the traditional rites, prayers, and sacrifices associated with the householder are especially important.

The third stage is that of retirement and retreat when the householder, "seeing his skin wrinkled and his hair white," takes to the forest as a **sadhu,** or ascetic, in search of self-control and spiritual insight. The *sadhu* spends his days fulfilling his new *dharma* through the study of sacred scripture and the performance of prescribed rituals.

The final stage of life is that of the homeless wanderer, the **sannyasin,** or recluse, who has no fixed abode, no possessions, and no obligations. He no longer performs sacrifices and other rites, and he has abandoned all attachments to this world. He shaves his head and beard and puts on the redbrown robe of the **mendicant,** or beggar. The *Code of Manu* describes the renunciant:

> Delighting in what refers to the Soul, sitting in the postures prescribed by the Yoga, independent of external help, entirely abstaining from sensual enjoyments, with himself for his only companion, he shall live in this world, desiring the bliss of final liberation.[13]

It is only in this final stage of life that the orthodox Hindu finds himself freed of the obligatory duties that encompass his life from infancy to old age. However, all these actions and duties have but two purposes: knowledge of the soul and liberation from the rounds of births and deaths.

## Islam

We have remarked that the soul of Islam is to be found in its law rather than in its theology. The Muslim tradition is called *islām,* meaning "to commit" or "surrender" to Allah, who guides the faithful "in the straight path" (*Qur'an* I, 6). Islam, like all the great historical religions, can point to Muslim saints and sages who epitomize the way of radical faith, the way of devotion, or the mystical path. However, the heart of normative Islamic religion is located in the daily obedience of the faithful to the commands of God.

The term used by Islam is *Sharī'a,* which is law, morality, and religion, for in Islam the three are not distinguished. The *Sharī'a* is—like the Torah for Judaism—a complex of obligations governing personal, civil, political, and ritual activity. Islam speaks both of things to be believed (*imān*, or faith) and things to be done or works (*islām*). It is clear, however, that for the faithful Muslim, things to be done take precedence over theology. A Muslim's obligations are principally expressed in five explicit duties or *Pillars of the Faith.* The five "pillars" reflect the importance of the way of duty and action in a great religion.

Shahādah—*Confession*  The first "pillar" of *islām* is bearing witness to the faith by saying the Confession: "there is no god but God and Muhammad is the Messenger (or Apostle) of God." The Confession must be said intentionally, thoughtfully, and with full understanding of its truth. The pious Muslim will recite the *Shahādah* several times a day in prayer.

Salāt—*Prayer*  In Islam, prayer is primarily something that must be *done,* must be ritually performed, although Muslims also engage in private devotional prayer. There are five obligatory times of ritual prayer each day, each prayer having as its theme adoration and submission to God. The Muslim prays on arising, at midday, in the afternoon, immediately after sunset, and before retiring. The prayers vary in the number of ritual movements (*Rak'ah*) and appropriate recitations, but each begins and ends in an erect posture, with intervening bowings, prostrations, and recitations. The following is a description of some of the actions involved in the completion of one *Rak'ah*, so distinctive of *Salāt* in the Sunni tradition of Islam:

> Both hands are raised up to the ears in a standing position, with the face towards the *Qiblah* in Mecca, while the words *Allahu Akbar* [God is the greatest of all] are uttered. This is called the Takbir and is followed by a standing prayer and the recitation of the opening *surah* of the *Qur'an*. . . .
>
> Then, saying *Allahu Akbar* the worshipper lowers his head down, so that the palms of the hands reach the knees. In this position, which is called *Rukū*, phrases expressive of the divine glory and majesty are repeated at least three times: "Glory to my Lord the great."
>
> After this, the standing position is resumed, with the words: "God accepts him who gives praise to Him, O our Lord, thine is the praise."
>
> Then the worshipper prostrates [the first *Sijdah* prostration] himself, the toes of both feet, both knees, both hands, and the forehead touching the ground, and the following words expressing the divine greatness are uttered at least three times: "Glory to my Lord the most High."[14]

The worshipper then sits in a reverential position, which is followed by a second prostration (as described previously). This finishes one *Rak'ah*.

Noon prayer in the mosque—the place of prostration—on Friday is the time of congregational *Salāt*. The worshippers are called to prayer by a **muezzin,** usually from a tower or minaret. A sermon, often, but not necessarily, by an *Imām*, or spiritual leader, usually in the form of an exhortation, precedes the *Salāt*. The *Imām* also leads in the timing of the congregational prayers.

There is something majestic and powerful in the corporate action of the faithful joining in their largely mental or subvocal recitations and ritual prostrations toward Mecca. The essence of *Salāt* is this personal sense of awareness and intention on the part of the faithful as they "remember" God in humility and reverent awe. *Salāt* involves this heightened response to God's mercy and "refuge" that discourages mere perfunctory, heedless gestures.

**Zakāt—***Almsgiving*   The third "pillar," *Zakāt* (or almsgiving), is derived from a root meaning "to purify." The *Qur'an* is full of appeals for charity to the poor and oppressed, and the practice of *Zakāt* has become the foundation of Islam's tradition of social responsibility.

The *Zakāt* is obligatory and—while technically not a civil function but a "pillar" of *islām*—in modern, complex society often is implemented by civil authority. Over the centuries, interpretations regarding the obligatory rate of alms tax on crops, cattle, camels, other possessions, and income have varied.

As complex and legalistic as the administration of the *Zakāt* has become, its religious significance has remained foremost:

> The doctrine is that property is validated as a private right and enjoyment, provided a portion of it is devoted to the common need, in token of the corporate awareness that should characterize all personal possession. This paid portion "purifies," that is, legitimatizes, what is retained. Without this active conscience, retention and ownership would be impure and disqualified. The community has not only a stake in, but also a claim on, the individual's *amwal* or substance.[15]

Sawm—*Fasting during Ramadan*   The duty of fasting during the month of Ramadan (the ninth lunar month of the Islamic calendar) is the fourth and most rigorous obligation of the Muslim's religious life as set forth in the *Sharī'a*. Like the other "pillars," the fast is a physical as well as a spiritual action, or deed—a sacramental ritual. The fast involves total abstinence from food and drink during the daylight hours for the 28 days of Ramadan. When the fast falls during the heat of summer, the hardship of this obligation is intense.

Islam teaches that fasting nurtures self-discipline and compassion as well as a sense of our own frailty and dependence on God:

> The benefit of fasting is primarily in terms of character. The abstention from food and drink and the other material pleasures for the long hours between dawn and dusk during the month of Ramadan is an act of self-discipline by which an individual asserts his or her ability to gain control over material pleasures and habits. This is a triumph of mind over matter. The desire to quench thirst, to soften the pangs of hunger, or to light a cigarette, are placed in their proper perspective of things which can be postponed, and in some cases given up entirely. . . . There is a social dimension of equal importance. The community sense of those who fast and break their fast together is greatly heightened and a necessary element for concerted social action is added. . . . One who can afford food and yet abstains from it, is better able to understand the person who does not have the food because he or she cannot afford it. . . .[16]

Hajj—*Pilgrimage to Mecca*   The fifth religious obligation is pilgrimage to Mecca, the holiest shrine of Islam's faith. Every Muslim who is physically and financially able is obliged to make this pilgrimage at least once during his or her lifetime. The rites connected with the pilgrimage bind the Muslim with his or her brothers and sisters from all classes, nations, and races in a powerful sacrament of spiritual unity.

The pilgrimage involves a series of rituals. First, the pilgrim must undertake certain restraints, such as sexual abstinence. On approaching the city, the pilgrim greets Mecca with the cry, "Labbaika: 'Here am I, Lord, here am I.'" There follows the sevenfold circuit of the cube-shaped *Ka'bah* in the center of the mosque court. The pilgrim must try to kiss, or at least to touch, the sacred stone that is mounted on a corner of the *Ka'bah* and is the object of

Muslims at Friday prayer in a mosque in Kuwait. (*Source:* Kuwait Ministry of Information Office.)

solemn reverence. The climax of the pilgrimage comes between the eighth and tenth day with a journey from Mecca through Mina to Arafat 12 miles away. There, the pilgrim assembles with the others from noon to near sundown, a "standing in the presence of God." At sunset, the pilgrims move on to Muzdalīfah for the night. The next day, a symbolic "stoning" of Satan takes place at Mina. The 12-day pilgrimage ends with a ritual sacrifice of animals at Mina and the return to Mecca for a last circuit of the *Ka'bah*. The sense of excitement, of spiritual unity and camaraderie is recalled by a convert to Islam, Malcolm X, on returning from *Hajj*:

> We parked near the Great Mosque. We performed our ablution and entered. Pilgrims seemed to be on top of each other, there were so many, lying, sitting, sleeping, praying, walking. . . . Then I saw the *Ka'bah*, a huge block stone house in the middle of the Great Mosque. It was being circumambulated by thousands upon thousands of praying pilgrims, both sexes, every size, shape, color, and race in the world. I knew the prayer to be uttered when the pilgrim's eyes first perceive the *Ka'bah*. . . . My feeling there in the House of God was a numbness. My *mutawwif* led me in the crowd of praying, chanting pilgrims moving seven times round the *Ka'bah*. Some were bent and wizened with age. It was a sight that stamped itself on the brain. I saw incapacitated pilgrims being carried by others. Faces were enraptured in their faith.[17]

The religious obligations of a pious Muslim do not end with the "Five Pillars." The faithful are expected to conform their daily lives to the entire Islamic *Sharī'a,* which would include such things as prohibitions on drinking wine and eating pork; requirements of just actions in all commercial transactions; and as we have seen, participation in holy war (*jihād*), the war against Islam's enemies.

Like the "twice-born" classes of orthodox Hinduism, the Muslim's life is encompassed by daily religious obligations that, far from being a burden, give life its dignity, its sense of purpose and communal unity, and its feeling of joy in conforming to a divine and sacred law.

## Judaism

Christianity, at least until very recently, has placed great importance on belief and doctrine, on orthodoxy. Judaism, on the other hand, has given greater attention to correct practice (*ortho-praxis*). Judaism never established an official creed. Pious Jews differ widely on theological questions; what is central is a holy living as set forth in the Law, or Torah, and in the teachings of the biblical prophets. Judaism holds that an observant religious life prepares the way for the coming of the messianic age, God's kingdom on earth, when everything will be sanctified. It could be said that Judaism believes morality can be legislated, in the sense that habitual observance creates a complex of values and beliefs that, in turn, reinforces behavior.

The traditional path of life, or "way," prescribed for the religious Jew is, as we have seen, set forth in what is called the *halakhah*—the tradition of legal decisions and prescriptive rules of the rabbis concerning every aspect of Jewish observance. *Halakhah* is the way the Jew shapes his or her daily routine into a pattern of sanctity. It is the way to redemption. The hallowing of everyday activities—including eating, work, and sexual relations—means that for the Jew there can be no sharp separation of the sacred and the secular; the sacred impinges on every situation of life and under all circumstances. Since most activities are fenced by certain religious rules of observance, only a few examples can be mentioned here. Jews call their observance *mitzvah,* the pious response to God's command. Therefore, every act should, ideally, be preceded by the spoken intention that it be done "for the sake of Heaven."

The heart and soul of Jewish observance is the keeping of the Sabbath (*Shabbat*). On the Sabbath, a person must not work or engage in the usual mundane activities. It is a time of worship, rejoicing, and rest—a "taste of the world to come." The ritual of the *Shabbat* observance is here well described:

> How does the pious Jew keep the Sabbath? All week long, he looks forward to it, and the anticipation enhances the ordinary days. By Friday afternoon, he has bathed, put on his Sabbath garments, and set aside the affairs of the week. At home, his wife will have cleaned, cooked, arranged her finest table. The Sabbath comes at sunset, and leaves when three stars appear Saturday night.

After a brief service, the family comes together to enjoy its best meal of the week, a meal at which particular Sabbath foods are served. In the morning comes the Sabbath service, including a public reading from the Torah, the Five Books of Moses, and prophetic writings, and an additional service in memory of the Temple sacrifices on Sabbaths of old. Then home for lunch, and very commonly, a Sabbath nap, the sweetest part of the day. As the day wanes, the synagogue calls for a late afternoon service, and then comes a ceremony, *havdalah*, "separation," effected with spices, wine, and candlelight, between the holy time of the Sabbath and the ordinary time of the weekday.[18]

In addition to Sabbath observance, the traditional Jew also observes the several festivals that mark the seasons of the Jewish calendar year and commemorate significant events in Jewish history. The festivals mentioned here are the major holidays observed by Orthodox, Conservative, and Reform Judaism, the three principal twentieth-century movements.

*Rosh Hashanah* is the beginning of the year, New Year's Day, a fall festival originally associated with the harvest but now initiating a time of the Days of Awe, a week of remembrance, judgment, and penitence. This period culminates in **Yom Kippur**, the **Day of Atonement**, the holiest day of the year, in which Jews confess their faults and ask for the forgiveness of God and their fellows (see Chapter 4). It is a 24-hour period of fasting and prayer, punctuated by confession. *Yom Kippur* is followed by *Sukkot*, a time of joy and thanksgiving, originally an autumn agricultural feast called the "festival of ingathering." God's preservation and shelter are symbolized by the construction of a booth or hut, covered with branches, fruits, and flowers, in which the family eats its meals. The hut now reminds the Jew that God made his people dwell in booths when he rescued them from Egypt and preserved them in their wanderings in the wilderness.

Two other principal festivals are *Pessah* (Passover) and *Shabuot*. **Passover** is not only a traditional spring festival celebrating the new life but also a festival of freedom commemorating the Exodus of Israel from bondage in Egypt. The central ritual is the Passover *seder*, or family service, at table on the eve of the holiday. The father presides and, as he relates the story of deliverance, several symbols are present at the table as graphic reminders of both the renewal of life given by God (an egg and vegetable greens) and the suffering and cost of the Exodus. The latter is represented by a dish of salt, symbolizing both the tears of slavery and the saltiness of the Red Sea; bitter herbs again remind those present of their earlier slavery; and *matzah*—or unleavened bread, baked like a cracker from flour and water—symbolizes the fact that the Israelites had to leave Egypt without preparation and had to take with them only unleavened bread.

The festival of *Shabuot*, or the Feast of Weeks (Pentecost), comes seven weeks after Passover and marks the end of the grain harvest and the sacrifice of first fruits. The rabbis later connected *Shabuot* with the giving of the commandments, or Torah, to Moses on Mount Sinai. Today, it is the day in which children are confirmed in a synagogue service to a life dedicated to the Torah.

Jewish life is also punctuated by a series of religious rites of passage—including the circumcision (*brit milah*) of the male child on the eighth day after birth, and the advent of puberty, at which time the young boy undergoes the rite of **bar mitzvah** (*bar* means "son," or "subject to," and *mitzvah* means God's commandment), a sign of allegiance to the Torah. Many congregations today have instituted a similar rite (*bat mitzvah*) for girls. In addition, there are, of course, rites prescribed for a traditional wedding as well as for sickness, funerals, and mourning. However, the observance that is perhaps most distinctive of Judaism, what can be called its "condensed symbol," is that associated with the *dietary laws*.

We know that most of the dietary observances followed today by traditional Jews have their origin in ancient taboos associated with hygiene. Yet they are also perceived by the devout as laws given by God to sanctify life. Furthermore, they are an outward sign of a community of faith, an observance that helps bind the community around ancient practices. Observance of the dietary rules varies among modern practicing Jews. The Orthodox make every effort to observe these laws strictly, often at great personal inconvenience, indeed sacrifice. However, many Jews observe a **kosher** (fit and proper) table in their home but not when eating away from home. Others observe only some laws, such as the prohibition against eating pork, as a symbol of their participation in the community.

To the outsider, the meticulous following of the dietary laws, whose original meaning often is obscure, may well appear to be an obsolete irrelevance. However, to the observant Jew, these requirements are meant to make God's presence known in one of life's fundamental activities. In carrying out this *mitzvah*, the Jew is made joyful in the knowledge that he or she is hallowing the day in following God's command. To be real, of course, commandment must be accompanied by faith and devotion. Commandment without devotion is dead.

## The Way of Meditation and Insight

The three paths to salvation previously discussed are ways followed by millions of devout believers in all the major faiths. They are the *exoteric*, or common, means to salvation. The way of meditation and insight is an ancient path that also is open to all who are willing to follow its demanding discipline. However, just because of its rigorous conditions, it remains the *esoteric* way, that is, one pursued by a spiritual elite. Our Western word *meditation* does not adequately convey the meaning of the word in Hindu Sanskrit or Buddhist Pali. Meditation in these religions means a regimen of mental cultivation and development that proceeds, as we will see, through a series of moral and physical disciplines to the higher levels of mindfulness, concentration, and wisdom, or insight-enlightenment.

Those who follow this way believe that insight is absolutely crucial for the achievement of genuine spiritual freedom and release. But it is insight of a particular kind: enlightenment regarding the illusory division between subject and object, and between the self and the Ultimate. We select as examples two notable paths of meditation: (1) classical Yoga, expounded by the Indian sage Patañjali (second century B.C.E.) in his *Yoga Sutras* and, building on the techniques of Yoga, (2) the Eightfold Path of Theravada Buddhism.

## The Yoga Techniques of Patañjali

*Yoga* (meaning "to yoke or join") is the physical and mental discipline, conjoined with certain philosophical principles, that constitutes one of the six orthodox philosophies of India. The yoga system was refined and combined with the *Samkhya philosophy* by *Patañjali*. Briefly, according to Samkhya (the oldest philosophy of India), the world is constituted by two uncreated, eternal substances: *prakrti*, or indestructible matter, and *purusha*, or the infinite number of individual souls. The soul's entanglement in matter is the cause of its fall into misery and suffering, due to its immersion in what is mutable or changing. Suffering, then, is due to a "want of discrimination," a failure to recognize the essential difference between soul and matter. Deliverance is the "discriminating knowledge" of the absolute difference between these eternal realities. Samkhya describes the human situation and its "fall"; Yoga elaborates the techniques for the soul's release.

According to Patañjali, the soul's emancipation from illusion is achieved only through struggle, more particularly through **ascetic** techniques and meditation that alone can abolish our normal, illusory consciousness. Yoga begins then in action, or ascetic practices, that lead on to concentration, meditation and, ultimately, wisdom. The point of departure is concentration on a single object, which can block or break the circuit or stream of the normal conscious and subconscious mind. However, concentration can be achieved only if the body is suitably prepared. Therefore, physiology plays a critical role in yoga. The body must be pure and without strain; the breathing must be rhythmical. The first four steps in the yogic technique prepare the body and mind for concentration. The first preliminary step involves the *yamas* ("restraints"), the five desire-killing vows: to abstain from killing living things (*ahimsa*), from lying, from stealing, from sensuality (unchastity), and from acquisitiveness. Along with these restraints, the yogi must practice a series of disciplines including physical cleanliness, ascetic mortifications, study, and devotion.

Yogic technique proper begins with the third step, *asana*, sitting in the proper posture. The **hathayoga** sutras describe innumerable possible *asanas*. The most famous of these postures is the lotus position, with the right foot on the left thigh and the left foot on the right thigh, with the chin resting on the chest and eyes focused on the nose. The purpose is to reduce physical effort and strain, and to achieve a sense of physical weightlessness so that consciousness is no longer troubled by the presence of the body.

The fourth step is the breathing discipline that eliminates respiratory effort and, again, reduces bodily activity to a few rhythmical processes. Now

An Indian seated in motionless concentration in the lotus position. The senses are withdrawn from external distractions preparatory to *samadhi,* union or superconsciousness. (*Source:* Courtesy of Stock, Boston, Inc.)

the yogi approaches the state of consciousness peculiar to sleep and the fifth step, the withdrawal of all senses from external objects. Mircea Eliade describes this withdrawal:

> Motionless, cadencing his respiration, fixing his eyes and his attention on a single point, the yogi experimentally steps outside the profane modality of existence. He begins to become autonomous in relation to the cosmos; he is no longer troubled by outer tensions; sensory activity no longer projects him outward toward the objects of the senses; the psychomental stream is no longer governed by distractions, automatisms, and memory: He is "concentrated," "unified." This withdrawal beyond the cosmos is accompanied by a plunge into the depths of himself . . . [He] surrounds himself with increasingly powerful defences—in a word, he becomes invulnerable.[19]

The yogi no longer is distracted and troubled by sensory activity and now can concentrate the mind, which is the beginning of the final, closely linked exercises leading to release. Concentration is fixation of *thought* on a single point with the help of an external object. It brings the mind to rest by emptying it of all else. It is called "conscious *samadhi,*" or *samadhi* "with support." The mind is like the calm surface of a pond. The transition from concentration to meditation requires no new technique. Meditation is the seventh step and is described by Patañjali as "a current of unified thought," free from all uncontrolled objects or associations. In meditation, a person is not conscious of consciousness; however, in meditation the yogi can be interrupted by stimuli. In the eighth and final stage of *samadhi* "without supports," the yogi is invulnerable. The word *samadhi* means union, absorption, a full comprehension of being. It is spoken of as an unconscious trance, but this conveys too negative an impression. *Samadhi* is a state of superconsciousness. While it presupposes all the earlier disciplines and is not a gift of grace, it comes nevertheless without effort. It is like a rapture. Eliade describes it as follows:

> It would be wrong to regard this way of being of the spirit as a mere "trance" in which consciousness was devoid of all content. [It] is not the "absolute void." . . . For, on the contrary, the consciousness is saturated at that moment by a direct and total intuition of being. . . . The yogi attains to deliverance: a "death in life." He is *jivanmukta*, "the man delivered in life." He no longer lives in time and under the control of time, but in an eternal present.[20]

The paradoxical nature of the release (*moksha*) achieved by *samadhi*, the "emptying" of being that at the same time is the "filling" of being in union or unity, is compared with other goals of salvation below. Suffice it to say here that it is one type of "rebirth" into a new, yet primordial sacred order.

### Theravada Buddhism

We learned in Chapter 9 that in Theravada Buddhism, liberation from suffering (*dukkha*) comes through the cessation of craving (*tanha*), which is the cause of human unease and pain. The Fourth Noble Truth preached by the Buddha was the way leading to cessation of suffering, what he called the **Eightfold Path** leading to **Nirvana**. This Middle Path (because it avoids the extremes of either pleasure-seeking or ascetic self-mortification) is a form of spiritual formation or therapy consisting of eight components:

1. Right understanding
2. Right aspiration
3. Right speech
4. Right action
5. Right livelihood
6. Right effort
7. Right mindfulness
8. Right concentration

The eight elements in Buddha's path to enlightenment are not practiced in the above numerical order; rather, they are developed together, each assisting in the cultivation of the others. Together, they promote the three essentials of Buddhist discipline: *ethical conduct*, especially compassion (*karuna*); *mental discipline* (*samadhi*); and *wisdom* (*prajna*). Buddha insisted on the preliminary discipline of right association, since a person cannot expect to develop attitudes conducive to concentration and wisdom if he or she associates with others whose habits thwart spiritual progress.

Right understanding involves a deep or "penetrating" knowledge of the Four Noble Truths because these truths explain things as they really are, free of all illusion. Right aspiration involves a single-minded intention to be free of selfishness and desire, ill-will, and violence. Right speech, action, and livelihood are especially conducive to ethical conduct. Right speech includes abstention from (1) telling lies, (2) engaging in slander and backbiting, (3) using harsh and abusive language, and (4) indulging in idle speech and gossip. Disciples must become aware of how often they deviate from true and compassionate speech and why they do so. Right action involves a person's motives and intentions as well as outward behavior. Especially important is abstention from killing, stealing, and illegitimate sexual intercourse. A person's actions should be helpful and contribute to the welfare of others. Right livelihood reveals the radical character of Buddha's message. The disciple cannot expect to achieve liberation while engaging in a livelihood that brings harm and suffering to others. Five trades are specifically prohibited: trading in arms, in living beings, in flesh, in intoxicating drinks, and in poison. Neither may a person engage in military service or the work of a hunter. All permitted trades must be engaged in without deceit or usury (i.e., lending money for interest). The moral conduct that is here called for is an indispensable basis for all further spiritual development.

Mental discipline is included in the final three categories of the Eightfold Path: Right effort, mindfulness, and concentration. Effort calls attention to the fact that liberation requires tremendous willpower and perseverance, especially in preventing and suppressing evil thoughts and actions, and in nurturing and maintaining good thoughts and actions. But effort must not be hurried and fretful. It must be like the ox pulling itself out of deep mire; effort involves patience, a single-minded diligence without anxiety.

The Buddha admonished his disciples: "Be mindful!" Right-mindfulness is not an occult mystical state. By mindfulness, the Buddha meant *attentiveness*, a diligent awareness regarding the activities of the body, the sensations, and the mind. To be mindful is to increase the intensity and quality of attention, to see things as they really are, purged of all falsehood. The numerous forms of mental discipline or meditation are discussed in detail by the Buddha in the discourse entitled *Satipatthanasutta (The Setting Up of Mindfulness)*. It includes meditation on breathing and prescribes the yogic posture of sitting cross-legged. This and other yogic disciplines are proposed to develop concentration in preparation for the several stages of deep meditation necessary for achieving "penetration" or liberating insight, including the realization of Nirvana. In the fourth stage of meditation all sensations have disappeared and the person rests in a state of equanimity and pure awareness. Illusion and craving are now overcome. With the extinction of desire (*tanha*) and attachment, the Absolute Truth, Nirvana, is realized: "deathlessness, peace, the unchanging state."

While the ways proposed by Pantañjali and the Buddha are based on different and even conflicting metaphysical doctrines, they are one in insisting that the path to salvation is through the cultivation of the mind by meditation and in the achievement of insight or enlightenment. It is a strenuous discipline of self-help. During the last days of his life, the Buddha underlined this point:

> And whosoever, Ananda . . . shall be an island unto themselves, a refuge unto themselves, shall betake themselves of no eternal refuge, but holding fast to the truth as their island and refuge. . . . it is they, Ananda, who shall reach the very topmost height—but they must be anxious to learn.[21]

At the beginning of this chapter, we noted that the religions of the world offer a variety of "ways" or paths of deliverance from the suffering, the moral guilt, estrangement, and finitude that characterize human life. Furthermore, we noted that the great traditions include, in one form or another, all the classic ways—that is, of faith, devotion, disciplined action or duty, and meditation and spiritual insight. The "ways" are not exclusive, and the life of any single believer—especially the great saints and sages—may reflect all these patterns of religious experience and response. However, each way does often appeal to a quite different religious need and spiritual temperament. Therefore, it is quite natural that some persons and some cultural settings would regard a particular path or discipline as especially responsive to their religious requirements and their understanding of Ultimate Reality.

Having looked at several specific examples of these classic "ways," we are now prepared to examine the actual goals of salvation or enlightenment that are envisioned by the world's religions, for they, too, are various.

## *Goals of Salvation and Liberation*

In the Latin West, the word *salvus* was used to suggest that salvation is a process of healing, of making whole. However, the biblical Hebrew word that is most commonly translated as salvation implies a lack of constraint and conveys the sense of a deliverance or redemption. **Salvation,** then, is the process of being delivered, redeemed, or liberated from an enemy, danger, sin, pollution, finitude, or "the Devil's barter"—whatever is considered evil or threatening.

The phenomenologist Gerardus van der Leeuw describes salvation as "Power experienced as Good." He points out that it implies a range of concepts such as "whole, complete, perfect, healthy, strong, vigorous, well-being, as contrasted with suffering and misery, and in some connections bliss, both earthly and heavenly."[22] The breadth of meaning conveyed by salvation is extraordinarily wide. In addition, the experience of salvation can be considered from a number of perspectives. Many religions understand it as both a personal and a cosmic process or event. Moreover, salvation is both a present reality and a future hope; it is described as involving not only the individual but also the community. Furthermore, it is a condition portrayed as both this-worldly and as a wholly transcendent, other-worldly state of affairs.

Despite the numerous meanings that can be given to the word *salvation,* one thing stands out as certain. Salvation or liberation is the essential goal of religion. Religion is the means, the vehicle, or the process by which we are delivered from the profane world's disorder, meaninglessness, and evil. It is religion that redeems us from social chaos and establishes our cosmos. On the personal level, it is the means by which we are freed from all those conditions that threaten and limit our very being. Salvation is so central to the nature of religion that one writer has defined religion simply as "a means to ultimate transformation."[23] Religion involves much more, of course, but personal and cosmic salvation is its fundamental purpose and goal.

Our analysis of salvation begins with entirely this-worldly, humanistic conceptions—for example, in the contemporary psychotherapeutic "cure of souls" and in some Eastern spiritual therapies, such as Zen Buddhism. A second form of salvation looks beyond personal psychic wholeness to a future but *this-worldly* liberation of the entire social order through the coming of a Utopian or Messianic Age. A very different conception of salvation is found in those religions that look to salvation in a future *other-worldly* afterlife, conceived either as a rather insubstantial "shade" of the physical self, as a disembodied immortal soul, or as one or another form of resurrected body. We will review these various ideas in ancient Egypt and Greece, as well as in Judaism and Christianity at the beginnings of the Christian movement. Belief in a Heaven and a Hell is not, of course, uniquely Christian or even Western, and we will look at depictions of Paradise in Muslim and in Mahayana Buddhist scriptures, as well as in Christianity. The mystical, yet rather different, concepts of the Beatific Vision and of Eternal Life as a present reality are also examined.

The last mode of salvation explored is that associated with various types of monism, for example, in Hindu Vedanta and in certain interpretations of Buddhist Nirvana. In both instances, meditation and concentration are seen as leading to the release or to the absorption of the self in union with Brahman or Nirvana—a state of perfect emptiness, of imperturbable and inexpressible bliss.

## Psychic Wholeness and a Healthy Social Order

We begin with concepts of salvation that are radically this-worldly, nontheistic, and entirely humanistic. Many thoughtful contemporaries reject the belief that the amelioration of evil and human sorrow is dependent on powers or agents that are transcendent of human life itself. Nor do they believe that hope should be placed in a future, other-worldly salvation. The cosmos as such, they believe, is meaningless—the accidental collocation of atoms—and all is finally destined to extinction. This view is expressed with feeling and force by Bertrand Russell in his celebrated essay "A Free Man's Worship":

> No heroism, no intensity of thought and feeling, can preserve an individual life beyond the grave; that all the labours of the ages, all the devotion, all the inspiration, all the noonday brightness of human genius, are destined to extinction in the vast death of the solar system, and that the whole temple of man's achievement must inevitably be buried beneath the debris of a universe in ruins—all these things, if not quite beyond dispute, are yet so nearly certain, that no philosophy which rejects them can hope to stand.[24]

The cosmic pessimism of Russell's vision did not and has not inevitably given rise to personal or even historical despair. On the contrary, it has shocked many persons into an acute need to shape their own meaning in life. "I for one," writes the philosopher E. D. Klemke, "am *glad* that the universe has no meaning, for thereby is *man all the more glorious*. I willingly accept the fact that external meaning is non-existent . . . for this leaves me free to *forge my own meaning*."[25]

For Russell and Klemke, the amelioration of personal suffering and social conflict rests entirely on the application of human reason and creativity. However, it would be stretching the word to claim that Russell's humanistic creed is religious. His confidence in the improvement of individual life is cautious, and his hope for society is equally guarded, if not altogether skeptical. Russell's convictions are thoroughly humanistic but hardly utopian.

There are humanists, however, who hold out a vision of the future for individuals and society that is both deeply spiritual and **utopian.** The twentieth century in the West has witnessed what Philip Rieff calls "the triumph of the therapeutic," the transference of the "cure of souls" from a priest to the psychotherapist and from the church to the "encounter group." The latter, like the former, offers opportunities for confession, resistance to temptation ("ego strength"), heightened awareness, and reconciliation with one's fellows. Psychological therapy appears to offer our scientific age a means of liberation and healing without the traditional theological constraints of dogma and church authority, or belief in a life after death. Salvation is here and is now. Erich Fromm refers to the religious dimensions of the psychoanalytic cure of souls as those that enable the individual "to gain the faculty to see the truth, to love, to become free and responsible . . . the wondering, the marveling, the becoming aware of life and of one's own existence."[26]

The religious character of the therapeutic movement is evident in organizations such as Transcendental Meditation, est, the Esalen institutes, "T" groups, Transactional analysis, Integrity therapy, Scientology, and numerous other forms of popular therapy. Closely related to these spiritual psychologies is the new interest in Eastern religions, especially Yoga, Taoism, and Zen. What they share in common is the romantic feeling of the pleasure to be found in the joys of the body and the earth, a confidence in the feelings, a positive attitude, an interest in the present, and a distrust of institutional religion and what they see as the inhibitions or "uptightness" of the Protestant work ethic. Among the gurus of the new therapeutic are Alan Watts (Zen), Fritz Perls (Gestalt therapy), Ida Rolf (massage therapy), Carl Rogers (sensitivity training), and **Abraham Maslow** ("peak experiences").

Maslow (1908–1970) is a leader of the movement known as "humanistic psychology." While he is critical of traditional religious supernaturalism, he recognizes that the human process of growth and "self-actualization" involves certain *"peak experiences."* These transcendent occasions that bring life new insight, joy, and creativity, are not unlike those experiences described by the great religious mystics. In fact, Maslow believes that the older reports of prophets and saints "phrased in terms of supernatural revelation, were, in fact perfectly natural human peak-experiences."[27] The mystic ecstasy of a St. Teresa and the "peak experience" of a mother flooded with joy as she holds her newborn infant, are essentially the same—what Maslow calls the "core-religious experience," or "transcendent experience." According to Maslow, most persons, but not all, experience peak or transcendent moments that are not simply "emotional highs" but genuinely cognitive, transformative events. These spiritual experiences are triggered, however, by entirely natural, even everyday occasions, such as engaging in an athletic contest, listening to waves crash against a rocky shore, watching a dance performance, or tending a flower garden. For Maslow, religion must be taken out of the narrow context of institutional churches, clergy, and dogma—a single department of life—and be recognized as a quality or state of mind achievable in almost any activity.

In his study of the peak experiences of a large number of individuals, Maslow discovered that they have many of the characteristics we associate with traditional religious experience. For example, "the whole universe is perceived as an integrated and unified whole . . . all of one piece and that one has a place in it . . . one belongs to it." This is accompanied by a new, total kind of visual concentration in which "things become equally important rather than ranged in a hierarchy from very important to quite important." The recognition of everything as equally valuable holds also for people: "The person is unique, the person is sacred, one person in principle is worth as much as any other person." This new cognition also "allows the individual to become more objective and detached, ego-transcending, self-forgetful, egoless, unselfish." Maslow furthermore has found that peak experiences change a person's sense of time and space. This person "may feel a day passing as if it were minutes or also a minute so intensely lived that it might feel like a day or a year or an eternity even."[28] The emotions of wonder, awe, humility, gratitude, creature feeling, and exaltation are often reported as the after effect of these unique occasions.

Maslow insists that genuine knowledge is attained in peak experiences. It is a new awareness that permanently affects a person's attitude toward life and death, "valuing reality in a different way, seeing things from a new perspective . . . the miraculous 'suchness' of things . . . which contrasts with what can only be called 'normal blindness.' " These natural peak experiences can therefore teach values and virtues previously thought to be the unique province of traditional religion: acceptance, unselfishness, seeing things under the aspect of eternity, reverence, love, and innocence.

Maslow believes that a psychologically healthy society is possible, and he envisions a utopia called Eupsychia. It will be brought about by a widescale application of psychotherapy.

> I am saying that if you examine human beings fairly, you will find that they themselves have innate knowledge of and yearning for goodness and beauty. . . . Our task is to create an environment where more and more of these innate instincts can find expression. This is what would characterize Eupsychia.[29]

A number of therapists also have discovered an ally in Eastern spiritual techniques and meditation. Erich Fromm, for example, sees important resemblances between psychoanalysis and Zen Buddhism. The essence of **Zen** is *satori,* enlightenment or the acquiring of a new point of view. D. T. Suzuki, the foremost interpreter of Zen to the West, defines *satori* as "an intuitive looking into the nature of things in contradistinction to the analytical or logical understanding of it. . . . Or we may say that with *satori* our entire surroundings are viewed from quite an unexpected angle of perception."[30]

*Satori* is a flashing, momentary intuition, like an uncoerced discovery that, like Maslow's peak experiences, overcomes our normal dualistic perception of the world, transforming the entire personality. While not fully explicable, the instantaneous experience of *satori* is both authoritative and affirmative. It produces a sense of great release, joy, and exaltation that accompanies the breaking up of a person's dualistic, egocentric, acquisitive orientation. Suzuki describes the peculiar effect of *satori* as follows:

> All your mental activities will now be working in a different key, which will be more satisfying, more peaceful, more full of joy than anything you ever experienced before. The tone of life will be altered. . . . The spring flower will look prettier, and the mountain stream runs cooler and more transparent.[31]

Struck by the similarities between Suzuki's description of Zen and psychoanalysis, Erich Fromm characterizes the psychic import of *satori* in the following terms:

> I would say that it is a state in which the person is completely tuned to the reality outside and inside of him, a stage in which he is fully aware of it and fully grasps it. *He* is aware of it—that is, not his brain, nor any other part of his organism, but *he,* the whole man. He is aware of *it;* not as an object over there which he grasps with his thought, but *it,* the flower, the dog, the man, in its, or his, full reality. He who awakes is open and responsive to the world, and he can be open and responsive because he has given up holding on to himself as a thing, and thus has become empty and ready to receive. To be enlightened means "the full awakening of the total personality to reality" . . . to have attained a fully "productive orientation."[32]

The goal of salvation proposed by Maslow, Fromm, and other therapists concerned with "self-actualization" is thoroughly humanistic and this-
worldly. Salvation is achieved not by recourse to transcendent powers or a
sacred code of behavior but by calling on a person's own innate rational and
creative resources. For these spiritual therapies, the deepest level of human
healing and liberation takes place in the unleashing of the human potential
for goodness and community responsibility, all of which come with genuine
self-knowledge.

## A Messianic, or Utopian, Age

There are religious faiths, both traditional and secular, that look beyond
the mere psychic healing of individuals to a future, this-worldly redemption
of the social order itself through the coming of a Messianic, or Golden Age.
What these religions share is a view of salvation that is *future, this-worldly,*
and *communal.* This salvational type was previously described in the discussion of revolutionary millenarianism—for example, see the Melanesian
Cargo Cults in Chapter 10. One other example will, therefore, suffice here:
ancient Israelite eschatology.

*Eschatology* has to do with the end, or goal (the *telos*), of personal life
or of history and not simply with its temporal conclusion (*finis*). Since the eschaton is often depicted as occurring in the future, eschatological beliefs are
frequently mythological, that is, imaginative visions derived from past experience and present convictions about the nature of God or Ultimate Reality,
and about humanity and the historical process. Whether consciously or not,
as self-transcendent beings, we take some attitude toward the *telos* of life and
history. In fact, the philosopher Nikolai Berdyaev ventured to claim that "it is
only the future which gives human life meaning in the present." In any case,
it is true that we do not decide *whether* we will have an eschatology; rather,
we decide *which* convictions about life's goal we will embrace as most congruent with our experience and our deepest hopes.

## Ancient Israel's Messianic Hope

It sometimes comes as a surprise to learn that the ancient Israelites did
not hold a belief in individual life after physical death in the sense of personal self-awareness. They did, of course, believe in redemption, and it was
a belief founded on certain religious convictions. Early Israel believed, first,
that God had created the world for a purpose. The creation is essentially
good but, because of Israel's "hardness of heart," it had forsworn God's purpose and his covenant commandments. Israel's God, Yahweh, had therefore
afflicted Israel with "the rod" of his righteous anger: foreign oppression,
even exile from the holy land of Palestine. Nevertheless, Yahweh's loving-
kindness and his covenant with Israel were not forsaken, for he had favored
Israel as his chosen instrument, "a light unto the nations," to bring redemption and peace to the world. God's purpose for creation could not, therefore,

be frustrated forever; God's redemption would come in some future time. While Israel's hope for a future, earthly kingdom of peace and prosperity was complex and various, it took two distinct forms in the period between the great prophets of the eighth century B.C.E. and the domination of Israel by the Persians, Greeks, and Romans after 500 B.C.E. The earliest expression of Israelite eschatology is basically *nationalistic*.

*Israel's Nationalistic Hope*    Israel's national hope was shaped by the belief in what was called the *"day of Yahweh."* Initially, it was conceived as a period of unbroken prosperity and glory inaugurated by Yahweh's victorious overthrow of Israel's enemies. It was Israel's duty to worship Yahweh and Yahweh's duty to protect Israel. In the eighth century, however, this rather simple idea gave way to the prophetic vision of a coming kingdom of God comprised only of an ethically regenerated Israelite nation, a community joined together by its devotion to the divine Commandments. Prophets such as Amos, Jeremiah, and Isaiah stood in the Temple and before the kings, and rebuked the people for their unfaithfulness to the Covenant. They proclaimed that for Israel the "day of Yahweh" would not be light but darkness—a time of judgment on the nation. The land would be burned up; the people would be as fuel for a fire (Isaiah 9:19).

> And the haughtiness of man shall be humbled,
>     and the pride of men shall be brought low,
> And Yahweh alone will be exalted in that day.
>
> —*(Isaiah 2:17)*

However, Yahweh's purpose was not simply destructive. Through the nation's suffering, Isaiah saw Yahweh purging the moral dross so that Jerusalem might become a place of true righteousness:

> I will turn my hand against you
>     and will smelt away your dross
>     as with lye
>     and remove all your alloy.
>
> And I will restore your judges as at the first,
>     and your counselors as at the beginning.
>
> Afterwards you shall be called the city
>     of righteousness,
>     the faithful city.
>
> Zion shall be redeemed by justice,
>     and those in her who repent,
>     by righteousness.
>
> —*(Isaiah 1:25–27)*

Beyond the wrath of the day of Yahweh, the great pre-exilic prophets saw the dawn of a new era, inspired by the pious remnant of the nation

Israel. They looked to God's agent, "the anointed one," a king who would come and restore the nation to its earlier glory under the great King David. The nations of the earth would beat their swords into ploughshares, and the desert would blossom like a rose.

*Israel's Apocalyptic Hope* With the Exile of the Jews to Babylon (593 B.C.E.), a shift in Israel's eschatological hope began to take place. Israel's earlier "foes from the north" were now envisioned as the hosts of Gog, that is, the mysterious forces of cosmic evil. The warfare with evil now is perceived as the final battle of history.

The prophetic oracles of the later postexilic writers are called *apocalyptic* (from the Greek *apokalyptein,* meaning "to uncover or reveal"). They are a form of eschatological vision that is especially prominent during times of persecution and historical pessimism. The postexilic Jews had become increasingly doubtful about Israel's worldly glory as, again and again, Israel felt her hopes crushed by the Persians, then by the Greeks under the Seleucid kings, and finally by the Romans with Pompey's conquest of Jerusalem in 63 B.C.E. Under the influence of these historical disasters, Jewish writers began to modify Israel's earlier nationalistic, optimistic eschatology into a vast, imaginative, pessimistic vision of the end time.

According to these apocalyptic writers, who were influenced by Persian dualism (see Chapter 7), this earth or "the present age," the scene of so much misery and suffering, is now under the dominion of evil powers, with Satan as their head. The Powers of Darkness are successfully warring against Yahweh and the angels of light. However, this present, evil state of affairs will not continue forever; God will intervene and vindicate his kingly rule. But, humanly speaking, there is nothing that can be done; God alone is able to destroy the powers that rule this present, evil age. The apocalyptic prophets were certain that the turning point between this age and the new aeon was near at hand; this age was moving relentlessly toward its predetermined final encounter and the victory of God's kingdom. According to these writers, it was vitally important to recognize the signs of the approaching end. It would be heralded, for example, by a series of "messianic woes" when satanic evil would reach a climax in the coming of an anti-Messiah. Nature would run amuck; there would be fire on the earth, unnatural births, and cosmic disturbances (IV Ezra 5:4:12). Finally, the end would come when Satan is defeated and the faithful are rescued and exalted. *The Assumption of Moses,* a work contemporary with the New Testament, is a particularly good example of Jewish apocalyptic:

> And then his [God's] kingdom shall appear throughout all
>    his creation,
> And then Satan shall be no more.
> And sorrow shall depart with him.
> Then the hands of the angel shall be filled
> Who has been appointed chief,

And he shall forthwith avenge them of their enemies.
For the Heavenly One will arise from his royal throne,
And he will go forth from his holy habitation
With indignation and wrath on account of his sons.
And the earth shall tremble: to its confines shall it
    be shaken.
And the high mountains shall be made low
And the hills shall be shaken and fall.
And the horns of the sun shall be broken and he
    shall be turned into darkness;
And the moon shall not give her light, and be turned
    wholly into blood. . . .
And the fountains of waters shall fail,
And the rivers shall dry up.
For the Most High will arise, the Eternal God alone,
And he will appear to punish the Gentiles,
And he will destroy all their idols.
Then thou, O Israel, shalt be happy. . . .
And God will exalt thee,
And he will cause thee to approach to the heaven of the stars,
In the place of their habitation.
And thou shalt look from on high and shalt see thy enemies
    in Gehenna,
And thou shalt recognize them and rejoice,
And thou shalt give thanks and confess thy Creator.

—*(10:1–10)*

The *Last Judgment* is vividly portrayed in apocalyptic writings such as Daniel and IV Ezra. God comes forth as the "Ancient of Days," and he takes his seat on the throne, surrounded by his court of angels. The books that record the deeds of persons are brought in and the judgment is given. The righteous are raised to participate in the eternal messianic kingdom. The writers portray the life of the righteous variously. In Daniel, the kingdom is on earth, but in other writers it is depicted as the New Jerusalem brought down from Heaven. In I Enoch, the abode of the righteous is entirely transcendent in Heaven above. The fate of the ungodly is also variously portrayed, but in each case no longer as a neutral abode of the departed but rather as a place of eternal punishment: Sheol, Gehenna, the Furnace, or Abyss of Fire.

The agent of salvation also takes on new forms. A new savior emerges, a heavenly, supernatural figure called the *Son of Man* (Enoch 46:1–6, 48:2–10; and IV Ezra 13), who comes to inaugurate the new age. In Daniel 7, the "one like unto a son of man" is a corporate figure symbolizing the "saints of the Most High," the righteous and faithful martyrs who bear witness that God is inaugurating his messianic kingdom in the end time.

We can see in these postexilic Jewish apocalyptic writings the appearance of themes—Son of Man, Last Judgment, Resurrection, and Heaven and Hell—that are common to early Christian literature, for example, in the Gospels and the Book of Revelation. These concepts certainly reflect a more radically transcendent and cosmic Jewish eschatology than was present in

Israel's earlier nationalistic hope. However, the record shows that many schools of thought struggled within Judaism in the century before the Christian era. This-worldly, political messianism competes with more dualistic, cosmic visions, as is evident in the war of the Jewish **Maccabean** revolutionaries (168 B.C.E.) and the presence of the political **Zealot** party in Palestine in the first century of the Christian era. A psalm from the late Maccabean period reflects the continuing influence of Jewish political messianism:

> Behold, O Lord, and raise up unto
>    them their king, the son of David,
> All the time in which thou seest, O God, that he may
>    reign over Israel, thy servant.
> And gird him with strength, that he may
>    shatter unrighteous rulers,
> And that he may purge Jerusalem from nations
>    that trample her down to destruction.
>                   —*(Psalms of Solomon 15:21–25)*

At the dawn of the Christian era there arose a Jewish party called the Pharisees that, like the earlier **Hasidim,** practiced a strict devotion to the Law—including the dietary rules—that separated the Jewish community from the Gentile world. The Pharisees believed that Moses had laid down a body of oral law that was meant to guide the interpretation of the written Torah. This oral law, codified in the **Mishnah,** was later expanded into a vast library known as the **Talmud.** It was this Pharisaic or Talmudic Judaism that became the normative Judaism of the postbiblical era—and remains so today in Orthodoxy. Like the ancient Hasidim of Daniel's time, Talmudic Judaism looks with longing for the coming of the *Messianic Age.* However, Orthodoxy's devotion to the Torah has caused it to stand apart from radical forms of apocalypticism and political messianism. Furthermore, unlike certain movements within Christianity, Jewish belief in the resurrection of the body and a future life has not usually been thought of apart from participation in a redeemed messianic community. While the end time of history may look beyond the powers of history itself for the redemption inaugurated by the Messiah, the kingdom of God is essentially this-worldly. This is reflected in Israel's confidence that the coming Messianic Age will bring forth a new creation, a perfected world of redeemed men and women.

## Resurrection, Immortality, and Eternal Life

We do not give the activity much thought, but a unique feature of human life is the practice of burying our own dead. The practice suggests the special importance of death in human consciousness. Indeed, there is evidence from the caves near Peking that a half-million years ago our prehominoid forebearers possessed some sense of a life after death. Neanderthal and Cro-Magnon prehumans placed food and implements on their graves, and in the

Neolithic Age, the chieftain was often buried with his wives and slaves. These practices show that our ancestors assumed some kind of afterlife. However, the earliest forms of survival were not what we think of today as an immortal soul or mind distinct from the body or a resurrected body. What survived was a "*shade*," an insubstantial shadow image or double of the body. The common prehistoric view is described as follows:

> The shade was assumed to continue after death, generally in a dim underworld beneath the level of the graves, which were sometimes thought of as entrances to the nether world. The dead were often thought of as potentially dangerous to the living and needing to be either placated or tricked into quiescence. Sometimes, however, a chief or leader was imagined to go to a distant part of the earth, or up into the sky, and was venerated and perhaps in due course worshipped as a god. Some tribes have believed in a happier hunting ground beyond the grave. . . . But the much more general belief was in a descent into the lower world in which the shade carried on a gradually fading life until eventually it passed out of memory and existence. This was not a conception of eternal life, or immortality, but of ghostly survival . . . there was no thought of positive immortality.[33]

This lower world was called **Hades** or **Sheol,** a rather joyless underworld where the shade lived a half-conscious, twilight existence. In Homer's *Iliad,* the unhappy shade of Patroklos in Hades appears to Achilleus who in sorrow describes Patroklos's sad state as a soul or image with no real heart or life in it. All night long, the phantom of Patroklos stood over Achilleus lamentating and mourning. The Hebrew Sheol was similarly a dark, underworld cavern or pit, so cheerless and unwelcome that Job could cry:

> Let me alone, that I may find a little comfort
> before I go whence I shall not return,
> to the land of gloom and deep darkness,
> the land of gloom and chaos
> where light is as darkness.
>
> —*(Job 10:20–22)*

The use of words like *lamentation* and *gloom* might give the impression that Hades and Sheol were places of divine judgment and punishment like Hell, but this is not the case. In early Greek and Hebrew writings, Hades and Sheol represent a neutral underworld where the shades of the dead persisted, regretfully, at least for a time. Generally speaking, there was little sense of an ethical judgment of the dead, one in which the wicked suffered retribution in Hell and the pious enjoyed the delights of a heavenly bliss. It was simply taken for granted that the self survives physical death. Since it was not a condition to which a person looked forward and had nothing to do with a person's moral rectitude or spiritual effort, existence in Hades or Sheol could hardly be regarded as a state of salvation or liberation, a genuine immortality or eternal life. Such a conception was present, however, in the Pyramid Texts in ancient Egypt as early as the third millennium B.C.E., long before Homer and the earliest Hebrew poets.

## Immortality in Ancient Egypt and Greece

It was in Egypt that belief in a judgment of the dead and the related concepts of Heaven and Hell are first clearly recorded. The idea that a person's future life after death is conditioned by the person's present moral conduct is expressed in the Instruction for King Merikabe (Tenth Dynasty, circa 2150–2060 B.C.E.), in a warning given by a father to his son:

> The judges who judge the sinner, thou knowest, that they are not mild in that day, when they judge the miserable one, in the hour when the decision is accomplished. . . . Trust not in the length of years: they look upon the duration of a life as but an hour. Man remains after death and his deeds will be laid before him. . . . But who comes to them, not having sinned, he will be there as a god, free-striding as the Lord of Eternity.[34]

The later *Book of the Dead* vividly portrays the judgment carried out by the god Osiris, in which a man's heart is weighed in a scale against the feather of Maat, symbolizing truth. The text includes an impressively long list of 36 "negative confessions" in which the man pleads his sinlessness:

> I have not committed evil against men . . .
> I have not blasphemed a god . . .
> I have not killed . . .
> I have not defamed a slave to his superior . . .
> I have not defiled myself . . . [and so forth.][35]

The universal character of judgment and mention of the future abode of the righteous is described on a later tomb inscription of the priest Petosiris:

> The West is the abode of those without fault. Happy is he who arrives there! But none enters therein whose heart is not right in the deed of Maat. There is no distinction between rich and poor; he only counts who is found to be without fault when the balance and its burdens stand before the Lord of Eternity [the god Thoth].[36]

The Egyptian conception of life after death was a true immortality, but it was a future existence realistically conceived—that is, lifelike. The afterlife was not represented as a disembodied soul or mind, or as a resurrected spiritual body; rather, it was the survival as *ba*, an animated existence free from the human corpse but possessing the characteristics of real earthly life.

A quite different conception of an immortal soul emerged in Greece among the Eleusinian, Dionysian, and Orphic **mystery religions,** and within the philosophical schools. It reflects a radical dualism, both between the soul and its material body, and between this earth and the soul's heavenly home. For example, the later Greek Orphic cults taught a belief not only in the soul's immortality but also in the soul's transmigration—its fall from Heaven into its earthly embodiment and its return to its heavenly home.

The Orphic philosopher Pythagoras (circa 531 B.C.E.) taught that divine and immortal souls had fallen into material bodies in which they were now imprisoned. Salvation involved the cultic removal of the soul's taint, its rescue from its fallen state, and its return to its heavenly home. This Greek dualism had a significant influence on early Christianity (as did Jewish apocalyptic eschatology), but its influence was felt even earlier in the philosophy of Socrates and Plato. In his dialogue *Cratylus*, Plato writes,

> Some say that the body (*soma*) is the tomb (*sema*) of the soul, as if the soul in this present life were buried. . . . I think it most likely that the name was given by the followers of Orpheus, with the idea that the soul is undergoing whatever penalty it has incurred, and is enclosed in the body, as in a sort of prison-house, for safe-keeping . . . until the penalty it owes is discharged. . . .[37]

Plato's account of the soul's immortal, divine destiny is, however, divested of much of the earlier Orphic ritual and mystery. It is portrayed simply as life's most urgent moral challenge, namely, the perfecting of the human soul. According to Socrates and Plato, it is the philosopher's task—not that of an other-worldly savior—to free the soul from its bondage to the corruptible body and the world of mere appearances so that it may enjoy its true and eternal destiny. In the *Phaedo*, Socrates points out the mortal seriousness that is implied in a belief in the soul's immortality:

> But there is a further point, gentlemen, which deserves your attention. If the soul is immortal, it demands our care not only for that part of time which we call life, but for all time; and indeed it would seem now that it will be extremely dangerous to neglect it. If death were a release from everything, it would be a boon for the wicked, because by dying they would be released not only from the body but also from their own wickedness together with the soul; but as it is,

A last judgment, "the weighing of the heart," from the Egyptian *Book of the Dead*. Behind the scales, the scribal god Thoth records the verdict. At the extreme right, a monster waits to devour the unjust soul. (*Source:* Courtesy of the Trustees of the British Museum. Copyright The British Museum.)

since the soul is clearly immortal, it can have no escape or security from evil except by becoming as good and wise as it possibly can. For it takes nothing with it to the next world except its education and training.[38]

## Postbiblical Judaism and Christianity

We have observed that in the postexilic period (sixth century B.C.E.), Judaism's hope for salvation shifted from a this-worldly nationalism to an other-worldly apocalypticism, with its attendant concepts of a resurrection, judgment, Heaven, and Hell. Especially significant was the emergence of the complex idea of resurrection. We noted that in the postexilic period, resurrection was conceived sometimes as the establishment of the community of the righteous in a kingdom on earth; sometimes as a wholly renewed earth, a New Jerusalem; and sometimes as a purely spiritual, angelic body raised directly to Heaven.

All these ideas were current in Judaism at the beginning of the Christian era, but prominent was the belief in the *resurrection of a spiritual body.* Jesus appears to have accepted this belief. It is reflected in his controversy with the Sadducees where he asserts that "when they rise from the dead, they neither marry nor are given in marriage, but are like angels in heaven" (Mark 12:25). St. Paul, too, makes a distinction between the natural, fleshly body and the resurrected spiritual body (*soma pneumatikon*):

> There are celestial bodies and there are terrestrial bodies; but the glory of the celestial is one, and the glory of the terrestrial is another. . . . So it is with the resurrection of the dead. What is sown is perishable, what is raised is imperishable. It is sown in dishonour, it is raised in glory. . . . It is sown a physical body, it is raised a spiritual body. If there is a physical body, there is also a spiritual body.
> —*(I Corinthians 15:40–44)*

The New Testament texts that speak of the redeemed—the resurrected body—introduce two puzzles that the texts themselves do not easily resolve and that have produced an ongoing scholarly debate. The one issue is whether the spiritual resurrection involves a transformed body (both individual and corporate) here on earth—a new earth—or is to be understood as a heavenly body. The second question is whether the resurrection (and judgment) occurs immediately following the death of the individual or whether it is to come in some future time, at the "general resurrection" that precedes the Last Judgment. The New Testament passages reflect a tension between salvation (resurrection) conceived as present and as future. The tension is present in the teachings of Jesus. He clearly proclaims a future judgment and Kingdom, as when he speaks of the Son of man coming in his glory, and that "before him all the nations will be gathered and he shall separate them from one another, as a shepherd divides his sheep from the goats" (Matthew 25:31–32). On the other hand, Jesus proclaims God's Kingdom as already a present reality in his healing the sick, raising the dead, and casting out the devils (Matthew 11:3ff, 12:28; Luke 10:18, 11:20). In the parable of Dives and Lazarus, Jesus speaks of Lazarus, the righteous beggar, as immediately carried off by the angels "into Abraham's bosom," or Heaven, and the rich man dying and, in the torments of Hell, lifting up his eyes and seeing Lazarus in Heaven and crying for Abraham's mercy (Luke 16:22–23).

It appears that for Jesus and the early Christians salvation was understood in terms of the resurrection of the spiritual body and, furthermore, that they considered it as "already fulfilled" for those who were "in Christ"—that is, those who had died to the old self and were now raised to a life in Christ who had inaugurated the new age. Paul writes, "Behold *now* is the day of salvation" (II Corinthians 6:2); old things have passed away, those in Christ are "new creatures." The Fourth Gospel similarly speaks of the eschaton as realized, as a present reality. John records Jesus as proclaiming, "Verily, verily I say unto you, He that heareth my word, and believeth on him that sent me, hath everlasting life, and shall not come into condemnation; but is passed from death to life" (John 5:24).

This having been said, it is nevertheless true that the New Testament also envisions the Kingdom of God as a future event, as "not yet consummated." The Christian is thus living "between the times"—salvation is already present, but it is yet to be fulfilled on the Last Day. This tension between salvation as a present reality for those "in Christ" or "in Paradise" immediately on death and an entirely future salvation realized at the time of the Last Judgment has remained through the centuries.

After the second century C.E., however, interest in Christ's second coming and the coming of the general resurrection and final judgment faded in the popular consciousness. It was to be reawakened in times of social suffering and injustice, as we have seen, for example, in the preaching of Protestant millenarianists in the sixteenth century. However, by the early medieval period, the belief that each individual was judged at the time of death and the soul translated immediately to its eternal reward or punishment became the prevailing view.

Belief in a future life in **Heaven** or in **Hell** has been of decisive importance in shaping the Western moral imagination—at least until recently. The classic portrayals of Hell—in Dante's *Divine Comedy*, for example—describe the fate of the damned in the most vivid imagery. In fact, the portrayal of the suffering of the damned in some second-rate Christian literature is so graphic as to be morally offensive. In a literary master like Dante, however, the *Inferno* serves as a ghastly and horrific moral parable. Dante depicts Hell as a dark and frightening abyss: a steaming and stinking place, with howling winds, frightening cold, frenzied, tortured bodies, shrieking, and groaning. He portrays each sinner being punished in a manner appropriate to his or her sin.

In the Christian tradition, Heaven is not painted—with some exceptions—in quite the vivid colors as is Hell. In fact, with the decline of belief in a literal Hell in modern times, Christian discourse about a heavenly life has been rather guarded. In traditional devotional literature and in hymns, the picture of Heaven took two forms. One is the more homely vision of the family of saints reunited in Paradise. It is a place of light, peace, and joy, with no more sorrow or pain, where the faithful join in worship before the Throne of God. Such representations of Heaven, or Paradise, are not unique to Christianity; they are common in all theistic religions, including Islam and Mahayana Buddhism. Islamic eschatology is similar in certain respects to that in the Bible. It portrays a trumpeter announcing the Judgment Day; the angels bringing forth the Throne of the Lord, and the opening of the Book of Deeds. The unbelievers and the unrighteous are cast into the eternal fire of Gehenna, and the righteous are translated to Paradise, "the Gardens of Bliss." No subjects are mentioned more frequently in the *Qur'an* than are the Day of Judgment, Gehenna, and Paradise. And in Islamic literature, they are described in the most vivid language, none more so than Paradise. The following is a vision of Allah in Paradise. It describes in rich imagery Allah's palace garden and the joys of the heavenly feast:

> This [Allah's palace] gate is of green emerald and over it are curtains of light of such brightness as almost to destroy the sight. . . . Its soil is of finest musk and saffron and ambergris, its stones of jacinths and jewels, its little pebbles and rubble are of gold, while on its banks are trees whose limbs hang down, whose branches are low, whose fruits are within easy reach, whose birds sing sweetly, whose colours shine brightly, whose flowers blossom in splendour, and from which comes a breeze [so delightful] as to reduce to insignificance all other delights.
>
> Then orders will be given that they [the righteous] be served the finest kinds of fruit such as they never before have seen, and they will eat of these fruits and enjoy thereof as much as they desire. . . . Then orders will be given for them to be clothed with garments [of honor] the like of which they have not seen even in Paradise; and of such splendour and beauty as they have never before had for their delight. . . . So they will fall down before their Lord in prostration and deep humility saying: "Glory be to Thee, O our Lord. In Thy praise Thou art blessed and exalted, and blessed is Thy name."[39]

Earlier we observed that the Mahayana Buddhist schools made provision for the fact that not all individuals are capable of achieving liberation by the difficult road of transcendental meditation and wisdom. The new path took the form of faith and devotion to personal Buddhas and Bodhisattva saviors. In the Pure Land schools of China and Japan, these saviors occupy numerous Paradises, or Pure Lands, where the faithful are reborn. The most famous is the **Western Paradise of the Buddha Amitabha.** A favorite subject of religious art, Amitabha (Amida) is depicted seated on a lotus throne in the Western Heaven, flanked by his attendant Bodhisattvas, including Kuan-yin, the Goddess of Mercy. The following extract is from the popular Sanskrit *Description of the Happy Land* (second century C.E.):

> 15. This world Sukhavati [the Pure Land], Ananda, which is the world system of the Lord Amitabha, is rich and prosperous, comfortable, fertile, delightful and crowded with many Gods and men. And in this world system, Ananda, there are no hells, no animals, no ghosts, no Asuras, and none of the inauspicious places of rebirth. . . .

"The Last Judgement" by Jan Van Eyck, 1441. Christ appears as Judge, accompanied by his saints. The dead rise from their graves on earth, the righteous ascending to Heaven and the unrighteous descending to eternal Hell. (*Source:* Jan Van Eyck, "The Last Judgement." Oil on Canvas. Courtesy of The Metropolitan Museum of Art, Fletcher Fund, 1993 (33.92b))

16. And that world system Sukhavati, Ananda, emits many fragrant odours, it is rich in a great variety of flowers and fruits, adorned with jewel trees, which are frequented by flocks of various birds and sweet voices. . . .

18. And nowhere in the world-system Sukhavati does one hear of anything unwholesome, nowhere of the hindrances, nowhere of the states of punishment,

the states of woe and the bad destinies, nowhere of suffering. And that, Ananda, is the reason why this world-system is called the "Happy Name."[40]

A rather different and less familial conception of the heavenly life is given in depictions of the *Beatific Vision*. It has played an important role in Roman Catholic piety and is the image of paradise envisioned by the great Christian mystics. As the words imply, the Beatific Vision is the direct, unmediated vision of the Godhead. In traditional Catholic spirituality, there are levels of sanctity as well as levels of punishment, and the direct vision of God is reserved for the highest purity. It is the simultaneous intellectual perception of all things in God, an Eternal Present. It is not a vision of nature transfigured, as in Zen Buddhist *satori* or nature mysticism; rather, it is a direct vision of God, of Infinite Love, face to face.

In the Beatific Vision, the self is united with God and yet is *not* God, in contrast to the isolation or extinction of the self in Vedānta and other forms of monistic liberation. The self dies to the old ego and is transformed into a new creature, "oned with God."

Practitioners of the contemplative life point out that a foretaste of the Beatific Vision is achievable here and now when the personal will becomes one with the divine will. When this occurs, *Eternal Life*—or Paul's experience that "it is no longer I who live, but Christ who lives in me" (Galatians 2:20)—is not a condition of the soul translated to an other-worldly heaven but instead is a present, perfected or divinely transformed existence, wholly devoted to the divine will.

The contemplative does not leave the world but enters into it as a servant of the divine will. The test of a genuine contemplative vision, attested to by all theistic mystics, is a transformed, egoless life in the world, penetrated by the divine spirit. It is, writes the Catholic monk Thomas Merton (1915–1968),

> an experience of mystical renewal, an inner transformation brought about entirely by the power of God's merciful love, implying the "death" of the self-centered and self-sufficient ego and the appearance of a new and liberated self who lives and acts "in the Spirit."[41]

To this point, we have surveyed a variety of representations of salvation that are common to theistic belief. It remains to describe the most radical form of self-transcendence. This is the monistic conception of liberation in which personal identity is extinguished or overcome in a state of nondualism—in which *atman* and Brahman are One. This is best illustrated in Hindu Advaita Vedanta philosophy and in some interpretations of Buddhist Nirvana.

## *Samādhi* and Nirvana

In Chapter 7, we noted the movement in Indian religion from polytheism to pantheism and monism, especially in the *Upanishads*. In these texts, the unifying principle of the universe is called Brahman, the ultimate sacred

Amida (Amitabha) descending from the Western Paradise, accompanied by 25 protective Bodhisattvas. Amida is embarked on a journey to assist the souls of devotees. (*Source:* Raigo, "Amida descending from the Western Paradise." Courtesy of The Seattle Art Museum, Eugene Fuller Memorial Collection, 34.117.)

power or world-ground. Since the power that works in everything cannot consist in parts or be subject to change, according to some Indian sages, it follows that everything is essentially Brahman, entire and indivisible. Ultimately, nothing exists other than Brahman, including the soul (*atman*) that *is* Brahman: Atman and Brahman are One. There is only the One, without a second. Vedanta philosophy expressed this monistic doctrine with utterances such as "I am Brahman" and "Thou are That."

### Hindu *Samādhi*

As we have seen, the philosopher Śankara was the formative and most influential exponent of a thoroughgoing nondualism (*advaita*). He taught the nonexistence of the self as a separate entity. According to Śankara, belief in finite individuality is due to *avidya* (ignorance of reality), and the goal of *Advaita Vedānta* is release (*moksha*) from the illusion of a self or "I" and union with the Infinite without individual consciousness.

To achieve the self's *moksha,* we have seen that Vedānta proposes a series of ascetic disciplines similar to those required in Sankhya-Yoga. Beginning with certain moral rules regarding such things as unselfishness and bodily cleanliness, it proceeds to disciplined postures of the body, to breathing exercises, to concentration, and to meditation. If successful, the candidate then progresses to the final goal of *samādhi,* or perfect absorption. The word *samādhi* means "to put together," "to unite," or "to compose." Vedānta, however, does distinguish two kinds of *samādhi*: (1) *savikalpa samādhi,* which is absorption with full consciousness of the duality of the perceiver and the perceived, and (2) *nirvikalpa samādhi,* perfect nondual absorption, which is totally devoid of any consciousness of a distinction between perceiver and perceived. In the first instance, the self remains aware of the blissful union with Brahman. As in the case of the Christian Beatific Vision, the subject enjoys the supreme ecstasy of union with the Infinite. However, this is not the highest goal in *nirvikalpa samādhi,* the One-without-a-second. Since it is the One without predicates, and therefore ineffable, it is the bliss of silence.

*Nirvikalpa samādhi* comes only when the mind is at complete rest, reposed in the changeless One: "As a lamp sheltered from the wind, that does not flicker." This final state, being without distinctions or predicates, is ineffable. And yet Vedānta uses many images to attempt to suggest it. One is the image of salt in water: "Just as when salt has been dissolved in water the salt is no longer perceived separately and the water alone remains, so likewise the mental state that has taken the form of Brahman, the one-without-a-second, is no longer perceived, only the Self remains."[42]

The liberated person would be entirely freed of the phenomenal world if it were not for the momentum of *karmic* actions that continue to carry him or her along. The liberated person therefore remains associated with a body, but in an imperturbable state of changeless serenity. Past, present, and future time are transcended; the person is indifferent to all actions, good or evil.

Being imperturbable, the liberated *sow* no new *karma,* and, therefore, the effects of the residual past *karma* slowly fade. When the vestigial shell of the body falls away in death, the liberated person achieves a supreme isolation, a "bodiless liberation." According to the *Vedantasara,* "then at last, when the remainder of karma has been exhausted . . . the life-breath dissolves into the Highest Brahman, which is inward Bliss."[43]

### Buddhist Nirvana

The paths to liberation taken by the Indian yogi and the Buddhist monk share certain family resemblances. Both emphasize the discipline of "sitting" or meditation. Both perceive liberation as a "release" or "extinction" of the illusory, phenomenal self. And yet for all these similarities, Buddhist Nirvana is described in what appears to be more positive, world-affirming terms.

The goal of the Theravadin *arahant,* or fully enlightened one, is the Absolute Noble Truth of *Nirvana.* According to Buddhism, this Absolute Truth is that there is nothing absolute in the entire world. Everything is conditioned, changing, and impermanent, including the "self." To realize this truth without illusion involves the extinction of craving and the cessation of desire, which is Nirvana. The *Sanyuttanikāya* speaks of Nirvana simply as "the stopping of becoming" and as "the getting rid of craving."

It would be incorrect, however, to think of Nirvana as the *result* of the extinction of craving. Nirvana is neither the cause nor the effect of anything. Nirvana *is;* it is unconditioned. This point is made by Buddha's disciple Nagasena in the famous dialogue *Questions of King Milinda.* It is possible to point out the path to the realization of Nirvana but, Nagasena insists, it is not possible to show a cause for its production:

> "Could a man, who with his natural strength has crossed in a boat over the great ocean, get to the farther shore?" "Yes, he could"—"But could that man with his natural strength bring the farther shore of the great ocean here?" "No, he could not."—"Just so one can point out the way to the realization of Nirvana, but one cannot show a cause for its production. And what is the reason for that? Because the dharma, Nirvana, is unconditioned . . . not made by anything."[44]

Because it is unconditioned, Nirvana is beyond all conception and description. Buddha refused every request for a positive description, insisting that it was "incomprehensible, indescribable."

Because Nirvana is literally inconceivable and the Pali word for Nirvana (*Nibbāna*) means "blowing out" or "extinction" (of a lamp), Nirvana is often thought of as a purely negative state, a nothingness. However, such a nihilistic view is a misconception, as is frequently pointed out by Theravadin scholars. While Nirvana is extinction, it is important to recognize that it is the negation of lust, hatred, illusion—the extinction of the finite self or ego-consciousness. While often using negations to describe it, Buddha nevertheless speaks of Nirvana as a positive reality: "O bhikkhus, there is the unborn, ungrown, and unconditioned. Since there *is* the unborn, ungrown, and unconditioned, there *is* escape from the born, grown, and conditioned."[45] Similarly, the *Sanyutta-nikāya* describes Nirvana in a series of positive terms, including "the stable," "the excellent," "the blissful," "the security," "the cave of shelter," "the stronghold," and "the refuge."[46]

Since the *arahant* has purified the mind and no longer craves either becoming *or* extinction, he or she clings to nothing in the world, knows that all is impermanent. The *arahant* has realized Absolute Truth, Nirvana, in this life itself:

> He who has realized the Truth, Nirvana, is the happiest being in the world. He is free from all "complexes" and obsessions, the worries and troubles that

torment others. His mental health is perfect. He does not repent the past, nor does he brood over the future. He lives fully in the present. . . . He is joyful, exultant . . . free from anxiety, serene, and peaceful. And he is free from selfish desire, hatred, ignorance, conceit, pride, and all such "defilements. . . ." His service to others is of the purest, for he has no thought of self. He gains nothing, accumulates nothing, not even anything spiritual, because he is free from the illusion of Self, and the "thirst" for becoming.[47]

Theravadin schools do differ, however, in their view of what happens to the *arahant* after death. One view holds that the *arahant* has no reexistence, even in Nirvana, after death.

The old craving exhausted, no fresh craving rises,
Freed from the thought of future becoming
They like barren seeds do not spring again,
But are blown out just like a lamp.[48]

According to this interpretation, at death the *arahant* is freed from the round of *samsara*, or rebirth, and is fully extinct. Nirvana, then, is a purely blissful psychological state of the living *arahant*. A person has realized Nirvana when he or she has extinguished the "self" of the Five Aggregates that cause craving and pain.

The alternative view denies that Nirvana is simply a psychological state of the living *arahant;* rather, it is the infinite supramundane Reality to which the *arahant* is joined or oned at death. In death, the "self" is dissolved, leaving only the "unborn," the "not-become," the "not-compounded." This conception is thoroughly monistic. It is the state of undifferentiated unity. It is deathlessness, perfect emptiness, and not the immortal soul's ecstatic Beatific Vision.

From this review of concepts of salvation or liberation, certain resemblances can be seen in the blissful sense of liberation and egolessness produced by "peak experiences," in Zen *satori*, in eternal "life in Christ," in Buddhist Nirvana, and in the Beatific Vision. And yet there appear to be unbridgeable differences between the theist's conception of an immortal soul or resurrected body reunited with the divine through the loving action of a transcendent, personal God and the atheistic or monistic doctrines of liberation which hold that the soul and God are, finally, One and the same and all else is pure illusion. But, even here, in current interreligious dialogue the question is raised whether it is possible to reconcile even these apparent contrary claims.

## NOTES

1. Martin Luther, *A Commentary on St. Paul's Epistle to the Galatians.* Cited in Philip S. Watson, *Let God Be God* (Philadelphia, 1947).

2. Ibid., p. 141.

3. Ibid., 47–48.

4. *Shinshu Shōgyō, Zensho* Vol. II (Kyoto, 1953), 527, cited in Alfred Bloom, *Shinran's Gospel of Pure Grace* (Tucson, 1965), 29. I am dependent on Bloom's excellent study for my exposition of Shinran's teaching.

5. Winston King, *Introduction to Religion: A Phenomenological Approach* (New York, 1968), 337. King's analysis of the "discipline of devotion" has been helpful at this point.

6. E. Allison Peers, trans. and ed., *The Complete Works of Saint Teresa*, Vol. I (New York, 1946), 119f., 121.

7. A. J. Arberry, *Sufism* (New York, 1950), 53ff., 62.

8. Edward C. Dimock, Jr., and Denise Levertov, trans., *In Praise of Krishna* (New York, 1967), 56f., 65f.

9. *Bhagavad Gita*, Vol. I, 40–42, cited in Ainslie T. Embree, *The Hindu Tradition* (New York, 1966), 83–84.

10. *Manu Smriti*, Vol. X, cited in ibid., 94.

11. *Manu Smriti*, Vols. I and X, cited in ibid., 79–80.

12. *Manu Smriti*, Vol. I, cited in ibid., 85–86.

13. Embree, *Hindu Tradition*, 93.

14. Sirdar Iqbal Ali Shah, *Lights of Asia* (London, 1934), 29f.

15. Kenneth Cragg, *The House of Islam* (Belmont, Calif., 1969), 48.

16. Kemal A. Faruki, *Islam, Today and Tomorrow* (Karachi, 1974), 264ff. Cited in Cragg, *House of Islam*, 55–56.

17. Malcolm X, *The Autobiography of Malcolm X* (New York, 1965), 327f., 341–42.

18. Jacob Neusner, *The Way of Torah: An Introduction to Judaism* (Belmont, Calif., 1970), 27.

19. Mircea Eliade, *Patanjali and Yoga* (New York, 1975), 81–82.

20. Ibid., 113–14.

21. *Maha-parinbbana-sutta.* Cited in Nyanaponika Thera, *The Heart of Buddhist Meditation* (London, 1969), 83–84.

22. Gerardus van der Leeuw, *Religion in Essence and Manifestation,* Vol. I (New York, 1963), 101.

23. Frederick J. Streng, *Understanding Religious Life* (Belmont, Calif., 1985), 2.

24. Bertrand Russell, *Mysticism and Logic* (London, 1918), 47–48.

25. E. D. Klemke, "Living Without Appeal," in *The Meaning of Life,* ed. E. D. Klemke (New York, 1981), 172.

26. Erich Fromm, *Psychoanalysis and Religion* (New Haven, Conn., 1950), 93–94.

27. Abraham Maslow, *Religions, Values, and Peak Experiences* (Columbus, Ohio, 1964), 20.

28. Ibid., 60–65.

29. Abraham H. Maslow, "Eupsychia—The Good Society," *Journal of Humanistic Psychology,* Vol. I (Fall 1961), 6.

30. D. T. Suzuki, *Zen Buddhism* (New York, 1956), 84.

31. D. T. Suzuki, *Introduction to Zen Buddhism* (London, 1949), 97–98.

32. Erich Fromm and D. T. Suzuki, *Zen Buddhism and Psychoanalysis* (New York, 1960), 115–116.

33. John Hick, *Death and Eternal Life* (New York, 1976), 56. Hick's study has been a valuable guide and resource for this segment.

34. S. G. F. Brandon, *Man and His Destiny in the Great Religions* (Toronto, 1962), 52.

35. Ibid., 53.
36. Ibid., 56.
37. *Cratylus*, 400b. Cited in Brandon, *Man and His Destiny*, 186.
38. *Phaedo*, 207c.
39. Arthur Jeffrey, *Islam: Muhammad and His Religion* (New York, 1958), 98–103.
40. *Sukhavativyuka*, Chaps. 15–18. Cited in Edward Conze et al., *Buddhist Texts Through the Ages* (New York, 1964), 202–4.
41. Thomas Merton, *Contemplative Prayer* (New York, 1969), 110.
42. *Vedantasara of Sàdananda*. Cited in Heinrich Zimmer, *Philosophies of India* (New York, 1957), 432.
43. Zimmer, *Philosophies of India*, 446.
44. Edward Conze, ed., *Buddhist Scriptures* (Baltimore, Md., 1968), 158–59.
45. *Udana*, 80. Cited in W. Rahula, *What the Buddha Taught*, 37.
46. *Sanyutta-Nikāya*, IV. Cited in Hick, *Death and Eternal Life*, 435.
47. Rahula, *What the Buddha Taught* (New York, 1962), 43.
48. *Sutta-Nipata*, 235. Cited in Hick, *Death and Eternal Life*, 436.

## KEY WORDS

faith (as *assensus* and *fiducia*)
Martin Luther
Mahayana Buddhism
Theravada Buddhism
Bodhisattva
Amida Buddhism
Shinran
the way of devotion
St. Teresa of Avila
ecstasy
*bhakti*
ortho-praxis
Code of Manu
Hindu dharma
the four castes (*varnas*)
the four stages (*ashramas*)
islām
*Sharī'a*
the Five Pillars of the Faith
*halakhah*
*mitzvah*
*Yom Kippur* (Day of Atonement)
Passover
seder
*bar mitzvah*
kosher

yoga
Samkhya philosophy
Patañjali
*samadhi*
*dukkha*
*tanha*
the Eightfold Path
Nirvana
salvation
Abraham Maslow
"peak experiences"
*Zen satori*
eschatogy (messianic)
the "day of Yahweh"
apocalyptic
Last Judgment
Son of Man
Messianic Age
the "shade"
Hades or Sheol
resurrection of the spiritual body
Heaven and Hell
the Western Paradise of the Buddha Amitabha
Beatific Vision (in Christianity)
Eternal Life

Advaita Vedānta                                *nirvikalpa samādhi*
*moksha*                                       *arahant*
*samādhi*                                      Nirvana

## REVIEW QUESTIONS

1. Describe the major features of Luther's experience of being liberated and "made righteous" by grace through faith. Include his understanding of the role of the law—that is, good works that are commanded—of grace, and of the true motivation for doing good works.

2. Describe the several features that characterize the way of devotion discussed in this chapter.

3. The lives of the three "twice-born" castes of Hinduism are encompassed by numerous social and ceremonial duties, all of which are devoted to knowledge and liberation. Describe the four classes, or castes, of Hinduism and the four stages of life that are elaborated in the Hindu *Code of Manu*.

4. The Islamic tradition includes all of the classic "ways" to salvation, but it is viewed as normatively a religion of *Sharī'a*, of ethical and ritual duty. Describe the five "pillars," or principal obligations, expected of the faithful Muslim.

5. In Judaism, redemption or the sanctifying of life is by means of *halakhah*, that is, those laws and commands relating to all aspects of life, including the keeping of the Sabbath and the yearly festivals. Indicate the main features of some of the Jewish observances and what they signify or commemorate.

6. The way of action or obligation is based, in part, on the insight that we humans are shaped by our daily or habitual gestures and activities. Would you agree that religious enlightenment or the sanctifying of life would be difficult, if not impossible, without the routine of sacred obligation?

7. The way of meditation and insight is a difficult path requiring a series of physical and mental disciplines. Without having to refer to every step (or the Sanskrit and Pali terms), describe the major practices or components of Patañjali's yoga technique to achieve *samādhi*, and the Buddha's Fourth Noble Truth, that is, the Eightfold Path to Nirvana.

8. How does *eschatology* relate to *soteriology*?

9. What analogies, if any, do you see between such "therapeutic" experiences as Maslow's "peak experiences" or Zen enlightenment and more traditional religious experience?

10. Characterize Israel's early, this-worldly political hope. How does it differ from the apocalyptic motifs that begin to appear in Israelite prophecy after the Babylonian exile?

11. Theistic religions have conceived of salvation in this-worldly terms and also in terms of a postmortem life of a personal soul or a resurrected body. Contrast such concepts of survival as *ba*, the Greek immortality of the soul, the biblical resurrection of the body, and eternal life. How do earlier portrayals of Sheol differ from later depictions of Hell? How does the heavenly Beatific Vision differ from more familial portrayals of Paradise or Heaven in the Christian and Islamic traditions?

12. The highest goal of Hindu Vedantic liberation is *nirvikalpa samādhi*, or perfect, nondual absorption. Can you indicate how *samādhi* differs from either the Beatific Vision or a dreamless sleep or trance?

13. What is Nirvana? How is the term *extinction* to be understood in Theravada Buddhism?

## SUGGESTIONS FOR FURTHER READING

*For general discussions of the classic ways of faith, devotion, obligation or duty, and insight, see the following:*

KING, WINSTON. *Introduction to Religion.* New York: Harper & Row, 1968, Chaps. 12–15.

STRENG, FREDERICK. *Understanding Religious Life.* Belmont, Calif.: Wadsworth Publishing, 1985, Chaps. 2–5.

*For the way of grace through faith, see the following:*

BLOOM, ALFRED. *Shinran's Gospel of Pure Grace.* Tucson: University of Arizona Press, 1965.

DILLENBERGER, JOHN. ed. *Martin Luther: Selections from His Writings.* New York: Doubleday, 1961. See, in particular, "Commentary on St. Paul's Epistle to the Galatians," "The Freedom of a Christian," and "Two Kinds of Righteousness."

JAMES, WILLIAM. *The Varieties of Religious Experience.* New York: Collier Books, 1961, Chaps. 9–10.

*For the way of devotion, see the following:*

CHADWICK, OWEN. *Western Asceticism.* Philadelphia: Westminster Press, 1958. Selections on the way of ascetism in Christian piety.

EMBREE, A. T. *The Hindu Tradition.* Part Four, "The Traditions and the People's Faith." New York: Random House, 1966.

KINSLEY, DAVID. "Devotion," in Mircea Eliade, *The Encyclopedia of Religion*, 4. Macmillan , 1987, pp. 321–26. See Bibliography.

PADWICK, CONSTANCE E. *Muslim Devotions.* London: SPCK, 1961.

RAMANUJAN, A. K. *Hymns for Drowning.* Princeton, N.J.: Princeton University Press, 1981. Hindu devotional hymns and overview of Hindu devotion.

SCHIMMEL, ANNEMARIE. *Mystical Dimensions of Islam.* Chapel Hill: University of North Carolina Press, 1975.

*For the way of religious obligation and duty, see the following:*

"The Dharmasastras." In *The Cultural Heritage of India.* 2nd ed. Calcutta: Ramakrishna Mission, 1962.

MARTIN, RICHARD. *Islam: A Cultural Perspective.* Englewood Cliffs, N.J.: Prentice Hall, 1982.

TREPP, LEO. *Judaism: Development and Life.* Part III, "Life as Mitzvah." Belmont, Calif.: Wadsworth Publishing, 1982.

*For the way of meditation and mystical insight, see the following:*

ARBERRY, A. J. *Sufism.* London: Allen and Unwin, 1950.

DASGUPTA, SURENDRANATH. *Hindu Mysticism.* Chicago: Open Court Publishers, 1927.

ELIADE, MIRCEA. *Patanjali and Yoga.* New York: Schocken Books, 1975.

JAMES, WILLIAM. *The Varieties of Religious Experience.* New York: Collier Books, 1961, Chaps. 16–17.

KAPLEAU, PHILIP. *The Three Pillars of Zen.* New York: Harper & Row, 1966. Examples of Zen training and enlightenment.

SCHIMMEL, ANNEMARIE. *Mystic Dimensions of Islam.* Chapel Hill: University of North Carolina Press, 1975.

SCHOLEM, GERSHOM. *Major Trends in Jewish Mysticism.* New York: Schocken Books, 1961.

THERA, NYANAPONIKA. *The Heart of Buddhist Meditation.* London: Rider, 1969. Exposition of Theravada meditation.

UNDERHILL, EVELYN. *Mysticism.* New York: Dutton, 1961.

ZAEHNER, R. C. *Mysticism: Sacred and Profane.* Oxford: Oxford University Press, 1957.

*For general accounts of salvation and life after death in the world's religions, see the following:*

BRANDON, S. G. F. *The Judgment of the Dead.* New York: Scribner's, 1969.

———. *Man and His Destiny in the Great Religions.* Toronto: University of Toronto Press, 1962.

HICK, JOHN H. *Death and Eternal Life.* San Francisco: Harper & Row, 1976. This study is especially thorough and lucid, and includes a valuable bibliography.

*For conceptions of eschatology, resurrection, immortality, and eternal life in the Abrahamic religions, see the following:*

CHARLES, R. H. *Eschatology: The Doctrine of the Future Life in Israel, Judaism, and Christianity.* New York: Schocken Books, 1963.

CULLMANN, OSCAR. *Immortality of the Soul or Resurrection of the Dead?* New York: Macmillan, 1958.

DAHL, M. E. *The Resurrection of the Body.* London: SCM Press, 1962.

NICKELSBURG, GEORGE W. E., JR. *Resurrection, Immortality, and Eternal Life in Intertestamental Judaism.* Cambridge, Mass.: Harvard University Press, 1973.

RUSSELL, D. S. *The Method and Message of Jewish Apocalyptic.* Philadelphia: Westminster Press, 1964.

SMITH, JANE I., and YVONNE Y. HADDAD. *The Islamic Understanding of Death and Resurrection.* Albany, N.Y.: SUNY Press, 1981.

*For conceptions of liberation in Hinduism and Buddhism, see the following:*

ELIADE, MIRCEA. *Yoga: Immortality and Freedom.* Princeton, N.J.: Princeton University Press, 1969.

O'FLAHERTY, WENDY D., ed. *Karma and Rebirth in Classical Indian Traditions.* Berkeley: University of California Press, 1980.

RAHULA, WALPOLA. *Anatta and Nibbana.* Kandy, Ceylon: Buddhist Publication Society, 1971.

———. *What the Buddha Taught.* New York: Grove Press, 1959.

SUZUKI, D. T. *Zen Buddhism.* New York: Doubleday, 1956.

ZIMMER, HEINRICH. *Philosophies of India.* New York: Meridian Books, 1957.

*For comparative studies of mysticism, see the following:*

OTTO, RUDOLF. *Mysticism: East and West.* New York: Meridian Books, 1957.

SUZUKI, D. T. *Mysticism: Christian and Buddhist.* New York: Collier, 1962.

SUZUKI, D. T., E. FROMM, AND R. DEMARTINO. *Zen Buddhism and Psychoanalysis.* New York: Grove Press, 1960.

UNDERHILL, EVELYN. *Mysticism.* New York: Dutton, 1961. First published in 1911.

ZAEHNER, R. C. *Mysticism: Sacred and Profane.* New York: Oxford University Press, 1961.

*For nontraditional and secular ways to salvation or liberation, see the following:*

HEELAS, PAUL. *The New Age Movement.* Oxford: Blackwell, 1996.

LEONARD, G. B. *Education and Ecstasy.* New York: Delacorte Press, 1968.

LIFTON, ROBERT J. *Revolutionary Immortality: Mao Tse-tung and the Chinese Cultural Revolution.* New York: Alfred A. Knopf, 1968.

MASLOW, ABRAHAM H. *Religions, Values, and Peak Experiences.* Columbus: Ohio State University Press, 1964.

NEEDLEMAN, JACOB. *The New Religions.* New York: Crossroads, 1984.

# Part IV

# *The Sacred and the Secular in Modernity*

# 13

# *The Sacred and the Secular in Modernity*

## Overview

In this book we have explored the question of what religion *is* compared to other spheres of human life, such as economics or government, and we have explored how it is studied and the issues encountered in this exploration. We then examined the universal *forms* of religious experience and expression, such as religious language and symbolism, ritual, and scripture. We then analyzed six fundamental components that make up a religious worldview, including concepts of deity, cosmogony, theodicy, and differing views of salvation or liberation.

In this concluding chapter we examine the sacred, i.e., the religions, as they face the challenges of modernity in a world characterized by the secularization of many institutions such as the state and education. At the same time, we see the influence of pluralism and globalization as they impact on the world's centuries-old religious traditions. The religions now face unprecedented, complex questions and threats to long-revered beliefs and practices. Here we will explore three themes that characterize this new situation facing religious life in this new millennium. One is the fact of the secularization of many of our institutions that previously were integral to the life of communities, such as education, law, and government. Second, we will show, however, that the notion of a uniform and inevitable process of secularization is now widely disputed, as evidenced by both the increase of recent movements of religious revitalization in most areas of the world, as well as the emergence of, often alarming, zealous Fundamentalist movements in Christianity in North and South America and Africa, in Islam worldwide, and even in Judaism, Hinduism, and Buddhism. Many of these new Fundamentalist movements are hardly distinguishable from long pent-up ethnic and nationalist aspirations in these same areas of the world.

Our third topic is an examination of the way that many of the great world religions have not sought to reject wholesale the contributions of modernity but, rather, have attempted to *reconceive* aspects of their traditions in the light of modern advances in the sciences and technology, but also in view of the important modern, often Western, challenges in such fields as moral philosophy, law, economics, and political thought. The demand for greater political, economic, and social equality, justice, and opportunity has been especially crucial. Here we will illustrate, with one example, how two religions today have attempted to develop, even change, long-standing beliefs and practices in response to these new threats. That crucial issue is the role of women in both religious and civic life.

## Secularization and Pluralism

The beginning of a new millennium is accompanied by speculation about what the next century and the future beyond that will bring. In what ways may our institutions and our personal lives be radically altered? The future of religion is a special case in point, because modernity has already unleashed social and cultural forces that have profoundly influenced, and changed, religious institutions, beliefs, and practices. Two features of our contemporary world are especially significant because of their impact on religion and its role in the future. One is the *secularization* of our social institutions and patterns of behavior; the other is the growth of cultural and religious *pluralism* and diversity.

The word *secularization* came into use in the West at a time of the Peace of Westphalia in 1648. It referred to the process of transferring lands and possessions from ecclesiastical to civil control. That is a clue to one important index of the secularizing process at work in the modern world: the structural *differentiation* and *specialization* of institutions and their roles in society. Since the middle of the seventeenth century in the West, there has been an ever-increasing distinction between the realms of politics and government and of religion. The same has occurred, gradually but relentlessly, in the spheres of economics, law, medicine, and finally in education. Increasingly, religion has become a *single* department in society alongside many others. Today, religion, or the church, no longer is *the* pervasive and determinate influence that it once was in earlier centuries.

Many observers believe that these factors are clear signs of a constriction of religion from its earlier dominant place in the functioning of social institutions and social behavior in many societies today. This secularizing process is described by a sociologist:

> Whereas social control once relied heavily on religiously defined rewards and punishments; whereas social policies ... at one time needed supernatural

endorsement, or at least the endorsement of those who were recognized as the agents of the supernatural; and whereas revealed faith once specified the boundaries of true learning—now, all of these functions have been superseded. Authority is now established by constitutions. Social control is increasingly a matter of law rather than from a consensual moral code, and law becomes increasingly technical and decreasingly moral, while effective sanctions are physical and fiscal rather than threats or blandishments about the afterlife. . . . Religion has lost its presidency over other institutions.[1]

Other students of religion tend to see this so-called process of secularization rather differently. They do not interpret the modern specialization and differentiation of social institutions as a sign of religion's last hour. First, they point to numerous studies that have shown not only the persistence of religion but also the rapid growth of new religious groups recently in many parts of the world, including in highly technological, urban societies. Also there is a surge of new "revitalization" movements in traditional Islam, Buddhism, and Christianity. These realities have led some observers to propose that what is occurring in modern highly developed societies is not religious *decline*, but rather a significant *change* in the patterns of religious life. While religious life and institutions are, in fact, progressively differentiated from other institutions of society, especially in the West, this has, some would argue, enhanced a more *personal* religious awareness and autonomy. We have seen this type of religious *change* in the emergence of the New Age religious movements discussed in Chapter 6. This new type of private, often eclectic, religiosity does not register easily on standard surveys of religious belief and practice. More significantly, the population estimates at the beginning and the end of the twentieth century suggest no steep decline in religious belief and practice beyond northern Europe—quite the contrary. For example, it was estimated that in 1900 there were, worldwide, approximately 560 million Christians, 200 million Muslims, 200 million Hindus, and 127 million Buddhists. The rough estimates in 2000 were about 2.1 billion Christians, 1.2 billion Muslims (a steep increase), 860 million Hindus, and 360 million Buddhists.

The second and more important feature that will certainly shape our human institutions and behavior in the new millennium is the rapid *globalization* of our lives and the ways in which we will perceive and understand our world. And closely related to this phenomenon is, of course, a growing religious *pluralism*. We are confronted today with multiple, diverse, and often competing belief systems and values.

It was pointed out in Chapter 1 that the modern technological revolution of the past 200 years, and the simultaneous knowledge explosion, has greatly intensified our sense that this small planet is populated by highly diverse, seemingly discordant, and often violently conflicting groups with opposing beliefs and ways of life. Religion is, once again in this new millennium, the storm center of these tensions and quarrels. As the historian of religion Wilfred Cantwell Smith has written,

Religion poses a general human problem because it disrupts community. It does so with a new force in the modern world because divergent traditions that in the past did and could develop separately . . . are today face to face. . . . Different civilizations have in the past either ignored each other or fought each other; very occasionally in tiny ways perhaps they met each other. Today they not only meet but interpenetrate; they meet not only each other, but jointly meet joint problems, and must jointly try to solve them. They must collaborate. Perhaps the single most important challenge that mankind faces in our day is the need to turn our nascent world society into a world community.[2]

The tragic consequences of Smith's remark that "religious diversity disrupts community" are all too apparent in the Middle East, in Pakistan, India, and Kashmir, in Serbia and Kosovo, and in Northern Ireland, to name only a few of the world's trouble spots. We are living in a situation unprecedented in human history.

This raises the perplexing question of how we are to understand the relationships among the world's religions. Does our new knowledge simply accentuate the differences and possible ongoing discord among the world's faiths? Or does it point to the essential, underlying similarities? These questions have been much debated of late and our responses are not merely the concern of scholars; they also involve the most serious social and political consequences. Indeed, in the long run the way in which these questions are resolved will be decisive in determining our human future.

## The Reactions of Religious Fundamentalisms Today

Religious Fundamentalism is a worldwide phenomenon today. The word *Fundamentalism* is complex and it conveys meanings that not all groups and movements called Fundamentalist are willing to accept. Many Jews and Muslims, for example, reject this term as not accurately describing their conservative or even extreme reactionary movements. They contend, correctly, that the name *Fundamentalist* is associated with a twentieth-century movement in American Protestantism that has spread to other, largely English-speaking, areas of the world.

While this is true, it is also correct to say that it now has become the widely adopted term used to describe those reactionary religious movements in the contemporary world that are, in general, opposed to modernization, especially as it poses profound threats to and betrayal of what these groups see as the true and essential doctrines and practices of their religious traditions. Therefore, if properly qualified with regard to, say, Protestant Christianity in America, Shi'ite Islam in Iran, or reactionary Jewish movements in Israel, the term *Fundamentalism* is an appropriate one to use for these religious groups. And they are currently a very important phenomenon on the world scene, both religiously and geopolitically, since many are venting deep political grievances and zealously support nationalist aspirations. It is also true that the significance of some of these groups extends far beyond their numerical strength, although the future import of a number of these movements may be considered questionable.

# The Characteristics of Contemporary Religious Fundamentalism

The Fundamentalist movements today are distinctive, be it the **Islamic Shi'ites** of Iran, the Jewish **Gush Emunim** ("Bloc of the Faithful") in Israel, or the followers of the Fundamentalist TV evangelist, Pat Robertson, in the United States. Nonetheless, Fundamentalism does reveal certain related features that most of these movements share in common, most strikingly their response to the dangers that modernity poses to their traditional religious, moral, and civic life. All of the groups recognize that this threat must be rigorously resisted by whatever means are available, although some reject physical violence. They are, basically, resistance movements.

Second, and related, these groups look back to a traditional religious culture in the past that they view as the pure and normative expression of doctrine and practice. Usually, this vision of a pure and unadulterated tradition is given in a revealed decree by God—through an inerrant, even eternally begotten, Word or text such as the Torah, the Bible, or the Qu'ran. And it is this divinely ordained worldview and way of life that is now seen as being assaulted, and this strikes fear and even rage in the Fundamentalists' heart and mind. Often the "Great Offender" is seen not as an outsider (e.g., the modern secularist [as evil as they may seem]) but rather as the revisionist and modernizer *within* the religious community who attempts to reinterpret the pure, eternally revealed worldview and practice by applying to it the insights and knowledge derived from modern scientific (the Big Bang, Darwinian evolution) and historical (biblical criticism) investigations. These "acids of modernity" are perceived as not only corrosively weakening the tradition but, ultimately, its death-blow, the very loss of their world.

It is not surprising that another feature of present-day Fundamentalisms is, then, the feelings of being dispossessed of their heritage and of being hemmed-in, of resentment, all of which issues in frustration, anger, and the urge to strike back. The Fundamentalist groups are unlike many other conservative religious minorities (e.g., the Amish, who attempt to be isolated and are quietistic). Rather, the Fundamentalists are fervently *counteractive*, often militant in their reaction to these modern threats. Another feature is that the multiple dangers that these groups face provoke them to reify or abstract these threats into a living and singularly *evil* object. For the American Fundamentalists it is the Anti-Messiah, the great Beast of the Book of Revelation, Leviathan, identified as Russia during the Communist threat, and more recently, as Iraq's Saddham Hussein. For the Ayatollah Khomeini in Iran in the 1970s, and for **al-Qa'ida** today, "the Great Satan" is the United States.

While most individuals and all societies require authoritative standards—laws, social rules, accepted claims about knowledge—it is characteristic of contemporary Fundamentalist groups that this demand for authority is maximized, to the point that it is required that the sources of authority must be recognized as inerrant and unquestioned. To deny the

Bible or the Shar'ia, or the charismatic leader, or the Imam ("Leader") absolute authority is to open the floodgates to questions, doubts, and the slip-
pery slope to relativism and chaos. The Fundamentalists deny that there are
any gray areas, any ambivalences, any compromises. They tend to be dualistic: Everything must be black or white, right or wrong, God or Satan. The
world is therefore perceived as a battleground, and life understood as a constant warfare against the ever-present heretic and infidel. This, of course,
instills something like a communal paranoia, distrust, and militancy.

With this brief introduction to the general features of contemporary
religious Fundamentalism, it will be helpful to illustrate this important,
worldwide phenomenon with two specific examples that are given much attention in the media: Protestant Fundamentalism in America and Islamic
Fundamentalism in the Middle East.

### American Protestant Fundamentalism

The term *Fundamentalism* was, for almost a century, associated with a
movement within several Protestant denominations in the United States in
the late nineteenth century. It reached its zenith in the 1920s. The Fundamentalist religious impulse persisted in numerous smaller Protestant sects but
rarely in the larger Protestant denominations (for example, the Episcopal,
Methodist, Lutheran, and Presbyterian churches). More recently, however, a
Fundamentalist faction has won control of the Southern Baptist Convention.

The roots of Fundamentalism lie in Protestant Orthodoxy and American Puritanism of the seventeenth and eighteenth centuries, and also in the
Protestant evangelical religious revivals of the nineteenth century. The latter
proved to have a significant influence on both American religious and social
life. It was, however, Fundamentalism's distinctive view of a wholly inerrant
Bible that remains the bedrock and the source of the Fundamentalist's message. While there were some eminent scholars and theologians associated
with the movement, most Fundamentalist groups take little, if any, interest in
the long history of the Christian Church and its scholarly achievements; the
Bible alone, inerrant and free of scholarly study and ecclesiastical commentary, is entirely sufficient. A series of Fundamentalist Bible conferences were
held in the late nineteenth century, most notably that at Niagara in 1905. It
issued a statement of belief which later came to be known as "the five points
of Fundamentalism": the verbal inerrancy of the Bible, the Divinity of Jesus
Christ, the Virgin Birth, the substitutionary theory of the Atonement, the
bodily resurrection and the bodily return of Christ in the future.

A high point of this early history of American Fundamentalism was the
period 1905–1920. It saw the founding of the World Christian Fundamentals
Association (1919) and the publication of *The Fundamentals: A Testimony of
Truth* (1910–1915), twelve brief manifestos that were sent free to three million
Protestant leaders in the United States. The targets of these earlier Fundamen-
talists were the purported "heretical" teachings of all progressive Christian

churchmen, the application of historical-critical methods to the study of the Bible, and the scientific claims of Darwinian evolution. We will see that these issues remain important; however, the Fundamentalist movement today exhibits important new characteristics and concerns. And it is to these that we turn, for they display features that are present as well in Fundamentalist movements elsewhere in the world today.

In the past, many ultra-conservative and even Fundamentalist groups sought to remove themselves from the dominant secular society of "nonbelievers." A feature of contemporary American Fundamentalism is, rather, its active engagement with, and appropriation of, aspects of modern secular culture (for example, the most innovative technology and mass communications that are used not only for evangelistic purposes but also for an active engagement in politics in the effort to "win back America"). This feature is evident in the programs of Jerry Falwell, one of the leading Fundamentalist "televangelists" in America today.

Jerry Falwell began his ministry to a tiny independent Baptist congregation in Lynchburg, Virginia, in 1956 in the storehouse of an abandoned soda factory. By 1988 the congregation of his Thomas Road Baptist Church numbered 18,000 with a total annual income of more than $60 million. Falwell was trained as an engineer, and he proved to be skilled in adapting current technology in the service of the mass communication of his fundamentalist message. He recognized that the younger generation was now being shaped by television, which, he judged, was fostering a disrespect for the traditional family, an ethical relativism, sexual license, and the values of a growing secular humanism. Falwell embraced the power of the media to counter these perceived threats.

In 1971 Falwell created Liberty Baptist College, later Liberty University, with a wide offering of accredited programs. Thousands of its graduates were prepared to insure a future for Falwell's fundamentalist worldview and sociopolitical philosophy. At the time, Falwell wrote of the creation of "a spiritual army of young people who are pro-life, pro-moral, and pro-American . . . a generation of young people who can carry this nation into the twenty-first century with dynamic Christian leadership."[3]

The bedrock of the new Fundamentalist worldview is, of course, the older doctrine of an inerrant, authoritative Bible. The alternatives, it would appear, are either an infallible truth or a relativistic chaos. Also distinctive of recent American Fundamentalism is the appeal to a *premillenarian* interpretation of the Bible as it applies to the events of contemporary history. Premillenarianism teaches that history is rapidly moving toward its climax. The period before Jesus' personal, bodily coming to Earth will see unprecedented wickedness, unbelief, and horrific wars and natural disasters that are prophesied in specific prophetic texts (e.g., Daniel, Ezekiel, and the Book of Revelation) in the Bible. The thousand-year millennial reign of Christ on Earth will *not*, however, occur until *after* these earthly Tribulations for they are the *sign* of his imminent return.

Falwell, and other Fundamentalist leaders such as Pat Robertson of television's 700 Club, are among the leading American Fundamentalists today who preach this premillenial view of the world and its present religious and political importance. While this message energizes the effort to convert lost souls, it also gives followers a certainty that they, unlike others, have the key to contemporary historical events, namely, that the world is doomed.

It should be noted that Falwell does hold out hope for America, despite his world-historical pessimism, for he sees America as given a special "manifest destiny." He believes that if true believers take action now America may experience a reprieve:

> I believe that if we trust in God and pray . . . lead the battle to outlaw abortion . . . take our stand against pornography . . . against the breakdown of the traditional family in America . . . [and] the promotion of homosexual marriges, as we stand up for strong national defense so that this country can survive . . . I think there is hope that God may one more time bless America.[4]

Many Fundamentalists, both in America and the Middle East, are fervent nationalists. In the 1980s Falwell spoke of an imminent nuclear holocaust prophesied as inevitable. It would follow Russia's invasion of Israel. Of the coming Tribulation and the Battle of Armageddon, which will occur on the plains of Megiddo in Palestine, Falwell reported, "God only knows how many human beings will be wiped out . . . but they will be wiped out." However, with the success of his political organization, Moral Majority, Inc., Falwell qualified himself and reported that Armageddon might be long delayed.[5]

Two things are striking about this popular premillenarian view of history. First, America itself is often viewed as being given a special privilege as a providential "holy commonwealth," a view that is traceable to the New England Puritans. Second, and related, is the premillennialist's readiness to see the world dualistically—a sharp line being drawn between what is true or false, right or wrong, God or Satan, the righteous remnant or the pagan or heretical "other." Also the "Evil one" is clearly specified, even personified: the Pope, Stalin, Saddam Hussein; but also prochoice defenders of therapeutic abortion, gays and lesbians, the federal court system in the United States, the American Civil Liberties Union, all depending on the context. It is of interest that since the late 1970s, the Iranian Shi'ite Fundamentalists similarly see America as the "Great Satan."

Another distinctive feature of contemporary American Fundamentalism is that, while it freely appropriates advances in technology, it strongly opposes those theories and conclusions of the sciences that it sees as challenging biblical teaching, especially the account of Creation in the Book of Genesis (some Fundamentalists would say a Creation in one week) and human origins and nature (descended from a single *historical* pair, Adam and Eve). This opposition has taken the form of what is called **Creation Science** (see Chapter 8) and its primary adversary, biological evolution. The defense of biblical creationism has a long history, but its current "scientific" form

Jerry Falwell, the Baptist evangelist noted for his Fundamentalist and premillenial view of contemporary world events, is shown here on his television program exhorting a host of listeners for prayers and financial support. (*Source:* Courtesy of Magnum Photos/Steve McCurry.)

dates to the publication in 1961 of a massive, and influential, work entitled *The Genesis Flood*. It was written by Henry M. Morris, a hydraulic engineer, and his associate, a Fundamentalist Old Testament professor.[6]

*The Genesis Flood* defends the view that the earth and its inhabitants were created in six twenty-four-hour days. The earth itself is no more than ten thousand years old. The historical datings of the geological and paleontological sciences are explained by the disruptions caused by the universal Flood depicted in Genesis 6–8. The authors also argue that neither human pain and death, nor the second law of thermodynamics (entropy of the universe causing its heat-death), were present in the world until *after* the biblical Fall of Adam.[7]

The special aim of Morris's Institute for Creation Science (1972) is to clarify the role of "scientific creationism," namely, to demonstrate how the new knowledge garnered by the natural sciences can serve to validate the biblical creationist cosmology as taught by the Fundamentalists. The prototype of this enterprise is the Institute of Creation Science (ICR) textbook, *Scientific Creationism* (1974), edited by Morris. The aim of its Public School Edition is to sanction the teaching of "scientific creationism" in the public schools alongside the mainstream theory of biological evolution.[8]

In the early 1980s the legislatures of both Arkansas and Louisiana approved statutes allowing for the teaching of "scientific creationism" in their public schools. However, these laws were overturned in 1985 by a federal judge who ruled that Creation Science clearly includes specific religious beliefs, and therefore teaching it in the public schools amounted to teaching the doctrines of "a particular religious sect or group of sects."[9] In 1987 the U.S. Supreme Court definitively struck down the Louisiana statute, thus concluding this particular church-state struggle.[10]

It is important to note that this scientific issue here encompasses very broad dimensions of modern life; it is not simply an academic dispute about the interpretation of the Bible or the validity of scientific hypotheses. It raises deep questions about, for example, law and the Constitution, religion's role in education, politics, and medicine. This points to a further characteristic of this new Fundamentalism, the fact that every aspect of life is to be shaped by the Bible and its moral and social worldview—with the assistance of legal measures or state support, if possible.

The Fundamentalists' political action, even militancy, produced considerable social conflict. It introduced what is now called the "Culture Wars." In the late 1970s numerous Fundamentalist leaders such as Jerry Falwell and Pat Robertson joined forces with noted political figures to form organizations— for example, the Moral Majority, Inc.—to initiate programs of political action. This involved a broadening of the range of issues addressed, such as social welfare legislation, national defense, women's rights, and foreign policy (for example, the United States' support for Israel in the Middle East conflict). What concerns many citizens is not the Fundamentalists' new enthusiasm for engagement in the political sphere but the blurring, or tacit opposition to, the separation of church and state.

It must be said that recent decisions of U.S. courts and government agencies have, understandably, raised concerns among many religious groups. The outlawing of prayers in public schools; *Roe v. Wade* (1973), which legalized abortion; challenges to the tax-exempt status of religious institutions; the extension of civil marriage to same-sex couples, all of these actions are troubling to many, but what has concerned other citizens—both religious and secular—are the frequent overtones of support by Fundamentalists for *theocratic* measures, such as explicit state support for religious programs or government advocacy of specific moral doctrines.

These "Culture Wars" increasingly have raised the public rhetoric on both sides, one calling the other "arrogant and self-righteous" and "treacherous." Each claims that its beliefs are in accord with true American traditions and principles and that the other is an "enemy of the country," a menacing challenge to those values. Both see the other as a "totalitarian threat."[11]

This chapter of the current struggle between traditional religion and the currents of modernity has, not infrequently, driven some American Fundamentalist groups (and others worldwide) to adopt militant, even terrorist, tactics, including bombings and murder. One American example is Operation Rescue, led by Randall Terry. This group has carried out extreme actions in its opposition to laws that it considers anti-Christian, particularly abortion.

Terry and his followers assert that America should "function as a Christian nation." Two other radical Fundamentalist militants are Eric Robert Rudolph and Timothy McVeigh. Rudolph's anger was directed at abortion clinics in Alabama and Georgia, which he bombed; he also bombed a lesbian bar and the 1996 Olympic Games there, killing a police officer. Rudolph judged the Games to be pro-gay. He was captured by federal agents in 2003, found guilty of murder, and given the death penalty. Like others who have used violence, Rudolph was associated with the ideology of *Christian Identity.*

Timothy McVeigh, the convicted bomber of the federal building in Oklahoma City in April 1995, was also associated with Christian Identity. McVeigh killed hundreds, including children. In 1997 he was sentenced to death and later executed in a federal prison. McVeigh was especially influenced by the novel *The Turner Diaries,* a book that holds ideas similar to Christian Identity and contains essentially a blueprint of McVeigh's own attack on the federal building. The Christian Identity group does not think that the Tribulation of the Last Days will take place in the Middle East, as do many Fundamentalists; rather, it will occur in America itself, where the current forces of satanic evil will be engaged by Christian warriors.

Unlike Fundamentalists such as Jerry Falwell and Pat Robertson, the Christian Identity groups are vehemently anti-Semitic and do not support Israel and Zionism. Also, they are smaller, more militant, and more isolationist. Christian Identity does, however, share the worldview of other Christian Fundamentalist groups, such as the Reconstruction movement, which, while not wed to violence, concurs that Christians are engaged in a colossal battle with satanic powers, a belief that justifies the use of militant action. The Reconstructionists also hold that their aim is the establishment of a *theocratic* Christian state and civilization under the strict law of God.[12] On this theme, many American Fundamentalists mirror some of the socio-political ideals and goals of the Islamic Fundamentalists, such as those held by the radical Iranian theocrat, the Imam Ayatollah Khomeini, and those similarly held by the leaders of the Taliban in Afghanistan more recently. What they want is a government that enforces their religious, moral and social vision.

## Contemporary Islamic Fundamentalism

*Modernization and Islamic Revitalization*   The history of Islam's response to Western modernization has followed a very different path from that of Christianity and Judaism. This can be explained in large measure by the fact that for the Islamic world modernization is synonymous with Westernization, which means that Islam, since the twelfth century, has been shaped by Western religious and political forces, foremost among them the Crusades and European imperialism, as well as more recent forms of neoimperialism that have posed both political and religious threats.

Related to the aforementioned factors, however, is adherence to what has been reinforced over the centuries as the standard or traditional Islamic worldview, one that has widely remained in place since Medieval times. This tradition has categorized as "unthinkable" much of the philosophical and scientific thinking that has so profoundly changed the West. Comparing this to the importance of our Western historical consciousness on, for example, the study of the Bible by Western Jewish and Christian scholars, a prominent writer on Islam points to the contrary response in Islam:

> Today ideological control confirms this unthinkable for everything connected with Islam. It is always impossible to think the historicity of the Qur'an, of the Hadith, of the Shari'a. . . . That is why "the resurgence" of Islam . . . is taking place on the basis of an immense *unthought* accumulated over centuries . . . Muslims themselves are stumbling against the "unthinkable" and the "unthought" as over obstacles bequeathed by their own history, and in this there is one of the deep but secret reasons for so many current problems.[13]

Contemporary traditional and, more important, radical fundamentalist Islam has embraced this worldview and the unchangeableness and finality of the Qur'an and the Shar'ia. This is true not only with regard to matters scientific and historical but also to the ancient rules and laws bearing on human life and social conduct. In traditional Islamic theology the word used to describe heresy is "innovation" (*bid'a*); and the true way is "the beaten track" or the customs (*sunna*) of Muhammed and the ancestors. The prime enemy of the present radical Islamicists is not, therefore, the enemies without. Rather, their wrath is directed more violently against the "innovators" and compromisers within who have "poisoned" Muslim society. This has included the Shah of Iran, overthrown by the Khomeini revolution in 1979, and President Anwar Sadat of Egypt, who was assassinated in 1981 by the Egyptian Organization for Holy War. He was killed for attempting to separate the state from the control of Islamic law and for his condemnation of the Iranian revolution as a "crime against Islam."

Some of the recent movements of radical Islam have been state sponsored, often because it was felt necessary to appeal to popular religious sentiment; other movements, such as those discussed here, are genuine religious uprisings against the state itself, which, for these movements, is apostate since it has denied the authority of Holy Law. They also see the West as complicit in its support of these corrupt regimes and, therefore, the evil source of the erosion of traditional Islamic customs and civic life. This often has resulted in militant hostility toward much of Western culture and its values. This is also based on a deep frustration and humiliation at being dominated and misused by these Western "enemies of God."

One recent commentator on radical Islamism points to the two basic assumptions that fuel these movements: First,

> they assume that Islam and the West are locked in an ongoing battle, dating back to the early days of Islam, which is heavily influenced by the legacy of the Crusades and European colonialism, and which today is the product of

a Judaeo-Christian conspiracy . . . the result of superpower neocolonialism [American intrusion in the Middle East and beyond] and the power of Zionism [in Israel]. . . . Second, these radical movements assume that Islam is not simply an ideological alternative for Muslim societies but a theological and political imperative. Since Islam is God's command, implementation must be immediate, not gradual, and the obligation to do so is incumbent on all true Muslims.[14]

*Contemporary Islamic Fundamentalist Leaders and Movements* As mentioned earlier, recent radical Islamic movements look to the Qur'an and the Sunna or traditions of the Prophet (see Chapter 11) as the sources by which they can carry out their "renewal" (*tafdid*), that is, a faithfulness to God's revelation and an authentic Islam. In pursuing this renewal, these movements glorify the struggle, sacrifices, and victories of the great successors to the Prophet as role models for their present battle. Their goal is, then, to reconstitute an Islamic state and, thereby, overthrow all of the policies and practices that have engendered moral decadence and impiety, injustice, and the erosion of Islam's way of life.

What is also characteristic of this new, radical Islamism (but also of earlier movements of "renewal") is the principle of *ijtihad* or the right of the leader of the renewal, the *mujaddid* or "soldier of God," to engage in independent analysis and judgment on the *Qur'an* and the Sunna. The *mujaddid* is not bound by the interpretation of the legal experts or of the schools of interpretation that have been advanced after the time of Muhammad. This allows the new leader to legitimize teachings that may be especially needed under current conditions that are rife with compromise and indifference and that threaten "true" Islamic belief and practice. These leaders of the Fundamentalist resurgence characteristically focus on certain texts and traditions in an effort to justify their own judgments; for example, concerning what constitutes the obligation of *jihad* (holy war) in a particular circumstance.

The ideology of many of the present leaders of militant Islamism worldwide is shaped by teachers whose writings and lives have given inspiration and direction to the policies and the militant, often terrorist, tactics of groups such as the al Jihad (Egypt), Hamas (Palestine), Hizbollah (Lebanon), Jamaat-i-Islami (Pakistan), and Osama bin Laden's al Qa'ida (now spread throught much of the Muslim world). First among these pioneers of fundamentalist Islam today is Muhammad ibn 'Abd al-Wahhab (1703–1792), who began a reform movement on the Arabian peninsula, the features of which now are known as *Wahhabism.*

During Muhammad Wahhab's time, the learned Muslim scholars in this area of the Middle East tended to tolerate superstitious religious beliefs and practices as well as to compromise the notion of one inerrant interpretation of the *Qur'an* and Sunna as being "unthinkable." Muhammad ibn 'Abd al-Wahhab rigorously challenged all this; he demanded a strict adherence to the traditional practices taught in the *Qur'an* as well as a political system that would protect these fundamental obligations. These are themes that reflect the strict traditionalism of many **Sunni Muslims** today. Ibn 'Abd al Wahhab also attacked the *ulama* (learned scholars) who had come to adhere to latter-day (i.e., medieval) interpretations of Islam as authoritative. He advocated *ijtihad*, the use of this independent judgment in interpreting the *Qur'an*, justified by renouncing those later "innovations" and returning to the authentic scriptural source. Ibn 'Abd al-Wahhab converted the ruling prince Ibn Sa'ud and together established and expanded the Saudi Arabian kingdom and its religious-political ideology. The Saudi kingdom, soon to be rich in oil reserves, increasingly entrenched Wahhabism as its official doctrine. This has meant that militant Wahhabist groups in the oil-rich Arabian Peninsula have often had at their disposal great financial resources to spread the ideology of fundamentalist Islamism beyond the borders of the Saudi kingdom.

A great force in contemporary Islamic fundamentalism is the role of the Muslim Brotherhood founded in Egypt by Hasan al Banna (1906–1949). It, too, is a resurgent movement devoted to a return to the fundamentals of the tradition. Its mission has proved more suitable to the conditions of life in urban Muslim settings, such as Cairo, than did conservative Wahhabism. While Hasan al Banna and others have consistently resisted the use of force and violence, factions within the Muslim Brotherhood have embraced the use of terrorist tactics. This development in Egypt is epitomized in the career and influence of Sayyid Qutb.

The young Sayyid Qutb (1906–1966) received a modern education and was an admirer of Western culture. Early in his career in Cairo he worked for the Ministry of Public Instruction while also writing poetry and literary criticism. At this same time, however, Qutb was attempting to reconcile his liberal views, influenced by the West, with his growing appreciation of Islam's unique social and communal values in contrast to both the West's secular separation of religion and the state and Communism's atheism. This tension was resolved after Qutb visited the United States in the late 1940s. There he encountered what he later was fiercely to attack as "Western decadence." In an influential essay, *Milestones*, he summarizes his view of the United States:

> Look at this capitalism with its monopolies and usury . . . at this individual freedom, devoid of human sympathy and responsibility for relatives except under force of law; at this materialistic attitude which deadens the spirit; at this behaviour, like animals, which you call "free mixing of the sexes"; at this vulgarity which you call "emancipation of women"; at this evil and fanatic racial discrimination.[15]

Note that Qutb's moral "puritanism" is similar to that of the American Fundamentalists, but his social and political views are a world apart, contrasting Islam's civic and political values with what he saw as the libertarian license, competition, and greed in American capitalism and democracy. He also saw America's support for Israel and the contempt for Arabs revealed in the media. He was increasingly drawn to the work of the Muslim Brotherhood and became its most influential thinker and publicist. With his Muslim brothers he now directed his attacks on the corrupt regime of the Egyptian President Gamal Abdel Nassar.

When the Muslim Brotherhood was banned in 1954, Qutb was imprisoned with many of his comrades. In prison he was radicalized. It is reported that he was tortured during his ten-year imprisonment, but, despite his failing health, he was able to write some of his most revolutionary and influential works. These largely outlined the ideology and tactics of an Islamic "renewal" based on the teachings of the *Qur'an* on all aspects of life—social, political, and economic. Qutb's writings were directed to the struggle (jihad) against the forces of the *jahiliyyah*, that is, the surrounding Muslim society of willful ignorance, political compromise and heretical practice—and for abolition of what Qutb called "manmade" laws and those Muslim political regimes that upheld them.

In his final book, *Ma'alim fi al-Tariq* (*Signposts on the Road*, 1964), Qutb spoke of the temptations of the *jahiliyyah*: its social pressures and its modern behavior and allures.[16] Qutb also came to insist on jihad as armed struggle as the only alternative and the obligation of all Muslims against the "enemies of God."

Qutb's prison writings were used against him, and he was charged by a military tribunal with attempting to overthrow the Egyptian government. He was found guilty, sentenced to death, and hanged in August 1966. Many radical Islamists see him as a warrior hero, in the line of the great martyrs for the faith. They also seek to sustain his vision of a renewed and purified Islam—and the necessity of armed struggle, indeed if necessary, a revolutionary and violent *jihad* to accomplish it.

Qutb's ideology and rhetorical power were echoed in the speeches of the leader of the Iranian revolution, the Ayatollah (a title referring to an honored Shi'ite jurisprudent) Ruhollah **Khomeini** (1907–1989). He strikingly pronounced, "Islam is politics or it is nothing." Khomeini early studied classical Persian poetry, but as a young man was tutored by a series of **Shi'ite** religious scholars and settled in the Shi'ite "Vatican," the city of Qom to study Islamic jurisprudence, philosophy, and mysticism. A rather unique feature of Khomeini's later teachings and leadership is his strict adherence to the Shari'a joined with a mystical illuminism regarding the Perfect Man (i.e., Muhammad, and the later Imams [the Prophet's successors and the *valis* or guardians], who carry on the mission of the Prophet). Khomeini quotes leading Islamic mystics who hold that "the Perfect Man is the holder of the chain of existence, with which the cycle is completed . . . He is God's great sign, created in God's image."[17]

Khomeini's followers in the Iranian revolution saw him as that long-expected Imam, successor to the role of Cosmic Guardianship. For Khomeini this combined a legal guardianship with charismatic leadership, and this allowed him to relinquish or supersede customary Islamic·jurisprudence when necessary for the sake of preserving Islamic government. In his authoritative treatise *Islamic Government*, Khomeini speaks of the unique authority of the Guardianship given to the jurisprudent (*faqih*) or expert in Islamic law. The jurisprudent, Khomeini insists, "has the same authority that the Most Noble Messenger (Muhammad) and the Imam had."[18] Furthermore, Article I of the Constitution of the Islamic Republic of Iran refers to Imam Khomeini as the eminent *marja'i taqlig* (Leader), which explains his extraordinary authority.

Khomeini also called for waging of jihad worldwide against religious and political enemies who threatened the authentic Muslim life and its institutions:

> Give the people Islam, then, for the school of jihad, the religion of struggle; let them amend themselves and transform themselves into a powerful force, so

The Ayatollah Khomeini, returning to Iran from exile in 1979, is greeted by the supporters of his radical Islamist revolution and the newly approved Islamic Republic. (*Source:* Courtesy of Camera Press.)

that they may overthrow the tyrannical regime imperialism has imposed on us and set up an Islamic government.[19]

Khomeini's most important legacy to contemporary radical Islamism is his dominant role in establishing, after the revolution of 1978–1979, a plan of government based on the strict teachings of the *Qur'an* and Sunna, specifically for the execution of God's ordinances. The scope of the governance by the *faqih* covers every aspect of a Muslim's life in an effort to transform society into a holy commonwealth. As Khomeini underlines in his treatise, Islamic law embraces the whole of life and

> amounts to a complete social system. In this system of laws, all the needs of man have been met; his dealings with his neighbors, fellow citizens, and clan, as well as his children and relatives; the concerns of private and marital life; regulations concerning war and peace; penal and commercial law; and regulations pertaining to trade and agriculture. . . . It is obvious, then, how much care Islam devotes to government . . . with the goal of creating conditions conducive to the production of morally upright and virtuous human beings.[20]

Khomeini has had a profound influence on later radical Islamic *mujahidin* ("soldiers of God"), for example, on the extremist Hizbollah ("Party of God") organization in Lebanon that, after Israel's occupation of southern Lebanon (1982–1985), looked to Iran as its revolutionary model. In its manifesto Hizbollah makes this clear:

> We the sons of Hizbullah's nation, whose God has given victory in Iran and which has established the nucleus of the world's central Islamic state, abide by the orders of a single wise and just command currently embodied in the supreme Ayatollah Khumaini. We have opted for religion, freedom and dignity over humiliation and constant submission to America and its allies and Zionism. . . . We have risen to liberate our country, to drive out the imperialists . . . and to take our fate in our own hands.[21]

Sunni Muslims also embraced a more radical jihadist ideology in the last quarter of the twentieth century. One of the leaders is Ayman al-Zawahiri, an Egyptian surgeon who came from a prominent Cairo family. His disillusionment over a growing Egyptian secularism and the humiliating Arab defeat in the 1967 Arab-Israeli war radicalized him and he joined the violent Islamic Jihad. He soon became one of the leaders and was imprisoned. Later, he joined with **Osama bin Laden** in Afghanistan, recruiting and training Muslims for jihad against the occupying Russians. He became, in effect, Osama bin Laden's mentor and closest strategist. It is believed that al-Zawahiri planned the deadly attack on fifty-eight tourists in Luxor, Egypt, in 1997. He was also instrumental in merging Islamic Jihad with al-Qa'ida; and he is considered to be responsible, with bin Laden, for broadening **al-Qa'ida's** jihad globally from the Middle East to South Asia, and especially against America. Some believe it was al-Zawahiri who devised the

September 11, 2001, attacks in the United States on the World Trade Center and the Pentagon.

Osama bin Laden grew up a shy but privileged son of a rich Saudi family in Riyadh, Saudi Arabia. At university he became more serious about his religion and about events in the Gulf, but especially important was the impression of the ultra-conservative and puritanical Wahhabi tradition which had been dominant in Saudi Arabia since its beginning. As we have seen, Wahhabism emphasized a fundamentalist interpretation of the *Qur'an* and Sunna and resisted all that it considered to be un-Islamic, its weapon being the obligation of jihad. Bin Laden's worldview was further shaped by his teacher, Dr. Abdullah Azzam, who advocated a militant ideology of global Islamic jihad. He wrote,

> This duty will not end with victory in Afghanistan; jihad will remain an individual obligation until all other lands that were Muslim are returned to us so that Islam will reign again: before us lie Palestine . . . Lebanon . . . Somalia, the Philippines, Burma, . . . and Andalusia (southern Spain).[22]

The 1970s proved to be a period of great renewal among a number of radical Islamic *mujahidin* and extreme jihadists, and Osama bin Laden was caught up in this great revival (*tajdid*). When the Saudi king allowed American troops to occupy Saudi Arabia after the first Gulf War, bin Laden became an even more zealous "soldier of God." Back in Afghanistan, he supported the Taliban in its efforts to impose its own strict vision of Islam. In August 1996 bin Laden issued a Declaration of Jihad against American forces in the Arabian peninsula and declared his support for revolutionary jihadist groups worldwide.

In concluding this examination of Fundamentalism in both the United States and the Middle East, it can be instructive to compare two responses to the horrific extermination of thousands of innocent people in New York City on September 11, 2001. One response was that of Osama bin Laden; the other that of Jerry Falwell. Both the Muslim leader and the Christian preacher interpret this event as the expression of Divine wrath against an enemy of God. In a videotaped address bin Laden affirms this conviction: "Here is America struck by God Almighty . . . so that its greatest buildings are destroyed. Grace and gratitude to God . . . God has blessed a group of vanguard Muslims . . . to destroy America."[23]

Falwell sees the strike on New York as God's warning to America and directed against the enemies within:

> We have insulted God at the highest levels of our government. And then we say "why does this happen?" . . . Well, why it's happening is that God Almighty is lifting his protection from us . . . I believe that the pagans, and the abortionists, and the feminists, and the gays and lesbians . . . all of them who have tried to secularize America [are responsible]. I point the finger in their face and say: "You helped this [September 11] happen."[24]

Both Osama bin Laden and Jerry Falwell know who is God's enemy, and they both claim to possess the blueprint for God's holy commonwealth on earth. It is this vision of history that the Fundamentalists propose in our increasingly global and pluralistic society. And it raises a series of crucial questions about the future of the great religions in our world today. The Fundamentalists essentially offer two visions of the future. One is the expectation of an imminent Apocalypse. The American Fundamentalist editor of *Endtime* magazine believes that Saddam Hussein "fits like hand in glove" the destroyer agent depicted in the biblical Armageddon. And he predicts that a "nuclear holocaust will take the lives of 2 billion people, the 'one-third of mankind' stated in the [Book of] Revelation."[25] The alternative vision is for the establishment of a theocratic-type society in which their perceived model of God's Law will maximally guide the lives of families, society, and the state.

It is regrettable that in response to the current Fundamentalist religious challenges to pluralism, democracy, and basic civil liberties, some governments and secular organizations now seem to be calling for an equally dangerous alternative, namely, a radical secular state in which long-honored religious customs and obligations are threatened. This is not new, of course. Only fifty years ago, the Communist government in dominantly Roman Catholic Poland restricted all religious activities to church buildings, seminaries were closed, and the state required approval of all appointments of Catholic bishops. In the Russian Constitution, all religious ceremonies or religious displays in public or private institutions were prohibited and religious groups were under constant surveillance and their activities greatly restricted. During the Khruschchev regime in the late 1950s, teachers in Russian schools were directed to attack religious beliefs and atheistic education was instituted in all the schools.

In Albania, a largely Muslim country with substantial numbers of Eastern Orthodox and Roman Catholic Christians, the state constitution declared in 1967 that "The State recognizes no religion and supports atheistic propaganda for the purpose of implanting the scientific materialist outlook in people" (Article 37). Here, then, is a state moving from the separation of religion and the state to *officially* restricting the free exercise of religion for the purpose of *eliminating* religion.

One might respond that these are extreme cases, but they are also rather recent examples of what a powerful government guided by a secular and, perhaps, even an overt or covert hostility to religion, can do to restrict the free practice of religion in a society. In December 2003, President Jacques Chirac of France, called for a law—later made law by the government—banning the wearing of "conspicuous" religious symbols in French public schools. This included large crosses for Christians, head scarves for Muslim girls, and skull caps worn by orthodox Jewish boys. Unmentioned in this proposal is the fact that head scarves and skull caps are not simply a preferred religious expression or religiously "ostentatious"; rather, they are, respectively, religious obligations for orthodox Muslim girls and Jewish boys.

A young girl wearing her head scarf, with the French flag and the words "liberty, equality" painted on her face. She is protesting a law banning Islamic head scarves and other religious insignia in the French public schools. (*Source:* Courtesy of the Associated Press.)

What some would consider a broader, more serious theme is the French report's call for the state to reassert its right to pronounce how religion influences public life in France, which, according to the report, includes the ideal of secularism and the "solemn adoption" of a "charter of secularism."

Critics of this French proposal rightly ask, What does such a "secular charter" intend? Is it a strict application of the separation doctrine as, for example, the legal prohibition against a government establishment of religion or the explicit support of religion? Or does a "charter of secularism" imply, as one French critic noted, a form of "secular fundamentalism"?

What many religious communities find troubling today is that it appears that two ideologies are dominating the discussion of religion and its role in public life. One is, of course, the increase in the efforts of conservative and especially Fundamentalist groups to demand that government support, directly or indirectly, the beliefs and practices through state sponsorship of certain expressions of religion in civic life, or outright legal measures or financial aid through, for example, subsidies for activities such as schools and social services.

The other ideology, peculiar to modernity, is, as we have seen, secularism which can, explicitly or in more concealed ways, inhibit or even suppress the free, public expression of religion by legal and other means. What is lost in this battle is the recognition that most religious communities today resist both militant secularism and the theocratic vision of the Fundamentalists. What they want, rather, is a healthy freedom in society not only for individuals and communities to practice their religions according to their own consciences, but also for them to be given a free voice in the community's civic life, in what has come to be called "the Public Square."

These religious communities also recognize the positive values of modernity, its pluralism, freedom of expression, and the equal treatment of other religious groups, civic rights, and opportunities for all, whether the "other" be of another religion, race, or gender. The modern embrace of these values by many of the great religions needs not only to be appreciated, but it must also be recognized that often these principles and values are not only congruent with but are advanced by these religious communities themselves, frequently against the opposition of the larger society or the state.

One thing we learned in this study is that religion is not one unrelated aspect of a person's or a community's life. On the contrary, a religion touches and informs every dimension of life—familial, sexual, social, political, economic. Religious belief and practice entail an entire "form of life" or worldview. It raises the deepest questions about life's meaning and purpose—to whom or what is one's final loyalty to be given, and, in consequence, how one should live one's life.

It is no surprise, then, that religious communities take their beliefs, values, and practices with profound seriousness—and that they are not easily questioned, or compromised, or dismissed. But modernity has shaken the foundations of *some* of these religions, hence some have tenaciously, even militantly, resisted change. Others have, quite rightly, moved slowly but have, over time, reconceived deeply held beliefs and practices in the light of modern knowledge and experience. And often they have done this without conceding or compromising their foundational religious beliefs and values. Rather, many religious traditions have come to see, through their encounter with modern experience, important dimensions of their own faith not only more clearly but also more deeply, more truly.

It is not possible to explore in detail how, in various ways, religious traditions have developed and reconceived their ideas and practices in the encounter with modernity. We can, however, conclude this discussion by selecting one salient example of this process, namely, the changing role of women in both Christianity and Islam. We have learned in Chapter 6 how profoundly religion is shaped by its natural and social environment; and how, contrarily, religion deeply influences a culture in all of its aspects. This is strikingly true of the role of women in religion. Patriarchy (the social organization dominated by the father and males) was dominant in much of the ancient Near East after about 3000 B.C.E., and it shaped the understanding of the status and roles of women in Judaism, Christianity, and Islam. Yet there are important sources in these religions that have, over time, also challenged and changed these perceptions, as we shall see.

## The Role of Women in Modern Christianity

Over the past two millennia the role of women in Christianity has been shaped by a general worldview dominated by patriarchy and its institutions. Patriarchy was pervasive in ancient Greco-Roman culture but earlier as well in the institutions of the ancient Israelites. It is important to note, however, that the critique of patriarchy and the traditional portrayals of women's roles emerged not only from the modern expansion of women's education, civil rights, voting privileges, and economic opportunities. Rather, it emerged through a discernment of sources, largely biblical, within Christianity itself that has profoundly challenged the dominance of patriarchy; moreover, it has focused on women's dignity and equality as beings created in the Divine image (*imago Dei*). These, largely biblical, sources reveal, then, that women are neither derivative of men, nor do men represent a normative humanity to which women must be subordinate.

But this was not the dominant reading of the Bible in Christian history until lately. Especially crucial for the traditional Christian view of women were the stories of the Creation of Adam and Eve and the Fall in Genesis and St. Paul's depiction of women in his New Testament letters. The traditional reading of Adam and Eve (in Genesis 2:7 and 21–23, Revised Standard Version [RSV]) reads,

> Then the Lord God formed man of dust from the ground and breathed into his nostrils the breath of life; and man became a living being . . . So the Lord caused a deep sleep to fall upon the man, and while he slept took one of his ribs and closed up its place with flesh; and the rib which the Lord God had taken from the man he made into woman and brought her to man. Then the man said, "This at last is bone of my bones and flesh of my flesh; she shall be called Woman because she is taken out of man."

This passage, it was held, depicts woman as derivative, hence inferior to man and meant to serve as his helper and wife. Moreover, because of Eve's having succumbed to temptation in the Fall, all women are to be punished, one form of it being the pain of childbirth, the other subjection to man ("To the women [the Lord] said, 'I will greatly multiply your pain in childbearing. . . . Yet your desire shall be for your husband, and he shall rule over you.'" Genesis 3:6, RSV).

The value given to celibacy over marriage by the Apostle Paul, and his appeal in I Corinthians 11:7–9 to support both woman's derivation from and service to man, and her obedience owed man (Ephesians 5:23–24, Colossians 3:18) profoundly influenced the Christian conception of women's status and role for centuries. What is especially disturbing about the weight given to these texts is their broader social impact on the lives of women. It not only excluded women from leadership roles in the Christian Church but gave support for civic laws that allowed men to have custody of their wives and control of their children, denied married women the right to property, gave men the right to their wives' labor and earnings, and generally opposed any genuine autonomy for women. When women began to counter this widely held view of women as being intrinsic to the Bible and Christianity, they recognized, as we will see, that the crux of the issue was that biblical monotheism habitually portrayed God exclusively in male patriarchal language and images, most notably by the title "God the Father."

The protest of Christian women and their male defenders was late coming. With a few exceptions, it received slight notice until the late nineteenth century, and it was only in the latter decades of the twentieth century that feminist scholars and theologians were able to bring about a revolution in the Christian churches with regard to women's status and roles. Perhaps the best known feminist pioneer is the American Elizabeth Cady Stanton (1815–1902), who, between 1895 and 1898, published *The Woman's Bible* in two volumes. It consisted of a series of Bible commentaries written by women (the majority of them by Stanton herself) demonstrating the position of women in both the Old and New Testament—the demeaning and brutal depictions, and the extraordinary exclusion of women in these texts, but also demonstrating the leading roles of women in the Bible and their spiritual contributions. In dealing with the biblical authors, such as the Apostle Paul, Stanton could be both witty and telling. On Paul's obsession with how women wear their hair, she wrote, "It appears very trifling for men, commissioned to do so great a work on earth, to give so much thought to the toilets of women."[26]

In countering the claims of a dominant Christian patriarchy, women writers used many strategies. Concerning the crucial appeal to the Bible, they showed that many texts were misinterpreted by male scholars, often because they were later shown to be wrong or mistaken in terms of current knowledge of the text. They also appealed to countertexts. For example, they showed that there are two Creation stores in Genesis and the second, dominant, one (Genesis 2:7, 21–23) is countered by the first (Genesis 1:26–27), where the original human being is described as both male and female: "Then God said, 'Let us make humankind in our own image, according to our likeness . . . So God created humankind in his image, in the image of God he created them; male and female he created them" (Genesis 1:26a–27, New Revised Standard Version [NRSV]). Scholars also began to demonstrate the selective bias in the male choice of texts and the flagrant biases of some male translations of the Bible, especially in translations having to do with women's roles. Also, they highlighted the obviously important roles of women in the Bible, from female judges to missionaries and to deacons in the earliest

Christian churches. Women also have been successful in insisting that new translations of the Bible, such as the New Revised Standard Version, and new prayer books and liturgies, use more inclusive language.

Brief mention of the work of a few prominent Christian women scholars and theologians will give a sense of both their radical challenge and the importance of their contributions to the Christian churches today. A crucial moment for many religious feminists was the publication in 1973 of Mary Daly's (b. 1928) powerful attack on patriarchy, *Beyond God the Father*, in which she declared, "If God is male, then male is God."[27] Another influential text for Christian feminists today is *In Memory of Her* (1983) by the leading feminist New Testament scholar **Elizabeth Schüssler Fiorenza** (b. 1938). Her work is critical, in part, because she insists that the feminist reform of Christianity finds its legitimacy in the earliest traditions regarding Jesus and his community. In these sources, Schüssler Fiorenza sees Jesus and his companions as offering a new vision, a radical call for a "discipleship of equals," that later was compromised by the Apostle Paul and other Christian leaders as they confronted the dominance of patriarchy in the Greco-Roman world where they carried out their missionary work.

The key to Schüssler Fiorenza's reconception of Jesus' message is found in the Gospel of Mark's account of the woman who anointed Jesus with precious oil before his death and burial. In this passage Jesus replies to the woman's action by declaring, "And truly, I say to you, wherever the gospel is preached in the whole world, what she has done will be told in memory of her." (Mark 14:9). The story exemplifies the fact that Jesus' gospel had at its center this politically subversive message of a "discipleship of equals" that was later concealed or eliminated. Schüssler Fiorenza thus contends,

> Whereas according to Mark the leading male disciples do not understand the suffering messiahship of Jesus, reject it, and finally abandon him, the women disciples who have followed him . . . suddenly emerge as the true disciples in the passion narrative . . . who have understood that his ministry was not rule and kingly glory but service, *diakonia*. . . . The unnamed woman who names Jesus with a prophetic sign-action [anointing] in Mark's Gospel is the paradigm for the true disciple.[28]

Christian feminists are called upon "to reclaim their sufferings and struggles in and through the subversive power of the 'remembered past.' "[29]

Central to Schüssler Fiorenza's biblical analysis is her affirmation that this liberating, yet demanding, vision of Christian discipleship is addressed not only to women; it constitutes a radical call for the liberation of men from misogyny, or mistreatment of women, as well as a liberation from prejudice against all those of other races or class and to service to the poor and outcasts of this world.

Basic to Christian, as well as Jewish and Muslim women, is the problem that monotheism perceives God as Lord or Father, that is, as Male. This is the theme of another influential Christian feminist scholar, **Elizabeth A. Johnson,** author of *The Mystery of God in Feminist Theological Discourse* (1994). Johnson enforces the point that a religion's *conception* of God influences its whole understanding of experience and the social world. And God seen as Father supports an androcentric, or male centered, worldview—and therefore must be challenged since it supports a dualistic anthropology that sustains the false perception of women as inferior.

Johnson then demonstrates how the language used to describe God has differed over the millennia, even in Christianity. The early Church Fathers and Eastern Christian writers, as well as Islamic theologians, have been especially aware of the dangers of **anthropomorphism**. Johnson insists that "there is no timeless speech about God."[30] Human terms and metaphors change in the effort to describe the grandeur and mystery of the wholly transcendent Divine. Those who are filled with horror at speaking of God in other than male language fail to recognize that to use any *gender* language about God cannot be literal; we use analogies and metaphors to point to some feature of the eternal and ineffable.[31]

Johnson suggests that because the term *Father* has, over the centuries of exclusive use, been taken literally it borders on idolatry:

> Insofar as male dominant language is honored as the only or the supremely fitting way of speaking about God, it absolutizes a single set of metaphors and thus obscures the height and depth and length and breadth of divine mystery. Thus it does damage to the very truth of God that theology is supposed to cherish and promote.[32]

Johnson sees the overemphasis on Jesus' maleness as also legitimizing male social structures in, for example, the Roman Catholic Church itself. This can be seen in the celibate male priesthood and the Pope in Rome who is viewed as *the* representative of the Patriarch "above." Johnson remarks on the significance of an excessive attention to Jesus' gender:

> When Jesus' maleness, which belongs to his historical identity, is interpreted to be essential to his redeeming function and identity [as the Christ], then the Christ serves as a religious tool for marginalizing and excluding women. . . . As stated in an official [Catholic] argument against women's ordination, for example, men, thanks to their "natural resemblance" [to Jesus] enjoy a capacity for closer identification with Christ than do women.[33]

Johnson points out that Jesus' gender is simply one of several "historical particularities" of his person; others are his "racial characteristics, linguistic heritage [and] social class."[34] It follows for her, as for Schüssler Fiorenza, that recognition of these "historical particularities" not only negates a major source of the marginalization of women; it also makes clear the incorporation of all Christians, male and female, in the body of Christ, the Church.

It is clear to these Christian feminists that the obstacle to women's full humanity and equality in society and, especially, in the Christian Church, has been the heritage of a male-dominant anthropology that has been pervasive in Christianity, but that can be challenged and, it is argued, is contrary to the true message of Jesus and his early followers. Islam, too, has a history of the marginalization of women and is based on a similar androcentric worldview. We close this discussion with a brief look at efforts of women in the modern Islamic world to carry out a similar challenge to this ideology as not consistent with the true message of the Prophet and the early tradition.

## The Role of Women in Islam

The place of women in Islam is a complex history and frequently distorted in the West. Prior to the sixth century C.E., Arabia was the only land in the Middle East in which patriarchal marriage was not institutionalized. About the time of the birth of Muhammad (c. 570), marriage was matrilineal. This does not imply that women held greater power; for example, it appears that infanticide was confined to girls. Nonetheless, Muhammad's first wife, Khadija, reveals the autonomy that other women enjoyed before Muhammad. His later followers, especially, institutionalized patriarchal practices. Muhammad was employed by Khadija, a widowed businesswoman, as leader of her caravan. She proposed to and married him. She was forty and he only twenty-five, and they remained in this monogamous marriage until her death twenty-five years later. She also assisted and supported him in his early religious activities. Furthermore, in Muhammad's day women attended the mosque and took part in the services on feast days. They also listened to Muhammad's discourses and had the right to speak out and give opinions about his comments. There is also evidence that his second wife, Aisha, and other women made contributions to the important *Hadith* or traditions about Muhammad. It is clear that the roles of women and marriage practices varied in pre-Islamic Arabia and even during Muhammad's life as a religious leader.

It is also evident, however, that, particularly after his first wife's death, practices already present, such as seclusion of women, polygamy, and maintaining a harem—all limiting the autonomy and the roles of women—were later adopted by Muhammad. His successors solidified these customs, which radically changed the relations between the sexes and legitimized the males' right to control the lives of Muslim women.[35]

Because Muhammad lived in a time when gender roles were rather fluid, and Arabic patriarchal practices were not yet hardened, many passages in the Qur'an express or imply a moral egalitarianism between the sexes. Common spiritual obligations are addressed equally to both sexes; and women are addressed directly. However, as Islam spread to other lands in the Middle East, where patriarchy and misogynist, or hateful, attitudes toward women were already entrenched, Islamic law and custom reflected these practices.

It was during the Abbasid dynasty (750–1258 C.E.) that women's role in Islamic religion and society was substantially diminished and proscribed. As a result, women had little, if any, influence on the increasing body of textual material—jurisprudence, theology, and commentaries on the Qur'an. These male texts of this period became the central prescriptive texts of Islam. They became *the* infallible Law. The practices of seclusion, polygamy, easy divorce for men, concubinage (living with a man though not married), female slavery, and the harem became traditional; and this led to the further abuse and degradation of women.

It was only in the nineteenth century that Islamic communities in the Middle East began to feel the winds of social change. Some of this was due to contacts with Western colonial social practices (some negative regarding women), but mainly from internal efforts to recover and restore Islamic traditions prior to the long Abbasid period. For largely economic reasons, some Islamic leaders began to recommend that women be better educated, some in the already existing European missionary schools. This spurred the growth of Muslim schools for girls and the encouragement of their larger role in society. In 1867 an important Turkish Muslim writer published an article arguing for women's rights:

> Our women are now seen as serving no useful purpose in mankind other than having children; they are considered simply as serving for pleasure like jewels. But they constitute half and perhaps more than half of our species. Preventing them from contributing to the sustenance and improvement of others . . . infringes the basic rule of public cooperation to such a degree as that our national society is stricken like a human body that is paralyzed on one side. Yet women are not inferior to men in their intellectual and physical capacities. In ancient times women shared in all men's activities. . . . Many evil consequences result from [the present] position of women.[36]

The new impulse for reform came from political figures but also writers, frequently women, who espoused women's liberation and a greater social and economic role for women. They appealed to earlier texts and traditions that revealed women as devout leaders and exemplars of women's role in society and that showed that divorce, polygamy, and seclusion were not essentials of Islam. This activity was especially true of writers in Egypt and Turkey. In the early decades of the twentieth century women feminists became more visible and more organized politically, although changing civil laws embodying patriarchal practices was still far in the future. These early feminists also differed. Some called for more radical secular reforms that reflected Western political and social models. Others called for women's liberation from some egregious patriarchal practices but rejected a wholesale imposition of Western customs.

This latter position is characteristic of **Malak Hifni Nassaf** (1886–1918), an Egyptian feminist who, however, opposed the immediate unveiling of women as not in their best interests since it could put them in a position of shame and even danger. Furthermore, wearing a veil can signify modesty rather than submissiveness. Even some contemporary militant Muslim feminists, who also oppose calls for Westernization, agree that the veil can be a sign of pride in a distinctive Islamic manner of dress. Nassaf gave priority to women's educational opportunities and reform in marriage laws and customs such as early marriage of girls, polygamy, and men's license to divorce. On polygamy she wrote,

> It [co-wife] is a terrible word—my pen almost halts in writing it—women's mortal enemy.... How many hearts has it broken...homes destroyed.... [It is] a terrible word laden with savagery and selfishness.... Bear in mind as you amuse yourself with your new bride you cause another's despair.[37]

Recent feminist Muslim scholars find, as do Christian women biblical scholars, that one must take into account *who* and *when* and, perhaps, *why* the all-male interpreters of scripture (the Qur'an) and Sunna of the Prophet chose particular texts as normative or read them in a particular androcentric way. They find, too, that these male interpreted texts are far from neutral or objective. Rather, they are read and then interpreted *through* their own male social and cultural experience.

*Amina Wadud-Muhsin*, an African American Muslim feminist, has pointed out these interpretive realities and their significance. She speaks of the text (e.g., the Qur'an) and the "prior text," the latter being the "perspectives" of the one who is doing the interpretation. She further argues that, although women have been excluded from the role of interpreter, this does not exclude them from the *message* that lies within the text. The message of the text does not change; what changes is only the "prior text." Wadud-Muhsin then proceeds to argue for the validity of new insights on the text, hence new interpretations. These plural readings do not mean, she points out, that the Qur'an is itself in its basic principles variant. What changes is "the capacity and particularity of the understanding of these principles."[38]

Wadud-Muhsin points out the importance of this with regard to gender. A new reading of the Qur'an, for example, will bring to light the error of reading patriarchy into depictions of God and also traditional notions of women's inferior status. One error of traditional patriarchal interpretation is "interpreting Qur'anic solutions for particular problems as if they were universal principles."[39] This would be similar to applying St. Paul's admonitions about women's headwear in Corinth late in the first century C.E. to women of the twenty-first century. Furthermore, cultural preconceptions predetermine traditional patriarchal exegesis. Wadud-Muhsin shows how this is true in the traditional gendering of God as masculine, whereas the Qur'an itself does not genderize God as either masculine or feminine, nor does it sanction it. Similarly, the Qur'an's account of the human creation as originating in "two existing forms of a single reality"[40] does not establish a hierarchy but rather a binary unity and complimentarity analogous to God's own self.

Furthermore, as Riffat Hassan argues,

None of the thirty or so passages which describe the creation of humanity by God in a variety of ways is there any statement which could be interpreted as asserting or suggesting that man was created *prior to* woman or that woman was created *from man.* In fact there are some passages which could—from a purely grammatical/linguistic point of view—be interpreted as stating that the first creation was feminine, not masculine.[41] [italics added]

So much for male priority or male superiority. These feminist writers also show that God's creation does not assume that only man is appointed God's vice-regent on Earth. As Wadud-Muhsin concludes, "Man and women are two categories of the human species given the same or equal consideration and endowed with the same or equal potential."[42]

*Fatima Mernissi* (b. 1940) is a Moroccan sociologist and one of the most important Muslim feminists. She grew up in a harem.[43] In *The Veil and the Male Elite: A Feminist Interpretation of Women's Rights in Islam* (1991) she proposes a new and, perhaps, more formidable theory regarding the root of Islamic patriarchy and subjugation of women. Islam, she argues, is not anti-woman, nor does it regard women as inferior. Quite the contrary. Since the Prophet Muhammad made the Muslim family the crucial unit of society (an innovation), this important heterosexual unit elevated women to a new power and danger. How? This deep sexual unit "constitutes a direct threat to man's allegiance to Allah, which requires the unconditional investment of all his [husband's] energies, thoughts and feelings in his God."[44]

The guard against this powerful danger is the crucial role of family law in Islam since the time of the Prophet. The threat that modern women pose is not, then, educational, civic, and political rights, but the demand for radical change in the fundamental traditional relationship in marriage, a relationship that moderates and even contains the repression of women's autonomy and power. As Mernissi argues, "The whole organization of social interaction and spatial configuration can be understood in terms of women's . . . power. The social order then appears as an attempt to subjugate her power and neutralize its disruptive effects."[45]

If Mernissi is right, then the struggle for the extension of women's rights and equality may be far more difficult than some have hoped. However, her bringing this central issue to the fore has both deepened the issue but also intensified the debate. It is clear, however, that largely due to the resurgence of traditional, especially militant Fundamentalist, Islam, the progress made for women by moderate Islamic writers and jurisprudents has been turned back in places like Iran and Afghanistan. However, even in the Muslim societies profoundly affected by the Iranian revolution there are signs of hope. Recently, 100 women (of a group of 502) in Afghanistan participated in the deliberations over the new constitution, although the limits that may be imposed on full equality with men is still contested and is opposed by the traditionalists. Similarly in Iran, gradual changes have taken place since 1979.

Many clerics uphold traditionalist views, but others are seriously making efforts to offer a more balanced and open view. And there are some clerics who are calling for even a more radical rethinking about the role of women. In many areas of the Islamic world, women's lives and role in society have clearly improved and the debate remains open.

This discussion has used the issue of gender and the role of women to exemplify the impact of modernity on religion and how changes have taken place not only from without but very often from within these great religions themselves. This has occurred through a fresh appropriation of their own authoritative resources. The examples of this process could be extended to other areas, such as the growth of democratic institutions, the relations between church and state, economic policy, and advances in social-service policies and programs. The point to be made is that religion remains a vital and, in some areas of the world, a dominant influence in society and on its institutions—despite the inroads of secularization. One would hope that the future would see neither the hegemony of religious Fundamentalism nor that of a militant secular ideology but rather the opportunity for these religious communities to continue, as in the past, to play a crucial role in their societies.

## NOTES

1. Bryan Wilson, "Secularization: The Inherited Model," in *The Sacred in a Secular Age,* ed. Phillip E. Hammond (Berkeley: University of California Press, 1985), 14–15.
2. Wilfred Cantwell Smith, "The Christian in a Religious Plural World," in *Christianity and Other Religions,* ed. John Hick and Brian Hebblethwaite (Philadelphia: Fortress Press, 1980), 94–95.
3. Jerry Falwell, with E. Dobson and E. Hinson, *The Fundamentalist Phenomenon: The Resurgence of Conservative Christianity* (Garden City: Doubleday, 1981), 219.
4. Quoted in Susan Harding, "Imagining the Last Days: The Politics of Apocalyptic Language," in Martin E. Marty and R. Scott Appleby (eds.), *Accounting for Fundamentalism* (Chicago: University of Chicago Press, 1994), 70.
5. See Paul Boyer, *When Time Shall Be No More: Prophecy Belief in Modern American Culture* (Cambridge: Harvard University Press, 1992), 137f.
6. For a superb discussion of contemporary Creation Science, on which I am dependent, see James Moore, "The Creationist Cosmos of Protestant Fundamentalism," in Martin E. Marty and R. Scott Appleby, *Fundamentalism and Society: Reclaiming Science, the Family, and Education* (Chicago: University of Chicago Press, 1993), Chapter 3.
7. J. Moore, *op cit.,* 47–48.
8. J. Moore, *op cit.,* 50–51.
9. See "Supreme Court Strikes Down Creation Science Statute," *Congressional Quarterly Weekly Report* 45 (1987), 1303.
10. On this, see James Davison Hunter, *Culture Wars: The Struggle to Define America* (New York: Basic Books, 1991), especially Chapters 4–5.
11. For an excellent, up-to-date discussion of the militant Fundamentalist movements in America, see Mark Juergensmeyer, *Terror in the Mind of God: The Global*

*Rise of Religious Violence* (California: University of California Press, 2003), Chapter 2. This book also covers militant Fundamentalism in Islam, Judaism, Sikhism, and Buddhism and discusses what these movements have in common.

12. Muhammad Arkoun, *Islamochristiana*, XII (1986), 159.

13. W. Montgomery Watt, *Islamic Fundamentalism and Modernity* (London and New York: Routledge, 1989), 1–2.

14. John L. Esposito, *The Islamic Threat: Myth or Reality?* (New York and Oxford: Oxford University Press, 1992), 19.

15. Sayyid Qutb, *Milestones* (Stuttgart: Ernst Klett Printers, 1978), 261.

16. Sayyid Qutb, *Ma'alim fi al Tariq* (Cairo: Dar al Shurug, 1988).

17. R. Khomeini, *Kashf-al-Asrar* (n.p. and n.d.), 8–10. Quoted in Bager Moin, "Khomeini's Search for Perfection: Theory and Reality," in Ali Rahnema, ed., *Pioneers of Islamic Revival* (London: Zed Books Ltd., 1994), 73.

18. R. Khomeini, "Islamic Government," trans. and ed. Hamar Algar, in *Islam and Revolution* (Berkeley: Mizan Press, 1981), 63.

19. Ruhollah Khomeini, *Islam and Revolution: Writings and Declarations of Imam Khomeini*, trans. Hamid Algar (Berkeley: Mizan Press, 1983), 75–76.

20. R. Khomeini, *Islamic Government, op cit.*

21. Robin Wright, "Lebanon," in Shireen T. Hunter, ed., *The Politics of Islamic Revivalism* (Bloomington: Indiana University Press, 1988), 66.

22. As quoted in Peter L. Bergen, *Holy War Inc.: Inside the Secret World of Osama bin Laden* (New York: Free Press, 2002), 53.

23. "Osama bin Laden Videotaped Address, October 7, 2001," in Bruce Lincoln, *Holy Terrors: Thinking about Religion after September 11* (Chicago: University of Chicago Press, 2003), 102.

24. "Transcript of Pat Robertson's Broadcast Interview with Jerry Falwell on the 700 Club, September 13, 2001," in B. Lincoln, *Holy Terrors, op cit.*, 104, 106.

25. Quoted in "Is the Second Coming Near? Some Interpreters See Biblical Prophecies Being Fulfilled in the War in Iraq," *Daily Press* (VA), March 22, 2003, D-10.

26. Elizabeth Cady Stanton, *The Woman's Bible*, II (Edinburgh: Polygon Books, 1985 [original 1885]), 112.

27. Mary Daly, *Beyond God the Father* (Boston: Beacon Press, 1973), 19.

28. Elizabeth Schüssler Fiorenza, *In Memory of Her: A Feminist Theological Reconstruction of Christian Origins* (New York: Crossroads, 1983), XIV.

29. *Ibid.*, 41.

30. Elizabeth A. Johnson, *She Who Is: The Mystery of God in Feminist Theological Discourse* (New York: Crossroads, 1994), 6.

31. *Ibid.*, Ch. 5.

32. *Ibid.*, 18.

33. *Ibid.*

34. *Ibid.*, 166.

35. Several studies have been helpful in understanding the early history of the role of women in Arabia and in the early centuries of Islam; especially helpful is Leila Ahmed, *Women and Gender: Historical Roots of a Modern Debate* (New Haven: Yale University Press, 1992).

36. Bernard Lewis, *A Middle East Mosaic: Fragments of Life, Letters and History* (New York, 2000), 192. Also cited in B. Lewis, *What Went Wrong? The Clash between Islam and Modernity in the Middle East* (New York, 2002), 70.

37. Bahithat al Badiyya, *Al-nisa'iyyat* . . . (Cairo, 1925) I, 41. Quoted in L. Ahmed, *op cit.*, 182.
38. Amina Wadud, *Qur'an and Women: Rereading the Sacred Text from a Woman's Perspecitve*, 2nd ed. (Oxford: Oxford University Press, 1999), 5.
39. A. Wadud, *ibid.*, 99.
40. A. Wadud, *ibid.*, 21.
41. Riffat Hassan, "An Islamic Perspective," in *Sexuality: A Reader*, ed. Karen Lebacqz (Cleveland, Oh.: The Pilgrim Press, 1999), 345.
42. A. Wadud, *op cit.*, 15. On the same issues, see also the excellent book by Asma Barlas, *"Believing Women" in Islam: Unreading Patriarchal Interpretations of the Qur'an* (Austin: University of Texas Press, 2002), especially Chapter 5.
43. See her interesting autobiographical account in *Dreams of Trespass: Tales of a Moroccan Girlhood* (New York: Addison-Wesley, 1994).
44. Fatima Mernissi, *Beyond the Veil and the Male Elite* (New York: Addison-Wesley, 1991), 8.
45. F. Mernissi, *ibid.*, 33.

## KEY WORDS

| | |
|---|---|
| secularization | Sayyid Qutb |
| Fundamentalism | Ayatollah Ruhollah Khomeini |
| Jerry Falwell | Osama bin Laden |
| Premillenarian | Elizabeth Schüssler Fiorenza |
| Creation Science | Elizabeth A. Johnson |
| theocratic | Malak Hifri Nassaf |
| *jihad* | Amina Wadud-Muhsin |
| Wahhabism | Fatima Mernissi |

## REVIEW QUESTIONS

1. Describe what factors in the modern world have contributed to the secularization process that has narrowed the scope of religion in some societies. What factors have caused scholars to question the secularization thesis?
2. Characterize the common features of the new Protestant Fundamentalism in America and the resurgent Islamic Fundamentalism in the Middle East.
3. Describe the characteristics of the American Fundamentalists' premillenarian view of history. What is its religious and political significance?
4. Why do contemporary radical Islamists equate modernization with Westernization?
5. What doctrine in Protestant and Islamic Fundamentalism might contribute to their resistance to "innovation" or new interpretations?
6. Characterize some of the major themes in, for example, the writings of Sayyid Qutb and the Ayatollah Ruhollah Khomeini.
7. Try to summarize some of the major themes in the Christian feminists' arguments against religious patriarchy. What is your assessment of these arguments?
8. What kind of evidence do the Islamist feminists offer regarding the Qur'an in their critique of religious and social patriarchy?

9. Do you see the spread of Fundamentalism worldwide as a danger? Why or why not? What is your own view of the relationship between religion (the church, mosque, etc.) and the modern state?

## SUGGESTIONS FOR FURTHER READING

*For discussions of the secularization thesis and its critics, see*

BELL, DANIEL. "The Return of the Sacred." In *The Winding Passage.* Cambridge, Mass.: ABT Books, 1980.

BERGER, PETER L. *The Sacred Canopy.* New York: Doubleday, 1967. Chapters 5, 6, 7.

————. "The Desecularization of the World: A Global Overview." In *The Desecularization of the World: Resurgent Religion and World Politics,* ed. Peter L. Berger. Washington, D.C.: Ethics and Public Policy Center, 1999. (Studies countering the secularization thesis.)

DOBBELAERE, KAREL. "Secularization: A Multi-Dimensional Concept." *Current Sociology* 29, no. 2 (summer 1981). (An overview of studies with an extensive bibliography.)

FENN, RICHARD. *Toward a Theory of Secularization.* Storrs, Conn.: Society for the Scientific Study of Religion, 1978. (Theoretical discussion of the secularization thesis.)

MARTIN, DAVID. *A General Theory of Secularization.* New York: Harper & Row, 1978. (Secularization in various cultural and political contexts.)

WILSON, BRYAN. "Secularization: The Inherited Model." In *The Sacred in a Secular Age,* ed. Phillip E. Hammond (Berkeley: University of California Press, 1985).

*For studies of worldwide Fundamentalism, see*

ARMSTRONG, KAREN. *The Battle for God: A History of Fundamentalism.* New York: Ballantine Books, 2001. (An extensive, highly informative account of the beginnings and modern developments of Fundamentalism in the Abrahamic religions—Judaism, Christianity, and Islam.)

JUERGENSMEYER, MARK. *Terror in the Mind of God: The Global Rise of Religious Violence,* 3rd ed. Berkeley: University of California Press, 2003. (Interviews with and discussion about contemporary religious terrorists in Christianity, Judaism, Islam, Sikhism, and Japanese Buddhism. Also a fine discussion of the features that characterize the religious terrorists.)

KEPPEL, GILLES. *The Revenge of God: The Resurgence of Islam, Christianity and Judaism in the Modern World.* Trans. by Alan Braley. University Park: The Pennsylvania State University Press, 1995. (While not covering recent developments, this is a good, readable introduction to the subject.)

LAWRENCE, BRUCE. *Defenders of God: The Fundamentalist Revolt Against the Modern World.* New York: Harper & Row, 1989. (An excellent study of movements prior to the first Gulf War.)

MARTY, MARTIN E. AND R. SCOTT APPLEBY. *The Glory and the Power: The Fundamentalist Challenge to the Modern World.* Boston: Beacon Press, 1992. (An excellent, brief introduction to the phenomenon of modern Fundamentalism in Protestantism, Israel, and Islam. It serves as the companion to the television series on PBS.)

————. *The Fundamentalism Project,* 5 vols. Chicago: The University of Chicago Press, 1991–1996. (A rich collection of studies by noted scholars on aspects of modern worldwide Fundamentalism. The most important source of information and analysis of movements from North America and Europe to Latin America, Africa, the Middle East, and the whole of Asia. See especially the first three volumes on *Fundamentalism Observed* [1991], *Fundamentalisms and Society* [1993], and *Fundamentalisms and the State* [1993].)

*For studies of American Protestant Fundamentalism, see the works of Armstrong, Juergensmeyer, and Marty and Appleby cited previously, as well as*

AMMERMAN, NANCY T. *Bible Believers: Fundamentalists in the Modern World.* New Brunswick: Rutgers University Press, 1987.

BOYER, PAUL. *When Time Shall Be No More: Prophecy Belief in Modern American Culture.* Cambridge: Harvard University Press, 1994. (Traces, in interesting detail, the role in contemporary American life of Fundamentalist prophecy belief about the end of the world and the political significance of that belief.)

CARPENTER, JOEL. *Revive Us Again: The Reawakening of American Fundamentalism.* New York: Oxford University Press, 1997. (An excellent account of contemporary American Fundamentalism by a sympathetic scholar.)

HARDING, SUSAN. *The Book of Jerry Falwell: Fundamentalist Language and Politics.* Princeton, N.J.: Princeton University Press, 2000. (A study of one of the most influential Fundamentalist preachers in America and his religious and political significance.)

HUNTER, JAMES DAVISON. *Culture Wars: The Struggle to Define America.* New York: Basic Books, 1991. (An interesting account by a sociologist of the fierce cultural struggle of Protestant Fundamentalists, as well as Orthodox Jews and Catholics, against modern attitudes and political actions as they bear on matters of the family, sexuality, education, popular culture, and the media.)

*For studies of Islamic Fundamentalism, see the books by Armstrong, Juergensmeyer, Keppel, and Marty cited previously, as well as the following:*

ESPOSITO, JOHN L. *The Islamic Threat: Myth or Reality?* New York: Oxford University Press, 1992. (An excellent analysis of the origins and factors involved in the recent Islamic resurgence and its relation to the West.)

————. *Unholy War: Terror in the Name of Islam.* New York: Oxford University Press, 2003. (An up-to-date, authoritative, and lucid guide to how Islamic jihad ideology has led to recent "Islamic rage" and terror.)

LEWIS, BERNARD. *What Went Wrong? The Clash between Islam and Modernity in the Middle East.* New York: HarperCollins, 2002. (A valuable accounting, by an authority on Islam, of Islam's response to the West as a result of the West's influence and domination.)

————. *The Crisis of Islam: Holy War and Holy Terror.* New York: Modern Library, 2003. (A highly readable overview of the history, particularly in the twentieth century, of events leading up to the recent Islamic terrorism and the attacks on the United States.)

RAHNEMA, ALI. ed. *Pioneers of Islamic Revival.* London: Zed Books, 1994. (Brief but excellent studies of leaders such as Khomeini, al-Banna, and Qutb.)

*For studies of women and modernity in Christianity, see*

DALY, MARY. *The Church and the Second Sex.* Boston: Beacon Press, 1968.

————. *Beyond God the Father.* Boston: Beacon Press, 1973. (These two influential books show Daly's development from an appeal for "equality" and "partnership" with men in the Roman Catholic Church to a more radical attack on patriarchal religion in general.)

JOHNSON, ELIZABETH A. *She Who Is: The Mystery of God in Feminist Theological Discourse*. New York: Crossroads, 1994. (Challenges the Bible's patriarchal anthropology and defends viewing God as female.)

MCFAGUE, SALLIE. *Models of God: Theology for an Ecological, Nuclear Age*. Philadelphia: Westminster Press, 1987. (A critique of "imperialist, triumphalist" metaphors for God, proposing feminine metaphors as more appropriate, especially in view of our present ecological awareness.)

RUETHER, ROSEMARY. *Sexism and God-Talk: Towards a Feminist Theology*. London: SCM Press, 1983. (One of the earliest efforts to develop a feminist theology, using women's experience as a source of biblical and theological interpretation.)

SCHÜSSLER FIORENZA, ELIZABETH. *In Memory of Her: A Feminist Theological Reconstruction of Christian Origins*. New York: Crossroads, 1983. (Important work by the most influential feminist New Testament scholar calling for reform based on the earliest traditions of Jesus and Christian origins.)

STANTON, ELIZABETH CADY. *The Woman's Bible*. Edinburgh: Polygon Books, 1985. (Originally published in 1885) (A commentary on the Bible by a nineteenth-century forerunner of contemporary religious feminists, detailing the often extraordinarily derogatory depiction of women in the Bible, as well as the noble portraits of them as leaders.)

*For studies of women and modernity in Islam, see*

AHMED, LEILA. *Women and Gender in Islam: Historical Roots of a Modern Debate*. New Haven: Yale University Press, 1992. (An excellent, highly readable introduction to this complex subject.)

BARLAS, ASMA. *"Believing Women" in Islam: Unreading Patriarchal Interpretations of the Qur'an*. Austin: University of Texas Press, 2002. (A valuable, but more sophisticated, rereading of the Qur'an, arguing that it affirms the complete equality of the sexes—and what that implies.)

BORRESEN, KARI AND KARI VOGT. *Women's Studies of the Christian and Islamic Traditions: Ancient, Medieval and Renaissance Foremothers*. Dordrecht, Holland: Kluwer Academic Publishers, 1993. (A valuable resource for both traditions covering the pre-Modern period.)

HADDAD, YVONNE Y. "Islam, Women and Revolution in Twentieth Century Arab Thought." In *Women, Religion and Social Change*, ed. Yvonne Y. Haddad and Ellison B. Findly. Albany: State University of New York Press, 1985.

MERNISSI, FATIMA. *The Veil and the Male Elite*. London: Zed, 1996. (A Moroccan feminist's argument that women's segregation in Islam is the institutionalization of authoritarianism by the manipulation of its sacred texts.)

STOWASSER, BARBARA F. *Women in the Qur'an, Traditions, and Interpretation*. New York: Oxford University Press, 1994. (Presents both Qur'anic statements on women and medieval, modern, and contemporary exegesis and interpretations.)

# Glossary

**agnosticism** From the Greek *a* ("not") and the base of *gignoskein* ("to know"); applies to any proposition (but usually with respect to God) for which evidence for belief or dogmatic unbelief is insufficient.

**al-Qa'ida ("the base")** A radical Islamist movement created and financially supported by Osama bin Laden in 1991 to liberate Afghanistan from the Soviet Russian occupation. It has since become a worldwide jihadist movement associated with terrorism.

**Amish** The followers of Jacob Ammann (1656?–1730?) in Berne, Switzerland, who broke from the Protestant Swiss Brethren. Under persecution they migrated to Pennsylvania as early as 1727 and spread to Ohio, Indiana, and Ontario, Canada. Noted for their conservative views and lifestyle, the Old Order Amish wear distinctive dress and reject many modern conveniences such as electricity and automobiles.

**amulet** An object that is carried on a person or is displayed in a home or place of business to ward off or repel disease, evil, or the assaults of demonic spirits.

**analogy** A similarity between things otherwise unlike. Because religions often refer to things (gods, a future life, and so forth) that lie beyond finite experience, they must speak of these things by analogy. For example, the word *good* when applied to God is neither the same as nor entirely different from goodness when applied to humans. *Good* is here used analogically.

**animism** From the Latin *anima,* meaning "soul"; the belief that all things possess a soul or spirit—that is, all reality is animate. Introduced by E. B. Tylor to refer to what he conceived to be the earliest form of religion.

**anomie** From the Greek *anomia,* meaning "lawlessness"; popularized in the study of religion by Emile Durkheim, it has to do with a condition of the individual or society in which normal order is dissolving or absent, bringing a state of disorientation, anxiety, and chaos.

**anthropomorphism**  Meaning "of human form"; used for the attribution of human qualities to the divine or God. Often used critically as the conceiving of God or the gods in too-human form.

**antinomian**  From the Greek *anti* ("against") and *nomos* ("law"); describes those religious groups or individuals who hold the doctrine that they are freed from and above the law that remains binding on others. Antinomian sects have threatened Christianity from time to time through the centuries.

**apocalypse**  From the Greek *apokalypsis,* meaning "revelation"; associated with a class of Jewish and Christian literature that purports to reveal, in highly symbolic language, what is to happen in the future.

**archetypal**  Original pattern, or model, from which other things—such as institutions, beliefs, and behavior—are patterned. In many religions, it is important to follow the model of behavior established by God or the gods "in the beginning."

**ascetic**  Generally refers to a person who lives an austere and self-denying life. In many religions, refers to a special group of devotees who lead a life of contemplation and self-denial, such as monks or hermits.

*ashramas*  One of the four "stages of life" in Hinduism. The practice of withdrawal from the world in which one lives as a holy recluse; an ashram is a community dwelling place where those who have withdrawn can gather around a guru, or teacher, to study and meditate.

**atonement**  At-one-ment. Especially prominent in Judaism and Christianity; a representative sacrifice of the life of a victim (symbolized by its outpoured blood), to serve as an expiation (see p. 394) for an individual or a community to cover an offense to God or gods.

**bar mitzvah**  Means "Son of the Commandment"; applied to a Jewish boy on his thirteenth birthday when, in a synagogue ceremony, he takes on his religious responsibilities in the community. The boy thereafter has certain prerogatives, such as the reading of the Torah, is held accountable for his own sins, and is commanded to fast on the Day of Atonement.

*bhakti*  Sanskrit word meaning "devotion"; the path to God or liberation in Hinduism that stresses love and devotion to a deity rather than study or ritual obligation. The way of devotion is classically outlined in the *Bhagavad Gita.*

**Calvinism**  Expression of Protestant Christianity that traces its doctrines and practices to the teachings of the Reformer John Calvin (1509–1564). These include the sovereignty of God, election or predestination, original sin, the irresistibility of grace, and a deep sense of calling in our secular occupation.

**catharsis**  A cleansing or a purging; in religion, one important function is the act of purification that is necessary if we are to be right with or in the presence of the sacred. Also serves to purge the emotions.

**cosmogony**   Refers to those stories or theories that have to do with the birth or creation of the world or universe.

**cosmological proof**   One of the classical proofs of the existence of God arguing that the world is not self-explanatory and requires an infinite (noncontingent) being, God, as its explanation. The contingency of the world requires a first cause, a necessary being.

**cosmology**   Derived from the Greek words meaning "doctrine of the world"; has to do with the branch of philosophical or scientific speculation that deals with the origin and structure of the world.

**Christian Identity**   Radical American Fundamentalist groups who seek to merge Christianity and the state into a theocratic society ruled by religious laws. It is deeply anti-Semitic and recently has been centered on the Aryan Nations compound in Idaho.

**Cro-Magnon**   Term that designates the first group of fully evolved representatives of *Homo sapiens,* who entered Europe from the Middle East between 42,000 and 30,000 B.C.E.

**deism**   From the Latin *deus* ("god"); applies to a movement of thought in the seventeenth and eighteenth centuries in Europe that held a belief in one God who creates the world but who does not intervene directly in its ongoing functioning. God allows the world to operate by the natural laws he originally established. The deist God is a transcendent Creator but is not immanent in the world.

**denomination**   A form of religious institution distinctive of Protestant Christianity and often contrasted with both state-established churches and religious sects. Common in pluralistic societies like the United States where no church is established by law or privileged by the state and each religious group receives equal treatment before the law. Resemble churches in that they are usually large and inclusive across socioeconomic lines, and their members are not alienated from the larger society.

*dharma*   In the Hindu tradition, means "sacred law"; set forth in numerous texts such as the Code of Manu, which has to do with caste duties and obligations. A caste member who does her *dharma* acquires good *karma.* In Buddhism, refers to the teachings of Buddha—for example, the Four Noble Truths.

**epiphany**   From the Greek, meaning "manifestation" of a god or divine power. In Christianity, the feast of Epiphany, or Manifestation of Christ, is celebrated on January 6.

**eschatology**   From the Greek *eschatos,* meaning the "last things"; the understanding of nature, of human life, and of history in terms of their goals or destinies. Often associated with beliefs concerning life after death, judgment, and Heaven and Hell.

**ethnocentric**   Assumption that a person's own race or culture is normative or superior to others.

**etiological**   Used in religion to designate those doctrines or myths that describe and explain the origin of something—for example, the world, human institutions, or beliefs.

**Eucharist**   The chief sacrament of Christianity, derived from the Last Supper of Jesus and his disciples that was celebrated the evening before Jesus' crucifixion. Believers partake of the bread and wine in remembrance of Jesus Christ and his sacrifice.

**evangelical**   Christians of any Protestant church or sect who place great importance on a conscious, personal conversion to Christ rather than on becoming a Christian through birth or baptism.

**exegesis**   The analysis of a passage of a text, in this case sacred texts, in an effort to understand or to offer commentary on the meaning of the passage. Exegesis involves examining many questions regarding the text, such as its historical and literary context, the lexical or correct understanding of the words, its grammar, structure, and form or genre, its audience, and so on.

**existential**   Those beliefs or actions that focus on personal existence in contrast to those matters that are impersonal or indifferent to the person. Existentialism is concerned with protesting against positions that view the person as an object of purely rational or scientific analysis. It emphasizes the "subjective"—things such as finitude, guilt, suffering, and death that cannot be approached in the manner of scientific problem solving—and the ambiguities of life that arise from our unique human freedom.

**exorcist**   Priest or magician who practices exorcism, or the expelling of evil spirits by the use of a special ritual or formula or the use of a holy name.

**expiation**   Making right by some ritual act or offering for the injury or sin done to some other person or god; closely related to atonement (see p. 392) and propitiation (see p. 398), expiation involves an act of sacrifice to remove pollution or sin.

**fetish**   Derived from the Portuguese *feitico,* meaning "skillfully made"; in religion, refers to various objects, either natural or artificial, that are endowed with supernatural magical power or virtue and are capable of averting evil or bringing good.

**fideism**   From the Latin *fides,* meaning "faith"; associated with those who believe that faith must precede reason with regard to knowledge of God and that reason alone is incapable of producing genuine knowledge of God.

**Functionalism**   Method applied to the study of religion that is not interested in the history or evolution of religions but rather focuses on how religion functions in a particular social structure or cultural context—for example, what role(s) a particular religious ritual plays in the social life of a tribe.

**genetic fallacy** Logical error of judging the nature, value, or truth of a religion based on a description or analysis of its origin or earliest expression.

**Gnosticism** A type of religious phenomenon that is found in the ancient world, especially in the Hellenistic period (300 B.C.E.–200 C.E.), and largely influenced by Platonic and Zoroastinian dualism. The word *gnosticism* is from the Greek word meaning "knowledge" (*gnosis*), but conveys the idea of a secret knowledge or revelation that will free the soul from its imprisonment in the body and this evil world and return it to its heavenly home. Orthodox Judaism and Christianity saw it as a dangerous heresy.

**guru** In Hinduism, a spiritual teacher or guide who instructs his followers on the path to liberation.

**Gush Emunim ("Block of the Faithful")** A radical Jewish Fundamentalist group of several thousand in Israel that began in the 1970s to settle in the Palestinian territories, contrary to the Israeli government's orders. Its Zionist goal is the entire restoration of the ancient biblical Land of Israel.

**halakhah** In Hebrew "that by which one walks" or the body of jurisprudence, ethical duties, and ceremonial observances that for Orthodox Judaism is binding as the word of God. The main sources of *halakhah* are the Hebrew Bible, the Talmud, and a large body of *responsa*.

**Hasidim (or Chasidim)** From the Hebrew *hasid*, meaning "pietist"; a party among the Jews of Palestine who opposed the hellenizing of Judaism in the second century B.C.E. and were the backbone of Jewish resistance. In modern times, associated with an ultra-orthodox Jewish movement whose members refuse to wear modern Western clothing and whose members dress as their ancestors in the ghettos of eastern Europe. Their piety is marked by a mystical joy and intensity.

*hathayoga* One of the four types of yoga; stresses the discipline of the body as the means to liberation.

**henotheism** From the Greek for "one" and "god"; ascribed to Max Müller, who used it to describe that form of religion in which one god is supreme but others exist; in contrast to monotheism, in which only one god exists.

**hermeneutics** The art or science concerned with the conditions and methods required to understand the meaning of a written text. In contrast to *exegesis* (see above), hermeneutics broadly concerns itself with the preconditions that make understanding possible. A specific hermeneutics involves the particular preconditions that are necessary to understand a distinctive text, such as a biblical book or a Buddhist *sutra* or teaching.

**hierophany** Proposed by Mircea Eliade to designate any act or manifestation of the sacred; literally means something sacred showing itself to us.

**Hutterite Brethren**   An Anabaptist (meaning "re-baptizer") group originating in the sixteenth century in Switzerland but, due to persecution, found asylum in Moravia in 1529 under the leadership of Jacob Hutter. Later the Hutterites migrated to Canada and the United States. Their communities are called Bruderhofs and they hold property in common and practice pacifism.

**icon**   From the Greek *eikon*, meaning "image" or "likeness"; a symbolic sacred image, usually painted on flat wood panels or canvas, that materially embodies a spiritual meaning and power. They are sacramental in that they make present the sacred or the divine and are venerated in Eastern Orthodox Christian churches.

**Kaddish**   Jewish public prayer that is characterized by the praise and glorification of God, and by hope in the establishment of God's kingdom on earth; also used as a mourner's prayer, it is recited at the graveside of close relatives and in the synagogue.

**lectionary**   A book that contains a table of readings from the Bible to be read in public worship. Particular passages or lessons are apportioned for use on particular days, usually on a two- or three-year cycle.

**legend**   Story about the past that is popularly taken to be historical and that does have some historical basis but includes elements of the fictitious and even fabulous.

**logos**   In Greek, translated as "word," "speech," "discourse," or "reason"; used by the Stoics to refer to the divine Reason or God. The Jewish writer Philo identified the creative, divine word of the Hebrew scriptures with the logos of the Stoics. In the Gospel of John and in the early Church, it was identified with the Son of the Christian Trinity.

**Maccabean**   Name given to the patriotic Jewish warriors in the second century B.C.E., named after their leader, Judas Maccabeus, who resisted pagan (Greek) practices. The story is told in I Maccabees and is celebrated in the Jewish Festival of Hanukkah.

**Mana**   Polynesian term for the impersonal supernatural force to which certain primal peoples attribute good or evil fortune or magical power.

*mandala*   A symmetrical diagram, circular or square; symbolic representation of the universe, reality, or those energies depicted as deities, demons, Bodhisattvas, and the Buddha. Used in meditation practices in some schools of Buddhism.

*mantra*   A sacred sound of one syllable or more. In Hinduism, repeated during meditation in order to empty the mind in preparation for liberation; in Buddhism, expresses the essence of some transcendental power or being such as the Buddha or Bodhisattva. The most famous is the syllable *OM*.

**masochism**   Broadly associated with the feeling of pleasure that a person derives from being abused or dominated by another person or institution.

**mendicant**   A beggar; in many religions, such as Christianity and Buddhism, the act of begging for alms is (or was) a high form of the spiritual life and discipline.

**millenarianism**   First appears in the New Testament Book of Revelation (Chapter 20) in connection with the final struggle between God and Satan and the second coming of Christ in the immediate future, all of which precede the millennium—the 1,000-year reign of the Messiah. Used, however, to describe a large variety of Christian and non-Christian apocalyptic (see p. 392) movements that expect a redeemer to inaugurate a Utopian Age. Often used interchangeably with "messianism" or "messianic movements."

**Mishnah**   From the Hebrew, meaning "to repeat"; the collection of oral Jewish law, in contrast to the written Law, or Torah, that was compiled by Rabbi Judah Ha-Nasi, circa 200 C.E. Six divisions of the Mishnah cover laws of agriculture, festivals, women, marriage, and so forth. Together with the Gemara, commentary on the Mishnah, it forms the bases of the Talmud.

*moksha*   From Sanskrit, meaning "liberation" in Hinduism; liberation from the round of birth, death, and rebirth. Various classical schools of Hinduism define in different ways what constitutes liberation and the methods of achieving it.

**monism**   From the Greek, meaning "one"; applied to those doctrines that teach that only one being exists, as differentiated from pantheism, which teaches that all beings are divine or that God is in everything. Especially associated with Indian nondualism or Advaita Vedanta.

**monotheism**   Belief in one personal, transcendent Creator God as opposed to belief in many gods. Judaism, Islam, and Christianity are examples of monotheistic religions.

*mudra*   A symbolic gesture or position of the hands in Hinduism and Buddhism; each *mudra* signifies a mood, virtue, or spiritual quality.

*muezzin*   Official in Islamic countries who calls the summons to prayer; in large mosques, he speaks from a tower called a minaret.

**mystery religions**   Associated especially with the secret religious cults of ancient Greece and Rome that practiced rites of initiation involving purification, the revealing of secret teachings and symbols, and a sacramental meal of communion with a person's fellows and with the divinity. The chief Greek cults were the Eleusinian and Orphic mysteries.

**Neanderthal**   A type of prehistoric man from the middle Paleolithic (see p. 398) age, whose remains were found in a cave in the Neanderthal Valley near Dusseldorf, Germany.

**Neolithic**   The New Stone Age that began about 8000–7000 B.C.E. in the Middle East and about 4000–3000 B.C.E. in Europe. It was followed by the Bronze Age.

**Nichiren**  A Japanese Buddhist reformer (1222–1282 C.E.) and the sect named after him, which incorporates aspects of Buddhism and Shintoism, the indigenous national religion of Japan. Nichiren believed true Buddhism was found in the *Lotus Sutra* and that other forms of Buddhism were in error. A uniquely militant and zealous expression of Buddhism.

**normative**  The measure or standard by which other beliefs or practices are to be judged.

**Oedipus complex**  The theory of the psychoanalyst Sigmund Freud that children (particularly boys) have an unconscious tendency to be attached to the parent of the opposite sex and to show hostility toward to other parent. Freud used the theory to explain certain social facts, including religion.

**omnipotent**  From the Latin *omni* ("all") and *potens* ("powerful"), meaning "all-powerful"; traditionally ascribed to God in Western monotheism is his having unlimited power and authority.

**omniscient**  Having infinite knowledge; knowing all things is traditionally ascribed to God in the Western monotheistic religions.

**ontological**  The nature of being; the branch of philosophy that investigates the nature, the essential properties, and the relations of being.

**Paleolithic**  The Old Stone Age that began with the appearance of the earliest toolmakers and extended to about 10,000–8000 B.C.E. It is characterized by the making of stone tools and weapons and by hunting and food-gathering.

**pantheism**  From the Greek, *pan* ("all") and *theos* ("god"); the doctrine that all that exists is God and God is all in all. God and nature are interchangeable terms.

**pantheon**  From the Greek, meaning "all the gods"; designates all the gods of a society taken collectively. Derives from the great Pantheon at Rome, a temple built in 27 B.C.E. and dedicated to all the gods.

**Pharisees**  In Hebrew meaning "separated ones." A Jewish religious party first recorded at the time of the Maccabean revolt (c. 135 B.C.E.). They exercised significant religious influence, especially among the common people and, unlike another party, the Sadducees, they allowed interpretations of the Mosaic law to fit different situations.

**polytheism**  Recognition and worship of more than one god; conceives of sacred power as being manifested in diverse forms.

**predestinarian**  A person who holds the belief in predestination—the doctrine that God, from the beginning, has determined the ultimate destiny of every human being, some to salvation and others to damnation.

**propitiation**  Act of appeasing, pacifying, or making favorable, often through some form of sacrifice to a deity.

**proselytize**  Engaging in the effort of persuading or converting a person from one religion or opinion to another; a proselyte is one who has been converted from one religion to another.

**rabbinic** Things that pertain to Jewish rabbis or teachers, their writings, opinions, and so forth.

**reliquary** A small box, container, or shrine used to hold or exhibit a religious relic, such as the bones of a saint.

**revivalism** A characteristic of certain religious groups, especially within Protestant Christianity, that emphasizes the importance of a personal, emotional conversion and commitment to Christ; effected through "revivals," evangelistic meetings, or even longer periods of religious fervor, in which a religious awakening and conversion of individuals is sought.

*sadhu* In the Hindu tradition, a wandering holy man who is devoted fully to achieving *moksha*, or liberation.

**saga** A heroic narrative about either a historical or a legendary figure. Classic sagas were those recorded in Ireland in the twelfth and thirteenth centuries.

*sannyasin* In Hinduism, a person who has renounced the world and its possessions and has become an ascetic (see p. 392), seeking liberation through prayer and meditation.

**shamans** A distinct class of religious specialists found among the native Americans, Eskimos, and the tribes of South and Southeast Asia; undergo strenuous initiations by which they gain control over the spirits and are able to use them in healing and in flights to the spirit world.

**Shi'i** One of the two great sects of Islam consisting of partisans or followers of Ali, the cousin and son-in-law of Muhammad. The Shi'ites maintain that Ali, the fourth of the caliphs, was the first Imam, the rightful successor of Muhammad as leader of the Umma or Islamic community. Shi'ites are the dominant Islamic community in Iran.

**Sikhism** A religion that originated in the Punjab region of north India in the sixteenth century C.E. as an offshoot of a *bhakti* (see above) cult of Hinduism. The word *Sikh* is derived from both Pali and Sanskrit and means "disciple." The Sikhs are the disciples of 10 *gurus* (see above) beginning with Nanak (1469–1539) and ending with Gobind Singh (1666–1708). The fifth *guru*, Arfan (1563–1606), consolidated the Sikh community, broke its connections with the Hindus and Muslims, and set it on its own course.

**Sufi** A Muslim mystic who teaches that salvation comes through a personal union with Allah and sometimes expresses views differing significantly from mainstream Islamic teachings; devotion often expressed in intense, passionate poetry.

**Sunnis** One of the two great sects of Islam, followers of the tradition (*sunna*)—as found in the life and teachings of the Prophet Muhammad—and the *Qur'an* as the authoritative sources. The Sunni represent a moderate, centrist position and is the largest of the sectarian Islamic communities.

**superego**  One of the three functional parts (with the id and ego) of the human personality as understood by Freud; originates in the child's identification with parents and others and serves as an internal censor of behavior. Embraces both the conscious and the unconscious conscience.

**syncretism**  In religion, the effort to bring together into a synthesis or harmony different beliefs or practices from several religious traditions to create a new union.

**taboo**  English form of the Polynesian word meaning "marked off" or "prohibited"; associated with a sacred—that is, dangerous—object or person who is not to be touched or approached for fear of supernatural contagion.

**talisman**  A magical object that is believed to guarantee good fortune, health, and other benefits. A talisman is often worn concealed on the person or in a dwelling. They are the counterpart of amulets (see above) that are used to protect against disease or evil.

**Talmud**  From Hebrew, meaning "learning" or "teaching"; an encyclopedic collection of the Jewish oral law consisting of the Mishnah (see above) and Gemara. Compiled between the first century and the end of the fifth century C.E., it is the highest legal authority in Judaism after the five books of the written Torah.

**theocratic**  Of or under a theocracy—the rule of a state or a society by God or by priests or God's representatives who claim to rule by divine authority.

**theodicy**  From the Greek *theos* ("god") and *dike* ("justice"); introduced by the philosopher Leibniz to designate the problem of justifying the goodness and power of God in view of the evil in the world. Used more broadly by social scientists to describe any legitimation of an ideology or world view in the face of the threat of chaos and meaninglessness.

**theophany**  The temporal and spatial manifestation of God or gods in some tangible, perceptual form; occurs in many religions, ancient and modern.

**tonsure**  The rite of clipping the hair or shaving the head to denote admission of a candidate to a religious order, often to a life of a monk.

**totemism**  Adopted from the Ojibwa Indian language for the widespread practice of associating human tribes or classes with animals or plants, from which the group is descended or has some close relationship. Some writers claim that the group worships the totem animal and that totemism is the earliest form of religion. These theories are now widely disputed.

*Tripitaka*  Sanskrit word used to designate the Buddhist sacred canon of writings.

**typology**  The study of types—for example, of religious phenomena such as forms of sacrifice and types of deity.

**usury** The exacting of interest on a loan or debt. Before the rise of modern capitalism, Judaism, Christianity, and Islam forbade the practice of usury (see Exodus 22:25; Deuteronomy 23:19f) from biblical times through the Middle Ages and even beyond.

**utilitarian** A philosophical and ethical position that identifies right ethical actions with the effort to maintain the greatest good and happiness for the greatest number of people. It arose in the late eighteenth century and in the early and mid-nineteenth century; it was very influential and associated with the English philosophers Jeremy Bentham and John Stuart Mill.

**utopian** A view that envisions an ideal or near-perfect world or social order. The word was first used by Sir Thomas More in his book *Utopia* (1516) and derived from the Greek meaning "no place." It was, however, used to suggest a good or ideal place. In religion, utopian prophecies are often associated with messianic-millenarian groups who look to the overthrow of the evil powers and the coming of a new and ideal social order here on earth.

*varna* Sanskrit word meaning "colors," or the four classes or divisions of society in Hinduism; the foundation of the caste system. The top three classes (Brahmans, Ksatriyas, Vaisyas) are the "twice-born" because they undergo initiations according to the sacred law.

**Wahhabism** The teachings of the Arab theologian Muhammad ibn 'Abd al-Wahhab, which insisted on a purification and renewal of Islam by strict adherence to the authentic Islam of the founding Prophet Muhammad. It has profoundly influenced contemporary Sunni Islamic traditionalists and Fundamentalists.

**Wicca** A New Age feminist movement that has adapted pre-Christian religious witchcraft practices into a benevolent religion oriented toward the harnessing of the feminine principle and energy present in nature for healing and social betterment.

**Zealots** An ultranationalistic Jewish sect in Palestine who led the first war against Rome in 67–68 C.E.; disappeared after the fall of Jerusalem (70 C.E.).

# Index

## A

Abortion, Jewish view, 290–92
Action and salvation
 Hinduism, 312–14
 Islam, 314–18
 Judaism, 318–20
Aggression, relationship to ritual, 98–99
Ahura Mazda and Ahriman, 176–78
Agnosticism, 25
*Akitu* festival, 93–94
Al-Ghazali, 187, 267
Allport, Gordon, 24
Almsgiving, Islam, 315–16
Alpert, Richard, 224
Amida Buddhism, 306–308
 characteristics of, 307–308
 salvation, Shinran on, 306–308
Amos (Hebrew prophet), 286–87
*An-atta*, not-self doctrine, Theravada
 Buddhism, 235
Ancestor worship
 natural religious communities
 and, 139
Animism, 39
Anthropology, 21–23
Anthropomorphism, 188
*Apatheia*, 227, 228

Apocalypse
 apocalyptic writings, 332*ff.*
 characteristics, 332
 final judgment, 333–34
Aquinas, Thomas, 230, 280–81
Arahant, 345–46
Archetypes, 11
 myth, Jungian view, 71–73
Aristotle, cosmological proof of God, 190
Asceity of God, 188–89
Ascetic methods, 321–22
*Ashramas*, 312–14
Atonement
 and sacrifice, 96–98
 *Yom Kippur* as example, 97–98, 319
Augustine, Saint, 232–34
Avalokitesvara, 276
*Axis mundi*, 47*ff.*

## B

Babylonians
 *akitu* festival, 93–94
 creation, concept of, 203*ff.*
*Bar/bat mitzvah*, 320
Beatific Vision, 342
Benedictine rule, 145
Berger, Peter, 247, 249

**403**

*Bhagavad Gita,* 43–44
   on caste, 312
*Bhakti,* 310
Bible,
   Christian, 111, 114–16, 127*ff.*
   Jewish, 110, 113–14
*Birth of the Gods, The* (Swanson), 136
Bodhisattva, 275–77
Book of Changes, 175–76
*Book of the Dead,* 336
*Book of the Infinite Love* (de la
      Touche), 310
Book of Job, 261*ff.*
   suffering in
      and God's sovereignty, 265–67
      as result of sin, 261–62
      as test, 262–63
*Brahman,* union with, 180–82
Buddhism,
   forms of
      Amida Buddhism, 306–308
      Mahayana Buddhism, 306–307
      Theravada Buddhism, 234–38
   Four Noble Truths, 235–38
   *karma-samsara* theodicy, 258–60
   Nirvana, 344–46
   paradise in, 340–41
   rejection of cosmogony, 213–15
   scripture in, 122–27
      *stupa* as sacred place, 48–51
      *See also* specific topics
Burkert, Walter, 98

**C**

Caillois, Roger, 41
Calvin, John, 129, 267
Cargo Cults, 254–55
   John Frum Cargo Cult, 254–55
   this-worldly theodicy, 251*ff.*
Charisma, 142, 282–88
   and religious leaders, 142, 282–83
Christian Identity, 365
Christianity
   and creation story, 210–13
   on human nature, 229–34
      Genesis, 210–12
      human/God likenesses, 230–31
      non-Roman Catholic view, 231

      self-transcendence concept, 231
      sin, 231–34
   life after death, 338–40, 341, 342
   and monotheism, 185–91
   scripture in, 111, 115–16, 118, 127–32
Cicero, 276
Code of Manu, 312–14
Collective unconscious and myth,
      Jungian view, 72–73
*Collegia pietatis,* 144
*Communitas* and life-cycle rituals, 85–87
Confession, Islam, 314
Confucianism, 238–43
   ancestor worship, 242
   education in, 239–40
   Five Great Relationships, 242
   on human problem, 238–43
   *Li,* doctrine of, 238*ff.*
   Mandate of Heaven, 238, 239
   moral ideal, *chun-tzu,* 242–43
   and natural law, 276–79
   rectification of names in, 241–42
   scripture in, 106–107, 112
   *yin* and *yang* in, 175–76
Confucius, 238–43
Contraception, Catholic view, 281
Conversionist sects, 148
Corporate personality, 250
Cosmogonic myth
   creation by decree or from nothing,
      209–13
      Genesis, 210–13
      Mayan example, 209–10
   divine craftsman and creation,
      207–209
      Greek example, 207–209
   emergence from primal substance
      (creation), 199
   meaning of, 196
   practical basis of, 197–98
   primal chaos and creation by conflict,
      202–206
      Babylonian mythology, 202–206
      Egyptian example, 202–203
      Taoist concept, 206–207
   primal male/female and sexual
      union, 200–202
      Japanese *Kojiki/Nihongi* example,
      200–202

rejection of concept, 213–15
  Buddhism, 214–15
  Jainism, 213–14
  twentieth century, 215*ff.*
    Anthropic Principle, 217–18
    Creation Science, 218–19
    Freudian view, 216
  waters, emergent of life from, 202
    Egyptian example, 199
Creation. *See* Cosmogony
Creation Science, 218–19, 362–64
Creativity of God, 190–91
Cults
  characteristics of, 150*ff.*
  communal/political and moral
      dualism, 158–59
    Unification Church as example,
      156–59
  New Age movements,
      characteristics of, 151–54

**D**

Dahomey tribe, 139
De la Touche, Mother Louise
      Margaret, 210
Daly, Mary, 378
Deism, 190
Demiurge, Plato's, 208–209
Denomination, 147, 148
Devotionalism, 308–11
  characteristics of, 308*ff.*
  devotional mysticism, 308*ff.*
    Krishna, Ramakrishna, 308
    Saint Teresa of Avila, experience of,
      309–10
    Sufi, 310
  erotic, 310–11
  in Hinduism, 308, 310
  negative views of, 308
  revivalism, 310
Dewey, John, 5, 7
*Dharma*, 258, 259, 312–14
  *Dharma Shastras*, 312, 313
  and duty, 312–14
  *Manu Smriti*, 312–14
Dietary laws, Judaism, 320
*Divine Comedy* (Dante), 339
Doctrines, and models, 74–77

*Do-ut-des* and sacrifice, 95–96
Dualism, 175–79
  of cosmic struggle, 176–79
    Gnosticism, 178
    Manicheanism, 178–79
    theodicy, Mandeans, 178–79
    Zoroastrianism, 176–78
  *yin/yang* dualism, 175–76
*Dukku* in Theravada Buddhism,
      236–38, 323
Durkheim, Emile, 10, 22, 136

**E**

Ecclesia (church), 144
*Ecclesiola in ecclesia,* 144
Egoistic sin, 231*ff.*
Egyptians
  creation, concept of, 199, 202–203
  life after death, 336
Eightfold Path in Theravada Buddhism,
      323–24
Eliade, Mircea, 46–48
*Enuma elish,* 203–206
Epictetus, 227, 228, 229
Eschatology. *See* Salvation (goals of)
Eternal life, 342
Ethnocentric view, 13
Evangelical, 14
Evans-Pritchard, E.E., 17–18
Existential questions of people, 11
Exorcists, 91
Expiation (atonement), 96–97
  *Yom Kippur* as example, 97–98

**F**

Faith and salvation, 302–308
Falsification principle, 25–26
Falwell, Jerry, 361–62, 364, 365
*Fascinans,* experience of, 42–43
Fasting during Ramadan, Islam, 316
Festinger, Leon, 255
Fideism, 25
Filial piety, 242
Fish as sacred symbol, 62–64
Flew, Anthony, 25–26
Founded religions, 141*ff.*
  activities after death of prophet, 142–43

Founded religions—*Cont.*
  disciples in, 142
  leader/prophet in, 142
  versus natural religious
        communities, 141
Freud, Sigmund, 5, 7, 23–24
  civilization, concept of, 216
  human problem, view of, 224
Fromm, Erich, 329–30
Frum, John, Cargo Cult, 254–55
Functionalist approach, 22–23
  and myths, 70–71
  and rituals, 82–83
Fundamentalism, 358–76
  American Protestant, 360–65
  characteristics, 359–60
  Islamic, 365–73
  use of term, 358
    leaders and movements, 367–72
    and modernity, 365–67
Funeral rites, 90

**G**

Gandhi, Mohandas K., 282–86
Geertz, Clifford, on definition of
        religion, 9
Genesis
  accounts of creation, 210–12
  on human nature, 229–30
Genetic fallacy, 7
Girard, René, 98–99
Gnosticism
  dualism of, 178
  Gnostic sects, 149
God
  and anthropomorphism, 188
  attributes of
    asceity, 188–89
    creativity, 190–91
    eternal, 189
    holiness, 187–88
    infinity, 188
    love/goodness, 191
    omnipotence, 186, 191
    omniscience, 186, 191
    one, 185–86, 188
  cosmological proof of, 190–91
  deistic concept of, 190

Grace, 303–305
  Protestantism, 303–305
Greece (ancient)
  creation, concept of, 207–209
  life after death, 335–37
Guru Granth Sahib, 111
Gush Emunim, 359

**H**

Hades, 335
*Halakhah*, 292, 318*ff.*
Hartshorne, Charles, 268
Hasidism, 144, 334
*Hathayoga*, 231*ff.*
Healing rituals, 91–92
  shaman illustration of, 91–92
Heaven
  Buddhist depiction of, 340–41
  Christian depiction of, 339–40, 341
  Islamic depiction of, 339–40
Hell, Christian depiction of, 339–40
Henotheism
  and ancient Israelite religion, 184–85
  compared to monotheism, 185–86
Hermeneutics, 27–28, 121*ff.*
  Buddhist, 122–27
  Christian, 127–32
Hick, John, 8
  on monotheistic theodicy, 264–65
Hierophany, 46*ff.*
Hinduism
  action and salvation: *dharma* and duty,
      312–14
    social obligations, stages of, 312–14
  *dharma*, 312–14
  erotic devotionalism, *bhakti*, 310
  *Karma*, 258–60
  *karma-samsara* theodicy, 258–60
  pantheism and monism, 179–83
  *samadhi*, union with Brahman, 343–44
  scripture in, 107–108, 118
  social classes of, 312–13
  stages of life in, 313–14
  *Upanishads*, 180–82
Historiography, 21
Hizbollah, 371
*Homo Ludens: A Study of the Play Element
    in Culture* (Huizinga), 83–84

Honen, 307
Hubbard, L. Ron, 154–56
Human problem
   Christianity, 229–43
   Confucisnism, 238–43
   Freudian view, 224
   Lorenz's view, 224
   Marxian view, 224, 225
   Plato's view, 225
   Stoicism, 226–29
   Theravada Buddhism, 234–38
Humanistic psychology
   Maslow's theory, 328–29
   therapies related to, 327–28
   Zen orientation, *satori*, 329–30
Hume, David, 261
Huss, John, 253
Hussites, theodicy of, 253–54

**I**

*I-Ching*, 175
*Idea of the Holy, The* (Otto), 42–54
Ijma, 294–95
*Imago Dei*, 230–31
*Imago mundi*, 230–31
Imam, 295
Immortality, 336–37
Individuation, Jungian view, 73
Infinity of God, 188
Initiation rites, 85*ff.*
   marriage and funeral, 90
   puberty, 87–88
   vocational initiation rites,
      88–89
Irenaeus, 264
Ishtar-Tammuz, 171
Isis, 170–71, 172
Islam, 293–97, 314–18
   action-duty in, 314–18
      almsgiving, 315–16
      confession, 314
      ethics, 293–97
      fasting during Ramadan, 316
      *jihad*, 295–97
      pilgrimage to Mecca, 316–17
      prayer, 314–15
   Day of Judgment, 340
   *Ka'ba* as sacred place, 47

   monotheism and, 387
   scripture in, 113, 293–95
Israel (ancient)
   apocalypse, 332–34
   creation, 210–13
   monotheism, 184–87
   Yahweh, development of, 184–86
Izanagi and Izanami, Japanese
   deities, 201–202

**J**

Jainism, rejection of cosmogony, 213–14
James, William, 23
Japanese Shinto, as national religion, 140
*Jihad*, 295–97, 367*ff.*
Job. *See* Book of Job
Johnson, Elizabeth A., 378–79
Judaism, 318–20
   creation and, 210–12
   dietary laws, 320
   ethics, 289–92
   festivals
      *Pessah*, 319
      *Rosh Hashanah*, 319
      *Shabuot*, 319
      *Sukkot*, 319
      *Yom Kippur*, 97–98, 319
   monotheism and, 184*ff.*
   Mount Zion as sacred place, 51–54
   resurrection concept in, 338
   rites of passage
      *bar/bat mitzvah*, 320
      circumcision, 320
   Sabbath (*Shabbat*), 318–19
   scriptures, 289–92
   Talmudic Judaism, 290
Jung, Carl, 23, 71–73
Jungian view of
   myth, 71–73
      archetypes, 72
      collective unconscious, 72
      individuation in, 73

**K**

*Ka'ba* as sacred space, 47
Kali, 173–74
Kannon (Kuan-yin), 276, 277

Kant, Immanuel, 5, 6
Karma
    concept of, 234–35
    *karma-samsara* theodicy, 258–60
        Buddhism, 259–60
*Khandhas,* Theravada Buddhism, 235
Khomeini, Ruhallah, 369–71
Kierkegaard, Soren, 288
Klemke, E.D., 327
*Kojiki,* 200–201

**L**

Ladin, Osama bin, 371–73
Lao Tzu, 279
Leo XIII, Pope, 280
Levy-Bruhl, Lucien, 250–51
*Li,* 238*ff.*
Life after death. *See* Salvation (goals of)
Liminal stage and life-cycle rituals, 85
Literary criticism, 20–21
Lorenz, Konrad, 98, 224
Love/goodness of God, 191
Lu Hsiang-shan, 279
Luther, Martin
    on Bible, 129
    on the fall, 231
    on salvation, 303–305
    theological orientation of, 303–305
Lutheranism
    *ecclesiola in ecclesia,* 144

**M**

Mahayana Buddhism
    *Bodhisattva* in, 276–77, 340, 343
    characteristics of, 340*ff.*
    salvation in, 340*ff.*
Malcolm X, 317
Malinowski, Bronislaw, 70–71
Mandala
    meaning of, 49
Mandeans, theodicy of, 257–58
Manicheanism, dualism of, 178–79
*Mantras,* 82, 109
Marduk and Ti'amat, Babylonian
        deities, 204–206
Marriage rites, 90
Martineau, James, 5

Marx, Karl, 5, 7, 224, 225
Maslow, Abraham, 328–29
Mass, Roman Catholic, ritualistic
        pattern of, 94–95
Mayans, creation, concept of, 209–10
McVeigh, Timothy, 365
Mecca, pilgrimage to, 316–17
Meditation/insight, 320*ff.*
    Theravada Buddhism, 323–24
    Yoga of Patanjali, 321–23
Mencius, 278–79
Mernissa, Fatima, 383
Messianic Age, Israel's messianic
        hope, 330–34
Metaphor, 64–65
    characteristics of, 64–65
    parable as extended metaphor, 65*ff.*
Millenarian movements, 252*ff.*
    this-worldly theodicy of, 251*ff.*
        Cargo Cults, 254–55
        Millerites, 255
        Taborites, 253–54
Millerites, this-worldly theodicy, 255
*Mishnah,* 334
*Mitzvah,* 289, 318*ff.*
Models and doctrines, 74–77
*Moksha,* 312, 344
Monasticism, 144–45
Monism. *See* Pantheism/monism
Monotheism, 5, 183–91
    ancient Israelites and Yahweh,
        184–86
    compared to deism, 190
    compared to henotheism, 184
    Egyptians, Ikhnaton, 183–84
    God, conception of, 187–91
Monotheistic theodicies, 260*ff.*
Moon, Sun Myung, 156–59
Morris, Henry M., 362–63
Mother goddesses, 169*ff.*
    characteristics of, 169–70
    Ishtar, 171
    Isis, 170–71, 172
    Kali, 173–74
    primitive cultures, 169–70
    *sakti* cults, 173
Mount Zion as sacred space, 51–53
Mountains as sacred space, 51–52
Mudras, 60–61

Muslim Brotherhood, 368–69
*Mysterium*, experience of, 42–45
Mystery cults (Orphic), 336–37
Mysticism
    devotional mysticism, 309–11
        Saint Teresa of Avila, 309
        Sufi, 310
    Theodicy of participation, 50–51
Myths, 68*ff.*
    cosmogonic myth, 196*ff.*
    definition of, 68
    functionalist approach, 70–71
    Jungian view, 71–73
    phenomenological approach,
        73–74
    in popular culture, 69–70
    as religious models, 69–70

**N**

Nassaf, Malak Hifni, 381–82
National religion, 138–40
    components of, 138–40
Natural law, 276–81
    in Confucianism, 276–79
    in Roman Catholicism, 279–81
Natural religious communities,
    138–40
    versus founded groups, 141
Neolithic Age
    creation, concept of, 198
New Age, 151–54
New Testament, life after death, 338–42
Niebuhr, Reinhold, 231
*Nihongi*, creation, concept of, 200–201
Nirvana
    Buddhism, concept of, 323, 324,
        344–46
Not-self doctrine, 235
Numinous, 42–44

**O**

Obligation, ethics of, 273–74
Omnipotent, God as, 186, 191
Omniscient, God as, 186, 191
*On Aggression* (Lorenz), 98
Original sin, 232–33
Otto, Rufolf, 5, 6, 42–43

**P**

*Pagoda* as sacred place, 48–51
Pantheism/monism, 179–82
    Hinduism, 179–82
    move from polytheism, 181
    natural mystical experience, 182
Parables, 65–68
    definition of, 65
    effectiveness, 66
    examples of
        "Visakha's Sorrow," 66–67
        workers in vineyard, 67
    as extended metaphor, 65
    features of, 65–66
Paradise
    in Buddhism, 340, 342, 343
    in Islam, 340
Patanajali, yoga of, 321–23
Paul, Saint, 303
Peak experiences, 328–29
*Pessah*, 319
Phenomenology and religion, 26–27
Philosophy, 24–26
    and religion, 24–26
        falsification principle as example,
            25–26
Pilgrimage to Mecca, Islam, 316–18
Pius XI, Pope, 281
Plato, 208–209, 225, 288, 337–38
    on creation, 208–209
    on human problem, 225
    on immortal soul, 337–38
    on ethics, 288
Play, relationship to ritual, 83–84
Pluralism, 356*ff.*
Polytheism, 166–74
    mother goddesses, 169–74
    sky gods, 168–69
    Zeus, 168–69
Prayer, Islam, 314–15
Prejudice and religion, study of, 24
Premillenarianism, 361–62
Process theology, theodicy of, 268–69
Propitiation, 4, 96
    and sacrifice, 96
Protestant ethic, 23
*Protestant Ethic and the Spirit of Capitalism*
    (Weber), 23

Psychoanalysis compared to Zen
Buddhism, 329–30
Psychology of religion, 23–24
religion/prejudice study,
example of, 24
Puberty initiation rites, 87–90
Pure Land. *See* Amida Buddhism

**Q**

Qa'ida, 21, 371–72
Qutb, Sayyid, 368–69

**R**

Race nation/nationality, natural
religious communities, 138–39
Ramakrishna, devotional mysticism of,
309–10
Rectification of names in Confucianism,
241–42
Reform/protest and religion
from within community, 143*ff.*
Catholic orders, examples of,
145–46
*ecclesiola in ecclesia,* 144
monasticism, 144–45
secession from church-type
community, 146–47
Religion
definitions of, 4–10
definitional difficulties, 5–10
study of and
anthropology, 20–23
historiography, 21
literary criticism, 20–21
phenomenology and religion, 26–27
philosophy of religion, 24–26
psychology of religion, 23–24
sociology of religion, 23–24
theology, 19–20
*Religion in Essence and Manifestation*
(van der Leeuw), 40
Religion and ethics, 273–300
charismatic leaders and moral
authority, 282–88
Amos as "ethical prophet," 286–87
Gandhi as "exemplary" leader,
282–85

cosmic or natural law as moral
authority, 276, 278–82
in Confucianism, 276–79
modern applications of Catholic
natural law theory, 281
in Roman Catholicism, 279–81
Saint Thomas Aquinas's teaching,
280–81
divine command and moral
obligation, 288–97
in Islamic law and ethics, 293–97
duty of *jihad,* 295–97
in Jewish law and ethics, 289–98
ethics of obligation, 274–75
ethics of virtue, 274–76
cardinal virtues, 274–76
Religious communities, 136*ff.*
cults, 149–59
founded religions, 141–43
natural religious communities,
138–40
reform/protest within, 143–45
*ecclesiola in ecclesia,* 144
monasticism, 144–45
reform from within community,
144–45
secession from church-type
community, 144–47
sects, 147–49
voluntary religious communities,
140–41
*See also* specific types of communities
Religious language
as metaphysical poetry, 75–76
Religious models, 74*ff.*
Religious symbols, 60*ff.*
language as symbolic, 59*ff.*
master-symbols, 62
Reliquaries, 48
Resurrection
Christianity, 338–39
Judaism, 338
Revolutionist sects, 149
Ricoeur, Paul, 74
Ritual(s), 80*ff.*
definition of, 81
functions of, 82–83
healing, 91–92
importance of, 81

life-cycle, types of, 85–90
  and *communitas*, 85–87
  funeral rites, 90
  and liminal (threshold) stage,
    85–86
  marriage rites, 90
  social puberty, 87–90
  vocational initiation rites, 88–90
play-oriented approach, 83–84
sacraments as, 99–101
and sacrifice, 95–99
  purpose of, 95–96, 98
  violence/aggression and sacred,
    98–99
  *Yom Kippur,* as example of,
    97–98
seasonal, types of, 92–95
Robertson, Pat, 364–65
Roman Catholicism
  Beatific Vision, 342
  Mass, ritualistic pattern of, 94–95
  monastic orders, 144–45
Rosh Hashanah, 319
Russell, Bertrand, 327

**S**

Sabbath (*Shabbat*), Judaism, 318–19
Sacraments
  characteristics of, 100–101
  definition of, 99
  as rituals, 99–101
Sacred power
  ambivalent response to, 40–41
  concept of, 40
  *fascinans,* experience of, 42–46
  *mysterium,* experience of, 42
  numinous
    examples of numinous experiences,
      42–46
  *tremendum,* experience of, 42–46
Sacred space, 46–52
  *axis mundi* in, 48*ff.*
  *ka'ba* as, 47
  Mount Zion as, 51–53
  mountains as, 51–52
  *stupa* as, 48–51
Sacred time, 53–54
Sacrifice, 95*ff.*

purposes of, 95*ff.*
  avoiding violence/aggression
    within, 98–99
  communal bond, 96
  *do-ut-des,* 95–96
  expiation (atonement), 96–98
    *Yom Kippur,* example of, 97–98
  propitiation, 95–96
  scapegoat in, 96–97
Saint Teresa of Avila, devotional
    mysticism of, 309–10
Sakti cults, 173
  action/obligation and
    features of action, 311–12
    Hinduism, 312–14
    Islam, 314–18
    Judaism, 318–20
  devotionalism, 308–11
  faith and grace, 302–308
  as goal of religion, 301–302, 325–26
  Luther, Martin, on, 303–305
  meditation/insight, 320–25
    Theravada Buddhism, 323–25
    Yoga of Patanjali, 321–23
  Shinran on, 306–308
  *See also* specific topics
Salvation (goals of), 325*ff.*
  Buddhism, Nirvana, 344–46
  Hinduism, Samadhi, 342–44
  humanistic approaches, 326–30
    Maslow's self-actualization, 328–30
    Zen-oriented approach, 329
  life after death
    ancient Egypt, 336
    ancient Greece, 335
    Beatific Vision, 342
    Buddhism, 340–41
    Islam, 340
    New Testament, 338–40, 342
    post-biblical Judaism, 338
    prehistoric view, 334–35
  Messianic/Utopian Age, 330–32
    Israel's Messianic Hope, 330*ff.*
Salvation (ways to), 301–24
*Samadhi,* 322–23, 342–44·
Samkhya philosophy, 321
*Sannyasin,* 314
*Satori,* insight, Zen Buddhism, 329
Scapegoat, meaning of, 96–97

Schleiermacher, Friedrich, 5, 6
Schüssler Fiorenza, Elizabeth, 378
Scientology, 154–56
Scripture, 104*ff.*
　authority and canonicity, 109–12
　in Buddhism, 122–127
　in Christianity, 111, 114–16, 127–32
　in Confucianism, 106–107
　features of, 104–105
　in Hinduism, 107–109
　interpretation of, 121–32
　in Islam, 106, 110, 113, 118
　in Judaism, 110, 113–14
　reception and uses, 116–21
　in Sikhism, 119–20
　use of term, 108–109
Seasonal rites, 92–95
　pattern of
　　*Akitu,* New Year festival as
　　　example, 93–94
　　Catholic Mass as example, 94–95
　purposes of, 92
Sects
　characteristics of, 147
　conversionist, 148
　denomination and, 147, 148
　gnostic, 149
　revolutionist, 149
　typologies of, 147
　utopian, 149
Secularization (and Pluralism), 356–58
Self-actualization, 330
Self-transcendence, human, 11, 231
Sexual union, creation concept, 200–202
*Shabuot,* 319–20
Shamans, 41, 91–92
　Healing ritual, example of, 91–92
*Shari'ah,* 293, 294, 314, 318
Shi'ites, other-worldly theodicy, 295
Shinran on salvation, 307–308
Shinto, and Japanese State, 140
Signs, purposes of, 59–60
Sikh
　scripture in, 119–20
Sin, 230–34
　concupiscence, 232
　egoistic sin, 231–32
　original sin, 232–34
　Saint Augustine on, 233–34

Sky gods, 168–69
　Zeus as example, 168–69
Smith, Wilfred Cantwell, 357–58
Smith, W. Robertson, 81–82
Social puberty, 87–90
Society and religion, reciprocal
　relation, 136–37
　*See also* Religious communities
Sociology of religion, 23
　Protestant ethic as example, 23
Socrates on immortal soul, 337–38
Space/place. *See* Sacred space
Spiro, Melford, 5, 6
Stanton, Elizabeth Cady, 377
Stoicism, 226–29
　*apatheia,* indifference, 227–28
　happiness, attainment of, 229
　human problems, view of, 226–29
　origins of, 226
　*Phusis,* nature, 226–28
*Stupa,* 48–51
　mandala and, 49
　parts of, 48–51
　as sacred space, 48
Suffering. *See* Book of Job
Sufi devotion, 310
*Sukkot,* 319
Sunna, 293–95
Suzuki, D.T., 329
Swanson, Guy, 136
Symbolic communication, 59*ff.*
　metaphor, 64–65
　models and doctrines, 74–77
　myths, 68–74
　parable, 65–68
　religious symbols, 60–64
　signs/symbols, purposes of, 59–60
　*See also* individual topics
Symbols
　presentational symbols, 60
　purposes of, 59–60
　representational symbols, 60
　*See also* Religious symbols

**T**

Taborites, this-worldly theodicy,
　253–54
Talmudic Judaism, 290–92, 334

*Tanha,* Theravada Buddhism, 323
Tao, 206–207, 278, 279
Taoism, creation, concept of,
    206–207
  *yin-yang,* 175–76
Tennyson, Alfred, Lord, 182
Teresa, Saint, 308, 309
Terry, Randall, 364–65
Thanatos, death-instinct, 216
Theocratic, 364, 365
Theodicy
  antitheodicy, 269
  dualism, 257–58
    Mandeans, 257
  *karma-samsara* theodicy, 258–60
    Buddhism, 259–60
    Hinduism, 258–59
  monotheistic theodicies, 260–68
    Book of Job, 261–63, 265–67
    process, 268–69
    of protest, 269–70
  need for, 249–50
  other-worldly theodicy, 255–56
    Shi'ites, 256
  of participation, 250–51
    in mysticism, 250–51
    in primal societies, 250
  this-worldly theodicy, 251–55
    Cargo Cults, 254–55
    Jewish concept, 251–52*ff.*
    millenarian movements, 252–54
    Millerites, 255
    Taborites, 253–54
  *See also* Book of Job
Theology, 19–20
Theravada Buddhism, 234–38
  *an-atta,* not-self doctrine, 235
  characteristics of, 234*ff.*
  *dharma,* 263
  *dukkha,* 236–37
  Eightfold Path, 235–36, 238
  on human existence, 234–38
  *karma,* 234–35
  *khandas,* 235
  Nirvana, 344–46
  *tanha,* 238
Tillich, Paul, 5, 54–55
*Timaeus* (Plato), 208–209
Time, sacred, 53–54

Tonsure, 87
Torah, 106, 289*ff.*
*Tremendum,* experience of, 42–43
*Trial of God* (Wiesel), 269–70
Turner, Victor, 85–86
Tylor, Edward B., 5, 6

**U**

*Upanishads,* 107, 180–81
Urban, W.M., 76
Utopian sect, 149
Unification Church, 156–59

**V**

Van der Leeuw, Gerardus, 40–41, 325
*Varieties of Religious Experience, The*
    (James), 23
*Vedanta,* 182
Vedas, 179–80
Violence, relationship to ritual, 98–99
*Violence and the Sacred* (Girard),
    98–99
Virtue, ethics of, 74–76
Vocational initiation rites, 88–90
  monk's initiation rite, 88–90
Voluntary religious communities, 140
  characteristics of, 141
  founded religions, 141–43

**W**

Wahhabism, 367–68
Wadud-Mushsin, Amina, 382–83
Weber, Max, 23, 137, 142, 147, 248, 258,
    282, 288
Weems, Renita, 130–32
*When Prophecy Fails* (Festinger), 255
Whitehead, Alfred North, 5, 6, 268
Wicca, 153
Wiesel, Elie, 269–70
Wilson, Bryan, 147–48
*Witchcraft, Oracles and Magic*
    (Evans-Pritchard), 17
Wittgenstein, Ludwig, 8
Women
  in Christianity, 376–80
  in Genesis (Book of), 376–77
  in Islam, 380–85

## Y

*Yahweh*
  day of Yahweh, 331–32
  development of, 184–86
*Yin-yang* dualism, 175–76
Yoga, 321–23
  *Hathayoga sutras,* 321
  Patanjali and, 321–23
  steps in yogic technique, 321–23
Yom Kippur
  as rite of atonement, 97–98, 319

## Z

Zarathustra, dualism of, 176–78
Zen Buddhism
  compared to psychoanalysis,
    329–30
  *Satori* as insight, 329
Zeus, story of, 161–69
Zoroastrianism, dualism of,
    176–78